THE DYNAMIC SOCIETY

'Professor Snooks has undertaken as ambitious a project as one could possibly conceive of . . . it is a stimulating work, and one which shows an immense amount of reading, and an organization of the material into an interesting and highly speculative, but fascinating structure.'

Douglass C. North, *Nobel Laureate in Economics*

In *The Dynamic Society* Graeme Snooks has set himself the highly ambitious task of exploring the driving force of global change over the past 2 million years. This path-breaking book is divided into three parts:

- Part I – outlines and explains the entire history of life on earth, by developing a fully dynamic model, not just of genetic change, but of the broader wave-like fluctuations of biological activity. Central to this is the dynamic role of the individual operating in a competitive environment.
- Part II – provides a critical review of current interpretations about the course of history and the forces driving it.
- Part III – develops an entirely new interpretation of the dynamics of human society over the past 2 million years. It analyses how individuals in a competitive environment generate growth by investing in the dynamic strategies of family multiplication, conquest, commerce, and technology. It argues that the rise and fall of societies is an outcome of the development and exhaustion of these strategies.

The author also employs his dynamic strategy model to discuss future outcomes for human society, controversially arguing that far from leading to ecological destruction, growth-inducing technological change is both necessary and liberating. Ultimately, the book demonstrates that dynamism, not stasis, is the essential condition of human society, as it is of life.

Graeme Donald Snooks is the Coghlan Professor and Head of the Department of Economic History at the Institute of Advanced Studies, Australian National University. He has published widely on a number of central issues in economic history and is editor of a number of prestigious book series and journals.

THE DYNAMIC SOCIETY

Exploring the sources of global change

Graeme Donald Snooks

London and New York

First published 1996
by Routledge
11 New Fetter Lane, London EC4P 4EE

Simultaneously published in the USA and Canada
by Routledge
29 West 35th Street, New York, NY 10001

Typeset in Garamond by Florencetype Ltd,
Stoodleigh, Devon
Printed and bound in Great Britain by
Redwood Books, Trowbridge, Wiltshire

British Library Cataloguing in Publication Data
A catalogue record for this book is available from the
British Library

Library of Congress Cataloguing in Publication Data
Snooks, G. D. (Graeme D.)
The dynamic society: exploring the sources of change/
Graeme D. Snooks.
p. cm.
Includes bibliographical references and index.
1. Economic history 2. Statics and dynamics (Social
sciences). 3. Social evolution. I. Title
HC21.S64 1996
330.9–dc20   95-40965
                                                           CIP

ISBN 0–415–13730–6 (hbk)
ISBN 0–415–13731–4 (pbk)

Dedicated to my sons
Adrian Graham and Roland William
who will inherit the future of
the Dynamic Society

CONTENTS

CONTENTS

Part III Wheel of fire

FIGURES

TABLES

PREFACE

In *Time's Arrow, Time's Cycle*, Stephen Gould, in following up an idea by Sigmund Freud, suggests that the increasing sophistication of human knowledge has gradually undermined man's 'original hope for our transcendent importance in the universe'. A number of discoveries have been particularly important in this respect. In the field of physics, Copernicus (1543) and Galileo (1632) showed, contrary to religious teaching, that the Earth was not the centre of the Universe. In the field of earth sciences, James Hutton (1785) and Charles Lyell (1830–1833) showed that geological time was not comfortingly short but unfathomably long with 'human habitation restricted to a millimicrosecond at the very end'. In the field of biology, Charles Darwin (1859) showed that mankind had not been created with dominion over the rest of life but had only relatively recently evolved from it. To Gould's list we can add a number of other discoveries that have profoundly changed the way we see our role in the Universe. In the field of prehistory, archaeologists from the mid-nineteenth century undermined the Biblical view that mankind appeared on Earth as recently as 4004 BC and that human society was fully formed from the beginning. More recently, in the fields of astronomy and physics there was the important discovery of an expanding universe (Slipher, 1924; Hubble, 1929) that began with the Big Bang (Gamow, 1952; Dicke *et al.*, 1965) and may eventually end by contracting in upon itself; and in microbiology there was the discovery of the structure of DNA (Watson and Crick, 1953) and the development of genetic engineering which opens the disturbing possibility of changing what we are. Each discovery has challenged mankind's age-old assumption of a special role in life.

What comforting but false notions remain? Currently the most cherished notion we hold about ourselves is the way we have transcended our origins through that uniquely human characteristic the intellect. Education and civilized culture, it is widely argued, have placed mankind above the great Darwinian struggle for life. Human society, we are told, is dominated not by base desires, but rather by intellectual ideas and altruism. Richard Dawkins, for example, concludes *The Selfish Gene* 'on a note of qualified hope' that 'we, alone on Earth, can rebel against the tyranny of the selfish replicaters' because of our unique 'capacity for conscious foresight' and our 'capacity for conscious genuine, disinterested, true altruism'. This widely held interpretation, I will argue, prevents us from seeing ourselves clearly. It is contrary to all the hard evidence we have about man's existence. It is necessary, therefore, to debunk this idea before we can understand the way human society has evolved over the past 2 million years. This tenacious myth has led social scientists to look for answers in the wrong places. Evolution of society is seen as a highly convoluted process, currently operating under the intellectual influence of mankind. But once we directly confront what we are as a species, we discover that the dynamics of human society is in fact a systematic process driven largely by fundamental human desires. We find that the dynamics of human society is no more complex than that of the rest of life on Earth. And its objectives and methods are certainly not unique. The complexity lies in the uniquely human institutional arrangements that facilitate the pursuit of mankind's desires.

We must, however, face the demonstrable but unpalatable truth that mankind is not predominantly altruistic and that human society is not driven by abstract ideas. We must face the fact, demonstrated in the following chapters, that mankind like the rest of life is basically self-seeking and that ideas are only effective when they are called upon to serve our basic needs. Once this truth is recognized, we will see that human society is not passively static and subject to the impact of external forces or to the intellectual manip- ulation of experts but is eternally dynamic and subject to the materialism of everyman. Accordingly, it is just not possible to engineer some sort of ecologically benign stationary state as suggested by the radical ecologists – at least not without setting in train an inevitable process of self-destruction. Instead the solution to current environmental problems must arise from the eternally dynamic character of human society. And this will require a revolution in the way we see ourselves.

This book is intended as a substantial contribution to an area of the social sciences in general and economics in particular – longrun dynamics – that has been largely ignored by the deductive theorist because of the limitations of the mathematical approach. To understand the dynamic process driving human society over the longrun we need to reconstruct and model real-world historical processes. This is the task of the analytical historian. The analysis presented here for the first time has been worked out over a number of years and in a number of books – particularly *Economics Without Time* (1993), *Portrait of the Family* (1994), *Was the Industrial Revolution Necessary?* (1994), and the present volume – by carefully reconstructing quantitative data on economic change and by examining the factual outlines of the fluctuating fortunes of major societies over very long periods of time. This has involved both time-consuming statistical estimation and a reliance upon the historical evidence provided by the vast labour of an army of dedicated scholars (to whom we all owe a debt of gratitude) working in many disciplines over many years. Only with the argument finalized and the penultimate draft written did I actively seek out those works that attempt to provide more general interpretations of the rise and fall of human society. These are much fewer in number than the careful factual reconstructions and do not have much in common with the new approach adopted here. In the final draft I attempted to show the points of similarity and contrast between my argument and the conventional wisdom. In matters of detail there are some areas of agreement with a few authors who have taken a more economic approach, but at the general level where I deal with the dynamic process of human society we have little in common. Disagreement over the issues raised, however, should not be taken to mean disrespect for their work. I endorse the Popperian view that a healthy science requires a critical approach to existing hypotheses – a view entirely consistent with a proper respect for their intellectual achievements.

My 'dynamic-strategy' model has led to a major reinterpretation of the reasons not only for the rise and fall of individual human societies but also for the detailed economic choices they have made. Most authors focus not on the fundamental economic forces driving the dynamic society but on sociopolitical institutions that emerge from these forces. And most find the idea of dynamic materialist man too shocking even to contemplate. The objective of this book is to explain the eternal dynamics of human society, not its changing – indeed ephemeral – sociopolitical forms. My view is that these institutional forms are merely the most efficient expression of the under-lying dynamic economic processes. The complex relationship between dynamic economic strategies and the resulting institutional forms is to be the subject of another book.

It may come as a surprise to some that a focus upon fundamental economic forces involving a central role for materialist man should lead to an uncom-promisingly humanist outcome. We are all aware that it is fashionable in intellectual circles today to downplay the positive role of humanity in the wider ecology. Mankind is seen in many quarters as the enemy of life on Earth. This seems to me to be a form of generic self-hate, involving a retreat from the real problems of life. In this study I draw attention to the great positive achievements of mankind down through the ages that should elicit our admiration rather than our masochistic hostility. Naturally we must be aware of our shortcomings and mistakes, but if we are to face the future with confidence we must understand and feel comfortable with what we are.

A major expression of the humanist spirit of this book is my argument that the dynamics of human society arises from the decision-making not just of small elites but of all members of society both male and female throughout the world. It will be argued that societal dynamics is an outcome of a vast groundswell of human actions and reactions to the world in which we find ourselves. Small elites who capture a disproportionate share of the surplus of human endeavour merely express the general desires of all humanity. The power of elites is very limited in the Dynamic Society and is exercised over distributional outcomes rather than the dynamic process of change. Small elites are able to exploit the groundswell of human desires only if they do not forget the limitations of their power and do not attempt to stand against the flow of humanity. To forget is to be swept away.

The people rather than the experts determine the dynamics of human society. The people provide the demand for ideas; ideas do not create their own demand. I will argue that the ideas of experts about the larger issues of life are shaped by the nature of the dynamic process rather than the other way round. Therefore, indirectly, the self-interested actions of the people operating within the constraints of their economic environment determine the world view of the experts. While this book is not a story about individuals because the individual does not drive the Dynamic Society, it *is* a story about humanity. This book is an affirmation of the remarkable spirit and inventiveness of the human race. It is also a story of hope based upon the common-sense of the average person, a story that rejects the fashionable counsels of despair by natural scientists who warn us of the chaos created by economic decision-makers and who ask us all to follow them beside the still waters.

A major theme in the book is that mankind and, hence, society are moved by biologically determined desires as well as human intellect. We understand and respond with both our rational and intuitive faculties through the use of ideas and images. Images make an appeal to that part of our being – human desires – than can be traced genetically to the beginning of life on Earth. This is the ground of the rationalization and pursuit of our desires. Ultimately, when the ideas have been forgotten, the images remain, powerful and evocative. Just as images emerge in the mind of man during the process of life, so they fight their way to the surface of our consciousness as we relive the past. Where images emerged in writing the chapters of the book, and where they succeeded in symbolizing the intellectual content, they were retained as italicized 'introductions'. Understanding operates at a number of levels and, as argued in Chapter 1, seeing is the beginning of understanding.

The Dynamic Society is the beginning of a larger research programme that aims to explore the ambitions, actions, and ideas of mankind which have given rise to the quintessential dynamic quality of human society over the past 2 million years and which will continue to drive it long into the future. Some important issues that can only be alluded to here will be explored in depth in subsequent work.

G.D. Snooks
Sevenoaks
Canberra

ACKNOWLEDGEMENTS

This book is the outcome of a relatively intensive and isolated period of research and writing. Accordingly, the scholars from many disciplines who have assisted me most have done so unknowingly through their written work. Their contribution has been acknowledged by reference to their publications in the text and the References. In as much as this work emerged from my earlier books, it was also influenced by the many people who generously commented upon them. They are acknowledged there. Also I was fortunate to receive generous encouragement and extensive critical comments on the penultimate version of the book from Douglass North, Mark Casson, and a number of anonymous referees.

I am delighted to be able to record the involvement of my sons Adrian and Roland in this work. Both have strong interests in the history and economics of modern and ancient societies. Together we have discussed some of the ideas that appear in these pages, which have been influenced by their youthful enthusiasm as well as their perceptive comments. The book is dedicated to them.

Once again I wish to acknowledge the essential practical support provided so expertly by my Department in the Institute of Advanced Studies at the Australian National University. Barry Howarth has made an important contribution to the book by keeping me supplied with an intimidating number of works on each subject I needed to investigate. The task of selecting the most appropriate publications for scrutiny was made so much easier by his broad knowledge of the history of oriental and ancient civilizations. And his general understanding of a number of languages made it possible to consult some key texts not published in English. He also collected data for many of the tables and figures, and compiled the index. The expert word-processing was, as always, cheerfully undertaken by Ann Howarth and Jeannie Haxell. Barbara Trewin, as well as organizing my time, took professional charge of formatting the text. Finally, Wayne Naughton was responsible for many of the statistical calculations and for the computer drawings. I wish to thank them all for their unstinting support. Without it *The Dynamic Society* would have taken much longer to complete.

ACKNOWLEDGEMENTS

It should be noted that bold phrases in the text have been included in a Glossary of New Terms and Concepts to be found at the end of the book.

1

CHARIOTS OF CHANGE

Behold there came four chariots out from between two mountains
. . . These are the four spirits of the heavens.

Zechariah, VI, 1, 5

In the beginning was the word. And the name of the word was change –
eternal change. The explosive beginning imparted an energy to matter that
has continued to drive our expanding universe ever since. It is a dynamic
that will continue forever, either in a universe that goes beyond the limits,
or in a universe that reaches its limits and contracts upon itself. To begin
again anew. It is a universe vibrant with energy from its greatest to its
smallest parts. Even life on a seemingly insignificant planet called Earth is
characterized by ceaseless change. The vehicles of this change are the various
species of animal and plant life, which are driven by individuals striving
with great determination to survive and, with survival, to consume. In the
eternal struggle to survive and prosper – a struggle that generates endless
change – the riders in the chariot adopt one of four strategies: procreation,
predation/conquest, genetic/technological change, and symbiosis/commerce.
These are the four chariots of Zechariah – the four spirits of the heavens.

This book is about the Dynamic Society of mankind. It explores the nature
and process of change in human society over very long periods of time. It asks
questions about the vehicle of change, about those who drive it, about its path
through time, and about its likely destination in the future. To understand the
dynamics of human society, we need to go back beyond the beginning of the
modern era, beyond the beginning of civilization, beyond even the beginning
of mankind. We need to begin at the very beginning – some 4 billion (4,000
million) years ago when the first signs of life on Earth emerged.

Why not focus upon the more recent past? Even the last few millennia?
The answer has had a major influence in shaping this work. In order to
understand the riders in the chariot of change – those who are driving the
dynamic society progressively forward – we need to understand their genetically determined nature. We need, in other words, to know the real nature
of mankind. And this requires an understanding of the nature of life itself.
We also need to understand the various strategies that riders in the chariot

have employed to achieve their dynamic goals which, in turn, requires an understanding of the entire sweep both of human society and of life itself. Yet even more importantly, we can only gain useful insight about the future by employing a very longrun approach to the past. The current myopic methods of prediction about the future of human civilization, it will be shown, are both flawed and misleading.

THE DYNAMICS OF LIFE AND SOCIETY

Until recently we knew little of the great longevity and continuity of life. And only since the time of Charles Darwin (1809–1882), barely more than a century ago, have we possessed any understanding of the mechanism by which it was achieved. While Darwin was the originator of the natural selection hypothesis, he was far from being the first to discuss evolution (Mayr, 1991). What is truly remarkable is that despite considerable intellectual effort by thousands of science's most talented and hardworking scholars, Darwin's central hypothesis remains as the only persuasive explanation of the evolution of life (Dawkins, 1986). Many have attempted to carve out reputations for themselves by disputing Darwin's thesis of natural selection, but none has succeeded. Once the excitement of each new attempt has died down, it has been seen by the scientific community merely as a gloss on Darwin's original hypothesis.

Neo-Darwinists claim that evolution involves a very gradual change in life's species owing to genetic mutation that occurs in a cumulative way through an intensive struggle for survival and reproduction. Only those individuals possessing a genetic advantage survive to pass it on to future generations. The rest are ruthlessly weeded out. According to that enthusiastic and highly persuasive interpreter of neo-Darwinism, Richard Dawkins (ibid.: 306–12), evolution is not a random process as some have claimed. Quite the opposite. Genetic change is non-random in the sense that it is the systematic outcome of a tenacious force within all life forms to survive, and only random in the sense that it can be either a cost or a benefit to the individual life form. It is only through the process of natural selection – whereby those who gain an advantage through mutation survive, and those who suffer a disadvantage are eliminated – that species change gradually by the slow accumulation of successful genetic changes. Life as we know it is such an improbable event that random chance would have given it no chance at all.

What is the driving force in Darwin's theory of evolution? It is the intense competition between life forms for the resources required for survival and, thereby, for reproduction. The former is more important than the latter. According to Darwin, this 'struggle for existence' involves intense competition between individuals in a particular species as well as with those from other species, and with its physical environment (Darwin, 1979: ch. 3). Darwin refers to this struggle as 'the war of nature' (ibid.: 459). Adopting

2

this metaphor, Dawkins (1986: 178) compares the struggle for life to an arms race: 'I regard arms races as of the utmost importance because it is largely arms races that have injected such "progressiveness" as there is in evolution'. And when discussing Darwin's theory of natural selection, Dawkins (ibid. 5, 313) says it is an 'unconscious, automatic process', it 'has no purpose in mind', and that it involves 'successful unconscious "choices"'. The individual life form is not concerned with ultimate ends but only with the immediate problem of life or death. Those who survive get to pass their genes on to the next generation. But the struggle for life comes first. Darwin, who regarded 'sexual selection' – which is based upon 'a struggle between the males for possession of the females' – as subsidiary to natural selection, argued that 'sexual selection will give its aid to ordinary selection, by assuring to the most vigorous and best adapted males the greatest number of offspring . . . [It] will also give characters useful to the males alone, in their struggles with other males' (Darwin, 1979: 442, 170). Hence the ever-present driving force in life is the struggle for survival in a hostile environment. Some socio-biologists, however, have subtly reinterpreted Darwin to downplay the 'struggle for existence' and to highlight the struggle for reproduction. Hence they claim (Trivers, 1985: 15) that 'natural selection refers to differential reproductive success in nature, where reproductive success is the number of surviving offspring produced'.

The fossil evidence, however, challenges the neo-Darwinian view that genetic change occurs at a very slow and relatively constant rate over extremely long periods of time as a result of natural selection. The evidence shows sharp breaks in fossil development. While the fossil record is clearly incomplete, some neo-Darwinists (Mayr, 1963) have attempted to explain it in terms of more rapid change taking place in small subgroups of a species that have become separated from the parent population. A more controversial and unorthodox attempt to explain the step-like pattern in the evidence is the 'punctuated equilibria' hypothesis of Eldredge and Gould (1972). They argue that stasis, or stability, rather than change is the normal state of affairs because any process of selection is 'stabilizing' rather than 'directional'. The stationary state is 'disturbed' or 'punctuated' only rarely by 'rapid and episodic events of speciation' that can be explained, not by natural selection, but by unusual environmental conditions ('allopatric speciation'). The physical science explanation of the 'punctuationists' contrasts with the economic explanation of Darwin.

In Chapter 4, I argue that this debate can be resolved: by recognizing that genetic change is only one of a number of **dynamic strategies** – including procreation, predation, and symbiosis as well as genetic change – that are 'pursued' by species competing for survival; by focusing not on evolution but on the development of life as a whole; and by isolating the driving force in life. What we require is not just a mechanism to explain genetic change, but a more comprehensive dynamic model that can show how the 'pursuit' of alternative strategies will produce both the step-like pattern in the fossil evidence and the wave-like pattern in the development of life as a whole. As we shall see, these patterns of genetic change and of life are similar to the patterns of technological change and of society, and they are generated by a similar dynamic mechanism.

The story of life in the round has many points in common with the story I have been telling for a number of years about the forces driving human society over the last few millennia (Snooks, 1990a; 1993a; 1994a; 1994b). This is a story, based firmly on quantitative evidence, about the competition between individuals within human society for material ends. It is a story in which the principal characters are motivated by an overwhelming desire to gain control over scarce resources – both natural and man-made – in order that they might increase their consumption, wealth and, thereby, power. This has involved, in the earliest period of human history, the gradual absorption of natural resources into economic production through family multiplication and, at a later stage, the application of new ideas to the ways in which economies were organized and their goods and services were produced. The driving force in this process of economic change is, what I have called, **materialist man** who persistently and ingeniously attempts to maximize his material advantage *over his lifetime*. It is a force that dominates the fortunes of the Dynamic Society, a force I propose to call **dynamic materialism**. As we shall see, this force is the outcome of individual decision-making and is in no way deterministic in the sense of involving historical inevitability. The dynamic objectives of economic decision-makers are pursued through the use of dynamic strategies encompassed by the four chariots of Zechariah: family multiplication, technological change, commerce, and conquest which, as we shall see, have their counterparts in the rest of life. These strategies are adopted according to their cost effectiveness and they are employed to increase material advantage at first by pioneering individuals but, owing to a mechanism I call **strategic imitation**, also by society as a whole. The dynamics of human society is the systematic outcome of the adoption and exhaustion of these distinctive strategies. And it is the exhaustion of dynamic strategies, not the scarcity of natural resources, that generates diminishing returns in the dynamic process.

In order to avoid confusion we must be clear about these central concepts from the very beginning. And we must be precise. Not only do we require an accurate characterization of human motivation, we also need to state it in a testable form. A vague discussion of utility maximization is virtually meaningless because it borders on the truistic – whatever people do is regarded as economically rational – and because it cannot be adequately tested. More useful is the bolder but potentially falsifiable hypothesis that the average decision-maker – not *all* decision-makers – attempts to maximize the probability of survival and material prosperity. By material prosperity I mean the accumulation and consumption of tangible goods and services. It is

4

also important here to distinguish between ends – the pursuit of material considerations – and means – either individual or cooperative (not be confused with 'altruistic') action. And we need to distinguish between human motivation and human activities involving adventure, entertainment, leisure, work, and family and cultural events. As will be explained in Chapter 7, the term 'materialist man' is used in preference to the economists' term 'economic man' because the former is a dynamic and realist concept while the latter is a static and analytical device.

The effect of these forces in human society was to drive the frontier of human settlement forward and the level of material living standards higher. This has been achieved through what I have called the great **technological paradigm shifts** (Chapter 9), involving the Palaeolithic Revolution (1.6 million years ago), the Neolithic Revolution (10,600 years ago), and the Industrial Revolution (200 years ago). In turn these paradigm shifts – which introduce major changes both in the economic system and in potential material living standards – have been driven by three great dynamic mechanisms, which owe their energy to the determination of human beings to survive and, having survived, to maximize their material advantage. The first of these is the 'primitive dynamic' that has been called here the **great dispersion**, by which unused natural resources are brought into production through family multiplication (Chapter 8). This dynamic process was responsible for modern humans migrating throughout the entire habitable world. The 'ancient dynamic' can be represented by, what I call here, the **great wheel of civilization**, which maps the path of material standards of living through a great circular motion of rise, stagnation, fall, and collapse for each successive society without any form of permanent progress (Chapter 12). This great wheel revolves slowly in space without gaining traction – without carrying human society from the plains of Sumer into the heady hills of affluence – because ancient civilization is trapped within a neolithic technological framework. The rise in material living standards beyond the neolithic base level is achieved by ancient societies through the pursuit of the dynamic strategies of conquest (Chapter 10) and/or commerce (Chapter 11); its stagnation occurs when these dynamic strategies have been exhausted; and its collapse is the result of being thrown back upon a neolithic revenue structure to finance the overexpanded empire's cost structure. Ultimately it crumbles. Yet with each turn of the wheel the Dynamic Society is brought closer to the technological limits of the neolithic paradigm through population expansion and the transmission of existing technical ideas.

The 'modern dynamic' is a process of linear, not circular, growth that can be represented by what I have elsewhere called (Snooks, 1993a; 1994b), the **great linear waves of economic change**, which describe very long upswings and downswings of about 300 years in duration around a growing very longrun trend. These great waves are driven by technological change (Chapter 9). While the modern pattern can be traced back a thousand years, it was only with the Industrial Revolution (Snooks, 1994b) that the great ancient wheel – the eternal recurrence of war and conquest – was finally broken. The dynamic society, therefore, is the great chariot of economic change, which is driven by materialist man. And it is this vehicle that is now carrying life of all kinds into the future. But there have been serious spills in the past, which may well occur again.

How close we are to the edge of darkness is taken up in the final chapter. There are some – the ecological engineers of the *Limits to Growth* and *Beyond the Limits* variety – who claim that we are very close to the abyss and argue that we should pull back immediately from the edge before it is too late. The present dominant growth-inducing technology strategy, they insist, should be outlawed and we should, under their guidance, seek to establish the stationary state. The conclusions of this book are very different. Using the 'dynamic-strategies' approach developed in Chapters 8 to 12, I attempt to show that if the technology strategy is outlawed, the eternal driving force within human society will adopt the only available alternative strategy – conquest. In this event, the technological progressiveness of the present would give way to the eternal recurrence of war and conquest. The great wheel of ancient civilization would replace the great linear waves of modern progress. This is demonstrated in the final chapter by modelling a world in which the Industrial Revolution never happened: what, we ask, would the world be like in AD 2000 without the Industrial Revolution? There can be little doubt we would see the emergence of a global empire based upon conquest that would have made even Augustus feel envious. Yet this is not to deny the current existence of severe environmental problems that can, must, and will be attended to. It is a proper balance between social and environmental goals that must be sought.

There are clearly strong parallels between the traditional story of life on Earth and my schematic account of dynamic change in human society. But, I hasten to add, this is not because I subscribe to any form of social Darwinism or, its more fashionable relative, economic evolutionism. Indeed, I will argue that the Darwinian hypothesis is incomplete and should be recast as a dynamic economic model. Only then can it explain the dynamics of life as opposed to the mechanics of genetic change. Both systems – of life and of human society – can be interpreted as dynamic systems that have produced accelerating waves of change over vast periods of time. These include the step-like pattern of genetic change, and the great technological paradigm shifts of the Dynamic Society. On the one hand, this dynamism generated a cumulative development of biological life, and on the other it led to the cumulative development of material standards of life – either actual or potential – in human society. The vehicle of biological change is the species, which is driven by the individual life form's instinctive struggle for survival using a variety of dynamic 'strategies' of which genetic change is but one. On the

6

other hand, the vehicle of economic change is human society, which is, and always has been, driven by the individual's determination, through the use of the dynamic strategies, to maximize their material returns.

In both cases, natural resource constraints – or rules of the game – are involved. For biological evolution, the constraints are dictated by physical and chemical laws that determine both the physical environment and the supply of natural resources. Biological evolution as a whole emerges from an interaction between individual life forms of one or more species and the environment. While variation in access to natural resources has been influenced by changes in the physical environment (Crawford and Marsh, 1989), it has probably depended more upon genetic changes (or changes in biological 'ideas'). In the Dynamic Society as a whole, natural resources can be accessed and extended by a change in technological ideas. Economic change involves an interaction between individuals mediated through institutions within society on the one hand, and the effective supply of natural resources on the other. Material maximization can be pursued in human society, because technological change makes it possible to accumulate a surplus in the form of productive capital. This possibility was not available to life forms before the Dynamic Society. Before the Dynamic Society, to survive was all. Everything else – reproduction and a precarious consumption – followed from this.

A dynamic model of life and society

We need a simple but robust model that can explain the emergence and development of life on Earth over the last 4 billion years. A model that can explain the dynamics of life both before and after the emergence of mankind. To build such a model requires a degree of poetic licence, to employ a metaphor that endows unthinking life forms with objectives and choices. In this spirit I propose an economic model – not a deductive model but an **existential model** or model of existence – which is developed in detail in Chapter 12. Briefly, this model emerged from my historical research undertaken for earlier books – particularly *Economics Without Time* (1993) and *Portrait of the Family* (1994) – as well as for this work. Hence it is not a preconceived model imposed upon the historical record, but rather a model that emerged from detailed historical research, which is the essence of an existential model. As a dynamic model it is concerned with the process of interaction between fundamental economic forces, decision-makers in competitive environments, the strategies they adopt, and the impact of those strategies on the material fabric of society. The model is self-starting and self-sustaining and responds positively and creatively to external shocks. It is concerned, therefore, with forces determining the way societies change. This dynamic model is contrasted with static models that focus upon either the conditions of equilibrium and the convergence to equilibrium, or on the conditions of the 'stages' of growth and of convergence to those 'stages'. Static models are concerned with outcomes and the structural conditions of society.

Our existential model can be characterized by four main features. First, it is a world populated by 'decision-making' individuals, who are motivated by an overwhelming desire to get the most out of their circumstances – to survive in the first instance and then to maximize their material well-being (or advantage) as surpluses emerge. The second feature involves a highly competitive environment in which individual life forms are unable to survive and prosper without intensive struggle. Third, the physical environment is capable of significant if slow change, both independent (such as ice ages, continental drift, and volcanic activity) and induced (such as the development of an oxygenated atmosphere during the early era dominated by blue-green algae, possible future greenhouse effect, etc.). Finally, and most crucially, the 'decision-making' individuals employ dynamic strategies – procreation, predation/conquest, genetic/technological change, and symbiosis/commerce – to achieve their objectives. The failure to realize that both biological and societal change are determined by strategies other than genetic and technological progress has led both natural and social scientists to misunderstand these respective dynamic processes. This has led to the puzzle in intellectual circles over how there could be growth, either biological or economic, during those very long periods of time without either genetic or technological change. The puzzles over 'stasis' in biological evolution and the 'stationary state' in economic progress are resolved in the following chapters.

These four ingredients can be combined into a general model in which maximizing individuals compete with each other for a finite supply of resources, the stock of which changes over time owing to exogeneous shocks and the induced effects of an evolving life process. Species expand their numbers while there are unused resources, but cease procreation when these are exhausted. Predation/conquest and the search for isolated environments are intuitive ways of dealing with the exhaustion of resources, whereas the introduction of new genetic or technological 'ideas' is a creative reaction to this competition. In the highly competitive phase those individuals with access to more successful ideas achieve their objectives of survival and maximization of material advantage. In the process there is a tendency to maximize the use of available ideas, both genetic and technological. Those who are unsuccessful either ultimately perish or exist at a low standard of living – the latter because they are useful to those who hold a monopoly of natural resources. The end result of this competitive process is either the development of life on Earth or of economic change, including expansion and growth, in human society. Those groups of individuals that are able to isolate themselves from the competitive mainstream languish until the isolation is eventually broken down and then they either perish or live on in poverty. This simple general model can be employed, therefore, to explain the dynamics of life on Earth in the past, present, and future. In the remainder of the book its various operations and complications will be explored.

During the phase of biological evolution that has dominated the history of life on this planet – for 99.999 per cent of the last 4 billion years – individual life forms operating within a highly competitive environment have struggled for existence in the face of a finite supply of natural resources (or nutrition). Without this eternal driving force located within individual life forms – a force that is instinctive rather than conscious – life would never have emerged let alone flourished over such a long passage of time. In the process of this struggle, the stock of 'ideas' applied to natural genetic engineering has increased significantly over very long periods of time. It has been argued (Eccles, 1989) that genetic change occurs on the relatively isolated margins of larger populations of a particular species, otherwise any advances will be diluted by the large and, hence, more conservative gene pool. If these genetic changes are of material advantage (and many will not be), they will spread through the larger population, through competitive struggle, when the small advanced group is reintroduced to the parent population. If this is true, it is a form of specialization and division of labour, which is a tactic that is also important in the dynamics of human society.

The outcome of this dynamic process is biological change or, as it is more commonly called, evolution. Involving, as it does, an interaction between a variety of competing life forms on the one hand, and a changing environment on the other, over extremely long periods of time, change is expressed in great steps of biological progress. But this is only part of the story. The step-like profile is a description only of the progress of genetic change for a species or group of species, it is not a profile of the progress of biological life which is the outcome of a range of dynamic strategies of which genetic change is only one. In Chapter 4 I argue that, in order to explain the emergence of life on Earth, we should focus not on the genetic change of species but on the progress of life as a whole which proceeds via a number of great waves covering vast periods of time. These great waves of biological change include the eras of blue-green algae, of the primitive marine and land animals, of the dinosaurs, and of the mammals including mankind. The usual scientific explanation of these waves is cast in terms of an interaction between genetic change and changing supplies of natural resources which drives the upsurgence of life; and in terms of catastrophic physical occurrences such as volcanic activity and cosmic events, which lead to the sudden collapse of dominant life forms.

A new argument is presented in this book. The upsurge in life is seen as an outcome of the competitive 'pursuit' by individual life forms of a range of dynamic strategies not just genetic change; and the collapse is the inevitable outcome of the exhaustion of these strategies. While external events can enhance the growth surge and hasten the collapse, this wave-like dynamic process is driven by internal forces and would occur even in the absence of outside shocks. And the reason that genetic change has a step-like profile – relatively sudden development followed by much longer periods of stagnation – is because there are long periods of time when individual life forms find it more efficient to pursue non-genetic dynamic strategies. The 'genetic step' and the 'biological wave' are, after all, mutually consistent.

During the subsequent era dominated by the Dynamic Society – which is relatively recent in the experience of life on this planet, covering only 0.001 per cent of the last 4 billion years – individual humans living in a competitive social environment struggled initially for bare survival, as all life had done for billions of years. As the outcome of this competition became more predictable – only relatively recently and only for a limited part of the world's human population – the struggle for survival became a struggle to maximize material advantage or well-being. This was made possible, after the Neolithic Revolution about 10,600 years ago, by a unique ability to accumulate productive capital and administrative assets embodying productive ideas. Those who were successful in this race for resources were able to pass on their wealth (and, later, human capital) culturally, rather than genetically, to their children. Those who failed either died prematurely or were reduced to poverty and subservience.

Ideas in the Dynamic Society are generated by a specialized elite often withdrawing from the larger population to do so. But not all ideas are immediately applicable. Indeed, only a very small proportion of ideas produced by a particular generation of experts are also applied economically during that era. The determining factor is whether the mass of economic decision-makers are able to use these ideas to maximize their material advantage. Hence, the great mass of economic decision-makers provide the drive for the Dynamic Society (and even many of the practical ideas), while the relatively small elite of experts plays a more passive role by providing the ideas required for progress once the momentum is under way. This is why individuals are unable to have any effect upon the Dynamic Society unless the mass of economic decision-makers, which responds to changing fundamental economic forces, can profitably employ their ideas. The 'great man in history' is the one who got this complex timing right, not the one who attempted to move the masses.

The impact of new ideas on economic organization and production is felt within the Dynamic Society by a reduction in the costs of transacting economic activities and business (transactions costs) and/or an increase in productivity in the production of goods and services in both the household and the market sector. Both developments are responsible for what we know as economic growth, which should be thought of as an increase in total income (household plus market) per household rather than the usual but more limiting definition of GDP per capita (Snooks, 1994a). These institutional and productive improvements, however, are the outcome of the various dynamic strategies of materialist man. And as suggested already, the longrun growth path taken by the Dynamic Society, during the past millennium, is not one of gradual change, but rather of a series of great waves of economic change of some 300 years in duration.

These great waves have been shaped by the interaction of population growth and 'technological change' (in its widest sense), together with the stock of natural resources. Relatively rapid growth of population and average living standards – at rates that make the process of evolution look as if it were standing still – were experienced as the application of new ideas to society enabled a more intensive use of natural resources (including labour services). This upswing could be quite an extended affair, lasting for a century or more. Only once a particular technological advance was exhausted would population growth impinge on resources, thereby reducing living standards and bringing economic and population growth to a halt. This new equilibrium between population and natural resources would persist until the introduction of a new technological advance, generally on the foundations built by a slow increase in capital stock (in towns, cities, ports, transport, and communications) that embodied slight changes in technology (a bit like the gradual accumulation of directional genetic mutation). Eventually a threshold level of embodied technical ideas is reached and a new rapid upswing of growth is initiated. While this is an endogenous model of very longrun growth via great waves of economic change, this system was also subjected to external shocks – such as disease, war, and sudden changes in the physical environment – that caused further shorter-run fluctuations.

But technological change is only one of mankind's dynamic strategies. It was the dominant strategy during the major technological revolutions during the palaeolithic, neolithic, and modern periods. In the vast periods of time between these great revolutions, the technological foundations of human society remained stationary or changed only very slowly. These are the **great steps of human progress**, which is a pattern of technological change resembling the 'punctuated equilibria' hypothesis for genetic evolution. In those periods when underlying economic conditions did not favour the technology strategy, economic decision-makers employed the alternative dynamic strategies of commerce/colonization and conquest to increase their material standards of living. These strategies drove the great wheel of civilization, and with every rotation the Dynamic Society approached more closely the limits of the neolithic technological paradigm.

It will be clear that this model is concerned with the fundamental economic forces underlying the dynamics of human society rather than with the determinants of institutional complexity. The latter is the subject of a future book. Here we wish only to explain why human societies grow, stagnate, and sometimes collapse. The argument in this book is that while cultural feedback does occur, the dynamic process essentially is determined by more basic forces. In *The Dynamic Society* I attempt to show that societal dynamics can be explained largely through predictable changes in fundamental economic forces. These I have called the 'primary dynamic mechanism'. Institutional forces are a systematic reaction to the primary mechanism through what I have called the 'secondary mechanism'. This secondary mechanism accounts for the complexity of society.

Hence our model is concerned with dynamic causal relationships not with the institutional contexts for, or the facilitation of, economic decision-making. In other words, while the model explains the mechanism by which dynamic strategies emerge and are eventually exhausted, it does not deal in any detail with the institutional arrangements that arise in response to these dynamic strategies. As with the objective of any scientific model, it constitutes an explanation rather than a description of reality. And because I wish to explain the dynamic mechanism of human society rather than its institutional complexity, this work cannot be regarded as more reductionist than any reasonable attempt to explain reality with the assistance of a theoretical model.

Intellectualism and reality

A possible response to this explanation of the dynamics of both human society and life might be: why has it not been proposed before? My answer is that there exists a great gulf between intellectualism and reality. Reality is often an affront to the self-perception of educated people. It was not uncommon in the past for influential thinkers to find Darwinism difficult to accept, not because of religious considerations, but because it appeared to contradict the high intellectual achievement and social dignity they thought man had achieved. This attitude has a long history, beginning with Darwin's co-discoverer of natural selection, Alfred Russel Wallace. At an early stage, Wallace believed that intellect prevailed over natural selection, and at a later stage he argued that human destiny was determined by the guidance of higher spiritual powers. Others like G.B. Shaw and, more recently, Arthur Koestler have also expressed a dislike for the materialism of Darwinism. They appear to prefer a personal version of Lamarckism, in which characteristics acquired by hard work and diligence can be passed on to future generations. Shaw wrote (Dawkins 1986: 291): 'There is a hideous fatalism about it [natural selection], a ghastly and damnable reduction of beauty and intelligence, strength and purpose, of honor and aspiration.' In commenting upon the difficulty that some intellectuals have with Darwinism, Dawkins (ibid.: 250) claims that there are those who 'find the idea of natural selection unacceptably harsh and ruthless; others confuse natural selection with randomness, and hence "meaninglessness", which offends their dignity'. Intellectual pride, it would seem, prevented them embracing the reality of life.

12

In a similar way, a major message of *The Dynamic Society*, namely that the driving force is provided by an overwhelming desire to maximize material advantage, is both distasteful and unacceptable to many people. Intellectuals disinterested in economics flatly reject the concept of economic man because, they claim, it contradicts the intellectual, cultural, and spiritual aspirations and attainments of mankind. Human beings, they insist, are motivated by higher considerations, such as the good of the group, and their behaviour is 'altruistic' rather than 'selfish'. I have called this characterization 'moral man' to contrast it with 'materialist man' the economic maximizer. A major difficulty with this suggestion, apart from its contradiction of the real-world evidence that will be introduced in Chapter 7, is that these intellectuals are left without a driving force in human society. What is it, we might ask, that has persistently driven humanity to compete so ferociously with other species and with its own kind during the past 2 to 3 million years (since *Homo habilis*)? What accounts for its remarkable success? What is this fire in its belly, if it is not the overwhelming desire to survive and prosper? They have yet to provide a persuasive answer. None of this, however, is meant to deny that certain individuals are self-sacrificing, just that they are not typical. None of this is meant to deny that most individuals are happy to help others during times of plenty, just that when they are forced by competition to make a choice between themselves and others the majority – not all – will choose themselves.

Even some economists, who live in a world of abstract ideas rather than of reality, have suggested that under certain circumstances, humanity is motivated by altruism (Snooks, 1994a: 42–6). But is the desire to help others such a powerful and persistent force that it could have driven our species from total insignificance to become the dominant and destructive force that we are today? Many of these economists would probably argue, without any evidence, that the inherent nature responsible for driving mankind into our modern age has been redirected through education. I will argue that no such change has taken place, nor could it have occurred because mankind's nature has been genetically determined, and that what is taken to be altruism is merely the strategy of maximizing individual material well-being through the well-being of the group to which they belong. And it will not change in the future because in a competitive world the struggle for survival and prosperity will be with us always.

But the most fascinating case of the rejection of materialism as the central driving force in human society is to be found in the natural sciences. The neo-Darwinists tell us constantly that all species have been shaped by natural selection, which leads to the maximization of reproduction. They vigorously reject as heresy the anti-Darwinism of Lamarckism, which suggests that acquired physical characteristics can be passed on to future generations. Despite this, many natural scientists appear to believe that what I have called 'natural man' has been replaced in the modern period by 'intellectual man', who is capable of overthrowing his former genetically determined nature through education and intellectual will. We are told that so-called 'cultural evolution' based upon intellectual ideas has replaced biological evolution based upon natural selection.

This is a view that also began with Wallace, who believed that the intellect of mankind prevails over selection (Desmond and Moore, 1991: 522). It is a view that has been readily adopted by a range of natural scientists including Ehrlich (1990), Suzuki (1990), and even Dawkins (1989). Dawkins is a particularly interesting example. In *The Selfish Gene*, the cold hard logic he applies to explaining evolution breaks down entirely when he considers human society. In a romantic act of faith, Dawkins (ibid.: 200–1) concludes by claiming: 'We, alone on earth, can rebel against the tyranny of the selfish replicators'. We can, he asserts, override the genetically determined survival/ materialistic mentality that has been built into us over at least the last 4 million years. But he provides no argument, let alone evidence, for how this is to be done. Perhaps he should calculate the probability of that eventuality as he has so effectively done the probability of life on Earth.

While it appears to be true that the related ideas of natural selection and dynamic materialism are both an affront to the intellectual and cultural dignity of mankind, I am convinced that there is something more fundamental involved. Today, most intellectuals and educated people have become accustomed to the idea that natural selection led to the emergence of our species, and a diminishing number would feel the outrage of Shaw. But the idea of materialist man is still unsettling for many intellectuals. I suspect that the main reason for this opposition is not so much for the slur it casts upon the perceived intellectuality of humanity, but rather the challenge it poses to the ideas they may cherish for its role in society. Most intellectuals appear to harbour the fantasy that they, or at least their kind, can influence the course of events in human society. Many believe that all it needs to change the world is for a few good minds to get together and agree on what should be done.

This is the ultimate intellectual fantasy. As I hope to show, ideas are only influential, and then only in a passive sense, when the great mass of decision-makers, who are driven by biological desires and are responsive to fundamental changes in the economy, use these ideas in an attempt to improve their material advantage. Ideas do not drive the Dynamic Society, they merely facilitate the changes that are already under way – changes driven by materialist man in response to shifts in fundamental economic forces of relative factor endowments and relative prices. Ideas, and those responsible for them, must wait until they are called upon by those who drive the chariot of change.

THE DYNAMIC INTERPRETERS

The very existence of life on Earth is remarkable. But even more remarkable is the fact that one small part of life can reflect upon its own highly improbable origins and development. While humanity's ability to do so has increased steadily down through the millennia, it has grown exponentially during the last century or so. Modern methods of intellectual inquiry in some disciplines in both the natural (physics and chemistry) and social (economics) sciences have reached a high level of technical sophistication. This has been achieved by the relatively recent development of deductive models expressed in mathematical form (Snooks, 1994a: 5–8). These elegantly abstract models, which are routinely employed for predictive rather than explanatory purposes, have become accepted as the standard to which all scientists should aspire. Those disciplines that do *not* do so – namely ecology, biology, and materialist history – have been criticized for their perverse backwardness (Peters, 1991; Keynes, 1891).

But are we not being led astray by the abstract model builders? A central premise in this book is that while the essentially inductive approach of biology and materialist history may limit the precision, elegance, and technical predictive power of these disciplines, they do employ the method required to ask questions about, and to explain, the big issues of life and society that are beyond the scope of the more technical disciplines. Instead of just dealing with the smaller shortrun issues of life or society (which are of course worth dealing with), the disciplines of biology and materialist history (defined broadly to include economic prehistory) are capable of focusing upon the very longrun dynamics of biological and economic change that have dominated our past and will dominate our future.

Biology and materialist history can successfully examine the dynamics of life and of society because they are able to piece together the extant evidence of life to reconstruct the patterns of change over long periods of time and they are able to develop general explanations of these patterns. In this study, the reconstructed patterns of biological and economic change have been called **dynamic timescapes**, and the general explanations of these patterns have been called **existential models** or models of existence (Snooks, 1994a: 2–5). Dynamic timescapes are those portraits of reality provided by a visual representation of longrun quantitative data. These portraits emerge from the statistical outlines of the course taken by both biological life and human society over vast expanses of time. They *show* us the nature of real-world relationships. And *seeing* is the beginning of understanding. They provide a glimpse of dynamic processes operating in life and in society, and are the building blocks of existential models. Elsewhere I have used the metaphor of the photograph album to explain this method – materialist history as photorealism (ibid.: 8–11). Existential models are empirical models of reality (or existence) and can be contrasted with the logical models of physics and economics, which are merely constructs of the mind. Deductive models are powerful tools which can be employed selectively in the reconstruction of dynamic processes, but they are limited by the range of issues they can examine. As existential models are based upon dynamic timescapes, they can liberate us from the limitations of deductive thought. They set free the imagination to range over the actual patterns of existence. And in these patterns of existence we shall see the dynamic processes of reality.

While existential models lack the mathematical rigour and technical predictive power of the logical models of physics and economics, they provide us with an understanding of the longrun dynamic processes that are driving human society out of the past and into the future. And the future of human society will be dominated by the big problems of human motivation, population growth, increases in living standards, the depletion of natural resources under our present technological paradigm, and the damage to an environment that has provided the cradle for life over billions of years. Only existential models can provide the answers we need, as deductive models have little to say about the big issues which often escape their attention entirely. Having made this essential point, it needs to be said that there is no simple dichotomy between the inductive and deductive methods, as each is used in support of the other. I have merely been talking of relativities.

To suggest a working partnership between biology and materialist history may be regarded as surprising to some. Only recently have *systematic* attempts been made to cut across the divide between the natural and social sciences (Foster, 1994). This should not be interpreted as saying that both disciplines should borrow concepts from each other – the evolutionary economists have attempted this with only limited success – just that together they can encompass the entire evolution of life on Earth. What I hope to show is that these two disciplines are closely related through the methods they employ, the types of issues they are capable of addressing (not that they always rise above the trivia of empirical detail), and the influence on both of political economy. Biology and materialist history have much in common. They are the dynamic interpreters of life on Earth.

The book is divided into three parts. Part I, entitled *The tide of time*, focuses upon the dynamics of life on Earth over the past 4 billion years. In 'Game of life' (Chapter 2) and 'Players in the game' (Chapter 3), a distinction is drawn between the largely passive but changing physical conditions of life and the central dynamic role played by individuals operating in a competitive environment. In Chapter 4, entitled 'Dynamics of being', the progress of biological life, via what I have called the great waves of life, are outlined and explained. This economic explanation attempts to turn Darwin's natural selection hypothesis – an explanation of genetic change – into a fully dynamic model of the process of life on Earth. It is an explanation that encompasses the Darwinian.

Part II, entitled *Shadow of the tower*, provides an outline of the current interpretations – many of them mutually inconsistent – made by experts in the natural and social sciences about the driving force in history and the progressive nature of human society. The 'Tower of Babel' (Chapter 5)

16

discusses the many different and incompatible interpretations by experts about the emergence of human society, and 'Quest for meaning' (Chapter 6) surveys the different roles they ascribe to decision-makers in history. This provides an essential backdrop against which the new model in this book should be viewed.

Part III, entitled *Wheel of fire*, attempts to provide an entirely new explanation of the dynamics of human society over the past 2 million years. 'Riders in the chariot' (Chapter 7) shows materialist man, who attempts to maximize lifetime material advantage by pursuing one or more of the dynamic strategies, to be the driving force in human history. This is followed in the next four chapters (8 to 11) by an examination of the four main dynamic strategies employed by society's decision-makers. 'Family of man' (Chapter 8) deals with the family multiplication strategy adopted as a dominant device by palaeolithic societies to increase their command over resources. 'Maker of the wheel' (Chapter 9) shows how and why the technology strategy has been employed in history. 'Horsemen of war' (Chapter 10) and 'Conjurers of commerce' (Chapter 11) focus upon the dynamic strategies of conquest and commerce by which ancient civilizations were able to raise their populations and living standards beyond the restrictions of neolithic technology. And it is shown that the cost of this form of progress for ancient societies was ultimate collapse. Then in 'The Dynamic Society' (Chapter 12) we retrace the path taken by human society over the past 2 million years – the great steps of human progress – and provide a systematic and internally consistent empirical explanation (or existential model). Finally, in 'Edge of darkness?' (Chapter 13), we explore the receding image of the future reflected in the mirror of the past to see where human society might be heading. We show what would happen if, as the ecological engineers advise, growth-inducing technological change were terminated, and conclude that the Dynamic Society must follow its eternal course or face Armageddon.

PART I
THE TIDE OF TIME

2

GAME OF LIFE

This world: a monster of energy that does not grow bigger or smaller, that does not expend itself but only transforms itself.

(Nietzsche, *The Will to Power*, 1885)

The world is a seething monster. Untamed and unrepentant. In the beginning, breathing fire and brimstone, the Earth refused to hide its contempt for life. Its violent energy knew no bounds, throwing up fiery mountains and raining molten rock, splitting the heavens with continuous electrical storms, and creating a poisonous atmosphere from its foul breath. But all this violence was inwardly directed. By controlling its fiery temperament the Earth could tempt organic life to begin building colonies and to grow confident about its future. It could then play bizarre games with these life forms by shifting the land masses and redefining the seas – by bringing the land together, breaking it apart again so as to send related life forms in entirely different directions and, much later, reintroducing them. Just when life was feeling composed and content, the Earth could split the ground asunder, unleash its molten core, cause temperatures and seas to rise or, if that failed to have the desired effect, to bring on an ice-age and falling seas. And, as a further shock tactic, there was always fire. But gradually life asserted its independence through man who is now capable of defying the Earth. Life and Earth are not partners as each is driven by its own internal forces; each attempting, unsuccessfully, to tame the other.

From the time mankind first learnt to speak, probably about 45,000 years ago, we have told stories – stories for entertainment and instruction around the campfire. The most complex and fascinating story ever told is about life on Earth. While this story has taken many forms in different places and at different times down through the millennia, it has only recently begun to be told with any precision. And even now there are many uncertainties, many missing events and episodes, many revisions, many remaining mysteries. But it is a story that grows in complexity each time it is retold. A story, curiously,

21

that we never grow tired of hearing. While it is not possible to do justice to the story of life in a few brief chapters, an attempt has been made in this book to reveal something of its fascination. It also serves as a foundation on which the later chapters about the Dynamic Society have been constructed.

The story of life on Earth is usually told as a sequence of different life forms, both beautiful and bizarre, that mysteriously emerge, unfold, battle for survival, and then disappear, to be replaced by equally fascinating species – endlessly. Usually, this passing parade of life, which takes place over vast periods of time, is explained as an outcome of cataclysmic events in the form of major climatic changes, of the rise and fall of the seas, of violent volcanic reminders of the Earth's beginnings, and of the planet's collision with space debris. It is a story told by natural scientists expert on the physical and chemical conditions of life. Natural selection may be invoked to explain how life forms change during their sojourn on Earth, but both their first timid emergence from the wings and their final disappearance from central stage are told with cataclysmic rhetoric – of crashing asteroids and exploding volcanoes.

What is missing from this story is a concern with the internal dynamics of life. Life on Earth, we are told, is the plaything of physical and chemical forces. In contrast, the story I attempt to tell in this book is that, while life on Earth clearly operates within physical constraints which from time to time are powerfully intrusive, it has a dynamic of its own. This dynamic is not only the most interesting part of the story, it is the part that explains how and why life has been able to adapt to, and prosper in, a physical world that pulsates to a different rhythm.

THE GAME

The story in this book is about the game of life. Like any serious game it has a set of well-defined rules, a number of highly motivated players, and a set of rewards and penalties. The basic rules of our game – the greatest game of all – are set by the physical and chemical conditions of life. With the emergence of mankind we must add to these basic physical rules the more ephemeral 'rules' of human society which are not externally generated but evolve from within the game to facilitate the objectives of the players. If physical rules define the nature of the game of life, social 'rules' represent agreements between the players as to how they will work together to exploit the game and their opposition. From time to time the basic rules change, in a way that may appear arbitrary to the players, if they think about it at all, but they adjust to the changes and go on with the game. Sometimes the physical rules may even change owing to the activity of the players, with the game becoming interactive. The players are the various life forms on Earth that are inextricably caught up in this highly competitive game. It is highly competitive because the winner takes all – life and all its sensual pleasures – while the loser loses all, through poverty and death. Yet despite the fierce struggle involved, there is no end to the number of individuals and species willing to take the place of those who cannot keep up.

The vitality and excitement of the game, therefore, are provided by the players, who develop strategies that will maximize their ability to survive and to obtain a material advantage. They, and not the rules – the physical conditions of life – provide the game's driving force. And this driving force, together with the ingenious ways in which the players attempt to turn the rules to their own advantage (by, for example, exploiting sources of chemical nutrients), provides the game of life with a dynamic quality that is largely responsible for the emergence and evolution of life forms over the last 4 billion years.

The game of life can be compared with highly professional games played in human society. Those who wish to play a professional game must accept the historically determined rules and have the abilities required to handle the highly competitive conditions under which play occurs. The history of any professional game – from chariot races in the ancient world to modern codes of football – shows that it is the players who provide the drive in response to the financial rewards associated with 'surviving' (remaining in the team) and winning. The higher the rewards, the greater the competition, and the more fierce the struggle between players who wish to maximize their material returns. While individual players struggle fiercely with one another to get into the team, once they have been selected they can only maximize their individual material returns by working cooperatively. As we shall see, this has major implications for the argument about 'altruistic' and 'selfish' behaviour. But there is always scope for individuals to employ opportunistic tactics to capture a larger than average share of the winning team's spoils.

In professional games, the basic rules merely provide the context for the competitive struggle. They may influence some of the responses of the players, but it is the individual drive in a competitive environment that is responsible for developing particular strategies and employing them to defeat the opposing team. Even changes to the existing rules, sometimes 'arbitrary' and sometimes induced by the strategies of the players, merely provide a different set of obstacles that the players have to overcome in their overwhelming desire to win. Players and teams merely change their strategies – change the means to a given end.

In the early history of any professional game, before the financial incentives were significant, individuals played for fun or for 'glory'. Players came in all shapes and sizes, and the difference between winning and losing was often a matter of will-power or big-heartedness. As the financial rewards – i.e. the competition – increased, so too did the seriousness with which the game was played. At some stage will-power was no longer sufficient, and the teams began to look closely at the ideal physical and intellectual characteristics. Players without these requirements were weeded out and replaced by those who had the necessary competitive advantage. This is the equivalent of genetic change. As the competition increased with further money being channelled into the game (particularly with the sale of television rights), the physical clashes became more ferocious. This required further, more radical changes in the structure of players, involving – once the limits of biological change had been reached – the adoption of body padding and helmets. This is the equivalent of technological change, and it enabled individuals and teams to throw themselves even harder into the conflict in order to survive both in the team and in the competition and to enjoy the fruits of success.

It is the ambitious individual players operating in a competitive environment who produce both 'genetic' and technological change that provides the game with its essential dynamic. Rules are required if the game is to be played at all, but these rules, or even changes in them, cannot provide the driving force, merely the context.

THE RULES

Rules for the game of life began with Time, some 15 billion years ago.[1] The story most often told today about the origin of the Universe – which has effectively replaced the creation story – is widely known as the Big Bang hypothesis. This story – which is not without its inconsistencies – is about what happened to a mere pinprick of spacetime, existing in a timeless medium, when it began to expand. Our expanding mini-universe gave rise to immense energy and heat and, when the fabric of spacetime was torn apart, the monolithic electronuclear force broke into three separate cosmic forces: the electric force, the nuclear force, and the weak force (or radio-activity). The huge thermonuclear explosion that occurred provided the matter out of which billions of galaxies of stars were ultimately formed as it was thrown across billions of light-years at great speeds and at very high temperatures.

As the Universe expanded it cooled, forming clumps of gases that eventually developed into galaxies. In these emerging galaxies, billions of stars appeared, and around these stars revolved concentrations of gas, ice, and radioactive dust. Of these billions of galaxies one is known as the Milky Way, and in one of its spiral-shaped arms is a star known as the Sun, and in this apparently insignificant solar system is a planet called Earth. The Earth was finally formed about 4.5 billion years ago and, on this planet, organic life emerged about 4 billion years ago.

The 500 million years after the Earth was formed were of crucial importance, because during this period the physical and chemical conditions from which primitive life forms emerged were laid down. In this period the rules of the game of life were established. It took much of this time for the temperature on Earth to fall below boiling point, and for the condensing water vapour to fall as rain, further cooling the planet. Thus began an important shaping influence – weathering – that helped to build the early continents

24

and has continued ever since. And all the while, the cooling process generated convection currents in the molten core, which exercised powerful influences upon the Earth's crust, causing it to shift, buckle, and give way to the upward thrust of rivers of molten rock.

At first the rains filled the many craters left by meteorites, but eventually these growing bodies of surface water ran together forming the first oceans – oceans that were rich in chemicals such as sodium, potassium, ammonium, phosphates, carbonates, chlorides, nitrates, and sulphates (Crawford and Marsh, 1989: 46). These rich warm waters provided an excellent medium for the chemical reactions that finally turned simple carbon and nitrogen molecules into complex organic molecules. Such a transformation was assisted by the presence of large quantities of carbon-rich debris carried from the asteroid belt to the Earth's surface by comets, together with the continuous electrical storms and the heat and ultraviolet rays of the Sun. When life finally emerged on Earth it was a primitive anaerobic form – because of the absence of significant quantities of free oxygen – usually referred to as bacteria and blue-green algae (proalgae). But this will be left until we deal with the players in the game of life.

The chemical conditions of life

A more general discussion of the chemical conditions of life follows quite naturally from a discussion of the Earth's atmosphere. Chemical compounds and chemical laws, which have their origins in the great forces unleashed at the beginnings of the Universe, have been, and are, essential elements in the emergence and maintenance of life. On the one hand, the planet's chemistry provides the basic building blocks of life and determines the conditions under which they can be put together to construct organisms. And on the other, chemical substances supply the nutrients required to maintain these organisms.

The basic chemicals involved in life are the different arrangements of carbon, hydrogen, oxygen, nitrogen, phosphorus, and sulphur. Of these, carbon is the basis of life on Earth. Carbon is more flexible than most other elements as it can make more bonds (four rather than two), thereby increasing the range of opportunities for creating more complex structures. Carbon atoms can link up with others of its own kind, together with the other main elements of life in order to build a variety of organic structures or compounds. While I have neither the expertise nor space to pursue technical matters further, it must be emphasized that 'there are very precise rules governing what will join up with what, how many atoms of one element can join with another, and the strength of the union' (Crawford and Marsh, 1989: 49). Evolving life *must* operate within these rules. But it should be realized that these rules are very general in the sense that they merely define the universe of possible life forms – and these are very large – that could exist. The actual

25

development path through that universe is determined by the drive of individual organisms together with the competitive circumstances in which they find themselves. This is brought out very clearly and ingeniously by Richard Dawkins in *The Blind Watchmaker* (1986).

In addition to providing the building blocks and the building code of life, chemical substances also supply the sustenance of life – chemical nutrients. While oxygen, the foremost of these, is an essential element in sustaining animal life, it has been produced (largely through photosynthesis) by life itself – plants in the seas and on the land. The role of other chemical nutrients is to provide the energy required by all life forms. As is well known, plants receive energy directly from the Sun, and, through the process of photosynthesis, use this energy, together with chemical nutrients in the soil, water, and atmosphere to generate cell growth and, as a byproduct, oxygen. Animals, however, are not able to obtain chemical energy directly from the Sun, although sunlight is important in enabling them to produce vitamin D and for maintaining the body temperature of reptiles. To gain access to chemical energy, which includes fats, protein, sugar, and cellulose, animals must consume plants or other animals that feed on plants. Because they use oxygen to break down plants, animals are more efficient in their quest of nutrients. This ability in turn has enabled later (or higher) life forms to exploit available resources by taking short cuts via specialization. Carnivores, for example, have avoided the necessity of devoting a large part of their brain capacity to organizing the production of essential fatty acids in their own bodies by eating herbivores who do that for them. This releases both brain capacity and time (eating grass literally takes all day) to be devoted to other activities – activities that include the biological development of more complex nervous systems to provide a competitive edge in the struggle for survival and, in the case of man, the cultural development of human society.

While this is well known, it has recently been given a new slant by Crawford and Marsh in *The Driving Force* (1989). They argue that chemical substances have always constituted an active, rather than a passive, factor in biological evolution. Indeed, as the title of their book suggests, they believe that the chemical conditions of life, and especially nutrition, amount to *the* driving force in life. Their argument, as will be explained in more detail in later chapters, is categorically rejected in this book. It is true that chemical substances provide the basic building blocks of life, but they determine only the universe of possible life forms that could exist on Earth, although not all at the same time because they are so numerous. The actual development path of life, however, depends upon the 'motivating' force of organisms together with the nature of competition between them. It is also true that chemical substances supply the nutrients required by organisms to sustain life, but it is the organisms that generate the demand for these nutrients and which, through a process of competition, develop strategies and tactics to maximize their access to these nutrients. One of these tactics involves specialization. Specialization of higher life forms (the players) is not directed by the supply of nutrients (part of the rules), rather it is a competitive tactic of the players in the game of life. There is ample evidence, as will be provided in later chapters, to show that supply-side forces, such as nutrients, are passive, while demand-side forces are active and dominant. Crawford and Marsh (1989) have presented a supply-side explanation, with no demand – and hence no driving-force – element.

Chemical substances and laws, therefore, are part of the rules of the game. The drive is provided by the players in a competitive environment. But, of course, there is an interaction between the players and the rules of life.

Forming an atmosphere

The atmosphere on Earth today, which currently supports an abundance of animal and plant life, is very different to the one in which the first primitive life emerged. That first atmosphere was probably provided both by volcanic gases and by icy objects drawn into Earth's gravitational field from outer space (Cloud, 1988: 39–40). The same is true of the hydrosphere. To retain both, the Earth had to be massive enough to provide sufficient gravitational force, and it had to maintain an orbital distance from the Sun that would neither vaporize the water content (or prevent carbon dioxide being absorbed from the atmosphere by the excessive formation of limestone and dolomite), nor turn it to ice. The balance is a delicate one, as can be seen from the inhospitably hot Venus and icy Mars.

The early (or Hadean) atmosphere was rich in carbon dioxide, water vapour, nitrogen, and various 'reduced gases', but lacked any free oxygen. It was, what is called, anoxic or neutral. Contrary to popular belief, this was just the atmosphere required for the emergence of life, because the oxidizing effect of oxygen is poisonous to life forms that have not had time to evolve complex processes of transporting small amounts of it around the body. Ultimately this was achieved in plants through chlorophyll and in animals through haemoglobin (Crawford and Marsh, 1989: 81). It is paradoxical that oxygen is both essential and highly poisonous to virtually all life currently on Earth.

It was in this anoxic environment that the first bacteria and, later, blue-green algae emerged and flourished for at least 2 billion years. This highly anaerobic life form, however, very gradually polluted its own environment by absorbing carbon dioxide and producing free oxygen by photosynthesis. It is also likely that some free oxygen was generated by photolysis, whereby transient oxygen is released by sunlight splitting water molecules (Cloud, 1988: 229). While free oxygen in the atmosphere was built up slowly at first, owing to its absorption by other chemical compounds it increased quite rapidly from about 700 to 370 million years ago, during which time animal life first appeared in the seas and finally made the transition to the land, and when blue-green algae went into rapid and permanent decline. In effect, the action of the first living forms changed the oxygen content of the atmosphere to the point where animal life could emerge from these early bacterial life forms.

The dynamics of the Earth

By 4.5 billion years ago, the Earth's crust had formed. The world's oldest rocks – discovered in the Pilbara region of Western Australia, the Baberton Mountains of Swaziland, the Morton Gneiss in Minnesota, and the volcanic rock of West Greenland – have been dated as 3.5 to 3.8 billion years old, while moon rocks analysed by US space probes are over 4 billion years old. Radiometric techniques, based upon the known rates of decay of radioactive atoms, have been used to divine the age of these ancient rock formations. By the time these rocks had been formed, the Earth had developed an iron core, and the dynamo motions in the molten outer sector of this core produced a magnetic field and a radiation-shielding magnetosphere (Cloud, 1988: 44).

While the Earth had been fully formed some 4 billion years ago, this was not the end of its development, only its beginning. It was not until about 700 million years ago (the end of the Proterozoic period) that the present continental mass (but not location) had been achieved, owing to the long process of mountain building and weathering. Indeed, the forces that had their origin in the Big Bang have continued to shape the Earth's physical character throughout the history of the planet. The Earth has an inner dynamic of its own. As the urbane geologist Preston Cloud has written, in poetic mood (ibid.: 117):

> If time can be said to flow, history can be said to pulse, to surge, to syncopate. And, while it is true that the prevailing rhythms and punctuating surges of Earth's crustal and biologic evolution denote the flow of planetary history at a given place or region, time continues unaffected.

The history of the Earth is ever-changing and it pulsates to the rhythms generated by the beginning of the Universe itself.

A study of the physical history of the Earth involves a study of plate tectonics – the changing location of the main landmasses or continents and the forces that move them. The continents drift, but not freely (ibid.: 215): 'Instead they ride on the backs of lithospheric plates as fixed and integral parts of those plates, their motions limited by tight packing and the rules of spherical geometry.' When this was first realized in the early to mid-1960s, the study of geology was revolutionized. The plates on the surface of the Earth move, grow, disappear, and slip past one another. In turn this changes the position, shape, and size of the continents; it transforms the oceans; it

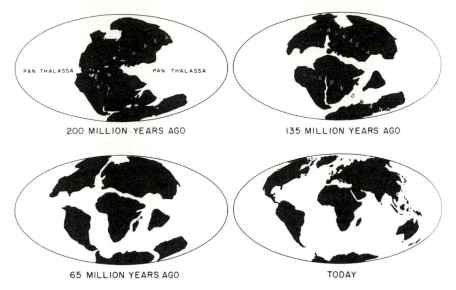

200 MILLION YEARS AGO

135 MILLION YEARS AGO

65 MILLION YEARS AGO

TODAY

Figure 2.1 Evolution of the continents

Source: R.S. Dietz and J.C. Holden, 'The breakup of Pangaea', *Scientific American*, 223(4), pp. 34, 36. Illustrations by Tom Prentiss. © Scientific American Inc., 1970. All rights reserved. Reproduced with permission.

produces folded mountains in the collision zones and volcanic mountains in the 'subduction' zones where one plate slips under another (e.g. the western coast of USA); and it generates earthquakes in these zones. All this is a result of the cooling of the Earth's interior by convection, which leads periodically to the upwelling of hot convection currents that come close to the surface. There are some geologists, like Preston Cloud (ibid.: 216), who see plate tectonics as providing a general theory of the changing Earth.

Possibly the most striking outcome of plate tectonics is the role of continental drift in isolating life forms for very long periods of time and then eventually bringing some of them back into contact again. For the past 3.3 billion years the continents have been emerging, drifting, and crashing into each other. Not long after animal life (jellyfish, seaworms, etc.) had emerged in the oceans, it is generally thought that a supercontinent called Gondwana – consisting of parts of what are now Australia, Antarctica (which straddled the Equator!), Arabia, Africa, and South America – was formed by plate tectonics. North America, Europe, and Asia were still separate entities. This was about 650 million years ago. By the time of the dinosaurs, say 200 million years ago, most of the world's landmass had been joined together (see Figure 2.1), to form the greatest supercontinent of them all – Pangaea, consisting of the ancient Gondwana and the newer Laurasia. With a single supercontinent came a single superocean, that has been called Panthalassa. From this high point in continent building, Pangaea began to break up again, creating a number of new and smaller oceans. By the time the dinosaurs had disappeared, about 65 million years ago, all the major continents had moved far apart, with the Americas moving towards each other, Africa closing in on Eurasia, India still some distance from the Asian mainland, and Australia drifting towards the Equator. Each continent carried a wide variety of fauna and flora passengers that were evolving in isolation, unaware of the fate that awaited them. About 15 to 20 million years later, the continents as we know them had largely come into being and the plant and animal species, including the primate ancestors of man, were confronting a range of new competitors. The rules of the game of life had rudely changed once more.

The mountain building associated with plate tectonics can be seen in Figure 2.2. This graph suggests that the main phases of mountain building were:

- 2,800 to 2,300 million years (myrs): this involved the first main phase of mountain building (equivalent to that in the modern period) associated with the building of the first supercontinent called Kenora, involving North America and Europe.
- 2,200 to 1,500 myrs: when the second supercontinent called Amazonia (South America) was formed.
- 1,400 to 800 myrs: when the third supercontinent, Baikalia (Asia), emerged.
- c.650 myrs: Gondwana.
- c.300 myrs: Laurasia.
- 300–200 myrs: Pangaea.
- 100–50 myrs: when the existing continents were being formed.

These changes are astonishing. But what we must remember is that they took place over a period of more than 3 billion years. Continental drift occurred very slowly and, accordingly, changes to the rules of the game of life took place equally slowly. Nevertheless, the changing physical environment produced changing landmasses that alternatively isolated and brought together different life forms; it changed the nature of the oceans; it created new mountain ranges, which were subsequently weathered away; and it changed local climates – all *very* gradually. While geologists such as Preston Cloud (1988: 399) see plate tectonics as the 'forcing factor' in biological change, I will argue that it merely amounted to a gradual change in the rules of the game. The only thing 'forcing' individual life forms to play this game was the overwhelming desire to survive. This came from within rather than without.

Climatic change

Plate tectonics together with variations in the Earth's orbit around the Sun have played an important role in shaping the climate of our evolving planet.

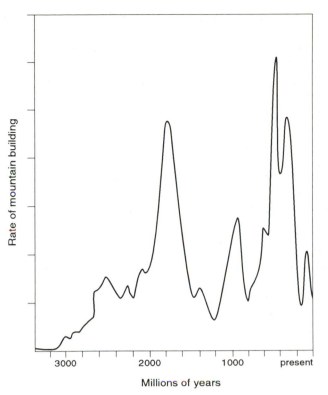

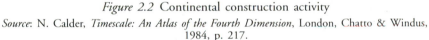

Figure 2.2 Continental construction activity

Source: N. Calder, *Timescale: An Atlas of the Fourth Dimension*, London, Chatto & Windus, 1984, p. 217.

While there are various approximate climatic chronologies detailing historical periods as hot/warm/cold and dry/humid/wet, these are a little tedious. In any case we need to be very careful about these generalizations. Rather than wading through a swamp of dates and climatic details, Figure 2.3, which shows the changing sea levels over the last 700 million years, provides a visual impression of climatic changes over very long periods of time. World temperatures, and hence length of growing season, are a mirror image of sea levels (Cloud, 1988: 324).

Climate defines the conditions under which the various animal species have lived and 'worked', together with the quantity and quality of land available for the hunting, gathering, and, later, the growing of food. The nature of the 'work' environment depended upon the rainfall, the temperatures, the level of the seas, the extent of the permanent snow fields and glaciation. For these reasons, the amount of suitable land available for 'production' contracted

31

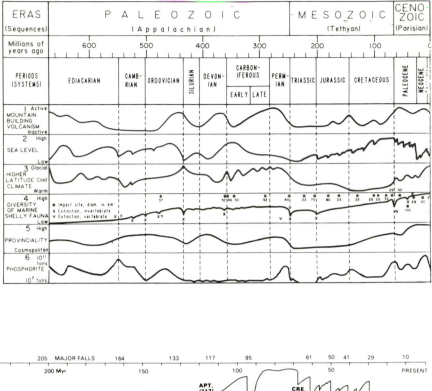

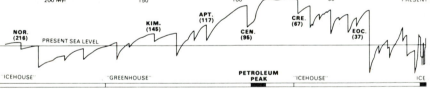

Figure 2.3 The changing rules of the game – the last 700 million years
(a) The physical conditions of life – the last 700 million years

Source: A.J. Boucot, 'Does evolution take place in a vacuum? II', *Journal of Paleontology*, 57(1), 1983, p. 8. Reproduced by permission of the secretary of the Paleontology Society (USA).

(b) Sea levels – the last 200 million years

Notes: 'The events marked with abbreviations are catastrophes or turnovers in life, namely the Norian, Kimmeridgian, Aptian, Cenomanian, Cretaceous terminal, and Eocene terminal; note that they were typically associated with minor falls in sea level. Data are from Exxon (P.R. Vail *et al.*) with dates adjusted to conform with the geological time-scale adopted here. The 123 Myr event is added (Gulf Oil). The heights of the sea are not precisely specified, but they ranged about two hundred metres above and below the present sea level.'

Source: N. Calder, *Timescale: An Atlas of the Fourth Dimension*, London, Chatto & Windus, 1984, p. 276. Reproduced by permission of the Author.

during the colder drier periods and expanded during the warmer wetter periods. Changes in climate, therefore, changed the rules of the game of life.

The general picture provided by Figure 2.3a suggests that over the last 700 million years – the period during which animal life first emerged and developed to the stage where it could reflect upon its origins – the wavelike motion of the world's seas achieved five peaks at about 650, 570, 450, 350, and 90 million years ago. These were the warmer wetter periods in the planet's history – considerably more so than at present. These fluctuations do not appear highly correlated with the development of life on Earth, particularly during the long decline (100 million years) into the cold era from about 340 to 240 million years before present (BP) when animal life, both in the sea and on the land, was growing rapidly in diversity and in extent.

Greater detail about sea-level changes during the last 200 million years is provided in the 'seascape' presented in Figure 2.3b. From around 240 million years BP – the low point in the longest cold period in the planet's history – sea levels rose gradually until about 110 million years BP, then increased more rapidly to a plateau between 90 to 67 million years BP (when they were 200 to 300 metres higher than at present), gradually fell to 29 million years BP, then declined suddenly to a level similar to that at the present, albeit with 'short' sharp fluctuations.

The usual argument that changing sea levels – indeed of climate generally – constituted a 'forcing factor' in the changes of life on Earth is not very persuasive. While these changes may have provided difficulties for some species and advantages for others, they took place over such long periods of time that it is hard to imagine that they would have had a major determining influence on life. These changes constitute a very gradual change in the rules of the game, not the driving force which comes from the individual life forms. A further interesting point concerns the current debate about a possible greenhouse effect. The last 30 million years have been a relatively cold period with relatively low sea levels. As we have seen, the preceding 100 million years were much warmer with far higher sea levels. This suggests that any possible future problem will be economic rather than biological – it is not a question about ability to adapt, but the economic cost of doing so in a relatively short period of time.

To examine the environmental background to the age of mankind, we need to focus more closely upon climatic change over the past 3 million years. During this period there have been thirty-five separate episodes that have been called 'ice ages', which have alternated in a cyclical manner with contrasting warmer periods. The last of these ice ages occurred between 72 and 10.3 thousand years ago, with interludes of milder weather. Figure 2.4 provides a picture of the changing sea levels over the past 135,000 years. The warmer period that saw the rise of agriculture and the civilization based upon it – the last 10,000 years – is comparable to that about 120,000 years ago. In between, particularly cold periods included the following (years BP): 110,000; 87,000;

33

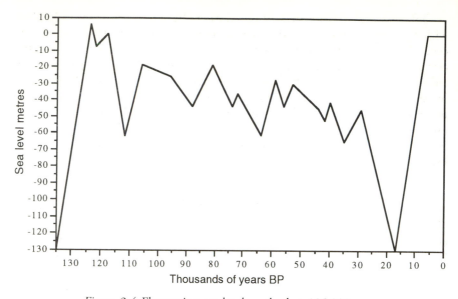

Figure 2.4 Fluctuating sea levels – the last 135,000 years

Source: N.G. Butlin, 'The palaeoeconomic history of Aboriginal migration', *Australian Economic History Review*, 30(1), 1989, p.92. © Economic History Society of Australia and New Zealand, 1990. Reproduced by permission of the editor.

75,000–65,000; 55,000; 42,000; 35,000; and particularly 17,000. The significance of these periods of lower sea levels lies in the opportunities they provided for man and animals to travel more easily from landmasses previously separated by the seas (e.g. Southeast Asia–Australia and Siberia–Alaska). While the return of warmer weather during the last 10 millennia coincided with the Neolithic Revolution, I will argue that endogenous forces – the pressure of population on natural resources, and the accumulation of technological change – were more important to human society.

More recently – 10,000 years ago to the present – climate can be briefly sketched as follows: after a warmer spell at the end of the last ice age, there was a sharp cooling about 5,800 years BP, then a sharp warming about 4,900 years BP, followed by a long cool period until around 1,000 years ago (Calder, 1984: 214–15). Cycles are like Russian dolls, there is always a shorter-term series within each episode of the longer-term series. The last millennium is no exception: the period AD 950 to AD 1100 was relatively warm enabling, amongst other things, the settlement of Greenland; there was a distinct cold phase, following moderate fluctuations, in the mid-fifteenth century; this was followed by another warmer period from 1470 to 1560; then from 1560 until 1850 there was the 'little ice age' (Loyn, 1989: 93; Grove, 1990). Since the mid-nineteenth century we have enjoyed a warmer climatic phase.

Only some of the warmer phases during the last millennium coincided with upswings in European GDP per capita during the eleventh and sixteenth centuries. The obvious contradiction is the Industrial Revolution – which also involved an unprecedented increase in agricultural productivity – coinciding as it did with the 'little ice age'. There is no doubt that fluctuations in climate did influence agricultural labour productivity, but this had only a marginal influence on endogenous (internal) changes. Probably the main outcome was the change in the type of agricultural commodities grown – sure evidence of the adaptive abilities of humanity. The driving force came from within human society.

Natural catastrophe

Natural catastrophe, which includes both large-scale volcanic eruptions and cosmic impacts, is a favourite explanation of those who see life on Earth as being driven by random physical events. The argument in this book, however, is that although major cataclysmic events acted as external shocks on living systems, these living systems possess a dynamic of their own, driven by individual organisms operating within competitive environments. Even without external shocks these living systems would have produced cycles based upon the exploitation and exhaustion of dynamic strategies.

Over the past 250 million years, there appear to have been two major volcanic events that could be regarded as cataclysmic. The first occurred at the beginning of this period – at a time when the supercontinent Pangaea was forming – in what is now known as Siberia. A huge outpouring of lava has left its traces in the basaltic rocks that form the Siberian Traps adjoining Lake Baikal, which are several kilometres thick and about 2,500 kilometres wide. These are the largest of all flood basalts on Earth. The argument advanced by natural scientists is that the dust and sulphur particles thrown high into the air during these eruptions not only blocked out the Sun causing climatic cooling – and hence an expansion of polar ice and a falling of sea levels – but also caused acid rain. Both had potentially harmful effects upon life on the land and in the seas (Campbell *et al.*, 1992).

The other great volcanic event is supposed to have occurred about 65 million years ago in what is now India, when it was an island continent midway between Africa and its future destiny with Asia. Although not on the same scale as the Siberian eruptions, it did leave a great pile of basalt rock known as the Deccan Traps which covers an area in excess of 1 million square kilometres (Crawford and Marsh, 1989: 139). Similar claims have been made for its impact on climate and its destruction of life (50 per cent of all species), including the extinction of the dinosaurs.

Lesser volcanic events have taken place since the end of the age of the dinosaurs. For example, 16 myrs in central Oregon; 14 myrs in the Hawaiian chain and elsewhere; and 4 to 3 myrs globally. During the age of man the largest single eruption appears to have been in Sumatra 73,000 years ago, which threw 100 times as much dust into the air as the eruption at Krakatoa in AD 1883. Further large eruptions, which possibly caused some climatic cooling, occurred 9,640 years ago (unidentified), 6,400 years ago in Oregon, and 3,470 years ago in the Aegean Sea near Crete (Calder, 1984: 285). More recent were the eruptions of Vesuvius in Italy in AD 79, Fuji in Japan in 1707, Tambora in Indonesia in 1815 (the largest since that in Oregon some 7,000 years earlier), Mt St Helens 1842–1857, Krakatoa in Indonesia 1883, Mt Katmai in Alaska in 1912, and relatively minor events since, mainly at Mt St Helens (Cloud, 1988: 462). The more recent eruptions had only local effects.

Cosmic impacts also have the potential to cause considerable damage and to affect the climate by the blanketing dust thrown into the atmosphere. It has been suggested that asteroids a kilometre wide hit the Earth, on average, every 250,000 years; those 5 kilometres wide impact every 20 million years; and those 15 kilometres wide impact every 100 million years. The destructive potential of these rare cosmic events is conveyed in the suggestion (Calder, 1984: 219) that the impact of a kilometre asteroid would be equivalent to a 100,000 megaton explosion of TNT, which would blast out a crater about 20 kilometres in diameter.

With this benchmark in mind, we can conclude from the available evidence on crater size (conveniently summarized by Calder, ibid.: 219–20) that no asteroid larger than 1 kilometre appears to have fallen on the land surface of the Earth in the last 10 to 15 million years. During this relatively recent period, there have been noticeably large impacts at Bosumtivi in Africa (1.3 myrs), Australasia (730,000 years ago), Arizona (25,000 years) with the largest crater of 1.2 kilometres, and Siberia (Tunguska) with an impact equivalent to 12 megatons of TNT (AD 1908).

From the beginning of Earth down to 15 million years BP, many large comets and asteroids hit the land surface. The impact of a live comet is even greater than a 'dead' asteroid, because of the greater speed of the collision. Before 3.9 billion years BP the Earth had to withstand a barrage of cosmic impacts, which thereafter abated. The main evidence is available from about 2.0 billion years ago with craters of up to 140 kilometres wide. There are also suggestions, based not upon craters but upon thin worldwide layers of the rare element iridium, that cosmic impacts were particularly prevalent about 65 million years ago, when dinosaurs vanished from the fossil record (Alvarez *et al.*, 1980), and possibly 250 million years ago when over 60 per cent of all species on Earth appear to have died (Rampino, 1992). In fact, Rampino has gone to the unnecessary extreme of suggesting that a gigantic bombardment of the Earth by cosmic bodies may even have been responsible for breaking up the supercontinent Gondwana and for precipitating the Siberian eruption – unnecessary because the forces of plate tectonics are

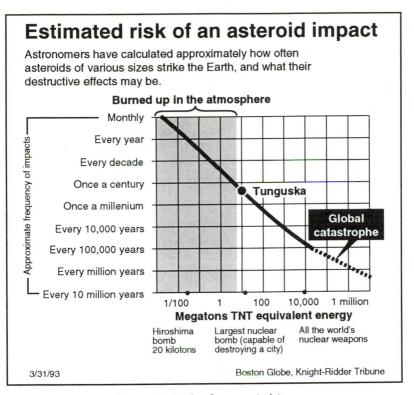

Figure 2.5 Risk of an asteriod impact
Source: *Boston Globe*, 31 March 1993. Reprinted courtesy of the Boston Globe.

sufficient cause. Also the use of iridium as evidence of asteroid impact is flawed, because this rare element is also associated with volcanic eruptions.

It is interesting that other scientists (such as David Morrison) at NASA's Ames Research Centre are now (March 1993) using these asteroid theories to argue that in order to avoid similar problems from a 'doomsday rock', the US needs to spend $US200 million over the next twenty years to study the problem. Figure 2.5, which is based upon data concerning asteroid impacts in the past, has been employed by natural scientists to extrapolate their doomsday message into the future. It is unlikely that a similar sum of money will ever be devoted to the more serious problem of the internal dynamics of life – a problem, as we shall see, which has been largely responsible for the destruction of the major life forms on Earth over the last 3 billion years and could well cause the destruction of life in the future.

It is fascinating to reflect that the natural sciences play host to the same arguments as the social sciences about the importance of exogenous and endogenous forces. The late Preston Cloud, as we have seen, was an enthusiastic advocate of the idea that the planet Earth possesses an internal rhythm, centred on the physical forces driving plate tectonics, which is suffi-cient to explain the 'drift' of continents, mountain building, volcanic action, and even climate. In his view of the evolving planet, cosmic events are only random shocks which have been responsible for a mere 10 per cent of changes to life on Earth (Cloud, 1988: 402). Clearly, there are other natural scientists, such as Walter Alvarez and Michael Rampino, who believe that random cosmic events have driven the Earth's major physical changes. What they have in common is the belief that physical events drive biological develop-ment. In a similar way, there are social scientists who maintain that human society is driven by external forces, such as environmental conditions and disease – that society is the plaything of forces beyond the boundaries of human influence. The 'cosmic' view, whether held by natural or social scien-tists, is rejected in this book in favour of endogenously driven biological life and human society, albeit one subject from time to time to external shocks. Life is not just a straw in the wind.

Social contracts

A fundamental distinction must be made between the basic physical rules that provide the foundations for the game of life and the agreements reached between players as to how the game should be played. The physical conditions of life are exogenously determined and are largely independent of the game, whereas social contracts are developed by the players to facilitate the strategies and tactics they adopt to achieve their common and individual objectives. Unlike the physical rules, these social agreements have no existence indepen-dently of the strategies and tactics that they are designed to facilitate. They are not binding rules in the same sense as the physical conditions of life.

Social contracts take a variety of explicit and implicit forms. Explicit agree-ments that influence the interaction between individuals include the consti-tution of a society, its political and legal system, its system of property rights, and its system of rules regulating the interaction of buyers and sellers in markets for commodities (rules concerning tariffs, subsidies, prices, trade practices, and transport arrangements) and for factors (rules concerning wages, immigration, land ownership and sales, financial arrangements, foreign investment, federal–state financial relations). And implicit agreements include unwritten conventions, traditions, and codes of behaviour that are adopted by human agents. As these social contracts are employed to facilitate the changing strategies of decision-makers, they vary quite considerably over time and space. For this reason they cannot be listed separately in detail. Nor should they be viewed apart from the human strategies and tactics that gave rise to them.

Of central importance to the game of life are the strategies adopted by opposing teams. These strategies, which are the central focus of the book, are a response to the physical conditions of life. They change as the game progresses owing to a fundamental interaction between human agents and the Earth's natural resources. And as the strategies change, so too do the agreements between the players. It is the strategies that come first. While the primary objective of the players is to work together to win the game – it is the only way individuals can achieve their objectives – they also strive for individual glory within the team in order to gain a greater than average share of the rewards going to the winning side. Particularly ambitious and skilful individuals employ a range of tactics not only in an attempt to maintain their dominance but also to challenge dominant individuals. These tactics define the relationships between the team's leaders and its followers.

The strategies and tactics adopted by the players to exploit the physical rules, the opposition, and each other determine the dynamics of the game – how the game develops over time. And it is this fundamental dynamic process that drives the change in social contracts of various kinds between the players. Accordingly, this book will focus on the fundamental dynamics of the game rather than on the changing agreements between the players. It is essential to discover the nature and role of the dynamic strategies and dynamic tactics before exploring the interaction between them and the resulting social contracts. That interaction is the subject of a further work.

NOTE

1 This conclusion is based upon well-established estimates of the Hubble constant – the relationship between the velocity at which galaxies are receding and their distance – giving a range of 8–20 billion years since the Big Bang; and upon estimates of the age – 15 billion years – of the oldest stars. (Throughout the book 1 billion = 1,000 million.) Recently (*Nature*, 27 October 1994) the refurbished Hubble space telescope has provided new data to revise the Hubble constant, which suggests that the Big Bang occurred 8–12 billion years ago – somewhat less than the current estimate of the age of the oldest stars. If this new estimate of the Hubble constant is confirmed, the story we tell about the Big Bang may change once more. This should not surprise us as we have been continuously modifying our explanation of life over the past 45,000 years.

3

PLAYERS IN THE GAME

Struggling to utter the voice of Man.

(Blake, *Vala*, 1797)

The game has been declared. Bring on the players. For without the players, who make up that endless parade of life passing through aeons of time, the story about the game of life would never have been told around the campfires. While the physical conditions of the planet provide the rules for the game of life, they neither guarantee that the game will ever be played, nor determine how it will be played. That is up to the players, who provide the game with its vitality, enterprise, and enthusiasm. The players give life and, more particularly, human society, its dynamic quality. From their struggle arose the voice of Man.

The pattern of life on Earth is constantly changing. And in the variety and brilliant beauty of its forms, life is truly kaleidoscopic. It began billions of years ago as single cellular bacterium in the primeval seas, gradually increasing in complexity as it struggled for survival against a hostile physical environment and other predatory life forms. In these fertile seas plant forms gave rise to animal forms and, as the available resources became increasingly exploited, both began to colonize the land. On the land, in the face of fierce competition, all life forms continued to change, but it was the animal branch that proved to be more flexible and to offer greater scope for development. Eventually, about 2 to 3 million years ago, there emerged from this endless struggle for survival a large-brained primate which began to fashion tools and, much later, to use speech in exploiting its environment. Once all the natural resources available to it through the traditional practices of hunting and gathering had been exhausted, mankind began to domesticate the surrounding plant and animal life, to store surplus food, to build villages, and to develop complex urban cultures. Technological progress, however, proved to be elusive and did not become dominant again until some 10,000 years later with the Industrial Revolution and beyond. But when it came again it came to stay. This eternal dynamic quality is bestowed by the players in the game of life.

40

THE EMERGENCE OF LIFE ON EARTH

It is generally accepted that life on Earth began about 4 billion years ago, although the oldest fossil evidence for stromatolites – colonies of bacteria – suggests a date of about 3.5 billion years ago (Cloud, 1988: 42). The dominant life form prior to the emergence of animals was the so-called blue-green algae (a type of bacteria), which can be found in the fossil record between 2.0 and 2.8 billion years ago. Blue-green algae evolved from the early eubacteria and gradually spread throughout the primeval seas, apparently reaching a peak around 1.0 billion years ago, before the oxygen they produced by photosynthesis sent them into permanent decline (Crawford and Marsh, 1989: 66). The increase in free oxygen down through aeons of time is charted approximately in Figure 3.1.

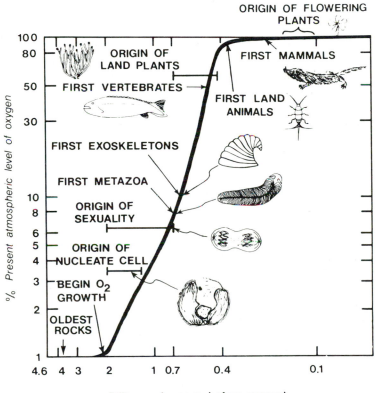

Figure 3.1 Build-up of Earth's free oxygen

Source: P. Cloud, *Oasis in Space: Earth History from the Beginning*, NY/London, W.W. Norton & Co. © Preston Cloud, 1988. Reproduced by permission of Janice G. Cloud, executor.

41

With the increase in free oxygen, to about 3 per cent of the present level, the nucleate or eukaryotic cell emerged from the single prokaryotic cellular blue-green algae. The nucleate cell is more complex than the prokaryotic cell, possessing functionally specialized subcellular units separated by membranes. While the eukaryotic cells were the foundations of later and higher life forms, they appear to have played a minor role in life until the blue-green algae went into a relatively sudden decline from about 1,000 million years ago. Both developments were largely a function of the level of oxygen – about 8 per cent of the present level – required for the rapid growth of plant and animal life (which separated about this time), and of a decline in competition for chemicals on the part of blue-green algae which were poisoned by a level of oxygen over about 6 per cent. The first true multicellular plants, called metaphytes, were the micro-seaweeds that appeared around 1.3 billion years ago, and the larger seaweeds about 1.0 billion years ago. Animals (metazoa) did not emerge in the primeval seas until about 700 million years BP, but then gained momentum as the Earth's free oxygen level rose more steeply. At this time the seas swarmed with the earliest animals including jellyfish, corals, molluscs, echinoderms, trilobites, orthopods, brachiopods, beard worms, moss animals, and sponges. The first vertebrates – jawless fishes – appeared at about 510 myrs (with an oxygen level about 50 per cent of the present), which in turn gave rise to the jawed fishes that eventually emerged from the seas as amphibians at about 370 myrs, when the oxygen level was more than 80 per cent of that at the present. Primitive reptiles – with water-retaining skins, more efficient jaws, and the ability to lay eggs – evolved from a branch of the amphibians at about 313 myrs, which in turn gave rise to: mammal-like reptiles, a small branch of which evolved into true mammals at about 216 myrs when oxygen levels were about the same as at present; and to land dinosaurs at about 235 myrs, and to airborne reptiles, some of which developed into true birds at about 150 myrs. With the touch of drama that one might have expected from such wonderfully bizarre creatures, the dinosaurs and winged reptiles disappeared about 65 myrs ago.

After the mass dinosaur extinction, mammals developed rapidly from the ancestral type which is sometimes described as a small shrew-like animal. This was the age of the mammals. By 125 myrs, the pouched marsupials had hopped off from the ancestors of the placental mammals, just in time to be isolated in South America, until it joined up with North America at about 3 myrs, and Australia, until it approached Southeast Asia making possible the immigration of man (about 60,000 years ago) and the dingo (about 4,000 years ago). The modern placental mammals appear to have originated in Asia at about 114 myrs and migrated into Europe and the Americas. It is usually argued that hoofed mammals diverged at about 100 myrs, preprimates at about 95 myrs, and the ancestors of carnivores and bats by 90 myrs ago. Of the preprimates, rodents and lagomorphs (hares and rabbits) separated from the primate line at about 85 myrs.

Not surprisingly, our interest in this Genesis-like genealogy grows as the evolutionary process approaches closer to our own line. The first fossil primates have been dated at 69 myrs, before the final extinction of the dinosaurs, at about the time premonkeys split from prosimians (lemurs). At about 35 myrs the premonkey lines split into Old World and New World monkeys, while ancestral apes diverged from Old World monkeys at 21 myrs; the ancestral apes saw off the lesser apes at 12 to 16 myrs, the orangutans at 10 myrs, and the chimpanzees and gorillas at 5 myrs (some – Easteal, 1995 – wish to reduce this to 3.5–4 myrs).

Now to our own family tree. The fossilized *Dryopithecus* is probably the common ancestor of modern pongids (apes) and hominids (ape-man and man). This ancestral ape, which flourished over a wide territory in Kenya, Hungary, Greece, Turkey, and India, emerged over 20 million years ago and disappeared outside Africa at about 5 myrs. Only in East Africa did it evolve, at about 4.4 myrs, into a more advanced form – the ape-man *Australopithecus*, which suggests how precarious the line of succession to modern man has been. Finally, man (*Homo habilis*) evolved from ape-man at about 2–3 myrs. In turn, *Homo habilis* gave rise to *Homo erectus* (1.6 myrs), to *Homo sapiens neanderthalensis* (120,000 years), and *Homo sapiens sapiens* (100,000 years).

The development of life on Earth, therefore, appears to have gone through a number of distinct long-term phases. Four major phases can be identified after primitive bacteria-like organisms first emerged about 4 billion years ago: the 1.6 billion years dominated by blue-green algae (until about 1,000 myrs); the 600 million years following the decline of blue-green algae, which was dominated by the expansion of animal life in the sea and on the land; the 185 million years after the mass extinction of early animal life at about 245 myrs, which was dominated by reptiles and, later, dinosaurs on the land, in the seas, and in the air; and, finally, the 60 million years following the extinction of the dinosaurs, which was dominated by birds, mammals, and, lastly, man. These phases of life are examined in greater detail in Chapter 4, which is concerned with the dynamic processes of life.

These are the major phases of life that have dominated the Earth. It is of interest to see if a macrobiological view, say in terms of number of either species or families, confirms this general great-wave pattern that we have discerned in the evidence of biological change. The most sensitive measure of what we are looking for would be the number of species (weighted by the number of individuals), but, as far as I am aware, the best measures we have are the numbers of families of marine and land animals, as shown in Figure 3.2. Our timescape of life is really a picture showing the fluctuating diversity of life over the past 700 million years. There was little diversity before that time owing to the dominance of blue-green algae. What our timescape shows is, as expected, a number of surges in the diversity of life:

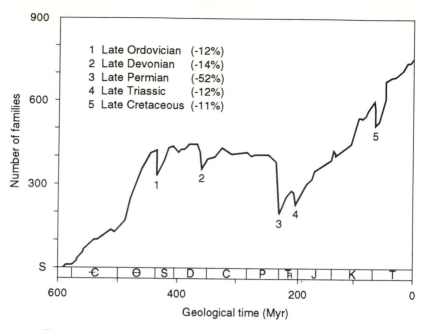

Figure 3.2 Family numbers for marine and land organisms – the last
800 million years
(a) Marine organisms

Source: D.M. Raup and J.J. Sepkoski, 'Mass extinctions in the marine fossil record',
Science, vol. 215 (19 March 1992), p. 1502. Reproduced with permission.

between 670 and 245 myrs, which was terminated by a sharp decline in the number of families (which was even greater in terms of the number of species); a new phase from 245 to 65 myrs, which was also more distinct in terms of numbers of species; and a final very rapid phase of growth of biological diversity over the last 65 million years. As we have seen before, there are cycles within cycles, with troughs at 435 myrs, 370 myrs, 215 myrs, 25 myrs, and 2 myrs. It is to be hoped that, in terms of biological diversity, life on Earth will not end as it began, under the suffocating influence of one dominant species.

Buried within these major phases of biological change, which are characterized by a competitive struggle between the dominant species and the species that would be dominant, is a struggle *within* individual life forms. This is a hidden struggle between antibodies within individuals of the dominant species, and the invaders of inner-space called micro-organisms. This struggle is known by man as disease. While the ravages of disease are popularly thought of as an external force – a little like the impact of volcanoes and

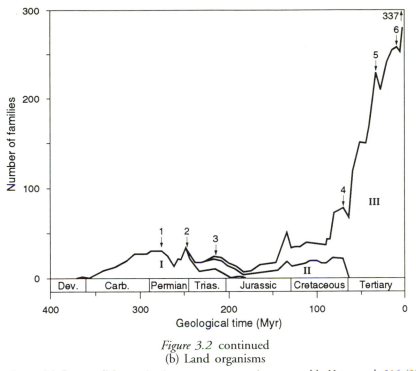

Figure 3.2 continued
(b) Land organisms

Source: M. Benton, 'Mass extinction among non-marine tetrapods', *Nature*, vol. 316 (29 August 1985), p. 811. Reproduced with permission.

asteroids – they are, in fact, part of the struggle for survival between different life forms. Because we cannot see this struggle taking place – at least not without the assistance of the microscope – the assumption often made (particularly by social scientists) is that it is external to the dynamics of life. In fact, this hidden struggle plays its part in the fluctuating fortunes of dominant species and may even be involved in determining the major phases of biological change.

The invisible invaders include particular forms of bacteria, viruses, and micro-parasites that attack the cells of most higher life forms. As we have seen, bacteria, which are microscopic unicellular plants, have a very long history of life on Earth. Their ancestors were the dominant form of life for the planet's first few billion years, and they have adapted a little too well to a world dominated by higher animal life forms. Viruses are very simple organisms that are even smaller than bacteria, consisting mainly of nucleic acid clothed by a coat of protein, and can exist only within living cells. Curiously, in the first great outburst of life, viruses were the bane of the dominant forms of bacteria. While man has recently learnt to destroy bacteria with penicillin and more advanced antibiotics, viruses can only be eliminated by the body's natural defences, although these can be stimulated by natural or artificial exposure to the virus in non-lethal doses. What we rather loosely call 'disease', therefore, is an important, if invisible, player in the game of life, and should not be associated with the inorganically derived rules of life discussed in Chapter 2.

THE ASCENT OF MAN

The transition from early ape-man, who had a brain capacity no larger than that of modern chimpanzees, to modern man, who has a-brain capacity some 3.4 times larger, in just 4.4 million years, is truly remarkable. The time taken for the ascent of man is only a fraction (about 0.1 per cent) of the period of life on Earth, or even of the time that the dinosaurs existed (about 2.6 per cent). Quite clearly, the momentum of evolution has been accelerating – a theme to which we shall return in the next chapter. The story of the ascent of man is now known in general outline, but there is room for genuine disagreement at the detailed level. It is a story that is continuously changing at a rapid rate as new discoveries are made. Even the version told here has gone through a number of revisions during the writing of this book.

It is important to realize that a number of branches of ape-men emerged some 4.4 million years ago, and that they all paid the penalty of failing to continue to develop – ultimate extinction, almost certainly at the hands of more advanced hominids. While today more advanced technology is employed as a weapon of war, in the beginning more advanced genetics served the same purpose. The most recent palaeoanthropological discovery (White *et al.*, 1994) suggests that the earliest ape-man, *Australopithecus ramidus*, with a brain capacity no larger than a modern chimpanzee, emerged in Ethiopia from the modern pongids (apes) about 4.4 million years ago, and was displaced by *Australopithecus afarensis* ('Lucy') 1 million years later. *Australopithecus afarensis*, with a brain capacity about 8 per cent greater than that of a chimpanzee, disappeared from the fossil record about 2.5 million years ago, after living for 1 million years in East Africa. His successor (although this distinction has been debated) *Australopithecus africanus* appears to have given rise to three main branches of hominids, *Australopithecus robustus* in South Africa and *Australopithecus boisei* in East Africa – both about 3 million years ago – and *Homo habilis* about 2–3 million years ago. The former two branches of ape-men disappeared not long after *Homo habilis* emerged, as did *Australopithecus africanus* itself (Eccles, 1989: 20). The coincidence is too great to ignore. Early humans in competing aggressively for natural resources almost certainly eliminated their rivals, who had failed to develop further during their 1 million years or so in Africa. As *Australopithecus africanus* numbered probably only a few thousand at any point in time (ibid.: 95), this would not have been difficult to achieve for a new form of ape with a brain capacity about 40 per cent greater than its rivals. This struggle for resources, with the winner taking all, is a continuing theme throughout the story of life on Earth. The chapter on mankind is no different.

In his discussion of the transition from ape-man to man, John Eccles (1989: 21, 23) writes:

> What can we say in our obituary notice for *Australopithecus africanus*? After its initial great success with its bipedal walking, and all the advantages and dangers of this terrestrial life, it lapsed into an evolutionary stasis . . . Its extinction would have been the end of hominid evolution. Survival was enough, and, to wait for the dawn of a genetic revolution, the origin of the large-brained *Homo habilis*.

But this waiting for a second coming was the waiting for extinction at the hand of the transcendent being – the first in the line of man.

The first true human beings, *Homo habilis*, appear to have emerged in East Africa about 2–3 million years ago. Unlike *Australopithecus africanus*, who also walked on two legs, *Homo habilis* used small chipped flakes of stone to cut the flesh from dead animals, for they were scavengers rather than hunters. While their brain capacity was about 40 per cent greater than that of the last ape-men, it was still only half the size of that of modern humans, and far less complex (ibid.: 15, 21). Nevertheless, the structure of the economy and society of early man bore a close resemblance to that of modern man before the neolithic age, and of hunter–gatherer societies down to the present. They formed small kinship groups in which the males supplied meat through competition with other scavengers, and the females gathered fruit, nuts, and roots (Calder, 1984: 140–1; Leakey and Lewin, 1992). Specialization according to comparative advantage, which is the foundation of modern society, was well established in the primitive society of early mankind.

Homo habilis dominated its habitat for up to 800,000 years – only 33 per cent of the reign of the ape-men, but longer than the presence of modern humans by a factor of 8 – before it was supplanted by *Homo erectus*, who appears in the fossil record in eastern Africa at least by 1.6 million years ago. Once again there was a significant increase in brain size – this time by about 37 per cent over *Homo habilis* – but, more importantly, the structure of the brain had become more complex, particularly in the area of problem-solving and primitive language (Eccles, 1989: 95). This growing complexity can be seen in mankind's new role – that of hunter rather than scavenger. It was a change as revolutionary in the history of mankind, and of life, as the much later development of agriculture about 10,600 years BP. This new role is reflected in the new tools fashioned and adopted by 'upright' man. In addition to small cutting flakes, *Homo erectus* employed a hand axe with a deadly looking point and, from about 1.4 myrs, used fire for cooking and perhaps to encourage the extension of new grasslands. These stone tools, together with wooden spears, were used to hunt large game such as rhinos, elephants, bison, and horses – and, no doubt, *Homo habilis* as well as each other. In this way they were able to survive in relatively small numbers over a range of climates, from tropical to glacial, and of geographical territories, from mountains to plains. Even major changes in climate, such as the ice ages, did not pose insurmountable problems. They played the game of life with distinction.

After these major developments in the human economy, little further technological change appears in the fossil record for the next million years. But this does not mean that human society was static. As can be seen from Table 3.1, population increased gradually from about 125,000 people 1 million years ago, to about 1 million people before *Homo erectus* was succeeded by *Homo sapiens* about 300,000 years ago. And in the process, mankind spread throughout Africa, Asia (1 myrs), Europe (0.45 myrs), and Australia (0.06 myrs). This has been called the 'great dispersion', and was a major achievement in itself. In the following chapters I will argue that this geographical expansion of *Homo erectus* was the response of a dynamic and competitive society to the abundant supply of unused natural resources that were made available by the new hunting technology. They did not improve their technology because they did not need to improve it to expand their families at an acceptable standard of living even under competitive conditions. They just moved into new regions. It was not until these natural resources were fully used, that competitive pressures built up to the point where human tribes could only survive if they had the advantage of new 'ideas', either genetic or technological.

A major breakthrough finally came about 300,000 years ago when the prototype of modern man, 'archaic' *Homo sapiens*, first emerged in Europe, probably as a result of growing competition for big game in smaller isolated valleys or regions. Archaic man had a larger (by about one-third), more complex brain than *Homo erectus*, and this was applied to the manufacture of more efficient stone tools (using the Levallois technique which extracted long flints from within a suitable rock), to a greater control over the animals they hunted, and to a greater management of their living environment (Calder, 1984: 151). The change in lifestyle is reflected in the changing facial features of *Homo sapiens* (archaic), who had a smaller jaw and teeth. Once again the old version of *Homo* disappears from the fossil record when the new version establishes itself.

With greater intellectual ability, modern humans were able to exploit their environment more effectively than did their predecessors. As they were able to compete more effectively with non-human species, their numbers grew more rapidly, which in turn placed greater pressure more quickly on natural resources. Hence the next breakthrough did not take over a million years, as it had between *Homo erectus* and *Homo sapiens* (archaic), but only 180,000 years. Around 120,000 years ago, a surprisingly large-brained version of *Homo sapiens* called *Neanderthalensis* (Neanderthal man) appeared in Europe. While

Table 3.1 World population estimates for the species *Homo* –
the last million years (millions)

Year	(1)	(2)	(3)	(4)
−1000000	0.125	0.125	0.125	
−100000	1	1	1	
−23000	3.34	3.34	3.34	
−10000	4	4	4	
−8000	7.5	7.5	7.5	
−4000		7	86.5	
−3000		14		
−2000		27		
−1000		50		
−500		100		
−200		150		153
1	250	170	133	225
200		190		252
400	250	190		257
500		190		206
600	237	200		207
700		210		208
800	261	220		206
900		240		224
1000	280	265		222
1100		320		253
1200	384	360		299
1300		360		400
1340	378			417
1400		350		431
1500	427	425		442
1600	500	545		375
1650	545	545	545	461
1700		610		578
1750	770	720	728	
1800	900	900	906	680
1850	1,200	1,200		771
1900	1,668	1,625	1,610	954
1920	1,811			1,241
1930	2,070			1,634
1940	2,295			
1950	2,516	2,500		
1955			2,400	
1960	3,020			2,530
1965	3,336			
1970	3,698			
1975	4,079	3,900		
1980	4,448			3,637
1985	4,851			
1990	5,292			

Sources: (1) Composite of Calder (1984), Cipolla (1974), Clark
(1977), Durand (1977), Livi-Bacci (1992), and UN (1973)
(2) McEvedy and Jones (1978)
(3) Deevey (1960)
(4) Biraben (1979)

its brain was about 10 per cent larger than that of modern man it was not as complex – it did not have our analytical or language power. These people, who were strong, stocky, and big boned, were able to adapt easily to the last ice age that began about 72,000 years ago. Neanderthal family groups dwelt in caves and were accomplished big-game hunters. They also developed a conspicuous culture, decorating themselves and their caves, and burying their dead with care and with ritual. The fact that they were the first humans to bury their dead in this way suggests that they were also the first to begin to form questions in their minds – as they probably did not have the power of fluent speech – about life, death, and the universe. Theirs was a difficult but a manageable and satisfying life. Neanderthal man took life in his stride, but he did not strive for more.

Life for Neanderthal man was shattered about 50,000 years ago when out of the south came a frightening new group of men – *Homo sapiens sapiens* or modern man. With our more complex brain, that conferred greater analytical power and the power over fluent speech, modern man appears to have reached Europe about 35,000 years ago, overwhelming Neanderthal man there within about 1,000 years. Yet again the old version disappears in the fossil record at the same time that the new version arrives. Neanderthal society paid dearly for its complacency, only dominating its habitat for about 90,000 years – half that achieved by *Homo erectus*. The acceleration of genetic change appears to have been a function of mankind's growing 'control' over nature, which permitted a more rapid growth of population. In turn this quickened the pace by which natural resource use achieved full exploitation with a given level of genetic/technological 'ideas'.

Modern man, according to many anthropologists, emerged in Africa about 100,000 years ago, and gradually spread out from there to replace all earlier species in the rest of the world (Groves, 1994). Some molecular biologists using mitochondrial DNA rather than fossil remains (Penny *et al.*, 1994) and some linguists (Nichols, 1994) have recently argued that this may have occurred some 200,000 years ago. In contradistinction to this 'replacement' hypothesis, some anthropologists (Thorne and Raymond, 1989) claim that Africa was not the only source of origin for modern man. *Homo erectus*, they argue, not only spread around the accessible world, but also evolved separately into modern man. This 'regional' theory, however, appears to be losing support. Nevertheless, with his more complex brain modern man developed, for the first time in human history, the ability to talk and communicate easily and fluently (Eccles, 1989: 166–7). The structure of the mouth also changed, but this was much less important than the development of the speech areas of the brain. It is not possible to exaggerate the importance of this crucial genetic change. To talk fluently is to think systematically. Only by being able to communicate effectively – and this reaches its highest point in the use of symbols, both words and mathematics, that can be written down – can we produce and maintain (through rote learning) a more profound knowledge than that possessed by speechless humans. And with this knowledge, modern humans changed their world.

This new knowledge was the basis not only for a new technology, but for a more efficient economic and social structure. The whole world lay before us, and we adapted to all geographical and climatic regions with relative ease. We developed new techniques for manufacturing stone tools that were really stone razors with longer blades and sharper cutting edges; we developed calendars and recorded the phases of the moon on bone objects about 35,000 years ago; we developed trade routes throughout Eurasia; we constructed more effective shelters; we fashioned a rich culture, carving figures in available materials such as bone, ivory, coal, and stone, and firing aesthetically pleasing ceramic objects; we painted works of art and learning on our cave walls (at least 30,000 years ago in Australia, 17,000 years ago at Lascaux in France); we buried our dead with elaborate ritual; we dressed in elaborately decorated clothing of jackets, trousers, caps, and moccasins at least 25,000 years ago. We were at the beginning of a radical new phase in the story of life on Earth.

Modern humans are great hunters. So great, that by about 17,000 years ago we finally eliminated the megafauna in Australia; between 17,000 and 10,000 years ago in Europe, we saw off the woolly mammoth, the woolly rhino, the musk ox, the steppe bison, the giant Irish elk among others; and between 11,000 and 10,000 years ago in North and South America, we hunted much of the big game to extinction. The modern romantic myth that the hunter–gatherers did not degrade their environment is just not true. In those parts of the world where competition between human tribes was intense, we were forced to develop an entirely new economic system – agriculture and domesticated animal husbandry – in order to survive; whereas in those isolated parts of the world, where competition was not intense, such as Australasia and North America, it was more cost-effective to reduce the pressure on natural resources by population control. The difference, I suggest, is merely a function of different degrees of competition, not of different cultures. We are all part of the same big family.

The success of early modern man is reflected in the growth of global population. Between the breakout of modern man about 50,000 years ago and the Neolithic Revolution about 10,600 years ago, the global human population increased from approximately 1–3 million to 6–10 million – a fourfold increase in 30,000–40,000 years. This absolute and relative increase in population was unprecedented in the history of the human race. In the first 2 million years population increased by less than a million people, whereas in the 40,000 years before the Neolithic Revolution population increased by about 6 million people. By this stage in the evolution of life on Earth it looked as if nature's latest experiment with large-brained mammals would be successful. Yet, nothing that had been achieved to this stage in the story of life on Earth could have prepared the timeless observer for what was to come – human civilization.

51

THE CIVILIZATION OF MAN

Human civilization emerged gradually but surely between 12,000 and 8,000 years ago. It began with the domestication of animals and the sowing of unusually large grass seeds at a time when much of the big game in Europe, Asia, and North Africa had been eliminated. A new way had to be found in this competitive part of the world if human society was to continue to survive and expand. The first animals to be domesticated were the wolf in Asia (12,000 years ago), and goats and sheep in Iran (11,000 years ago); and the first systematic 'gardening' (rather than farming) took place in conjunction with tending of goats and sheep (for their milk, wool, and meat) in the rift valley of Jordan about 10,600 years ago. The main crops at that time were emmer wheat and barley, which had, by process of *artificial* selection, evolved from the wild grasses of the region. In this new economic system, the men of the village were responsible for taming – also by a process of *artificial* selection, based upon culling all the aggressive animals – and tending the goats and sheep; and the women, who gathered the grass seeds, were probably responsible for the casual experiments by which these grasses evolved into wheat and barley. The men continued to hunt and fish, as they have done ever since, although in recent times more for pleasure than out of necessity. These animal and plant experiments became the economic basis of what is thought to be the world's first town at Jericho, which consisted of a tightly packed huddle of clay buildings for human and animal habitation as well as for grain storage, surrounded by a wall about 4 metres high.

Here we have the beginning of the Neolithic Revolution – a revolution both in terms of the unprecedented speed at which this change was taking place and in the way human society was being transformed. This momentous sequence of events – there was no single event – changed forever the nature of life on Earth. In more than 3 billion years, no other dominant species had been able to domesticate both plants and animals for its own benefit; no other species had been able to transform the basis of progressive genetic mutation from *natural* selection to *artificial* selection. More specifically, this economic revolution changed the nature of human society. Instead of small kinship groups, of perhaps thirty to fifty people, scattered across the face of the globe in search of fresh fields of plants and animals, the foundations had been laid for the gathering together of large numbers of peoples, unrelated as well as related, in towns, cities, and ultimately civilizations. From this revolutionary form of economic activity emerged an unprecedented type of human endeavour – record-keeping using clay tokens as symbols for objects in the real world, together with marks denoting the numbers of these objects. This was the beginning of financial accounting that quite quickly became the basis both of a sophisticated state taxation system and of the first writing – cuneiform – in the civilization of Sumer in lower Mesopotamia.

But this was still a few thousand years in the future. Ten millennia ago this economic system, and the social institutions built upon it, was no more than an experiment born out of economic necessity. It involved no more than a few thousand people from a global population of about 8 million who were still following the hunting–fishing–gathering traditions of mankind that had been handed down from parents to children for about 1.6 million years. It was, however, an experiment that worked and spread throughout the Fertile Crescent. A second town called Mureybet, for example, was built upon experiments with einkorn wheat and the, by now, familiar goats and sheep. And around 8,800 years ago the world's first city, called Çatal Hüyük, with a population of about 5,000 people was constructed in Anatolia. Çatal Hüyük, with its cluster of houses and artistically decorated shrines, gave birth to the first truly urban culture that included the weaving of cloth; the manufacture of bread, drink, pottery, and domestic objects; and led to trade in grain and obsidian. By this time cattle had also been domesticated, both as a source of milk and meat, and of agricultural power.

It was an experiment that also broke out independently in a number of different parts of the world, but all for the same reason, the progressive exhaustion of the palaeolithic technological paradigm, and the need to gain a competitive advantage. In China and Southeast Asia, towns based upon the cultivation of rice, using the water buffalo, and the domestication of pigs had emerged by 9,000 years ago. And 7,700 years ago, a primitive corn, which had been developed through – in Darwin's words – 'variation under domestication', from the wild teosinte grass, was being cultivated in Mesoamerica. The experiment, therefore, was no accident or result of human fancy. It was the outcome of systematic economic forces. The success of the experiment is seen in its widespread emulation, as it travelled gradually along active trade routes between the Fertile Crescent and Europe, North Africa, and Asia; and from Mesoamerica into parts of North and South America. Between 8,700 and 7,500 years ago, agriculture spread throughout central and Western Europe along the trade routes of the Danube and the Rhine; by 8,000 years BP the Indus Valley had been reached; and by 7,000 BP the Nile Valley was practising mixed agriculture. Irrigation techniques became an integral part of this agricultural economy which, by then, was no longer an experiment. Of ancient Pangaea only Australia, which dreamed on in its isolation, remained immune. The success of this experiment is reflected in a global population that had increased by this time to something in excess of 10 million.

The surpluses generated by urban societies produced a demand for more sophisticated domestic goods and for weapons of war. Intense competition between urban societies began to express itself in escalating military conflict. The battles that broke out between rival towns and cities replaced earlier tribal, and often, ritualistic skirmishes. For the first time the surpluses generated by agriculture – which, rats willing, could be stored – allowed some members of the community to specialize in non-productive, but not non-economic, activities such as religion and war. These surpluses also provided a reason for war – plunder. In contrast, hunter–gatherer groups could not afford to engage in serious warfare because, like all hunting animals, serious wounding meant the impoverishment and, eventually, the extinction of the family group. Only urbanized societies could afford to gamble in this way with the lives of their young men. Specialist warriors, particularly in a large community, were expendable. And, in any case, palaeolithic society was not able to generate and store surpluses that made war profitable. Not surprisingly, the first objects produced from the smelting of copper and bronze (initially a copper-arsenic alloy) were axe and spear heads, appearing around 6,500 years ago in Eastern Europe. This was the beginning of the bronze age which lasted until around 3,200 years BP, when supplanted progressively by the age of iron.

The pioneering civilization

The world's first civilization, or highly urbanized culture, emerged in lower Mesopotamia about 6,000 years ago. This was the Sumerian civilization, bounded by the Tigris and Euphrates Rivers, which flourished between 3,800 and 2,000 years before Christ (BC). In this story we have become accustomed to the slow evolution of life on Earth over 4 billion years, and even of man over 2 million years, all as a result of the application of genetic 'ideas' to organic life under conditions of competition and natural selection. Hence the relatively rapid changes in economic, political, social, and cultural structures that occurred in the world's first civilization are bewildering. Within only 112 generations a great civilization rose, flowered, peaked, and fell. And in that time, indeed much less than that time, the Sumerians created a complex economy upon which was based a sophisticated and literate culture that possessed well-developed social, artistic, religious, and political institutions (Crawford, 1991).

The economy of the land of Sumer was based upon mixed agriculture – the growing of grains and the raising of livestock – using techniques of ploughing and irrigation that were to remain essentially unchanged, apart from agricultural modifications introduced into Europe after about AD 700, until the Industrial Revolution. It also involved the manufacture of a wide range of commodities such as textiles, pottery, metal goods (largely copper and lead), leather and wooden products, jewellery, tools, and weapons of war; together with service activities such as architecture, engineering, building, art, bureaucracy, and religion. While transactions within the economy were not based upon money (demonstrating that financial institutions are only of secondary economic importance), exchange was facilitated by expressing market prices in terms of copper and, later, of silver which became a medium of exchange. Coins were an Anatolian invention that occurred as late as 650 BC. The economy was based upon a sophisticated degree of specialization both within and between the independent and highly competitive cities of the Sumerian plain which, in addition to increasing labour productivity, was the basis for a flourishing intercity trade as well as long-distance trade with the civilizations of the Nile and Indus. The cities of the plain imported raw materials such as copper, lead, tin, timber, stone, beads, precious stones, and stone bowls; and they exported grain and leather products.

The standard of living in the cities of Sumer was surprisingly high – surprising because, only 4,000 years before, human tribes lived as they had lived from the dawn of mankind, pursuing a subsistence lifestyle (Goldsmith, 1987: 11–12). In addition to large landowners and wealthy traders, there was a class of minor officials and professionals who were able to purchase luxury goods, such as richly adorned clothing, jewellery, domestic goods, spacious housing, and works of art. Needless to say, the cost of these expenditures was borne by the peasants and slaves who laboured long and hard in the fields and the workshops – longer and harder than they had worked as nomads. But the income of the wealthy was not just a redistribution of leisure time from the poor, it was also a product of economies of scale in production and organization, of higher labour productivity resulting from specialization and division of labour (the gender division of labour of nomadic tribes had been extended to various market activities), and of the introduction of new techniques of production (irrigation, ploughs and plough beasts, and the pottery wheel invented about 4000 BC), of transport (wheeled waggons from about 3500 BC, and ships), and of organization (state bureaucracy, record keeping, and writing).

With the surpluses generated through production and trade, the cities of Sumer were able to develop a sophisticated form of religion which appears to have given rise to a formal system of government with autocratic rules and a bureaucracy that used an effective system of writing – cuneiform on clay tablets – to record the raising and spending of taxes and revenues from state enterprises. Cuneiform writing – the first form of writing in the world – is thought to be based upon the clay tokens of commerce developed in the city of Çatal Hüyük to record commercial transactions. The priests recorded not only daily business transactions but also the positions of the stars and the movement of the planets. They did so in order to provide an authoritative analytical structure for forecasting the future. As discussed elsewhere (Snooks, 1993a: 95–106), this technical apparatus provided the mystery and status required of forecasters, who in fact relied more upon their detailed knowledge of history and current affairs when making practical predictions. They were at least as successful as the economic forecasters of today, who also rely upon the mystery of a technical craft. And their craft grew rapidly in sophistication. By 1800 BC the Babylonians were compiling star charts and mapping planetary movements which provided a data base extending over hundreds of years; by the eighth century BC they were analysing this data using mathematical techniques that were as sophisticated as those of Copernicus; and by the fourth century BC they were able to calculate the motion of the Sun with an accuracy not exceeded until our own century (Morris, 1985: 15).

Sumer achieved a considerable degree of technical competence in architecture and engineering responsible for the beautiful large public buildings that culminated in the great ziggurat of Ur. The Sumerians also possessed a well-established legal system, a written literature, and a range of impressive visual arts. An example of the literary and philosophical achievement is the Gilgamesh epic, in which mankind is seen striving, creating, but eventually perishing. The Sumerian hero Gilgamesh asks rhetorically (Pritchard, 1950: 79):

> Who, my friends is superior to death?
> Only the gods live forever under the sun.
> As for mankind, numbered are their days;
> Whatever they achieve is but the wind!

Sumer's technical achievements, based upon an effective economic system, enabled the intellectual elite to ponder the meaning of life and the universe they observed in the night skies. While they knew nothing of the amazing story of life on Earth, their questions were profound and provided the first building block in the intellectual structure that some 4,000 years later would begin to provide some of the answers to their questions.

The followers

Since Sumer a succession of civilizations has emerged – just like a new dominant species or family of species in the aeons before mankind – out of the ashes of former civilizations. In the process by which one civilization has replaced another before the modern age, there were refinements to the achievements of Sumer in things political, social, and cultural, but economic and technological progress before Europe in 1500 was not great. It was largely a matter of doing basically the same thing, possibly from a slightly higher base, in slightly different ways. While there was a great deal of imagination and drive causing each new civilization to rise rapidly and produce relatively high living standards for the ruling elites, the end result was the same in each case: the achievement of a peak of economic and cultural flowering, followed by stagnation, decline, and finally collapse. There appears to have been an increase in material standards of living within each civilization, but little increase between civilizations until the Industrial Revolution. Had this not been the case, economic living standards would be far higher today than they actually are. This process of economic change was like a great wheel spinning freely in space, without gaining traction. The axis of this great wheel was the technological basis provided by the Neolithic Revolution which, in the ancient period, was largely fixed.

As we shall see in Chapter 12, this **great wheel of civilization** did produce a dynamic in human society. While there was not a marked increase of GDP per capita between successive civilizations – although there were increases during the turn of the wheel of any particular civilization – there was economic expansion which is reflected in the growth of global population. During the 5,000 years before the modern age, the economic achievement of Sumer, together with the elaborations made in each successive civilization, were gradually extended throughout the world. Accordingly, the global population increased from 10 million during the time of Sumer to about 500 million at the beginning of the European epoch (say AD 1500) – an increase in population by a factor of 50. This was the outcome of the slowly turning wheel of civilization. But it begs the question (that will be discussed at length in Chapter 12): why did the wheel of civilization turn freely without gaining traction? Essentially the answer is that it was not until the beginning of the European epoch that population achieved a level which exhausted the technological paradigm generated by the world's first civilization. Until the European epoch, the factor endowment of human society – the relationship between natural resources, capital, and labour – and hence relative factor prices, did not change fundamentally. When it did, the need to generate a new technological paradigm became imperative for survival and prosperity in a competitive world. Thus the Industrial Revolution was born.

I will here do no more than briefly mention the passing parade of human civilizations during the past 4,000 years since the fall of mighty Ur in the land of Sumer. The civilizations of the ancient Old World went through three main epochs: the pioneering civilizations of the Fertile Crescent; the Greek civilization in the east; and the Roman civilization in the west. As we have seen, the land of Sumer was the centre of the first flowering of the city-state, which had a considerable influence upon the succeeding Babylonian Empire and the early history of the contemporaneous Egyptian civilization on the River Nile. Babylon became heir to the cities of the plain after the declining Sumerian society was swept away by Semitic nomads. The language of the invaders replaced the Sumerian tongue which was reserved solely for sacred uses. Under the Babylonian king Hammurabi (1792–1750 BC), Mesopotamia enjoyed one last period of cultural glory – particularly the development of mathematics, astronomy, and law – before it fell to pieces and was overrun by further invaders.

The Egyptian civilization flourished, with a few ups and downs, between 3100 and 1700 BC. This was the period of the Old and Middle Kingdoms. Owing to its isolation, Egypt developed a novel cultural structure upon its more familiar irrigated agricultural foundations. A highly centralized economic system existed throughout these 1,400 years organized by a monarchy and priesthood located at Memphis just south of the Nile Delta. While agriculture was largely in private hands, the state controlled foreign trade, held large grain reserves in anticipation of natural disaster, and owned the extensive mines and quarries. This centralized society was based upon a highly sophisticated taxation system. Egyptian officials employed 'Nilometer' readings of the height of the ever reliable Nile to estimate the likely extent of flooding, and hence the probable harvest for every holding, for the forthcoming year. On these readings Egyptian officials based their annual taxation assessments. In addition the landed wealth of Egypt was surveyed every two years. With this surplus, the Egyptian state developed a highly complex, literate society that attracted the unwanted attention of each rising empire in the Old World. But unlike the culture of Sumer, Egypt had little influence upon succeeding civilizations.

While the pioneering Mesopotamian and Egyptian civilizations stumbled and were ultimately swept away by nomadic tribes, the seeds of civilization were sown and rejuvenated, and new urban societies – in Syria and Palestine, in Turkey (the Hittites), Crete (Minoan) and on the Greek mainland (Mycenaean) – sprang up for a brief season to take their place. Distinct, but possibly not entirely independent civilizations also emerged after the middle of the third millennium BC in the valleys of the Indus and the Yellow Rivers. The Harappan civilization, which flourished in the Indus Valley for a millennium between 2500 and 1500 BC, was the most extensive and highly urbanized of the period. Owing to the easy land and sea routes, it was probably influenced by the earlier Mesopotamian civilizations. Certainly it was finally brought to an end after a period of decline by invading Aryan charioteers. Northern China was even more isolated from the Fertile Crescent by 4,800 kilometres of steppe and semi-desert in the west, by the Himalayas in the south, and by a long and difficult sea voyage. While it is now thought that the development of farming in the middle of the third millennium BC was largely a local affair – particularly the growing of millet and barley – rice was introduced from Southeast Asia and wheat could have come from contact with the Fertile Crescent (Starr, 1991: 114). Some have been bold enough to suggest that early Chinese civilization in the second millennium BC may have been indirectly influenced by Aryan charioteers who reached the Altai Mountains in the heart of Asia by 1900 BC (Calder, 1984: 168). Whatever this influence, owing to their late start and relative isolation, the Orient failed to have any significant impact upon the West. Even the major achievements of the Sung period (AD 960–1279) were largely unknown in the West, at least until after the late-thirteenth-century visits of the Polos and after the European breakout of the early sixteenth century. But by then Europe had surpassed China in technology and science.

The second epoch involves an interaction between two empires in western Asia – the Assyrian (911–612 BC)/Persian (559–330 BC) civilizations and the Greek civilization (750–146 BC). The Assyrian civilization, which centred on the city of Ashur on the middle Tigris, was the world's first great empire – the earlier Akkadian Empire (2330–2230 BC) lasted only a few generations. Assyria played an important role in conserving the achievements, both technological and cultural, of the Sumerian civilization and transmitting them to other developing peoples such as the Greeks. The Greek world emerged from a long period (1100–750 BC) of isolation to develop into more than 200 completely independent city-states held together by a common language and a highly competitive tension. In the eighth century BC, the Greeks were attracted to the Assyrian culture and were strongly influenced by it. While the Greek city-states were based upon a highly labour-intensive form of agriculture, which experienced little technological change throughout their history, they did undergo a remarkable cultural flowering. When the natural resources available to a city were exhausted, the Greeks set up colonies elsewhere. Hence there was no pressure to introduce new techniques of production. As economic incentives did not encourage technological change, ambitious men went into the military, trade, scholarship, or the arts. In a highly competitive environment, scholarship and the arts flourished, particularly in the fifth century BC. After the destructive Peloponnesian Wars between Athens and Sparta (431–404 BC), Greek culture changed significantly and may have gone into permanent decline but for the revival that followed Alexander's conquest, by 330 BC, of the Persian Empire which extended in the east to the mountains bordering the Indus Valley. The resulting Hellenistic civilization was more urbane and cosmopolitan and less austerely rational than the classical age of the fifth century. Its intellectual and scientific achievements, however, were theoretical rather than applied because they lacked the basic technology to do so owing, it will be argued, not to a lack of ability or ideas but to the absence of economic incentives.

While Alexander's heirs were consolidating their achievements throughout western Asia and North Africa, a new force was rising in the West. The city-state of Rome, which dates back to about 800 BC, had overrun the entire Italian peninsula by 220 BC, and had embarked upon its expansion into the Mediterranean which it completed by 133 BC. In addition to its very considerable engineering, building, military, and bureaucratic achievements, the Roman Empire played an important role in distributing the benefits of civilization, which they had absorbed from Greek culture, to the lands bordering the Mediterranean. In effect, they passed on to Europe what the Sumerians had handed down to the Assyrians, and in turn what the Assyrians had communicated to the Persians and the Greeks. While each new civilization, particularly the Greek, added something of its own, these were but brilliant variations on a theme – a theme that remained in the consciousness of mankind to be revived in Renaissance Europe when it finally could find economic application. The remarkable intellectual achievements of the ancient world had transcended their economic usefulness and hence went into hibernation after an ailing Rome was sacked by the Vandals in AD 455. While the Western Roman Empire was replaced by a number of Germanic kingdoms (except for a brief period of unification with Constantinople in the sixth and seventh centuries), the Eastern Empire transformed itself into the Greek Byzantine Empire and continued until it was dismantled under the cunning supervision of Venice during the Fourth Crusade in 1204.

While it is essential to include the civilizations of Mesoamerica in this survey, they had little influence upon our own civilization because of their complete isolation from the Old World. When contact was finally made between the two hemispheres after 1492, the New World civilizations were destroyed by disease and war. The agricultural base of Mesoamerican civilization began about 7,000 years ago with the domestication of corn, turkeys, and dogs. Settled villages, which appeared 4,000 years ago, had spread throughout Mexico by 3,000 years BP. Craftsmen in these villages manufactured pottery, baskets, and food products. Some 3,250 years ago emerged the first Mesoamerican civilization, the Olmec culture, which was ruled by a military and priestly elite for some seven or eight centuries before it collapsed and was reclaimed by the jungle. Although there is no direct record, it is thought from the evidence of later cultures that the Olmecs may have developed a system of writing and a calendar of 365 days (Thorne and Raymond, 1989: 241).

The Olmecs were replaced by the Maya, whose civilization was expanding rapidly some 2,750 years ago. Ultimately they spread by conquest throughout the lowlands of central America. At its height between AD 300 and 900 the Mayan civilization was a highly sophisticated urban society that was literate, artistic, innovative, and learned in science and mathematics. All this on the surplus that could be generated by irrigated agriculture, trade, and conquest. But like the civilizations of the Old World, once the dominant strategy of conquest was exhausted, the empire collapsed (in AD 900). Other Mesoamerican civilizations include the sophisticated society based upon the city of Teotihuacan which 1,600 years ago had a population of 125,000 people; the Toltec in central Mexico about AD 1000; and the last Mesoamerican civilization, the Aztec which, like the Inca civilization in South America, was destroyed by the Spanish in the early sixteenth century. The Aztec Empire was at its height between AD 1326 and 1519, with a population of about 10 million, and a great capital city, Tenochtitlan (later Mexico City), built upon islands in a lake, with a population of 100,000 people. We will never know for certain if the Aztec civilization would have collapsed like all its predecessors, but it is highly probable. They certainly believed that they were part of the fifth and final creation of the universe, and that their civilization would collapse unless they could appease the Sun god through continuous human sacrifice.

Islam, which was a major creative force in the Mediterranean and the Fertile Crescent between 650 and 1200, had a greater influence upon Western Europe. The Arabs, who were united spiritually and politically by Mohammed in the early seventh century, expanded rapidly under his influence, and by 650 they controlled the former Persian Empire. By 737 the Umayyad Caliphate had advanced to the Black Sea in the east, North Africa in the south, and most of Spain and part of France in the west. But this was the high-water mark of united Arab rule. After 800 the Abbasid Caliphate broke up into independent dynasties, and from about 1000 the Muslim world was on the retreat, first in Spain and then in the former Persian Empire. By 1200 the Arabs held only the southern third of Spain; a century later they had only a toehold in Granada; and by the end of the Middle Ages they were finally expelled from Europe. Yet while the Arab world shrank, Islam continued to flourish as a religious, if not an innovative, cultural and technological force under the Ottomans.

Between 700 and 1200 the Islamic world developed a sophisticated culture with a synthesis of ideas and practices from classical antiquity, Asia, and Africa (Mokyr, 1990: 39). Theirs was a highly literate and scholarly society responsible for a number of significant advances in knowledge and technology ranging from mathematics to improvements in power generation, textile production, mechanical engineering, industrial chemicals, and metal working. But, while Islam had been an important medium for the transmission of ideas as Western Europe began its rise to economic prominence, by 1200 it had little more to provide, apart from adding to the competitive environment experienced by the West.

Interest finally shifts to Europe during the last millennium or so, and in particular to England, a small country that, nevertheless, was the first to experience changes in the fundamental economic forces that created the Industrial Revolution. The European tribes and, later, kingdoms were slow to adopt the achievements of classical civilization. By AD 800–900 unified kingdoms were emerging in France, Germany, and England, which absorbed classical ideas through the institution of the Roman Church and blended these with their earlier Germanic culture. Between 1000 and 1300 these kingdoms experienced a flowering of their own cultures based upon a rapid economic and population growth. During this time their feudal structures began to break down as factor markets emerged and commodity markets were widened. In northern Italy and Flanders urbanization, which fed on trade between East and West, re-emerged in the West and its citizens began to remember and appreciate the cultural achievements of the ancient and Islamic worlds. And at the same time the agricultural methods of Rome were adapted to the different conditions of northern Europe (Mokyr, 1990).

This considerable development of economy and society was disrupted by the onset of the Black Death in 1347, which emerged like the chariots of old out of the East, and retarded economic and social change for a further 150 years. Despite the deathly grip of pestilence, the economic system of Western Europe continued to change, even though the outcome in material terms was suppressed. After 1500, when pestilence's grip was loosened, and there was a breakout of Europeans into the rest of the world, population and living standards in the West increased rapidly. By the sixteenth century Western Europe had clearly surpassed the economic and scientific achievements of the ancient world and was on the verge of a new era of economic and cultural development. By the early seventeenth century the impressive but relatively brief burst of progress had broken itself against the ceiling of an exhausted technological paradigm that stretched back to the Neolithic Revolution. Further progress required a new paradigm, which was finally achieved between 1780 and 1830 and became known as the Industrial Revolution (Snooks, 1994b).

The essential characteristic of this modern economic transformation was the application of a new technology required to substitute inorganic fuels and materials for those of an organic nature. This was a response to changing relative factor prices as organic materials became relatively more expensive and capital funded from the profits of commerce and colonization became less expensive relative to labour. But the driving force, as we shall see in later chapters, was the need to create greater economic space in which to generate greater material standards of living now that the space provided by the neolithic technological paradigm was being used to capacity. So successful was this effort that a new technological paradigm was introduced which enabled further sustained growth of real GDP per capita, population, and urban culture. Without this paradigm breakthrough, as I will show in Chapter 13, Western civilization would have slipped back into the ancient pattern described by the great wheel of civilization – the eternal recurrence of war and conquest.

Today there are signs that human society once more is approaching the limits of its technological paradigm. The urgent question for the immediate future is whether the Dynamic Society will be able to break through these limits as it has always done, or whether it will retreat from them as the ecological engineers claim it must. This is the challenge faced in the rest of this book.

4

DYNAMICS OF BEING

The essential thing in the life process is precisely the tremendous shaping, form-creating force working from within which *utilizes* and *exploits* 'external circumstances'.

(Nietzsche, *The Will to Power*, 1883–8)

Life on Earth is a long, sheer, but continuous thread that stretches back from the present to its origins about 4 billion years ago. This is of fundamental importance. It is the continuity of life before and after the emergence of mankind that has helped to shape the nature of the Dynamic Society. The dynamics of the age of man owes much to the dynamics of earlier eras of biological change, because of the progressive or accumulating relationship between each great wave of evolution, and because of the long-established genetically determined nature of man who is the driving force behind human progress – the rider in the chariot of change. And this continuity emerges from within rather than from without. When we gathered around the campfires and listened wide-eyed to the tales of the storytellers – of exploding mountains and crashing stars – we looked in the wrong direction. We looked outwards to the heavens rather than inwards to ourselves. For all their drama, random cataclysmic events could not have sustained and shaped life over billions of years. The life force comes not from without but from within.

To explore this the greatest of all subjects we need to review modern theories of evolution to see what they have to say about the dynamics of life, and then to interpret the progressively accumulating **great waves of biological change** by employing an endogenous model. The validity of this approach rests on two great foundation stones – that the dynamic paths of evolution and human society have much in common, and that evolution is an economic rather than a 'physical' problem. While no attempt is made to provide any new evidence concerning biological evolution, that evidence is presented and discussed from a different perspective. An attempt has been made, therefore, to apply economic thinking to an issue that has been dominated by scientific thinking. This novel perspective helps both to sort out conflicting views amongst natural scientists and, more importantly, to demonstrate the great continuity in the dynamics of life both before and since the emergence of mankind, and to show that the driving force in life comes from within rather than without. In the process, a more general explanation of the dynamics of life is outlined. This explanation is assisted by employing, at times, the rhetorical device of endowing non-human species with objectives and rational responses to changing circumstances. It is meant to imply no more than the fact that individuals, owing to their genetic inheritance, act as if this were true.

DARWINIAN DYNAMICS AND BEYOND

Much has been written about evolution during the last century in academic and commercial presses, but the basic mechanism of biological progress – natural selection through the struggle for existence – published by Darwin in 1859 stands firm if not unchallenged. The main contributions since Darwin's *The Origin of Species* include the development of the relatively new field of genetics, and various elaborations of the original argument to encompass the subsequent increase in the fossil record. What we want to know is how Darwin and those natural scientists who have come after him view the dynamics of biological change.

Darwin's theory of natural selection

Let us begin at the beginning. Darwin emphasized the centrality of gradual change over very long periods of time to his view of evolution; periods of time that were so vast that they could not be fully comprehended by the mind of man. He wrote (1979: 453): 'The mind cannot possibly grasp the full meaning of the term of a hundred million years; it cannot add up and perceive the full effects of many slight variations, accumulated during an almost infinite number of generations.' Since Darwin's time the origin of life has been pushed back to 4 billion years, forty times the period he had in mind – a fact no less difficult to comprehend. Darwin would have been fascinated but not surprised.

In the last chapter of his revolutionary book – perhaps the greatest book of the modern era – Darwin summarizes his view of the nature of the evolutionary process (ibid.: 444–5):

> As natural selection acts solely by accumulating slight, successive, favourable variations, it can produce no great or sudden modification; it can act only by very short and slow steps . . . [N]ature is prodigal in variety, though niggard in innovation.

This should not be taken to mean that Darwin viewed evolution as occurring always at the same rate. While he did believe that the rate of evolution would be fairly constant if the 'conditions of life' (both physical and competitive) remained unchanged, he also realized that there were circumstances in which it would vary from slow to 'slow in an extreme degree'. What he did not believe was that biological change would occur rapidly. In concluding *Origin* (ibid.: 457–8), Darwin wrote:

> As species are produced and exterminated by slowly acting and still existing causes, and not by miraculous acts of creation and by catastrophes; and as the most important of all causes of organic change is one which is almost independent of altered and perhaps suddenly altered physical conditions, namely, the mutual relation of organism to organism – the improvement of one being entailing the improvement or the extermination of others; it follows, that the amount of organic change in the fossils of consecutive formations probably serves as a fair measure of the lapse of actual time. A number of species, however, keeping in a body might remain for a long period unchanged, whilst within this same period, several of these species, by migrating into new countries and coming into competition with foreign associates, might become modified; so that we must not overrate the accuracy of organic change as a measure of time. During early periods of the earth's history, when the forms of life were probably fewer and simpler, the rate of change was probably slower; and at the first dawn of life, when very few forms of the simplest structure existed, the rate of change may have been slow in an extreme degree.

While he did not expect wide variations in the rate of biological change, such variations – as Richard Dawkins (1986: ch. 3) has argued – are not inconsistent with his theory of selection through a struggle for existence. We should also note that Darwin rejected the hypothesis, now currently fashionable, that the rise and fall of species were due to catastrophes.

Yet did Darwin develop a dynamic model of the growth of biological activity? The answer, I believe, is: no. What he provided was a persuasive hypothesis about the mechanism of biological change – natural selection operating through the struggle for survival in a physical environment (as a secondary factor) that was both hostile and occasionally subject to change. While this is an important starting point, it does not constitute a full dynamic model. Darwin did not, for example, elaborate on the nature of the driving force required in any dynamic system. Although it is implicit in his discussion of struggle and selection, which are merely outcomes of the driving force, he does not explain the nature of the impetus. But it is clear, as we saw in Chapter 1, that Darwin regarded the unconscious desire to survive as the overwhelming driving force in life. Only with survival can individuals attempt to indulge their other, subsidiary desires, such as physical dominance and sexual pleasure. There is no hint in *The Origin of Species* of the modern preoccupation of sociobiologists with maximizing reproduction – or, taking this idea to a logical extreme, maximizing the spread of one's genes – because Darwin understood that it could never be the driving force in life. Sociobiologists like Trivers (1985) have played down the role of economics (competition for scarce resources) in Darwin, in favour of sociology (inter-action between individuals).

Darwin had no clear idea about the development path of life on Earth – owing, of course, to the poverty of the fossil record available to him – and, as a consequence, he had no mechanism for explaining fluctuations or cycles in the evolutionary process. In the absence of satisfactory evidence he preferred to think of it progressing in a slow and steady manner. Natural selection is only (and this was a very big only!) an explanation of organic change of the various species, and not an explanation of the general dynamics of life. To bring this point closer to our time, the theory of natural selection could be compared with a theory of technological change rather than with a theory of the dynamics of human society. Technological change, like natural selection, is only part of the wider dynamic process and its role has varied considerably over time.

Since Darwin

Has a clearer and more complete model of the dynamics of biological change been articulated by natural scientists since Darwin's time? Some scholars have suggested that Darwin's insistence on very gradual change is not reflected even in the more extensive fossil record that is available today (Eldredge, 1986). Darwin, as is well known, constantly complained about the imperfect fossil record (Darwin, 1979: ch. 9). Today, mainstream Darwinists also blame the fossil record, but their arguments are more sophisticated. Mayr (1963) has suggested that sharp breaks in the evidence are the result of a process by which a small population becomes geographically separated from the parent species and, under different competitive and physical conditions over a long period of time, experiences more rapid genetic change thereby giving rise to a new species. Eventually the breakaway population rejoins the ancestral species and, as it has a competitive edge, eliminates the original population. The fossil record, therefore, will show a sharp break in the evolution of this species. Intermediate types are to be found elsewhere. This explanation is within the spirit of Darwin's discussion of isolation in *The Origin of Species* (ibid.: 150).

More recently, Eldredge and Gould (1972), in order to explain their perception of the fossil record, have developed this mainstream Darwinian explanation into what they like to think of as an alternative hypothesis to natural selection called 'punctuated equilibria'. They claim that genetic change in a small local population at the margin of the geographic range of its parent species may occur at a much faster rate than envisaged by Darwin and his followers. This they associate with the emergence of new species ('speciation').

66

Hence long periods of 'stasis' or equilibrium, which they regard as the normal condition of life, are interrupted by relatively rapid change. Eldredge and Gould (1972: 82) explain:

> The history of life is more adequately represented by a picture [a theory] of 'punctuated equilibria' than by the notion of phyletic gradualism. The history of evolution is not one of stately unfolding, but a story of homeostatic equilibria, disturbed only 'rarely' . . . by rapid and episodic events of speciation.

As there is some confusion in the literature as to what Eldredge and Gould mean by punctuated equilibria we will let them speak for themselves. In reflecting upon their influential article, Niles Eldredge (1986: 120, 128) wrote: 'At its simplest, punctuated equilibria entails the recognition of stasis and the realization that patterns of change in the fossil record are best explained by allopatric [geographical] speciation'; and 'Gould and I claimed that stasis – nonchange – is the dominant evolutionary theme in the fossil record . . . Adaptive change is relatively rare, and usually associated with speciation, thus typically rather rapid'.

In other words, evolution is the outcome of the emergence of new species in geographical regions isolated from the parent population, rather than the slow but gradual genetic change of that population through time. Further, variation in physical conditions appears to be central to their hypothesis about the emergence of new species. Eldredge (ibid.: 118, 149) suggests that, in the process of speciation, 'geography seemed to be the key', and, again, that the 'environmental conditions' in which local populations live is the 'trigger that releases a rapid phase of adaptive modification'. He even claims (ibid.: 150) that species rather than individuals are 'discrete, semi-independent actors in the evolutionary drama', and proposes that evolution is the outcome of a 'higher-level sorting principle in nature' – higher than Darwin's principle of natural selection – called 'species selection'. Other 'punctuationists' have even suggested that these episodes of rapid organic change could result from a series of 'catastrophic stochastic genetic events' (Carson, 1975: 88). The hypothesis of the 'punctuationists', therefore, emphasizes the priority of non-systematic physical forces over the economic forces that are the hallmark of Darwinism.

An attempt has been made by other natural scientists, such as Richard Dawkins (1986), to show that the 'punctuationists' are really in the mainstream of Darwinism. Dawkins argues that their hypothesis involves taking a mainstream idea – 'periphera isolates' – and pushing it to an extreme. But, even their extreme version provides only 'a minor gloss on Darwinism'. The punctuationists, he argues, are gradualists in the traditional Darwinian sense – in that genetic change must go through a large number of very small steps – although they believe that the evidence shows this to have occurred in brief bursts of tens to hundreds of thousands of years. Dawkins also dismisses the suggestions of catastrophic and stochastic influences as rhetorical flour-ishes, but he agrees that their emphasis on stasis as something positive – as an active resistance to evolutionary change rather than just an absence of change – is non-Darwinian and is 'quite probably wrong'.

A matter that the critics of the punctuationists do not mention is of consid-erable importance in this book. They fail to mention that the punctuationist push is really an attempt, either conscious or not, to replace the economic explanation in Darwin's theory of evolution with a purely physical explana-tion. Also what these critics miss is that the punctuationist hypothesis is an attempt to replace the basics of a dynamic and systematic explanation of biological change with an unsystematic and curiously static explanation. In Darwinism the normal condition is change, albeit of a straightforward kind, whereas in 'punctuationism' the normal condition is stasis or equilibrium punctuated from time to time by unsystematic random events. Gone is the Darwinian driving force within individual organisms, gone is the competition that gave rise to this driving force; and gone are the conditions of scarcity – a matter for economics – that gave rise to competition. Basically, the punctuationists have presented a lifeless picture of life.

But they have suggested the possibility of a well-defined pattern in evo-lution – certainly at the species, and possibly higher, level – even though they have implicitly denied that it is a continuous dynamic process. Stability is the norm until it is disturbed by unsystematic events such as geographic isolation or random change in the environment. According to this view there is no systematic driving force in evolution. This has lent support to the ever-popular but crude physical explanations of life as the outcome of random catastrophic events in the form of crashing stars and exploding mountains. Also, the punctuationist view of evolution appears to be basically a microbiological view of individual species rather than a macrobiological view of the expansion of all life on Earth. Later in this chapter an attempt will be made to combine the more recent fossil evidence – which suggests a step-like pattern of genetic change – with a more general model of the dynamics of life.

A physical science takeover?

Quite recently a more macro approach has been taken to the evolution of life. Crawford and Marsh, in a most inappropriately named book *The Driving Force* (1989) – it should have been called 'The Constraining Force' – have attempted to undertake a more systematic analysis of biological change. Regrettably, their starting point is similar to that of the punctuationists, to whom they refer with approval. While proclaiming a belief in the role, albeit secondary, of natural selection in evolution, they effectively contradict them-selves by insisting that the driving force in this process lies not in the mech-anism of struggle and selection, but in the alleged dynamics of the physical and chemical conditions of life. What they are not prepared to say is that by removing the driving force from Darwin's struggle/selection mechanism is to destroy it entirely. In effect, what they attempt to do, completely unsuccessfully, is to breathe life into punctuationism by endowing the physical world with an active driving force.

Crawford and Marsh (1989: 33) take up where the punctuationists leave off:

> The point put forward by the Punctuationists is that whilst they consider selection an adequate sorting out mechanism, they do not see it as the direct cause or origin of the 'punctuations': clearly there must be another driving force in operation.

In seeking an alternative driving force to that in Darwinism, they advance the flawed hypothesis of 'substrate-driven' change. Basically, their argument is that sudden changes in the physical environment, namely the supply of chemical substances or nutrients, are responsible for genetic change. This is a supply-side argument which assumes that organisms passively consume the nutrients that are actively supplied to, or forced upon, them. They do not realize, as Darwin certainly did, that the pressure to employ resources must come from the demand side – from individual life forms caught up in the deadly struggle for life. The environment is not the driving force, but rather the physical constraints – the rules of the game – within which life operates according to a dynamic of its own. Naturally, the constraints will change from time to time, and the individual life forms will interact with that environment, but the motive force must come from the individual in competition with other individuals. Without this organic driving force there will be no dynamic system either biological or social. Accordingly, Crawford and Marsh's sustained attempt to produce a dynamic system without an organic driving force was doomed to failure at the very outset.

While I do not wish to devote much space to this flawed theory, it has a persuasive quality that may have diverted some readers. Also the arguments I develop here are relevant to any similar attack upon Darwinism by physical scientists. But it must be acknowledged that Crawford and Marsh do recognize the need to describe a development path and do at least attempt to discuss the dynamics of life, even if it turns out to be a discussion of the food of life. The positive aspect of this critical evaluation is that it helps to set the stage for my economic interpretation of evolution. Crawford and Marsh's argument can be characterized in four main points.

1 They claim, quite wrongly, that Darwinism is based on chance, via random genetic change. Although familiar with Dawkins' (1986: ch. 1) prior refutation of this criticism of Darwin, they ignore it almost entirely. Dawkins argues that genetic mutation is random only with respect to its costs and benefits to the individual and species, and that it is non-random in the sense that it is caused by systematic events (such as x-rays, cosmic rays,

radioactive substances, and chemicals) which do not just happen, that it occurs at different rates for different genes, that it is directionally biased, and that it is constrained by the existing processes of embryology (Dawkins, 1986: 306–12). Also, Dawkins argues that life as we know it is so highly improbable that it could not have occurred in a random way or through 'single-step' selection. Rather it was a non-random process of 'cumulative selection' in which 'chance is filtered cumulatively by selection, step by step, over many generations' (ibid.: 288). Crawford and Marsh reject this argument – they have little in common with what they call 'socio-biologists' whom they distinguish from 'real' natural scientists – on the flimsy grounds that while it can explain the difference between species, it cannot explain the origin of life: 'The difference between one species and the next is tiny in comparison with the difference between the presence and absence of life' (Crawford and Marsh, 1989: 4). This of course misses the point entirely, as Darwin did not attempt to explain the beginning of life, only its evolution: in the last sentence of *Origin* (Darwin, 1979: 459–60) Darwin leaves the beginning of life up in the air, with life 'having been originally breathed into a few forms or into one'. They go on regardless to conclude that biological change is due not to chance but to chemical laws.

2 Crawford and Marsh claim incorrectly (see Dawkins, 1986) that Darwin, unlike his followers, was aware that organic variation arose from both selection and 'conditions', but that he did not understand conditions, and hence placed too much weight on selection. In other words, they believe that Darwin was influenced excessively by the economists of his day and insufficiently by the physical scientists. They claim (Crawford and Marsh, 1989: 33), quite mysteriously, that: 'The important distinction between selection and substrate-driven change is that the mechanism of the latter is active or propelling, whereas "selection" is passive, effecting a sorting out process.' In similar vein, they refer to the chemical conditions of life as 'environmental stimulation', as the 'initiator', the 'impulse', the 'driving force', and as 'coercive'.

There are at least three problems with this hypothesis. First, they regard natural selection as a passive sorting device, because they do not appear to appreciate, as Darwin did and the myriad of his followers do, that natural selection operated through the competitive struggle for existence. It is the intense 'desire' to live, and the competitive struggle to do so in a world of scarce resources, that provides the active component in Darwin's system. Natural selection – life or death – allows the successful combatants to pass on their genetic advantage to future generations. As argued in *Origin* (Darwin, 1979: 133):

> natural selection is daily and hourly scrutinising, throughout the world, every variation, even the slightest; rejecting that which is bad,

preserving and adding up all that is good; silently and insensibly working, whenever and wherever opportunity offers, at the improvement of each organic being in relation to its organic and inorganic conditions of life.

Darwin's struggle-selection mechanism is hardly a passive device! Crawford and Marsh's failure to appreciate the real nature of this mechanism is reflected in their confession at the end of their book (1989: 257) that they see evolution as 'the product of a more generous world' than the world of Darwinism.

Second, they do not recognize, or at least do not mention, the important fact that theirs is a supply-side explanation of evolution with no demand component. They claim, in other words, that the mere supply of chemical resources or nutrients is able to force biological change. More specifically, they assert that the shift of animal life forms from the sea to the land was driven by the abundance of land; that the availability of various essential chemicals (e.g. vitamin B12, essential fatty acids, etc.) forced the speed and direction of evolution; that the specialization of higher mammals was driven by the availability of fatty acids in lower animals when consumed. But all this evidence, and more, actually supports the reverse argument. The mere existence (or supply) of nutrients does not guarantee that they will be used. Resources will only be used if there is an active demand for them. The old saying is true: you can lead a horse to water but you cannot make it drink! For example, the widespread shift of animal life from the sea to the land would not have taken place unless the competition in the sea for resources, for at least some species, was intense. If life in the seas was easy, why shift to the land given the attendant costs of an unfamiliar and possibly even more dangerous environment? In fact, Crawford and Marsh's claim that resources were 'abundant' on the land is relative, and only makes sense in terms of a comparison with conditions in the sea which, logically speaking, must have been less abundant. Similarly, why would the evolving 'higher' mammals bother to specialize unless they were driven to it by fierce competition? It is demand that provides the active principle and supply the passive principle in a dynamic relationship. This is not to say that supply cannot change independently, just that it will only be responded to if there is a willing consumer. No successful, longrun dynamic process can be set in motion and be maintained by supply-side variables if there is no active force on the demand side. The reverse hypothesis, however, is true. In fact, the scarcity of resources constitutes a powerful incentive for innovation, both genetic and technological.

Third, all the evidence supplied by Crawford and Marsh in their book only serves to demonstrate quite clearly that nutrients, which are scarce in the economic sense, act as a constraint on the development of life forms. This is, therefore, an economic problem: how to gain access to scarce resources, and how to allocate them within the kinship group in order to maximize the chance of survival. Unless this is done, because of the competition generated by scarcity, some individuals and species will be eliminated from the Earth. Hence the problem of biological evolution, like the problem of social evolution, is an economic problem rather than a 'physical' problem. But of course it does take place within a physical environment. Crawford and Marsh, like the punctuationists before them, have attempted, unsuccessfully, to take evolution out of economics, where Darwin placed it, and to put it in the natural sciences.

My point is that the natural sciences are concerned with the physical environment – the rules of the game of life if you wish – not with the strategy of the players who, driven by an intense 'desire' to survive, act out a deadly economic game involving scarce resources. The name of the game is Survival, and those who win are granted all the spoils – consumption, and sexual gratification – while those who lose, lose everything. Only by denying that resources are scarce can Crawford and Marsh pretend that the game of life is played out by physical laws. This would, of course, require that populations of all species always remain at very low levels so that resources are always abundant and that any individual who needs any resource can merely put out its hoof/claw/paw/hand to receive it. To the contrary, all available evidence shows that animal populations in competitive situations will expand to the limit of available resources relatively quickly, thereby eliminating abundance. Darwin (1979: 117), under the influence of Malthus, certainly appreciated this.

Fourth, all the evidence provided by Crawford and Marsh (1989) in an attempt to support their 'substrate-driven' hypothesis, actually supports Darwin's case. The relevant economic argument is that because resources are scarce, species use the most efficient manner possible to gain access to them. This is unwittingly borne out by the examples provided by Crawford and Marsh: with animal species adding on to existing body structures (from the first emergence of animal life about 1 billion years ago to the specialized nature of the human brain) that they have inherited; through specialized genetic development to occupy particular niches; and through specialized exploitation by one species of another (such as carnivores consuming herbivores to gain the fatty acids required for the development of their central nervous systems, rather than using scarce brain capacity to produce these fatty acids in their own bodies). The examples are many. We can conclude, therefore, that the individual life form provides the drive to use available resources (sources of nutrition) as economically as possible in order to maximize the probability of survival in a highly competitive world. Resource supplies act as a constraint on what can be achieved. Here we have the familiar economic problem of demand and supply.

3 The Crawford and Marsh argument becomes even more transparent when applied to the emergence of man and to human society. Their claim (ibid.: 188) is that: 'If the concept of substrate-driven change is valid there will be evidence in history and today of food changing man in shape and performance'. In order to apply their nutrition thesis to evolution and to the society of man, they (ibid.: 32) are forced to postulate a different approach to evolution which involves what they call 'plastic heredity' which 'may work ... through the suppression of one or more genes; or ... through the release of a genetic potential which had previously been suppressed'. In support they offer well-known evidence (even in the discipline of economic history) about the change in physique owing to increased nutrition and the change in physical well-being owing to a change in diet. What they overlook here is the fundamentally important fact – which is destructive of their thesis – that the relatively recent increase in nutrition and the change in diet are not independent of man. Quite the reverse. The change in eating habits is a direct product of technological change, which is driven by the demands of materialist man – or the general human desire to maximize what is perceived to be to their material advantage. Owing to our proximity in time to this matter, the real relationship between human drive and the change in nutrition is easily recognized. In a similar way, although its distance from us in time may make it more difficult to appreciate, chemical resources in those evolutionary epochs before the emergence of man were also strongly influenced by an intense 'desire' of life forms to survive.

4 Hence, Crawford and Marsh (ibid.: 35–6) propose a dynamic system in which the driving force or 'push' is provided by the physical environment, to which life forms merely respond passively. Actually, the model is internally inconsistent, because without the drive provided by living organisms it would be impossible to start, let alone maintain, the process. Nutritional opportunities, even if independent of the activities of life forms, cannot drive a dynamic life system. In other words, a life system cannot be driven by inorganic substances, especially if the life forms are denied an active, or even a predominant, role. Such a system could never work. They have, therefore, been unable to overthrow Darwin and to displace economics with physical science. The metaphor for their supply-side approach, mentioned in the last sentence of their book, is 'The figure of a human mother and child' – which they interpret as the supplier, and passive recipient, of chemical nutrients! To the contrary, the essence of life on Earth is the driving force provided by life itself under the condition of economic scarcity. If we are no longer at the mercy of the gods, we are certainly not the playthings of inorganic substances!

Yet while Crawford and Marsh do not provide a convincing case for an inorganic explanation of the origin of the species, they do spell out admirably the nature of Darwin's 'conditions of life'. This is an essential background against which to reconstruct the interaction of driving life forms with their physical environments.

THE GREAT WAVES OF LIFE

We have seen how the Darwinian perspective on the development path of evolution has been modified from one of gradual change at a fairly steady rate of progress (at least within fairly narrow limits) in *The Origin of Species* (1859) to the idea of 'punctuated equilibria' held by some evolutionists today. Unfortunately there has been no attempt to distinguish between the profile of genetic change and the contours of life. Hence we still do not have a clear idea of what this development path looks like. Accordingly, what I plan to do in this section is to employ the available evidence in the fossil record to sketch out a **timescape** for the dynamics of life, which should not be confused with a profile of genetic change. This will provide the basis in the next section for an **existential model** that can explain this pattern of existence.

The development path of life

The timescapes I wish to examine are presented in Figures 4.1 to 4.4 which are to be read from left to right. The first two figures are based upon the fossil record concerning the emergence and disappearance of different forms of plant and animal life over the last 3 billion years in the case of Figure 4.1 and the last 270 million years for Figure 4.2. As we saw in Chapter 2, there have been many fluctuations in the fortunes of life on Earth. In Figures 4.1 and 4.2 I have attempted to identify the longest swings in biological development, which I have called the great waves of life. An attempt has been made to identify the main turning points when one major form of life gave way to another – such as the decline of blue-green algae and the emergence of animal organisms; the emergence of dinosaurs as the dominant species; and the disappearance of dinosaurs and the ascendency of the mammals. Other setbacks such as the widespread extinctions around 435, 370, and 215 million years ago constitute major fluctuations within the great waves, just as more minor fluctuations can be recognized within the major fluctuations and so on. A similar attempt has been made in Chapter 12 to identify for human society the longest swings in economic development, within which can be found cycles within cycles.

Owing to the sophistication of modern fossil-dating methods, it is possible to provide a reasonably accurate picture of changes on the horizontal axes of Figures 4.1 and 4.2. The vertical axes, however, present a greater problem. What I wanted to achieve in the first two timescapes was a sense of expansion in the quantity of life on Earth – a sort of impossibly gigantic population census of all species adjusted for size and complexity. This was to be a

74

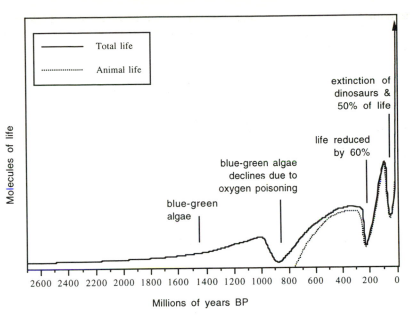

Figure 4.1 The great waves of life – the last 3 billion years

macro view of life on Earth, rather than the usual micro, or species, view. Accordingly, the vertical axis could be thought of as being a measure of the basic units of all life – the molecule. Needless to say, no precision could possibly be attained. None, however, is required; only a visual impression is being sought.

The *shape* of the timescape of biological life in Figures 4.1 and 4.2 is based upon evidence and inductive generalization. We have evidence for a number of major turning points, such as: the relatively rapid collapse in the dominant life forms of bacteria and blue-green algae around 1 billion years ago, which enabled the emergence of animal life; the sudden reduction by a massive 60 per cent of all animal and plant species around 250 million years ago, which led to the emergence of the dinosaurs; and the sudden disappearance of the dinosaurs (and three-quarters of all other species) around 65 million years ago, which gave mammals, and eventually man, their chance. While these relatively sudden disappearances of dominant life forms are said to have been caused by events exogenous (or external) to the dynamic process of life, the extent of the devastation they caused suggests that, on each occasion, the major life forms were under severe stress. Otherwise we might reasonably expect a higher survival rate than that shown in the fossil record. In addition it is known that, while the collapses may have been sudden, each of these dominant forms of life had long been in decline following very extended periods of dominance by the major species. As we know from contemporary studies (e.g. Elliott, 1986:143), introduced animal populations starting from a small base increase slowly at first, but then gain momentum and accelerate rapidly towards the ceiling provided by natural resources. It is proposed here that the increasing pressure on resources following the exhaustion of the dynamic strategies of the dominant species leads to a reduction in food per capita and hence a decline in the rate of growth of population, followed by stagnation and possibly absolute decline. In the process the animal population suffers the ravages of disease, famine, conflict, and death. Consequently, over such long periods of time we can expect populations to experience cycles of expansion, stagnation, and decline even in the absence of exogenous shocks.

The immediate visual impression provided by the timescape for the last 3 billion years, presented in Figure 4.1, is of a great wave-like motion of life on Earth surging across vast tracts of time. These are the great waves of biological change. Beginning some 4 billion years ago plant life, in the form of bacteria and, later (1.6 billion years ago), blue-green algae, spread gradually at first, and then increasingly rapidly, throughout the world. Paradoxically the very success of blue-green algae was responsible for polluting its own environment with oxygen – which was toxic to this life form – and sending it into permanent decline about 1,000 million years ago. This brought the first great wave of life to an end. But the very oxygen that caused this dominant life form's demise marked the beginning of a newly mutated form of life that depended upon oxygen – animal organisms. Hence, about 700 million years ago early animal life (metazoans) began to emerge, and by 500 million years before the present, a rapid acceleration of multicellular animal life was under way. This was the second great wave of life on Earth, which appears to have reached the limits of its physical environment in the sea and on the land after some 600 million years.

The third great wave of life was the era of the dinosaurs. Their opportunity came with the sudden and dramatic decline of the well-established animal and plant life throughout the world around 250 million years ago. Indeed, the fossil record suggests that over 60 per cent of all plants and animal species on Earth were wiped out. An earth scientist (Campbell *et al.*, 1992) at the Australian National University believes he has the answer to this remarkable event, in the form of a 'gigantic volcanic upheaval' in Siberia which coincided with the disappearance of virtually all life in the Permian era from the fossil record. According to Campbell, this upheaval produced great explosions that in turn gave rise to an 'enormous' output of sulphurous gas that formed a blanket in the upper atmosphere and shielded the planet from the Sun. The subsequent cooling of the Earth caused the polar caps to expand and the sea levels to fall by about 250 metres. The resulting unfavourable impact on food production was compounded by acid rain, as the sulphur reacted with the air, which led to further destruction of life on land and sea.

No doubt such an event would have had a major impact upon life on Earth, but it is also highly likely that, by around 250 million years BP, the second-wave plants and animals had exhausted the dynamic opportunities underlying their expansion, thereby rendering them particularly vulnerable to any exogenous event. We should be careful in assuming that the coincidence of a physical event with changes in the fossil record constitutes simple cause and effect. No doubt big physical events also correspond with the absence of significant change in the fossil record. Dynamic life systems, it must be realized, are capable of sizeable downturns and collapses that are internally generated.

The age of the dinosaurs also appears to have ended suddenly about 65 million years ago after an extended period of decline. Not only did the dinosaurs vanish, but so too did three-quarters of all other species. Once again we are treated in the literature to a variety of catastrophic causes, such as massive volcanic action, this time in the Deccan Traps of India – 'one of the largest piles of lava on earth' – and/or the possibility of an asteroid impact at Chicxulub on Mexico's Yucatan Peninsula (Crawford and Marsh, 1989: 139). The widely recognized problems with these catastrophe hypotheses are twofold: the decline, rather than the collapse, of dinosaurs occurred relatively slowly, possibly over millions of years; and the dust thrown up into the air by an asteroid impact or massive volcanic explosion would, it is generally agreed, have fallen back to Earth within six months, not long enough to reduce temperatures sufficiently to kill all dinosaurs. These catastrophe theories are clearly insufficient to explain the regular rise and fall of species. In order to salvage the asteroid theory, scientists at the US National Aeronautics and Space Administration (NASA) have recently (Chen *et al.*, 1994) suggested that the sulphur-rich rock formation around Chicxulub may provide the answer. They claim that the impact of the giant asteroid would have vaporized the sulphur in the rock, throwing more than 100 tonnes high into the air, thereby creating a dense haze of sulphuric acid that could have filtered out enough sunlight to reduce the surface temperature below zero for at least a decade. But, of course, while this could have contributed to the collapse of the dinosaurs it does not account for the long period of slow decline typical of a life system exhausting its dynamic strategies. Also the NASA scientists suggest that had the asteroid hit the Earth at any other place 'Dinosaurs could still be roaming the Earth'. This is quite a revealing statement because it is an admission that the catastrophe model is entirely random relying heavily on chance, and that these scientists do not appreciate the internal dynamics of life systems which are sufficient on their own to lead to the regular rise and fall of dominant species. Having exhausted their dynamic strategies more than 65 million years ago, there is no way that the giant dinosaurs could still be with us, even in the absence of cosmic catastrophe. A hypothesis more consistent with the evidence is that the dinosaurs and associated species, which were already in decline, suffered

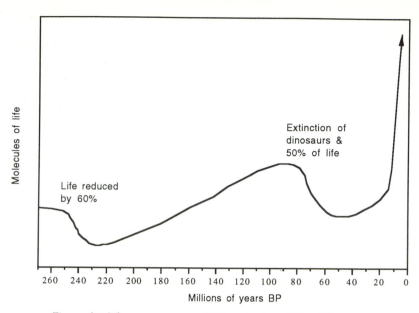

Figure 4.2 The great waves of life – the last 270 million years

from over-expansion owing to the exhaustion of their dynamic opportunities, and that a major catastrophic event (which has occurred more regularly than once every few hundred million years) may have been the last straw. The catastrophic explanations of changes in the fossil record come easily to natural scientists who are not accustomed to thinking in terms of endogenously (internally) driven life systems.

Whatever the primary cause, the disappearance of the dominant dinosaurs, together with many of the remaining species, left the way clear for a new range of plants and animals, including birds and mammals, which had first appeared almost 100 million years earlier but had only survived the age of the dinosaurs with difficulty. This gave rise to the fourth and, until now, final great wave of biological change. The last wave is the era of the mammals and of humans. So far the rate of growth of the last wave has been exponential in nature, but the great question is: for how much longer can this continue? Are we approaching the stage, which has been encountered at least three times before in the history of life on Earth, when the pressure of population on natural resources through the exhaustion of dynamic opportunities will irretrievably pollute our world? Will the predictions of natural scientists about the devastating impact of greenhouse gases come true? Will we, in a last desperate scramble for key natural resources, destroy much of life on Earth by a great nuclear winter? Or will the rational faculties of mankind prevent the 'disaster' that the blue-green algae was unable to prevent some 1 billion years ago? These issues will be taken up in the final chapter.

In order to see more clearly what has happened in the last two great waves, the timescape in Figure 4.1 has been redrawn with an extended horizontal scale. The wave-like motion of the last two eras of life can be seen even more clearly in Figure 4.2. It would seem that life on Earth embodies a fundamental dynamic tendency to proceed via great waves of change. As we shall discover in Chapter 12, great waves of change, although of much shorter duration, also characterize the manner in which the Dynamic Society has progressed.

The dynamic timescapes in Figures 4.1 and 4.2, therefore, show a series of great waves of biological change. But those waves are not independent of each other. Like the surging waves of a great ocean rushing onto a continental shore, there is a systematic relationship between them. The first great wave was about 1.6 billion years in duration, the second about 600 million years, the third about 185 million years, and the fourth, which is by no means complete, about 60 million years. For what it is worth, the declining duration of each wave represented in Figure 4.1 is a mathematical constant – each wave is about one-third as long as the one that preceded it. Also, the amplitude of the waves is increasing. There can be little doubt, therefore, that the momentum of life on Earth is accelerating. As can be seen from Figure 4.3, this increasing momentum of life is described by an exponential curve on an arithmetical scale and a straight line (log linear) on a logarithmic scale. This is Malthus's geometric rate of growth. In other words, Malthus's speculation about the growth of human population (which, it has turned out, is not universally true) is a good approximation for the growing intensity of the great waves of life. Either this is purely coincidental (certainly there are few observations) or it is powerful evidence that the great waves of biological change are largely endogenously determined, with the energy of each wave feeding into its successor, rather than the result of random natural catastrophes. What are the implications of this fascinating discovery? It appears to constitute an important law of life: that any dynamic life system (including human society) involving an accumulating stock of 'ideas' (either genetic or technological), where the output of 'ideas' in one phase (or wave) becomes the input of the next phase in which they are further transformed, will grow exponentially.

The ascent of man

The ascent of man, which cannot be detected in Figure 4.1, requires its own timescape. Figure 4.4 traces out the rising step-like path for mankind from the early ancestry of about 3 to 5 million years ago to *Homo sapiens sapiens*. A different type of data has been used to construct Figure 4.4, which has important implications for both the precision of the timescape and the story

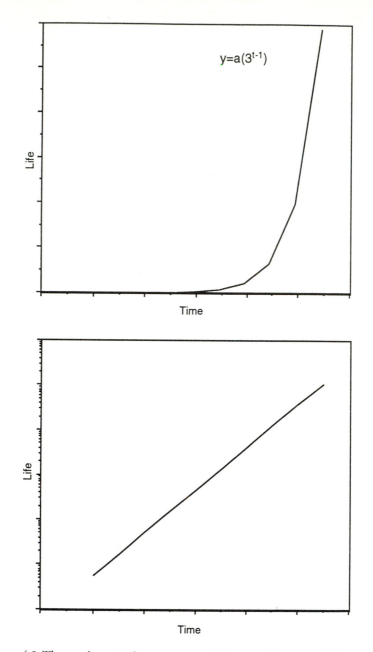

Figure 4.3 The mathematical momentum of life over the past 3 billion years as described in Figure 4.1
(a) Life on an arithmetic scale
(b) Life on a logarithmic scale

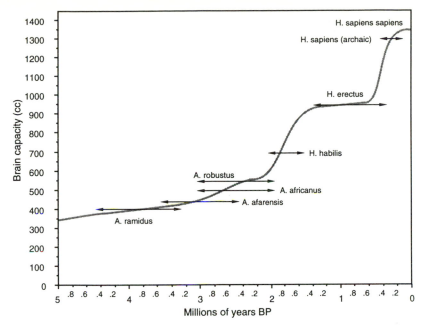

Figure 4.4 Ascending the intellectual staircase – the last 5 million years
Source: Drawn from data in Eccles (1989: 21), and in White *et al.* (1994).

that it tells. First, as both the horizontal and vertical axes are based upon fossil evidence – time on the former and brain capacity on the latter – this timescape is more precise than those in Figures 4.1 and 4.2. Second, when looking at the ascent of man, we are interested not only in the quantity of change – the global population of humans – but also its quality. The quality – the efficiency or productivity of the life form we call man – can be measured approximately by the size of the brain cavity of fossilized skulls. This can be used as a proxy for the quality or standard of life he enjoyed. But only approximately, because the add-on bits of the brain of modern man are themselves more efficient owing to their more specialized nature (Eccles, 1989: ch. 9). This growing brain capacity, and hence the efficiency with which man could achieve his objectives, is reflected – as discussed in Chapter 2 – in the improvement in the tools that were employed in the daily activity of survival. Curiously, in the case of early man there is less complete information on quantity (and what does exist is less reliable) than on quality.

The use of qualitative rather than quantitative data gives a picture that is essentially different to that in Figures 4.1 and 4.2. Instead of a pronounced series of waves, we see a step-like pattern of qualitative change. Man has ascended a moving intellectual staircase – a staircase that has accelerated as it has approached the present. The scattered population data available suggest, however, that if we had better information the familiar wave-like pattern of development would be clearly discernible. As can be seen in Figure 12.1, even the most heroic estimates of human population do not go back beyond 1 myrs BP: nevertheless, these data suggest that human population has progressed via three great waves of diminishing duration from 1 myrs to 10,000 years BP, from 10,000 to 2,000 years BP, and from 2,000 years ago to the present. The qualitative picture in Figure 4.4 shows that the ascent of man, like the development of life on Earth (and, as we shall see, like the progress of the Dynamic Society), has been achieved not steadily, but via a series of surges that have become more pronounced as they pass from the distant past to the present.

The interesting question is: what will the future bring? A specialist on brain development, John Eccles, claims that the evolution of the brain is complete, as it has been ever since the emergence of *Homo sapiens sapiens* some 100,000 years ago. His reasoning is that the process by which natural selection took place in the past is no longer operative because it is no longer possible for a small local population, which may experience favourable genetic change, to avoid the diluting effect of a large global gene pool. It is not possible in the modern world because no tribe or group of tribes could remain isolated for the required period of tens or hundreds of thousands of years. As Darwin insisted, genetic change is a slow, gradual process. Whether or not Eccles is correct, mankind has discovered a quicker process for improving efficiency, and hence their quality of life – technological change. Technological ideas have replaced genetic ideas in the ascent of man.

AN ECONOMIC INTERPRETATION OF THE DYNAMICS OF LIFE

The history of evolution as an idea clearly shows the contribution made to it by an inductively based political economy. Charles Darwin's thinking about evolution via struggle and natural selection owed a good deal to Thomas Robert Malthus's economic analysis of population (Desmond and Moore, 1991: 264–8). In Malthus's account, a rapidly growing population would eventually outstrip increases in the production of food, would lead to a struggle for resources, and would result in famine, disease, death, and war. Only the strong and powerful would gain: the weak and poor would suffer and die. This is one of the truly pivotal observations in the history of life and social sciences, and both fields have used the idea extensively. When discussing his concept of the 'struggle for existence', Darwin (1979: 117) openly acknowledged his debt to Malthus: 'It is the doctrine of Malthus applied with manifold force to the whole animal and vegetable kingdoms; for in this case there can be no artificial increase of food, and no prudential restraint from marriage.'

Although not publicly acknowledged by Darwin, Adam Smith, another great observer of, and thinker about, the human economy, had a major influence on his thinking. The key to Smith's explanation of the growing wealth of nations was the concept of specialization and division of labour that takes place within a competitive society. Darwin was familiar with this economic concept and with its operation in the world around him, particularly in the businesses in which he invested his wealth. But, according to his biographers, as he wished to avoid the political wrangles in which political economy was (and still is) involved, he thought it best not to acknowledge this influence. Desmond and Moore (1991: 420) describe this influence as follows:

> Darwin recognized that, just as industry expanded when the workers specialized, so did life. But Nature had the 'more efficient workshops'. He argued that natural selection would automatically increase the 'physiological division of labour' among animals caught in competitive situations. Stressful competition in overcrowded areas – what he called Nature's 'manufactory of species' – favoured variants that could exploit free niches. These individuals would seize on new opportunities, exploit the available openings on that spot.

Just as the concept of specialization played a central role in Smith's analysis of economic growth, so it played an important part in Darwin's explanation of organic change. And, more generally, the role of competition between individuals in Adam Smith also had a profound influence upon Darwin's concept of struggle for survival in nature – as did Smith's idea of the 'invisible hand' in coordinating the actions of the many individuals in society. Gould (1987: 7) reminds his fellow scientists: 'Culture can potentiate as well as constrain – as in Darwin's translation of Adam Smith's *laissez-faire* economic models into biology as the theory of natural selection'.

While economics has strongly influenced Darwinism, it has not been employed as a model of the entire dynamic system of biological change. Indeed, Darwinism itself is only an explanation of progressive genetic change in individual species. This, as suggested earlier, is equivalent to an explanation of technological change in a particular sector of the economy, which is a subset of any explanation of the dynamics of human society. The mechanism of struggle and selection, therefore, is only part of the model required to explain the timescape in Figure 4.1.

A new model

In this section I describe a simple economic model that can be used to analyse the dynamics of life on Earth over the last 4 billion years. This existential, rather than deductive, model was briefly outlined in Chapter 1. It has only four main requirements: 'decision-making' individuals who maximize their survival/material advantage objective; a highly competitive environment; a set of physical constraints capable of significant if slow change; and, most crucially, the pursuit by 'decision-making' individuals of a variety of dynamic strategies – multiplication, predation, symbiosis, and progressive genetic ideas – to achieve their objectives. 'Decision-making', of course, is done in an instinctive rather than an intellectual way as in human society. This rhetorical device facilitates model construction. The model's requirements will be discussed, together with the way it acts as a dynamic system. It is a model relevant to both biological change before the emergence of mankind and economic change since its arrival.

1 The first requirement of our model is a world populated with 'decision-making' individuals who are motivated by an overwhelming 'desire' (or instinct) to get the most out of life. This desire is a function of the nature of life on Earth, in that the individuals who have it survive to pass it on to future generations, while those who do not possess it die early, or at best, live on in poverty and impotence. Before the society of man, this motivation can be translated into an instinct to survive at all costs. From this, everything else follows, such as the pleasures of consumption, watchful idleness, and sexual gratification. The unconscious 'objective', therefore, is to maintain a state of existence, not to maximize consumption and sexual pleasure which are merely by-products of staying alive. In fact, an attempt to maximize the by-products of survival will endanger life itself through a loss of physical condition and excessive conflict with rivals. This overwhelming instinct to survive, therefore, is the potent driving force in life, which will exist from the beginning to the end of life on Earth.

It is essential to stress the importance of this requirement, because it appears to be the source of so much confusion, not only about the dynamics of biological change but also about the dynamics of human society. While Darwin recognized this (although he did not subject it to analysis), the recent 'pure science' push – namely the punctuationists and environmentalists – have missed its significance entirely. They either assume or explicitly claim that the driving force in evolution is provided by the physical environment, through catastrophic events or chemical substances. Or they twist the Darwinian idea of maximizing the probability of survival to become the maximization of reproduction. This requires further elaboration.

The limitations of the maximization of reproduction hypothesis can be illustrated by a random example of the study of animal behaviour – the springbok of the Kalahari (Attenborough, 1993). Attention focuses in that study upon the interesting territorial behaviour of the elite male springboks which make up about 10 per cent of the male population. All other males travel together in groups, while the females and 'lambs' herd together separately. In contrast, the elite solitary males stake out their territories in dry river beds and defend these against all comers including dangerous carnivores. The usual explanation is that this dangerous and solitary vigil is to maintain a territory that will attract herds of female springboks during the rutting season.

When the females do finally arrive our solitary male has to beat off challenges both from neighbouring springbok males, who have their own territories, and from the more dangerous roving males. This, we are told, is the explanation for his long and dangerous vigil. Clearly, this is a perilous business that can easily lead to death. Usually the neighbouring males are relatively easily driven off, but the roving males are a different matter. Eventually a younger and stronger roving male will displace the older territorial male. But if successful, our territorial male will mate with all the females he can herd together before some are attracted to his neighbours' territories. Finally, we are told, when the rains come and the former dry river beds are covered with lush grass, large herds of springbok (and other animals) are attracted to these key feeding areas. Interestingly, the territorial males appear unconcerned about these temporary invaders.

Upon closer inspection, the traditional reproduction story is not a persuasive explanation of the long, lonely, and dangerous vigil of the elite springbok male. What, for example, does the traditional story tell us about the gains made by the elite males from this behaviour? Apart from sexual gratification, little else. They do not receive companionship and they take no interest in the offspring. What, therefore, drives them to maximize the number of their offspring? There is no reason at all. It is not sufficient to respond by stating that only those species in which individuals – owing to their 'selected' genetic makeup – maximize their reproduction survive, because such a static mechanism possesses no active Darwinian driving force (the 'struggle for existence'). Without such a driving force, as Darwin was well aware, there would be no life to reproduce itself. A far better explanation of these observed facts is that all actors in this drama are acting as if they are attempting to maximize not reproduction but the probability of their own individual survival. Once again I will employ the rhetorical device that individuals in a species possess objectives and respond rationally to changing external circumstances.

The elite springbok males, like elite males in neolithic society, attempt to monopolize the best land to ensure their survival and, having survived (and only then), all the other pleasures it can provide. It is the dry river beds that grow the best grasses and receive all the runoff after the occasional rains. As this land is scarce, only a small proportion of males can hope to gain territories. These are the strongest males in the population who have to fight to gain and maintain their territories. It is not persuasive to argue that the bucks' long, lonely, and dangerous vigil is sexually inspired because that motivation is too indirect, too distant. Solitary males stake out territories on the best land because that is the best way to survive from day to day. Roving males fight life-and-death battles with territorial males towards the end of the dry season not primarily for access to the gathering females but because the supply of grasses elsewhere has been exhausted. If they fail to gain territories at this arid time of the year they could starve to death. They only fight to the death when food is scarce. This is why the roving males are more dangerous than neighbouring males who still have a share of the remaining grasses.

Meanwhile, the females and their offspring are attracted to the dry river beds at the end of the dry season primarily for the same reason as the roving males – supplies of grasses elsewhere have been exhausted. They are allowed by the territorial males to graze in the dry river beds in return for sexual favours, and they provide sexual favours in return for grazing rights. It is significant that the females do not provide sexual favours to the roving males who have no food with which to negotiate. The usual explanation is that they mate with the strongest males to ensure they have the strongest offspring. While females do mate with the strongest males, as Darwin (1979: 136) knew, this is merely an outcome of competition by both genders for access to scarce resources. It is not about sex but about economics. 'Sexual selection is', as Darwin (ibid.: 136) claimed, 'less rigorous than natural selection'.

Finally, the reason that the territorial males do not get agitated when the lush grasses brought on by the rains attract great herds of springbok to their territory is that there is food enough for all. But in the Kalahari this abundance does not last for long, and as grasses diminish the males return to fighting over territories. They must in order to survive. Survival is only a life and death issue when food is scarce. Life is driven by the struggle to survive and having survived – and only then – to the gratification of the senses. The naturalists' preoccupation should be redirected from sex towards the management of scarce resources!

2 The second requirement of our model is a highly competitive environment created by a range of life forms with the drive to generate an infinite demand for resources on the one hand with a world of finite resources on the other. This is the central economic problem of scarcity. In a world without scarcity, it is doubtful that life could have begun, and had it done so, evolution of any primitive life form would not have occurred. It is even likely that if scarcity suddenly ceased to exist, the Dynamic Society would grind quickly to a halt and go into decline because there would be no incentives to pursue the dynamic strategies that alone give rise to progress. Competition is the very essence of life on Earth.

The struggle between individuals for a finite supply of resources is the universally applicable Malthusian insight that is at the centre of Darwinism and must be at the centre of any discussion of the dynamics in human and non-human species. Malthus argued that as population would grow at a geometric rate and access to resources at only an arithmetic rate, the end result would be misery and death. Yet, he failed to realize two important matters. First, Malthus overlooked the possibility that this seemingly inevitable outcome could be postponed, if not eliminated, by the pursuit of a number of dynamic strategies through which a society could increase its material standards of living. The best known of these is the technology strategy. The application of technological ideas to economic organization and production makes it possible to use existing resources more intensively or, in other words, to generate a growing output from a given input of natural resources. In the case of life before man, survival, and possibly even expansion of population, of the successful species in the 'war of life' could be achieved by the introduction of new 'ideas' in the form of genetic 'engineering'. Needless to say, this has been a much slower process than technological change in human society. Second, Malthus failed to realize that, in an advanced and viable economy, family multiplication is a dynamic strategy that will only be employed when unused natural resources are available. When all natural resources are fully utilized (given the available technology), alternative dynamic strategies are adopted. This is also true of non-human species, and is not invalidated by the rapid expansion of some species in good seasons and the equally rapid reduction during bad seasons.

3 This discussion of strategies leads to the model's third requirement. Decision-makers attempt to maximize the probability of survival and material advantage by employing a range of positive dynamic strategies that includes multiplication, predation, symbiosis, and genetic change. There is also the negative strategy of isolation, which weakens the resilience of species and ultimately leads to extinction. In the animal world, multiplication is a useful strategy if unused resources exist, as there is safety in large numbers. Herbivores employ this survival strategy with great effectiveness, roving the plains in large herds. But this strategy may, as we have seen, get out of hand in good seasons and lead to large-scale starvation when seasons turn bad.

There are a number of ways that individuals and species can deal with declining resources. First there is predation – the animal equivalent of war and conquest – when individuals and species gain access to territories through physical conflict, as in our springbok example. Second, some species will search for a specialized niche – the animal equivalent of trade protection – such as the move of dolphins back into the seas. This is a negative strategy because the growing specialization of such species reduces their flexibility and long-term viability. Third, there is symbiosis – where one species derives its sustenance from another – which occurs in both the plant and animal kingdom. The best-known examples are that of carnivores preying upon herbivores; or of particular plants drawing sustenance from other plants. Symbiosis can be thought of as the equivalent to the commerce strategy in human society where merchants attempt to capture the gains from trade through monopoly arrangements.

Fourth, there is the accumulation of a stock of beneficial (or product-ive) 'ideas' that can be used by individuals to improve their prospects of survival or material advantage because they provide favourable access to natural resources. These 'ideas' are generated by a small, relatively isolated subgroup of the wider population under study, and can be either genetic or technological. These ideas can and will emerge at any time, but they will only be employed if they are generally perceived by individual 'decision-makers' as improving the efficiency with which their 'objectives' can be pursued. In the case of life before man, the process by which new genetic 'ideas' are adopted has been brilliantly explained by Darwin through his theory of natural selection. Only those genetic mutations that provide an individual life form with an edge in the battle for survi-val will be passed on to future generations because only their owners will survive. In the Dynamic Society, technological ideas are only applied to economic organization and production when it is anticipated by the great mass of decision-makers that the necessary investment (and hence deferred consumption) will significantly increase the efficiency of achieving their objective – the maximization of material advantage or well-being.

While the genetic paradigm in nature is the equivalent of the techno-logical paradigm in human society, there are limits to this comparison. In nature a genetic paradigm is specific to a particular set of species, whereas in human civilization a particular society can change its technological paradigm. Hence the change in genetic paradigm implies the replacement of one set of species by another.

4 The final requirement of our existential model, is that the physical environ-ment, which is the ultimate constraint on organic activity when – and only when – all the dynamic strategies have been exhausted, experiences both independent and induced change. Independent change includes all those events in the history of the Earth that are not caused by life form activities. These include changes in global climate, (which in extreme form have involved ice ages), significant volcanic activity, and natural events from outer space (such as the impacts of asteroids). Induced changes in the physical environment result from the activities of life forms, and include natural resource degradation, erosion, desertification, and atmos-pheric and climate changes due to the emissions of harmful gases. None of this is new. Around 1 billion years ago the dominant life form, blue-green algae, had managed to pollute its environment with oxygen and, as a result, went into permanent decline. This is an induced change and cannot be regarded as an independent motivating force as claimed by Crawford and Marsh (1989).

All life takes place within a physical environment that is subject to physical laws. But as far as the game of life is concerned, these laws merely provide the rules by which it is played. They define the boundaries within which the game is played and determine what type of moves are possible. But they do not determine when or how those moves are made, the strategy employed, or how ruthlessly or brilliantly the game is played. That is entirely the province of the organic players, who provide the game with its driving force.

These four requirements or variables can be combined into a dynamic model to explain the pattern of life as revealed by the timescapes in Figures 4.1 to 4.4. It is a dynamic model that can account for the expansion of dominant and supporting species, the development of growing crisis and downturn, and the collapse of these dominant forms of life. There are a number of interrelated sequences in this dynamic process of life.

1 The first dynamic sequence is characterized by expanding populations of the dominant (and associated) plant and/or animal species. We begin with relatively small populations in relation to available resources, as was the case at the beginning of life some 4 billion years ago and during the periods that followed the sudden (in geological terms) disappearance of major life forms on Earth around 250 and 65 million years ago. The obvious strategy is multiplication or reproduction. In these circumstances populations expand slowly at first, but gather momentum as they develop new colonies in previously unsettled areas. This expansion takes place with little improvement in the efficiency with which the species' 'objectives' are pursued and obtained. Competition in settled areas exists but it is relieved by the safety-valve of additional accessible resources. Before man, this meant that insufficient pressure existed to 'introduce' new genetic 'ideas'. Or, in more conventional terms, the fight for resources was not yet so intense that only the fittest survived – the less fit could move into new regions. This growth phase of the great wave of life corresponds with the long period of stasis in the genetic profile of the punctuationists. It is similar to the palaeolithic phase in human society. While human families could multiply by shifting to new regions where resources were under-utilized, there was no incentive to introduce new technological ideas which would increase the efficiency of natural resource utilization.

2 The second dynamic sequence occurs when all available resources are approaching full exploitation. For some time before this ceiling is attained, increasing difficulties will be experienced by individual life forms in gaining access to the resources they need to ensure survival. This pressure will increase the competition between individuals in the same species as well as between species. Some individuals will, as Darwin noted, seek out specialist niches in order to avoid excessive competition. This specialization – a strategy familiar to economists of the day – may be reinforced genetically. I want to suggest a fascinating example of this negative strategy of competition-avoidance which has close parallels with protective tactics employed by human societies at a later date. About 50 million years ago

89

some land mammals, the ancestors of whales and dolphins, returned to the sea. My suggestion is that this was the result of increasing competition among mammals – most notably with the early primates – along the fringes of the seas. This strategy was, in the short term (in terms of life on Earth), so successful that dolphins with their larger brains had little opposition in the seas. But in the longer term the strategy was disastrous. As they effectively avoided competition, there was no need to 'introduce' new genetic 'ideas' beyond those that enabled them to swim efficiently (at a time when the ancestors of man, and then man himself, were beginning to walk efficiently on two legs). While dolphins lived a relatively stressless and unchanging lifestyle, humans in their more competitive environment developed a relatively larger (in comparison with body weight) and more complex brain, which enabled them to build civilizations based upon the introduction of technological ideas to the organization and production of goods and services. When these land and marine mammal species finally came back into contact, it was a one-sided contest. The destiny of sea mammals now depends entirely upon the whims of mankind. While the avoidance of competition may appear successful in the shortrun, in the longrun it is nothing short of a disaster for the species concerned. There are parallels here with those human societies – Aboriginal Australians, the Indians of the more isolated parts of northern and southern America, and the inhabitants of islands in the Pacific – that developed in isolation from the highly competitive Eurasian and Mesoamerican tribes.

Those species that remained in the competitive mainstream of life employed their competitive advantage to win the struggle for survival against their less successful neighbours. This struggle for survival prompted animal species to adopt a number of different dynamic strategies. In the shorter term this led either to greater predatory activity to take over the territories of other animals, or to the attempt of one species to live symbiotically with another. The extent to which these strategies are successful delays the 'adoption' of genetic change and accounts for the apparent equilibrium, or stasis, found in the fossil record. In the longer term, however, the most effective strategy is genetic change.

The manner in which genetic change was achieved, apart from the need for a competitive environment, is still not entirely clear. The neo-Darwinian view is that progressive genetic change occurs in small sub-groups isolated from the diluting effects of the large parent-population's gene pool. Such a situation, however, will only produce accumulating genetic change if the small local population has to struggle hard for survival, presumably against individuals from other species with whom they are unable to produce offspring. Whatever the exact mechanism, intense competition led, in effect, to the application of new 'ideas' to genetic engineering in order to improve the efficiency of successful individuals and species in achieving their primary 'objective' of survival. This generated an acceleration of genetic change relative to the long period of genetic equilibrium when the species found it more effective to use other dynamic strategies. In other words, the 'dynamic strategy' model can explain the fossil evidence that has so worried the punctuationists. The apparent longrun stasis (probably *very* slow genetic change) occurs when it is more 'cost' effective for individuals to employ non-genetic strategies. It must, however, be borne in mind that the 'punctuated equilibrium' (or genetic paradigm) profile – which is the equivalent of the technological paradigm profile in human society – is not an outline of the expansion of life (or of the great waves of biological change) but only of the genetic strategy. The expansion of life can and does occur when there is no genetic change. This has been a source of considerable confusion in the past.

3   We now come to the third dynamic sequence. This emerges when all the dynamic strategies that can be employed by the dominant species in their upward path have been exhausted. This is what I have called the **strategic crisis** which, as explained in Chapter 12, is a more general concept than the Malthusian population crisis. During this sequence the dominant species, which have become highly specialized and inflexible, have 'explored' all the possibilities in their genetic paradigm. The only way in which a new genetic paradigm can emerge is for the old dominant species to collapse and for opportunistic species waiting in the wings to take their place on centre stage by employing the various dynamic strategies including genetic change. The changeover occurs when the old dominant species pursue the only course open to them in a highly competitive environment – excessive predation. A major species, such as the carnivorous dinosaurs, will be able to increase its numbers and dominance on the Earth by specializing in excessive predation. This will involve not only depending entirely for nutrition upon the killing of other species, but also using this strategy aggressively to extend their territorial range. Over hundreds of thousands of years this strategy will become genetically reinforced. Once the capacity for further territorial expansion has been exhausted and the former external food source has been eliminated, these highly specialized and inflexible predators will turn upon each other. During this final phase of cannibalism they literally tear each other and their environment to pieces. Excessive predation destroys the former balance between the forces of order (herd instinct) and chaos (individual aggression). It also destroys the balance between life and physical environment. In the resulting war of the giants their whole genetic paradigm collapses. While this could occur in the absence of an external shock, such a shock would exacerbate a crisis and may cause it to become unstable. Chaos may, like the upward momentum, become self-generating. Individuals respond 'rationally', in a world where order is not possible, by highly predatory activity. Not until the dominant species (or civilization) have fought themselves to a standstill can order be attained. Then it may be too late, because the way has

been cleared for an eventual takeover by a new set of species that have been watching from the wings, and waiting for their opportunity.

A new wave of life will be generated owing to the emergence of new species which are not highly specialized and still possess considerable potential for change. This potential is explored under the pressure of competition and the struggle for survival by using various dynamic strategies. Initially, because of the vacuum left by the disappearance of earlier dominant species, the emerging groups will employ the simple multiplication strategy until all unutilized natural resources have been exploited. To achieve continued success requires the development of further strategies including predation, symbiosis, and, ultimately when other strategies have been exhausted, genetic change. But eventually, this new wave of life, which will involve many species going through similar processes, will reach the limits of their genetic paradigms, and they will stagnate, decline, strike out ruthlessly, and collapse. Only man has been able to transcend this genetic paradigm collapse, by substituting the technological paradigm shift for the genetic paradigm shift. In human society the technological paradigm shift provides continuity for the species man, but in the pre-human world a genetic paradigm shift involved both the collapse of the old dominant species that had carried the old paradigm to this stage, and the emergence of new dominant species to carry the new genetic paradigm forward.

Here we have an internal mechanism for generating extremely long cycles – a dynamic mechanism underlying the great waves of biological change. Once under way, change, fed by greater access to resources and a natural form of 'genetic engineering', becomes exponential in nature as the outputs of one dynamic sequence become the inputs of the next. While new genetic 'ideas' and other non-genetic strategies will prolong this acceleration, eventually the entire genetic paradigm of the dominant species is exhausted and a strategic crisis occurs. The strategic crisis finally breaks the upward momentum, which leads to the decline and collapse of the old dominant species to make way for the rise of the new.

Explaining the accelerating pace of life

This model has been used to explain the essential characteristic of the great waves of life in Figure 4.1. It explains the upward surge – slow at first and then, after gathering momentum, explosively upward – the crisis, the downturn, and the complete collapse that precedes any further expansionary phase. But it can also be used to explain the cumulative energy exhibited by each successive great wave of biological life.

Each great wave begins at a higher level of genetic 'efficiency' than the last. As life is continuous, we never go back to the beginning. As life is continuous, we never 'forget' the past genetic experience. Instead, new genetic changes build upon the structures that have brought us to this stage. The collapse of one set of dominant species not only clears the way for a new set of species, but for a new set of species that have gained in genetic 'knowledge'. In effect, the genetic output of one great wave becomes the genetic input of the next great wave, during which further progressive genetic change is realized. Hence each new wave surges more rapidly than its predecessor – it achieves a higher level of activity in a shorter period of time. This is the cumulative effect of positive feedback in genetic 'ideas'. As we shall see, a similar process underlies the Dynamic Society.

This dynamic process is so fundamentally important that it requires further exploration. A few familiar illustrations of what this process is like and what it is not like may help. Owing to the continuity of life, the development of genetic 'ideas' is like a positive feedback system. The output of one generation becomes the input of the next. The development path, in the upward phase, approximates an exponential curve – slow at first, it gradually gathers momentum until it eventually takes off almost vertically. What, in our experience, does this resemble?

What it does *not* resemble is individual human experience. Because human reproduction, like that of all higher life forms, is not a cloning process, the acquired knowledge of a lifetime dies with the individual. Human experience has no continuity of existence. Each new generation has to start from the beginning – learning to walk, talk, and to build up a store of both general and specialized knowledge – although access to institutionalized experience (via education and training) does help to speed up the process. Accordingly, a large proportion of an individual's life is spent in acquiring the level of knowledge and experience achieved by her/his parents' generation. An individual at the frontiers of human knowledge, for example, may take forty-five years to surpass the level reached by an earlier generation of intellectuals in his field. This is about 60 per cent of the average lifespan. Or put another way, the amount of formal training and experience involved – from the beginning of schooling to 45 years of age – is about the same length as the individual's working life and about double the remaining period (twenty years) in the workforce. Is there little wonder that the development of knowledge is such a slow process? Imagine how much faster it would be if each new generation automatically acquired at birth the knowledge and experience of earlier generations. This is what distinguishes human knowledge from genetic knowledge.

Genetic progress is more like cybernetic development. Both involve a continuity of existence. The 'genetic' output of each generation of computers becomes the basis for further developments that are embodied in the next generation. The development path of computers is also similar to that of biological evolution. After the first crude electronic computer was built by J.P. Eckert and J.W. Mauchly in 1946, development was slow at first, owing partly to the general level of development in electronic technology, but during the 1960s this development began to accelerate and thereafter followed an exponential growth path. Just like life, the world of cybernetics is very competitive, with high rewards for successful computer companies and bankruptcy for the unsuccessful. There has been an interaction between computer development and the electronic environment, but the driving force has always been materialist man. Because of the continuity of cybernetic 'life', just as with biological life, computers can now do tasks that were beyond the wildest imagination of the early pioneers. The great contrast between cybernetic and biological life, of course, is the speed with which 'genetic' change occurs in the functioning of computers.

The dynamic model developed in this chapter can also explain the accelerating ascent of man outlined in Figure 4.4. We should recall that this timescape shows the changing efficiency/productivity of mankind, rather than their progressive colonization of the planet. Nevertheless, a population graph would show a similar progression. The growing intensity of the waves (or steps) by which mankind made its ascent over the last 3 million years is due to the interactive effect of accumulating genetic change. Once again we see the importance of continuity of life and of positive genetic feedback.

An examination of evolution – or the dynamics of life – from an economic perspective has produced some interesting insights. While this approach may be surprising, even shocking, to those who have long regarded evolution as the monopoly of the natural scientist, it should be realized – as Darwin did – that evolution is essentially an economic rather than a physical problem. It involves a struggle by individuals to gain access to scarce natural resources, in order to achieve their primary 'objective' of survival. In order to increase the efficiency of achieving this end, individuals and species effectively maximize the input of resources and genetic 'ideas' by employing a range of dynamic strategies. It is an economic rather than a physical problem, even though it occurs within an environment dominated by physical laws. A major difference between the approach adopted here and that usually employed by natural scientists is that my focus has been on *the* output (the growth of life activities) and a range of inputs (resulting from all the dynamic strategies) rather than on just *one* input called genetic change. The difference in approach is similar to that between an analysis of technological change (usually measured by GDP per factor input) on the one hand and the expansion of human society (usually measured by GDP) on the other. I have focused upon the great waves of biological change together with a dynamic model that can explain this process. As we shall see in Chapter 12, a similar model can be employed to explain the Dynamic Society of man.

The fascinating discovery of this chapter is that the progress of life takes the form of great waves of biological change that occur with a systematically increasing intensity over time. Each successive wave of life generates a greater amplitude but a shorter wave length than the one preceding it. Each great wave is about one-third of the length of the wave it succeeds. In other words, the momentum of life is increasing in geometric fashion. This appears to be a fundamental law of life – the law of cumulative genetic change – which is due to the positive feedback of genetic (and, in human society, techno-logical) change. It can be explained by the essential continuity of life.

PART II

SHADOW OF THE TOWER

5

TOWER OF BABEL

Therefore is the name of it called Babel; because the Lord did there confound the language of all the earth: and from thence did the Lord scatter them abroad upon the face of all the earth.

(Genesis, XI, 9)

The people of the cities of the plain had much to be proud about. In little more than a dozen generations simple Mesopotamian farmers, not long separated from the surrounding nomadic tribes, had transformed their primitive communities into sophisticated urban societies. The world's first civilization. The cities of Sumer had, within recorded history, become thriving centres of industry, trade, religion, art, science, and literature. The priests of the cities gazed into the night skies and, as they tracked the bright heavenly bodies, pondered the meaning of the Universe. So intent were they on reaching out to the stars they forgot that their feet were planted in mud. So intent were they on reaching a higher understanding that they built a great tower out of the mud of the plain – a tower called Babel. Looking down from the night sky Yahweh saw the intellectual pride of the citizens of Sumer and caused them to speak many languages and to be scattered throughout the Earth.

Change is the most commanding characteristic of human society. Human society, like the whole history of life on Earth, is forever waxing and waning, rising and falling. It is never static. Yet despite the constancy of change, it is a state of being that is imperfectly understood. There is no consensus about the driving force in human society, or about the dynamic process by which it is constantly being transformed. The Dynamic Society is an enigma. In order to discover why this is so we need to survey the various attempts made to deal with this issue of issues. We need to investigate the stories told by those who live within the shadow of the Tower of Babel.

While natural scientists have a relatively unified outlook, they are forced to abandon their expertise at the point in evolution when modern man emerged about 100 thousand years ago. Those scientists interested in the future of life on Earth must be prepared to ignore – or deal inadequately with – 100 millennia of the most momentous change the planet has ever experienced. Social scientists, on the other hand, who are experts on some aspect of human organization, but rarely on its entirety, have never managed to reach a consensus about the forces driving society, let alone the dynamic process of transformation. Some even deny that there is a driving force: life to them is not a game but a lottery. The ivory tower, therefore, bears a close resemblance to the Biblical Tower of Babel in the land of Sumer.

Modern scholars interested in the progress of human society speak in many different tongues. While there has always been a tendency towards specialization in intellectual activities based upon individual comparative advantage, it was possible, until a hundred years ago, for individuals to keep abreast of the major developments in most fields of human enquiry. As late as the mid-nineteenth century, the naturalist Charles Darwin was sufficiently widely read in the social sciences to receive inspiration from the work of the classical economists Adam Smith (1723–1790) and Thomas Robert Malthus (1766–1834). And economists such as John Stuart Mill (1806–1873) and Alfred Marshall (1842–1924) had interests that extended well beyond the boundaries of political economy. Mill was an intellectual in the broadest sense, writing widely on logic, philosophy, political theory, population, and literature; while Marshall, who was very well read in history and the natural sciences, thought that economics should have drawn methodological inspiration from biology rather than physics, and had plans (unfulfilled) to develop a dynamic theory of society.

The explosion of knowledge, and the development of specialized and highly technical methods of analysis – using both mathematics and statistics – in the twentieth century, made it increasingly difficult for scholars to achieve expertise in more than one or two specialized fields. Of course, this explosion of knowledge was in part (on the supply side) due to the economies generated by intellectual specialization based upon comparative advantage. In the process, natural scientists became unfamiliar with the work of social scientists and vice versa; and, within these broad categories, scholarly studies fragmented into a large number of small, highly specialized disciplines and subdisciplines. This modern trend has proceeded so far that no major research economist can hope to keep up with work published in areas other than his or her own small part of the entire discipline. The same is true in the natural sciences. How many leading biologists today are familiar with, let alone inspired by, the work of leading economists? And how many Nobel Laureates in economics have attempted to introduce ideas from the natural sciences in their work? The silence is profound.

We all stand in the shadow of the Tower, speaking languages that only a handful of the initiated understand. Few even notice the predicament, as each group of specialized scholars is busily pushing their own barrow. Not surprisingly there is no persuasive overview of the dynamics of human society, just partial and static pictures of parts of the larger structure. The great challenge for us all, therefore, is to emerge from the shadow in order to capture an overall picture of the Dynamic Society.

THE LANGUAGES OF SCIENCE

Although natural scientists do not possess a well-formulated view of the dynamics of human society, they have, from time to time, drawn parallels between genetic change and 'cultural' change, and between the operation of a self-regulating machine and the dynamics of society. The biological analogy can be *illustrated* – for there is insufficient space in this chapter to be more comprehensive – by reference to Richard Dawkins' work *The Selfish Gene*, and the mechanical analogy by reference to the recent book by Meadows *et al.* entitled *Beyond the Limits*. The purpose throughout this chapter is to show how and why our fragmented disciplines fail to analyse the entire dynamic process of human society, not to target and denigrate the work of individual authors, all of whom have made a major contribution to their chosen field of study.

The biological analogy

The analogy between genetic and cultural evolution has often been made – by Popper (1972), Stebbins (1982), and Eccles (1989) among others. There are some scientists (Gould, 1987: 18), however, who believe that comparisons between biological evolution and cultural change have 'done vastly more harm than good' and should be abandoned. I am sympathetic with this view. If an argument cannot be made in a simple direct way it is doubtful that a complex analogy will help. Nevertheless, those scientists who see value in this type of exposition highlight the contrast between the rates of genetic and cultural evolution, and assert that biological evolution with its deadly, and slightly unsavoury, struggle for survival, has been displaced by cultural evolution with its 'altruistic' basis. Ironically, modern social biologists, who embrace Darwin's 'economic' explanation of genetic change, abandon it when exploring human society. Cultural change, in effect, is given a life of its own. Ideas are seen as inhabiting a 'world of human creativity' – the World 3 of Popper – in which subjective thought processes achieve an objective status. While the world of ideas interacts indirectly with the world of 'physical objects and states', through the world of 'states of consciousness', it operates according to laws of its own (Eccles, 1989: 72–4, 218–25). The medium for this dynamic process is the human brain, rather than the economic market. To the economist, although there are exceptions, this conception of cultural development, which is divorced from material change, appears disembodied and other-worldly.

Richard Dawkins, who shares the Popperian perspective, provides a striking example of the way natural scientists view cultural change. As Dawkins is aware that genetic evolution was displaced as the prime mover in life by cultural evolution with the emergence of modern man some 100,000 years ago, he is keen to find ways of extending the influence of Darwinism into the era of human society. He argues that the age-old biological replicator, the gene, has been replaced by a new cultural replicator, the strangely named 'meme'. The 'meme', according to Dawkins (1989: 192), is a unit of cultural transmission or imitation, and can include ideas, tunes, catch-phrases, clothes fashions, and technology. He claims that '[j]ust as genes propagate them-selves in the gene pool by leaping from body to body via sperms or eggs, so memes propagate themselves in the meme pool by leaping from brain to brain via a process which, in the broad sense, can be called imitation'. While all memes can replicate, some are more successful – have higher survival rates – than others. But Dawkins is unable to explain why some memes survive better than others. It is at this point that his argument, as he himself implies, breaks down. Dawkins (ibid.: 196) admits:

> There is a problem here concerning the nature of competition. Where there is sexual reproduction, each gene is competing with its own alleles – rivals for the same chromosomal slot. Memes seem to have nothing equivalent to chromosomes, and nothing equivalent to alleles.

Analogies of this type, as we shall see again later in this chapter when discussing technological change, always break down and cause at least as much confusion as insight.

Dawkins' analysis of cultural change is seriously flawed for a host of reasons. First, culture is seen in terms of disembodied ideas, divorced from economic progress and the materialist drive of mankind. It will be argued in Chapter 12 that cultural changes are driven not by ideas but by fundamental economic forces to which the mass of people respond opportunistically. Second, the focus of the analysis is inappropriate. Dawkins, in common with other natural scientists, focuses upon the emergence of ideas (invention) rather than the application of ideas to the material world (innovation). This is a fundamental problem because, while many weird and wonderful ideas may emerge in the mind of man, only those ideas that are applied to the real world are influential in the dynamics of human society. In fact, the equivalent of biological change in the natural world (which results from the 'application' of new genetic material) is economic change in human society (which results from the appli-cation of technical ideas to the material world). The essence of the comparison with genetic change, therefore, is that technological change (in its broadest sense) and not the transmission of ideas from brain to brain, drives human society. Natural scientists, therefore, have focused upon the wrong variables in this instance.

This brings us to the third major problem with Dawkins' analysis, which raises questions about the entire focus of his book. In *The Selfish Gene*, Dawkins employs a rhetorical device that is calculated to shock his readers.

Despite the occasional disclaimer, he has written about Darwinian evolution as if genes were 'conscious, purposeful agents', who are attempting to maximize their chances of survival. An effective way of achieving this aim, according to Dawkins, is for one group of genes to compete against other groups of genes by building 'gene machines', or individual life forms. While this unusual, indeed startling perspective captures and holds our attention, it is not ultimately persuasive. It is highly unlikely that Darwin would, as Dawkins likes to believe, have found this approach useful in explaining biological evolution. While it does provide some insights, it also misleads both the book's readers and, ultimately, its author. It is a good example of an exciting medium obscuring the fundamentally important message.

The reality of life is that individual organisms rather than individual genes struggle with each other in competitive situations for survival. If it is seen in this way, as Darwin intended that it should, a comparison of the respective *roles* of biological change in life and economic (and cultural) change in human society can be clearly made. As I argued earlier, it is the individual life form locked in a competitive struggle that takes advantage of either genetic or technological change to maximize its chances of survival and of material advantage. Actually, as shown elsewhere in this book, genetic and technological change are only two of a variety of strategies that individuals can employ in pursuing their objectives. Only by taking this wider view can we place ideas back into the material fabric of human society where they belong.

The mechanical analogy

The engineering analogy between the machine and the society of man is more complex technically than the biological analogy and, hence, more seductive. There have been a number of attempts by natural scientists and engineers – both physical and managerial – to model 'dynamically' the contemporary economy in order to make predictions (usually called 'scenarios') about the future (Forrester, 1961; 1968; 1973). These models, which have been developed by systems analysts, employ an extensive network of *assumed* interrelationships between societal variables that are *thought* to be important, together with computer simulation methods. The detailed and highly technical nature of these models makes them inaccessible to the general reader, who is merely presented with a range of possible alternatives, or scenarios, based upon changes in the values given to the main variables. These technicalities and details also obscure the fact that simulated models are not based upon coherent dynamic theories nor upon longrun dynamic historical processes, but rather they are *ad hoc* in nature and reflect the guesses (informed or not) that the model-builders are prepared to make. And they seem to be prepared to make many curious, and even empirically incorrect, guesses (Adelman 1987: 341 on Forrester, 1973). The reason these models are *ad hoc* and highly subjective, despite parading their scientific credentials, is that economists have been unable, as I show later in this chapter, to develop satisfactory dynamic models of the economy. They are concerned not with *processes* but only with *outcomes*. Hence computer simulation models are not dynamic, and never will be until they are based upon internally consistent models that deal with processes as well as outcomes. They generate the results that their authors predetermine by the guesses they make about the nature of key interrelationships. Computer simulation models merely provide an aura of objectivity to predetermined subjective views about the world.

Probably the best-known model of this kind is the one used to write the highly controversial *The Limits to Growth* (Meadows *et al.*, 1972) sponsored by the Club of Rome and, in revised form ('World3') used by the authors of the recent *Beyond the Limits* (Meadows *et al.*, 1992). The second of these books can be used to illustrate the mechanical analogy for societal dynamics. *Beyond the Limits* was written by three authors who regard themselves as environmentalists, who were trained in either biophysics or management, and who have specialized in the analysis and management of 'social' systems. It is not surprising, therefore, that they see human society in terms of mechanical systems that are mainly influenced by, and impact upon, the physical world. They are concerned to model the contemporary world in order to predict how that world will change in the future, and how it should be managed to achieve what they believe to be a desirable set of outcomes. The detailed 'model' – or set of interrelationships – they employ is mechanical in inspiration, is tightly constrained by the current physical conditions of life, and fails to capture the innovative spirit of man. Capitalists and consumers, for example, are treated as automatons who can be turned on (so that they compulsively multiply their wealth and consumption) or off (to eliminate growth) at will. (Meadows *et al.*, 1992: 118)

The author of the computer model ('World2') underlying *The Limits to Growth* (1972) and, in revised form ('World3'), *Beyond the Limits* is Jay Forrester, a management systems specialist who wrote an early textbook on systems analysis (Forrester, 1968). It is instructive to see where his inspiration comes from. Forrester stresses that applied science is a good background for management and bases his systems analysis upon mechanical engineering principles (1961: 5–6). His idea of a dynamic system is one characterized not by decision-making individuals, but by automatic feedback systems. This can be seen in the mechanical models Forrester employs to illustrate the way his computer systems operate – the thermostatically controlled boiler and the governor-operated engine. Hence his model of global human society is highly mechanistic and includes no role for flexible human agents. This is why their models tend to extravagantly 'overshoot' desirable targets. As the parameters are set mechanically, their models adjust crudely to changing conditions. In human society, serious 'overshooting' can only occur when individual human choice is eliminated, as in a totalitarian society like the former USSR. In a highly competitive society, human agents adjust relatively quickly to changing conditions.

'World3' in *Beyond the Limits* is a model with five sectors: 'persistent pollution'; 'nonrenewable resources'; population; agriculture (food production, land fertility, and land development and loss); and what they call the 'economy', consisting of industrial output, services output, and jobs. Each of these 'sectors' includes a large number of variables that are related to each other in an *ad hoc* and largely untested way. In other words, a large number of assumptions have to be made about the direction and the degree of the interrelationships between the variables isolated for study – assumptions that reflect the subjective and mechanistic views of the model builders. The totality of these relationships is not embodied in dynamic economic theory (although partial and static economic theory is used); nor have they been observed in longrun historical processes. Hence, the model reflects the intuition and values of its makers to an unhealthy degree. This is a serious problem for a technical model that claims a high degree of objectivity.

The authors of *Beyond the Limits* – the ecological engineers – see human society operating as a mechanical system within the limitations of its physical constraints and with little human drive or inspiration – a society that is highly destructive, but potentially 'manageable'. The model operates along the lines of a self-regulating physical system. It is 'driven' by the exponential growth of population and output, which eventually brings the system into contact with the physical limits (i.e. the 'carrying capacity' of the land) of human expansion at a desirable standard of living. Owing to feedback delays in this rapidly expanding system, it will 'overshoot' these limits, and will oscillate until a new equilibrium growth path is achieved, or until it collapses completely. The outcome depends upon whether the physical limits are irreversibly degraded, in which case 'erosive positive feedback' will cause unsupportable instability.

In the 'World3' model, the limits provided by natural resources are given greater importance than the unanalysed forces that drive exponential growth. Exponential growth is just an assumption of the model. As they say: 'To answer those questions [about how the 'crisis' will be resolved], we must look not at growth, but at the limits to growth' (Meadows *et al.*, 1992: 41). Technology, therefore, plays a very limited and mechanical role in their model. The authors reject the idea of a transforming technology – what I will call a new technological paradigm – and substitute for it an 'adaptive' technology that merely responds in a lagged fashion to environmental degradation. In this respect – prescribing a limited role for technology – the *Beyond the Limits* model is similar to the classical growth model of Thomas Robert Malthus and David Ricardo, and ignores the central role played by technology in the growth models of Joseph Schumpeter and the 'new' growth theorists of the present (Snooks, 1993a: 73–90). They appear to have overlooked the important lesson that can be learned from the example of Malthus and

Ricardo, who ignored the influence of technological change whilst in the very midst of the Industrial Revolution – one of only three great technological paradigm shifts in the history of mankind! The ecological engineers seem determined to ignore – indeed to prevent – the fourth paradigm shift.

The reason technology plays such a limited part in 'World3' is the absence of any role for human inspiration. They replace human drives with management 'choices' (Meadows *et al.*, 1992: 8, 12). Curiously, the driving force is mechanistic and is furnished by the assumed role of exponential growth, which actually *is* – not just described by – a mathematical equation! In the chapter entitled 'The driving force: exponential growth' they argue (ibid.: 14):

> Exponential growth is the driving force causing the human economy to approach the physical limits of the earth. It is culturally ingrained and structurally inherent in the global system, and the causal structure that produces it is at the core of the World3 model.

They see population growth and capital accumulation as the 'engines' of growth and as the 'underlying driving forces' (ibid.: 22, 100), rather than as the fuels that feed the engine of technological change. It is assumed that exponential growth of population and economy, rather than strategies employed by economic agents to maximize material advantage, is universal and inevitable. The only role for human agents in 'World3' is in managing the system to operate within its present physical limits in order to prevent 'overshoot' and collapse. The 'driving force' chapter is devoted to an explanation of what exponential growth means, rather than a discussion of the decision-making processes that are, in reality, driving it.

What does the *Beyond the Limits* model show? What are its outcomes? By changing a number of key assumptions, the authors employ their computer simulation model to track a variety of possible future outcomes for the global economy to the year 2100. The variables they report in graphical form are population, resources, food, industrial output, pollution, and a number of measures of material living standards including life expectancy, consumer goods per capita, food per capita, and services per capita. Thirteen outcomes, or 'scenarios', are presented in two series. The first series of seven scenarios, which are environmentally 'incorrect', begins with the 'World' holding to its 'historical' (since 1900) growth path as long as possible without major corrective action, and then including additively: a doubling of resources; pollution control; land yield enhancement; land erosion protection; resource efficiency technology; and a shorter time for implementing effective 'adaptive' technology (five rather than twenty years). The outcome of the first five scenarios is 'collapse' of population and production before AD 2100, while in the last two scenarios population and food output keep growing but only at the expense of significant reductions in material standards of living.

The second series of six scenarios, which are environmentally 'correct', starts at the same point and cumulatively adds: a family size limitation of two children after 1995; a ceiling on industrial output per capita 50 per cent higher than that in 1990; the introduction of technologies to conserve resources, protect agricultural land, increase land yield, and to attack pollution; advancing the starting point of all policies from 1990 to 1975; delaying all policies until 2015; and implementing all policies in 1975 but with higher targets for consumption standards. The outcomes are: 'collapse' for the first two scenarios; sustainability with a population of 7.7 billion at a 'comfortable' standard of living in the third; early rather than late implementation of preventative policies means the avoidance of either collapse or lower living standards (owing to a smaller stabilized population).

They conclude that immediate action should take place to limit family size, to limit consumption demands, and to implement conservation technologies so that the world can be *forced* to live within its present physical limits. Interestingly, in the course of all these simulations, and no doubt many more that were tried but not reported, no thought was given to pushing back the physical limits through the introduction of a new technological paradigm as has occurred three times in the history of mankind in the Palaeolithic (1.6 myrs), the Neolithic (10,600 years ago), and the Industrial (1780–1830) Revolutions. The reason, of course, is that they have chosen the wrong analogy. While an 'organic' society can transform itself into something even more wonderful, a 'mechanical' society must stay within its physical limits or blow itself apart.

But how is the world to be forced to live within the present physical limits rather than being permitted to respond creatively to them? As the book unfolds, the reader is increasingly driven to the conclusion that the immediate and effective action urged by the authors – to reduce consumption standards in the developed world (thereby allowing their increase in the Third World) and to implement corrective conservation technologies – could only occur if a global organization with real teeth exercised coercive power over the nations of the Earth. Surely the magnitude and urgency of the inevitable impending crisis that they present demands centralized coercion? The formal model does not allow for any alternative way of resolving the crisis: it expressly rejects the possibility of individuals responding to changing economic incentives in a creative way. Even the language employed by the authors suggests that centralized action is envisaged: they talk about what a sustainable 'society would decide', together with the type of choices that would 'serve social goals and enhance sustainability'; and suggest that '[i]t would certainly not permit the persistence of poverty' and that 'the remaining material growth possible . . . would logically be allocated to those who need it most' (Meadows *et al.*, 1992: 210–11). And their crowning example of successful conservation technologies – the replacement of CFCs – demonstrates, they claim, the need for scientific watchdogs who can persuade a body like the UN Environmental Program to pressure national governments to change their industrial policies *before* the problem 'produced any measurable damage to human health or to the economy' (ibid.: 155).

In the light of this expectation, the book's conclusion – that a sustainable society can be achieved not by coercive central control, but by individuals throughout the world believing the computer simulations reported in *Beyond the Limits* and rising as one person to adopt the restricted lifestyles advocated there – comes as a surprise. It is surprising because it is inconsistent with the critical urgency of the problem they project and with their formal analysis of that problem. It is surprising because there is nothing in their analysis to show why people will be motivated by abstract argument in lieu of economic incentives, but a great deal in their analysis to suggest the inevitability of systems *management*. There is, therefore, an inconsistency between their method and their ideology. The danger is that those more impressed by the methods of systems analysis and the ideas of social *management* presented throughout the book, rather than the inconsistent ideology tacked on at the end, may decide to take matters into their own hands.

The main limitation of *Beyond the Limits* is its non-historical, even anti-historical, stance. 'World3', which has been taken from the ahistorical science of systems analysis, owes nothing to an examination of real-world, longrun dynamic *processes*. And yet it claims to be able to track the dynamic global economy throughout the twenty-first century – a precariously long period even for the most realistic of models. Because the model is not appropriate to the problem under analysis, its conclusions cannot be regarded as valid. The authors of *Beyond the Limits* even draw attention, inadvertently, to this problem. They briefly (two pages out of three hundred) compare the present 'crisis' with the crises existing prior to the Neolithic Revolution about 10,000 years ago and prior to the Industrial Revolution a little over 200 years ago. They suggest that these first two revolutions (actually they were preceded by the hunting revolution some 1.6 million years ago) were resolved by the introduction of a new economic structure with a new technology. They conclude by insisting that the present crisis must be resolved by a revolution of sustainability rather than of technological transformation. This is, of course, a historical *non sequitur*.

It is a historical *non sequitur* because the Neolithic and Industrial Revolutions involved (as did that of hunting) major technological paradigm shifts in the face of physical limits to further expansion, whereas the misnamed 'sustainable revolution' will involve not the transcendence but rather the acquiescent acceptance of the current physical limits. Instead of modelling the competitive forces arising from the pressure of population on natural resources (owing to the exhaustion of conventional dynamic strategies) as an input into producing a new technological paradigm as history suggests, the authors of *Beyond the Limits* want human society to *manage* and eventually destroy those competitive pressures. They want human society to act *now* in order to live within the present physical constraints by destroying the driving force behind life, instead of using the driving force to transcend the present constraints – as has happened throughout the history of the Dynamic Society. The attempt to extinguish the spirit and ambition of man could only be undertaken by totalitarian means, and the only outcome would be the destruction of human society, a possibility discussed in the final chapter. It would be a bit like attempting to stop the world rotating. If it could actually be achieved, life on Earth as we know it would be destroyed.

The second anti-historical aspect of their model is that they treat human society as a global unit, rather than as an interacting set of regional units. This simplification, which has been adopted to make possible the computer simulations, actually denies the way in which technological paradigm shifts have occurred in the past, and will occur in the future. The paradigm shifts of the past have emerged first in small regions, and have then spread to the rest of the known world. The hunting revolution began in a small valley in East Africa; the Neolithic Revolution began in the Jordan Valley in the Old World and in the narrow Mesoamerican isthmus in the New World; and the Industrial Revolution began in the small country of England. Going back even further in time, biologists believed that genetic mutation responsible for creating new species occurred in small isolated populations on the margins of parent populations, which later returned to the ancestral lands and eliminated their forebears. This simplification in *Beyond the Limits* should not be regarded as just an analytical difficulty. If global authority were imposed, it could well prevent the seeds of the future technological revolution from being sown, just as the elimination of global isolation prevents the emergence of major new species through natural selection because of the continual dilution of genetic changes in the constantly mixing global gene pool. This is but part of the possible suppression of initiative that would occur at both the individual and regional levels.

The argument that we must act now or suffer global collapse is also anti-historical. *Beyond the Limits* does not take into account the acceleration of technological transformation over the course of history. The rate of technological implementation, as will be shown in Chapter 12, has been increasing at a rate approximating the geometric. It took hundreds of thousands of years for the hunting revolution to take hold; about 2,000 years in the case of the Neolithic Revolution; and about 100 years in the case of the Industrial Revolution. If this trend continues, it will require less than a generation to achieve any future technological transformation. Hence, while the required rate of change may be very rapid, so will be the response. History challenges the simple and dangerous view – dangerous to the freedom of mankind – that we are approaching an irreversible threshold.

Like most natural scientists, and many social scientists, the authors of *Beyond the Limits* view economic growth as a modern aberration. It is all part of their anti-historical approach. According to this view, rapid economic growth (of GDP per capita) has only appeared since the Industrial Revolution

(Meadows *et al.*, 1992: 3, 221). The implication is that just as economic growth has been turned on like a tap quite recently, it will be possible to turn it off again. As I will show in Chapter 12, economic growth is not a new phenomenon. It has been a persistent and systematic feature of human society since the emergence of civilization more than 6,000 years ago. Major surgery would be required to remove the driving force in human society which has generated economic growth throughout civilization. It is this possibility that is more of a threat to human society than any perceived future damage to the physical environment.

All this begs the question: why attempt to force/cajole human society to live within present physical constraints when history suggests that competitive pressure on these constraints will act to stimulate mankind to transcend them? The *Beyond the Limits* authors want to 'pull back' (ibid.: 9) rather than to crash through. Our answer has at least four dimensions. First, it is a matter of ideology, as environmentalists have shifted the focus of their interests from human society to the ecology. Humanism is fighting a hard battle for survival against environmentalism. Second, it is an attempt to impose order on the forces of chaos – to shackle the creative forces of life and to reduce risk. This is the instinct of those who fear change owing to doubts about their capacity to deal with it. Third, it is a matter of training. Natural scientists, engineers, and social managers are trained to believe that the physical conditions of life are more important than the individual driving force internal to life systems.

But finally, and possibly more importantly, the model employed in *Beyond the Limits*, like the simulated models sometimes employed in statistical economics (or econometrics), limit the vision of those who employ them. While deductive models can incorporate marginal changes in technology, they cannot handle technological paradigm shifts. What is the point, therefore, of running an endless number of simulated scenarios for the twenty-first century, on the assumption that the present physical limits are immutable, if there is likely to be a technological transformation during that period? Deductive models are useful for making projections over only the next few years, not the next century or so. When examining the response of human society to a major global ecological crisis over the next century, we must abandon *ad hoc* deductive models like 'World3' and fall back upon longrun existential models. A dynamic existential model is developed in Chapter 12.

THE LANGUAGES OF SOCIAL SCIENCE

Although social scientists specialize in the study of human society, there is no consensus among them about its dynamics. Different disciplines in the social sciences not only focus upon different aspects of human society, they also hold very different, indeed incompatible, views about what makes it work. It is as if they belong to entirely different and hostile tribes. Economists who have the most well-developed body of theory on human society, see society as the outcome of individuals in households and markets attempting to maximize material returns in various competitive situations. Economic rationality (that decision-makers will maximize their utility) is employed not to explain the driving force in human society, but merely to provide a deterministic solution for their mathematical models. Their view is largely static but, within their chosen boundaries, fairly comprehensive. Political science is concerned with the way political institutions and systems operate, and sociology focuses upon narrowly defined social institutions and relationships. As discussed in Chapter 6, each of these disciplines has a different, and largely inconsistent, attitude to the nature of motivation and decision-making in those various economic, political, and social systems. They also view these systems as operating largely independently of each other, although they will concede that there are interactions between them, but will not agree on the direction of causality.

While these social scientists focus largely upon the present and are concerned with possible outcomes and policies in the immediate future, historians are concerned with human society in the past. Historians, who are just as divided as the rest of their social science colleagues, tend to cluster into economic, social, and political groups. Accordingly, they have widely different ideas about how and why human society changes over time. To complete this sketch, other groupings in the social sciences, such as demography, geography, and various issue-related units, largely focus upon single issues (population and women's studies) or regions (American or Asian studies). This has only served to increase the fragmentation and the excluding languages of the social sciences.

The tribe of economics

Owing to physical limits and to the approach taken in this book, I will illustrate my argument by reference to interesting work conducted on societal dynamics in economics and history of various types. As with the discussion of the approach taken by natural scientists, this is meant to be illustrative rather than comprehensive.

As an abstract, deductive, and mathematical science, economics has focused upon shortrun comparative static analysis of individual markets and of the economy as a whole. Within this frame of reference, economics as an intellectual activity has been highly successful, although governments employing the advice of economists have been unable to prevent alternating shortrun bouts of inflation and balance-of-payments difficulties on the one hand, and unemployment and stagnation on the other. While these shortrun issues are important, they pale into insignificance when compared with the issues that economics cannot handle. The big issue facing human society today is how to resolve the growing problem of the pressure of population and economic growth on natural resources – of how a possible collapse of human society is to be avoided. This is an issue, as we have seen, about the dynamics of human society on both a regional and a global scale – an issue that transcends the shortrun equilibrium analysis favoured by economists. The problem for economists in this respect is that their discipline has very little to say about longrun dynamic processes.

'But,' our economist friend might object, 'the issue of economic growth has long been of interest in my profession. Formal economic models were first developed by Adam Smith, Thomas Robert Malthus, and David Ricardo (1772–1823) in the late eighteenth and early nineteenth centuries. This classical economic growth model describes a simple economy with a single sector, agriculture, and three socio-economic categories, landlords who receive rents, capitalists who receive profits, and workers who receive wages. In this model, an increase in profits will lead to further investment, which in turn increases the demand for labour and causes money wages to rise, which encourages an increase in population, which requires the cultivation of additional and less productive land, which leads to an increase in production costs and a reduction of profits and wages, which causes investment and population to decline so that eventually the stationary state is achieved. Economics is vitally concerned with the issue of growth.'

'True,' we might respond, 'economists have always demonstrated an interest in economic growth but, ironically, they have adopted a timeless, even an anti-real-world, approach to it. The fundamental flaw in the classical model is that its central assumptions were not closely related to the reality of the period – that of the Industrial Revolution – in which it was developed. Accordingly, the classical economists underestimated the role of both technological change and international trade in counteracting the eventual move to a steady-state equilibrium. Had the classical economists been better historians they would have realized that English feudal and medieval society experienced prolonged periods of rapid growth (in terms of GDP per capita) owing to technical and organizational change, and to international trade which enabled specialization according to comparative advantage. Essentially the classical economists focused upon the mechanism by which a basically static society returned to the stationary state after a growth surge generated by random external events.' With the mention of historical process our economist friend loses interest and returns to his computer.

The serious point that needs to be made is that the timeless approach of the classical economists distorted their view not only of the future, in which growth rather than stagnation was the norm, but also of the past. Their view of the past was obscured by the limitations of their simple abstract model. In the classical model, growth was a function of the proportion of the social surplus that found its way into the hands of capitalists, because landlords and workers, unlike capitalists, were *assumed* to use their incomes un-productively. Feudal and ancient societies, as we know, were dominated by landlords. Hence, the classical economists assumed – the great disease of economics – that very little of social surpluses in the past could have been invested productively and, accordingly, human society in the past must have been unenterprising and largely stationary. They did not realize that landowners in pre-industrial societies acted in an aggressively entrepreneurial way, investing surplus income and applying technical and organizational changes to their world. The classical economists viewed the past and future through the lenses of an abstract model that was based upon completely unrealistic and misleading assumptions. Unfortunately, this type of model has had a major influence on the way scholars in other disciplines view the pre-industrial world.

The dangers of ignoring historical processes can be illustrated time and again in the deductive approach to dynamic processes. An interesting compar-ison in this respect can be made between the classical model and the simu-lation model underlying *Beyond the Limits*. In both cases the model builders underestimated the role of technological change and the driving force behind it, because they failed to examine dynamic historical processes. The simple but apparently unpalatable fact is that economic change is a historical process – a process that takes place in real time rather than analytical time.

As the industrialized world defied the predictions of the classical growth model, it just faded away. Apart from the esoteric interests of the great Joseph Schumpeter (1883–1950), who attempted to explain economic growth by placing technological innovation and the entrepreneur at the very heart of his dynamic system (Snooks, 1993a: 77–9), economists lost interest in the question of growth until it was disrupted by the Great Depression of the 1930s. Modern growth theory – which ignored not only historical processes but also the work of economists in the past, particularly that of Schumpeter – began, under the influence of J.M. Keynes (1883–1946), with the concern that an equilibrium growth path might be very difficult to achieve and, as a result, the economy might become unstable and 'crash' as it had in the 1930s. Models were built (Harrod, 1939; Domar, 1946) which reflected these concerns. As these simple models attempted to show under what conditions either stable or unstable growth could be achieved, they focused not upon dynamic *processes* but upon dynamic *outcomes*. This is a feature that also characterizes the model in *Beyond the Limits* – a model that appears to have been influenced by the worst features of both classical and Keynesian growth theory.

Predictably, with the experience of abnormally high rates of growth during the 'golden age' of the 1950s and 1960s, the gloomy Keynesian models were abandoned and economists such as Trevor Swan (1956) and Robert Solow (1956) attempted to show why these models predicting unstable *outcomes* had been wrong, and how simple models predicting a stable or equilibrium growth path could be constructed. This saw the birth of the neoclassical growth model based upon the assumption of constant returns to scale, and in the following decade there was an explosion of specialist articles published by young economists attempting to make names for themselves (Solow later received the Nobel Prize in Economics) by exploiting all the possibilities of the neoclassical model. By the mid-1960s this burst of model building had run its course owing to the onset of diminishing intellectual returns. Once again these models were concerned not with processes but with outcomes: what type of model would generate the high growth outcome of the 1950s and 1960s, rather than the unstable outcome of the 1930s, or the stationary state thought by the classical economists to be the normal condition of human society? The *process* by which growth was actually achieved was ignored.

When economists eventually returned to building growth models in the late 1980s and early 1990s, they (like the classical economists) ignored the world around them which appeared, temporarily, to be heading towards the stationary state. They ignored this world by introducing the idea that, if we assume increasing returns to scale rather than decreasing returns (as did the classical economists) or constant returns (as did the neoclassicists), profits will not be driven down by continual investment and growth rates will increase indefinitely into the future. Encouragingly, they also attempted to include technological change in their models. This was the 'new' growth theory pioneered by Romer (1986) and Barro and Romer (1990).

Unfortunately, both the assumption and the resulting conclusion of the 'new' growth theory are anti-historical, and emerge from a misreading of recent (1800–1980) growth experience in the USA. As I attempt to show elsewhere (Snooks, 1993a: 84–7), growth rates have not been increasing progressively over the last two centuries, but rather have fluctuated cyclically. Needless to say, the 'new' growth theorists do not examine the record of growth over the very longrun, which shows (Figure 5.1) that over the last 1,000 years, English growth rates have gone through at least four long cycles and are not growing through time as economic scale (i.e. population) increases. Once again we can see how the outcomes of deductive models depend upon the assumptions that their builders make, and that these assumptions owe nothing to a study of historical processes, and may even ignore contemporary events. Once again deductive growth models are concerned not with *processes* but with *outcomes*. And, as for the genre as a whole, growth is treated not endogenously but as the result of exogenous changes. In order to model processes and observe outcomes that are determined by the past rather than by arbitrary or ephemeral assumptions, we need to build existential models – models of existence based upon historical experience.

While growth theory, which attempts to model the economy in a overarching way, has been the main focus of economists interested in dynamics, limited attention has been given by economists to simulation models of the type used in *Beyond the Limits* – limited mainly because of the messy *ad hoc*

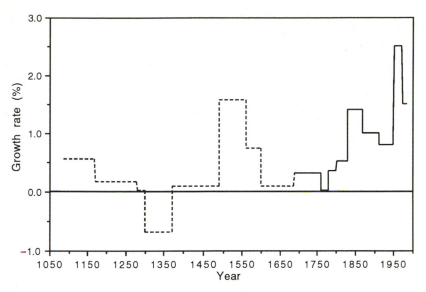

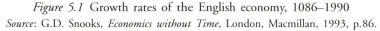

Figure 5.1 Growth rates of the English economy, 1086–1990
Source: G.D. Snooks, *Economics without Time*, London, Macmillan, 1993, p.86.

nature of these models. Economic theorists prefer to use models that show how the whole system works, rather than models that consist of unintegrated partial relationships. They are worried, and rightly so, about what a simulated model actually means. There is no way of conceptualizing these models. Econometricians – applied economists who employ statistical models to test economic relationships – are less worried by this issue, and have been prepared to employ computer simulation models in a number of applied areas such as economic planning and forecasting, interindustry economics, the study of business cycles (which appears to be undergoing a resurgence) and microanalytic systems. The techniques employed were originally imported from the fields of engineering and management, but have been modified to include relationships which, while still partial, have greater economic theoretic justification. But their methods are still highly *ad hoc*. The model builders keep changing the detailed relationships between variables until their statistical models can replicate changes in these variables over the past few decades. The theoretical arguments for the changes suggested are often less than convincing. And the overall meaning is lost. But even econometricians would not attempt to extrapolate results a century or more into the future as the authors of *Beyond the Limits* are prepared to do. This is definitely regarded as beyond the pale.

On the margins of mainstream neoclassical economics exist a number of dissident groups of economists interested in the dynamics of human society.

Principally these include the economic evolutionists and the self-styled post-Keynesians (really neo-Marxists). Of these the evolutionists are the most interesting and need to be taken most seriously. The evolutionists are serious deductive economists, albeit a rather disparate collection of individuals, who are highly critical of the optimizing and unique-equilibria framework employed by neoclassical theorists, and of the engineering approach underlying dynamic simulation (Witt, 1992; 1993). Indeed, they all reject the mechanical analogy of physics for the organic analogy of biology. In addition they are interested in the process, rather than just the outcome, of economic change, together with the role of economic agents in what they see as an endogenous process. The inspiration of this heterogeneous group of economists can be found in the fertile theorizing of Joseph Schumpeter (1883–1950), in the later social philosophy of the neo-Austrian economist Friedrich Hayek (1899–1992), in the work of behavioural theorists of the firm (emphasizing 'satisficing' rather than maximizing behaviour), in the 'old' institutionalism of T.B. Veblen (1857–1929), and in the work of those influenced by evolutionary biology (e.g. Nelson and Winter, 1982).

Our interest in this group concerns their attempt to understand economic dynamics by employing the deductive method. As far as the evolutionists are concerned, neoclassical economics makes the mistake of treating dynamics as a mechanical problem, of regarding economic agents as reactive rather than proactive, and of focusing upon the converging forces of equilibrium rather than the expansionary forces of disequilibrium. But while they reject the viewpoint and some of the techniques of neoclassicism, the evolutionists have no intention of rejecting the deductive for the inductive method.

Rather than investigating reality directly, the evolutionists have adopted various concepts and analytical frameworks used by other disciplines. The attitude appears to be that if the mainstream of their own discipline is unable to tackle dynamic issues deductively, then possibly the answer might be found in the deductive approaches of other traditions in economics, or even in other disciplines such as biology. This rather eclectic shopping around does not generate much confidence in eventual success. Indeed, I argue that, in the field of economic dynamics, the deductive approach is doomed to failure because it is unable to confront reality directly. Selected historical data are employed only to 'illustrate' rather than to test – in the Popperian sense of falsification – their deductive models. But at least it is an interesting attempt by deductive economists to breathe new life into their discipline.

The other main group of dissident economists regard themselves as post-Keynesian mainly on the grounds that they deal, in one way or another, with the role of consumer demand, an important element in the seminal work of John Maynard Keynes, *The General Theory of Employment, Interest and Money* (1936). But in reality they have more in common with neo-Marxists who view the evolution of human society as a dialectical process involving an interaction between the modes of production and the sociopolitical superstructure. In this way some have attempted to model the entire economic–sociopolitical process of change. Ironically, Keynes had no interest in historical processes, and made no attempt to go beyond the explanation of purely economic forces (Snooks, 1993a: 40). Some members of this group appear to be gravitating towards the standard of evolutionary economics as Marx is increasingly losing his attraction.

A recent exponent of this approach is Andrew Tylecote (1992). A self-styled post-Keynesian, he claims to have analysed the long wave – or Kondratieff cycle of fifty years – in the world economy over the past few centuries. This, however, is not his real focus. Rather than modelling the dynamic process of economic change, Tylecote attempts to explain the emergence of all major political, social, and economic crises experienced in the world since 1780. These crises include revolution, civil war, regional conflicts, global wars, ecological disasters, as well as depressions and recessions. While it is difficult but feasible to model the longrun process of economic change, it is impossible to employ a simple model to simultaneously explain economic, social, and political change.

The model of longrun cycles adopted by Tylecote was initially developed by Carlota Perez (1985) who is obviously in a neo-Marxist tradition. In this model long cycles emerge from an interaction between technological change and the 'sociopolitical framework' of a particular society. According to Perez, when new technological ideas are 'mismatched' with the old institutional framework, a process develops in which technological diffusion is inhibited, the economy turns down, and an institutional crisis occurs. In turn this generates institutional change favourable to the new technology – a 'rematch' occurs – which promotes rapid technological diffusion and economic expansion. Central to this model, but not integrated theoretically with it, are the long cycles of technological change which Perez calls technological 'styles' of the past two centuries.

Tylecote (1992: 184), who is aware that this model cannot explain 'the absence of any identifiable long wave in the first half of our period [1780–1880]', attempts to salvage it by attaching three extra elements. First, he extends Perez's discussion of institutional crisis from the 'depression crisis' discussed above to a number of political crises that can occur even in the upswing. Second, he takes his cue from the mechanical engineering models discussed earlier by adding to Perez's model a number of feedback processes – by which a move in one direction can generate forces operating in either the same or the reverse direction – including money, population, and inequality. The feedback process of inequality is where the Keynesian influence is felt because it involves a discussion of consumer demand which is inversely related to the level of profits. Together these feedback mechanisms are supposed to suppress the long cycle before the 1880s and to reinforce it thereafter. Finally, he throws in an entirely unrelated 'model' (really a stylized description) of changes in international power relationships by

G. Modelski which asserts a long cycle of 100 to 120 years. It is not clear at any stage how Tylecote is able to justify the coexistence of Perez's technological 'styles' cycle of fifty years with Modelski's international power cycle of 100–120 years – he just accepts both as part of the complex reality.

Tylecote (1992: 185) claims that the cycles in technological styles and in international power are regular, while the impacts of institutions and feedback processes change over time, becoming 'gradually more pro-cyclical'. This very loose collection of ideas is misleadingly called an 'evolutionary model' because its 'dynamics are mainly determined by economic, political and social institutions and that these, and their interactions, change over time' (ibid.: 183). Is it surprising that, owing to this 'flexibility', Tylecote claims that his 'model' can explain all unpredictable events? This is a model that is reformulated on every occasion to suit any change of circumstances. Clearly, the entire exercise is problematical. Any 'model' which needs to be continually adjusted to explain reality can, in reality, explain little and predict even less. It has little in common with the technically rigorous work of the evolutionary economists.

Most disappointing is the absence of any explanation of what feasibly can be explained – the longrun dynamic process of economic change. Tylecote adopts the mechanical engineering model in which economic growth is taken for granted and fluctuations are generated by feedback mechanisms – like those that characterize a thermostatically controlled heating system rather than an innovative social system. Accordingly, he makes no attempt to explain the driving force in the economy, why the new technological 'styles' emerge, or how the growth process occurs. Like the orthodox growth theorists and the ecological engineers, Tylecote is interested only in outcomes not processes. Also, as with the models of the ecological engineers, the feedback mechanisms are not only arbitrarily selected – how many other such possibilities could be regarded as 'appropriate' is not investigated – but also are mechanically determined with no adaptive role for economic agents. Many of these problems could have been avoided had an existentialist, rather than a deductive, approach to long cycles been adopted.

The tribes of history

Historians of various persuasions have attempted to account for the rise and fall of civilizations and, later, nation states. Sometimes historical interest has focused upon society's material fortunes, but more often on its non-material culture. Usually, attention is devoted specifically to a single region, a limited period of time, or single issues such as population or technological change; rarely is it directed to the global economy over the very longrun. Analytical studies of the dynamics of human society – as opposed to general surveys of world history – have always been rare and are definitely out of favour at the present.

The most broad-ranging historical studies are those that attempt to describe, and sometimes explain, the changes in important individual variables such as population and technology. By abstracting a single important variable from the complex fabric of human society, the task of describing change over long periods of time is simplified. But there is a significant cost, as this method can fragment and distort the overall picture. By abstracting one variable from the whole system, explanations tend to focus upon proximate causes that end up being largely truistic. Population growth, for example, is usually 'explained' in terms of demographic (fertility and mortality) and environmental forces. This merely begs the questions: what determines these 'sources' (rather than 'causes') of fertility and mortality; and what is the driving force that causes population to surge against these physical constraints? The same is true for studies of technological change, in which 'explanations' focus upon the 'sources' of technical ideas rather than the wider dynamic processes that involve technological change as one of a number of dynamic strategies for achieving the objectives of those driving the whole system. Also single-issue studies always end up treating that issue as the rationale of the whole system. The danger here is that a variable such as technological change is seen as an end in itself rather than a means to an end – a dynamic strategy – and may even be explained in terms of itself – pulling itself up by its own bootstraps. The same is true of most population studies. A few recent illustrations from major works in this tradition will suffice.

The recent book by Massimo Livi-Bacci entitled *A Concise History of World Population* presents an admirably clear statistical picture of a number of demographic topics. We are introduced to the sources of population growth, fertility and mortality; to the environmental constraints; and to the outcomes of these proximate causes from the distant past to the present. We are told that population growth results from an interaction of 'choice' (regarding marriage, reproduction, mobility, migration, and defence against disease) and 'constraint' (space, climate, and disease), and also how this simple 'model' can be used to explain population change during: the neolithic transition; the Black Death in Europe in 1346–1350; the tragedy of the American *Indios*; the success of the French Canadians; and the case of small islands like Ireland and Japan. We are informed about the Malthusian relationship between population growth and the productive services of land; and about the positive role of population pressure in development – Malthus on his head – an idea with a long history but which has recently been popularized by Ester Boserup (1965; 1981). We are shown the demographic statistics of Europe since the Industrial Revolution, and the contrasting experience of the Third World.

We are told, therefore, about demographic 'choices', but not about the driving force in society that leads to these choices. We are told that man is 'forced' by population pressure to adopt new technologies, but not how both are related to the overall dynamics of human society. We are told – as we

SHADOW OF THE TOWER

were told by the authors of *Beyond the Limits* – that physical conditions and external events (particularly disease) are more important than 'choices', because individuals must operate within these constraints. The single-issue approach is useful in exposing the main changes that are taking place, but it encounters difficulties of explanation because of its partial analyses. To resolve these difficulties, we need to develop a model of the dynamics of human society as a whole. Until then our picture of reality will be not only incomplete, but also misleading.

While the choice of population for study as a single issue may seem obvious, that of technological change requires more subtle justification. Although economic growth has, I will argue, characterized each epoch in human history, its causes are disputed. This applies particularly to the role of technological change. Much of the difference in opinion emerges from a failure of scholars to develop a common set of priorities and a common language. Some focus on the proximate causes of growth – such as institutions or technology – while others are concerned with ultimate causes – such as changes in relative factor prices. Each discipline has its own exclusive, and excluding, language. The social sciences flourish happily in the shadow of the Tower.

Joel Mokyr (1990: 3), for example, who has recently focused upon technological change as the key to economic growth, writes:

> The causes of economic growth – why some societies grew rich and others did not – have been pondered by economists, sociologists, historians, and philosophers for centuries. This book is another attempt to struggle with this issue of issues. It focuses on what I believe to have been one key ingredient of economic growth: technological creativity.

Mokyr attempts to throw light on economic growth indirectly by a study of technological change. Yet no matter how important technological change is in the growth process – and some would give it less emphasis than Mokyr – its study, like that of population, can only be a partial analysis; and a partial analysis inevitably leads to distortions in the picture of reality. Let me say at the outset, however, that while I disagree fundamentally with Mokyr's interpretation of the role of technological change, I admire the expert way in which he has examined changes in technique over the past two millennia.

Mokyr begins by providing a brief outline of significant inventions and innovations in classical antiquity, the Middle Ages, the Renaissance, the Industrial Revolution, and the later nineteenth century to the First World War. He accounts for these technical changes through a long list of 'factors that operated, consciously or otherwise, on the minds and actions of individuals in their lonely struggles with the laws of physics, chemistry, and biology' (ibid.: 155). These broad-ranging factors include: life expectancy, nutrition, attitudes to risk, environment, path dependency, labour costs, science, religion, values, institutions, resistance to innovation, politics and

120

the state, war, openness to new information, and demographic factors. Mokyr focuses, therefore, upon the supply of ideas rather than the demand for ideas, because he believes that derived demand for technology always exceeds supply, and hence there is nothing to explain from that side of the equation. Progress is a matter of removing obstacles to the emergence of new ideas. Also he emphasizes the role of technical ideas, more than economic forces, in stimulating further technical ideas: innovation cannot proceed without invention – hence, he argues, invention is of central importance. But, Mokyr admits, he has no overarching theory to explain technological change. It is a response to a large number – a veritable shopping list – of supply-side factors, which he employs in a discursive manner to explain technological progress since about 300 BC. Finally, he attempts to explain, in a general way, the process of technological change by analogy with biological evolution, in which, rather curiously, *techniques* are compared with *species* rather than with genes. In concluding, Mokyr (ibid.: 16) writes:

> The study of technological progress is therefore a study of exceptionalism, of cases in which as a result of rare circumstances, the normal tendency of societies to slide toward stasis and equilibrium was broken. The unprecedented prosperity enjoyed today by a substantial proportion of humanity stems from accidental factors to a degree greater than is commonly supposed. Moreover, technological progress is like a fragile and vulnerable plant, whose flourishing is not only dependent on the appropriate surroundings and climate, but whose life is always short. It is highly sensitive to the social and economic environment and can easily be arrested by relatively small external changes. If there is a lesson to be learned from the history of technology it is that Schumpetarian [i.e. technologically based] growth, like the other forms of economic growth, cannot and should not be taken for granted.

There are a number of comments that need to be made. First, the major problem confronting partial analysis is that the issue under study is often mistaken for the end itself, rather than the means to the real end. Boserup (1981: ix) appears to be more aware of this problem than Mokyr. In the above quote, and much of his analysis, there is a subtle tendency to equate technological change with 'progress'. An absence of technological change is interpreted as stasis or equilibrium, and a revival of technological change is taken to be evidence of growth. This is similar to the argument of the punctuationists (discussed in Chapter 4), who equated the profile of genetic change with the development path of life. Clearly, Mokyr has been influenced by their arguments. In the longrun, however, technological change is not a good proxy for economic progress (as Mokyr explicitly recognizes in parts of the book), as it is only one dynamic strategy employed by ambitious individuals who wish to maximize their material advantage. The other major strategies that have been employed over longer periods of time, as we shall see in Part III, include commerce, colonization, and conquest. It will be shown that despite the 'punctuated' nature of technological change over long periods of time, economic progress has proceeded via great waves of economic change. Hence, the danger to the Dynamic Society is not 'small external changes', in the 'social and economic environment' for technical ideas – i.e. the supply of inventions – but rather forces that restrict the driving force of materialist man and his various dynamic strategies.

Second, I disagree fundamentally with Mokyr (1990: 151) over his supply-side explanation of technological change. It is not correct, as I hope to show, that '[h]uman appetites being what they are, necessity is always there; the ability to satisfy it is not'. Nor is his statement elsewhere (Mokyr, 1993a: 61n) that '[e]conomists and historians alike have treated the common wisdom that necessity is the mother of invention with contempt' a happy one. Certainly Ken Sokoloff and Zorina Khan (1990) do not do so in their discussion of the role of markets in technological change in nineteenth-century America. And, as I show in the last half of this book, the wisdom of the common person may be closer to the truth than the contempt of intellectuals. The Tower of Babel casts a long shadow. Human desire to consume is always present, but the dynamic demand (which is very different to the market demand of Sokoloff and Khan and others) for the technological strategy, and hence of technical ideas, varies considerably through time and space. This is the key variable that must be explained. Essentially, technological change is one of a number of strategies that are employed by economic decision-makers to give them a competitive edge in the struggle for economic survival and material advantage. Where there is only a low level competitive environment, as in Aboriginal Australia before European settlement, the demand for technological change collapses or operates only occasionally at very low levels. In other words, it is essential to draw a clear distinction between the driving force and the dynamic strategy in achieving the objectives of those who make the economic decisions.

I will argue in later chapters that the main reason some periods experience only a low level.of technological change is that the objectives of economic agents can be more efficiently pursued by employing other dynamic strategies such as the exploitation of underemployed natural resources, commerce or conquest. In this context, it is not correct to say, as Mokyr (1990: 19) has done, that the ancient Greeks had 'no interest in growth', just because they did not adopt technology as a dominant strategy; rather they employed other dynamic strategies that were more economically efficient, such as colonization, commerce, and, when a comparative advantage was demonstrated (by Alexander the Great), imperial wars. And these strategies enabled the Greeks to increase their material standards of living above the base level provided by the neolithic agricultural system. They were very interested in growth, but not in technological change in the production of goods and services. Of course, the supply of technical ideas is important, as shown in

Chapter 9, but the available evidence makes it clear that it responds to the demand of those determining the dynamic strategy, rather than the other way round. Mokyr (ibid.: 44) imbues ideas with a drive of their own, as, for example, when he says that Islamic technical ideas 'ran out of steam'. Ideas, although they sometimes achieve a limited momentum of their own, are essentially passive. They are only adopted when the technological strategy is the most efficient dynamic option.

Third, a related point is that different value systems, religions, etc. should not be invoked to account for what can be explained by different dynamic strategies. My dynamic-strategy argument can be used to explain the apparent 'enigma' (ibid.: 29) of technology in classical antiquity, in which modest advances were achieved in transport, communication, war machines, and imperial administration, but not in agriculture or industry. Classical technical advances occurred in those areas of the ancient economy that were needed to support the dynamic strategies of colonization and conquest, not for increases in agricultural productivity. Quite clearly the limited degree of technological change that did occur was a response to demand generated by the dominant dynamic strategies of the ancient world. Similarly, medieval inventions were numerous, but were directed at applying the Neolithic Revolution to the very different climatic and soil conditions in northern Europe. Once again demand for new methods arising from the dynamic technological strategy was the determining factor in the rate of technological progress.

Fourth, the interesting attempt to use biological evolution as an analogy for technological change does not really work. While Mokyr's objective appears to be to clarify the *process* of technological change, he creates as much confusion as insight, particularly for the reader who has no special knowledge of genetic change. Also, the focus of the comparison is not appropriate – techniques are equated with species (rather than with genes), and firms with organisms. The focus, in other words, is on technological change as an end in itself rather than on economic 'progress' (or, in my terminology, the dynamics of human society) – techniques are treated as the end product of human endeavour. In the process, the 'innovating' individual – the driving force in the dynamic society – is entirely passed over.

A sure sign of the difficulties arising from this analogy, is the fact that Mokyr spends much of the last chapter explaining the numerous points at which the comparison breaks down. A more direct explanation of the process of technological change would have provided a clearer exposition. One has the sneaking feeling that this analogy was employed in the absence of an existential model to explain the role of technological change. Just in case someone is muttering something about people in glasshouses, I should emphasize that evolution has not been employed as an analogy for the *process* of technological change in this book. Instead I have attempted to develop a general model to explain not only the wider process of societal dynamics, but also the dynamics of life which encompasses the Darwinian hypothesis. In this dynamic model genetic change plays a role in the dynamics of life similar to that of technological change in the dynamics of human society – as one of a number of alternative strategies by which individuals could gain a competitive edge in the struggle for survival/material advantage. No analogy is involved because the dynamics of society and life have been totally recast. Also my approach allows a role for the dynamic individual whereas Mokyr's excludes such a role.

Fifth, it is not possible to agree with the emphasis Mokyr places upon the role of ideas, as opposed to the application of ideas, in both biological and economic change. Biologists focus upon genetic change rather than the dynamics of life, while Mokyr focuses upon technical ideas rather than upon the dynamic system that produces them. As I will argue later, ideas do not drive change, they only facilitate it. Ideas are of no economic importance until they become part of the competitive strategy of economic decision-makers. It is the demand for ideas – which fluctuates in the longrun owing to changing relative factor prices – rather than their supply that accounts for technological progress or stagnation. This is analysed in detail in Chapter 9.

Finally, on the basis of the findings in this book, we must reject Mokyr's view that the 'normal tendency' of human society is 'to slide towards stasis and equilibrium' which is 'broken' only by technological change during 'rare circumstances'. From our discussion in Chapter 4, it is clear that Mokyr has been strongly influenced by the punctuationists who attempted unsuccessfully to displace the economics in Darwin with a physical-science approach that emphasizes the dominant role in evolution of external physical circumstances. There is an interesting irony here. Like the punctuationists (but unlike Darwin) Mokyr not only neglects the internal driving force in living systems, but also ignores the distinction between the genetic profile and the development both of life on the one hand and the technological profile and the development path of human society on the other. If both the genetic and technological profiles or paradigms are 'punctuated', it is only because genetic/technological change is but one of a range of dynamic strategies that are adopted by life forms on a relative benefit–cost basis. Not only is strategic demand the determinant of technological (genetic) change, it is the reason that the normal condition of human society (life) involves constant flux. As we shall see in Chapter 12, the Dynamic Society is *eternally* dynamic.

This brings us to the historians concerned with the bigger picture – of the way certain civilizations change over time. They can be grouped into those interested in the rise and fall of ancient civilizations, and those who have searched for the antecedents of the rise of the West. Those interested in ancient civilizations have been attracted more to their collapse than to their rise, possibly because the fall of once mighty empires is more dramatic; possibly because it appears less difficult to understand – 'sudden' change is easier to detect and, hence, considered easier to explain than the long slow climb to the top; and possibly because many have begun to believe that the collapse of modern society is not that far away. Those who have focused upon the history of the rise of the West have not had the opportunity to explain its fall. But some live in hope!

There is much disagreement about the collapse of ancient civilizations. Indeed, there is even disagreement about the basic concepts of 'civilization' and 'collapse'. What constitutes civilization? Is it the cultural achievement, the political entity, or the economic system? To complicate the problem, what is meant by collapse? Is it political fragmentation (because rarely did everything end in ashes), or the decline in sociopolitical complexity, or the end of all the living cultural forms of the civilization, or the breakdown in the economic system that gave rise to the civilization? The answer is that, to scholars in the shadow of the Tower, it includes all these possibilities. Some scholars claim that civilization must be identified with the cultural achievement of a particular society, others that it is the political manifestation that is central, and others that the political and cultural forms are driven by the economic system. It is not surprising to learn, therefore, that some emphasize the political causes of collapse, some focus upon the decline and collapse of cultural values, some look to economic causes, some are impressed by exogenous shocks, and others want a bit of everything – those great shopping lists of history (Yoffee and Cowgill, 1988). Yet, despite the lack of consensus, historians of ancient civilizations have at least attempted to define what they wish to investigate.

A number of causes of collapse have been nominated in the literature. The political events include incompetent leadership, hierarchical power struggles, overextension of empire and bureaucratic mismanagement (Grant, 1976; Yoffee and Cowgill, 1988: ch. 11); the economic forces include disruption of trade, the loss of income, escalating costs of administration, growing costs of accountability, and increasing environmental damage (Levi, 1988: ch. 4; Finley, 1985; Yoffee and Cowgill, 1988: ch. 11); the decline in cultural values includes the neglect of the highest intellectual standards in favour of crass materialism (Starr, 1991); and the external events include war and disease. On the face of it, these are all reasonable candidates, depending upon what we are trying to explain, whether we are interested in proximate or ultimate causes, and whether we are happy with the shopping-list approach. If, however, our interest centres on the dynamics of human society, we will prefer to focus upon the ultimate causes of collapse – as all the rest merely respond to these – and we will want to develop an existential model to explain how civilizations rise and fall, possibly a number of times before they finally collapse. It is not good enough to say, as most historians do, that reality is so complex that it is impossible to provide a clear and simple explanation, and to offer instead another great shopping list of history in which every conceivable variable is given the same weighting. If reality were indeed this complex, the shopping lists would be of little assistance. Reality is complex, but it does not defy rigorous explanation. In this book I intend breaking with this tradition by proposing a dynamic model of 'ultimate' causation in which economic forces are responsible for turning the great wheel of civilization.

The most ambitious attempt to explain the collapse of complex societies in general terms has been made by Joseph Tainter (1988). He claims (ibid.: 209) that his work 'provides an overarching theoretical framework that unites diverse approaches, and it shows where connections exist among disparate views'. In evaluating this claim we should begin with his definition of collapse (ibid.: 193):

> Collapse is fundamentally a sudden, pronounced loss of an established level of sociopolitical complexity. A complex society that has collapsed is suddenly smaller, simpler, less stratified, and less socially differentiated. Specialization decreases and there is less centralized control. The flow of information drops, people trade and interact less, and there is overall lower coordination among individuals and groups. Economic activity drops to a commensurate level, while the arts and literature experience such a quantitative decline that a dark age often ensues. Population levels tend to drop, and for those who are left the known world shrinks.

This comprehensive description of collapse clearly reveals the non-economic nature of the process Tainter has in mind. The collapse of human society to Tainter is essentially a sociopolitical process in which economic activity merely responds to the change in organizational structure.

Because Tainter is only interested in the collapse of complex societies, he does not construct a comprehensive model of societal change that can explain the rise as well as the fall of civilization. But we can draw out some of his less formal views about the evolution of human society. According to Tainter, post-neolithic society is a sociopolitical system that has evolved in 'complexity' in response to an endless series of external problems. He claims (ibid.: 195) that the 'problems with which the universe can confront any society are, for practical purposes, infinite in number and endless in variety'. Human society according to this interpretation, is a 'complex adaptive' or 'problem-solving' system manipulated by a political and social elite.

Problem-solving, the main function of sociopolitical entities, requires access to unused or new resources in order to develop more sophisticated organizational structures. The more external problems a society faces the more complex it becomes in an organizational sense. Tainter (ibid.: 193) claims that '[e]ach society represents a point along a continuum from least to most complex'. In other words, the sociopolitical complexity of society is driven by a series of external problems: a society under pressure 'responds to stress

126

by increasing complexity' (ibid.: 120). Problem-solving, we are told, involves higher organizational costs, and it confers benefits in terms of resolved problems. But, '[o]nce a complex society enters the stage of declining marginal returns, collapse becomes a mathematical likelihood, requiring little more than sufficient passage of time to make probable an insurmountable calamity' (ibid.: 195). Tainter (ibid.: 150) goes on to say: 'when a complex society enters a situation of declining marginal returns, collapse can occur from one or both of two reasons: lack of sufficient reserves with which to meet stress surges, and alienation of the over-taxed support population'. He rules out the possibility of achieving equilibrium – the classical stationary state – but does not provide a persuasive theoretical reason. Declining marginal returns, he asserts, lead directly and inevitably to sociopolitical collapse.

By employing the well-known economic principle of diminishing marginal returns, Tainter has merely adopted the adjustment mechanism employed by the classical economists – Ricardo and Malthus, discussed earlier in this chapter – to explain how a society could make the transition from economic growth to the equilibrium position known as the stationary state. Diminishing returns is an *assumption* found in all economic growth models from the classical economists of the early nineteenth century to the neoclassical economists of the 1960s and 1970s as well as in orthodox production theory. The considerable effort that Tainter devotes to illustrating this basic principle in economics, therefore, is hardly necessary. He does, however, provide a new twist by applying this adjustment mechanism – it is not a model of the dynamic process – not to the economy, but to sociopolitical structures.

Does this model of collapse meet the claims made for it by Tainter? In the first place, how universal is the desire or need to increase organizational complexity? As Tainter (ibid.: 198) admits himself, complex societies are 'recent in human history'. For the great majority of the past 2 million years human society demonstrated absolutely no move towards sociopolitical complexity but, as shown in Chapter 8, it did exhibit a considerable economic dynamic capability. Hence the *universal* characteristic of human society is not sociopolitical complexity but economic change. This is true not only for the period before the Neolithic Revolution but also since then. Accordingly, Tainter's focus upon organizational rather than economic change is misplaced. Organizational change responds to fundamental economic change. It is economic change that we must explain.

We also need to ask what could possibly motivate decision-makers in Tainter's world of complexity. His view of complex human societies is that they respond to external problems by investing in further complexity. In other words, his world of complexity is peopled by risk-averse decision-makers. While a risk-averse strategy can be employed in isolated communities, it is not possible in a highly competitive environment where decision-makers are struggling to survive and to maximize their material advantage. In a highly competitive environment this is achieved by investing in one or more of the dynamic strategies. Complexity, or lack of it, is a response to the nature of the dynamic strategies employed. Prior to the Neolithic Revolution the dominant dynamic strategy of family multiplication and migration required no increase in organizational complexity, whereas since the Neolithic Revolution, the successful dynamic strategies of conquest, commerce and, since the Industrial Revolution, technology have demanded a progressive increase in organizational complexity. The downturn and collapse of these societies resulted not from relatively high levels of organizational complexity, but from the exhaustion and non-renewability of specialized dominant dynamic strategies.

This brings us to our final point. It is not possible to understand why ancient societies collapsed without understanding the dynamic economic process that enabled them to transcend the size and level of material advantage provided by the neolithic technological paradigm. Collapse, it is argued in this book, is an outcome of the dynamic process of economic change and can only be sensibly analysed in that context. Tainter does not model the process of growth and the way this leads to collapse, he merely suggests what happens after the unexamined and, hence, unknown forces of economic growth have been exhausted. In other words, he merely attempts to chart the downward path without understanding the underlying dynamic process of economic change.

Tainter claims that the well-known principle of diminishing marginal returns is the central cause of collapse in complex societies. This is not so. Diminishing marginal returns, just as the classical economists told us two centuries ago, merely cause a growing economy to decelerate and eventually to grind to a halt once marginal returns approach zero. This cannot, and has not, caused any rational society to collapse, contrary to Tainter's misplaced assertion about the mathematical probability of this event. The reason that collapse occurred regularly in ancient societies is that they attempted to transcend the optimum size – both in terms of population and real GDP per capita – of an economic system determined by the neolithic technological paradigm. That optimum size was probably in the vicinity of 5,000–30,000 people (an urbanized agricultural community) depending on the locality and time period, which was much larger than the optimum size determined by the palaeolithic paradigm of about 500 people (a tribe consisting of about twenty forager bands of about twenty-five people), and much smaller than the optimum size determined by the industrial paradigm in a range from about 15 million to more than a billion (the modern nation state).

In ancient societies the neolithic optimum was exceeded, both in terms of population and GDP per capita, by adopting a major non-technological dynamic strategy such as conquest or commerce. These non-technological strategies have the capability to increase the inflow of resources and income beyond that possible for a neolithic society. The resulting prosperity continues until the dominant strategy is exhausted and found to be non-renewable. This occurs when the costs of an extra (or marginal) unit of investment are equal to or greater than the extra benefit. It is here, as the classical economists showed, that diminishing marginal returns enter. But not for long. In those circumstances where the size of the economic system approximates the technological optimum, this will merely lead to the stationary state, even if only in the short-run. But for a society that has transcended the technological optimum, through conquest or commerce, this situation will lead to collapse, not through diminishing marginal returns but through a reversion to the revenue structure of a neolithic system while having to support the cost structure of a conquest (or commerce) empire. (In more technical terms: not a movement along the marginal revenue curve, but a large backward shift of that curve.)

The society will revert to a neolithic economic system because the inflow of income and resources from conquest or commerce is suddenly cut off. Hence the society is thrown back onto an income flow generated by the underlying agricultural system – a level of income that cannot finance or justify the existing level of population, living standards, or social overhead capital. Suddenly there is a large gap between revenues and expenditures. To close this gap the society needs to reduce dramatically its size, living standard, and social overhead capital to bring it into line with the neolithic technological optimum size. Clearly, no society will do this voluntarily. Instead the ruling elite will attempt to maintain its past gains by raising additional funds through taxes and devaluing the currency in the hope that, in the meantime, an economic solution will present itself. This merely unleashes the internal forces of chaos that eventually overwhelm those of order. The point to note is that none of this will occur in a society that has not attempted to transcend its technological optimum size, which is why in the modern era only irrational societies – such as Nazi Germany and Stalinist USSR – are likely to collapse.

While Tainter effectively describes the empirical events of collapse in the detailed case studies he selects – Rome, the southern lowland Maya, and the Chacoan – he does not explain its real causes. He mistakenly sees the collapse of ancient societies as an inevitable result – a mathematical probability – of diminishing marginal returns. It is not possible to understand the real causes of the collapse of societies unless we understand the wider dynamic process of which it is a part.

The last group of historians to be reviewed are those who wish to account for the rise of Western civilization. As can be seen from the titles of their books – *The Unbound Prometheus* (Landes, 1969), *The European Miracle* (Jones, 1981), *The Rise of the Western World* (North and Thomas, 1973), *Structure and Change in Economic History* (North, 1981), and *How the West Grew Rich* (Rosenberg and Birdzell, 1986) – they emphasize what they see as the uniqueness of this event. There is, they claim, something about the emergence of Western civilization that marks it off from all civilizations in the past. That something is the rapid and sustained rate of growth achieved through the accelerated pace of technological change. We have, they claim, thrown off the shackles of the past. What is it then that occurred in the runup to the Industrial Revolution that enabled Europe to remove the restraints on the innovative abilities of economic decision-makers?

The response to this question varies and, with the exception of North (1981), is generally couched in rather vague terms. Landes (1969) suggests that it is the release of Western Europe from the traditional values that had bound the innovative spirit of man in the past. Jones (1981; 1988) also nominates the restricting influence of traditional values, but his explanation is essentially political. He argues that the will to innovate has always been harboured in the breast of man, but that it has, until recently, been suppressed by the oppressive power of unproductive rent-seeking ruling elites except for brief flourishes such as Sung China. Only with the breakdown of the power of ruling elites owing to internal and external conflict does the innovative spirit rise to the surface. According to this interpretation, economic growth is the outcome of the removal of political barriers to change. Basically this type of supply-side explanation, in which strategic demand is unknowingly assumed to be constant, is a passive rather than a dynamic process. Other writers such as Kennedy (1989: 38) – whose work is discussed in the next chapter – have adopted the same theme.

Even more economically inclined historians (or historically inclined economists) like Rosenberg and Birdzell (1986: ch. 1), and Maddison (1982) are prepared to accept that political structures, religion, and traditional cultural values were largely instrumental in the alleged 'dismal' performance of European economies prior to 1700 and particularly before 1500. These explanations, however, are not systematic, and are little more than lists of possible causes. Only North and Thomas (1973) provide a systematic economic explanation of the rise of the West, in terms of the influence of emerging markets on the costs of doing business (i.e. transactions costs) and the role this plays in dismantling restrictive feudal structures. At one level this is a more persuasive argument because of its systematic nature, but it is somewhat narrowly focused upon institutions rather than fundamental economic forces and it begs the question as to why markets emerged. A more comprehensive dynamic model is required.

The most challenging of those modern economic historians or *historical economists* is Douglass North who, in *Structure and Change in Economic History* (1981), has provided a systematic explanation of the change in human organization since the Neolithic Revolution. His work has made a major contribution to our understanding of Western civilization. North was the first to suggest that an institutionally augmented neoclassical model can be employed to interpret the great sweep of Western history. He was the first to make sense of changing contractual arrangements in Western society and to suggest a mechanism for institutional change. He is one of the few who does not regard economic growth as a monopoly of the modern period. And he persuasively suggests that economic growth is an outcome not only of new technical ideas but also of new institutional ideas.

Yet North's analysis is diametrically opposite my own in terms of both methodology and interpretation. His method is deductive (he employs an augmented neoclassical model) whereas mine is inductive (I construct and employ an existential model). His model is comparatively static in nature and focuses upon supply-side forces, whereas my model is dynamic and emphasizes the demand side. He focuses upon the role of institutions in leading the growth process, whereas I focus upon the role of fundamental economic forces which determine both the progress of society and its institutional and ideological change. His model is open-ended as it is driven by exogenous forces (particularly population change), whereas my model is self-contained as the driving force (the ambitions of the dynamic strategist) is endogenous. His empirical verification is of an analogous nature, whereas I attempt to test formally the main features of my argument. We need to review these issues.

What is the nature of North's model? This question is not easily answered because his model is open-ended, because it possesses a number of *ad hoc* elements, because it changes over time, and because each of the three parts of his book (North, 1981) presents a slightly different variant. I have attempted to capture the main features of the model in the following four points.

1 The deductive economic model employed by North changes abruptly from period to period. For the pre-modern period he adopts an augmented classical model in which exogenous population growth runs into diminishing returns in the face of the fixed resource of land; and for the modern era he adopts an augmented neoclassical model which assumes constant returns to scale and embodies a highly elastic supply curve for knowledge (ibid.: 60). Both variations are extended by theories about institutions and ideology because he believes that the original models cannot explain the totality of the progress of Western society. His aim, he tells us (ibid.: 7), is 'to fill out the gaps in the neoclassical model'. As argued in Part III, I regard ideology as the domain of the dynamic tactics by which wealth and income are redistributed, not the domain of the dynamic strategies that drive the progress of society; and I regard institutional change as reactive rather than proactive.

2 In North's model of the pre-modern world, exogenously determined population growth leads to an increase in the ratio of labour to land, which in turn stimulates organizational change involving more sophisticated property rights and the reduction of transaction costs. This increases productivity in its own right and induces technological change, both of which promote the growth of GDP per capita. *Ad hoc* elements such as

the role of warfare also play a role by influencing the size and structure of political organization; and fortuitous changes in bargaining power prevent the effects of a reduction of population in Europe after 1300, and a failure to recover until about 1700, from reversing the organizational changes that North claims were generated by population growth between 800 and 1300. Not only does organizational change lead to secular growth, but 'it is the successes and failures in human organization that account for the progress and retrogression of societies' (ibid.: 59). To the contrary I argue that the rise and fall of societies are due to the adoption and exhaustion of the dynamic strategies.

3 The transformation from an agricultural to an industrial economic system, according to North, resulted from the 'structural transformation' that occurred during the 300 years before the Industrial Revolution. This organizational change led to an increase in the size of markets, which in turn had two major outcomes. First, it promoted an increase in specialization and division of labour which increased transaction costs, thereby acting as an inducement for further cost-reducing organizational change. Second, wider markets, together with changes in property rights that protected inventors and innovators (whereby the private rate of return is raised to the social rate), promoted technological change. It is this technological change, North argues, that we know as the Industrial Revolution. He also believes that the differential rates of growth as between nations is an outcome of their different systems of property rights. Yet the organizational changes that North claims gave rise to the Industrial Revolution, and that account for differences in growth rates between nations, do not appear to have been sufficient to prevent the relative decline of Britain during the twentieth century.

4 North regards the Industrial Revolution as merely preparatory to the 'Second Economic Revolution' which takes place from the late nineteenth century based upon a 'wedding of science and technology' which 'made the underlying assumption of neoclassical economics [constant returns] realizable' (ibid.: 171). It is the 'Second Revolution' rather than the Industrial Revolution that is comparable with the Neolithic Revolution on the grounds that '[b]oth entailed substantial institutional reorganization' (ibid.: 171). I argue that what the Neolithic and Industrial paradigm shifts have in common is a massive increase in the economic access to natural resources. As ideas respond to strategic demand there is no need to draw a fundamental distinction between the ideas of practical men and the ideas of scientists. It should be noted that population growth, the changing labour/land ratio, and warfare have been dropped from the model for the modern era.

North's decision to use a deductive rather than an inductive (existential) model poses a number of major difficulties. While mainstream economics has long been concerned with the issue of growth, it has been conspicuously unsuccessful in analysing it. This is largely because deductive theory is comparatively static in nature and because it focuses upon the supply side to the exclusion of demand. North inherits the same problems. It is for this reason that his historical interpretation is curiously static and that he has a supply-side explanation of the progress of Western society. Also as his model has deductive origins, the need to test it empirically is of paramount importance. In fact, North undertakes no formal testing of his hypotheses, and his 'historical essays' largely involve descriptions of organizational differences in time and space. There is an abstract quality about these 'stereotyped scenarios' which, he admits, are 'banal and self-evident' (ibid.: 116, 120). He makes no attempt to reconstruct and analyse the dynamic process.

As will be seen in Part III, by testing the major assumptions and interpretations of my own dynamic model I do unintentionally refute a number of key elements in North's model. A critical test of North's theory of the role of institutions and ideology is contained in the regression model I employ to examine the causes of the 'new revolution' of the second half of the twentieth century – the massive shift of married females from the household to the market. It is critical because the feminist and neoclassical (Becker, 1991) interpretations include a major ideological and institutional component. In Chapter 8, I am able to explain 98 per cent of the increase in this major structural shift solely in terms of changes in both the ratio of capital to labour and the gender wage ratio. This leaves little room for ideology or institutional arrangements, which merely responded to facilitate and to rationalize what amounted to a fundamental economic change in modern society.

All the evidence in this book supports the hypothesis that the progress of human society is the outcome of decision-makers attempting to achieve their objectives by responding to relative factor prices and investing in a range of dynamic strategies. This primary mechanism of dynamic materialism also drives the secondary mechanism of institutional or structural change. The various static institutional constraints in North's work are dealt with by me as the dynamic tactics of order and chaos. Metaphorically speaking, if the charioteer is the driving force in society and the paths he takes into the highlands of prosperity are the dynamic strategies, then the non-mechanical aspects of chariot design are the organizational structure of society, which sometimes influence the efficiency but not the motivation or direction of the race. And the jostling for position in the chariot is part of the dynamic tactics of order and chaos – a dynamic version of rules, regulations, and ideology. This will be explained further in a future work.

Finally we need to consider the old school of historical economists – now out of fashion – that saw the emergence of Western civilization as proceeding through a number of historical stages. This group includes members of the German historical school of economics, such as Karl Knies (1821–1898) and

Gustav von Schmoller (1838–1917), together with Karl Marx (1818–1883) and, more recently, W.W. Rostow. Each of these scholars has been more interested in the different economic systems or stages through which changing societies have passed than in the underlying dynamic process. They have focused, in other words, on the changing forms of economic organization – upon the nature of different economic systems – rather than upon the processes of change. Marx (1957–1961), for example, focused upon the forms of feudalism, capitalism, and beyond, while Rostow (1960) focused upon the traditional society, the preconditions for take-off, the take-off itself, the drive to maturity, the phase of high mass-consumption, and beyond. It is true that both authors developed mechanisms to explain economic change – for Marx it was dialectical materialism and for Rostow the leading-sector approach – but this was merely a way of getting from one particular stage to the next. The transition mechanisms in both models are specific to each stage and are unable to explain the growth of societies in the longer term. These authors, in other words, did not build general dynamic models that can transcend all stages. In essence they focus upon the convergence of societies to particular organizational forms rather than on the more general dynamic process of human society – a process by which the driving force interacts with key variables to produce a continuous sequence of increasing income and wealth.

By focusing upon stages or organizational forms, these historians were preoccupied with outcomes rather than economic processes. These historical theories, therefore, are little more than a set of suggestive staging posts through which societies are supposed to progress. Essentially the stages approach is a static approach. It is no more dynamic than the approach taken by mainstream economists who focus upon the convergence to equilibrium. The historical record, however, shows that in competitive societies there are no static stages or organizational forms. There is only change. We need, therefore, to focus upon the underlying process of economic change, not upon idealized organizational structures frozen in time. The organizational structures are, in fact, ephemeral – they change even before there is time to describe and define their shape – whereas the growth processes are continuous and eternal.

A major reason for this preoccupation with stages and organizational forms is the failure to realize that economic growth – in terms of real GDP per capita – has been an integral part of all competitive societies in the past, even the distant past. In this book I suggest that the nature of the longrun growth process can be approached by examining economic change in major nations over millennia past. Hopefully, this approach – which focuses on the continuity of longrun dynamic processes rather than on a series of static organizational cross-sections – will be a more viable alternative than the stages approach.

Most of the arguments used to explain the rise of Western civilization focus on supply-side forces. The impetus for growth, in other words, is not a result of a demand for the implements of change, but a result of conditions favouring their supply. Things happen because, for some external reason or other, barriers to their happening are removed: seas rise and fall; rivers are diverted by natural events; climate changes; wars cease; diseases disappear; political oppression collapses; traditional values, institutions, and religions break down; and the opposition to new ideas evaporates. Always mankind's role is passive. We merely respond to changing physical and cultural environments, albeit in an opportunistic way. We never take an active role. Mankind is merely a captive of life. We do not purposefully attempt to achieve our objectives by adopting strategies in order to actively exploit our environment. Forces on the demand side – the active exercise of preferences – are rarely invoked by social scientists, even economists, to explain change. Indeed, the current fashion in most fields of mainstream economics is anti-demand and pro-supply.

Possibly the most extreme form of this supply-side approach has been adopted by demographic historians interested in the emergence of the modern world. Some (Lee, 1973) argue that the longrun fortunes of human society are determined by random exogenous (external) shocks. Basically, the argument is that population growth is determined by exogenous shocks such as climate, pests, epidemics, political events, and wars through their impact upon mortality and fertility; and that the resulting population change drives real wages (or real GDP per capita) inversely. Society, therefore, is driven from without rather than from within – and not in any systematic way. In this explanation, upswings in real wages and real GDP per capita (i.e. economic growth) are driven by a fall in population determined by forces external to society; while a downswing in real wages (negative growth) is driven by an increase in population. This implies that longrun changes in human society, both past and future, are not the result of systematic internal forces, but of random external shocks – of what statisticians call 'white noise'. Life is just a lottery.

This arid and anti-humanist interpretation is the logical extreme to which those in the shadow of the Tower have been tending for some time. And not just of social scientists. It also includes natural scientists who view life on Earth as being determined largely by random cosmic events. Indeed, social scientists were probably influenced in this respect – Lee (1993: 2), for example, refers approvingly to the work in 'animal population biology' – by the natural scientists.

Modern Western scholarship therefore has not been able to achieve any consensus about the dynamic nature of human society, apart from the disturbing view that it is being tossed about on the cumulative waves of chance. There exists no persuasive dynamic model that can be employed to explain the past or to offer satisfactory suggestions as to the big issues facing mankind in the future. The black-box simulation models employed by the ecological engineers are not only inadequate, they are positively dangerous if taken seriously. Everyone has a view, and each view is different in substance, form, and language. While change and, particularly, economic growth is, and has always been, the defining characteristic of human society, we are unable to explain it – in many cases we have even refused to admit that epochs other than our own have been able to achieve it. A major reason – as we shall see in the next chapter – is the absence of any consensus among those who work within the shadow of the Tower about the forces that drive human society.

6

QUEST FOR MEANING

Why have you exerted yourself? What have you achieved?
You have made yourself weary for lack of sleep,
You only fill your flesh with grief,
You only bring the distant day (of reckoning) closer
Mankind's fame is cut down like reeds in a reed bed.
(*Epic of Gilgamesh*, 2nd millennium BC)

*Around the campfires of the desert caravans and on the long sea voyages to
the Indus Valley they tell a tale about a hero called Gilgamesh, a Sumerian
king in the third millennium BC. It is a tale about the quest for meaning.
About Gilgamesh and his wild friend Enkidu who, with youthful energy
and indiscretion, pursue fame and immortality. Gilgamesh and Enkidu reck-
lessly scale the greatest mountains, bravely tackle lions in the mountain passes,
and heroically confront and kill the great monster Humbaba in his pine
forest. Their zeal knows no limits. They even foolishly seize the bull of heaven
and slay it. The gods are angry. Gilgamesh and Enkidu have gone too far.
They have challenged the deities themselves and must be punished for their
arrogance. There is a great debate in the heavens. Finally it is decided that
the wild Enkidu, close friend and companion of Gilgamesh, must die.
Distraught by his friend's death and fearing for his own life, Gilgamesh
leaves the mountain heights for Sumer's plain where he wanders endlessly
calling into question the wisdom of striving for anything in this world. On
one of his long-distance journeys Gilgamesh meets the sage Ut-napishtim,
who tells him to stop worrying about immortality, to accept life as it is, and
to extract as much from it as possible. Ut-napishtim says to Gilgamesh:*

> *Death is inevitable at some time, both for Gilgamesh and for a fool
> But a throne is set down for you in the Assembly.
> To a fool is given dregs instead of butter . . .*

*Those around the desert campfires and under a sea-misted moon, who are
going about their lucrative business of commerce, nod in silent approval.*

137

There are those who seek meaning in human history on the mountain tops, and those who find it on the plains. Their quest is the driving force in history. Although many suggestions have been made, there is little consensus on this central issue. Some have suggested that the driving force is imposed upon human society from the outside through accumulating random shocks or major changes in the physical environment. Others reject the idea that human society is driven by some great cosmic lottery and maintain that we should investigate man and his society. Yet even here there is disagreement. Does mankind respond to spiritual, intellectual, political, or economic forces? Each has its supporters among those in the shadow of the Tower.

In whatever way these forces of change are identified and interpreted, it is clear that they have somehow involved human decision-makers. Accordingly, I will review the various ideas about the forces driving society in terms of the roles human agents are thought to have played. This can most effectively be outlined in terms of polar cases. The contrasting roles of mankind can be thought of in terms of passive versus active man, of natural versus cultural man, and of moral/political versus economic man. This characterization encompasses the main protagonists in the sciences and humanities on this centrally important issue. The intellectual traditions in the sciences and humanities provide a kaleidoscopic view of the nature of mankind. It is a colourful but very fragmented view. Owing to the very different perspectives from which mankind is seen by the various intellectual traditions, it is not surprising there are a variety of views about the past and future of human society. We need to see these views clearly before considering the nature of mankind revealed in Part III by our study of the past.

PASSIVE VERSUS ACTIVE MAN

The characterization of human beings as passive agents in life is widespread and transcends the usual boundaries between the sciences and humanities. According to this view human agents, who may act either rationally or irrationally, merely respond in a reactive way to forces that are outside their control. They are merely swept along by the tide of time and have no controlling influence over the longrun changes in society. Passive man has been portrayed either as the victim of accumulating random events or as the beneficiary of positive changes in the physical environment. This role contrasts starkly with the characterization of active man, who not only responds to external change, but who also takes the initiative and actively changes his society and his world. Active man is the subject of subsequent sections of this chapter and includes natural, cultural, intellectual, moral/political, and economic man.

There is a pervasive school of modern thought that argues that the rise and fall of human society is the product of accumulating random shocks. This view emerges whenever academic technicians, particularly statisticians, come to dominate a discipline. Representatives of this school can be found in the social, as well as the natural, sciences. Owing to their command over statistical and mathematical techniques they are often regarded as being at the leading edge of their respective disciplines. This is particularly unfortunate because their interest is not in explaining changes in human society, but in providing a quantitative basis for predicting changes in the future (as explained in Pagan, 1993). Prediction, in their minds, becomes explanation. It is a black-box approach to life. It matters little that we fail to understand why something is happening provided we can replicate what has taken place in the recent past and predict what will happen in the future.

This approach to reality is highly misleading. In neglecting to explain the forces driving the system under study, the academic technicians cannot hope to analyse the big issues facing society today. An approach that views society from the outside has little time for human decision-making. A recent example of work in technical historical demography makes this point quite clearly. After years of studying population and real-wage fluctuations over the very longrun, Ronald Lee (1993: 1) concludes that '[l]ong waves in European demographic history do not arise from homeostasis [i.e., Malthusian-type self-regulation] and may simply reflect the demographic cumulation of random shocks, rather than a cyclic driving force'. This conclusion explains little. Human beings are just passive agents in the path of the tide of time and, as such, are not considered important in the lifeless 'statistical' processes that are of interest to academic technicians. The longrun fluctuations experienced by human society are merely the product of outrageous fortune. Merely a matter of chance. And as such they can be reproduced by random statistical processes. This type of approach amounts to nothing less than the dehumanization of human society.

Rather than being the victim of outrageous fortune, man is sometimes seen as the beneficiary of fortuitous, if systematic, changes in the environment. According to this view, the driving force in both life and human society is a systematic outcome of the dynamics of the Universe, not of random events. Society is driven by a dynamic physical environment. The most enthusiastic champions of this thesis, as seen in Chapter 4, are Crawford and Marsh in their book *The Driving Force* (1989). They focus upon the chemistry of the planet which has its origin in the beginning of the Universe. These chemical elements supply the nutrients – the food – for all living organisms including mankind. Their thesis is deterministic in the sense that the supply of nutrients depends upon systematic and unchanging chemical and physical laws – laws over which mankind has no control. The supply of chemicals on Earth provide, according to Crawford and Marsh, *the* 'driving force' in life to which all organisms respond. Evolution, including that of human beings, is 'substrate-driven'. In other words, the physical conditions of life are 'active' forces in evolution, while individual organisms and species are 'passive' or reactive.

The views of Crawford and Marsh about the prime mover in life are fairly reflected in the following extracts from their book. They begin (ibid.: 18) with a sweeping flourish:

> Malthus and Darwin recognised that food and space were the ultimate determinants of population size, but neither of them recognised the food and space factor as the initiator, the forward driving force of populations. Neither did they recognise that it was not just the amount of food that matters, but also its chemistry.

And when pulling the threads of their argument together they write (ibid.: 37):

> We could sum up our approach by saying that we see all life forms and their evolution as examples of physics and chemistry in action. The process can be considered as a series of chemical reactions in which genetics, organisms and their environments interact. Variability occurs in both genetics and chemistry but the evidence indicates that, of the two, chemistry is the more coercive.

In their thesis, chemistry is the 'impulse' or 'initiator', the 'directing force', and *the* 'driving force' in life (ibid.: 18, 21). In claiming a new way of looking at evolution they say (ibid.: 33): 'The important distinction between selection and substrate-driven change is that the mechanism of the latter is active or propelling, whereas "selection" is passive, effecting a sorting out process after the change has taken place.' This is to replace the distasteful economic basis for natural selection with an explanation derived from physical science.

For Crawford and Marsh, what is true of life in general is also true of human evolution and human history. Their claim is that 'human evolution, like that of previous epochs, was substrate-driven', and that '[i]f the concept of substrate-driven change is valid there will be evidence in history and today of food changing man in shape and performance' (ibid.: 187–8). In warming to this theme, they write (ibid.: 189–90):

> Civilisations . . . were stimulated, or checked, by food, energy and raw materials. As in evolution, two great influences can be seen at work: the driving force of nutrition followed later by the struggle for resources which favours some and, in the end, destroys those that can no longer find their necessities in the environment they have helped to shape.

And they claim (ibid.: 249) that 'nutritional chemistry was, and is still, a fundamental evolutionary force'.

What of the future? Like many other natural scientists, Crawford and Marsh believe that recent advances in science have, for the first time, given mankind control over the physical conditions of life. They confidently claim (ibid.: 252): 'Now that we know, we can respond'. The 'we', of course, are the natural scientists. They recognize, however, that it is still a matter of persuading the rest of mankind of the truth of this science-based vision of the future. As they see it, mankind needs to abandon its immature preoccupation with material things: 'The problem is that *Homo sapiens* has yet to reach adulthood. In his relationship with his parent planet, *Homo sapiens* is still a child that has not learnt to look after his pocket money' (ibid.: 253). This alleged ignorance on the part of the vast bulk of mankind, particularly before the great scientific enlightenment, reinforces their view that physical conditions rather than man are the driving force in history. While the natural scientist is the interpreter of the physical driving force, the economist is the false prophet who merely obscures the truth. As they say (ibid.: 253): 'For our future success, economic theory must accept its biological and planetary responsibility.' The social scientist must follow the lead of the natural scientist. Indeed, it is a call to humanity to place itself under the controlling influence of science: 'biological considerations ought to direct agricultural policies world-wide, yet in reality the aim of "agricultural development" is often pursued for different reasons' – reasons such as economic gain (ibid.: 256). Clearly, what they do not appreciate is that the 'ignorant' mass of humanity which, in their view, is passively waiting for enlightenment, is the very force that is driving human civilization now as it has always driven it. It is the intellectuals, not just scientists, who are out of step with the march of human civilization.

They conclude this discussion in a euphoric manner (1989: 257):

> Were we shaped by a concentration of random events, unpredictable and unpatterned, or are we rather the latest creation of a universe governed everywhere and always by the [physical] laws of its own development; laws which through science we, its creatures, can hope to understand and use in shaping our own destiny?

As the environment rather than mankind is the driving force in history, Crawford and Marsh insist that we focus upon the active physical world rather than the passive occupants of that world. Indeed, their concluding symbol of the future is 'the figure of a human mother and child' (ibid.: 258) – mother Earth feeding the passive child of humanity in her arms, with the wise and protective medical scientist looking on.

There could be no clearer rejection of the dynamic role of human beings fighting for survival and material gain. This symbol is the answer to their rhetorical question (ibid.: 257):

> Are we what we are because of a long process of selection involving the unceasing war of all against all in which the survivors demonstrate their 'fitness' by wiping out their rivals? Or are we instead the product of a more generous world, whose children are called into existence by

the wealth of new opportunities which at certain critical moments she presents to them?

Mankind, according to this view, is the passive beneficiary of a bounteous world. As this book demonstrates, nothing could be further from the truth.

The ecological engineers of the *Beyond the Limits* variety also see the vast majority of mankind as passive and in need of leadership from the physical scientist and the systems engineer. As shown in Chapter 5, the computer simulation models – 'World2' and 'World3' – underlying the analysis and prediction in both *The Limits to Growth* (1972) and *Beyond the Limits* (1992) are based upon engineering feedback systems which provide no role for the innovating decision-maker. The driving force in these models is merely an *assumption* of exponential growth. As the authors say (Meadows *et al.*, 1992: 14):

> Exponential growth is the driving force causing the human economy to approach the physical limits of the earth. It is culturally ingrained and structurally inherent in the global system, and the causal structure that produces it is at the core of the World3 model.

No justification is provided for this central assumption. It is just assumed that human society attempts to maximize the *rate* of economic growth because it is a part of the culture of modern capitalist society to do so. The implication is that to change this assumption it would be necessary merely to change the culture of modern society rather than the genetic nature of mankind. This they have in common with other natural scientists. Economic growth in this model is generated not by the dynamic strategies identified in this book but by mechanical feedback processes of the type displayed by thermostatically controlled heating systems.

As there are no innovative human agents in their model of the global economy, it just grinds on in a mechanical way. The economic – and hence social and political – outcomes are prisoners of the mechanical system devised by these ecological engineers. Accordingly, it is not possible for the predictions of this model to break out of predetermined mechanical confines. Such an approach provides a dehumanized view of human society, which denies the demonstrable energy, innovativeness, and plain common sense of human beings. It is not hard to understand why the predictions of the ecological engineers are filled with gloom and doom. We would expect a machine-like world to grind on regardless of its actions, and ultimately to destroy not only the physical but also the social environment. Such a view of human society is a denial of the human spirit.

The only role for human agents in the world of *Beyond the Limits* is in managing the real world as if it were a mechanical model. Systems managers, it is argued, are required to prevent the real world experiencing the 'overshoot' and collapse predicted by their simple engineering systems. This can be achieved by turning off economic growth – largely by substituting restorative technology for growth-inducing technology – and shutting down population expansion. While they claim this can be done by telling people about the gloom and doom ahead, it is unlikely to occur without coercion on a massive scale.

Hence the ecological engineers' view of the world is one in which human agents are largely passive and unable to manage a destructive global machine that is out of control. Control can only be reestablished by expert and benevolent systems managers who can instruct the world how to live within its technological limits. The expert is triumphant over the people. In effect this amounts to shackling the innovative spirit of mankind to prevent us crashing through these limits into a new technological paradigm, as has occurred at similarly critical periods in the past.

NATURAL VERSUS CULTURAL MAN

Some natural scientists, mainly 'sociobiologists', do see a more active role for decision-makers in human evolution and history. To define their view of the nature and motivation of mankind, I here use the term 'natural' man.

A convenient starting point is the view of the well-known biologist Paul Ehrlich. In his recent bestseller *The Population Explosion* (1990: 186), Ehrlich claims that the human mind 'evolved as a tool for keeping us alive, and maximizing our reproduction'. According to this interpretation, natural man is motivated by the paramount desire to survive and to maximize the number of his offspring. But while natural man has prevailed for some 2 million years, he has recently changed his spots. Since the scientific enlightenment, mankind has been able to alter its basic drive. Natural man has transcended his biological nature and has become, what I have called, 'cultural' man. While we will return to this remarkable 'transformation' in human nature later in the chapter, at this point we need to explore the biological basis for the view that the driving force in the evolution of mankind is the overwhelming desire to maximize reproduction.

It is a view that has emerged from the Darwinian theory of evolution. Evolutionary biologists appear to focus on either the gene, the individual, the social group, or the species, and each faction stoutly defends its choice. This is similar to the conflict in the social sciences between those who maintain that human evolution is driven by ideas (for a recent attempt to draw parallels with the role of the gene in biological evolution, see Mokyr, 1990), individuals (economic man), or social groups ('moral' man). The view that either genes or ideas play a driving role is a curious one and will be discussed later.

At this point we need to explore how biologists have rationalized the idea of maximizing reproduction. We begin by exploring the interesting argument presented by Richard Dawkins, the neo-Darwinian populist, in *The Selfish Gene*. Essentially, Dawkins' argument is that when life first emerged some 4 billion years ago it consisted of molecules floating freely in the primeval seas. Eventually molecules that he calls 'replicators', which had the ability to produce copies of themselves, were formed. These replicators are portrayed as complex chains of building-block molecules that attract compatible individual building blocks arranged in a way that mimics the replicator. As the replicators spread throughout the congenial seas, the smaller building-block molecules become increasingly scarce. This produced a competitive environment for the various replicator varieties as they struggled blindly for survival. During this competitive struggling, replicators attempted to break down chemically the structure of their rivals and to use the newly released building blocks to make further copies of themselves.

To defend themselves against aggressive rivals, some replicators built walls of protein around themselves and thereby formed cells. According to Dawkins (1989: 19), this began the development of 'containers, vehicles for their continued existence. The replicators that survived were the ones that built *survival machines* for themselves to live in . . . Survival machines got bigger and more elaborate, and the process was cumulative and progressive'. Eventually these 'survival machines' turned into you and me. With his usual rhetorical flourish, Dawkins writes (ibid.: 19–20):

> Four thousand million years on, what was to be the fate of the ancient replicators? They did not die out, for they are past masters of the survival arts. But do not look for them floating loose in the sea; they gave up that cavalier freedom long ago. Now they swarm in huge colonies, safe inside gigantic lumbering robots, sealed off from the outside world, communicating with it by tortuous indirect routes, manipulating it by remote control. They are in you and in me; they created us, body and mind; and their preservation is the ultimate rationale for our existence. They have come a long way, those replicators. Now they go by the name of genes, and we are their survival machines.

While the use of this brilliantly extended metaphor is calculated to shock and stimulate interest – which it does most successfully – it nevertheless betrays the non-humanistic way in which many natural scientists view human society. And it completely overlooks the real driving force. According to this view, the individual acts in a way that maximizes the survival of its component genes. The gene is seen as 'immortal' in the sense that exact copies are passed forever from individual to individual – whereas these individual organisms are mortal. Man, in other words, is the transitory vessel – the 'lumbering robot' – that carries the immortal genes. This is, however, merely a fascinating intellectual game called 'how far can we get by pretending that genes wish to maximize their reproduction and are able to build survival machines to do so?' While it does provide a basis for the view that the driving determination of organisms to survive is genetically determined, and gives a persuasive explanation of the evolution of simple cells in the primeval seas, it breaks down when it comes to explain the struggle between 'decision-making' individuals for survival and material gain, particularly in human society.

How does this argument work in human society? Dawkins, expounding the ideas of W.D. Hamilton (1964), presents the 'kin selection' hypothesis, whereby 'gene selfishness' paradoxically brings about a limited degree of 'individual altruism'. He argues that genes 'attempt' to maximize their influence in the gene pool by programming individuals to undertake, in effect, benefit–cost calculations based upon the degree of their genetic 'relatedness' to other individuals. Such an index, Dawkins (1989: 91) tells us, 'expresses the chance of a gene being shared between two relatives'. It can be constructed by first identifying the common ancestors between two individuals and then calculating the 'generation distance' from individual A to the common ancestor, and then back to individual B. In the case of identical twins who share the same genetic structure, the relatedness is equal to unity. For siblings it is, on average, ½ because half the genes possessed by one brother will be found in his sibling. It is also ½ between parent and child, and ¼ for grandparents and grandchildren, aunts/uncles, and nieces/nephews. And to complete the scale, it is ⅛ for first cousins, $\frac{1}{32}$ for second cousins, $\frac{1}{128}$ for third cousins. By the time we get to third cousins, Dawkins (ibid.: 92) tells us, 'we are getting down near the baseline probability that a particular gene possessed by A will be shared by any random individual taken from the population'.

With perfect information and a copy of this index of genetic relatedness, individual organisms could attempt to maximize the spread of their genes. This involves individuals attempting to assist other individuals according to the genetic relationship between them. An identical twin would be treated as oneself; one would be indifferent as between parents, children, and siblings; and all the foregoing would be more important than grandparents, grandchildren, aunts/uncles, and nieces/nephews, all of whom would be treated equally. A qualification, which takes the average lifespan of individuals in any of these egalitarian categories into account, is usually introduced. Children, for example, will receive more care and support than parents, because they have longer to live. Although not stated by biologists, this is implicit recognition of the variation in rates of return on investment in time and effort. All this makes the complex calculations required by neoclassical economic man seem quite simple.

An obvious problem with this genetic approach is that the mate of any individual making these calculations should be no more important than any other member of the opposite sex selected at random from the population. Why then do individuals devote so much time to their sexual partners? The answer is obvious, and has nothing to do with an index of genetic relatedness. Also, it is highly improbable that one would treat an identical twin as oneself, or treat a sibling as one's child (even if both were the same age). Dawkins attempts to resolve this difficulty by introducing a further index – the 'index of certainty'. He argues (ibid.: 105), not very convincingly, that:

> [a]lthough the parent/child relationship is no closer genetically than the brother/sister relationship, its certainty is greater. It is normally possible to be much more certain who your children are than who your brothers are. And you can be more certain still who you yourself are!

This uncertainty about close genetic relationships leads to 'selfish' rather than 'altruistic' individual behaviour, we are told, even where the degree of genetic relatedness is the same.

This argument is unconvincing and unnecessarily complex. To recapitulate, Dawkins advocates the 'genetic relatedness index', which cannot be applied until we qualify it with another measuring stick – the average length of remaining life. But even this adjustment is not enough. We have to combine the mortality-qualified genetic relatedness index with a further index of certainty. In other words, the genetic relatedness hypothesis, which is based upon perfect information, can only be regarded as operational in a world in which information is imperfect! But even then it cannot handle the care that human individuals devote to their sexual partners, or to adopted children. This would, no doubt, require a further index. In other words, the genetic relatedness hypothesis is able to tell us very little about human relationships and would be a hopeless practical guide for those wanting to know how to treat those around them. In Chapter 7 I develop a simple hypothesis that can explain human relationships without reference to genetic relationships, a hypothesis based upon the **economic distance** between individuals – the degree to which other individuals are necessary to maximize our own material advantage.

If for the purposes of exposition we temporarily accept the genetic related-ness hypothesis, we need to ask why individual organisms would wish to maximize their reproduction. Dawkins' answer (ibid.: 88) is that individuals wish to maximize the propagation of their own genetic makeup: 'what is a single selfish gene trying to do? It is trying to get more numerous in the gene pool. Basically it does this by helping to program the bodies in which it finds itself to survive and reproduce.' One way of doing this is by program-ming individuals carrying the same gene to act altruistically to each other.

When discussing biological evolution, the natural scientist is usually objective and rigorous, but as soon as the focus falls upon modern man, these admirable qualities vanish. If we return, for example, to Ehrlich's recent work (1990: 192–3), we are told that modern man, unlike his earlier counterpart, pays 'more or less heed to "maximising your reproduction" message engraved in their genes – in part because there's much less danger that their children won't survive to reproduce. Cultural evolution clearly can override biological evolution.' He passes very lightly over what is a fundamental problem. If the maximization of reproduction is really 'engraved' in our genes, and if this has been such a powerful force over billions of years, how is it possible that modern man has been able to transcend it? If it is merely a matter of discretion, why did not other species achieve it millions of years ago? If the answer to this question is that it required the development of a large brain, why did not the dolphins, who have larger brains than man, do it 10 million years ago when they returned to the seas? If the answer to this question is that it is the brain/body ratio which is critical, why did not squirrels, which have a similar brain/body ratio to man, do it? If the answer to this question is that there is something unique about man, why did not man do it when he first emerged about 2–3 million years ago, or at least when *Homo sapiens sapiens* emerged about 100,000 years ago? And if the answer to this question is that man needed first to develop a sophisticated culture, why are the sophisticated cultures of China and India generating exponential rates of population growth; and why were relatively unsophisticated cultures such as Aboriginal Australia and Eskimo Alaska able to achieve static populations for tens of thousands of years?

Surely a more satisfactory explanation is that what is engraved in our genes is not the maximization of reproduction, but the maximization of something very different. I have already suggested that what is, and has always been, maximized is the probability of survival; everything else – consumption, sexual gratification, power, and social relationships – flows from this. Once survival has been ensured the objective is to maximize material gain in order to enjoy the pleasures of life to the full. The difference between these two hypotheses amounts to the difference between focusing upon the 'immortal' gene and upon the mortal individual. To focus upon the lowest level of all is not to encapsulate everything else. As will be shown in the next chapter, we must treat the decision-making individual as the central agent in the Dynamic Society. In this context, the attempt to maximize reproduction may actually minimize the probability of survival of the individual and the society. That is why human society, operating under competitive economic conditions, has always attempted to control its population, not to maximize it. The same may well be true of other species. But more of this in the next chapter.

Richard Dawkins, who goes to a great deal of effort to make the point that individuals and the genes they carry are driven by a blind compulsion to maximize their reproduction, also assumes without evidence or much argument that mankind can escape its genetic heritage. After a very brief survey of the range of family relationships in human society today, Dawkins (1989: 164) concludes: 'What this astonishing variety suggests is that man's way of life is largely determined by culture rather than genes'. Biology is declared redundant: 'for an understanding of the evolution of modern man, we must begin by throwing out the gene as the sole basis of our ideas of evolution' (ibid.: 191). After an unconvincing attempt to use genetic evolution as an analogy to 'explain' cultural development – ideas or 'memes' are seen as playing the same role in society as genes in life – he concludes (ibid.: 200–1):

> We have the power to defy the selfish genes of our birth and, if necessary, the selfish memes of our indoctrination. We can even discuss ways of deliberately cultivating and nurturing pure, disinterested altruism – something that has no place in nature, something that has never existed before in the whole history of the world. We were built as gene machines and cultivated as meme machines, but we have the power to turn against our creators. We, alone on earth, can rebel against the tyranny of the selfish replicators.

Like Ehrlich, Dawkins gives no argument or evidence – other than the existence of different cultural forms which, in fact, reflect different economic structures – in support of this rhetorical flourish. It is the product of romantic wishful thinking. It is merely assumed that mankind can transcend billions of years of genetic change and thousands of years of cultural development by doing, no less, than changing its nature through intellectual will-power. Natural man is to be replaced by cultural man. This is a theme that is common to most natural scientists and many social scientists.

While I intend addressing these issues in the following chapter, it should be said at this stage that the argument of natural scientists about cultural development completely misses the point. This is hardly surprising because, by their own admission, biology must be thrown out when it comes to discussing modern man – and that extends over 100,000 years back into the past. Cultural development, which includes technological and institutional change, can only be explained in an economic framework in which human beings are attempting to maximize their material advantage, rather than in a pseudo-biological framework in which the counterpart of genes – ideas – are attempting to maximize their numbers in the wider pool of ideas! Biological models are just not appropriate to a study of human society. We need, as will be shown in the next chapter, to examine the economic conditions that determine the spread of ideas, and we need to understand the role of materialist man – who is a dynamic version of economic man – in this process.

Underlying this alleged transition from natural to cultural man is a change in the behaviour of human beings from selfishness to altruism. There are a variety of attitudes among natural scientists to the complex issue of human behaviour. Some argue that while 'selfishness' dominated biological evolution, 'altruism' began evolving culturally from the very beginning of human society. Others suggest that even in humans, selfishness is genetically determined and can only be transcended through education and intellectual will-power. Altruism, according to this view, is the ultimate goal of civilization. Overall, it is generally believed that the nature and behaviour of modern man either has or can be transformed.

John Eccles (1989: 114–16) takes the view that altruism – by which he means 'a particular type of moral behaviour by a person who is attempting to do good for others without thinking of any personal advantage that might accrue' – has evolved in human society. He claims that the 'first traces' of intentional altruistic behaviour in the whole history of life on Earth can be seen in 'the food-sharing at communal living sites' of early hominids. Further evidence, he claims, can be found in Neanderthal burial customs about 80,000 years ago; in the evidence for severely incapacitated Neanderthal individuals who were kept alive by their community; in the Epic of Gilgamesh written in Sumer more than 4,000 years ago (a curious misreading of this source); and in his observation that modern '*normal* human life is a tissue of altruistic acts'. Accordingly, he concludes: 'Cultural evolution . . . takes over from biological evolution and soon becomes crucial in natural selection, not only because of the wealth of technological innovations, but also because of the creation and development of the values'. He draws, however, a sharp distinction between the intentional altruism of humans and the 'accidental' altruism of other animals, which he claims is often cited by 'sociobiologists' like Richard Dawkins.

Richard Dawkins' central theme in *The Selfish Gene* (1989: 1) is 'to examine the biology of selfishness and altruism'. He claims to be interested not in motives, although he certainly discusses these, but only in behavioural outcomes. His argument (ibid.: 2–3) in this respect is

> that a predominant quality to be expected in a successful gene is ruthless selfishness. This gene selfishness will usually give rise to selfishness in individual behaviour. However . . . there are special circumstances in which a gene can achieve its own selfish goals best by fostering a limited form of altruism at the level of individual animals . . . [but be] warned that if you wish, as I do, to build a society in which individuals cooperate generously and unselfishly towards a common good, you can expect little help from biological nature. Let us try to *teach* generosity and altruism, because we are born selfish.

While 'kin selection' leads only to a limited form of altruism, Dawkins is optimistic that we can teach ourselves to be altruistic even to individuals who are not genetically related to us. He claims (ibid.: 3), without evidence or argument, that:

> Our genes may instruct us to be selfish, but we are not necessarily compelled to obey them all our lives. It may just be more difficult to learn altruism than it would if we were genetically programmed to be altruistic. Among animals, man is uniquely dominated by culture, by influences learned and handed down.

This is at the beginning of his book. By the end he is wildly optimistic, claiming (ibid.: 200–1), as we have seen earlier, that '[w]e have the power to defy the selfish genes of our birth'.

In the endnotes to the second edition of *The Selfish Gene*, Dawkins protests that this enthusiastic affirmation of the triumph of altruism over selfishness – of cultural over natural man – is not inconsistent, as his critics have claimed, with the rest of the book. But this is clearly not the case. For 4 billion years, evolution was dominated by the overwhelmingly powerful driving force of self-interest, which he argues is genetically determined. Suddenly, in the last instant of existence, mankind is able to transcend this ingrained instinct for survival. For those who do not believe in miracles, this appears to be a funda- mental inconsistency. And even if such a miracle occurred and man overcame his instinct for survival, would not that miracle quickly lead to his own destruction? It appears impossible to have it both ways. The problem is that human motivation is regarded as a subject of faith rather than of evidence. We shall appeal to evidence in the next chapter.

Finally, we should briefly consider the views of physical (rather than biolog- ical) scientists, such as Crawford and Marsh. They are not directly concerned with the issue of 'selfish' versus 'altruistic' behaviour, precisely because they downplay the Darwinian theory of scarcity, competitive struggle, and natural selection – that part of the theory of evolution that can be traced back to the social, rather than natural, sciences. They see the driving force in terms not of the replicator or individual, but of the changing supply of chemical resources. Therefore the transformation of human nature is not from natural to cultural man but from passive to cultural man. In their view, while mankind – indeed the whole of life – has in the past been driven by the supply of nutrients, we have now reached the stage where we can take charge of this driving force and use it for our own purposes. In their view this trans- formation has behavioural implications, because the boundless generosity of the physical world can be employed in an equally generous manner (Crawford and Marsh, 1989: 257). Suddenly passive man is transformed into cultural man who 'has the ability to do the right thing' (ibid.: 256). So the benign behaviour of passive man becomes, through the harnessing of the laws of the universe by scientists, an instrument of enlightened intervention.

MORAL/POLITICAL VERSUS ECONOMIC MAN

The social sciences and humanities have their equivalent of behavioural types that inhabit the scientific world. The dominant behavioural type to be found in explorations of the past is what I have called 'moral' man – from the Latin *moralis*, meaning custom – whose behaviour is dominated by what have been variously called traditional values, or community rules, or custom. Moral man acts as he does because things have always been done in that way. He is unimaginative and unenterprising. He learns his values and ideas at his parents' side, and passes these values and ideas unchanged on to his children. He is the favourite peasant character in histories of the medieval period, and is usually contrasted with the landowner, that representative of the tiny ruling elite, who is violent, rapacious, spendthrift, and subject to the social disease of conspicuous consumption. The latter may attempt to maximize the exercise of personal power (political man) but does not attempt to maximize material return (economic man). These two, moral and political man, are locked together in a predatory relationship. It is this predatory relationship that some (Jones, 1981) argue is responsible for the economic stagnation – according to their perception – of most pre-modern societies. Only when the predatory relationship broke down did economic growth occur and modern society emerge. This interpretation, we shall see, cannot be sustained.

Moral man lives in a world without economic growth. Populations fluctuate and may even increase over the longrun, but there is no sustained increase in living standards as measured by GDP per capita. And populations increase only because of external shocks which influence mortality and, to a lesser extent, fertility. Any shortrun gains that may be made in real wages are eroded by increases in population. This is a view that elsewhere I have attempted to challenge (Snooks, 1993a; 1994b). Moral man is the humanities equivalent of passive man in the physical sciences. He responds stoically to changes in the physical and cultural environment. He does not take risks and does not initiate change. He certainly is not a driving force in medieval society – how could he be in view of the conventional wisdom that medieval society was not going anywhere anyway? Both medieval society and moral man are merely carried along by the ebb and flow of the tide of time.

Political man, on the other hand, attempts to maximize his power over others. This, it is argued, can be seen in pre-modern societies and, during the twentieth century, in various totalitarian systems. To some, it is the desire for political power that is the driving force in cultural or sociopolitical evolution, with the economic system in train. Also it is seen as defining the changing power relationships between nations. It is to these matters that we now turn.

Curiously, as we approach the modern age – from the time of the Renaissance – there is a change in the nature of man portrayed in historical writings. The revival of classical learning appears to have paved the way for a new approach towards the world around us. Moral man is somehow transformed by historians into intellectual or philosophical man, the originator of ideas. And armed with these new ideas, intellectual or philosophical man is able to gain mastery over his environment and to change the world forever, as witnessed by the French Revolution and the Industrial Revolution.

Many writers, however, are ambivalent about the changes that have been wrought by ideas in the modern world. While they are certain about the beneficial role of intellectual ideas, they are suspicious about those groups in society, known as capitalists, who exploit both these ideas and those who work in their factories or mines. Many historians see capitalists of the modern period as they see landowners of the medieval period – as rapacious and self-serving if not indolent and spendthrift. Somehow capitalists have perverted, as well as exploited, the ideas of intellectual man. Nevertheless, intellectual man continues to be seen as a force capable of changing human society for the better, while the capitalists and the economists who advise them and their political representatives have been seen as distasteful opportunists who are always attempting to grab a piece of the action. Intellectual man is also seen as being motivated by altruistic rather than selfish impulses. More recently, environmentalists have taken up this theme and have portrayed capitalists and economists as the enemies of the planet because of their alleged role in inventing and perpetuating economic growth.

In the modern world, ideas are seen as the prime mover in society just as custom dominated the medieval world. Intellectual or philosophical man in the humanities is equivalent to cultural man in the sciences. Indeed, the parallels are fascinating. In both cases, the dawn of the modern world marks a sharp discontinuity in the nature, and hence the role, of mankind – a change from passive victim to enlightened interventionist. Exactly what accounts for this change is never really explained. It is almost as if the new learning had a life of its own.

These attitudes in historical scholarship have been influenced by two main characteristics of the profession – the influence of the church during the pioneering phase of modern historiography, and the non-social-science methodology it has employed. The early traditions of English history, for example, were established by clerics or high churchmen at Oxbridge in the third quarter of the nineteenth century, either directly as in the case of William Stubbs (1825–1901), Lord Acton (1834–1902), and William Cunningham (1849–1919), or indirectly under their influence. These Anglican clerics and churchmen rejected the notions that mankind arose from 'lower' life forms through evolution, and that it was motivated by the materialistic considerations that blindly drove non-human species (Desmond and Moore, 1991: 494–8). As God was in control of human history, it was characterized by the highest aspirations of man (religion, politics, law, culture, and an ordered existence) rather than its lowest and most sordid aspirations (materialism and an unseemly struggle for life). In this view, history is the product of religious and political activity, while matters of business and economy are, like sex, sordid and subservient to those higher callings. This clerical view was reinforced by the influence of the classical Greek writers who focused upon war, politics, and philosophy to the exclusion of material considerations (precisely because war and not technological change was the basis of the ancient dynamic). Only the separate caste of prehistorians, who are strongly influenced by the economic nature of the archaeological evidence, have taken a more materialist approach to the past (Trigger, 1978: 54). But then archaeology is a grubby business!

Even before the professionalization of the subject in the late nineteenth century, historical publications focused on political and legal issues. History was regarded as the product of lofty ideals rather than lowly desires. The idea that the English people were descended not from Geoffrey of Monmouth's Trojans but from 'savages' was difficult for cultivated people to accept even by the late seventeenth century (Kenyon, 1993: 16–17). Before David Hume's *History of England* (1754–62), we are told, 'history was still regarded at best as a moral or political exemplar, or as a means of civilized recreation' (Kenyon, 1993: 44). The only historian who dared to view the progress of human ideas and, hence, of society in terms of self-interest rather than higher concerns, was Henry Thomas Buckle (1821–1862). He was the first English historian who attempted to employ history to discover scientifically the laws governing the progress of human society. The first two volumes of his *The History of Civilization in England* were published between 1857 and 1861. Buckle became an overnight sensation and may have competed successfully with Darwin (*Origins*, 1859) for public attention had he not died prematurely.

What is interesting here is the reaction of the leading historians of the day to Buckle's work. The eccentric Carlyle dismissed it out of hand. But R.H. Froude (1818–1894), who as an old man followed E.A. Freeman in the Regius chair of history at Oxford, gave Buckle's work more considered attention. He indignantly rejected Buckle's claim that man was governed by self-interest rather than much higher considerations of 'truth and justice'. Life, he believed, was a noble struggle between 'good and evil' (in Kenyon, 1993: 120). Similarly Lord Acton, who followed John Seeley to the Regius chair of modern history at Cambridge in 1895, was, like churchmen of all persuasions, 'deeply affronted by Buckle's materialism and his hostility to religion'. He said of Buckle's *History* (in Kenyon, 1993: 117):

> We may rejoice that the true character of an infidel philosophy has been brought to light by the monstrous and absurd results to which it has led this writer, who has succeeded in extending its principles to the history of civilisation only at the sacrifice of every quality which makes a history great.

Acton believed that history, of which he wrote very little, should deal with the higher things of life: '[I]t is the office of historical science to maintain morality as the sole impartial criterion of men and things, and the only one on which honest minds can be made to agree' (in Kenyon, 1993: 139). The disturbing idea that mankind, like other animal species, is driven by desire rather than ideas was totally unacceptable to learned Englishmen at the end of the Victorian era.

This was the background to the emergence of professional history in Oxbridge in the last quarter of the nineteenth century. History did not become part of the undergraduate curriculum until 1853 in Oxford and 1870 in Cambridge and, even then, was an appendage to legal studies. Independence from law had to wait until 1872 at Oxford and 1875 at Cambridge. William Stubbs, who accepted the Regius chair of modern history at Oxford in 1866, was the first English academic to introduce the serious study of history. He is regarded as the first professional historian and, as such, had a profound influence on the study of history over the following century.

Like most historians of the age, Stubbs was interested in the evolution of political institutions, particularly of the constitutional relationship between government and the people (but only those actively involved politically). This was seen as the essence of emerging nations. The shaping influences in this political process, according to Stubbs (1880, I: 1), were threefold: the national character; external influences in the form of law, religion, language, and custom; and the institutions of 'the people'. In Western Europe, the 'dominant principle' in this interaction was the 'Germanic influence'. The institutional differences between England, Germany, France, and Spain resulted from the differential interaction between this 'paternal' principle and the imperial influence in matters of law, religion, language, and custom. In Stubbs's view (ibid.: 11), England was 'the purest product of their primitive [Germanic] instinct'. Hence, the main focus of Victorian historiography was on government and its relationship with its electorate, and the evolution of this relationship depended upon cultural and institutional influences. Materialism played no part. Stubbs, a Tory churchman, rejected the idea of individual self-interest for higher national aspirations. He regarded the Magna Carta, for example, as 'no selfish exaction of privilege [by the barons] for themselves', and claimed that 'the people for whom they acted were on their side' (in Kenyon, 1993: 158). In this, Stubbs was supported by John Seeley, Regius professor at Cambridge, who rejected the 'vulgar view of politics which sinks them into a mere struggle of interests and parties' (in Kenyon, 1993: 178). Unlike Greek historians, those in Victorian England were not concerned with the real forces driving society. While Greek writers focused upon the role of war – the key ancient dynamic strategy – Victorian historians refused to acknowledge the economic forces transforming English society.

Modern English history is constructed upon these traditions, even though most contemporary historians reject the idea of history being controlled by God. The influence of Stubbs on the writing of British history extended long after his resignation in 1884 from the Regius chair to become bishop first of Chester and later of Oxford, and even beyond his death in 1901. John Kenyon (1993: 154) tells us:

> With 'The Norman Conquest' and 'Henry V' on the list of special subjects, and his *Select Charters*, first published in 1870, on the list of

basic set books, his shadow still lies across the Oxford School of Modern History in 1980.

Other historians, such as Norman Cantor and David Knowles, claimed in the late 1960s that Stubbs' *Constitutional History of England* was still relevant and influential. Although the impact of Darwin's theory of evolution severed the link between religion and science in a way that changed the nature of science forever, the preoccupations of historians were slower to change. History still considers that the quest of mankind is more intellectual/cultural/spiritual than materialistic and it still emphasizes the primacy of political and cultural (including social) activities and processes. Eminent historians such as Geoffrey Elton still proclaim the essential political nature of history. One even occasionally hears about the quest of mankind for grace before death (Clark, 1985: 62).

This view has been so strong that even a famous representative of economic (i.e. materialist) history – John Clapham (1873–1946) – felt compelled in his inaugural lecture at Cambridge in 1929 to say to other non-economic historians: 'I am no rival. Yours is the higher work. I want to help.' Even just prior to his death twenty years later, Clapham (1949, Preface) wrote: 'Of all varieties of history the economic is the most fundamental. Not the most important: foundations exist to carry better things ... Economic advance is not the same as human progress'. It was impossible, therefore, even for the foremost English economic historian of the interwar period to cast off the influence of his early Cambridge training under the Revd William Cunningham, who largely wrote political history for political economists. Nevertheless, Clapham adopted a more materialist approach than the rest of his economic history colleagues who preferred social (cultural) to economic (materialist) history. But the majority explicitly rejected the concept that man was primarily motivated by sordid matters such as material gain. The concept of rational economic man was, and still is, hotly contested whenever it raised its ugly head.

Elsewhere, particularly in Germany, there was a more robust tradition in historical materialism. Throughout the nineteenth century the German historical school of economics provided, in the hands of Bruno Hildebrand (1812–1878) and Gustav Schmoller (1838–1917), a strongly materialist view of history – of the way nations proceeded through various economic stages. The leading exponent of materialist history, however, was Karl Marx. Marx viewed historical evolution as the product of economic change, and economic change as the result of the struggle between the classes who owned the factors of production, namely capital and labour. Hence, the mechanism of change in Marx's analysis is the struggle between two broad classes, while the process of change involved the accumulation of capital, the reduction of profit rates, the reduction of real wages, the increase in unemployment, the generation of increasingly severe economic fluctuations, class warfare, the collapse of the old socio-economic system, and the emergence of a new system. Despite the flaws in its economic logic, Marx's materialist interpretation of history was unique in the nineteenth century.

There was no room, however, for Marx's materialist interpretation of history in English historiography. General history in England was even less interested in materialist considerations than was economic history. When Marxism did gain popularity with some English historians, particularly between the 1930s and 1970s, it did so only in a transformed state – a state transformed from economics into politics and class struggle. In effect, the materialist core of Marxism had to be stripped away to make it palatable to English historiography. As discussed in the next chapter, English intellectuals were unable to give up the belief that ideas rather than materialism drives history – that, in effect, intellectuals matter.

The other major characteristic of English historiography is that, owing to a largely non-social-science approach, it focuses upon individuals or small groups rather than upon society as a whole. Accordingly, it deals with exceptional individuals or groups together with their atypical values. Hence, much history that has been written in this way imputes unrepresentative behaviour to the wider social group – behaviour that stems allegedly from a non-materialist, even altruistic, motivation. Since the 1960s there has been an increasing trend in historical writing to focus upon 'the people' – history from below – rather than exceptional individuals. But this often involves historians taking a great deal of the old intellectual baggage with them and, hence, of imposing inappropriate concepts and values upon 'the people'. Also the methodology is often inappropriate, as it involves generalizing from small and unrepresentative samples of letters, diaries and other documents rather than from the use of quantitative techniques using data for entire groups or classes.

Historiography in the USA has taken a more middle-of-the-road approach than that in England which has ranged from non-economic to anti-economic. Much political history in the USA (Hollister, 1982; Levi, 1988; Fleming, 1991) has a strong economic flavour. They see a relationship between economics and politics and regard economic motivation as playing a role – even if limited – in human affairs. This appears to be due in part to the relative newness of a society (as in Australia) still in touch with its economic origins, and in part to a greater market orientation of US society. Institutional reasons also appear to be involved. Economic history has never been a separate discipline in US universities, unlike the UK, with the result that economic history is taught in history as well as economics departments. Also many US graduate students from the late nineteenth century undertook further studies in Europe, particularly in Germany which had developed a more materialist approach to history (Snooks, 1993a: ch. 4). German scholars viewed history as an alternative source of economic generalization to deductive British economics with its unacceptable free trade implications.

The US approach can be illustrated using three important examples: Chester Starr and Moses Finley for classical antiquity, and Paul Kennedy for the modern period. As will be discussed in detail in Chapter 11, Starr (1977) examines the role of commerce in Greek economic and social growth during the period 800–500 BC. He shows that trade was initiated and financed by Greek aristocrats from their agricultural surpluses but that increasingly after 600 BC they withdrew to attend to their political duties, leaving the field to the despised non-aristocratic groups and to foreigners.

Starr is willing to grant that the aristocrats (and others) were interested in profits but only as a means to an end – to provide them with the modest wealth they required to partake fully of the leisured pursuits of their class in literature, art, war, and politics. He explains (ibid.: 52): 'True, neither in trade and colonization nor in foreign military service were men of the leading classes motivated solely by economic factors'. And again (ibid.: 53):

> The leading classes were most directly moved by social and political reasons. Theognis talks much of wealth and poverty, but when one considers carefully his references riches are to be held in order that their owner be respected and have power ... Concentration purely on economic advantage continued to be generally frowned on ... Solon, thus, asserted that he would not exchange virtue (*arete*) for wealth ... Yet even he, in the famous interview with Croesus, specified as one quality of Tellus' glory the fact that he spent a life 'in which our people look upon as comfort'; and Phocylides could prize first a living, thereafter virtue.

As can be seen, Starr flits uneasily between the insistence that the aristocrats were involved in economic activities, that they *did* invest their agricultural surpluses and that they *did* value wealth on the one hand, and the less well-established assertion that they were largely driven by social and political forces. As most scholars in this tradition argue, wealth was merely a means to an end – pursuit of the leisured lifestyle of their class – and the means could be, and was, sacrificed to the end. The only problem with this argument is that once this objective was achieved, all economic change would cease, which clearly was not the case for Greece in this period. A similar view about ancient Rome is adopted by Moses Finley (1985: 147) who asserts: 'So long as an acceptable life-style could be maintained, however that was defined, other values held the stage'. The general view about ancient man is that he was definitely not economic man. Only recently (Rathbone, 1991), as will be discussed in Chapter 7, has this view been challenged. In Chapter 11, when discussing Greek commerce, I will argue that this uneasiness can be resolved in favour of materialist man.

The most recent devotee of this attitude to the motivation of humanity is Paul Kennedy in his widely read *The Rise and Fall of the Great Powers* (1989). While Kennedy was trained in Australia and the UK, he wrote this book in the USA, and is clearly in the more middle-of-the-road tradition. Basically his objective in that book is to explain the continual shifts in the relative political and military power of nations. His view is that the main objective of the larger nations is to maximize their political influence in the world. In Kennedy's own words, each nation attempts 'to enhance its power and influence internationally' (ibid.: 696). While his hypothesis is simple and obvious, it is not very precise. He claims that the relative political and military power of nations '*over the longer term*' depends upon their relative economic wealth. This is hardly a contentious issue. Nevertheless, Kennedy qualifies the suggested relationship by claiming that it is lagged over time, although the nature of the lag is not specified; and by suggesting that he is '*not* arguing that economics determines every event, or is the sole reason for the success and failure of each nation'. He then provides a historical shopping list of 'other things' that influence relative international power for which there is 'much evidence', including 'geography, military organization, national morale, the alliance system, and many other [unspecified] factors' (ibid.: xxvi–xxvii). It is hard to know what to make of this. Does he mean that these other variables can explain a sizeable proportion of the relative power of nations and, if so, what proportion? Or does he merely mean that the relationship between power and economics is stochastic rather than exact? He does not say.

In other words, Kennedy has developed a hypothesis that cannot be easily tested or refuted. One gains the impression that it is really a device to structure a simple story about the rise and fall of the political influence of nations. As Kennedy says, his book provides 'a large body of detailed facts and commentaries to those scholars in that discipline [political science] who are investigating the larger patterns of war and change in the international order'. It is, therefore, a hook on which to hang a number of historical case studies about war and diplomacy. His story is that nations rise and fall in relation to each other, according to their relative economic prosperity (and a host of 'other things') and that this prosperity can be adversely affected by the political scramble if conducted through war.

The economy, therefore, is seen as a constraining influence upon the political ambitions of statesmen. In other words, the driving force in the rise and fall of the Great Powers is the desire of political leaders to maximize the influence of the nation rather than its material well-being, presumably on the grounds that political advantage will, on average, be pursued at the cost of material advantage (otherwise it is all about economic maximization). This is what I have characterized as political man as opposed to economic man. While Kennedy does not elaborate on this issue, what he appears to have in mind is political decision-making undertaken at the national level by national leaders. There is, however, a major problem with this view of human motivation apart from a lack of evidence. Even if, for the sake of argument, one accepts that national leaders attempt to maximize national political influence (rather than material advantage), one discovers the discredited Great Man view of history thinly disguised. For example, Kennedy concludes his book with the statement (ibid.: 698):

> To paraphrase Bismarck's famous remark, all of these powers are travelling on 'the stream of Time', which they can 'neither create nor direct', but upon which they can 'steer with more or less skill and experience'. How they emerge from that voyage depends, to a large degree, upon the wisdom of the governments in Washington, Moscow, Tokyo, Peking, and the various European capitals.

It is, however, just not possible to translate the idea of political maximization at the national level into the idea of political man at the individual level. It is not at all persuasive to imply or argue that the overriding objective of the vast majority of individual citizens is to maximize the political role of their nation on the international scene. This is hardly the motivation that keeps the average person going through each day of each week, year after year. This contrasts starkly with the concept of materialist man, which makes sense at both the individual and national (even international) levels. The desire of the vast majority of individuals to maximize their own material advantage can easily be translated – as shown in Chapter 7 – into maximization of the nation's material advantage. The story about political man is a story about the Great Man in history, whereas the story about materialist man is a story about Everyman.

We should also note that Kennedy is not committed to the idea that political decision-makers are driven by consistent objectives. Indeed, he is willing to explain changing political outcomes in terms of changing fundamental objectives. He explains (ibid.: xxv):

> Most of the historical examples covered here suggest that there is a noticeable 'lag time' between the trajectory of a state's relative economic strength and the trajectory of its military/territorial influence. Once again, the reason for this is not difficult to grasp. An economically expanding power . . . may well prefer to become rich rather than to spend heavily on armaments. A half-century later, priorities may well have altered.

This suggests that he sees the desires for getting rich and for achieving military glory as alternative objectives, despite the fact that this means alternating between materialist man and political man. This is enough to cause his hypothesis to collapse completely. By switching objectives, military and political power could be just as much an instrument of the desire for the maximization of national economic advantage, as economic power could be an instrument for the maximization of military and political power. Kennedy appears to lose the plot of his story at this point.

Further, Kennedy (ibid.: xxii–xxiv) suggests that, owing to the complexity of reality, it is not possible to derive a model to explain the rise and fall of nations: 'the problem which historians – as opposed to political scientists – have in grappling with general theories is that the evidence of the past is almost always too varied to allow for "hard" scientific conclusions'. This view is rejected throughout my book. Reality is not too complex; the evidence is not too varied. History can be used as a source of generalization. We need to identify correctly the driving force in history and to show – to model – how this force operates to achieve its objectives. Kennedy is not only unclear about the objectives of decision-makers and what constitutes the driving force, he appears unwilling to specify the relationship between key variables with any precision. Clearly, specified empirical models are essential if one wishes, as Kennedy apparently does, to say anything sensible about the future.

Kennedy's generalizations, therefore, do not tell us very much. It is hardly novel or contentious to say that there is some sort of relationship between relative economic power between nations and their power and influence in the world. If economic wealth and progress is a major determinant of international political influence, then it would have been interesting to have been told something about the determinants and process of economic change and how this was connected with military operations and political influence. Indeed, Kennedy's silences tell us more than his conclusions. It is curious in a book that attempts to analyse the rise and fall of the Great Powers over the last five hundred years, and to offer some thoughts about the twenty-first century, that the collapse of the USSR within a few years of the book's publication is not seriously considered as an option. After evaluating the economic problems faced by the USSR in the late 1980s, Kennedy (ibid.: 663–4) concludes:

> However one assesses the military strength of the USSR at the moment, therefore, the prospect of its being only the fourth or fifth among the great productive centres of the world by the early twenty-first century cannot but worry the Soviet leadership, simply because of the implications for long-term Russian power.
>
> This does *not* mean that the USSR is close to collapse, any more than it should be viewed as a country of almost supernatural strength. It *does* mean that it is facing awkward choices.

Kennedy fails this crucial test because he appears to have no clear idea of the driving force in society and no empirically generated model of the economic processes that led to the USSR's fall. Those who analysed the economic performance of the USSR – such as Goldman, *USSR in Crisis* (1983) – knew for a decade before the event that the collapse of the USSR was imminent because of the gross inefficiencies of large, centrally determined economic systems. In particular these systems do not provide an appropriate incentive system to give full rein to the technology strategy which is the central dynamic of modern societies. Prediction is the best test of the explanatory power of this type of analysis. But in this respect – although not in terms of his admirable historical discussion of the political history of the West between 1500 and the 1980s (if not to 2000) – Kennedy's analysis has been found wanting.

'Political man' is also a useful characterization of the view of the driving force in ancient society held by a significant proportion of the profession of archaeology. Sociopolitical or cultural evolution is seen in terms of the attempt by ruling elites to gain control over key economic resources in order to exercise power over the rest of the population. This has varied from control over large-scale irrigation systems (Reade, 1991: 37) to control over the production and distribution of goods such as food and other necessities that are required by society as a whole.

A representative example of this type of interpretation is provided by the distinguished Mesoamericanist William Sanders (1984: 276–7), who tells us:

> The evolution of social systems is essentially a process of increasing inequities of political power, that is, the power of human beings over other human beings. In fact, I would argue that the desire for political power is the driving force behind cultural evolution. This process is found in all human groups, and, in essence, there are no real egalitarian societies. What happens in cultural evolution essentially is an increase of opportunities to expand this type of behavior; one of the most effective methods to achieve this expansion is control over the production and distribution of goods – that sector of human behavior that we refer to as the economy. The higher the input of the resource, in terms of consumption rates per capita, and the greater the use throughout the social groups, the greater the potential of control in increasing political power . . . Following this model, the control of food staples is the most important economic variable.

In other words, the ruling elite attempts to control the means of production and distribution in order to maximize personal political power over others rather than to maximize material advantage. Could it be, however, that the reverse is true? That materialists seek and use political power in order to protect and extend their economic interests? We have already seen that early neolithic towns which accumulated agricultural surpluses attractive to surrounding nomads also had to organize themselves militarily to defend these surpluses.

Before leaving politics for economics, we should briefly consider what I have called philosophical man. In a recent book provocatively entitled *The End of History and the Last Man*, Francis Fukuyama has resurrected Hegel's metaphysical interpretation of 'universal history' written around decision-makers who, by adopting their own rules of behaviour, are able to transcend their 'animal nature' and make free moral choices. This is a very explicit rejection of the struggle for either political power or material advantage.

Fukuyama characterizes Hegel's theory of history in the following selective terms. The overwhelming desire to be recognized as human beings with dignity led early man to battle with each other for 'prestige'. The outcome of this conflict was a society divided into two classes: a class of masters who were willing to risk their lives for prestige, and a class of slaves who were not willing to do so. Yet this division satisfied neither master nor slave in their 'struggle for recognition'. Hence a fundamental contradiction existed in this sociopolitical relationship, which provided the driving force for the development of further stages in history. Not until the French Revolution, when 'universal and reciprocal recognition' was finally achieved, could the contradiction in human society be resolved. This removed the dynamic in Hegelian historical evolution and, thereby, led to the end of history in the sense that no further sociopolitical change could occur. The desire for recognition had finally been achieved. This is the prime example of what we might call philosophical history.

Surprisingly, Fukuyama takes seriously Hegel's philosophical and anti-empirical theory of history, in which men, even great men, are merely the unconscious agents of Hegel's 'World Spirit'. He is able to do so because his attempt to resurrect Hegel is based not upon historical reconstruction but rather on a discussion of political philosophy. Essentially the book is a discourse between Fukuyama and political philosophers such as Kant, Hegel, Hobbes, Locke, Rousseau, and Nietzsche. No attempt is made to substantiate empirically the naïve claims made about the concept of 'struggle for recognition', the Hegelian dialectic in universal history, or the late twentieth-century realization of the end of history and the Nietzschean last man. As I attempt to demonstrate empirically in Part III, there can be no final stage in the Dynamic Society, no end to history, because the fundamental condition of human society is eternal change. History is not a teleological process.

While no serious attempt at historical verification is made by Fukuyama, his work can be used to illustrate the curious idea of philosophical man. Our main interest here is the example it provides of the difficulty many intellectuals have in accepting the true genetically determined nature of man. It is part of a tradition which insists, without any real-world evidence, that man is ruled more by intellect than desire. A tradition which claims that human society is driven by ideas.

Fukuyama (1992: xii) states the book's objective rhetorically when he asks: 'Whether, at the end of the twentieth century, it makes sense for us once again to speak of a coherent and directional History of mankind that will eventually lead the greater part of humanity to liberal democracy'. The answer is in the affirmative. He wishes, in other words, to explain sociopolitical change rather than the economic dynamics of society. There is, he argues, an approximate correlation between modern industrialization, which is driven by the unexplained emergence of 'natural science', and the development of liberal democracy. But, Fukuyama claims, this cannot explain either pre-modern sociopolitical change or why some modern industrialized nations turned to totalitarianism – 'economic interpretations of history are incomplete and unsatisfying' (ibid.: xvi). (This may well be because he does not develop an economic explanation.) Accordingly, he explicitly rejects economic man in favour of philosophical man, who is involved in a 'struggle for recognition' which arises from his very soul. Fukuyama (ibid.: 162) concludes that 'the desire for recognition' is 'the primary motor driving human history'; and again that 'recognition is the central problem of politics' (ibid.: xxi). Unfortunately he provides no evidence for any of this. He appears to confuse the ambitions of a tiny minority of intellectuals like himself with the objectives of all mankind.

It does not occur to Fukuyama that there might be a dynamic economic process underlying the unexplained modern emergence of 'natural science', which also operated throughout pre-modern times. As I will demonstrate empirically in the rest of this book such a dynamic process has always existed in human society, and it has been driven by economically rational decision-makers concerned not with 'prestige' or 'recognition' but with survival and material advantage. Philosophical man is a myth constructed by an insignificantly small group of intellectuals who are convinced that social progress depends entirely upon them.

This brings us to the view of mankind held by economists. The central behavioural assumption underlying economic theory is that of economic rationality which is embodied in *Homo economicus* or economic man. Economic man, however, is not a dynamic force in society, but rather an abstract collection of preferences and rational choices concerning consumption and production. Economic theorists have divorced these behavioural outcomes from more fundamental human motivational impulses. Hence, economic man is disembodied and has no real-world substance – he is little more than a cardboard cut-out. As economic theory is concerned primarily with shortrun static, rather than longrun dynamic, analysis, its concept of economic man reflects that preoccupation. *Homo economicus* is not a dynamic force. He does not aggressively adopt dynamic strategies, he merely expresses preferences for goods and services, and coolly maximizes his profits, consumption, or utility. And he does this secure in the perfection of his knowledge of the world and in the bewildering speed and unerringness of his rational calculations. Owing to its myopic and static theoretical analysis, therefore, mainstream economics has lost touch with the wellspring of economic change. This concept of *Homo economicus* is one of static economic man and contrasts with the dynamic, real-world decision-maker in Part III of this book which, for purposes of differentiation, I have called materialist man. The relatively recent work on expectations, uncertainty, and limited information does not fundamentally alter the rationality assumption underlying mainstream economic theory.

Static economic man has much in common with passive man discussed above. He responds to changes in the physical and cultural environment rather than actively attempting to alter it himself. This reaction only occurs when economic conditions – as reflected in the relative prices of goods and services – change. But unlike the scientist and humanist, the economist regards human behaviour as essentially unchanging. To the economist, modern man is not different to pre-modern man; only the economic circumstances, and hence the nature of the responses, differ. If medieval man does not act entrepreneurially, it is not because he is economically irrational, but because the prevailing economic conditions do not provide the necessary incentives. The essence of economic man is that he is reactive rather than proactive.

While economists usually assume that 'selfish' behaviour dominates the market sector, some, such as the Nobel Prize winner Gary Becker (1991), have argued that 'altruistic' behaviour rules the household. The idea of 'altruism' in economics is not new as it has been discussed earlier by other economists including Boulding (1973) and Phelps (1975). Becker's contribution has been to draw a sharp distinction between 'selfishness' in the market and 'altruism' in the home. In the chapter on the 'family of man' I argue that Becker's dichotomy is false and is based upon an inappropriate use of the terms 'selfish' and 'altruistic'. The word 'selfish' implies abnormal behaviour, and is inappropriate as a description of the normal human behaviour involved in attempting to maximize either profits or consumer satisfaction. Selfish behaviour occurs when an individual pursues self-interest to an irrational extreme and (ironically), in the process, fails to maximize his/her utility owing to the hostility this generates in others. In the generally accepted sense of the word, it is not selfish to maximize one's individual utility through individual action. Nor is it altruistic to cooperate with other people (related or not) in order to maximize individual utility even if, in the process, one's self-interested action leads to an increase in the utility of other people. The point that Becker appears to overlook is that individual and cooperative actions are just different *means* applied in different circumstances to achieve the same, unchanging *end* – the maximization of individual utility.

It will have become clear that this discussion of 'selfish' and 'altruistic' behaviour is also relevant to the arguments of natural scientists and humanists on this subject. We have seen that the typical view of both biological and physical scientists is that while selfish behaviour dominated biological evolution before the emergence of mankind, altruism either has been an outcome of human evolution or will be in the immediate future. But, as with economists, natural scientists have confused means with ends.

The emergence of family groups, tribes, nations, and civilizations is not the result of altruism, but of the best way to achieve individual objectives. An economist – if he/she were interested in the issue – would argue that economies of scale, arising from the specialization of individuals according to comparative advantage can explain the growth of larger social groups since the Neolithic Revolution. It is not a response to the desire to do good for others. Also, the fact that society protects the infirm, the injured, and the destitute likewise is not the result of the emergence of altruism, but rather the desire of individuals to take out insurance against future accidents. In other words, if we develop systems to protect the infirm, then these systems will protect us when we eventually fall into that category. If, however, the cost of that insurance rises too rapidly, in terms of the rate of tax required to finance social welfare, then individuals will want to substitute individual for communal action. This was the reason for the success of 'economic rationalism' (which is not to be confused with the concept of economic rationality as a form of decision-making behaviour) in the West during the 1980s.

This is not to say that certain individuals are not genuinely altruistic, self-sacrificing, suicidal, or totally irrational, just that they are not typical and do not drive human society. It is pointless to quote individual examples of altruism, because it is the average response of entire societies – and of the whole of human society throughout time – that we need to examine. As I attempt to show in the next chapter, human nature is unchanging. There has been no sudden, or even gradual, transformation of human behaviour during the entire history of human civilization let alone the last few generations. And the force that drives mankind is similar to the force that has always driven life – the overwhelming desire to survive and to enjoy to the maximum all the material satisfaction that follows from life. This extremely powerful force has survived many crises, both internal and external, over billions of years, and it is unlikely to be overridden or reversed in the future. Man's superior intellect merely makes it possible to pursue the age-old objectives more skilfully than other species are able to do. This is why we have come to dominate them and our world. What we have not been able to dominate are the internal impulses that drive us.

Despite the eloquent and passionate attention given to the fundamental nature of mankind and the natural environment, there is little agreement about the forces driving human society. The fragmented nature of scholarship has generated irreconcilably different views on this the central issue for the Dynamic Society. Yet not all of these views are equally comfortable with the evidence. For one reason or another their authors have preferred to seek meaning in human history on the mountain tops rather than in the plains. As will be suggested in the next chapter, in order to discover the driving force in history we need to take a hard long look at what humans do, not at what they say they do. We need to observe carefully the riders in the chariot of change.

PART III
WHEEL OF FIRE

7

RIDERS IN THE CHARIOT

Seizing the chariots of the morning, go outfleeting ride, afar into the
zenith high, bending thy furious course.

Blake, *Vala*, 1797

*From a halo of light and dust emerges a racing chariot glinting dully in
the rays of a rising sun. As the horses thunder past, two shadowy riders
can be seen staring grim-faced towards the distant hills. One, the charioteer,
relentlessly drives horse and chariot on into the unknown. He sees only his
own immediate interests, constantly changing direction as new paths open
up before him. He is racing against time and against fierce competitors.
Sometimes he achieves the high ground, leaving the plain behind. Sometimes
he takes the wrong path and, flying over the brink, crashes into the ravine
below, smashing the chariot and breaking the wheel of civilization. Those
who reach the high ground of prosperity generally rely on more than
intuition. There is another rider in the chariot. Standing beside the driver
is one who lifts his eyes from the path and looks ahead, making suggestions
about which direction to take. This is the navigator, who has time to reflect
upon the tortuous path from the plain into the mountains, time to look
at the sun's progress in the sky, and time to devise plans about where they
should be going. But the driver, staring intently into an uncertain future,
does not always accept this advice, often with good reason. He is the driver.
He is in control of the chariot. He makes up his own mind.*

There are many views about the unseen driving force in human society. These
diverse views include the mutually exclusive ideas of man as the plaything
of forces beyond his control and of man as an active agent of change in the
world. But even scholars who argue for a more active role for humanity see
that role changing in response to cultural developments within society. Man,
according to this view, is not as independent and influential as he appears
at first sight. It is suggested in earlier chapters that these views are unable
to explain the changing fortunes of human society since its emergence. This

169

chapter presents an essentially new view of the driving force in human society, which I have called **dynamic materialism**. It is a view that places mankind at the centre of our story about the Dynamic Society. In this story, mankind is driven by its genetically determined nature, which is unmodified by historical changes in its environment, either physical or cultural. In this story, the unchanging materialistic nature of humanity is the incredibly powerful force that drives, and has always driven, the Dynamic Society.

But just who are the riders in the chariot of change? What is their nature, and what is their role? Two main figures can be seen. Both share the same general purpose, but serve very different specific roles. They possess a unity and a diversity. Each rider is motivated by the same internal impulses, but each contributes differently to the dynamics of human society. Metaphorically speaking, the riders include the charioteer and the navigator. The charioteer – the driver – is the representative of all those people in society who make effective decisions, either directly or indirectly, about the use of economic resources and the returns from their use. This includes the vast bulk of society today who make critical decisions in their households about the balance of their expenditures between children, consumer goods, and savings, and about the balance of their time between the market, the household, and leisure. Even in feudal times, when they had little scope for effective economic decision-making, their overwhelming desire to survive and make the best of their material circumstances supported the superstructure of economic decision-making made by the feudal elite. The elite could not rule without the acquiescence, albeit grudging, of all the people. The driver, who is enlisted from the entire membership of humanity, is responsible for perceiving and investing in the dynamic strategies that charge human society with a boundless energy. The navigator, on the other hand, symbolizes those in society who provide the ideas and advice about the direction we are travelling and where they think we should go in the future. While there are others in the chariot who have merely come along for the ride, they are in an insignificant minority and will not be discussed here.

Our chariot metaphor can be extended to encompass not only the strategies and tactics of the Dynamic Society but also its many institutional forms. The constant jostling to be seen between the various riders in the chariot are the dynamic tactics of order and chaos. A balance between them is required because excessive order leads to stability at the expense of speed, and excessive chaos to speed at the cost of stability. The driver, as we have seen, is responsible for the dynamic strategies, which include the technical design of the chariot and the choice of pathways to the highlands of affluence. Further elaboration of the first is required because we must distinguish between matters technological and organizational. Those aspects of chariot design – the axle, wheel, and harness – concerned with speed and stability are the technological foundations of society. As these change, so too do growth and economic fluctuations. Other aspects of design influence the institutional structure of society. Some of these, such as the personalized motifs and trappings, are purely cosmetic like the external cultural forms of different societies, while others, such as the chariot's internal fittings, contribute to the comfort of the riders in the chariot and, hence, to the efficiency of this race against time. The chariot, like society, is merely the vehicle of change. And the horses? They are the natural resources of society.

THE CHARIOTEER

The driving force in human society – the driver in the chariot of change – is a dynamic version of economic man that, in order to avoid misunderstanding, I have called **materialist man**. This concept should not be confused with the economic man employed by the economic theorist. That is static economic man, which is merely the underlying behavioural assumption in theoretical economics, and amounts to little more than an abstract collection of preferences and maximizing choices. Such an assumption is required for the mathematical solution of economic problems. Static economic man is barely a shadow of reality, and is incapable of driving anything.

Materialist man attempts, over the course of a lifetime, to maximize his material advantage. This does not require perfect knowledge or sophisticated abilities to calculate rapidly the costs and benefits of a variety of possible decision-making alternatives – as does the concept of static economic man in neoclassical economics – just that he is capable of gathering sufficient information about the real world to make sensible decisions. That mankind does make sensible decisions is reflected in the great civilizations for which he is responsible. An important method for economizing on gathering and processing information about reality is provided by mankind's amazing instinct – an instinct we share with other species – for imitating the desirable and successful actions of others. This matter, which I have called **strategic imitation**, is discussed in greater detail in Chapter 8. It does not mean that materialist man will attempt to maximize his material advantage in every situation, just that he attempts to do so in the longer term. Those determined to squeeze blood out of every stone fail to maximize in the longer term because they alienate everyone around them. Maximization requires cooperation. It does not mean that every individual in society is a materialist, only that the majority – the statistical average – are. There is room, therefore, for the eccentric, the suicidal, and the irrational, but only limited room otherwise their society will itself fail to prosper and, ultimately, to survive. It does not mean that mistakes are never made, just that individuals learn from their mistakes and adjust their decision-making. It does not mean that motives such as power, security, leisure, and adventure are unimportant, just that, on average, these can best be achieved through the maximization of material advantage; and that, if there is a conflict between them, it will be resolved in favour of materialism. It does not deny man's involvement in cooperative

171

or social activities, just that these activities are in certain circumstances the best way of maximizing individual material advantage. It does not mean that people who cooperate in this way cannot feel deep affection for each other, just that when their individual interests come into serious conflict they are resolved by individuals according to their self-interest, which may turn affection and love into envy and hatred. It does not mean that all societies behave in the same way in similar situations, just that their behaviour will vary according to the degree of competition that they face.

Materialist man, therefore, can be seen all around us, struggling to maximize his career prospects, his income, his assets both individual and family, and his satisfaction from the consumption of goods and services both market and household. He can appear relaxed and benign when not under competitive pressure, but as the pressure increases he becomes more tense, aggressive, and competitive. Amicable relationships with associates will become brittle and may even be swept aside, to be replaced by a competitive tension that may ultimately break out into open hostilities. The balance in society between cooperation and competition, between order and chaos, is always fragile. Yet in moments of reflection, materialist man appears to feel guilty about his self-centredness and, when there is little danger of material loss, attempts to salve his conscience by doing good works. While it is never a serious challenge to man's materialist objectives, the ritual appears to be important to his self-image. And this self-image, which is used to mask the less appealing aspects of human nature, makes it difficult for materialist man to see himself objectively.

What could possibly account for man the materialistic maximizer? The answer is quite straightforward, but the implications are so disturbing to many intellectuals that they refuse to accept it. Instead, they attempt, as we have seen, to transform the unpalatable truth into a more accommodating explanation. I will argue, based upon the evidence in Part I, that the answer to this fundamentally important question is that human nature is genetically determined and, despite many protestations by intellectuals to the contrary, it is unchanging. And unchangeable.

In order to survive over the last few million years man had to be a materialist. It was impossible to be anything else. The process of survival has shaped human nature, which is genetically fixed. Mankind had to maximize its material advantage because there was the ever-present danger that if one individual, family, tribe, or even species (such as *Homo erectus* or *Homo sapiens neanderthalensis*) failed to maximize their material advantage, they would be driven to the edge of subsistence and beyond by those that did maximize. The records of archaeology and history provide abundant evidence of this. It is no coincidence that when a more advanced species of mankind emerged, the earlier species disappeared from the fossil record; or that whenever two unequally matched societies came into conflict, the economically less powerful society (Harappan, Carthaginian, Greek, Aztec, Inca, American Indian, Australian Aboriginal) was destroyed.

Those in a highly competitive world that did not maximize their material advantage did not survive to pass on their less self-centred genes or less aggressively competitive society to future generations. Prehistory involved a very intense struggle for survival, in the face of a hostile world, over millions of years. The end result of this prehistoric struggle was a species genetically well adapted to meet every conceivable competitive situation. And the historical period down to the present made, is making, and will continue to make, heavy demands – in the form of wars, disease, and changes to the physical environment – on these genetic characteristics which are designed for survival in a highly competitive and hostile world. In fact, this genetically acquired characteristic is the most important in mankind's survival tool-kit. If we possess all the other necessary survival characteristics – good eyesight, physical skills, intelligence, and imagination – but lack the desire to maximize, ultimately we will, in a competitive environment, be eliminated. While the other survival characteristics are important, materialistic drive is *essential*.

Modern man is heir to this long genetic conditioning that goes back to the very beginning of life on Earth. We are driven by a desire to maximize material well-being even when it is no longer a matter of immediate survival. This can be seen in the scramble to accumulate ever larger fortunes in the modern world both by individuals and by nations. A survey of the world's richest people, undertaken in mid-1993 by *Forbes* magazine, suggests that the world's top ten richest individuals and families had a combined net worth (assets not income) of about $US80,000 million, which is about 21 per cent of the GDP and 7.3 per cent of the net capital stock of Australia, a country in 1993 of 17.6 million people. This is advanced as a measure, not of average experience, but of the insatiable desire to accumulate material possessions. There is no shortage of aspirants for a position on the top rung of the income ladder. The disparity in individual wealth is echoed by the unequal distribution of the wealth of nations throughout the world. The average GDP per capita of the leading Westernized nations (EU, USA, Japan) is greater than that of the poorest fourteen Third World nations by a factor of 138. And there is every reason to believe that both individuals and nations are furiously competing in order to widen rather than to close this wealth gap (Maddison, 1994). There is just no evidence to support the view held by many natural and social scientists that modern man has been able to override his genetically determined nature through cultural development.

Darwinian evolutionists provide the greatest paradox in their interpretation of the nature of man. They have told us, some eloquently, that all species of life have been shaped by natural selection – by the struggle of life and the survival of the fittest. They reject as heresy the anti-Darwinian interpretation of the neo-Lamarckians, who claim that man can consciously pass on acquired physical characteristics to future generations as an act of human will. Yet they feel able to claim, in the teeth of all available evidence, that in the modern era 'natural' man – who has been shaped over millions of years to be self-centred – has been, or can be, transformed through education into 'cultural' man, who is supposed to act altruistically.

This is a major contradiction. How is it possible to change a genetically acquired drive through intellectual willpower? We are not told. Nor are we provided with any evidence that such a transformation has taken place. Indeed, the evidence is all on the materialist side of the argument. The disparities of individual and national wealth are only one source. Strip away the buffers of modern society, expose the naked competition never far from the surface, and watch the way normal societies react – with aggressive, even brutally violent attempts to protect their material way of life. Eastern Europe in the early 1990s is sad evidence for this argument.

Why has the obvious – which is staring us all in the face – been rejected for so long by those who write books? Why is the idea of materialism as the major driving force in society so difficult for intellectuals to accept? Why is it always referred to scathingly (Kennedy, 1989: xxvi) as 'crude economic determinism'? The answer appears to be threefold. First, misunderstanding arises in many instances because of the difficulty of viewing mankind in a disinterested and objective way, owing to the fact that the observer is also the observed. Objectivity requires the rare ability to achieve emotional distance from oneself. Second, materialism is an affront to the intellectual pretensions of many educated people. They would prefer to live in a world where mountains could be moved, if not by faith, at least by ideas, rather than by base desires. It is fascinating that even the most complex economic explanation – usually far more sophisticated than alternative non-economic explanations – is automatically branded as 'crude'. This is done partly in defence against powerful logical economic arguments for which they have no answer, and partly because economic explanations focus upon things material rather than things intellectual – on the satisfaction of animal desires rather than on the quest for cultivated ideas. Curiously all discussion of economic motivation is branded as 'economic determinism', as if all economic explanations override man's free will, which is thought to aspire to higher things. The truth, that many intellectuals do not wish to face, is that the vast majority of human beings – but not all – are expressing their free will in pursuing materialistic objectives. This cannot possibly be regarded as determinism because it does not involve any suggestion of inevitability. If they wish individuals can, and do, opt out. To brand arguments about economic motivation as 'crude economic determinism' is illogical and nonsensical – a mere intellectual affectation. Finally, and perhaps more importantly, intellectuals reject economic man in favour of cultural man because they wish to maximize their own influence in society. If ideas are seen to be of secondary importance, then their status in society will decline. They will lose prestige, influence, and income. They have much to lose if the materialists are generally seen to be correct. Intellectuals, despite their inevitable protestations, are not immune to the self-interest of human nature.

No doubt some will attempt to dismiss this argument about the materialistic basis of mankind's motivation by claiming that it amounts to biological determinism. To make such an accusation is not the same as providing either a knock-down argument or falsifying evidence. Indeed, it is not even clear what such a critic might mean by this statement. If they mean that it implies inevitability or the denial of individual freedom, then they are wrong. We must distinguish between a nature that is determined (i.e. caused) by biology, and a nature that has no choice owing to biological determinism. I mean the first and not the second. The record of history is littered with the ruins of those individuals and societies who denied self-interest, and perished. While our biologically determined nature provides us with the ability to survive, we can always choose to ignore it. Individuals, and societies, always retain that freedom. But there is always a cost which, in the longer term, cannot be avoided. If they merely mean that mankind's survival depends upon a genetically determined self-interest, then they are not making a serious objection. Only those who – on average and in the longrun – freely choose to pursue their material interests survive and prosper in our competitive world. As we shall see, the history of the Dynamic Society is the history of successful materialists, not unsuccessful moralists. And only a successful society can subsidize non-material activities.

Yet this is not to say that the test of economic rationality is success or failure. Whether or not societies survive is an outcome that depends on other factors (including luck) as well as rationality. The only proper test of rationality concerns the perceived objectives of decision-makers. What we want to know is whether a group of decision-makers were attempting to maximize their material advantage or were systematically and consciously pursuing objectives that significantly undermined their prosperity. The former (such as Rome, Aboriginal Australia, Teotihuacan, or Domesday England) are economically rational, while the latter (such as Nazi Germany in its pursuit of racial purity and racial dominance, and the USSR in its pursuit of the aberrant political objectives of the hierarchy of the Bolshivik Party) are irrational. While it is possible for economically rational societies to fail owing to critical mistakes or to invasion by unknown and more advanced societies (such as Aboriginal Australia, the Aztecs, and the Incas), the collapse of irrational societies (such as Nazi Germany and the USSR) is both highly probable and predictable. In this chapter I have devised a number of ways to test empirically the revealed objectives of economic rationality in human society.

A model of dynamic materialist man

To explore the driving force in human society we need to develop a simple model of dynamic materialist man. Through this model we will see how economic decision-makers operate in open and closed economies and how they employ individualistic and cooperative tactics to achieve their objectives. In turn, this will provide the dynamic context for my 'concentric spheres model' of human behaviour.

The nature of materialist man's behaviour and his influence on society depends upon the degree to which an economy is open or closed to outside competition. There are two extreme cases: the completely closed economy, such as the Australian Aboriginal economy for the tens of thousands of years prior to white settlement in 1788; and a largely open economy, such as Britain after the Industrial Revolution. These are, of course, only tendencies; there are no absolute states in human society. Even the Australian Aboriginal economy before 1788, which was the world's most isolated society, had long witnessed unsystematic landings by Europeans along the north-west and northern coasts, and latterly on the southern tip and eastern edge of the continent, together with age-old seasonal visits from Southeast Asian fishermen. Moreover, the British economy did not fully achieve its briefly held ideal of *laissez-faire* in international (or domestic) economic matters. Also in all societies there is a constant tension between the forces of order (the attempt of established elites to protect their wealth and power) and chaos (the attempt by those outside the protected circle to break in). The battle between these forces was certainly raging in English society after 1788, and was probably present, although to a radically different degree, in Australian Aboriginal society before 1788. As these two societies were involved in a fatal clash in Australia after 1788, they provide an appropriate illustration of my argument.

In the closed economy of Aboriginal Australia before 1788 there had been little or no external competition or pressure for tens of thousands of years. Indeed, in those parts of Australia – particularly Tasmania after it was isolated from the mainland by rising seas about 12,000 years ago – where even irregular and unsystematic contact with outsiders passed unnoticed, the coastline of Australia must have seemed like the edge of the world. Under these isolated conditions, economic materialism manifested itself in an entirely different way to that in Europe. Without the continuous stimulus of outside competition, it was economically rational – using an intuitive benefit–cost calculus – to attempt to maximize immediate material returns by establishing a system dominated by order and consensus. By employing a traditional technology – that changed imperceptibly from generation to generation and only gradually from century to century and even from millennium to millennium – and by deliberately controlling population to prevent it from exceeding accessible natural resources (food, hides, wood, etc.) Aboriginal tribes were able to achieve, on average, a comfortable lifestyle with an adequate and healthy diet, with considerable leisure (they may have worked as little as five hours per day), and with a rich cultural life (Snooks, 1994a: 136–8). What they lacked was a living standard that included material assets and fixed capital, either private or public. It has been very roughly estimated that, just prior to white settlement in 1788, Aboriginal GDP per capita might have been about half that in England, although this appears to be on the high side (Butlin, 1993). A significant improvement in the Aboriginal living standard would have required considerable extra effort (with a corresponding reduction in leisure) both in developing and applying a radically new technology and in working longer hours and probably in a more regimented way.

Clearly, without the external threat of invasion, the benefit to be gained from such a radical change would not have been worth the cost of the extra effort involved. Australia's original inhabitants had developed a workable system down through the millennia in which the marginal utility of work and leisure was in *very*, very longrun equilibrium. Only the real threat of dispossession and destruction of their way of life – as has always existed in Europe – could change their intuitive benefit–cost calculation in favour of economic development. What was lacking in Aboriginal Australia was not the ability to respond creatively to changing circumstances – there is ample evidence of this – but rather the competitive incentive to transform their rational benefit–cost calculation. This is why those authors (Thorne and Raymond, 1989: 147) who interpret the stone eel and fish traps as indicating that Aboriginal Australia was on the verge of a Neolithic Revolution are completely mistaken.

Aboriginal society, however, had not always operated within the context of very longrun equilibrium. Beginning with the period of migration, possibly some 60,000 or more years ago, Aboriginal people gradually spread throughout the Australian continent. This process of economic expansion involved an increase in the number of Aboriginal 'households' (or family units) through procreation so as to exploit unutilized natural resources (Snooks, 1994a: 136–8). The driving force behind family multiplication was the attempt to maximize family 'income', and hence individual income, in order to maximize the probability of survival. Family income could be maximized over time – the goal of *dynamic* materialist man – by producing children who would eventually form family units of their own and thereby increase the **economic resilience** of the extended family group or tribe. This behaviour was based upon a benefit–cost calculation – the discounted future benefit of an extra family unit had to be balanced against the cost in household time and resources involved in raising an extra child. While there was easy access to unused natural resources, the numbers of 'households' would increase and the frontier of Aboriginal occupation of the land would expand. But once all the natural resources of Australia had been fully utilized with the technology possessed by this hunter–gatherer society – a stage reached some tens of thousands of years before European settlement – the production of children was limited in order to prevent a reduction of living standards.

Although economic expansion gave way to the stationary state, the economic motivation remained unchanged – the maximization of family/tribal, and hence individual, material returns.

The contrast between Aboriginal Australia and England in the late eighteenth century is stark. European tribes had experienced the threat of wars and invasions for thousands of years before 1788. Tribes from Eurasia came, saw, conquered, settled, traded and, in their turn, were overrun. In the process, networks of trade were developed, which were based upon shipping links in the Mediterranean, the North Sea, and the great rivers of Europe. Enterprising adventurers and traders even went as far afield as China, India, Southeast Asia and the Americas. In this context the existence of aggressive competition transformed the primeval benefit–cost calculus faced by early European societies concerning the introduction of new techniques of production, the increase in population, and the accumulation of fixed capital. As this dynamic process involved economic as well as population growth, the nature of household choice was widened to include an increase in levels of consumption as well as an increase in family units or households. None the less, the objectives were just the same as those in Aboriginal society – the maximization of material gain over the lifetime of the individual. The outcome of this process of economic change, at least until after the Industrial Revolution, was to increase the economic resilience and power of European societies rather than to increase the living standards (except those of the ruling elites) of its populations. And it is this increase in economic resilience that has been critical to the survival of the open European society.

When these two societies – the European and the Australian Aboriginal – finally met in 1788, inevitably it was the closed culture that was destroyed. Clearly, Aboriginal decision-making could not factor this eventuality into their primeval benefit–cost calculus, because they had no idea that, 20,000 kilometres away a potential aggressor was, within the forge of intense and continuous competition, unconsciously steeling itself down through the millennia for just such a meeting. Aboriginal society, in company with other closed societies around the world, paid tragically for its isolation. Yet within its isolation Aboriginal society acted rationally.

Intense competition is not a comfortable condition, particularly for those who are unable to match the best performers. It is quite understandable that those who are unable to keep up the pace attempt to cut themselves off from the mainstream to create an artificially isolated environment. This falls between the two extremes of natural isolation experienced by Australian Aboriginal society and the intense open competition of Western society. It can be achieved by small groups of people setting up colonies in isolated regions (many idealistic communities set up in the New World from Europe and Australia) or by established societies cutting themselves off from the outside world (such as China and Japan after the Western breakout) or by establishing tariff protection and a system of subsidies. Instead of attempting to keep up with the best performers these closed societies attempt to protect themselves from them. This negative cost-minimizing strategy can be found not only in human society but also in other species that attempt to find their own specialized niche in life. While this approach may pay off in the shortrun, it merely reduces economic resilience – or the power to survive – in the longrun as it renders that society even less able to compete with the best performers. Ultimately the self-imposed exiles will be forced to face reality and their society will collapse entirely. There is only one longrun outcome for the risk-averse strategist – extinction.

Any attempt to explain the nature of historical, or dynamic materialist, man must take into account the diverse circumstances that human society has encountered. While the ever-present goal is to maximize individual material advantage, the ways in which this can be achieved are extremely varied, as is suggested by the number of different economic systems that have existed in the past. I have already suggested that the operation of materialist man in open and closed societies can lead to entirely different, but rational, outcomes in terms of the structure of society and economy, the allocation of time between work and leisure, the introduction of new ideas to the process of production, and the nature of economic performance. Elsewhere (Snooks, 1993a: 206–30) I have discussed the role played by materialist man in a competitive feudal society in generating a surplus that was employed (a) to extend the economy's infrastructure; (b) to introduce new productive and organizational techniques; and (c) to widen the extent and influence of commodity and factor markets. In the process, this system of feudalism was transferred into mercantile, and then industrial, capitalism. It was this industrial capitalist system that was introduced into Australia after 1788.

The degree to which the individual needs to cooperate with others in order to maximize his or her utility varies with the type of economic system under consideration. In a completely closed society, such as pre-1788 Aboriginal Australia, the economy will be based upon an extensive set of cooperative relationships. The decision-making individual was only able to maximize his utility by taking into consideration the utility of other members in the kinship group. This is not to deny the rivalry that existed between different kinship groups over adjoining land and the game thereon, or that this rivalry sometimes ended in raiding and in ritualistic (and occasionally serious) combat. As with other species that live by hunting, conflict tends to be ritualistic because even relatively minor wounds can lead to death through infection of a few key providers, which in turn could endanger the entire kinship group. And in hunter–gatherer societies there is no surplus to attract potential conquerors. At the other extreme, in modern Westernized societies, there is greater scope for individuals to pursue their own self-interest with less extensive cooperation with others. Nevertheless, one should not over-emphasize individualistic behaviour, because, even in the most modern society, widespread cooperation is required to maximize individual utility, not only in the home, but also in the factory, shop, and office. And of course, in between these two extremes, such as feudal Europe, cooperation (in the form of monopsonistic behaviour) was required both within and between manors for individual economic decision-makers to achieve their objectives. But at the same time there was also considerable individual initiative on the part of medieval decision-makers, which often led to open conflict between manorial lords (Snooks, 1993a: ch. 6). Many other examples could be provided.

Within different sectors of an individual economic system, a mix of cooperative and individualistic behaviour can be detected. Indeed, it is difficult to imagine any economic sector in any real economic system in which one type of behaviour dominated the other. Cooperation provides stability while competition provides the dynamics in human society. Individualism and cooperation exist in both the market and household sectors of the modern (or indeed the ancient) economy. Firms, just as much as homes, require cooperative effort between members in order to maximize individual incomes by maximizing firm profits. This is not diminished – to the contrary it is actually enhanced – by the competition between firms in the market sector. And, for that matter, households also compete with each other – although in an informal way – just as aggressively as firms in the market. But the essential point I wish to make is that whenever there is a conflict between individual and group objectives, individuals will attempt to break free from the group.

The upshot of this discussion of materialist man in history is that we require a simple model of behaviour that can encompass the interaction between individualistic and cooperative ways of maximizing individual utility. As materialist man is not schizophrenic, we need a model of behaviour that is holistic rather than dualistic – that can explain decision-making in closed and open economies, as well as in market and non-market sectors.

Elsewhere (Snooks, 1994a: ch. 3) I proposed a simple model in which the individual is at the centre of a set of concentric circles or spheres that define the varying strength of cooperative relationships between him and all other individuals and groups in society. The strength of the economic relationship between the central individual and any other individual or group – which could be measured by what I have called the **economic distance** between them – will depend upon how essential they are to the maximization of his utility. Those aspects of his objective function that require the greatest cooperation – such as the generation of love, companionship, and children – will be located on circles or spheres with the shortest economic distance from the centre. But even in this case the economic distance will be greater than zero, implying that the average individual will always discriminate between himself and even those closest to him. For the typical individual, spouse and children will occupy the sphere closest to the centre, with other relatives, friends, workmates, neighbours, members of various religious and social clubs, other members of his socio-economic group, city, state, nation, group of nations, etc., occupying those concentric spheres that progressively radiate out from the centre. As the economic distance – a measure of the importance of others, in maximizing the central individual's utility – between the centre and each sphere increases, the degree of cooperation between them diminishes.

There is always tension between the centre and the periphery no matter how short the economic distance may be, because all personal relationships are built up by the central individual during his or her lifetime in order to maximize his or her utility. While one must cooperate with others to maximize a joint objective function in order, in turn, to maximize individual utility, other cooperating individuals are still perceived to be a constraint on what one can achieve. Hence the persistence of tension in economic and social relationships. And the degree of tension appears to be inversely related to the economic distance, with most conflict and violence occurring between people who are closely associated with each other. This is not a static model of behaviour. Individuals and groups on the various spheres are constantly changing, in response to changing economic circumstances. And the economic distance between these spheres of relationships, and even the order of those spheres, will change over time. Hence while mankind's overwhelming objective is to maximize individual material returns, the means to this end involve a combination of individual and group competition. We form, dissolve, and reform groupings at the various levels of the outwardly radiating concentric spheres in the struggle for life and prosperity. Clearly, not all competition occurs on an individual basis, but all cooperation is part of the struggle of individuals to achieve their materialist objectives. Ultimately the individual is on his/her own.

This concentric spheres model of human behaviour, which focuses upon the individual at the centre of decision-making processes, can be contrasted with the behavioural principle in earlier explanations of the transformation of human society discussed in Chapter 6. Two models will be briefly considered: Karl Marx's dialectical materialism and W.W. Rostow's so-called 'dynamic' theory of production involving leading sectors. This model is also seen as a more persuasive explanation of the nature of cooperation in families, incorrectly called 'altruism', than in the neoclassical model of Gary Becker and the 'kin selection' model of sociobiologists. Further discussion of the latter can be left to Chapter 8 entitled 'The family of man'.

The models of Marx and Rostow will be reviewed here. The dynamic force in Marx's (1957–1961) analysis is the material interests of, and political clash between, two classes – the ruling elite (aristocrats or capitalists) and the emerging class (middle class or working class). As it turned out, Marx's analysis encountered difficulties because he focused upon the wrong level of decision-making – the dominant classes rather than the individual. As history has shown, if individuals in the emerging class can gain access to the surplus they generate, then they will not attempt to destroy the prevailing economic system. A more relevant focus is that at the individual decision-making level. It is individual dynamic materialism rather than class dialectical materialism that drives human society.

Rostow (1960), in his stages-of-economic-growth hypothesis, goes beyond Marx. He denies that individual economic advantage is a 'dominant' motive and unsuccessfully attempts to replace individual material maximization with social 'acts of balance' between a number of economic and non-economic considerations, including national culture, family, leisure, adventure, and power. There is, in other words, no single driving force. Instead, Rostow envisages mankind being motivated by a complex array of economic, social, and political considerations that operate at a societal rather than an individual (or class) level. An array of considerations so complex and diverse that, according to Rostow, they could not possibly have emerged from the simple overwhelming desire of all life to survive. Quite the opposite is, I believe, true. Survival requires the maximization of individual material advantage. From this everything else follows. Rostow does not entertain the fact that non-economic considerations can best be achieved by first maximizing material advantage. In contrast, my concentric spheres model can explain all these considerations in terms of individual material self-interest.

The concentric-spheres model of decision-making is workable at both the individual and aggregated level – which could be regional, national, or international. In Chapter 6 it was argued that the model of political man underlying the analysis of political scientists and political historians is seriously flawed, not only because of a lack of supporting evidence, but also because it is not possible to translate the idea of a national leadership attempting to maximize military and political influence on the international stage to the individual level. But there is no problem in this respect with the concept of the material maximizer. The regional, national, and international levels involve different aggregations of individual material maximization each with its own characteristic interactive dynamic. If, for example, the underlying economic conditions favour commercial activities, individual decision-makers will compete with one another in exploiting this opportunity by investing in small-scale trading activities. If these individual ventures are successful, existing trading firms will extend their activities and new entrants will be attracted. This is strategic imitation in operation. As the wealth of merchant groups increases, they will have a growing influence upon political institutions which direct government revenues towards the construction of commercial infrastructure such as wharves, loading and storage facilities, and land transport to carry bulky goods. Governments, which will include merchants and their friends, will be lobbied by the merchant community to negotiate, or extract by force, favourable trading relationships with other countries. In this way, individuals following their own self-interest give rise to commercial policies at the regional, national, and international levels. The same is true in other circumstances where the prevailing economic conditions favour investments in technological change, colonization, or conquest as dominant national policies.

A possible difficulty that the careful reader might experience with this argument is the decision of a state to embark upon conquest as a method of maximizing material advantage. Clearly, individuals cannot embark upon wars of conquest. In Chapter 10 it will be shown that those societies success-fully pursuing conquest as the dominant strategy to increase their material advantage – such as Assyria, Macedonia, and Rome – began doing so right from the beginning when they were composed of small groups of tribes. These tribes, which responded to the decision-making of family heads, had limited options for economic expansion other than through conquest because they possessed limited good land, and they were crowded out of commerce and colonization by surrounding superpowers. And, because of the intensely competitive environment, if they did not expand they would be swept aside by neighbouring tribes. In these circumstances the decision of individuals within this tribal society regularly to raid and plunder the surrounding tribes is easily understood. Tribes that were successful in their early attempts at conquest were able to develop relatively wealthy towns, cities, kingdoms, or republics. This profitable success attracted a host of followers – the strategic imitation mechanism – who attempted to share in the gains from raiding. After an extended incubation period these conquest societies eventually broke out of their local environments and carried their economic policies of conquest, with a rapidity that surprised their contemporaries, to other parts of the world. And in the process the political organization of society was transformed from a tribal structure into a kingdom, or even into a republic, and a system of occasional raids was transformed into the dynamic strategy of conquest. The conquest strategy as a dominant method of increasing material advantage, therefore, has generally begun with small groups of individuals, expanding to the national level only as the initial communities grew to that stage. Wars of conquest are fought by entire nations not just the ruling elites, because all groups in society stand to gain materially.

Throughout this book dominant national economic policies that arise from the pursuit of material self-interest have been called **dynamic strategies**. They are not imposed from above but are built up from below. Hence when I talk about a nation or civilization employing the commerce strategy, I merely mean that the majority of economic decision-makers in that country have responded to the prevailing economic conditions that make investment in commercial activities more profitable than that in conquest or technological change. As the majority of economic decision-makers invest in a particular type of economic activity, their governments support and enhance that invest-ment. A dominant strategy does not preclude other economic activities, but these are secondary or even supporting strategies. The commerce strategy of

Venice, for example, required support from investments in technology, colonization, and even war and conquest.

The nature of rational decision-making as envisaged in this work may be clarified by touching briefly upon the subject of a future book – the relationship between reason and desire. In essence this is a matter of whether 'rational' action – action that is aimed at the maximization of material advantage – requires conscious thought. The historical research in this study has led me to the view that rational action is a response to biological drives – to be referred to as desires – for survival and the satisfaction of the senses. This appears to be an outcome of the evolutionary struggle for survival. These drives, or desires, appear to have occurred instinctively in mankind's early ancestors and in more primitive forms of life, even simple molecules fighting for survival in the primeval seas (such as Dawkins' initial 'selfish genes').

While being more complex, the circumstances of mankind are basically the same as those for the rest of nature. The driving force in human society is generated by our biological desires, while the major method of satisfying them is provided by our intellectual faculties along with other physical characteristics such as manual dexterity, the ability to walk and run on two legs, our effective eyesight, and our ability to speak. In other words, our intellect is one of a number of tools, albeit the most impressive, for devising ways to pursue our desires more effectively. The only difference between mankind and all other animal species on Earth is that we consciously devise ways to indulge our senses. Hence, while 'rational' action does not require conscious thought, it is greatly facilitated by the human intellect.

So far we have pictured the driver in the chariot of change as a unitary being. While there is a oneness of purpose in materialist man – survival and the maximization of material advantage – there is, as we shall see, a duality of tactics. We must emphasize the difference between the tactics and the strategies. While the broader dynamic strategies are determined by the degree and nature of competition (and hence the costs and benefits of various strategies), the tactics have a genetic as well as an economic basis.

The two main tactical categories employed by materialist man in the pursuit of his objectives are order and chaos. The tactic I have called 'chaos' involves the use of aggression to destabilize the current system and to throw one's competitors off balance in order to take charge of the situation. The tactic called 'order' involves the use of organizational abilities to set up orderly structures and procedures that can be manipulated by our tactician to achieve his/her objectives. While both tacticians are aggressive in competitive situations, the one creating chaos is more aggressive than the one creating order. This is, therefore, not an absolute, but a relative, state.

The tactics employed by materialist man have a genetic basis. Individuals are born with the ability to produce specific hormones – such as the male hormone testosterone and the female hormone oestrogen – that are passed into the bloodstream to stimulate our organs into action. The balance between different types of hormones that are secreted determine, amongst other things, the degree of aggression in response to external stimuli. This varies both within and between gender. In any competitive situation there are those who are naturally more aggressive than others. This is where economics comes in. Owing to comparative advantage, those who are relatively more aggressive will tend to specialize in the 'chaos' tactic, whereas those who are less aggressive will tend to specialize in the 'order' tactic. I stress that this is a relative not an absolute concept. As the category of tactics employed depends upon relative aggressiveness, individuals will change tactics according to the situation in which they find themselves. On one occasion they may be in the relatively more aggressive category and on another they may be in a less aggressive category. It is not economically rational to employ the same tactic in all situations.

The relative aggressiveness concept is useful in understanding the behaviour of individuals and groups in society, and in sorting out ends from means. Those individuals and groups who are relatively more aggressive will have a comparative advantage in conflict situations, whereas those who are relatively less aggressive will have a comparative advantage in more orderly situations. The relatively more aggressive group will be more likely to resort to risky individual action aimed at creating chaos by temporarily breaking down the existing order and, in the confusion of conflict, picking up the reins of power. The actual tactics employed will include radical reforms, rebellion, riots, and radical ideology (Marxism, fascism, or new religious ideals). On the other hand, the relatively less aggressive group will be more likely to attempt to maintain, or create, order through cooperative rather than individual action. They attempt to keep the existing system together because they – individually and as a group – will lose more than they will gain if it collapses. The tactics of order will include enforceable rules and regulations together with ideology, particularly of establishment values and religion. It should be noted that the static constraints on individual behaviour (the freerider problem) that concern the institutionalist critic of neoclassical economics (North, 1981; Hayek, 1988) are not an issue here. In my model a dynamic balance is achieved through a struggle between those who wish to enforce order (or compliance) and those who wish to resist (at least until they become part of the ruling elite) – a struggle between order and chaos. This is a struggle for power over the distribution of income and wealth generated by the dominant dynamic strategy. Issues of the state and of ideology are encompassed by this dynamic framework, and they will be explored more fully in a future volume.

This concept of order and chaos also enables us to distinguish between means and ends. Some scholars have used the existence both of order and cooperative behaviour as evidence of moral man rather than economic man. This, however, is a confusion of means with ends. The pursuit of order, and the cooperation necessary to achieve it, is a means of obtaining the universal objective of survival and material maximization. It is not a matter of altruism.

While different degrees of aggressiveness can be detected within each gender, the most obvious difference can be seen between males and females as broad categories. This is not meant to deny that some females are more aggressive than some males, just that on average males are significantly more aggressive than females and that this has a genetic basis. Accordingly, in society as a whole, males tend to employ the chaos tactic, and females tend to employ the order tactic. This is reinforced by differences in physical strength between males and females. This hypothesis contradicts the currently fashionable claim of scientists that differences in gender behaviour are the result of differential brain function (Gur *et al.*, 1995). There is some evidence for my 'tactical' view. A reflection of the differences in gender aggressiveness can be seen clearly in road accident statistics. Even in the 'liberated' 1970s and 1980s in Australia, females never accounted for more than one-third of total traffic accident fatalities (Knott, 1994). The aggression of males was deadly on the roads. Also, in an Australian survey of consumer satisfaction in 1993, only 36 per cent of men were 'very satisfied with life' in this most orderly of societies compared with 43 per cent of women. Order tends to frustrate aggressive tendencies.

A clear example of the change in gender fortunes in a period of chaos is provided by William the Conqueror's Domesday Book. In Domesday Book (1086) it is possible to compare the gender basis of ownership of manors before and after the Conquest in 1066. By the end of Edward the Confessor's reign, about 5 per cent of the rateable value ('hidage') of land was held by female tenants-in-chief owing to the process of inheritance in an orderly society (Meyer, 1991). But in the turmoil of conquest and rebellion, all property passed to male warriors, with females being completely dispossessed through confiscation, forced marriages with Norman warriors, or trust arrangements with the Crown (Stafford, 1994). Only once economic and political stability had been regained in the twelfth century did the independent wealth of women recover and surpass pre-Conquest levels (Holt, 1982–1985). Many other examples of the dominant role of men in conflict could be provided, including the civil war in Yugoslavia in the early 1990s.

The important conclusion that can be drawn from this discussion is that a balance between the forces of order and chaos is required in the Dynamic Society. If this balance is seriously upset in a particular society, or in human society as a whole, it will go into either temporary or permanent decline. If the forces of chaos get out of hand – as they did in Athens and Sparta in the fifth century BC, and in the former Yugoslavia in the early 1990s – then the society will tear itself apart. Collapse will come quickly. If the forces of order and oppression gain control, then society will become increasingly unenterprising, isolationist, and moribund, like the USSR after the 1950s.

Eventually – and this may take a number of generations – the society will be unable to keep up with the outside world and will either collapse under the weight of its own inertia (the USSR in the late 1980s) or be taken over by its neighbours (Anglo-Saxon England in 1066).

A balance between order and chaos is essential. This is the basis for the 'two in one' nature of materialist man – of the oneness of purpose and the duality of tactics of our driver in the chariot of change. The balance between these two tactical approaches accounts for the success of mankind. Indeed, without this balance it is unlikely that the human race would have emerged, or that the Dynamic Society would exist.

The evidence for materialist man

It is one thing to present an argument about the driving force in history, and quite another to provide the necessary evidence to support it. This is one of those subjects on which evidence in the literature is conspicuously absent. Indeed, it is a major reason why the proliferation of different views about the driving force has existed for so long.

There are different forms of evidence concerning the revealed objectives of decision-makers that can be used to support the view in this book that the driving force in history is essentially one of dynamic materialism. If the dynamic materialism hypothesis is correct, we would expect to find a number of very specific outcomes in the era of human civilization. We would expect to find evidence of:

- competition operating through commodity and factor markets and through open hostilities (I focus here on the former);
- a close and systematic relationship between the inputs and outputs of economic decision-making;
- persistent economic growth (of real GDP per capita) throughout history.

We would expect to find, in other words, interacting evidence of competition, of rational economic decision-making, and of economic progress in the very longrun. The available evidence on these matters will be briefly reviewed.

There is considerable evidence on the widespread existence of competitive markets in the past. While this evidence may not be considered conclusive in itself, it can demonstrate whether economic decision-makers have been subject to competitive forces over long periods of time. Competitive forces are, as we have seen, essential for the emergence of materialist man. In the absence of these forces, owing to isolation, rational economic decision-makers will opt for the stationary state. This evidence, therefore, is a critical test of the dynamic materialism hypothesis in the era since the emergence of human civilization. Before that time competition for land resources and game largely took the form of tribal conflict, a subject discussed in Chapter 10.

187

The emergence of markets, and hence of competitive economic forces, occurred with the development of the first urban societies in the Fertile Crescent of the Old World about 9,000 years ago, and in the Mesoamerican isthmus of the New World about 4,000 years ago. As the ancient civilizations in both worlds flourished, domestic and foreign markets for commodities and, to a lesser extent, factors (land, labour, and capital) developed. This will be analysed in detail in Chapter 11. In this way a structure for competitive economic forces, operating through the price mechanism, emerged. This structure provided the opportunity for risk-takers to invest time and capital (by abstaining from present consumption) in order to increase their consumption, wealth, and power in the future. To maximize, in other words, material advantage over their lifetime – the hallmark of materialist man.

With the collapse of the Western Roman Empire there was a reduction in the operation of formal markets in Rome's former sphere of influence. Of course, the Eastern Empire centred on Constantinople still played an important role in the economies of Europe and Asia Minor. It is often argued that, in Western and northern Europe in the millennium after the fall of Rome, competitive market forces virtually disappeared. This is not true. There is abundant evidence of extensive trade within Europe, as well as between Europe and Asia Minor during the early Middle Ages of AD 500–1000 (Hollister, 1982). But it is true that the first hard evidence – apart from the coin hoards – on the extent of domestic and international markets is that of Domesday Book in 1086, which can be used to test our hypothesis about materialist man.

Domesday Book is unique. As it has no equal until the mid-twentieth century, we are forced to focus our attention upon England. But it should be realized that as England was part of a highly competitive Western Europe, the results from this country have wider relevance. Basically, Domesday Book is a set of official national accounts that can be used to calculate not only the GDP, but also the market structure of England in 1086 (Snooks, 1993a: ch. 5). What we want to know is how far commercialization had spread throughout England by the late eleventh century. We know from existing literature that for England (and other Western European countries) there was extensive internal and international trade between the eighth and eleventh centuries. There is, for example, evidence of an active European trade in textiles, raw wool, metals (iron and lead), salt, horses, and agricultural goods such as dairy products and grain. This trade, undertaken at first by Frisian and later by Scandinavian seamen and merchants, linked England with all parts of the Continent. The late Anglo-Saxon economy had trading connections with Scandinavia, Flanders (and from there to Cologne and Bruges), southern Europe and the Mediterranean. In response to this commerce with Europe, a number of English coastal towns, such as London, Southampton, Dover, Hull, and Ipswich, developed into thriving ports, occupied by a rapidly emerging merchant class in the tenth and eleventh centuries. As the king imposed tolls upon ships entering these ports, he was keen to encourage this development. The main exports from England in the mid-eleventh century included both craft and agricultural products. Indeed, fine English craftwork, in the form of metalwork (particularly silver), embroidery, fine textiles, and manuscripts, appears to have been in considerable demand throughout Europe. In addition there were exports of agricultural products, mainly wool but also grain, cheese, butter, oil, honey, and salt. Imports, on the other hand, appear to have consisted mainly of luxury goods that could not be produced on the manor or in the borough. These imports included silks, finely dyed textiles and garments, gold and precious stones, glass, wine, oil, ivory, tin, bronze, copper, and sulphur. Other less exotic imports included military equipment, timber, furs, hides, and fish.

We also know that the manorial lords needed to market their surplus in order to provide cash to meet substantial taxes, both feudal and national (amounting to about one-third of manorial income), to purchase military equipment and warhorses, and to satisfy their desire for elegant building materials (glass) and luxuries, fittings, clothing, and investment in productive rural and urban assets. Yet to gauge how extensive the market really was in 1086, we need quantitative evidence. This is available in the form of sectoral estimates of GDP that I have constructed from the data in Domesday Book (Table 7.1).

From this table an estimate can be made of the value of net demesne output (i.e. after the deduction of seed, fodder, and other intermediate goods) that entered the market. While a number of assumptions had to be made, it may not be very far from the mark to say that about 60 per cent of net demesne output in 1086 was marketed. Also as primary produce to the value of £44,134 passed through an urban sector which contributed only £10,708 to GDP, the bulk (possibly as high as three-quarters, even if we assume that *all* urban income was spent on domestic rural goods) of this marketed surplus

Table 7.1 The national income of feudal England, 1086

1.	National income (£)		
	1.1	Manorial income	
	1.1.1	Recorded counties	
		• demesne economy	71,573
		• subsistence economy	51,306
	1.1.2	Omitted counties	3,034
	1.2	Burghal income	10,708
	1.3	Total	136,621
2	Per capita income (shillings)		1.785

Notes: Non-recorded income estimated on the assumption that the average household size was 5.0 people, and that slaves were recorded in the same way as the rest of the population (i.e. as household heads).
Source and methods: See Snooks (1993a: ch. 5).

Table 7.2 Market and subsistence sectors in the feudal economy of
England, 1086

	£	%	£	%
Market				
• rural[1]	44,134	32.3		
• urban[2]	10,708	7.8		
			54,842	40.1
Subsistence/sustenance				
• tenants-in-chief	12,878	9.4		
• free peasants	16,328	12.0		
• unfree peasants and slaves	52,573	38.5		
			81,779	59.9
Total			136,621	100.0

Notes: 1 Rural income, both market and subsistence, includes omitted counties
on a *pro rata* basis.
2 All urban income has been treated as market income.
Source: Snooks (1993a, ch: 5).

(or 20 to 24 per cent of GDP) must have been exported (Snooks, 1995).
Certainly these conclusions are consistent with the indirect evidence of market
activity discussed above. All this evidence, therefore, points to the conclusion
that the feudal economy of England was substantially open to market
influences and must have been capable of responding to them.

The national accounts in Table 7.1 can be reorganized to determine the
relative importance of the market and the subsistence/sustenance sectors.
Table 7.2 suggests that 40 per cent of the entire economy was involved in
market activities and 60 per cent in subsistence. In turn the market sector
was dominated by manorial agriculture, amounting to almost one-third of
GDP, and the subsistence sector was dominated by the dependent peasant
sector, amounting to almost 40 per cent of GDP. But even more importantly,
the major economic decision-makers operated within a market-dominated
environment. In other words, even though the market was restricted to about
40 per cent of the economy, it was in this sector that all the major economic
decisions in England were made. These results challenge the conventional
wisdom (Abel, 1980: 5), which insists upon only a very limited role for
market forces at this time.

This estimate of the size of the market sector in the feudal economy of
England can be placed within a wider historical context by making a comparison with modern Third World economies and with the ancient world. In
the mid-twentieth century, the market economy accounted for about 50 per
cent of GDP in Africa and 60 per cent of household consumption in India
(Goldsmith, 1984). While there is no direct evidence for the Roman Empire
at the beginning of the Christian era, Goldsmith (1984: 274–5) is prepared

to hazard an informed guess, that 'the monetization ratio of national product is unlikely to have been as high as one-half'. If this is so, it would appear that the relative size of the market sector in the English feudal economy was only marginally less than that in both the early Roman Empire and Third World economies in the mid-twentieth century.

The commodity market, which was well established by the late eleventh century, continued to spread throughout the English (and European) economy during the following centuries until by the late seventeenth century the market dominated all aspects of English economic life. Others have shown how towns increased in number and in size and how growing market trans-actions were facilitated by an increase in the supply of money in circulation per capita (Persson, 1988; Britnell, 1995). But the most significant and neglected aspect of changing commodity markets during these six centuries was the change in the socio-economic structure of these markets. In 1086 the unfree peasantry was effectively excluded from the market sector by an oppressive feudal military elite. The commercialized sector was the demesne sector (which included the free peasants) rather than the dependent, or subsis-tence, sector. The Conquest reversed any growth in peasant market partici-pation that had occurred in the first half of the eleventh century. Only after the decline of feudalism in subsequent centuries did the peasantry emerge again in the market economy (Hilton, 1983). Between 1086 and 1300 factor markets for labour and capital – which I have argued led to the breakdown of feudalism (Snooks, 1995) – emerged for the first time in post-Roman Britain. The unfree peasants and slaves became either small tenants of manorial lords or landless labourers for hire on a piecework basis. Local land markets developed, and capital markets emerged (Harvey, 1984; McCloskey and Nash, 1984). These changes in commodity and factor markets reduced the costs of doing business (costs of transactions) – of obtaining land, labour, and capital, and of buying and selling commodities.

While the English and other European economies were held in the vice-like grip of epidemic and war between 1347 and the late fifteenth century, their economic structures continued to change with the extension of both commodity and factor markets. But these changes paled in comparison with those of the sixteenth century, when there was a rapid growth of towns and markets in England together with a rapid extension of trade with the rest of Europe and with the New World. This century saw the first breakout by the Europeans into the wider world (Phillips, 1988). England, together with the Netherlands, was in a good position to exploit the commercial expansion of Europe and, indirectly through Spain, of the New World. For the 150 years before 1500, the English export of raw wool declined from 28,302 to 8,149 bags per annum, while woollen cloth increased from 3,024 to 13,891 equivalent bags (Bridbury, 1962). But from 1500 to 1550 the number of 'shortcloths' increased 2.7-fold from 49,000 to 133,000 (Fisher, 1954). The main buyer was Germany who, owing to a collapse of Italian production,

191

could no longer purchase woollen cloth from its former suppliers. English products were particularly competitive in this period owing to the Tudor devaluation of the pound between 1522 and 1550. While woollen exports declined in importance after 1550 owing to changing conditions of demand and supply on the Continent, other exports took their place including non-woollen textiles, iron, lead, military equipment, and glass. Iron production in England, for example, increased from 5,000 tons per annum in 1550 to 18,000 tons in 1600 and 24,000 tons in 1700; coal production increased from 0.21 to 1.5 million tons between 1550 and 1630, and had reached 11 million tons by 1800. British involvement in international trade also began to expand in the sixteenth and seventeenth centuries, with the total tonnage of merchant shipping rising from 50,000 to 340,000 tons between 1572 and 1686 (Cipolla, 1976: 256–73). It was during the sixteenth century that the foundations for mercantile capitalism were constructed.

Competitive economic forces, therefore, were well entrenched even during the high-tide of feudalism in Europe. The market in the eleventh century was as large as it needed to be to accommodate the all-embracing economic activities of the small ruling elites. Markets grew as the *proportion* of the population – and hence the proportion of total output – that was involved in formal (or market) economic decision-making increased. The market, in other words, was appropriate to the organizational structure of feudal society and did not operate as a brake upon it. All economic decision-makers were fully exposed to highly competitive economic forces. The only question is: did these economic decision-makers respond to these forces in an entrepreneurial way, or did they waste their opportunities through riotous living, as is usually asserted by historians (Snooks, 1994b: 43–8)?

The mere existence of market forces in an economic system may not be regarded as sufficient evidence that economic agents respond effectively to the material incentives that these markets provide. We have been told repeatedly by historians (Round, 1895; Darby, 1977), and by economists in the classical tradition (Mill, 1848; Cunningham, 1882), that the ruling elite in the Middle Ages preferred to ignore market signals by consuming rather than investing the surpluses they extracted from the peasantry. Indeed, we are expected to believe that medieval man, unlike his modern counterpart, was 'moral' man (who followed the rules of custom) rather than materialist man (who follows the dictates of the market). Some have challenged this wisdom but, owing to the lack of hard evidence, their ideas have made little headway (McCloskey, 1976).

The hard evidence, however, is available in Domesday Book to test this issue directly. It enables us to answer the fundamental question: were the economic decision-makers in Domesday England – and by implication Western Europe – prisoners of custom, or were they primarily motivated by individual self-interest? Were, in other words, feudal tenants-in-chief (which includes free peasants holding their land of the king) economically rational? This is a critical test of the existence of materialist man. Most historians acknowledge, albeit reluctantly, that modern Western man attempts to maximize his material advantage, but deny that this was the case in pre-modern times, and particularly in feudal societies. Elsewhere I have marshalled the detailed data in Domesday Book to test statistically three key aspects of the dynamic materialism hypothesis (Snooks, 1993a: ch. 6). These issues include: the economic behaviour of the state in relation to its system of taxation; the economic behaviour of manorial lords; and the nature of the process of manorial production. The traditional interpretation of these issues has been used to support the idea of moral man and to reject that of materialist man (Snooks, 1990b).

The conventional wisdom claimed that the taxation system known as Danegeld, which existed for almost 200 years from 991, was 'artificial' in that there was no systematic relationship between the tax assessments on the one hand and either manorial income or resources on the other. In other words, it is argued that this non-feudal tax was based not rationally upon capacity to pay but rather arbitrarily upon the whims of the king. This argument dates back to J.H. Round in the 1890s. Second, it is argued that there was no relationship between manorial resources and manorial output. This implies that investment in the form of additional ploughbeasts or meadowland was undertaken without expecting any financial return from it in terms of increased output. What farmer or businessman today would do the same? Third, it is argued that the manorial system of production was inflexible and was operated according to unchanging customary rules.

By computerizing the data in Domesday Book and formally testing these hypotheses, we (Snooks and McDonald, 1986; Snooks, 1993a: ch. 6) were able to demonstrate overwhelmingly that the conventional wisdom on these issues was wrong in every respect. As these results are widely known I will discuss them briefly here. It was shown that the taxation system was economically rational – the tax assessments were very closely related to both the income ($R^2 = 0.81$) and the resources ($R^2 = 0.79$) of the manors – and was directed at maximizing the king's net tax revenue. These results are very persuasive – we can explain between 79 and 81 per cent of the variation in tax assessments by the variation in manorial income or manorial resources. Taxation, therefore, was not the result of an absolute monarch wilfully exercising his arbitrary power, but of a prudent king grappling with the economic and political realities of his time in order to advance his material interests. Power is about economics. The success of Danegeld is reflected in its survival for almost 200 years. Compare this with an irrational English taxation system – Mrs Thatcher's poll tax, which was an inequitable tax based not upon capacity to pay but on each individual irrespective of income. It aroused so much opposition, as any irrational tax is bound to do, that within seven months of its introduction in England and Wales (April 1990), Mrs

Thatcher was forced to resign as Prime Minister and the tax was radically changed. William the Conqueror would not have been surprised. Only the economically rational, barring accidents, can hope to survive and to achieve their objectives.

Also, the statistical results at the manorial level show that there was a very close relationship between manorial inputs and outputs ($R^2 = 0.81$), and that manorial production ($R^2 = 0.97$) was not a prisoner of custom, but rather a flexible and competitive system that responded effectively to market signals. It is quite remarkable that we can explain 97 per cent of the variation in production between English manors in 1086 using manorial inputs and a simple (CES) production model. We can do no better with similar studies in the 1990s. The economy of feudal England was, therefore, a far more flexible and rational system than the conventional wisdom would have us believe. And this system was driven at both the macro and micro levels by individuals who quite clearly were successfully attempting to maximize their material advantage. In other words, the ruling elite in medieval England were not members of a mythical class of idle rich who squandered their incomes on riotous living and conspicuous consumption, but were prudent and entrepreneurial businessmen who also had a constrained taste for the luxuries of life. The same was true of the rest of Western Europe which, together with England, was locked in a highly competitive and deadly struggle.

Finally, we need to reflect upon the nature of the 'growth' of GDP per capita that is presented and discussed in Chapter 12. Longrun systematic increases in material living standards are the clearest indication we have of the existence of materialist man. Longrun growth requires a determined and persistent effort successfully to implement dynamic strategies that are going to maximize material advantage over the lifetime of economic decision-makers. This requires the investment of considerable time together with physical and human capital in risky ventures to implement the commerce, conquest, and technological strategies discussed in the rest of the book. Economic growth has been a persistent feature of Western civilization over the past millennium, and has taken place via the great waves of economic change that have been recently identified (Snooks, 1993a: ch. 7). Economic growth in England (see Figure 5.1) during the period 1000 to 1200 rose to levels (0.6 per cent per annum) slightly in excess of those (0.4–0.5 per cent per annum) achieved during the Industrial Revolution (1780–1830). Those (1.3 per cent per annum) in the sixteenth century exceeded growth rates in any subsequent period with the exception of the 1950s and 1960s (2.5 per cent per annum) (ibid.: 247–8). Persistent economic growth is the final and most conclusive block of evidence in our jigsaw puzzle of dynamic materialism. We have been able to employ hard evidence to show that (a) highly competitive market forces have existed in the past, even during the high tide of feudalism;

(b) even feudal kings and landholders acted so as to maximize their material returns in response to competitive market forces; and (c) this resulted in persistent and quite rapid economic growth during the very longrun. The case, therefore, for materialist man as the driving force in pre-modern European history is very strong, whereas that for non-materialist man is neither proven nor provable.

Unfortunately, we do not have such extensive evidence for classical antiquity, but what evidence we do have points in the direction of materialist man. Until very recently the traditional wisdom insisted that the ancient world not only had no interest in maximizing its material advantage, it even lacked the ability to do so. It was claimed that economic decision-makers did not possess sufficient data in an appropriate form to make economically rational decisions. Moses Finley (1985: 181), who has long cast a daunting shadow over ancient history, asserts: 'Graeco-Roman bookkeeping was exceedingly rudimentary, essentially restricted to a listing of receipts and expenditures, from which it was impossible to determine the profitability or otherwise of any single activity in a polyculture.' This judgement – which implies that the ancients, who were able to build up and maintain world-wide empires, were totally inept in accounting practices – is based upon earlier (1930s) studies of rather fragmentary evidence. The most recent study of Roman accounts based upon a more complete recovery of estate accounts, however, tells a different story.

Dominic Rathbone (1991) in a recent study of a 'huge collection of documents' on papyrus relating to the 'Appianus estate' located in the Fayum area of Roman Egypt in the third century AD has been able to challenge successfully the traditional wisdom. Far from being a simple list of receipts and expenditures, the Appianus documents constitute a complex system of interlocking financial records – a 'sophisticated system of accounting'. For each productive unit of the estate (*phrontis*) there are monthly cost data extracted from even more detailed records by each manager (*phrontistes*) and sent to the central administration. After a careful analysis of these accounts, Rathbone (1991: 369) tells us:

> My conclusions are that, although direct evidence is lacking, monetary profitability probably was calculated, but that the main purpose of the accounting system was to provide a check on the efficiency of production on the *phrontides* as measured in monetary terms.

These accounts were, Rathbone argues, used as 'an aid to the maintenance and improvement of the cost effectiveness of production in the future'.

Hence the Roman owner was in an excellent position to operate his estate in an economically rational way. And, as Rathbone demonstrates, there was every reason to do so because this estate was an economic rather than a social structure geared to the market, it was well integrated into the wider economy, and it depended upon credit from the banking system. Rathbone (1991: 387) concludes that the monthly accounts

> contained much data which could have been used as the basis for making economically rational decisions about future activities and practices. Whether they were used for these purposes cannot be proved, but the presentation of the information in a logically structured format which facilitated its analysis and the more general evidence for the attitudes and practices of the management of the Appianus estate imply that its accounting system was designed and used as an aid to economically rational management of the estate.

And we have every reason to believe that the Appianus estate was representative of the general approach to business in classical antiquity.

Finally, in more recent research, Rathbone (1994: 33) suggests that 'the central government of Ptolemaic Egypt had access to abundant information about the productive resources, especially agricultural and human, of its kingdom' and was also in a position to intervene in an economically rational way. While his arguments are persuasive, the final proof will require an examination of their actions as well as their procedures of the kind undertaken above for the medieval period. Yet there can be little doubt that materialist man was as active in classical antiquity as in medieval Europe.

What of the modern era? There are some who argue that modern man has been able to break with the past. That the forces that drove humanity in the past are no longer operative today. They argue that modern man in developed countries has been able, through cultural development, to override the previously overwhelming urge to maximize reproduction and, in the face of the looming population crisis, finally to limit the size of the family. This, they claim, has been achieved in affluent societies that have invested heavily in education and other cultural activities. This is seen as the triumph of intellectual man over natural man.

This view, however, is merely assertion. It is not based upon persuasive argument, nor upon hard evidence. The only evidence employed by those who adopt this view is the decline of the birth rate and the rate of population growth in Westernized countries – the so-called 'demographic transition' (Livi-Bacci, 1992: ch. 4). Some natural scientists interpret this 'demographic transition' as the outcome of a change in the motivation of man – from the maximization of reproduction to a more intelligent response to the problems of our time. The argument is as simple as that. No attempt has been made to analyse this 'transition' using hard evidence. The burden of proof has been left to others.

Hard evidence has already been marshalled in this chapter to show that in the past economic decision-makers have attempted – and been quite successful in the attempt – to maximize not reproduction but rather material

196

advantage. Had reproduction maximization been the driving force in history, longrun population growth would have been pursued at the expense of living standards. The important implication is that prior to the modern period there would have been no systematic increase in real GDP per capita. Clearly, this is wrong. Considerable growth in average living standards (GDP per capita) was achieved in human society before the nineteenth (or the seventeenth) century. My growth rate estimates over the past millennium demonstrate this. Even before I published these growth rate estimates (Snooks, 1990a), the non-materialists needed to explain the substantial gap in average *material* standards of living between the world's most advanced regions and the rest just prior to the Neolithic and the Industrial Revolutions. This income gap implies periods of substantial economic growth in some nations. An example of this gap is the difference between Britain and Aboriginal Australia when they confronted each other on the western edge of the Pacific in 1788. Such a gap would not have existed had the driving force in human society been the maximization of reproduction. To the contrary. Maximization of reproduction would have undermined the ability of the human race to survive, by placing unsupportable demands upon scarce resources. It is well known that palaeolithic societies – such as Australian Aborigines and American Eskimos – controlled their population to the extent that, in the absence of external competition, they achieved stable equilibrium of population and society over tens of thousands of years. This was to prevent a reduction of living standards and, hence, ultimate extinction. Natural man, therefore, is not merely an assertion, it is a myth.

The change in birth rates (relative to death rates) and rates of population growth in Westernized countries can be explained in terms of changes in fundamental economic forces rather than a change in human motivation. Materialist man is the same yesterday, today, and forever. Only the underlying economic conditions facing him have changed. And the so-called 'demographic transition' is an outcome of these economic changes and should not be regarded as the ultimate explanation of changes in living standards or of the remarkable post-Second World War shift of married women from the household into the market.

The 'demographic transformation', which is regarded as having occurred in Westernized societies since the Industrial Revolution, is not even a single response to a single shift in fundamental economic forces. The decline in birth rates was a response to a series of separate economic changes: the increase in material living standards from the Industrial Revolution to the early twentieth century; the introduction of labour-saving household equipment during the interwar period at a time when there was a limited widening of employment opportunities for women in the most advanced industrial countries; and the major change in economic structure after the 1940s which suddenly created a wide range of new jobs for which women had a comparative advantage.

The first of these changes – a sustained increase in real GDP per capita – resulted from the widespread adoption of a new technological paradigm during and after the Industrial Revolution. Higher material living standards significantly improved average nutrition and, hence, resistance to disease; and it led to the provision of infrastructure to eliminate disease (deep sewerage and piped water) and famine (food storage and fast transport systems). Hence, there was a decline in death rates, an increase in population, and a lagged reduction in birth rates so as to reattain the age-old average family size of five persons – which appears to have been the optimal size before the introduction of labour-saving household equipment in the 1920s (Snooks, 1994a: 63–5).

The size of the Western family began to decline significantly for the first time after the First World War, owing to the wider (but still limited) range of jobs available for females together with labour-saving electrical equipment that could be substituted for labour in the home. This was the first intimation of a change that was to accelerate and deepen suddenly after the 1940s. The suddenness was in part due to the pent-up economic forces arising from two decades of depression, war, and postwar reconstruction. This demographic change arose from a change in factor endowments and, hence, a change in the relative factor prices of capital and labour. As the price of capital relative to the price of labour began to fall, capital was substituted for labour in the market sector. In this way the physical requirements of market work declined and opened up in the most advanced industrial nations a range of jobs that had previously been closed to women. In turn this increased the opportunity cost for those families with married women staying at home producing and looking after children. Hence, the market sector's demand for married women increased, within limits, at a time when electrical household equipment was becoming available as a response to higher material living standards.

Not until after the 1940s did, what I have called, the **new economic revolution** occur (Snooks, 1994a: 110–12, 268–9). While it built upon changes tentatively emerging in the 1920s, it differed both quantitatively and qualitatively from the earlier period. The marked decline in the price of capital relative to labour, at a time of rapidly expanding international trade and of general prosperity, led to a major substitution in the market sector of capital – particularly self-regulating and, later, computerized equipment – for both 'heavy' physical labour and skilled labour. This generated for the first time an extensive market demand for 'lighter' and unskilled labour in which married females had a comparative advantage. At the same time, relatively cheap electrical household equipment was flooding the market. Hence, there was a major shift in demand for female labour – which significantly increased the cost for families of raising children – at a time when the range of consumer and leisure goods and services produced by the market increased dramatically. Not surprisingly there was a major movement of married women, largely on a part-time basis, from the household to the market. As can be seen in Figure 7.1, married female participation rates in Westernized countries increased threefold between 1950 and 1990, and family size declined for the first time in the entire history of human society from five to three people.

The argument presented here, therefore, is that the 'demographic transition' is a secondary phenomenon reflecting the responses of materialist man to fundamental economic change. It has absolutely nothing to do with any fanciful change in the motivation of human beings. Mankind has never attempted to maximize reproduction and has not recently and suddenly been able to override its genetically determined human nature through intellectual will-power. While human objectives remain unchanged, the dynamic strategies have been switched around.

Whatever the reaction to this argument, the only way to determine its explanatory power is to set up a few key hypotheses that can be tested using hard evidence. Elsewhere I have tested two simple models that are based upon historical experience: one explaining the change in household size and the other explaining the change in female participation rates using Australian data (Snooks, 1994a: 67–9, 85–8). Australia since the First World War can be taken to be representative of Westernized countries in this matter (see Figure 7.1). The model to explain changes in average household size from five people in 1920 to three in 1990 involves merely two explanatory variables, the capital/labour ratio, which is a measure of the fundamental changes taking place in the gender demand for labour, and the female/male wage rate, which is a measure of forces influencing the decisions made by households to distribute male and female labour between market and household work. The underlying argument is that the rapid increase in capital intensity of market sector production leads to a demand for 'lighter' and less skilled labour, in which females have a comparative advantage, in a wide range of manufacturing and service industries. This causes an increase in female relative to male wages, which in turn encourages a rational household to allocate more female labour to market work, to purchase labour-saving household equipment, to allocate more male labour to household work, and to have less children because of the increase in the opportunity cost (market wages forgone) of married females staying at home. This simple and unadorned model can explain 99 per cent of the change in household size in this period (ibid.: 68).

The second model attempts to explain the change in married female participation in the market sector in Australia between 1946 and 1990. This model, which is also straightforward, has three explanatory variables: the familiar capital/labour ratio; the annual change in female/male wage rates; and annual changes in the birth rate. Once again the capital/labour ratio is a measure of the gender demand for labour that depends upon fundamental changes in the technological base of society, and changes in the female/male wage ratio influence the gender division of labour in the household. Variations in

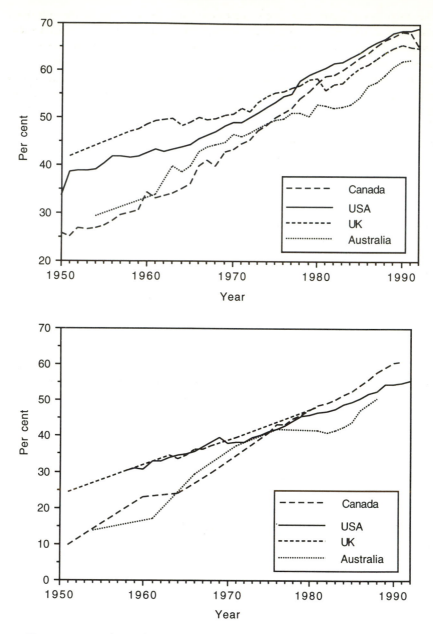

Figure 7.1 Female market participation in the Western world, 1950–1992
(a) All working-age women (15–64 years)
(b) Married women

Source: G.D. Snooks, *Portrait of the Family within the Total Economy*, Cambridge,
Cambridge University Press, 1994, p. 16.

the birth rate have also been included, not because it is the ultimate source of change, but merely as a medium through which changes of a more fundamental nature are communicated from the market sector to the household sector. This model can explain up to 98 per cent of the changes in married female participation shown in Figure 7.1; and 97 per cent of our explanation is due to changes in the gender demand for labour (the capital/ labour ratio). In other words, the radical change in female participation rates that occurred in the second half of the twentieth century in Western society was due to a major change in its technological foundations, and not to changing attitudes or motivation. The motivation of human decision-makers remained unchanged while social attitudes followed in the wake of economic necessity.

The hard evidence, therefore, demonstrates quite clearly that the decline in family size, or the decline in fertility rates, in Western society – the misnamed 'demographic transition' – was a response to changes in fundamental economic forces and not to a change in human nature or motivation. Human nature has been the great constant throughout the history of human society. That nature, that motivation, set in a competitive environment is what I have called dynamic materialism.

THE NAVIGATOR

The navigator deals in ideas rather than practicalities. These ideas embrace every facet of the physical and metaphysical worlds, including the natural sciences, engineering and technology, social sciences and humanities, philosophy and theology, astronomy and astrology. The specialist in ideas – the mystic, the witchdoctor, the astrologer, the scientist, the engineer, the social and behavioural scientist, the humanist, and the artist – is important to society, but not as important as is often thought. Some intellectuals imagine that they are the real charioteers – that their ideas are actually driving human society forward. In fact, they stand behind the driver and move forward only when called upon to do so. Even then they only whisper into the ear of the charioteer. And if their advice is not acceptable they are sent back again, often with a rude jolt.

The strategic demand for ideas

The driving force in society is the urgent desire to maximize the probability of survival and the achievement of material advantage. Both are interlinked and one cannot be achieved without the other. Economic decision-makers select the dynamic strategies that are best able to meet these objectives. And each strategy generates demand for a family of ideas. Geographical expansion arising from family multiplication requires at least rudimentary knowledge of: navigation, appropriate types of transport and communication, essential supplies, the terrain ahead, and how to appease the gods. In the face of a need for knowledge of this type, ideas have been forthcoming. The supply of ideas responds to the strategic demand for them. Some of these ideas may already exist but, because they are not part of daily economic life, may have lain dormant. They are remembered because they have been embodied in cultural life, such as wheeled toys in Mesoamerica or mechanical amusements in China and Europe before the Industrial Revolution (Landes, 1983). Other ideas have to be invented or reinvented. Of course the inability to meet the demand for particular useful ideas will limit or redirect a given strategy, but if the demand is great enough the incentives will be too high to ignore and eventually technical solutions will be forthcoming.

Conquest requires highly specialized knowledge about military equipment and machines, effective forms of transport for troops and their war gear, provisioning, communications, engineering, military organization including strategy and tactics, and effective forms of imperial organization and rule. And to ensure the regular supply of ideas on demand, it is necessary to develop permanent systems for the generation and dissemination of more general knowledge through institutions for research and education. This was realized by all ancient civilizations, particularly the Greek and Roman, and was the source of the cultural glories of those societies. The commerce strategy also generates a demand for ideas of various types including improvements in transport – sea, road, rail, and air – and communications, improvements in storage and loading facilities, and new ways of conducting business to reduce transactions costs. It also requires negotiating and diplomatic skills of the highest kind.

The technological strategy has generated a different set of demands for supporting ideas. It requires practical engineering knowledge, together with the general development of theoretical and applied ideas in science and engineering. The emphasis in these ideas is more on how natural resources can be exploited more efficiently in order to increase the productivity of the economic system, rather than how to pursue conquest more effectively. But as war is still a strategy of last resort in the technological era, and as science in the service of industry is a fertile source of ideas for war machines, it is a relative matter. Of course as the society, whatever its dynamic strategy, becomes more sophisticated and complex – whether ancient Greece or modern America – a demand is generated for ideas of a wider nature in the social and behavioural sciences and in the humanities.

This book focuses upon the dynamic-strategy process which calls forth the ideas required to achieve a certain end. These ideas come from either a pre-existing stock or emerge for the first time, both in response to strategic demand. Naturally the short-term response of ideas to strategic demand will be limited – limited by the capacity of a society to provide ideas of certain types. But, on the whole, this is not a major real-world problem, because strategic demand is not generated in a vacuum. A particular strategy is chosen because the society concerned has a comparative advantage in that area and believes that the means exist for travelling that path. In other words, the stock of ideas will influence the strategy chosen through the strategic benefit–cost calculation. But, as will be explored further in a future book, ideas do not drive the strategy, merely facilitate it. The driving force comes from the charioteer rather than the navigator.

Once a strategy has been proven successful, the society will continue to pursue it until there are clear indications – in the form of declining rates of return on the strategic investment – that it is not fulfilling their objectives. Hence, the ideas that are supplied become locked into a particular strategy. This is the reason that Greek and Roman civilization developed highly sophisticated ideas concerning imperial and military organization, military machines and equipment, construction, transport and communications; but that their economic technology languished. It was not a matter of the classical mind being better at the former type of ideas – which is the position taken by advocates of the view that ideas are the driving force in society – just that these were the ideas required to implement the conquest strategy. And the conquest strategy was chosen because it was a more cost-effective way of achieving the objectives of materialist man in classical times. Had they chosen the technology strategy then we can speculate that classical economic technology would have developed more rapidly than it did, as would those sciences required to facilitate it. And the history of the world would have been very different. But the choice of a successful strategy depends upon relative benefit–cost calculations, and the technology strategy was just not viable in the ancient period. Ideas can operate as a constraining force and even influence the shape of the dominant dynamic strategy, but they do not constitute the driving force. This position is diametrically opposed to the conventional wisdom (Mokyr, 1990).

Nevertheless, ideas can and do achieve a limited momentum of their own. Before this can occur, however, a society must be able to generate a surplus that can be used, either by individuals or the state, to finance the activities of those – usually known as intellectuals – who specialize in creating ideas. These intellectuals may be wealthy individuals who use their income to finance their intellectual interests, or they may be people with education but no wealth who are employed by the rich as tutors in their households or, later in history, by the state or private foundations in institutions of learning.

Initially, the ideas generated by intellectuals will, broadly speaking, be in areas that are considered relevant to their society. But as the intellectual environment of a society grows larger and more specialized, the terms of reference for the intellectuals become related less to the outside world and more to the internal dynamics of the intellectual world. Intellectuals develop their own objectives, which are pursued with as little reference to the outside world as is possible, and they have their own set of rewards including status, reputation, and influence, as well as income. A cultural flowering, which is often thought to mark the high point of a civilization, occurs when their world of ideas, fed by a successful dynamic strategy's surplus, achieves a considerable momentum of its own. But even this flowering takes place within the broader context of the dynamic strategy chosen by the society – a flowering which can be nipped in the bud by a disapproving society. The blooming of Greek culture in the fifth to fourth centuries BC, for example, involved ideas that had little direct relevance to the prevailing dynamic strategy of war and commerce (let alone technological change). And when it was discovered that it had little immediate relevance to Greece's conquest strategy, it was brought to a close. Rather than being the societal decline as traditionally portrayed, it was just the exercise of tighter control over intellectual and artistic ideas by the dynamic strategists.

The essential point to emphasize is that ideas can only achieve a momentum of their own within limits, both in scope and time. Intellectuals flourish on the profits of economic fortune. When surpluses are abundant, intellectuals achieve considerable independence. In the sunlight of prosperity a thousand flowers bloom. But when the economy is under stress, the paymaster is more careful with his funds and insists upon a more concrete and relevant rate of return on the investment of these hard-won surpluses. If the ideas being generated are not considered 'relevant' and do not appear to be contributing to the dynamic strategy of society, the intellectuals, quite properly, will be called to account.

This was clearly the case in most Western countries during the 1980s and 1990s. Real funding for universities in the Western world declined significantly over these two decades, and a closer supervision of ideas, to ensure that they are more 'relevant' to the perceived objectives of society, was imposed. The past also provides numerous examples of scholars whose ideas exceeded their societies' bounds of tolerance, and were censured – scholars such as Socrates and Galileo.

We also need to explode the myth that the intellectual world operates on a higher moral plane than the outside world. The internal dynamics of the world of ideas are driven by desires similar to those in the world of action – namely to survive (in the intellectual system) and to maximize material advantage (property rights in ideas, status, and advancement in their institution). The riders in the chariot are, after all, siblings. Intellectual communities even employ dynamic strategies that parallel those in the wider society. If, for example, the university system is overfunded and, hence, not very competitive (as in the 1960s throughout the Western world), academic leaders will employ the multiplication strategy and employ as many new staff members as possible, irrespective of their academic quality. By building up their empires, the more successful academic entrepreneurs gain greater control of resources in their institution.

204

On the other hand, if the system is highly competitive, intellectual leaders will aggressively employ a different set of strategies to achieve their objectives. The choice of strategy will depend upon the costs and benefits imposed by funding bodies. There is the 'conquest and colonization' strategy – where funding bodies do not closely supervise use of funds – in which the objective of leading academics or, more appropriately, feudal barons, is not to generate new ideas but, by excessive and aggressive critical attack in seminars, journals (particularly book reviews), and in references for grants and promotions, to prevent others from generating new ideas and also to bring them within their sphere of academic influence. Then there is the 'technological' strategy – when funding bodies establish regular reviews of performance – in which individuals attempt to achieve their objectives by acquiring highly technical, theoretical, mathematical, and statistical skills and by steering academic disciplines in highly specialized and technical directions. By doing so they are able not only to produce large quantities of technical papers with a minimum of intellectual effort – compared with their more empirical and real-world colleagues – but also to dominate the specialist journals, conferences, and policy forums. These are what I have elsewhere called the 'gameplayers', as opposed to the 'realists' of the academic world (Snooks, 1993a: 35–9). This is a distorting strategy, as it has led the intellectual world away from the direct observation and analysis of reality to an indirect theoretical and excessively technical approach.

Finally there is the commerce strategy, which emerges when the financial inputs are very closely related to individual items of academic output. In these circumstances contract research work is exchanged for piecework payment. The astute academic entrepreneur will mass-produce this work and attempt to earn supernormal profits by employing existing university infrastructure and undercutting the commercial competition; by developing highly technical and distinctive models with which the researcher's name is closely linked; and by developing products such as drugs, new genetic material, and high-tech machinery that multinational companies are prepared to purchase at high prices. Needless to say, this type of research is very closely related to the requirements of the dynamic strategies of the day – such as Archemedes' work on Alexander the Great's war machines and modern scientific work on highly sophisticated technology.

My point merely is that the world of ideas is similar to the world of action. It is driven by the same desires and it employs very similar strategies to society as a whole. And it owes its existence and very limited freedom to the society that supports it. If the intellectual world strays too far from the path determined for it by the dynamic strategies of society, it will inevitably be called to account, and that accounting may be painful for those who inhabit that other world. Of course, there is the minority in both the intellectual and real world who pursue their own idiosyncratic, even irrational, objectives. But they have little immediate impact upon reality.

Intellectuals on ideas

Some critics of modern society have, I will argue, misinterpreted the relationship between ideas and the progress of society. This involves two aspects. The first is that most intellectuals believe that ideas drive society; the second is that the intellectual world is or, at least, should be on a higher moral plane than the rest of society, and that it operates according to very different forms of motivation. The view that ideas are the central driving force in society has a long history and includes influential modern thinkers such as John Stuart Mill (1848), Karl Popper (1957; 1966; 1977), Ludwig von Mises (1958), and Friedrich Hayek (1952). Basically they argue that ideas both precede, and can be held responsible for, human action. For example, totalitarianism in the USSR, it is claimed, was due to a philosophical tradition that can be traced from Plato to Marx. And the way to change human actions is by changing their ideas.

Some critics even blame the intellectual class for the ills of the world. Such writers look back romantically to the origins of universities as a time when 'clerks' were motivated by higher moral values, and are critical of academics who deny the origins of their class and sell out to materialistic forces. Accordingly, the intelligentsia is berated whenever it cooperates with the outside world, when it falls short of some intellectual/moral ideal, and when it fails to prevent the world going off the rails. Julien Benda (1959: 143), for example, in *The Betrayal of the Intellectuals*, first published in 1927, argues:

> If I look at contemporary humanity from the point of view of its moral state as revealed by its political life, I see *(a)* A mass in whom realist passions in its two chief forms – class passion, national passion – has attained a degree of consciousness and organization hitherto unknown; *(b)* A body of men [intellectuals] who used to be in opposition to the realism of the masses, but who now, not only do not oppose it, but adopt it, proclaim its grandeur and morality.

It is this switch from the pursuit of spirituality and truth to the acceptance and support of the aspirations of the masses that Benda regarded as the betrayal of the intellectuals.

In similar vein, the distinguished central banker and humanitarian, Dr H.C. Coombs has written (Coombs, 1993: 119):

> Benda was right. Over the decades since he wrote, the intelligentsia has betrayed its social function and obligation to counter the prejudices and hatred which dominate Western societies . . .
>
> The intelligentsia has acquiesced and become the instrument for the subordination of the institutions of education, research and the critical analysis of our civilisation to the demands of the greedy, the selfish and the unscrupulous.

And yet in numbers and potential intellectual and spiritual significance the intelligentsia alone has the capacity to restore sanity to our civilisation . . . Unfortunately, it seems that intellectuals have chosen to entrust the effects of their ideas to the owners of resources and to those who exercise political power.

This approach, which is not uncommon among intellectuals, overrates the importance of ideas in society. It romanticizes the clerical origins of the intelligentsia, which were definitely not on a higher moral plane (Kadish, 1989; Kenyon, 1993). It fails to recognize that the intelligentsia is supported and controlled by society. In effect, the intellectual world depends upon the outcome of materialistic striving. And, as I have suggested, the intelligentsia is not, nor ever has been, 'above' materialism – which, according to the ascetic view, is regarded as greed. If sanity is to be 'restored' in this world, it will only occur when we recognize that oppression by powerful groups cannot be overcome by reforming human nature, but by removing the economic and social controls which have reduced competition between large numbers of competing groups. The greatest insanities the world has ever known have resulted from the seizure of economic and, hence, political power by small but powerful groups – whether they be religious or political fanatics – who are convinced that they know what is best for everyone else. We would do well to resist any attempt by intellectuals – either clerical or environmental – to restore the world to sanity.

An attempt has been made here to place mankind at the centre of the Dynamic Society. We present an essentially new view of the driving force in history called **dynamic materialism**. It is argued that humanity is driven by a genetically determined nature that is focused upon maximizing the probability of survival and prosperity. While there is unity of purpose, the tactical manoeuvres of materialist man emerge from a balance between order and chaos. The drive of materialist man gives rise to various dynamic strategies that, in turn, generate demands for the ideas required to facilitate them. And many of these ideas are provided by practical men and women. In effect, the ordinary decision-maker – the bulk of humanity – rather than the intellectual is the prime mover in history. The intellectual is the navigator who only becomes involved in the great chariot race when called upon to do so by the charioteer. While human ideas are important in a passive way, it is human desires that drive the Dynamic Society.

8

FAMILY OF MAN

The generation of men run on the tide of time.
                                        (Blake, *Milton*, 1804–1808)

The sky has cleared after the morning rain. Not of water that would have collected in the rock holes outside the cave, but of volcanic ash. The great mountain has been smoking for weeks, spewing out foul odours as well as hot ash. Now it is time to collect water from the river in the valley below. A family emerges from a small cave in the side of a hill and walks playfully down to the river rushing by. There are two adults and a child. The father leads the way holding his daughter's right hand; she swings their arms to and fro. The mother, laughing, follows closely behind, placing her feet carefully in his larger footprints deeply etched into the volcanic dust. By the time they turn back by a different path, it has begun to rain. Had they retraced their steps they would have noticed that the rain and sun had crystallized the soft volcanic pavement. Next morning they remain in their cave again as the great mountain smokes heavily. When they re-emerge in the afternoon they notice that their earlier footprints have disappeared under a protective blanket of ash. This very normal family outing occurred 3.6 million years ago in East Africa, and the tribe of 'people' to which they belonged is now known as Australopithecus africanus. *This was the tribe that gave rise, some 1 million years later, to the first family of true humans called* Homo habilis. *This is the portrait of the family of man etched upon the tide of time. The family is the rider in Zechariah's first chariot.*

Family multiplication is the primitive dynamic of human society. This age-old dynamic strategy has been employed by mankind for the past 2 million years to survive and prosper. It is a strategy involving the exploitation of unused natural resources at a given level of technology, through an increase in family numbers. Before the emergence of civilization, family multiplication was the dominant strategy of mankind, and thereafter it played a supporting role to the technological, commerce, and conquest strategies.

The impact of this primitive dynamic can be seen reflected in the distribution of the human race throughout the world. The great migrations of mankind began with *Homo erectus* about 1.6 million years ago, and by 15,000 years BP our species had successfully occupied most climatic and geographic types on the globe. Even the mighty Pacific Ocean had been conquered by the end of the first millennium AD. The only major part of the globe left uninhabited until recently was the extremely isolated and climatically hostile continent of Antarctica. This remarkable achievement, undertaken with the simplest of technologies, attests to the strength of the dynamic driving force within mankind.

THE DYNAMIC STRATEGIES OF MANKIND

This is the first chapter devoted to the dynamic strategies of mankind, which is the very core of my argument about the Dynamic Society. Before considering the first of these – the age-old strategy of family multiplication – we need to outline the way in which decision-makers in human society have attempted to maximize both survival and material advantage. There are, as suggested earlier, four main dynamic strategies: family multiplication, technology, conquest, and commerce, which have their equivalents in the non-human strategies of reproduction, genetic change, predation, and symbiosis. These are not the so-called 'strategies' of economic game theory which, according to accepted English usage, are only 'tactics'.

I have called these economic strategies 'dynamic' because they are deliberately used by mankind to increase material advantage *over the lifetime of the individual* and they lead, where successfully employed, to population increase, geographical expansion, and, in the case of the last three, to economic growth. Dynamic strategies, therefore, are central to the progress of human society. The first two – family multiplication and technology – are strategies that fortuitously increase not only the survival and material prospects of the society employing them but also that of mankind as a whole. It is fortuitous because decision-makers are only attempting to maximize their own material advantage and not that of other peoples. Conquest, however, is a zero-sum game. The gains made by the victor are at the expense of the vanquished. Yet even here, in the longer term, conquest may act as a vehicle for the transmission of higher standards of living and culture. The Roman Empire, for example, grew wealthy on plunder, but it also spread classical culture and technology to Western Europe, which not only enjoyed higher living standards in the longer term but went on to give rise to the Industrial Revolution. This transformation of human society would not have occurred without the ancient strategy of conquest. Commerce is a less clear-cut case than the other strategies. While expanding trade benefits all participants (although not equally), the societies actually employing commerce as a dynamic strategy are able to earn supernormal profits by capturing the lion's share of the gains from trade through monopoly arrangements. Those employing the commerce strategy live off those who have goods and services for exchange. It is equivalent to symbiosis in the natural world.

In the remaining chapters it will be argued that most successful societies specialize in a particular – a dominant – strategy. Palaeolithic societies employed the dominant strategy of family multiplication; in the civilizations of Akkad, Assyria, Macedonia, and Rome the dominant strategy was conquest; commerce was central to the success of the Greeks, the Phoenicians, Venetians, and the Western Europeans in the sixteenth century; and technological change has been the dominant dynamic of Western civilization since the Industrial Revolution. But the dominant strategy was not the sole strategy in any of these examples. To be successful, a dominant strategy needs support from other subsidiary strategies. Conquest, for example, requires technological and commercial support; commerce needs the assistance of technology and military action; technology always calls upon commerce and the military; and even family multiplication needed some support, even if minor, from technology and trade. And at times of crisis the supporting strategies – particularly conquest – may become society's leading focus in the shortrun, such as during Carthage's commercial phase (wars with the Greeks and Romans), and in Western Europe's technology phase (the great wars of the twentieth century).

In addition to the four main dynamic strategies, which are capable of supporting the emergence of highly successful civilizations, there are a number of dependent strategies. The first of these is colonization, which is really an extension of the family multiplication strategy in a world in which all known resources have been brought into production of one sort or another. For a particular society to expand into other locations in such a world, it must establish colonies and provide them with support and protection. Hence, for colonization to be successful it requires military support. While the military threat may only be implied, ultimately, as the native inhabitants become more assertive, force is generally used, although not always successfully (as with the Greek colonies in Italy when Rome was on the march). Colonization is also closely associated with trade. Many colonies were established in order to protect trading routes – as in the case of Sumerian colonies in upper Mesopotamia, and Greek colonies in Italy, Sicily, and the Black Sea region – and once established led to an even greater expansion of trade.

The other major dependent strategy – unable to exist on its own – is isolation. This strategy, however, is negative and has an unfortunate longer-run impact. It involves a policy of deliberate isolation from competitive forces, and can take a number of forms – the establishment of break-away societies in isolation from the rest of the world; the action of established societies to sever all contact with the mainstream of human society; and the use of trade protection also by established society to reduce the intrusion of external competition. These policies are negative because they arise from a desire for isolation from competition that is the forcing ground for growth in the Dynamic Society, and because they further weaken these retreating societies by leading to a loss of economic resilience or power to survive. Despite some shortrun benefits, it is a strategy that will lead ultimately to relative decline and, unless corrective action is taken, extinction.

The importance of these dynamic strategies is their ability to increase the material advantage of the societies employing them. Family multiplication is a way of maximizing the probability of survival by increasing control over natural resources through the extended family. It does not lead, however, to significant economic growth because it does not involve the systematic use of growth-inducing technology or commerce. Indeed, it is an economical substitute for growth-inducing strategies in a world with unused natural resources. The technological change involved is of the type that enables palaeolithic society to expand into new areas rather than that which increases real GDP per capita. On the other hand, the strategies adopted since the Neolithic Revolution are strategies of economic growth for the societies successfully employing them. The reason they have only been used since the Neolithic Revolution is that only since then has the scope for the family multiplication strategy been exhausted, and only since then have the necessary surpluses been available to invest in strategic infrastructure. And the structural and institutional changes that facilitate this economic growth – such as increasing specialization both within and between the market and household sectors (Snooks, 1994a: 14–21, 126–34) and changing property rights – must be treated (in a forthcoming volume) as a response to the dynamic strategies.

Central to the success of these dynamic strategies is investment in the physical and human capital required to undertake them. Dynamic strategies do not just happen. While this may appear obvious, it is generally overlooked or assumed away by those who favour supply-side explanations. In fact, dynamic strategies are the result of individuals responding to their economic environment in an effort to survive and prosper. To do so they abstain from present consumption and invest in a range of physical and human capital required to exploit the prevailing economic conditions. This is a conscious and positive act that involves considerable cost undertaken in the expectation of receiving a positive and sizeable rate of return on their investment in order to achieve a higher material standard of living in the future. Such an act requires confidence in the ability to understand what is happening in the world and to exploit this understanding to the full. It is important to sort out cause and effect here. Higher material standards of living (real GDP per capita) are both the object and – if successful – the effect of strategic investment, while the amount and type of investment depends upon the competitive environment and the factor endowment filtered through relative factor prices. We must not fall into the Keynesian trap of regarding aggregate demand (i.e. GDP per capita) as the driving force behind our dynamic strategies. Of course, mistakes are made in the perception of profitable opportunities and the execution of plans to exploit them, but the remarkable degree of success, as seen in the development of complex civilizations in the past and present, confirms that the Dynamic Society is driven from within by decision-makers who are both economically rational and effective.

The mechanism by which successful individual economic decision-making is transformed into the dynamic strategies of human society was touched upon in Chapter 7. It arises from that remarkable human instinct to imitate the successful actions of others. This imitation effect, which is responsible for amazing swings in fashion in human ideas and actions of all kinds, has been widely commented upon by a diverse range of acute observers of human society. Imitation, which is undertaken by the 'followers' in order to achieve their materialist objectives without costly search activity, would appear to be an important factor in the evolution of mankind. While originality in the few is highly prized, if it were the rule rather than the exception it would lead to chaos as there would be many leaders but no followers. In other words, imitation of successful original ideas by the people is a positive and laudable characteristic of mankind, not a characteristic to be derided as it often is by intellectuals (see Mises, 1958: 191–2).

I will provide just three examples of the use of the imitation effect by scholars. Joseph Schumpeter (1934) uses the imitation effect to great effect in his model of innovation and economic development, by suggesting that successful innovators who earned supernormal profits were quickly followed by a host of imitators all trying to capture some of these economic rents. Ludwig Mises (1958: 188–95) argues that the *ideas* of great men are able to transform society by being 'repeated' by 'common men' who 'do not have thoughts of their own'. And Richard Dawkins (1989: 192–4) believes that human ideas – which he rather idiosyncratically calls 'memes' – are able, just like genes, to 'propagate themselves in the meme pool by leaping from brain to brain via a process which, in the broad sense, can be called imitation', thereby leading to societal evolution.

The imitation effect as employed in this study is closer to that of Schumpeter than to that of either Mises or Dawkins. Indeed, in Chapter 7 I explicitly reject the hypothesis that some sort of intellectual mechanism is the source of growth in human society. Like Schumpeter I argue that what is imitated are the investment projects that generate supernormal profits. But rather than just seeing this imitation effect as driving the longrun, or Schumpeterian, cycle of about fifty years, I see it as generating the dynamic strategies – and not just of technological change – that are responsible for the rise and fall of civilizations. Hence I have called it the **strategic imitation** mechanism.

Successful 'strategic pioneers' respond to changes in relative factor prices by investing in new profitable economic opportunities. These opportunities may be exploited by the introduction of new technological ideas but, even more often in the past, they may be exploited by achieving a monopoly position in commerce, by planning and executing a raid on a neighbour, or simply by increasing family size and moving on to fertile but unutilized land. If these strategic pioneers are successful and earn supernormal profits they will be followed by a swarm of imitators at first in a limited locality, but eventually on a wide front, in order to share in the wealth of the original few. And if the success of these investment projects continues long enough, the tidal wave of 'strategic followers' will transform these new opportunities into a dynamic strategy of nationwide, or indeed civilization-wide, significance. Hence the desire of the common person to maximize his/her material advantage is achieved through the dynamic mechanism of strategic imitation. In the Dynamic Society, imitation is just as important as innovation.

Dynamic strategies are responsible not only for the growth of society, but also for its ultimate downturn. In the initial stages of implementing a dynamic strategy, a society will experience increasing returns to scale. Each new phase of the dynamic strategy will involve greater specialization and better ways of doing things which, in turn, will increase the strategic return on a society's investment and lead to increasing rates of economic growth. But there will come a point in the expansion of any society when its dominant dynamic strategy is beset by diminishing returns, owing to the increasing exploitation of its productive potential within a given technological paradigm, thereby causing growth to slow. This may be an extended process, but finally, when marginal returns on investment in a particular strategy are matched by marginal costs, growth will cease and even become negative. This is what I mean by the 'exhaustion' of a dominant dynamic strategy. Hence, in my model of dynamic materialism, the cessation of growth is a function of diminishing returns, not of scarce natural resources, but of exhausting dynamic strategies. Further growth of our society will depend upon the ability to rejuvenate old strategies or to substitute new strategies, not to increase the natural resource base. If, however, this cannot be achieved, and the forces of chaos overwhelm those of order, the society could collapse.

THE FAMILY MULTIPLICATION STRATEGY

The family is, and always has been, the central institution in human society. It is the prime source of economic motivation, the generator and regenerator of human resources, and the ultimate bestower of economic purpose. During the entire course of human history the dynamic role of the family in society has passed through at least four main phases. Until the beginning of urban living about 9,000 years ago, the extended family or forager band was the very centre of economic activity in larger tribal groups, and nuclear families constituted the core of the forager bands. The small forager bands, which consisted of four or five nuclear families, provided the economic

213

decision-making unit within early human 'society', and organized the hunting and gathering activities required for survival at a subsistence level (Quale, 1992). The wider 'locally functioning', or 'tribal', group of – perhaps twenty – interrelated forager bands formed the loose societal structure that provided: stability and continuity for the smaller family groups; a degree of security; the basis for an exchange of goods and gifts; and a framework for cultural activities. Naturally these societal groupings varied in size and interaction in different economic environments.

This economic structure changed dramatically after the Neolithic Revolution in the Old World about 10,600 years ago and in the New World about 7,700 years ago. With the development of urban life built upon a new agricultural foundation – about 9,000 years ago in the Fertile Crescent and about 4,000 years ago in Mesoamerica – came the division of labour and specialization on an occupational basis, together with the emergence of formal markets in which goods and services and factors of production (labour, land, and capital) were bought and sold. The family in this second phase was still the centre of the urban economy – with much of the goods and services consumed by the family being produced in the household – but a separate market sector had emerged. While these specialized goods and services were produced for sale in local and, ultimately, distant markets, they were mainly produced in household workshops rather than separate estab-lishments. This was true in the civilizations of both the Old and New Worlds. And in these new urban communities the family unit or household – rather than a group of related nuclear families – became the centre of economic decision-making.

Elsewhere I have argued that the market sector emerged in urban society because the family was unable to achieve the size necessary to enable special-ization of tasks and division of labour (Snooks, 1994a: 51–3). My argument is that family economic activity cannot be supervised in the same way as market activity (farm or workshop), because family household workers have non-economic rights (and responsibilities) as well as economic ones. And it is these non-economic rights arising from small cooperative family ventures that are violated under normal systems of supervision which are necessary if their size exceeds about five people. This is why, for example, in wealthy households the size of the paid domestic staff – which is really a market enclave operating within the household precincts – will be significantly larger than a household of family-related workers. As Gregory King (1936) has shown, in 1688 the size of English middle-class and working-class households ranged from four to five people, whereas the size of upper-class house-holds ranged from eight for 'gentlemen', thirteen for knights, sixteen for baronets, twenty for 'spiritual' lords, and forty for 'temporal' lords.

While economic systems of supervision, used to eliminate disruptive and dishonest behaviour, can be imposed on paid or enslaved domestic workers, the same system will rarely be tolerated by family-related household workers who have non-economic rights that emerged from small cooperative family activities. Hence, households of family-related workers have a small optimum size – historically about five people – whereas a household of paid or enslaved domestic workers can achieve a size that rivals the average size of many market establishments. Also, historically, to reduce the average family size below five persons would reduce the productivity of the family to uneconomic levels – levels that would fail to ensure the fulfilment of individual objectives and, hence, would cause the household to break down. Only since the introduction of electrical household equipment after the First World War, which has been substituted for married females who have entered the market workforce, has it been possible to maintain household productivity in the face of declining family size. Only in these circumstances can smaller, more efficient households maximize individual and family material objectives.

The third phase in the development of the family economy occurred during the Industrial Revolution. In England during the late seventeenth century, the household was the focus of economic activity for both males and females as they moved into and out of the market. Both male and female family members worked in and around the house without pay; they worked on any family land for both sustenance and the production of goods for the market; they took advantage of the common land to graze their animals; they sold the output from cottage industrial activity; they worked part-time for wages on nearby farms or in nearby towns; and they worked seasonally on the seas and in the mines. In all these part-time and seasonal activities by adults and children, males and females, the organizing principle was the family. There was, as there had always been, a gender division of labour in both the household and the market sectors, but it was based on a biologically determined comparative advantage, not on a market/male and household/female distinction. The female members of the family generally adopted a supportive role in which they assisted their husbands, fathers, and brothers in these various activities by undertaking less physically demanding – but, nevertheless, exhausting – tasks (John, 1980).

The British Industrial Revolution of the late eighteenth to early nineteenth centuries, however, changed the relationship between the household and the market and created a new gender division of labour. Many former household activities, both paid and unpaid, were taken over by specialized workshops (and farms) in the market sector. These market activities were undertaken on a larger and more specialized basis involving more capital and more embodied technical ideas. Hence there was an increase in the efficiency of production – which was the rationale for households contracting out many of its former activities to market establishments (Snooks, 1994a: 17–21). In the process, the market became the main determinant of the use of family time.

This is particularly evident in the new gender division of labour in the household and the market produced by the Industrial Revolution. During the second half of the nineteenth century, market work became regarded primarily as men's work, and household work was deemed to be women's work. This radical change was technologically rather than socially determined. In other words, the Industrial Revolution was based upon a technology in both the agricultural and industrial sectors that made heavy demands on physical strength. Lighter industries existed, but even here there were tasks – lifting and carrying – that could only be performed with the use of considerable physical effort. Human strength was essential to the success of the Industrial Revolution and its aftermath. Although all sectors of the USA economy experienced growing capital intensity during the interwar period, it was not until after the 1940s that there was a major substitution of automated – and, later, computerized – capital equipment for heavy and skilled labour. This led, for the first time in the history of the human race, to a large-scale expansion in the range of market jobs that were relatively undemanding in terms of physical strength and technical skills – jobs in which women had a comparative advantage (Snooks, 1994a: 78–83).

The fourth phase in the long history of the family economy, therefore, occurred during the second half of the twentieth century. This was nothing less than a **new economic revolution**. As we saw in Chapter 7, there was a major change in factor endowments and, hence, in relative factor prices, which encouraged the widespread adoption of labour-saving, fully automated and, later, computerized capital equipment. This fundamental shift in the technological base produced a change in the gender demand for labour and an increase in the female/male wage ratio. Western families had the incentive to alter their gender division of labour and, accordingly, married females left the household for the market (see Figure 7.1) and labour-saving electrical household equipment was adopted on a wide scale. These fundamental economic changes reduced the average size of the family from five in the early 1920s to three in the early 1990s – a reduction of 40 per cent. The significance of this change cannot be overemphasized. It was the first widespread and permanent change in average household size in human history stretching back before the Neolithic Revolution. It amounted to a reversal of the gender division of family labour that had occurred during the Industrial Revolution. And it accelerated the reduction in birth rates that is central to the so-called 'demographic transition'. The 'demographic transition' is, as shown in Chapter 7, a response to changes in fundamental economic forces.

These four phases in the development of the family economy – from a monopoly of economic activity in palaeolithic times to about one-third of total economic activity in modern times – have witnessed a significantly changing role for the family. None of this, however, diminishes the importance of the family in human society. The family may have contracted out many of its activities to market establishments in order to enjoy the fruits of higher productivity, but it is still the ultimate decision-making unit in the Total Economy. It is, and always has been, the central institution in human society.

What motivates the family?

To understand how the family economy works and how it interacts with the market sector over time, we need to understand its ruling behavioural principle. To do so we build upon the discussion of materialist man in Chapter 7. Most writers on the family assert that its motivation is very different to that of decision-making units in the market. It is generally claimed by social scientists that the market is dominated by 'selfishness' and that the family is ruled by 'altruism'. While the view of some natural scientists about altruism being a major force throughout modern society has already been discussed, we need to tackle the idea that motivation in the household is radically different to that in the market.

If it were true that 'selfishness' dominated the market and 'altruism' the family, a number of improbable implications would arise.

- As the family is the central institution in Western society, it would follow that society is driven not by individuals attempting to maximize their own material interests, but largely by small groups attempting to assist each other at the expense of their own individual interests.
- As Third World countries are even more family oriented than Westernized countries, their societal objectives will be significantly different to those in the West.
- As the history of the human race has been dominated – up to 96 per cent – by the family economy, the major driving force over millions of years must have been self-sacrifice rather than the struggle for the survival of self. In other words, the early history of mankind must have been more caring and altruistic than life today. This suggests that the competitiveness of life has increased with growing prosperity – something like Darwinism in reverse!

These implications hardly fit the evidence about the emergence of mankind and human society presented in earlier chapters. It will also be shown that they cannot be supported by logical argument or empirical data.

Most discussion of the economic behaviour of the family has been impressionistic and has not been characterized by either intellectual rigour or hard evidence. An important exception, however, is the 1992 Nobel Prize winner in economics, Gary Becker. In an important book, *A Treatise on the Family* (1991), Becker explores the ruling behavioural principle in the family – an issue he explored years earlier (Becker, 1976). We can begin with Becker's (1991: 303) claim for his book. He writes:

> Sophisticated models tracing the economic effects of selfishness have been developed during the last 200 years as economic science has refined the insights of Adam Smith. Much is now known about the way selfishness allocates resources in different markets. Unfortunately, an analysis of equal sophistication has not been developed for altruism.

For it is 'altruism', Becker claims, that dominates family life. He also says:

> If I am correct that altruism dominates family behavior perhaps to the same extent as selfishness dominates market transactions, then altruism is much more important in economic life than is commonly understood. The pervasiveness of selfish behavior has been greatly exaggerated by the identification of economic activity with market transactions.

And he sums up this theme by stating: 'Even if altruism were confined to the family, it would still direct the allocation of a large fraction of all resources'. Other economists (Boulding, 1973; Phelps, 1975; Collard, 1978; Tullock, 1978; Frech, 1978; Samuelson, 1983) have attempted to analyse the concept of altruism, but it is Becker who makes a sharp distinction between 'selfishness' in the market and 'altruism' in the home.

In order to evaluate this claim, we need to understand exactly what Becker means by the words 'selfishness' and 'altruism'. 'Selfishness', according to Becker, is the principle that dominates market activity, with firms attempting to maximize profits and consumers attempting to maximize utility derived from the consumption of market goods. 'Selfishness' is equated with the maximization of *individual* utility. 'Altruistic', on the other hand, 'means that h's [first individual's] utility function depends positively on the well-being of w [second individual] . . . and "effectively" means that h's behavior is changed by his altruism' (Becker, 1991: 278). In other words, the altruist gains utility, or satisfaction, from seeing other family members increasing their utilities, and that this has an important influence on his/her economic decision-making. He further claims, without evidence, that while selfishness dominates market behaviour, altruism dominates household behaviour.

The implication of Becker's argument appears to be that rational economic man possesses two very different hats, one for work and the other for home; and that he behaves very differently when wearing one or other of these hats. This impression is reinforced by the introductory and concluding remarks in his altruism chapter, where he makes wide-ranging claims for the implications of these different behavioural responses. But, in the body of the chapter, Becker focuses entirely upon a number of narrow technical conditions of behaviour which he quite misleadingly calls 'selfish' and 'altruistic'. In other words, while he makes large claims for the implications of his altruism principle in society, his theoretical use of the term is narrowly and technically directed. As if in anticipation of this type of criticism, Becker (ibid.: 279) writes:

> Since an altruist maximizes his own utility (subject to his family income constraint), he might be called selfish, not altruistic, in terms of utility. Perhaps – but note that h also raises w's utility through his transfers to w. I am giving a definition of altruism that is relevant to behavior – to consumption and production choices – rather than giving a philosophical discussion of what 'really' motivates people.

But this is attempting to have one's cake and eat it too.

In *Portrait of the Family* (Snooks, 1994a: 42–6), I argued that Becker's technical definitions of 'selfish' and 'altruistic' are very different to the normal meaning attached to these words, and they are also inconsistent with the more general, and empirically unsupported, conclusions he draws from his analysis. As we saw in Chapter 7, the word 'selfish' implies abnormal behaviour, and is inappropriate as a description of the normal human behaviour involved in attempting to maximize either profits or the utility derived from consumption. Selfish behaviour only occurs when an individual pursues self-interest to an irrational extreme. It is not selfish to maximize one's individual utility through individual action. Nor is it altruistic to cooperate with other people, whether they are related or not, in order to maximize individual utility even if, in the process, an individual's self-interested action leads to an increase in the utility of other people. Indeed, to achieve one's materialistic objectives it may be necessary to buy support from others by increasing their material advantage. Individual and cooperative actions are just different *means* applied in different circumstances to achieve the same *end* – the maximization of individual utility.

This is not just an argument about the meaning of words. It is an attempt to resolve the confusion that Becker causes by inappropriately drawing wider implications from his technical analysis. The issue is very important and must be resolved because he gives the impression that households operate on fundamentally different principles to those governing the behaviour of firms. Becker (1991: 299) says, for example, that 'the same persons are altruistic in their families and selfish in their shops and firms'. A less confusing, and admittedly less exciting, term than 'altruism' is *'cooperation'* – cooperation between individuals in order to maximize their separate utility functions by maximizing their joint objective function. Such behaviour is as relevant for firms as it is for households. Indeed, it is difficult to imagine a successful firm composed of uncooperative individuals, precisely because their individual returns depend upon their ability to work together for the good of the group.

The motivation for the family and the market is, therefore, one and the same – to maximize material advantage. While the means may differ to a degree – although not by as much as Becker suggests – the ends are the same. It may be the case that individual maximization is achieved more often through cooperative behaviour in the family than in the firm, but we should not lose sight of the fact that it is individual motivation that drives both sectors. Materialist man is definitely not a Jekyll and Hyde character, depending upon whether he is in the home or the office. The Total Economy is not a dualistic, but rather an integrated, economy. We must resist being led into that seemingly endless confusion in the literature between ends and means.

In the light of a more integrated and holistic analysis, the contradictions that arise from a dualistic approach to human society just disappear. There is no conflict between the family economy and the market economy in modern Westernized societies; there is no motivational conflict between the Third World and the West; and it is just not true that the majority of human history has been dominated by self-sacrifice rather than self-interest. It is clear that if man were motivated primarily by self-sacrifice, the human race long ago would have lost the battle for survival. As Darwin was at pains to point out, one must survive in order to reproduce. This may be unpalatable to many but it is the inescapable reality of life and must be squarely faced.

Nor is it possible to support the concept of altruism in the family by reference to the arguments of sociobiologists about 'kin selection'. As we saw in Chapter 6, the basis of this idea is that the degree to which individuals are prepared to risk their own welfare to ensure the welfare of others depends upon the strength of the genetic relationship ('generation distance') between them. In the colourful language of Richard Dawkins (1989), altruism at the individual level is an outcome of selfishness at the gene level, whereby genes are attempting to maximize their numbers in the gene pool. This hypothesis is based upon the unproven assumption that there is a gene that 'makes' individuals help their relatives. Only if this is true will that gene, which is carried by all family members, prosper relative to the selfish gene. What I have attempted to show in Chapter 7 is that family relationships depend not upon the 'generation distance' between people sharing the same genes, but on the 'economic distance' between people sharing the same objective function. Individuals promote the interests of the group – whether it be family or firm – in order to maximize their own material advantage. A recent attempt (Bergstrom, 1995: 59) to apply kin selection to economic game theory has led to the construction of totally unrealistic and misleading models in which '[i]ndividuals do not consciously choose strategies [i.e. tactics]. Instead, their actions are programmed by their genetic structure.' Absurd models of this nature invariably emerge when deductive economists import models from other disciplines rather than employ the historical method.

The proponents of kin selection would find it difficult to explain the significant and growing frequency of males abandoning their own children along with their first wives, in order to raise the genetically unrelated children of their new wives. There is no such problem with my 'economic distance' argument. Owing to the materialist objectives of individuals, the current genetically unrelated family will occupy a concentric sphere with a shorter economic distance to the self than the earlier and genetically related family. The reason is that the new genetically unrelated family is more important to the individual's current material welfare than his former, genetically related family.

Nevertheless, affection and love are sentiments compatible with the cooperative economic relationships within families under normal conditions. In fact, these feelings make family cooperation easier to achieve. And in a relatively small number of cases self-sacrifice and other economically irrational actions can and do exist. It is fortunate that we are able to find fulfilment in what is materially necessary. The real test of these relationships, however, is to be found in periods of conflict, when individual family members are called upon to decide between their own material interests and those of the family. The few will always behave self-sacrificially, but the vast majority will always act in their own individual self-interest. That is why so many modern families, where independent sources of income are available to both partners, break down.

A dominant dynamic strategy

Family multiplication is the dominant dynamic strategy of palaeolithic societies. In this type of society a family leader could maximize his material returns by increasing the size of the family group, either as an extended family or as a closely related group of family units. This involved a deliberate increase in family labour in order to achieve greater control over natural resources and the 'income' derived from them. The outcome was to increase his probability of survival and, with survival, to consume. The maximization of the probability of survival, however, must not be confused with the maximization of reproduction. Too many offspring would reduce a family's economic resilience in the face of fluctuating climatic conditions by reducing the average consumption of its members to precarious levels. The number of children will increase only until the perceived benefit of an extra child (in terms of economic support in old age) is balanced by the cost (in terms of forgone current consumption of all other family members) of producing and maintaining that child.

Family reproduction underlies **economic expansion** – defined here as an increase in the number of households without any increase in real household income – which is the essence of the palaeolithic dynamic. This can occur either by a more intensive use of existing resources under the prevailing technology or, if all resources are fully employed, by bringing new natural resources into the palaeolithic system of production. Hence, as families grow and mature they give rise to further families in such a way that the frontier of human settlement on this planet expands. Settlement expansion occurs because each new household requires the same quantity and quality of natural resources if it is to enjoy a similar standard of living to the average of all other families. Elsewhere (Snooks, 1994a: 126–9) I have called this type of economic expansion **environmental dynamic change** (EDC), which is contrasted with **technological dynamic change** (TDC) arising from a more intensive use of existing resources through technical change which generates an increase in both the number of families *and* the real value of family 'income' even when all resources are fully utilized. This is the essence of the post-palaeolithic dynamic.

The growing utilization of the world's natural resources through family multiplication and migration involves deliberate and conscious decision-making. It also involves costs. These costs are, in effect, investments in both the creation of human labour and in the means required to migrate to other regions. Sometimes these relocation costs are minimal as access to adjacent land is direct, but at other times when natural barriers are encountered, the costs are quite considerable as the migration involves crossing large rivers, high mountain ranges, wide deserts, and deep oceans. To do so requires the acquisition of human and physical capital in the form of organizational and navigational skills, various means of primitive transport (canoes or rafts), together with the means of scaling mountains, cutting through dense undergrowth, and surviving parched deserts (tools, ropes, and carrying vessels). These costs and risks are undertaken in the expectation of discovering rich and unoccupied land. In this way the human race broke out of Africa and spread around the entire world.

The main constraint upon family multiplication, or environmental dynamic change, in a pre-market society with a given technology, is the quantity and quality of accessible natural resources. With the pressure of population on natural resources, marginal consumption will decline, and population growth will slow, cease, and possibly even reverse itself until a balance between population and resources is achieved. The duration of this equilibrium will depend upon the degree of competition. In completely isolated societies such as Aboriginal Australia it lasted for 20,000 years. But where tribes jostled for access to resources it led to the forging of a new technological paradigm called the Neolithic Revolution. Hence the *ultimate* constraining force is not Malthusian but strategic, involving the exhaustion of dynamic strategies not the exhaustion of physical resources. The real dynamic crisis is not the Malthusian crisis but the **strategic crisis**.

THE HISTORICAL ROLE OF THE FAMILY

Running on the tide of time

The process of family multiplication passed through a number of phases during the 2 million years down to the present. It began from a very small population base in East and South Africa. This was the era of *Homo habilis*, whose range was limited because he was a scavenger rather than a hunter. Existence was precarious and expansion was gradual and uncertain. But the speed and certainty of this expansion increased perceptibly with the emergence, at least 1.6 million years ago, of the larger brained *Homo erectus*, who had the ability and the tools to hunt. This was a great step forward, and it has been referred to here as the Palaeolithic (or hunting) Revolution. With this new technology, which was the response of a more intelligent species of man to the same conditions of life, *Homo erectus* was able to break out of Africa to colonize Asia Minor and the less bleak parts of Asia and Europe.

This was the 'great dispersion' of early men, which took place between 1.6 and 0.3 million years BP (see Figure 8.1).

During the great dispersion, the more accessible and fruitful lands were colonized first by small groups (probably numbering twenty to fifty) of mobile people. These lands included the Fertile Crescent, India, Southeast Asia, and China. It is thought that the groups may have initially followed a coastal route and only later struck inland (Thorne and Raymond, 1989: 16). In these lands there was an abundance of plants, fruits, and small animals. The cooler lands, where eking out an existence was more difficult, were left to last. But eventually the continued use of the family multiplication strategy led *Homo erectus* further north into the colder lands of Europe and Asia, where plant life and smaller, more easily captured animals were less abundant. Gathering fruits, berries, and roots that were more limited in supply, and hunting the larger, more dangerous animals, called upon greater manual and organizational skills. Greater effort was also required. But within an increasingly competitive environment *Homo erectus* made the effort and adapted to these more inhospitable conditions. He had little choice if he was to survive and prosper. It may have been this struggle to survive in a harsh environment that gave rise to Neanderthal man more than 120,000 years ago who, with a larger brain, was able to handle this difficult environment with greater ease.

About 100,000 years ago modern man emerged on the world stage from Africa (or both Africa and Asia). With a more complex, but not a larger, brain than his Neanderthal cousin, modern man swept all before him. As an intelligent and resourceful hunter, he tackled, and eventually exterminated, the largest animals that Africa, Europe, and Asia had to offer. He also eliminated earlier species of his own line of descent. There was no altruism here. Owing to a greater intelligence and power over speech, modern humans were able to colonize the rest of the world at a greater rate than had been experienced earlier (see Figure 8.1 – some dates vary from text). About 40,000 years ago human foraging bands moved into Siberia and from there into North America possibly 20,000 years ago. By 13,000 years BP they had reached the tip of South America. Also about 60,000 years ago *Homo sapiens sapiens* migrated to New Guinea and Australia in search of new land, most likely following and destroying more archaic forms of *Homo sapiens* who may have reached these regions about 100,000 (possibly even 140,000) years ago. Excavations in Australia show that both Java (heavier-featured types) and China (more delicately featured types) were sources of these migrations (ibid.: 46). From New Guinea, family groups embarked eastwards into the Pacific, reaching Fiji about 3,000 years ago, Tahiti about 2,000 years ago, Hawaii about 1,600 years ago, Easter Island about 1,500 years ago, and New Zealand about 1,000 years ago (ibid.).

This gradual expansion of the human race throughout the world stemmed from our adoption of the dynamic strategy of family multiplication with a

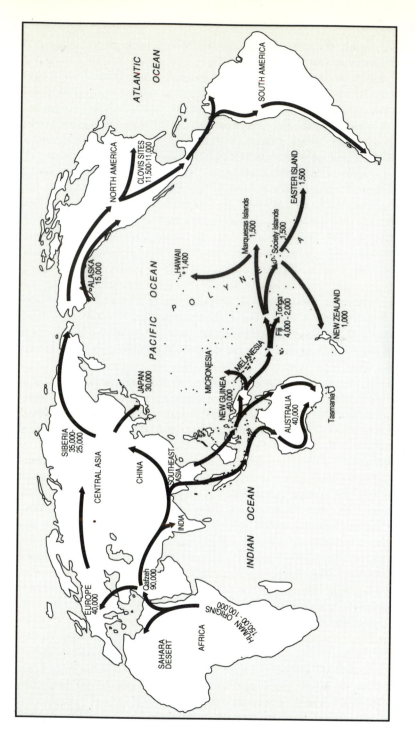

Figure 8.1 The 'great dispersion' of modern man (years before present)
Source: Drawn from data in Renfrew and Bahn (1991).

given level of living standards. It is important to stress that this process of family multiplication did not occur automatically, rather it was in response to the demand of family leaders for more labour to gain greater control over resources in order to achieve their materialistic objectives. It was a deliberate strategy and not an accidental outcome.

As each new species of mankind emerged, there was an increase in the ability to pursue this strategy faster and further. The technological base, the manual and organizational skills, and the level of material living standards were different for each species of man over this 2–3 million year period, as the emergence of each new species from life's competitive struggle to survive amounted to a quantitatively different response to the same set of environmental conditions owing to their different intellectual and, hence, physical capacities. Improvements in skill and technology, however, were a function not just of genetic change but also of economic change. This all occurred within the same type of economic system – hunting, scavenging, and gathering. Each new species of mankind was able to carry this economic system more quickly to previously inaccessible regions, and to gain access to larger animals, thereby increasing the density of their population. But their very success brought this economic system to an end, as the larger animals – the mega-fauna – were hunted to extinction 17,000–10,000 years ago in Europe and 11,000–10,000 years ago in the Americas. This increased the competition between hunting groups and, in those unique **funnels of transformation** – the Fertile Crescent and the Mesoamerican isthmus – led to the emergence of agriculture in the Old World about 10,600 years ago and the New World about 7,700 years ago. These 'funnels of transformation' are clearly illustrated in Figure 8.2.

The palaeolithic society of man, therefore, possessed an essential dynamic that transported it from its origins in East and South Africa about 2 to 3 million years ago to the ends of the Earth about 15,000 years ago. This great human odyssey of early hunter–gatherers, which transcended even the imagination of Homer, attests to the powerful dynamic nature of human society. It was pursued with great determination and persistence in order to maximize the probability of survival and, within a society that could not carry surpluses forward into the future, of material advantage. It took place through increasing the number of family units and, thereby, exploiting unused natural resources. It was achieved with only the simplest of technology – stone axe and blade, bow and arrow, throwing stick, club, carrying bag and container, and simple raft and canoe – but with considerable manual and organizational skills.

When the limits of settlement were reached – when the family multiplication strategy within palaeolithic society finally had been exhausted – there were two portentous outcomes. Where human society experienced highly competitive conditions, both in the Old World and the New World, the exhaustion of this age-old dynamic strategy provided the economic

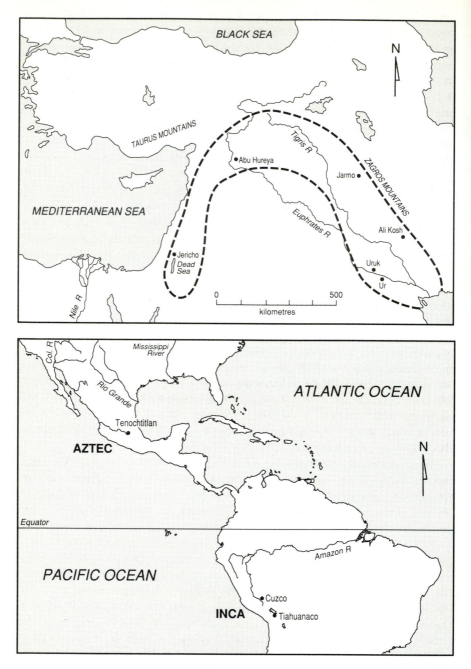

Figure 8.2 'Funnels of transformation' in the Old and New Worlds
(a) The Fertile Crescent (defined by broken line)
(b) The Mesoamerican isthmus

incentives that led to a new technological paradigm – the Neolithic (or agricultural) Revolution. But where human society was isolated from competitive conditions, extremely longrun equilibrium, or the stationary state, was achieved by abandoning the family multiplication strategy in favour of maintaining the existing family structure through population control. The stationary state, of course, does not mean the absence of change in the number or structure of families and kinship groups at various levels, just that these changes were largely limited by the extent of fluctuations in the physical and disease environments. Nor does it mean that these societies – which in Australia flourished in environments ranging from the tropical to the 'arctic' – were other than energetic or viable, just that this energy was of a zero-sum nature in the longrun. And it does not mean that palaeolithic societies were devoid of competition. In fact, owing to the relatively large number of families and tribes in a given region, there was sufficient low-level competition to maintain the viability of their economy, but not sufficient to transform it. This only occurred in the presence of a geographical 'funnel of trans-formation', as in the Fertile Crescent and the Mesoamerican isthmus. What it does mean, however, is that in the station-ary state mankind is at the mercy of changing external conditions and adjusts its role from the proactive to the reactive. But only in the extre-mely rare case of complete isolation.

An important aspect of the internal dynamics of an economy in longrun equilibrium is that technical change might be called forth to maintain population and living standards at the old levels in the face of deteriorating environmental conditions. This technical change, however, is subsidiary to the family-formation strategy. The same process occurs in modern society, since technical changes, which are subsidiary to the dominant technological strategy, are required to repair environmental damage to prevent a decline in both population and living standards.

Both the isolated and the competitive parts of human society, therefore, responded to their circumstances in an economically rational way. What was portentous about these two very different responses was that ultimately the barriers between these societies would be surmounted, and only one would survive.

The structure of the family in history

To show how the family multiplication strategy was employed by decision-makers in hunter–gatherer society, we need to examine the structure of their family economy. This can only be done here at a general level which, unfortunately, obscures the rich diversity of this type of society. While the basic technology was similar – involving the use of digging sticks; simple devices for catching and trapping fish, birds, and animals (stone and wooden fish and animal traps); simple shelters from the elements; rafts and canoes; stone axes and blades; bows and arrows, spears and throwing sticks; and carrying bags – the structure of the economy and society varied according to the nature of the environment. In regions where edible plants were abundant, as in the tropics, gathering activities constituted a much larger proportion of the Total Economy than did hunting. At the other extreme, where there was little or no plant life, as in the arctic, hunting activities dominated the Total Economy. In between these extremes, the structure of the economy – the balance between hunting, gathering, and 'household' activities (preparation of food and childrearing) – varied considerably.

For these reasons, the roles played by males and females in the Total Economy also varied widely. Where hunting and warfare were insignificant, the bulk of economic activities, primarily gathering and 'household', were undertaken by women. In these societies the status of women reached its highest point. While this never approached a matriarchal form, there are instances – as in the case of Hopi Indians – of matrilineal descent (Keesing, 1975). On the other hand, where hunting was the main economic activity – as in Inuit (Eskimo) communities – the contribution and status of males was clearly dominant. In these societies 'excess' female infants were systematically killed immediately following birth. In Inuit communities, as late as the 1930s, infanticide extended to about 40 per cent of female births (Ponting, 1991: 23). Different social structures also have an economic–ecological origin.

Despite this diversity of economy and society arising from different environmental conditions, the universality of the family multiplication strategy and the similarity of various versions of palaeolithic technology makes it possible to discuss the hunter–gatherer society in a general way.

What was the structure of the family of man prior to the Neolithic Revolution? When did something resembling the nuclear family first emerge? There are different views on this, but a major line of interpretation (Lovejoy, 1981: 348) suggests that 'the nuclear family and human sexual behavior may have had their ultimate origin long before the dawn of the Pleistocene'. As John Eccles (1989: 113) remarks, this involves 'a timing that would have placed it with the Australopithecines'. In other words, the nuclear family characterized the early stages of hominid evolution more than 3 million years ago, which is prior to the emergence of *Homo habilis*, the first true man. Keesing (1975: 134) also claims that: 'Even the late Australopithecines of two million years ago, and almost certainly *Homo erectus* of half a million years ago, are probably well on their way to a human-like family.' The best evidence for this is the set of *Australopithecus* family footprints frozen in volcanic rock laid down in East Africa about 3.6 million years ago (Eccles, 1989), which is the basis for the italicized introduction to this chapter.

The traditional interpretation of this early emergence of pair-bonding is that the nuclear family was the optimum evolutionary strategy for hominids because it maximized the probability of survival of hominid offspring

(Lovejoy, 1981: 348). This arrangement is regarded as central to the success of early hominids, who existed in such small numbers that every advantage had to be exploited if they were to survive as a species. A problem with this type of argument is that it possesses strong teleological overtones. Even if the Australopithecines, or the members of *Homo habilis*, understood the link between sexual intercourse and birth, it is unlikely that the possibility of more efficient parenting would have led to pair-bonding. What sort of incentive is this to male and female primates? A more persuasive argument is that family cooperation and formation is an effective way of maximizing individual material advantage. Hence, for pair-bonding to occur and be maintained, it had to provide significant benefits for both male and female participants. There can be little doubt that for the female and infant, the nuclear family provided protection, food, and assistance during the long years of child-rearing. And for the male it provided care and gathered food during periods of convalescence after the many injuries received during the dangerous activities of hunting and raiding (Quale, 1992: 27). In addition it would have become obvious that a gender division of labour based upon comparative advantage – with adult males responsible for the hunting and protection, and the adult females undertaking the gathering, child-rearing, and other 'household' activities – increased individual consumption for both partners. These mutual material benefits, which could only be ensured in a close relationship involving rights and responsibilities, were surely the early origin of the nuclear family. The widespread idea of the desire for maximization of reproduction is nothing more than a myth.

Needless to say, the nuclear family did not stand alone then, just as it does not stand alone today. It has been suggested that in the early history of mankind, nuclear families found benefits – in the form of hunting and security – by forming small forager bands. By about 100,000 years ago these forager bands may have included, on average, about fifteen to twenty-five men, women, and children. As these bands were based upon team hunting, which required close cooperation, the men were all family-related, whereas most of the women were from other bands or kinship groups to prevent inbreeding and to form alliances with a wider network of people (ibid.: 27). Each forager band, therefore, was linked to a number of other bands to form what have been called 'locally functioning groups' but which, for convenience, I will call 'tribes'. These bands, which were linked by marriage, usually shared a hunting territory, cooperated in large hunting drives, and met together each year for festivities and for gift exchanges (a form of disaster insurance, in my view, and the beginning of trade). In the case of Australian Aborigines, the bands were in the vicinity of twenty-five people and their tribe (or clan) included between seven and neneteen such bands, depending upon environmental conditions (ibid.: 29; Keesing, 1975: 79–84). This was the nature of palaeolithic society which revolved around the natural rhythms of hunting and gathering.

The evidence suggests that, for a basically monogamous group, the optimum size of a tribe was about 500 men, women, and children. A group of this size ensured 'enough women of childbearing age for a fairly equal ratio of men to women at the time of reproductive maturation and potential mating' (Quale, 1992: 30). A significantly larger group would impose unacceptable costs of organization on a relatively unsophisticated society. If the tribe were polygamous on either the male or female side, it could be smaller than 500 people, because a spouse would not be required for each adult. But it is unlikely that monogamy and polygamy would have been randomly distributed in a particular region, as the pressure to conform to a particular type of family relationship must have been intense, owing to the difficulty that the smaller polygamous group would experience in competing with the larger monogamous group.

While the evidence suggests that bilateral monogamy – where children relate equally to the families of both parents – was the norm in hunter–gatherer societies, this does not deny the existence of alternative family structures in special circumstances. There is nothing preordained or sacrosanct about the nuclear family, which should be viewed as a maximizing response to the general competitive conditions of life on Earth. It is the basic unit of cooperation required to maximize individual material advantage. Where special conditions prevail, both in terms of competition and physical environment, the unit of cooperation will differ from the monogamous norm. It is claimed, for example, that a form of gerontocracy emerged in Australian Aboriginal groups in the more arid central regions of the country as the climate became drier and, accordingly, experience and wisdom became more highly prized. This is also the case with forager groups in the more arid areas of West Africa, and along the southern shore of the Mediterranean to central Afghanistan. This form of family organization usually involved gerontocratic polygamy in which the old male tribal leaders monopolized all the young fertile women. Other arrangements can be found, but are minor and the result of special circumstances (Keesing, 1975).

It has been argued (Quale, 1992) that the dictates of survival in a competitive world led forager bands to strive for a balance in which there were 'three-actives-to-two-dependants'. While individual bands varied widely in size and structure, the typical band might include (ibid.: 35):

> five married couples (one in each decade from the late teens to the early 50s), four infants, three young children, three older children, two not-yet-married postpubertal young people, one widowed childless woman who had become a second wife to one of the older husbands, and two widowed parents of younger married people.

With the emergence of settled agricultural communities after about 8000 BC, forager bands linked to tribes gave way to households within villages or urban communities. At this stage, households rather than forager bands attempted to achieve the optimum ratio of 3 to 2 between workers and dependants. Such an arrangement might involve: husband and wife, two dependent children and a sibling of the paired group; or it might include a dependent parent rather than a second child. Of course, there would have been considerable variation of individual households around this average or typical nuclear family. As far as the size of the average family is concerned, the evidence suggests a remarkable consistency between widely separated regions and over very long periods of time. The average household size in forager and subsistence farming communities falls in the range 4.5 to 6.5 persons (Quale, 1992: 46–53). What is even more remarkable is that a household of about five persons appears to be the optimum size not only for pre-urban society, but for civilized society in the Old World from the Minoan civilization, c. 1600 BC (Castleden, 1990: 7) until the time of the First World War (Snooks, 1994a: 66) and in the Mayan civilization of the New World (Webster, 1977: 341). The dramatic change in family size from five to three people in the West since the First World War is, therefore, of great historical significance.

Against the background of this family structure we can more easily understand the process of family multiplication in palaeolithic society. An emerging forager band would gradually grow, both by absorbing surplus individuals from associated groups and through procreation. To do so it would be necessary for the growing band to migrate away from existing bands in order to take advantage of new natural resources. As the band approached the optimum size of about twenty-five people, breakaway nuclear families would create new bands, all the while expanding into new territory. Similarly, as the tribe, which expands with the addition of new bands, approaches the optimum size of about 500 people, the larger structure would divide and form new tribal boundaries involving new territories. In this way family units, forager bands, and larger tribes would have gradually spread across the habitable face of the Earth. This was the process of household multiplication – the dynamic of human society before the Neolithic Revolution.

While there were unused natural resources available, new family units would be formed, new forager bands would develop, and new tribes would emerge, because the leaders at all levels could, thereby, extract the greatest material advantage from the competitive world around them. More families and bands meant:

- more assistance with hunting and gathering;
- greater access to natural resources through kinship groups at various levels;
- more hunter/warriors to keep raiding parties at bay and to resolve difficulties over disputed territory by show of force;
- more goods, services, and people to extend one's influence throughout adjoining territories.

In effect, those making economic decisions within kinship groups at various levels, in their struggle for survival, generated a demand for new labour –

for family multiplication – to extend their influence geographically over natural resources.

In this competitive struggle, those who were successful achieved, what I have called, economic resilience – the power over natural resources and, hence, over survival. These successful individuals were the leaders who created new kinship groups at various levels. In contrast, those who were unsuccessful in this process of family multiplication – because of bad luck or bad decisions concerning spouse, territory, or tactics (either hunting or raiding) – lost the power of economic resilience. Their kinship groups at various levels would have fallen in size below economically viable numbers, and the rump would have been absorbed by newly developing groups or slaughtered in territorial disputes. Even in a state of abundant resources, survival was a matter of intense struggle – the unsuccessful were reduced to poverty and ultimately disappeared forever, while the successful flourished and passed on their genes, strategies, and tactics to the generations that followed.

The case of Aboriginal Australia

The manner in which the family multiplication strategy worked itself out can be seen quite clearly in the case of Aboriginal Australia. It is generally accepted that the first human inhabitants migrated to Australia from South-east Asia at least 40,000–50,000 years ago, and recent sedimentary evidence subjected to the optically stimulated luminescence (OSL) technique at the Australian National University (Roberts, *et al*, 1994) has pushed this back, with a high degree of probability, to 60,000 BP. Some (Thorne and Raymond, 1989: 49) appear comfortable with a beginning point as early as 100,000 years ago, while recent unconfirmed evidence (drill cores 80 kilometres off the coast of Cairns) has suggested that this might eventually be pushed back to 140,000 years. It is thought by some (Bowdler, 1977) that the original inhabitants, who were reinforced by small waves of new arrivals, initially occupied the northern coast of Australia and then, through the combined processes of family multiplication and immigration, moved south around the coastal fringes. In this way they could have reached Tasmania within one or two thousand years (Thorne and Raymond, 1989: 59). At the same time some bands and tribes would have moved inland where the environment was suitable – particularly along water courses – or where population pressure was 'intense'. Alternatively it has been argued (Birdsell, 1957) that the new arrivals radiated out relatively quickly in all directions from their entry point in Arnhem Land. The exact settlement routes may never be known, particularly as the coastal plains of that period are now under the sea.

As these relatively new arrivals faced an abundant supply of resources in a land both accessible and blessed with a relatively moderate climate, it is reasonable to expect that expansion through family multiplication would have reached the maximum rate possible in a palaeolithic society. In other words, the main period of population growth would have occurred during the first half of the period of Aboriginal occupation rather than the last few millennia as some (Beaton, 1983) have claimed. Certainly, the archaeological evidence suggests that by 20,000 years BP all parts of Australia had been inhabited. Habitation sites have been dated in Tasmania between 20,000 and 23,000 years ago, and in the (then) glacial uplands of south-eastern Australia about 20,000 years ago. Hence by about 20,000 years BP, the natural resources of Australia were probably fully exploited, given the palaeolithic technology available. As Australia was effectively isolated from outside competition, particularly after the final rising of the seas from 15,000 to 5,000 years ago, Aboriginal society was able to achieve an extremely longrun equilibrium between population and natural resources by abandoning the family multiplication strategy in favour of population control. At this time the population may have been roughly the same size as it was in 1788, which, according to Noel Butlin (1983; 1993), was about 1 million people. At this stage the system of land use would have stabilized but been subject to variation as the need arose from climatic and economic changes. While each tribe (or clan) had property rights over a reasonably clearly defined 'estate', it also had hunting rights over a larger range because of marriage relationships with other tribes. The combined area of the core estate and the surrounding area over which they could range has been called a 'domain' (Stanner, 1965). Naturally the size of these areas varied according to the nature of the climate, soils, and vegetation.

Equilibrium between population and natural resources does not imply that population numbers remained unchanged. Changes in climate, physical environment, and disease – particularly in response to the advances and contractions of the polar ice caps – would have generated fluctuations in population numbers and led to geographical advances and retreats. But this should not be thought of as a simple relationship. At any particular time, existing bands and tribes would have resisted the adverse pressure of climatic change by developing new skills and techniques in order to maintain their population levels and living standards.

Over the 7,000 years before British settlement the Australian climate, in the wake of the last ice age, became drier and the inland regions became more arid. While some of the mountainous regions became more accessible, the coastal strips were reduced in area, and the inland regions, became less productive. The hypothesis I wish to propose is that in order to maintain existing populations and living standards in inland regions it became necessary to develop new skills, new tools, and new organizational forms. These changes probably took place in the worst affected areas and then gradually spread elsewhere. This would account for the recent evidence of the development of more sophisticated tools during the last five millennia before British settlement (Mulvaney, 1987: 81–6). This modest increase in technology may, in

233

more productive areas, have actually permitted further family multiplication and, hence, population increase. Accordingly, even an economy experiencing the stationary state is dynamic – it takes imagination, skill, and flexibility to maintain a steady state in a changing environment.

In fact, the hypothesis presented here resolves the problem that some authors have had in reconciling the early (20,000 BP) achievement of a maximum level of population with the changes, albeit modest, in technology achieved towards the end of the period (Dingle, 1988: 49–55). It is neither persuasive nor necessary to argue, as Beaton (1983) has done, that population was caught in a low-level trap for about 40,000 years and then increased rapidly in the last 5,000 years. In fact, this is a totally unrealistic scenario which was not experienced elsewhere. As discussed in more detail later, palaeolithic societies elsewhere at the same stage of development increased their populations at rates of about 0.007 per cent per annum – a doubling every 9,500 years – rather than a rate approaching zero before 5,000 BP and an unrealistically high rate (thirteen times as high as that experienced by other palaeolithic societies) of 0.092 per cent per annum over the final five millennia as in the Beaton hypothesis. My estimates for population growth during the 40,000 years before 20,000 BP are similar to those observed in other palaeolithic societies facing abundant, unused natural resources.

It should be emphasized, however, that this modest improvement in skills, tools, and, possibly, organization, was subsidiary to the basic family multiplication strategy. It was used to maintain the achievement of the earlier family multiplication strategy, and its impact was merely to fine-tune their palaeolithic economic system, not to cause a technological paradigm shift. In very general terms this is similar to the purpose of technological change adopted in Europe during the Middle Ages – it was aimed at fine-tuning, or getting the most from, the agricultural system inherited from ancient civilizations. But it is extremely unlikely that this modest change in skills and tools would have led to a technological paradigm shift as it did in Europe in the late eighteenth century, because of an absence of the intense outside competition that existed in Europe throughout the Middle Ages. Aboriginal Australia in 1788 was not, as some have implied (Dingle, 1988: 55) on the brink of a major technological breakthrough. The forcing conditions just did not exist.

Most archaeologists are puzzled by the fact that Australia was the only continent not to experience a Neolithic Revolution. Thorne and Raymond (1989: 146), for example, write: 'The reasons why Australia was the only continent to miss out on the agricultural revolution is one of the most puzzling questions in the prehistory of this continent.' They are quite rightly reluctant to think that this was due to any inherent quality in the nature of Aboriginal man as a genetic type. Their response, somewhat inconsistently, is that Australian Aboriginals 'preferred a way of life that maximised the time they had available for other things' and that in 1788 they were 'on the verge of food production'. The first of these two inconsistent conclusions is unfortunate and the second is just plain wrong. To claim that Australian Aboriginals were different to all other ethnic groups in the world by maximizing leisure appears to be suggesting that they were unique – which, of course, they were not. Australian Aboriginal society, like all societies elsewhere, was attempting to maximize its material return. Owing to the absence of external competition, this meant maintaining their pre-neolithic economic system. There is no possibility that they were about to invest in a technological paradigm shift because the potential benefits (in the absence of external threat) were not worth the cost, in terms of longer working hours, of doing so. Had they attempted to introduce a Neolithic Revolution under these conditions, they would have been very different – they would have been irrational and they would have failed. The absence of external competition, however, does not imply that there was no internal competition. Clearly, internal competition did exist, as demonstrated by regular raiding activity, but as there was no 'funnel of transformation' in Australia this internal competition never became intense. It was sufficient to keep them on their toes and to maintain a viable palaeolithic system but not to drive them to innovate on a significant scale.

As a successful rational society with a satisfying culture, Aboriginal Australia had no reason to change its implicit economic calculus of benefits and costs concerning possible alternative economic systems. It just did not make any sense to undertake the onerous additional costs that a change of technological paradigm would require. In the absence of intense competition from without and within, there were no benefits that could match the potential increased costs – in terms of longer working hours, heavier and more onerous work, loss of independence, and greater inequality – of introducing an agricultural system. Such a change would not be seriously contemplated in a society that knew no other more wealthy and powerful than its own. Only when the European invasion came, suddenly, did the economic calculus change but, by then, it was too late. Aboriginal society had sensibly and rationally pursued their palaeolithic lifestyle because they had no way of knowing that 1788 would ever occur.

What does this historical experience imply both for the dynamics of Aboriginal society and for other palaeolithic societies? We can attempt to measure the rate of both population growth and technological change from about 60,000 years ago to the coming of the British. To do this we need to make a number of assumptions about: how many people were in Australia in 60,000 BP; the date at which all natural resources were fully utilized; the size of the Aboriginal population at that time; and the extent of technological change. It seems reasonable to assume that Aboriginal foragers were well established by 60,000 years BP owing to the possibility of migrations as early as 100,000 years BP. A minimal population estimate at that time might be about twenty tribes consisting of 400 bands, 2,000 families, and 10,000 men, women and children. At the rates of growth calculated in this exercise, a starting point of 10,000 people in 60,000 BP could have been achieved after only twenty-four years, or a generation, on the assumption that the first year of migration involved 200 people and that in each subsequent year this absolute inflow increased by a very modest 10 per cent of the initial number (simple interest) – owing to the slowly growing knowledge of this emigration by the parent population – and that each year's migrant intake increased its numbers (see below) by 0.012 per cent per annum (compound interest). As it turns out, within this framework of assumptions, migration increasing at a modest rate of simple interest accounted for 99.9 per cent of the total increase in population over this first generation of occupation in Australia. Now assume that this was the lucky generation that arrived in Australia before the seas reached their highest point in about 20,000 years cutting off further immigration (see Figure 2.4). By the time the seas fell again, some 25,000 years later, the descendants of the lucky generation were well established and could fend off any further waves of migrants, which would be regarded, by them, as foreign invaders.

Second, the available archaeological evidence suggests that Australia had been fully occupied by about 20,000 years BP. Third, at that time the population was probably about the same size as it was in 1788 when the British arrived. Recent work (Butlin, 1983; 1993) suggests this might have been about 1 million people – an estimate towards the upper end of the range of estimates. And, fourth, given the level of both material living standards (GDP per capita) and technology in 1788, it is highly unlikely that technical change increased by more than 10 per cent over the entire period.

With these assumptions we can estimate very approximate growth rates of population and technological change throughout Aboriginal history. During the 40,000 years when the strategy of family multiplication was in force – 60,000 to 20,000 years BP – population grew at a compound rate of 0.012 per cent per annum, which implies a doubling every 5,800 years. Clearly, it is not realistic to assume that there were no further migrations to Australia after the initial population of 10,000 people had arrived by 60,000 BP – although a well-established tribal system would have provided an effective barrier across the north of Australia – and, accordingly, this growth rate should be thought of as an upper bound for natural increase. But we would expect the rate of natural increase in Australia to tend towards the upper limit of population growth rates in palaeolithic societies because of the abundance of available resources, the absence of major physical barriers, and a less arid climate than at present. This, in fact, turns out to be the case. Robina Quale (1992: 28–9) claims that population growth rates were about 0.0056 per cent per annum about 50,000 years BP and 0.0111 per cent per annum about 20,000 years BP – an average of 0.0074 per cent per annum, which is about 60 per cent of my estimate for the growth rate of Australian

Aboriginal population over the entire period. Thereafter population would have retained a balance with a slowly changing stock of natural resources. If population growth is calculated over the entire period from 60,000 BP to AD 1788, the rate of growth drops to 0.008 per cent per annum, at a doubling every 8,750 years.

As the dynamic strategy of Aboriginal society was family formation between 60,000 and 20,000 years BP, we would not expect any significant change in human skills or technology during this period. There is evidence, however, for a modest improvement in skills and tools in the five millennia before 1788. While Aboriginal foraging bands had a balanced and nutritious diet, they had little in the way of material possessions – just a small range of essential tools and, except in rare circumstances (such as eel traps, fish weirs, and bird nets) little or no other capital equipment, and material living standards were minimal in 1788. Hence technological change had to be minimal, and was probably no more than 10 per cent over the entire period. This implies a compound rate of technological change over 60,000 years of 0.0001 per cent per annum.

On the basis of these guesstimates, therefore, the rate of technological change would have been no greater than 1 per cent of the rate of growth of family formation. Clearly, family multiplication was the overwhelmingly dominant dynamic strategy employed by Aboriginal society. This can be regarded as typical of hunter–gatherer societies in general.

Family multiplication has been the dynamic strategy of human society for the great majority (96 per cent) of human existence. The success and power of this strategy can be measured in terms of the spread of the human race throughout the world. But it had severe limitations. While it was able to provide a comfortable level of human well-being, it was unable to raise material living standards above a relatively low level. And it was unable to reduce infant mortality – unable to minimize the wastage of human life. This could only be achieved by new and unknown strategies of technology and commerce. These strategies were only economically viable when the family multiplication strategy had been exhausted and, in some regions – which I have called 'funnels of transformation' – a new and more intense form of competition had emerged. Those societies that adopted new strategies were able to raise material standards of living and increase their power of economic resilience. Those that failed to do so were ultimately destroyed.

9

MAKER OF THE WHEEL

A wheel of fire surrounding all the heavens.
(Blake, *Jerusalem*, 1804–1820)

There is, it is said by some but denied by others, a curious story written on a clay tablet found in Uruk (level IVA), which has been dated to about 3500 years BC. It reads: I am old. Nearing death. The truth needs to be written before it is too late. Throughout Sumer I am known as the maker of the wheel. I am treated with the reverence reserved for priests. I told them all that it came to me in a dream. A dream about a wheel of fire in the heavens. I told them that this miracle was my inspiration. I lied. My only inspiration was how to carry wheat more cheaply than my brother merchants from my city Uruk to other cities stranded by the shifting rivers. First I made a toy with four wheels. It amused my sons. Later I made four large solid wheels from wood which I fixed to my old sled using axles. It worked and I became rich. And famous. How could I tell them that it was gold and lapis lazuli that inspired me, rather than a vision from the gods. There is no wheel of fire in the heavens. No miracle. The maker of the wheel is the rider in Zechariah's second chariot.

The Neolithic Revolution changed the world forever. No longer did the dynamics of human society depend primarily upon the strategy of family multiplication. The Neolithic Revolution enabled the generation of agricultural surpluses that could support specialized urban activities of an economic and military kind. And the fruits of specialization together with the introduction of new production techniques were reflected in growing material standards of living. Civilization brought with it not only the possibility of economic growth as well as economic expansion, but also the possibility of large-scale war and conquest. Civilization gave rise to the horsemen of war as well as the maker of the wheel.

Needless to say, the emergence of civilization was a gradual process involving a large number of small, step-like phases of development. These phases appear to have included the collection and storage of wild seeds, the development of subsistence farming based upon sown crops and domesticated animals, the part-time production of crafted objects by subsistence farmers for sale in local markets, the emergence of specialized workshops within household precincts using family labour to produce commodities for both the household and the market, and finally the establishment of separate urban workshops producing goods and services solely for the market. The process was a revolution, but a revolution that occurred over thousands of years. While this seems slow when we look back from the present, it appears unbelievably rapid when we look forward from the time mankind first emerged on Earth. It was a revolution because it completely transformed the nature of human society and because it released three new dominant dynamic strategies – technology, commerce, and conquest. The three new strategies have driven civilization from that time forward.

THE TECHNOLOGICAL STRATEGY

Technology, in contrast to the technological strategy, is as old as the human race itself. It has long been used to distinguish early man from other members of the primate family. While it is no longer claimed that man is the only species to use tools, man *is* the only species able to fashion and employ a sophisticated technology to transform the world in order to extract more from nature than it is willing to offer. It is this which makes us unique. Technology defines mankind.

Technology has always been employed by humanity to improve its ability to survive and consume. But the role it has played has changed dramatically during the course of human history. To understand that role we need to draw a distinction between technology as a dominant strategy and technology as a supportive substrategy. As a supportive substrategy, technology has existed throughout human history; but as a dominant dynamic strategy, technology has been employed only during critical episodes that have led to technological paradigm shifts and during the modern era since the Industrial Revolution.

Technology as a dominant strategy

It is as a dominant strategy that technology commands our greatest attention. There are two dimensions to this role – the technological paradigm shift and the modern process of *continuing* technological change. The technological paradigm shift is a widespread human response – occurring in both the Old and New Worlds – to critical episodes in the relationship between population and natural resources owing to the exhaustion of the prevailing technological paradigm. A paradigm shift involves a technological transformation that provides, in a relatively short space of time – *when looking forwards rather than backwards* – a quantum leap in the access to the resources

of a niggardly natural world. Human society has experienced three technological paradigm shifts: the palaeolithic shift from scavenging to hunting; the
neolithic shift from hunting to agriculture; and the modern shift from agriculture to industrialization. While each of these shifts took time to work
itself out, it is only in the modern period that technological change has
become a continuing strategy – a continuing strategy that has had a sub-
ordinating influence on strategies, such as conquest and commerce, that have
been dominant in the past.

Exactly what is a technological paradigm shift? It involves a fundamental
change in the technological and, hence, economic foundations of human
society. This enables a quantum leap in the access of mankind to the hidden
bounty of natural resources and, in the process, profoundly transforms the
nature of society. The human outcome of a paradigm shift is no less profound
than the change in economic, social, and political organization, and includes
significant increases both in regional and world populations, and in the
material standards of living of these populations. While most of the technological, economic, and 'cultural' changes inherent in a paradigm shift will
be worked out at the beginning of the new economic era, there will be later
periods of technological fine-tuning as the new economic system is adapted
to different regions and as the ultimate possibilities of the paradigm are
progressively explored and exhausted through the expansion of population
(as a user of resources not as a driving force).

It is one thing to define what is meant by a shift in technological paradigm,
but quite another to explain why it emerged. The argument advanced in this
book is that a paradigm shift occurs in a competitive environment when the
old technological paradigm has been exhausted – when the existing strategies
of palaeolithic family multiplication and neolithic conquest are no longer
able to satisfy the material objectives of mankind. A major characteristic of
this paradigm exhaustion is the fundamental change in factor endowments
that are reflected by critical changes in relative factor prices: particularly of
a rise in the price of natural resources relative to both labour and capital,
and of a differential impact on the prices of various natural resources. This
provides powerful incentives in a competitive environment to substitute both
labour and capital for natural resources in the productive process, and of
'new' natural resources (such as fossil fuels and metals) for 'old' natural
resources (such as timber).

An essential ingredient in the process by which a paradigm shift occurs is
competition – the struggle between individuals, families, market organizations, and societal groupings at all levels for survival and material advantage.
It is this struggle that provides the need to respond to changing factor
endowments and prices by searching for new ways to achieve pressing human
objectives. If this competition could be avoided through isolation, there would
be no need to search for new and better ways to use natural resources. Instead

240

there would be a need to control the size of the isolated population in order to prevent a collapse of material standards of living. This stationary state, however, is not easy to achieve, and can only be reached under special conditions. We have seen, for example, that it was achieved in Aboriginal Australia only because of the extreme degree of isolation and the unusual geographical conditions – the absence of a constricting landform funnel through which peoples were forced to pass. Not only is this state of being difficult to achieve, its price for that society is also very high – ultimate de-stru-ction. The experience of both the Old and New Worlds was very different to Aboriginal Australia, at least until they came into contact after 1492.

Provided the old paradigm shift is approaching global exhaustion, it need not actually reach that absolute state before a technological paradigm shift occurs. It is sufficient that this exhaustion occur in a critical form in a restricted but central geographical area that is a major funnel for economic and social communication between various parts of the known world that are moving towards the paradigm ceiling. And it is essential that this strategic crisis be unrelieved by access to natural resources elsewhere. In other words, this strategic crisis is a true paradigm crisis. The resulting intense competition within a framework of paradigm exhaustion will produce an intense search for the techniques required to expose new hidden reserves of natural resources. This search will be directed by the change in factor endowments and prices. In the past, these **funnels of transformation** (Figure 8.2) have included the Rift Valley in East Africa during the shift to hunting; the Fertile Crescent in the Old World, and the Mesoamerican isthmus in the New World, during the shift to agriculture; and England, the gateway to Western Europe, during the shift to industrialization.

Once the paradigm shift has occurred in the central transformation funnel, the transmission of the new economic system to other areas is relatively rapid, at least when viewed forward rather than backward. The periphery will either follow the centre relatively quickly in adopting the new paradigm because of the competitive advantage acquired by the centre, or it will be taken over by the centre through conquest. Of course, there will be delays in this process owing to differences in the physical conditions as between the centre and the periphery, which will require further minor changes in technology to enable the implementation of the new paradigm. But it is unlikely that the periphery will achieve total paradigm exhaustion before the new paradigm is either hastily adopted or imposed upon them.

Those peoples at the centre of a technological paradigm shift clearly gain an advantage over those on the periphery. In these circumstances a paradigm shift quickly gives way to the conquest strategy. Evidence for this can be found in the rapid emergence of large empires after both the Neolithic and Industrial Revolutions. The difference between these two revolutions is that in the ancient world the conquest strategy came to dominate, whereas in the

241

modern world conquest has always been subordinate to the technology strategy, except for very short periods of time. Nevertheless, conquest is too tempting to be resisted by those societies in the vanguard of a paradigm shift. Will the future be any different? This will be discussed in the final chapter.

The timing and speed of the three paradigm shifts in human history is illuminating. Despite Albert Einstein's demonstration that time and speed depend upon the position of the observer, there is considerable confusion over whether what I have called paradigm shifts took place sufficiently quickly to be regarded as revolutionary. It will be shown in Chapter 12 that each paradigm shift occurred more rapidly than the last, and that the time lapse between them declined progressively. Despite the limited number of observations – only three revolutions – both relationships appear to be geometric in nature. The time taken for the technological shifts to occur involved hundreds of thousands of years for the Palaeolithic, 4,000 years for the Neolithic, and 100 years for the Industrial Revolutions. The intervals between the Palaeolithic and Neolithic Revolutions was about 1.6 million years, and between the Neolithic and Industrial Revolutions was about 10,000 years. And the time taken to carry each new paradigm around the known world was about 1.2 million years for the Palaeolithic Revolution, 3,000 plus years for the Old-World Neolithic Revolution, and 200 plus years for the Industrial Revolution.

That the timing and speed of the paradigm shifts is changing geometrically must surely be unsettling for those scholars whose criteria for the concept of 'revolution' is absolute – in the sense of a fixed rate of growth threshold – rather than relative in nature. Some argue that there was no such thing as the Industrial Revolution on the grounds that the rates of growth achieved in the UK between 1780 and 1830 were little faster than those in the first half of the seventeenth century and much slower than those in the nineteenth and twentieth centuries (Cameron, 1989). Of course, if the Industrial Revolution was not a revolution, then the much slower neolithic and palaeolithic paradigm shifts cannot possibly be thought of in these terms. In my opinion it is a fatal error to judge the past in terms of the present – of looking backward rather than forward. A revolutionary change must be evaluated in terms of what came before rather than what has happened since. The palaeolithic transformation was revolutionary in terms of what had occurred before, as were the neolithic and industrial transformations. We should only look backward in order to look forward (Snooks, 1994b: ch. 3).

In any case, the speed at which a paradigm shift takes place is not as important as the nature of the transformation itself. The speed depends on the sophistication of the technological network and the system of communications, not on the extent of the change in the existing system. The usual meaning of 'revolution' is: 'complete change, turning upside down, great reversal of conditions'. It is, therefore, the completeness of the change that is important rather than its speed. Each of the three paradigm shifts qualifies in this respect. In certain circumstances a complete change – a revolution – will be necessary just to maintain growth rates of GDP per capita rather than to increase them dramatically.

The idea that an economic revolution significantly increases growth rates is a misconception based upon the failure to realize that growth is not a modern but an ancient invention. European growth has not suddenly appeared or accelerated since the Industrial Revolution, rather it has gone through a number of great waves since the so-called 'Dark Ages'. The modern upsurge of economic growth is merely the third wave in the past millennium. And rates of growth achieved in Europe during the sixteenth century can rival those achieved during the nineteenth and twentieth centuries. The essence of a paradigm shift is the technological and economic transformation that is effected. In this respect there is absolutely no comparison between the sixteenth century and the Industrial Revolution. If timing and speed are significant at all, it is in terms of the geometrically declining interval between the timing of the paradigm shifts and of the exponential increase in the rate of the transformation. The significance lies in what it suggests about the future. Could, for example, the fourth paradigm shift be soon upon us? Will it occur within a space of time as short as a generation? And will the future involve a continuous paradigm revolution rather than just continuous technological change within the framework of a static paradigm? Could, in other words, the dynamic strategy take place within a *dynamic* paradigm?

Economic growth may not be a modern invention, but technological change as a *continuing* strategy certainly is. Since the last great paradigm shift, technological change has been the dominant dynamic strategy. While two hundred years is but a brief moment in the history of humanity, there are reasons to believe that technological change will continue to be the strategy of the future. Unless, that is, the ecological engineers are able to convince the United Nations to derail the Dynamic Society in a misguided attempt to 'save' the world ecology. Of course, the world ecology must be saved but not at the expense of a collapse in the Dynamic Society.

There are four reasons for believing that the technological strategy is here to stay. First, there is a continuous and continuing demand for the technological strategy largely because of the post-1940s shift in household demand from children to market consumer goods. The market, in responding to this structural change in household demand, continues to generate a wider demand for new technologies to produce new consumer goods. Diminishing utility in consumption can be put off indefinitely merely by the production of more complex and sophisticated consumer goods and services. This has been central to the decline in the family multiplication strategy in Westernized countries.

Second, modern society appears to be driven by an ever-changing set of factor endowments. This causes a continuous change in relative factor prices which, in a competitive environment, leads to continuing technological change. Third, for the first time in human history, the technological strategy has been institutionalized. This is the result of the establishment by developed nations of substantial public research facilities in science, engineering technology, and the social sciences, together with private research facilities by large corporations. This institutionalization of scientific and technological research provides a continuous supply of techniques that can be used by economic decision-makers *if required*. In other words, it reduces the cost of the technological strategy. But, it must be realized, the hallmark of a technological paradigm shift is the strategic demand for new technological and organizational ideas. It is this demand that has led to the institutionalization of technological change. The source of ideas – whether from practical inventors or highly trained scientists – has no causal significance. It is just a response to the dominant dynamic strategy of our time. This is why we cannot agree with Douglass North (1981: ch. 13) that the 'Second Revolution' is distinct from the Industrial Revolution and that it alone can be compared with the Neolithic Revolution. It was the Industrial Revolution, and its aftermath, that constituted a quantum leap in the access to natural resources.

Finally, the conquest strategy, as an alternative to the technological strategy, has become less attractive to the great powers of the modern world owing both to the smaller scope for achieving systematic increases in material living standards through conquest, and to the development of doomsday weapons. While smaller nations or ethnic groups continue to battle with conventional weapons for the more limited spoils of conquest, the great nations look on uneasily. Even the 'little wars' of the late twentieth century were restricted by UN interventions, even if indecisively.

What does the technological dynamic strategy involve? It involves the introduction of new ideas to the process of production and distribution in the market sector and to the economic system as a whole. These economic decisions – or this strategy – are made in the market sector in response to price signals that reflect fundamental changes in the resource endowment of society, in order to achieve the objectives of the ultimate consumer of all goods and services – the family (Snooks, 1994a). Hence there is both a market and a household dimension to economic change which, in Chapter 8, was called technological dynamic change (TDC) and included both economic expansion (household multiplication) and economic growth (increases in GDP, or GCI, per household).

To the household, TDC means an increase in market employment opportunities and an increase in real income. Indeed, it was because of the higher market productivity that the family, or household, first contracted out certain of its activities to the market sector as urban centres emerged following the Neolithic Revolution. The higher productivity provides the family with two choices. First, it enables the production of children who, in a growing market sector, will find employment, will establish new households, and will add to the income of the extended family group. This is the primitive process of economic change discussed in Chapter 8. Second, an increase in real market income enables the average household to increase its consumption of goods and services through higher real family wages. This is an opportunity not available in a pre-market world. The balance achieved between these two choices will emerge from a process in which families attempt to maximize their material advantage.

The market responds to its general economic environment in a manner that will maximize firm profits. In a competitive environment this will involve the introduction of new ideas to production and organization in order to improve product quality and/or reduce costs of production. And the way they do this will depend upon the changing factor endowments, and hence of relative factor prices, over time. This should not be thought of as a static concept. Entrepreneurs attempt to maximize their profits over their lifetime and this can only be achieved through growth. Decision-makers in the market sector, therefore, generate a longrun demand for new or recycled technical and organizational ideas. This is an essential point. This longrun demand by all decision-makers in society for appropriate technical ideas determines the technological dynamic strategy.

New technical and organizational ideas are supplied in response to a society's strategic demand. Strategies drive ideas; ideas do not drive strategies. Naturally this is a complex and highly interactive process, which depends fundamentally upon the demand generated by economic decision-makers. Materialist man is at the centre of the dynamic process. Remove strategic demand for new ideas and the dynamic process will break down, even if institutions on the supply side continue to churn out new ideas. If, on the other hand, the supply of new ideas stops for some institutional reason, but strategic demand for growth continues, society's entrepreneurs will either recycle existing ideas or, if the technological strategy is completely exhausted, will adopt new strategies, such as conquest. The driving force in a competitive world is unstoppable in the longer term. While not all ideas are demand-led – research institutions generate a momentum of their own – they will only be applied to the economy if a strategic demand for them exists. Materialistic decision-makers – the people – dominate the producers of ideas – the experts.

Technology as a subsidiary strategy

Technological change also plays an important, if secondary, role as a supportive substrategy to the dominant dynamic strategy. Technology is used in this way either to facilitate, support, or protect the dominant strategy. A number of illustrations from the palaeolithic, neolithic, and modern periods will explain what I have in mind.

In the palaeolithic period the dominant dynamic strategy was, as we have seen, family multiplication. This was a process in which new resources were exploited by increasing the size of nuclear families, foraging bands, and tribes to the point where new social units at each of these levels were established. In this way the human race set out from East Africa about 1.6 million years ago and gradually spread throughout the world. This great dispersion involved crossing rivers, lakes, seas, mountains, forests, deserts, tundra, and other physical obstacles. To do so it was necessary to develop: effective methods of transport and communications, including rafts and canoes, carrying devices, cutting and slashing tools, and long distance signalling; effective ways of combating a harsh environment, including clothing and fire; and effective methods of hunting and protection, including weapons of various types. It was also necessary to develop new skills for navigation, for the discovery of new sources of food and water, and for learning how to tackle new animals. All these techniques and skills, which were called forth by the dynamic strategy of family multiplication, are strategy-facilitating rather than growth-inducing. Also new techniques may be introduced by an isolated palaeolithic society in order to maintain its balance between population and resources in the face of climatic change. In those circumstances, technology is used only to support the existing dominant dynamic strategy.

In neolithic societies – which include all societies prior to the Industrial Revolution – there were a number of dimensions to the supporting role played by technological change. Technical and organizational ideas were pressed into duty by the dynamic strategy of conquest. Systematic conquest requires a continuous improvement in the weapons of war such as swords, daggers, spears, lances, armour for men and horses, guns, assault weapons (battering rams, assault towers, catapults, cannons, ships of war), and defensive weapons (shields, pikes, earthworks, castles, fortresses). It is also essential to improve the means of transporting men, horses, equipment, and supplies, together with the means of communications, particularly as the frontier of conquest moves steadily outward from the conqueror's home base. Sophisticated forms of organization and administration of the growing empire are also essential. Not only does this technology facilitate the dominant conquest strategy, it indirectly improves the efficiency of the domestic economy particularly through improvements in transport, communications, and public administration. Technological change, although not necessarily of the same kind, will be adopted by both the conqueror (say Rome) and those societies (say Germanic) that successfully resist conquest.

In a less direct way, technological change can be employed to support the conquest (or defence) strategy, by making the domestic economy more efficient. While these changes will be subordinated to the dominant strategy, they may enable the finetuning of the existing technological paradigm. This certainly occurred in the ancient civilizations of Greece, Rome, and China, but it was employed to a greater and more effective degree in Europe during the Middle Ages.

The main reason for technological advance in medieval Europe was to adapt the economic system of classical antiquity to the different climatic and physical conditions of Western and Northern Europe, and to the different conditions of war and conquest. After the collapse of the Western Roman Empire in the late fifth century AD, Europe consisted of a relatively large number of small, equally matched kingdoms and principalities which were geared for war. In highly competitive circumstances in which no single group could dominate, an effective military force needed a highly efficient domestic economy to provide the necessary resources. Generally speaking, a European kingdom could not achieve its material objectives by systematically acquiring resources through conquest. There were notable exceptions – including Charlemagne of France, Cnut of Denmark, William of Normandy, and English kings during the Hundred Years War – but even these were one-off affairs which did not provide a growing access to outside resources. In this process of fine-tuning the neolithic paradigm, European kingdoms gradually developed a new dynamic as a byproduct of the attempt to do as the ancients had done – to pursue a conquest strategy. Hence, technological change which began as a substrategy in the early medieval period gathered momentum and, by the late Middle Ages, emerged as a major if not dominant strategy in the leading kingdoms of Western Europe.

While the modern period saw the emergence of technology as the dominant strategy, a highly specialized branch of technology has more recently played a supportive role for the strategy as a whole. The dominant strategy involves a continuing attempt to make more efficient use of existing natural resources through the application of technology, largely embodied in capital equipment, to the process of production in both the market and household sectors. At the same time, a highly specialized branch of technology has been employed to repair the unintentional damage inflicted upon the environment by the dominant technological strategy. We need to distinguish, therefore, between the dominant technological strategy and the specialized restorative technology – often inappropriately called 'sustainable' – which is a facilitating substrategy. The distinction is important for two reasons. Owing to the pressure being placed upon natural resources as the dominant strategy carries modern society closer to paradigm exhaustion, increasing damage is being inflicted upon the environment. Restorative technology plays an essential role in repairing this damage and maintaining the viability of the Dynamic Society. This distinction is also important because many pressure groups in society have confused the restorative technology with the dominant technological strategy. This confusion is partly conscious and partly deliberate because these groups, particularly the ecological engineers, wish to replace the dominant strategy entirely with the restorative strategy. As discussed in Chapter 13, this would be self-defeating as it would undermine not only the Dynamic Society but also the wider ecology.

THE TECHNOLOGICAL FOUNDATIONS OF CIVILIZATION

Technological change, like economic growth, is an ancient invention. It can be traced back through our modern world to the Industrial Revolution; it can be seen as a major thread stretching back through the Middle Ages to the fall of Rome; it can be seen from time to time in the record of ancient civilizations back as far as the Neolithic Revolution; and it can be traced back through hunting societies to the time when mankind first emerged from its primate origins. While recognizing the very long record of technological change in human history, I wish to focus upon its nature and achievements since the development of civilization, a period of some 6,000 years. This is a period greatly influenced by the maker of the wheel.

The ancient world

The technical achievement of ancient civilization is generally misunderstood at both the popular and expert level. Graeco-Roman society is regarded as paradoxical. Commentators who have been dazzled by the philosophical, cultural, and administrative achievements of ancient Greece and Rome have long been puzzled by their limited technological advance. It will be suggested that this puzzlement, even disbelief, results from a misunderstanding of both the objectives and the dynamic strategy of Graeco-Roman society. Once it is understood that the dominant strategy was chosen on a benefit–cost basis from a number of other possible strategies in order to maximize *individual* material advantage, the issue of technology in classical antiquity ceases to appear paradoxical.

The conventional wisdom on this issue can be effectively summarized by a number of quotations from Moses Finley who, until his death in 1986, was a highly influential authority on the economic history of the ancient world. Even now his shadow lies upon the page of ancient history. Finley (1985: 108–9) tells us:

> They [the large landowners in Rome] were equally bound by a limited and fairly static technology, with the two-year fallow cycle as its base, and by the high costs of transport. These points need to be made explicitly because they are repeatedly challenged by modern scholars, not so much on the evidence as on psychological grounds, on a disbelief that Greeks and Romans should have been so incapable of 'simple' improvements. There were improvements of one kind or another in the course of antiquity, especially in the Roman classical period, in drainage and irrigation, in tools and mill-stones, in seed selection, but they were marginal, for, as our leading contemporary authority on Roman farming summed up the story, 'the patterns of land use and the methods of tillage remained unchanged. As in ancient industry,

248

new improvements were met by the transfer of old techniques.' But there is nothing mysterious about this 'stagnation', no serious reason for disbelief: large incomes, absenteeism and its accompanying psychology of the life of leisure, of land ownership as a non-occupation, and, when it was practised, letting or sub-letting in fragmented tenancies all combined to block any search for radical improvements.

And again Finley (ibid.: 146–7) claims:

The Greeks and Romans inherited a considerable body of techniques and empirical knowledge, which they exploited well insofar as it suited their particular values, and to which they added the gear and the screw, the rotary mill and the water-mill, glass-blowing, concrete, hollow bronze-casting, the lateen sail, and a few more. There were refinements and improvements in many spheres. But there were not many genuine innovations after the fourth or third century BC, and there were effective blocks ... We must remind ourselves time and again that the European experience since the late Middle Ages in technology, in the economy, and in the value systems that accompanied them, was unique in human history until the recent export trend commenced. Technical progress, economic growth, productivity, even efficiency have not been significant goals since the beginning of time. So long as an acceptable life-style could be maintained, however that was defined, other values held the stage.

More recent work in this tradition (Hopkins, 1983: x–xxi) confirms this basic 'primitive' model for the Roman economy, but suggests that it is 'sufficiently flexible' to incorporate a 'modest dynamic' owing to 'very modest' increases in agricultural productivity mainly due to 'the increased pressure of exploitation', and possibly (and this is regarded as 'more problematic' and involving 'no basic shift') to productivity increases in the urban sector.

In the first of Finley's passages our attention is drawn to the disbelief of 'modern scholars' about the surprisingly limited technological performance of the ancient Greeks and Romans, which he explains in terms of their very different system of social values. Indeed, he scolds them for projecting modern values onto ancient civilized man, whom he regards not as economic man but, in the jargon of economists, as 'satisficing' man – man who is content with achieving a satisfactory lifestyle and who, thereafter, strives no further. While Finley is correct in claiming that the attitude of classical antiquity should not come as a surprise, the reason he advances is wide of the mark. Ancient objectives were not different to modern objectives – the aim in both cases was to maximize material advantage. The difference lies in the strategies they employed to meet their objectives. Economic decision-makers in classical antiquity employed the conquest strategy (and the commerce strategy) rather than the technological strategy because the rate of return on investment in conquest was perceived to be greater. This does not mean that no techno-logical progress took place, just that it was not the dominant dynamic strategy, and that it was mainly directed towards facilitating or supporting the conquest strategy. Finley, of course, was fully aware that ancient civilizations used war to expand their empires, but he did not recognize that war was considered by them to be the best – on a benefit–cost basis – available strategy to achieve their material objectives.

At a more general level Finley is guilty of the very charge he levels against 'modern scholars' – of extrapolating present ideas on the past. Like many other scholars, Finley associates economic growth largely with technological change, and regards both as a modern invention. But he is wrong on both counts. Both economic growth and technological change are ancient inventions. Furthermore, economic growth is not uniquely dependent upon technological change, even when interpreted broadly. Economic growth is universally defined as an increase in real GDP per capita, and is usually thought of as an outcome of a process of production involving increases in one or other, or all, of technology, economies of scale, or specialization. But this is only the modern way of thinking about economic growth or increases in average material standards of living. The ancients also thought long and hard about their material standards of living – although they did not call it economic growth – and about the best way of maximizing them. They were very successful in increasing their material standards of living through a process that involved investment not so much in productive technology but in war and in commerce. As will be explained in Chapter 10, this was as much a process of economic growth – of increasing real material standards of living – for the conquest empire as the modern technological kind is for Western society today.

The dynamic-strategies approach developed in this book provides an entirely new perspective on the technological achievement of the ancient world. What we should be looking for are not innovations in production – although some innovations were clearly made – but innovations in waging war and in administering the resulting territories acquired. In the light of this approach there can be no disbelief in the technological record of ancient civilizations, nor do we need, as Finley has done, to see ancient man as a different species from modern economic man. In the same economic envi-ronment modern man would act in the same way as ancient man and vice versa.

One further comment on the above passages from Finley is called for. While conquest was the dominant dynamic strategy in the ancient world, it is just not true that technological progress had not been one of many 'signif-icant goals since the beginning of time'. The Neolithic Revolution, and the subsequent development of an agrarian economic system that could support the civilizations of classical antiquity, involved an unprecedented technological revolution in human history – when looking forward rather than backward in time. This was the outcome of a deliberate strategy on the part of economic decision-makers and did not happen by accident. Most of this technological advance was achieved prior to and within the pioneer civilization of Sumer and, later, was merely modified by the civilizations of Greece and Rome. Just because technological change in Greece and Rome was slow, one cannot conclude that previously it had not been an important objective or outcome. In the pioneering civilizations of both the Old and New Worlds – at least in their earlier phases – technological change must have been a dominant strategy otherwise these pioneering civilizations would not have emerged.

Histories of technological change in the classical world generally focus upon the advances made in Greek and Roman times in the fields of civil engineering and military technology (Finley, 1985; Mokyr, 1990; White, 1984). Much has been written about ancient roads, bridges, aqueducts, sewerage systems, public buildings and fortifications together with the use in this work (by the Romans) of cement and concrete (Hodges, 1970; Forbes, 1958). It is generally acknowledged, although the full significance is not recognized, that these technical achievements focused on urban (Hodges, 1970: 197) and military rather than 'economic' objectives (Mokyr, 1990: 21). As Mokyr (ibid.:20) writes: 'The Rome of 100 AD had better paved streets, sewage disposal, water supply, and fire protection than the capitals of civilized Europe in 1800.' Military equipment and machinery was the other major field of technological advance. Greek and Roman military engineers were responsible for inventing and building sophisticated catapults, battering rams, and siege towers, that employed a sophisticated knowledge of the pulley, gear, cam, and ratchet, as well as the lever, wedge, and screw (Hacker, 1968; Landels, 1978).

As we have come to expect, scholars have noted the sophistication of these engineering principles applied to war machines, and have expressed surprise and regret that the same principles were not employed in the general economy. That they were capable of doing so can be seen in the highly sophisticated astronomical machines such as the Greek Antikythera mechanism (Landes, 1983). The Greeks even mathematically analysed these machines (Hall, 1983: 13). In a recent evaluation, Mokyr (1990: 21–2) concludes: 'these insights were applied mostly to war machines and clever gadgets that were admired for their own sake but rarely put to useful purposes'. Yet he completely overlooks the fact that the ancients regarded war machines as eminently useful in facilitating their conquest strategy which was directed towards maximizing their material advantage.

By not recognizing this connection between military technology and the dominant dynamic strategy, Mokyr (ibid.: 21) omits an important area of ancient technology and is led to a new puzzle: 'Although military technology is not of major concern here, it is worth noting that Greek and Roman military technology provides one of the few areas of a successful collaboration between scientists and technology.' He does not, however, ask: why? The answer, of course, is that as military machines were a major input into the process of economic growth through systematic conquest, this was a high priority area of research for ancient civilizations – just as technical research is in our modern civilization. The same answer resolves Mokyr's (ibid.: 22–3) dilemma about the Antikythera mechanism: 'What the discovery shows,' he writes, 'is that classical civilization had the intellectual potential to create complicated technical devices. The question remains why so little of this potential was realized, and translated into economic progress.' Here technical progress is equated with economic progress. The ancients were able to achieve economic progress effectively enough through conquest.

Technological change in agriculture did occur, but not very rapidly or systematically. The basic system of agriculture in the Graeco-Roman world was inherited from earlier civilizations, with the main changes being limited to those needed to adapt the system to the local geographic and climatic conditions (White, 1984). Only in irrigation technology were significant changes made. In the non-agricultural sectors of the ancient economy some progress was made in mining – mainly pumping water from mines and extracting metals from ore – and metal working (Mokyr, 1990: 24). While shipping made limited progress, the designs adopted appear appropriate for use on the Mediterranean. Only when regular long sea voyages were required in the later Middle Ages did shipping design and construction change radically. Technical ideas are driven by the demands of dynamic strategy. In the ancient world, therefore, technology was used to facilitate and support the dominant conquest strategy.

The Middle Ages

The contrast between technological progress in the medieval and the classical worlds is quite stark and has occasioned considerable comment. Recently Mokyr (1990: 29–30) has expressed surprise about the difference between medieval 'creativity' and classical stasis:

> When all is said and done [about classical antiquity], it remains some-thing of an enigma why a commercial and sophisticated economy, heavily dependent on transportation and animate power, in which handicrafts and food-processing industries catered to a large urban population, failed to arrive at some rather obvious solutions to technical problems that must have bothered them. Many of these problems were resolved in the first centuries of what we now call the Middle Ages.

And, not to put too fine a point on it, he writes (ibid.: 31): 'When we compare the technological progress achieved in the seven centuries between 300 BC and 400 AD, with that of the seven centuries between 700 and 1400, prejudice against the Middle Ages dissipates rapidly.'

252

As tempting as a comparison of this nature may be, it is not valid as a means of evaluating the relative economic achievement of the ancient world and the rising West. It is the sort of comparison that contemporary scholars often make – a comparison that Finley (1985: 108–9) warns us about – which involves imposing the experience of the present upon the past. A habit of looking backwards rather than looking forwards. It is certainly not the sort of comparison that a scholar in the Middle Ages, aware of the achievements of the past, would have thought to make. Rather than basing a comparison upon a single growth input that played a very different role in the classical and medieval economic systems, we need to compare their growth outcomes – namely material standards of living. While strategies differed, objectives were the same – to maximize material advantage – and, hence, a comparison of outcomes is valid and useful. Such a comparison suggests that material living standards in Europe did not surpass those of ancient Rome until the rapid economic growth of the sixteenth century (Goldsmith, 1987: 19). Clearly, technological change is neither the only nor, in certain economic circumstances, the most efficient way of generating economic growth.

Why did the dynamic strategy in Europe change after the collapse of the Western Roman Empire in the late fifth century AD? The answer is to be found in the economic environment that developed in Western·Europe between AD 500 and 1000. From the early Middle Ages emerged a large number of highly, indeed murderously, competitive Western European kingdoms or principalities. This was a response to the extended decline and collapse of central authority in a world dominated by small regional warlords with tribal origins who sharpened their competitive edges against the monolithic grinding wheel of the Roman legions. Also within the Western Roman Empire the growing economic and political instability led to a decline in the authority and importance of urban areas, and hence central control, and the emergence of regional warlords using their rural estates as an economic base.

By AD 1000 the large number of kingdoms jostling for supremacy in the bid for economic and, hence, political power included the kingdoms of England, Scotland, France, Leon, Navarre, Burgundy, Norway, Sweden, Denmark; the German Empire (that incorporated Italy north of Naples); together with a number of duchies – of Brittany and of Normandy; the Earldom of Orkney; the County of Barcelona; the Lombard Principalities; and the lands of the Irish and Welsh (McEvedy, 1961). And these competing Western European kingdoms were, as a group, under pressure from the Islamic world (which occupied three-quarters of Spain), the Byzantine Empire in the south, the Hungarians and Poles in the east, and Russia in the northeast. Western Europe, therefore, was subjected to intense competition from within and without.

Western Europe was a veritable pressure-cooker of competition – a pressure-cooker that continued to boil, yet remained intact, down to the end of the Middle Ages. The degree of sustained pressurized competition was matched in the past only by the city-states of both Sumer and classical Greece. Intermittent internal competition did occur elsewhere – as in China 800–200 BC and AD 200–600, India before 1500, and the Islamic world 750–1500 – but it was not as intense or sustained. The main changes that occurred in Western Europe between 1000 and 1500 were the driving of the Arabs from Spain and of the Byzantine influence from Italy. By 1500, however, Western Europe had begun a new phase in its development – a boiling over into the rest of the world that was to continue with great energy for the next 450 years.

It was in the pressure-cooker of Western Europe between 1000 and 1500 that a new dominant dynamic strategy began to emerge – the technological strategy. But it was only a beginning that did not come fully into focus until the time of the British Industrial Revolution some 300 years later. The new strategy emerged from the new competitive conditions that can be contrasted with the monolithic structure of the Roman world. In the world of Rome there was but one dominant player for about 600 years before the fifth century AD; whereas in Western Europe during the 500 years before 1500 there were fifteen or more players who, being fairly equally matched, were able to resist the rise of an all-powerful conqueror from amongst their ranks. This was assisted by a system of fluid alliances against potentially dangerous kingdoms.

Rome had been able to increase its material living standards by a process of systematic conquest, colonization, and exploitation of new natural and human resources. A central aspect of the dynamic conquest process was the ability to finance further conquest-led growth from past conquest. The process of conquest-led growth, therefore, was self-sustaining. At an earlier time, the Greek states had been able to finance their wars with each other by commerce and colonization; and Alexander had used conquest to finance both further conquest in Persia and increases in material living standards back in Greece.

After the collapse of Rome in AD 476, the Germanic tribes overwhelmed Western Europe, pursuing the age-old strategy of conquest. But once these tribes, under the pressure of war, had established small kingdoms that were equally matched, conquest could not be relied upon to achieve systematically their materialistic objectives. Although the fragmented peoples of Europe were highly aggressive and geared for war, they, with a few exceptions, were not able to finance conquest, defence, and increases in material standards of living from past conquests. A new strategy had to be found. The exceptions included the Norman warlords William the Bastard (who conquered England in 1066 and used the proceeds to pursue territorial ambitions in France) and Robert Guiscard (who conquered Byzantine Italy between 1059–1071 and used the proceeds to attack the neighbouring Lombards in Italy and the Muslims in Sicily). At the same time the Castilians began their long campaign to force the Muslims from Spain, which was not finally achieved until 1492.

The momentum and proceeds from this success saw Spain gain control of the western end of the Mediterranean (including Sardinia, Sicily, and southern Italy), and lay claim to the heart of the New World, all within a generation of 1492. The new strategy was designed to extract the greatest possible surplus from their domestic economies by developing new techniques of production and organization to modify the economic system they had inherited from classical antiquity. In the beginning this was merely a substrategy to support the ancient strategy of conquest, but as it came to be seen, probably somewhat reluctantly, as providing more reliable surpluses, it eventually emerged in some kingdoms as a dominant strategy. This does not mean, however, that any of them gave up the idea of windfall gains from military aggression.

While Spain and Portugal at the very end of the Middle Ages looked back to the dynamic strategies of the ancient world, the rest of Western Europe was forced through the pressure of intense competition for survival and material gain to look forward to a new dominant strategy – the strategy of technological change. Before the Industrial Revolution, however, European kingdoms fluctuated in their attitude to the strategies of technology and conquest. For Western Europe as a whole it is probably best to regard them as dual strategies, with technology providing the steady longrun increase in real surpluses and conquest providing windfall gains (and losses). The two leaders of these competing strategies, Britain and Holland on the one hand and Spain and France on the other, tested each other's strength throughout the early modern period until, with the advent of the British Industrial Revolution, Spain and France were left struggling in the rear. Technology rather than conquest was to be the dynamic strategy of the future.

The central issue of the period 1000 to 1500, therefore, was how a large number of highly competitive kingdoms, which were fairly equally matched, could finance their desire for survival and territorial acquisition. Systematic conquest – the seductive legacy of the classical past – was out of the question. The only other possibility for Western European combatants was to generate greater surpluses through greater efficiency in their domestic economies and, for the fortunate few (Flanders and Venice), through commerce. Greater efficiency could be realistically achieved by the application of improved techniques of production in agriculture and industry; by access to wider markets, and hence the achievement of greater international specialization, through improvements in land and sea transport and port facilities; by greater specialization and division of labour; and by improvement in economic organization. As we shall see, all four sources of improved efficiency were systematically tackled by the kingdoms of Western Europe before 1500 and, in the process, there emerged a new dominant strategy that took the world by storm.

But what were the changes in commerce, organization, and techniques of production that saw Western Europe change from a feudal economic system in the eleventh century to a mercantile capitalist system in the sixteenth century? As discussed in Chapter 7, a major achievement of this period was the way in which European kingdoms organized their economies and societies. The importance of this change in economic organization lies in the substantial reduction of transactions costs between buyers and sellers of goods, services, and factors of production (land, labour, and capital) (North and Thomas, 1973). This institutional change involved an extension of both commodity and factor markets. While commodity markets were, as we have seen, well developed by the eleventh century – although between then and 1500 they were extended to include a greater proportion of total economic activity – markets for labour, capital, and land were virtually non-existent. In the eleventh century, for example, the only way to obtain additional scarce labour, in the absence of a formal labour market, was to grow or steal your own – by encouraging dependent peasants to expand their families, or to obtain slaves through raids on adjoining territory. Clearly, the costs of raising labour in this way were more expensive than employing labour through the formal markets that had emerged by 1500. The same was true for financial capital which, in the absence of well-developed capital markets, could only be raised through ploughed-back profits, through moneylenders at very high rates of interest, and through conquest. The nature of the former was restricted and the cost of the latter two was high and uncertain. With the emergence of factor markets – which was central to the breakdown of feudalism – entrepreneurs were able, more effectively, to mobilize resources to undertake large-scale ventures. Economic growth was the major outcome.

The pace of technological change also quickened during the 500 years before 1500. These centuries saw Western European kingdoms attempting to maximize the surplus that could be extracted from an agricultural system bequeathed by the ancient world. In effect, medieval Europe attempted to fine-tune the economic system that had emerged from the Neolithic Revolution and which had been carried forward by a series of ancient civilizations, including those in the Asian and Islamic worlds. Because they were not able to increase their surpluses as the ancients had done through systematic conquest, the kingdoms of Western Europe attempted to take this ancient economic system as far as it would go. It is not possible, therefore, to agree with Mokyr (1990: 31) that medieval Europe 'managed to break through a number of technological barriers that had held the Romans back'. The Romans were not held back by technological barriers because they had more cost-effective methods of achieving their objectives – at least until the conquest strategy was exhausted by about AD 138 and by then it was too late. Rome had pursued the conquest strategy to its ultimate conclusion and in the process became so highly specialized in its human, physical, and administrative capital that it was unable to develop a new dominant dynamic strategy before being overwhelmed by the forces of chaos. But this is the subject of the following chapter. The point that needs to be made here is that the Romans were not held back by supply-side barriers. They had chosen – on a benefit–cost basis – an entirely different, and brilliantly successful, path.

The main agricultural innovations in medieval Europe were directed towards modifying and adapting the inherited technology to environmental conditions very different to those of much of the Roman world, and in fine-tuning it to deliver the greatest possible surplus. A key innovation was the heavy plough drawn by a large team of (up to eight) oxen that could work the rich but heavy valley soils (White, 1962). This replaced the light Roman plough that was only effective on the lighter, drier soils of the valley slopes. This innovation was combined with the three-field rotation system (rather than the two-field Roman system), by which only one field was left fallow each year to allow regeneration.

Rather curiously it has been argued that the development of the heavy plough drawn by a large team of oxen was 'in part' responsible for the development of the manorial system, because '[f]ew peasants could afford to own such an expensive capital good' (Mokyr, 1990: 33). In reality this 'part' would have been very small, because alternative systems involving cooperation between peasants could have been developed. Domesday Book shows quite clearly that, within a manor, plough teams were designated as 'belonging to the men' (i.e. groups of unfree peasants) and that individual free peasants had property rights in individual oxen that were combined for ploughing on a cooperative basis (Snooks, 1993a: 171–4). Rather the manorial system was a response to an economic environment in which labour was a scarce factor of production that the warlords were keen to exploit by expropriating (quasi-rents) as much of their contribution to production as possible.

While ancient society substituted animal power for manpower wherever possible, medieval society substituted inanimate power. This was achieved by harnessing both waterpower more efficiently than the Romans and, for the first time in the West, windpower. Waterpower was more effectively utilized from the seventh to the tenth centuries through the development of the more efficient overshot (to replace the undershot) waterwheel together with better systems of gearing and better water control. Early medieval Europe was able, thereby, to use waterpower not only to grind grain, but also to manufacture a wide range of other products. As Mokyr (1990: 34) says: 'By about 1100, waterpower was used to drive fulling mills, breweries (to prepare beer mash), trip hammers, bellows, bark crushers, hemp treatment mills, cutlery grinders, wire drawers, and sawmills.' And in those regions not served by running water, windmills (introduced in the twelfth century) could serve the same purpose. Both types of mill underwent an almost continuous process of improvement throughout the pre-Industrial Revolution period.

Medieval society also improved the earlier use of animal power. Innovations responsible for 'harnessing' animal power more efficiently include the horse-shoe (by the ninth century), the stirrup (at some indeterminate time between the eighth and late eleventh centuries), the horse collar (also by the ninth century), and the horse harness. These innovations led gradually to the horse replacing oxen in ploughing and general draught work (pulling carts and waggons). By the end of the eleventh century the ratio of energy generated by animals as compared with water mills was 7 to 3 (Langdon, 1986: 19–20).

Other early medieval innovations included seagoing ships (not required by the Romans and hence not a barrier to progress) for both military (Viking longships) and economic (the *cog*) purposes. By 1300 carvel-built ships (using a timber skeleton), which were lighter and larger, had been developed. The outcome was better seaworthiness and faster, cheaper transportation. There were also improvements in sail and rigging design, which included the lateen and square sails which, by about 1400, could be employed in fully rigged, three-masted ships. This increased both seagoing manoeuvrability and speed. Also the sternpost rudder replaced the steering oars of ancient vessels, enabling more precise and less onerous sailing. Finally, navigation became a less risky enterprise enabling longer sea voyages, with the development of more reliable charts and navigating tables (thirteenth century), the compass (late twelfth century), and the astrolabe to measure latitude (mid-fifteenth century).

Innovations also occurred in the construction of public buildings and other social infrastructure; the development of the blast furnace – a larger, hotter furnace driven by waterpowered bellows – by the late fourteenth century; the printing press; the mechanical clock from the end of the thirteenth century, which introduced new standards and sophistication in the construction of machinery; better spinning and weaving machines; and improvements in the chemical basis of both manufacturing and war (Mokyr, 1990: 44–55).

Medieval Europe also adopted and adapted technology directly from the Asian and Islamic worlds. The main innovations from these sources were papermaking (China before AD 100) from the thirteenth century, which quickly replaced parchment; textile technology; mechanical engineering, particularly in hydraulics and waterpower; metallurgy; and chemical technology. But, as Mokyr (ibid.: 44) explains: 'Having pioneered power and chemical technologies, by the thirteenth century Islamic society began to show signs of backwardness', and 'by about 1200, the economies of western Europe had absorbed most of what Islam and the Orient had to offer. From then on, they pulled ahead mostly on their own steam.'

By 1500 Europe had equalled, if not exceeded, the technological achievement of any former or contemporary civilization (Lach, 1977: 400; Mokyr, 1990: 55). The West had been preceded by other contemporary societies – Islamic and Chinese – but it now surged ahead while the others fell behind. Why? The answer is to be found in the economic environment that had set Europe on its technological strategy course – a pressure-cooker competitive environment surrounded by larger powers and occupied by a large number of relatively small kingdoms locked in an intense struggle for survival. It was a difficult and dangerous environment, but it produced a technological paradigm shift that would not have been possible in the more isolated, rarefied, and relaxed environment in the Orient or even in the Islamic world. The Western European environment was unique in post-ancient society and it produced a unique outcome – the Industrial Revolution.

The age of commerce

The limits of the ancient agricultural technological paradigm were increasingly approached during the 250 years from the discovery of the New World in 1492 to the breakthrough of the Industrial Revolution. In England, for which we have the best quantitative data, this period witnessed a spectacular growth of real GDP per capita during the sixteenth century followed by stagnation in the early seventeenth century and, from then, very slow growth until the third quarter of the eighteenth century. During this period England was the archetypal Western European economy, as it led the way through the third great paradigm shift in human history. It should be realized that while Britain was the first industrial nation, the Industrial Revolution was a Western European revolution (Snooks, 1994b: 14–15). Britain did not get there first on its own. Had it not been Britain, another Western European nation would have led the way.

The competitive situation in Europe remained extremely intense as the various kingdoms struggled for economic advantage. There was a degree of consolidation with England absorbing Scotland, Wales, and Ireland. France had already reasserted control in Normandy and Brittany and had expelled the English before 1500, and during the mid-seventeenth century took control of Burgundy and Upper Baden; and the Spanish ruled the western Mediterranean between 1492 and 1700. Yet, at the same time, the various kingdoms in the German Empire – Austria, Prussia, Bavaria, Saxony, Hanover, and a large number of self-governing Western states – were continually struggling for supremacy. The German Empire was like a microcosm of Western Europe.

For up to a millennium the Western European kingdoms had been contained by their landlocked neighbours in this cauldron of competition. In the process these kingdoms had steadily but powerfully increased their economic resilience beyond that of their neighbours, and after 1500 the pressure-cooker began a great boilover that was not reversed until the Russian victories over Nazi Germany during the Second World War. Austria expanded over its borders into the former kingdom of Hungary from the mid-sixteenth century and into Poland in the late eighteenth century. German kingdoms increasingly exercised control over western Poland which, after fluctuating fortunes, became part of the larger kingdom of Prussia. Even more spectacularly, by the mid-eighteenth century Europe had developed a considerable empire in the New World and was making inroads into Africa and Asia. The Spanish occupied much of the east coasts of the Americas as well as the Philippines; the Portuguese held Brazil and had a presence on the west and east coasts of Africa as well as in India and Timor; the British occupied the eastern half of North America with a presence on the west coast of Africa, in India, and in the East and West Indies, as well as South and West Africa, and in Guyana; and the French, who had lost the scramble for North America and India to the British, had a limited involvement in the West Indies and in West Africa.

This sudden breakout of Europeans was the totally unanticipated result of a millennium of intense economic competition – a result of the European pressure-cooker that surprisingly did not blow up but which boiled over with great energy into the rest of the world. Europe was able to achieve this global expansion because of the steady improvement in the technology of production, transport, and economic organization that had been forced within the intense European environment.

But did this European boilover mean that they would abandon the newly emergent technology strategy, in favour of the ancient conquest strategy, just as it was building up a head of steam? As it turned out the answer was – no. Before the Industrial Revolution, no single European power gained anything like a monopoly of overseas possessions. During the course of a millennium, the various European kingdoms had become conditioned to a highly competitive strategy through which they generated domestic wealth to engage in a deadly struggle for survival and material gain. In doing so they achieved a remarkable dynamic balance – a balance that was maintained as they widened their struggle to include the rest of the world. The European boilover, therefore, merely widened the stage of European conflict.

It is true that the acquisition of overseas possessions increased the material living standards of the Europeans by providing them with access to new natural and human resources and new markets, just as had been experienced by the Greeks and Romans in the ancient world. But unlike the outcome of classical antiquity, in which Macedonia and then, later, Rome gained a monopoly over the conquest strategy, no single European kingdom was able to gain the upper hand. Accordingly, no single European kingdom could rely upon conquest as a method for achieving a sustained increase in material standards of living and, hence, of economic resilience. By dividing the world between them, they were all better off, but no one could dominate – no one could gain the monopoly of conquest achieved in classical antiquity. The competitive edge still had to be sought through greater technological, rather than geographical, control over natural resources. Even during the great European boilover, individual kingdoms, at least those at the leading edge, continued to pursue the technology and commerce strategies. Naturally, individual decision-makers did not think in these global terms. They did not need to. All they had to do was to follow their own self-interests to achieve the technological strategy outcome.

In economic terms, just how profitable was overseas venturing in this period? Surely the risks of overseas expansion were much higher than those associated with the development of new techniques at home. As it turned out the European acquisition of overseas possessions was achieved with a surprisingly low investment of capital and manpower owing to the limited opposition encountered from less technologically advanced and less disease-resistant societies. While the costs were low, the Europeans were happy to acquire what they could. But to fight costly wars far from home-base made little economic sense, as the French and British taxpayers discovered in the early to mid-eighteenth century in North America and in India.

An attempt by the British, who had ousted the French from North America by 1763, to recoup some of the cost of this folly, by taxing the American colonialists in 1765–1766, was thwarted by local opposition. A further attempt by the British at indirect taxation, through an East India tea-importing monopoly, provoked a rebellion (1773) that led, finally, to the formal Declaration of Independence of 1776. The subsequent series of skirmishes between 1776 and a Declaration of Peace in 1783 demonstrated the impossibility of a European power being able to occupy vast territories against determined opposition, particularly when supported by a rival European competitor, such as France (1781) who had earlier witnessed the effectiveness and efficiency of the British navy in dismantling much of her own empire. Overseas possessions added to the metropolitan material standard of living only if the cost of maintaining that possession was relatively low. While an efficient navy was essential to acquiring colonies, it was of limited use against determined land-based opposition. In the latter scenario, investment in technological change was more profitable than investment in conquest when the parties were equally matched.

Surprise is usually expressed that the period 1500 to 1750, which lies between the technologically fertile Middle Ages and Industrial Revolution, was devoid of major innovations. Yet, it is usually noted that this period is characterized by a large number of small changes – of fairly continuous modification – to the existing technological base of agriculture, manufacturing, transport, and communications.

How are we to explain this 'disappointing' period? Mokyr (1990: 57–8) suggests that: 'One explanation for the absence of discontinuous breakthroughs between 1500 and 1750 is that although there was no scarcity of bold and novel technical ideas, the constraints of workmanship and materials to turn them into reality became binding.' Once again Mokyr attempts to explain the rate of technological progress in terms of the supply of ideas and barriers to the implementation of these ideas. Once again I will argue that the main explanation comes from the demand side – from the dynamic strategy and its eventual exhaustion.

My argument is that technological change proceeded by a series of small steps in the two centuries before the Industrial Revolution because the limits to the existing technological paradigm were being increasingly approached.

Increasingly, advances in technique involved the finest of fine-tuning of the existing paradigm. While the scope for doing this had been relatively large before 1500, it declined exponentially thereafter as the old paradigm ceiling was approached increasingly closely. Not until there was a shift in the technological paradigm, which ultimately occurred during the Industrial Revolution, would there be further scope for discontinuous breakthroughs or leaps in technological change. And this would not occur until the factor endowments and, hence, relative factor prices passed a certain threshold level in a number of leading sectors in the British economy. This threshold was passed during the middle of the eighteenth century. The constraints on technological change, therefore, were of the most fundamental economic kind that affected the **strategic demand** for new technical ideas, rather than barriers to the supply of those ideas. The pressure was relieved temporarily by adopting the dominant strategy of commerce in the sixteenth century. But even this was exhausted by the early eighteenth century.

At a broader level of analysis, if the technological paradigm and dynamic-strategies arguments presented in this book are correct, we would expect a paradigm shift to be preceded by an extended period of time in which technological change takes place by small continuous steps rather than large discontinuous breakthroughs. Small changes are the result of society increasingly approaching the limits of the existing paradigm, and continuous technological change is the result of growing population pressure on natural resources and, hence, on material standards of living. This growing pressure can only be relieved by continuous modification of the existing technological paradigm because any single change at the end of a technological era can only be small.

Probably the most significant technological development in this period was a gradual shift in the basis of thermal power or energy from organic (timber) to inorganic (peat and coal) sources. While both peat and coal had long been used in some domestic and manufacturing activities, it was only after 1500 that these fossil fuels were adopted on a widespread basis. Nevertheless, before the Industrial Revolution it had not been possible in Europe to convert thermal energy or heat into kinetic energy or motive power, nor to use fossil fuels for the smelting of iron (Mokyr, 1990: 62). It is interesting to realize that coal had been used in Chinese blast furnaces to produce iron and steel from the fifth century AD (Temple, 1989: 68–9). In Europe, these two uses lay at the heart of the changes we know as the Industrial Revolution. Of the most advanced European countries, Holland, had large supples of peat, while England was well endowed with coal. And they both made extensive use of these energy sources before the Industrial Revolution.

Other improvements, which were introduced into agriculture, included new crops, stall feeding of cattle, and a reduction in the use of fallowing owing to increased supplies of animal fertilizer and increased use of nitrogen-fixing crops. Methods of generating inanimate motive power were also improved through the gradual perfection of the windmill, particularly in Holland and Italy. In industry there was, as we have seen, the widespread adoption of more efficient fuels, together with improvements in blast furnaces, rolling and slitting mills, textile machinery, and instrument and lathe making. Steady improvements occurred in mining in the form of better pumps, rock-blasting methods, underground transport, and haulage. Transport also improved with technical changes in shipping, navigation, and, on the land, the introduction of stage coaches for passengers. As far as overland transport of goods was concerned, rivers were still the most efficient medium (Mokyr, 1990: ch. 4).

Although there was considerable minor modification of the economic system that had emerged before 1500, technological change was gradually grinding to a halt. The process of fine-tuning a technological system that had been inherited from the Neolithic Revolution via classical antiquity had been taken about as far as it could go. By the early eighteenth century, the old paradigm had been virtually exhausted in those countries like England, Holland, and France who were in the vanguard of European civilization. In the case of England this can be seen reflected in the stagnation and very slow growth of real GDP per capita from 1601 to the mid-eighteenth century, which only picked up again as the Industrial Revolution gained momentum (Snooks, 1993a: 257). Had the Industrial Revolution not occurred when it did, we could anticipate that stagnation would have given way to economic decline and, in a highly competitive situation, to further military aggression to achieve through conquest what had been denied by an exhausted technological strategy.

A new technological paradigm

Traditionally the period 1760 to 1830 has been regarded as the British Industrial Revolution. This period witnessed a great surge in significant technological innovations in industry, agriculture, and motive power. It was the beginning of the modern phase of sustained and, eventually, rapid economic growth. Curiously, it has been referred to as 'the wave of gadgets' (Ashton, 1948: 58), 'the age of improvement' (McCloskey, 1981: 118), and 'the years of miracles' (Mokyr, 1990: 81). Others, however, have pointed out that economic growth in the period 1780 to 1830, while marginally faster than that in the first half of the eighteenth century, was quite slow in comparison with later periods (Crafts, 1985). Even more significantly, it has been shown (Snooks, 1990a; 1993a; 1994c) that there were periods in the past – such as 1086–1170 and 1492–1601 – when growth rates were as much as four times faster than those during the Industrial Revolution. Clearly, the distinctive characteristic of the Industrial Revolution should not be viewed in terms of the rates of economic growth. However, it can be thought of as the beginning of modern sustained economic growth that gradually built up to the high rates achieved in the periods 1830–1914 (1.2 per cent per annum) and 1950–1973 (2.5 per cent per annum), keeping in mind that the latter period was in part a response to a release from more than a generation of political and economic crisis.

Can this period be regarded as the 'age of improvement' or the 'years of miracles'? In fact, there was nothing miraculous about these years. It was the culmination of a millennium of intense struggle in the European pressure-cooker of competition. There was nothing sudden or mysterious about this technological transformation except for those unfamiliar with the longrun dynamic of Western Europe. Also the descriptive term 'the age of improvement' is ambiguous. Does it imply an improvement in technology, average living standards, income distribution, or an improvement in all three? In fact, the Industrial Revolution was only the beginning of a sustained improvement in these conditions, which did not become general in Europe until the second half of the nineteenth century, and not in other parts of the world until the twentieth century. Also it should not be taken to imply that there were no other comparable 'ages of improvement', because the Neolithic Revolution, the emergence of the classical civilizations, and even the technological changes that occurred in Europe during the Middle Ages have strong claims to such a title. Clearly, the Industrial Revolution was a complex process, but what marks it off from all other ages is that it involved a technological paradigm shift that ushered in the strategy of *continuing* technological change. It was the age of the technological strategy *par excellence*.

There has also been an extended debate over the nature of well-being during the Industrial Revolution. This debate includes pessimists (Hobsbawm, 1963) and optimists (Hartwell, 1963) and it has raged backwards and forwards in the past and probably will do so in the future (Snooks, 1994b: 11–14). The debate, however, is misconceived. The objective of economic decision-makers, who brought about the Industrial Revolution, was not an improvement in well-being, but an increase in economic resilience or an increase in the power over survival. Economic resilience, which can be validly measured by real GDP per capita, is the ultimate objective of a society involved in an intense competitive struggle for survival, as were the European kingdoms throughout the previous millennium. Well-being, on the other hand, which is impossible to measure objectively, is merely a by-product of the struggle to survive. While an improvement in material well-being can be generated by an increase in economic resilience, some would see non-material well-being (happiness, security, etc.) as depending upon an absence of competition which is the very wellspring of economic resilience. In this case, well-being and economic resilience will be in conflict. If non-material well-being is pursued too far by interventionist organizations, then economic resilience – the power to survive in a competitive world – will decline. Clearly, a balance should be maintained.

The nature of the Industrial Revolution and beyond is more familiar territory and need not detain us long. The technological innovations of this period were major and occurred in a number of mutually reinforcing sectors such as the motive power to drive the new machines; the iron and engineering works to build the new power engines, the new machines, and the new transport facilities; the new transport facilities to carry building materials and products efficiently over land as well as water; the mining of minerals and fossil fuels required by these new industries; and the agricultural surpluses to feed the rapidly growing urban areas.

What distinguished the Industrial Revolution from earlier periods of technological change was the concerted quantum leap occurring across a range of interacting sectors that were able to achieve sustained technological and economic change. This paradigm shift was not a supply-side response as many have suggested (Mokyr, 1990), but an outcome of a surge in demand for 'new' technical ideas by economic decision-makers implementing the new dominant strategy. These decision-makers were responding to changes in fundamental economic forces – particularly concerning factor endowments and relative factor prices – as well as to changing consumer demands as real GDP per capita rose. With the growing pressure of population on natural resources, as the old technological paradigm was progressively exhausted, came a rise in prices: of natural resources relative to labour; of labour relative to capital; and of organic relative to inorganic natural resources. In turn these changing relative factor prices led to the substitution: of capital and labour for natural resources; of capital (machines) for human and animal power; and of inorganic fuels and materials (coal and iron) for organic resources (charcoal and timber).

The major innovations of the Industrial Revolution are well known and include the steam engine, which had a long prehistory but was finally developed as a practical source of power by James Watt in 1774. This engine, which was subsequently improved by Richard Trevithick (high pressure capacity) in 1800 and John McNaught (the compound engine) in 1845, gradually replaced the waterwheel which, nevertheless, continued to attract the attention of improvers. By the second half of the nineteenth century the steam engine had been widely applied to urban and rural economic activity. By being able to convert thermal energy to kinetic energy efficiently, the steam engine transformed the contribution of fossil fuels to economic activity. For the first time in the history of humanity it was possible to generate motive power that did not depend on the muscle of humans and animals, organic sources, or on the elements of nature.

Major strides were also made in the production of iron and steel through the development of new furnaces and processes, such as Abraham Darby's use of coke in the blast furnace (1709), Benjamin Huntsman's coke and reverberatory ovens used to produce a higher quality steel (1740), Henry Cort's puddling and rolling process (1784), and James Neilson's hot blast technique (1829). These techniques reduced the costs (still relatively high) of iron and steel production, and enabled these key materials to be used more widely. In turn this increased the demand for coal, the mining of which became more efficient as the new technology being developed elsewhere was used for pumping, blasting, carrying, hauling, and transport. There were also important mechanical engineering innovations that enabled the working of iron and steel materials with the greater degree of precision required by the new steam engines and other machinery. The key innovations included planing and milling machines, screw-cutting machines, and lathes.

While these machine tool industries were essential innovations, it is not true, as Mokyr claims, that their previous absence had been a barrier to technological change in the medieval period. Mokyr (1990: 103–4) claims:

> It is only a mild exaggeration to say that Wilkinson and his colleagues, by actually being able to manufacture the required parts as specified by the inventor, made the difference between Watt and Trevithick on the one hand and Leonardo Da Vinci on the other.

The argument throughout this book is that economic change is driven by the dynamic strategies of economic decision-makers. When new methods are demanded by a particular strategy, the material incentives are such that these methods are generally forthcoming. The existence of a technical idea, on the other hand, is not sufficient to lead to its application to production. There must also be a strategic demand for this idea. Da Vinci's ideas about motive power were blocked not by problems of execution, but by the absence of demand for that technical solution. Strategic demand, not conditions of supply, is the major determinant of both technological change and economic growth.

These basic industrial techniques provided the foundations on which a range of new mass-consumer industries – which responded to growing material standards of living – were based. In the textile industry, for example, a rapid succession of innovations transformed the nature of production from a domestic to a factory activity producing woollen, cotton, and silk thread and cloth. The main innovations included Richard Arkwright's water frame (1769), James Hargreaves' spinning-jenny (1764), Samuel Crompton's 'mule' (1779), and Edmund Cartwright's power loom (1785). In addition there were many other innovations in industries such as ceramics, glass, paper-making, and food-processing and brewing, all of which reduced the costs of production and created mass markets for these products.

The technological change that has occurred since about 1850 has taken place within the technological paradigm shift that began with the Industrial Revolution. Since 1850 Western society has been exploring the possibilities inherent in this paradigm by pursuing a continuing technological strategy. This process has gone through two phases – the old economic revolution from about 1760 to the 1940s, and the **new economic revolution** since the 1940s (Snooks, 1994a: 14, 268).

The old economic revolution experienced a number of stages. The first of these, between 1760 and 1850, depended upon a relatively small enterprise basis in which the inventor of technical advances was closely related to the 'coal face' of productive activity and to the ownership of the firm. In the second stage, from the 1850s to the 1940s, enterprises grew into large private and public corporations in which the ownership was increasingly divorced from both the running of the business and the technical side, which were managed by specialized research departments staffed by paid professionals. In the second stage, therefore, the commitment to the technological strategy became institutionalized. This was reinforced by government and private investment in specialized scientific institutions undertaking pure scientific and technical research together with the education of research staff being demanded by business corporations. This was the mature phase of the technological strategy in which – for the first time in human civilization – science and practical technology became closely linked. Yet, innovative individuals continued to play a direct role in the technological strategy, often providing the most imaginative solutions to the problems it generated.

The new economic revolution – which has taken place within the paradigm introduced in the late eighteenth century – began to emerge in the interwar period, but only had a significant impact on the modern economy after the 1940s. As shown in Chapter 7, this period saw the application of electronic methods to the technology of the Industrial Revolution in response to a fundamental change in factor endowments and, hence, of relative factor prices – particularly an increase in the prices of skilled labour relative to capital, and of land relative to labour. The resulting substitution of automatic and, later, computerized capital equipment for skilled and heavy labour led to a revolution in the nature of both the market and the household: unskilled married females shifted from the household to the market in order to take over the type of jobs formerly done by skilled, and heavy unskilled, labour. In the household, electrical and, later, electronic equipment was substituted for the labour of married females who were working in the market sector (Snooks, 1994a: ch. 3). As a consequence of these economic changes, the average size of households fell dramatically and permanently for the first time in human history.

Technological development after 1850 went through two main phases: 1850 to 1914; and the 1920s to the 1990s. Even before the turn of the century the technology strategy had ceased to be the monopoly of Europe. Up to the First World War technological change involved the completion of those more sophisticated developments that had begun during the Industrial Revolution. This included improvements in the production of steel (the Bessemer/Kelly converter 1856/57, and the Siemens–Martin open hearth);

of chemicals (explosives, dyes, fertilizers, vulcanized rubber, and plastics); of steam railways (from 1825) and ships (from 1819); of electricity (from the 1870s) and the telegraph; and, in the area of personal transport and leisure, the bicycle (from the 1880s). Since the First World War a number of major new developments have occurred, including the internal combustion engine and the associated assembly-line techniques, mechanized farming, the aeroplane, electrical and electronic equipment for domestic and industrial use, telecommunications via satellite, and, since the early 1970s, the intrusion of computers into every aspect of our lives together with the development of biotechnology which promises to have a huge impact upon agriculture.

The outcome of continued technological change has been a rapid increase in efficiency that has enabled the creation of mass markets for an ever-widening range of consumer goods and services. In the process, the dream of materialist man throughout human history to be able to maximize economic satisfaction was being achieved. Or was it? It would seem that diminishing returns in consumption can be delayed indefinitely merely by continuously producing new, more complex, and more sophisticated goods and services. It would seem, therefore, that the human desire to maximize material advantage is limitless. The drive of materialist man, and the ingenuity of the maker of the wheel, will be with us forever.

The pattern of technological change during the entire history of human society has long puzzled social scientists. It has made major contributions to the progress of human society at both the global and regional levels during relatively brief periods, but has been inactive for vast expanses of intervening time. Only during the two centuries since the Industrial Revolution has technology become a continuous agent of economic change. While this pattern appears puzzling, it can be explained using the dynamic-strategy model developed in this book.

There have been three giant steps in the development of human society when technology has played a major transforming role – the Palaeolithic (hunting), the Neolithic (agriculture) and the Industrial/modern Revolutions. During each of these steps new ideas for production and organization enabled an exhausted technological paradigm to be transcended. With each technological paradigm shift, considerable potential was created for increasing material living standards by using more cost-efficient strategies such as conquest, commerce, and colonization. Only when the potential for improving living standards had been exhausted was technological change called upon once more to transcend the old paradigm. Within the long intervening expanses of time, however, it was employed by individual societies as a subsidiary strategy to support and facilitate the dominant strategies. But in this role technology did not change the nature of the prevailing economic system, only the instruments of the non-technological strategies. With the

Industrial Revolution the threshold, beyond which technological change permanently became the most cost-effective dynamic strategy available to materialist man, finally was passed. The maker of the wheel, like William Blake's Albion, was finally awakened from his fitful sleep.

10

HORSEMEN OF WAR

And there before my eyes was a white horse, and its rider held a bow. He was given a crown, and he rode forth, conquering and to conquer.
(Revelations, VI, 2)

A whirlwind came out of the east. From a swirling cloud of dust and thunder erupted wild men travelling fast on horseback shouting threateningly in a strange language. And bringing death. The whirlwind raged for a millennium and, in that time, reached as far west as Ireland, as far north as the Baltic, and as far south as the Mediterranean. But rather than dying away at the continent's edge, the whirlwind's intensity increased and turned east again. With the coming of the chariot the horsemen of war stormed into central Asia, India, and Iran. Only the ancient civilizations in Egypt and Mesopotamia, which also adopted the horse and chariot as an instrument of war, were able to resist the whirlwind. Finally, when the dust had settled, the world had changed forever. For the horsemen of war had come to stay. The conqueror is the rider in Zechariah's third chariot.

The Indo-European horsemen, who came from the steppes of Russia about 4,900 years ago, were not the first in human society to wage war, but they were the first to carry it so widely throughout the known world. War, in contrast to tribal raids, became a possibility only after the Neolithic Revolution, which gave birth to urban societies that used their agricultural surpluses to achieve specialization and division of labour. For the first time in the history of mankind, a specialized military class emerged. These warriors were employed not only to defend their city, but also to conquer neighbouring cities in order to gain extra agricultural land, labour in the form of slaves, fixed capital, and taxes. With these spoils of war the successful warrior state was able to increase its wealth and material standards of living. Archaeological evidence suggests that war began on a sporadic basis at the same time as urban society in the Fertile Crescent about 9,000 years ago;

that it became more systematic in Egypt and Sumer at least 5,600 years ago; and by 5,300 years ago it had become a major dynamic strategy in urban societies that were dominated by warrior kings and elite warrior classes. War and conquest were to dominate ancient civilization for the following four millennia, reaching their apogee in the Roman Empire.

While war is a relatively recent invention in human society, organized aggression using specialized weapons is as old as the human race itself. Hunting societies have always engaged in fierce raids against one another. And sometimes these raids have escalated into pitched battles. Palaeolithic conflict was generally an outcome of competition between equally matched groups over hunting rights, marriage complications, and retribution for past grievances. These raids and, occasionally, battles did not develop into wars because there was no economic surplus, except in the non-transferable form of leisure, either to support a warrior class or to provide a reason for conquest.

Leisure could not be readily converted into military activity because the security of the foraging band would be jeopardized if even a modest proportion of the part-time raiders was killed or badly injured. In any case, conquest could not be used to increase material living standards, because a foraging band had no use for more land than they could effectively hunt upon; because slaves had no value in a hunting society based upon the close teamwork of equals; because there was a limit to the number of captured wives that could be supported; and because rival bands had no surplus that could be taxed. Once limited hunting rights had been protected, sufficient wives had been procured (usually through peaceful means), various wrongs had been righted, and honour restored, the raids were brought to an end.

Balance was achieved and maintained in palaeolithic society through the existence of large numbers of small groups that were equally matched in economic power. (This was also true for certain periods beyond the neolithic barrier, as in Sumer, Greece, and medieval Europe.) If, however, one hunting group was significantly more resourceful – in all senses of the word – then it would gradually displace the other group through raiding and family multiplication. Equilibrium was more likely to be disturbed in the early history of mankind when unequal rates of genetic change meant that one subspecies had greater hunting and raiding abilities than another. In these circumstances, competition for adjoining territories would gradually lead – as the fossil evidence in Chapter 3 suggests – to the more intelligent and resourceful group taking over from the other through raiding and family multiplication. This was the dynamic of early human society.

Armed aggression, therefore, has been an inherent characteristic of human society over the past 2 million years. Before the Neolithic Revolution, conflict was persistent but remained on a small scale for economic rather than cultural reasons. Only with the development of urban societies based upon agriculture did the costs and benefits of armed aggression change in such a manner that

271

war could be used to meet the material objectives of human society. Henceforth, conquest became a dominant dynamic strategy for ancient civilizations in both the Old and New Worlds. And it is a strategy that has been employed regularly ever since.

CONQUEST AS A DYNAMIC STRATEGY

Conquest is synonymous with civilization. Civilization gave rise to conquest and conquest enabled the development of civilization. Western civilization in particular developed a philosophical and moral code based upon the heroic role of the warrior, and the greatest achievements of ancient culture celebrated the role of combat and conquest as seen in the Gilgamesh epic of Sumer, the *Iliad* of Homer, and the *Peloponnesian Wars* of Thucydides. This is a clear demonstration of the importance of the conquest strategy in the eyes of the ancients.

War and conquest, it has been suggested above, only became an economically viable strategy when urban societies were able to generate the agricultural surplus required both to finance a specialized military elite and to attract the close but predatory interest of surrounding nomads. During and immediately following the Neolithic Revolution, however, most small towns and cities would have been largely preoccupied with developing the technological bases of their societies. This involved the further development of grain types and domesticated animals, agricultural techniques, irrigation facilities, the development of specialized crafts and trades, and the construction of houses, public buildings, and city walls. Nevertheless, there was a need to develop a military capability in order to protect their fixed capital, stored food and raw materials, precious minerals, crafted products, animals, and agricultural lands from the surrounding tribesmen.

Jericho, the first town in the Fertile Crescent, was built with fortified walls some 4 metres high about 10,000 years ago. Many other towns emerged over the following millennium, during which time there must have been intermittent raids from the surrounding herdsmen and conflict amongst themselves. The first city, Çatal Hüyük, was built about 8,800 years ago, and other cities followed. From archaeological investigation it is clear that by 8,000 years BP some of these cities had been destroyed by wars. It would seem that the defensive military forces initially created to deter the unwanted attention of raiding tribesmen were soon used for more offensive military action against neighbouring cities. Within a few millennia of the Neolithic Revolution, war and conquest had become a strategy by which material living standards could periodically be increased. It was not, however, until the first pioneering civilizations arose about 6,000 years ago between the Tigris and Euphrates Rivers and on the Nile that this strategy became systematic and, within a few further centuries, that it became the dominant dynamic strategy of ancient civilizations for about 4,000 years.

What is the conquest strategy and why was it employed in preference to the technological strategy by ancient society once the new technological paradigm had been established? To answer this question we need to recognize that in classical antiquity war in general was not a random event caused by irrational impulses, but was pursued systematically in order to increase material advantage beyond the level that could be achieved through the prevailing neolithic economic system. This is not to argue, however, that some wars did not emerge from irrational forces, just that these were in a small minority because they merely led to self-annihilation. Conquest, in other words, was an integral part of the process of economic change. As a rational economic process, conquest involved both investment in the infrastructure of war and conquest and, for those who were successful, a return on this investment that made the strategy worthwhile.

Investment in the conquest strategy required the diversion of a significant part of the social surplus to, what most observers have wrongly regarded as, non-economic purposes. This may have begun as a defensive response, but the offensive possibilities would soon have become obvious. First and foremost it was necessary to finance a substantial army. This involved the development of a military elite in any society that decided to specialize in war and conquest. These elites gained great wealth and power in ancient civilizations and, in most cases, eventually controlled the destinies of these societies. The common soldier also specialized in military activities and was recruited both from among the citizenry and from conquered territories. This, however, did not preclude both the military elite and the common soldier from being engaged also in other economic activities on a part-time or occasional basis. The military elite were typically large landowners, while the rank and file were often engaged in peasant agriculture when not fighting with their neighbours. Considerable investment was also required to purchase military equipment, war machines, horses and chariots, and warships. Equipment included large numbers of personal armour, swords, daggers, spears, bows and arrows, and shields, while war machines included catapults, battering rams, and siege towers.

Investment on a large scale was also required in transport and communication infrastructure. This included the construction of roads and bridges throughout the conquest empire in order to move men and equipment to trouble spots with all possible speed. The efficiency with which this was done reached a peak in the Roman Empire where roads were built, not for the carriage of traded goods, but for rapidly marching infantry (Mokyr, 1990: 21). Not surprisingly, civil engineering became one of the great achievements of the Romans. Conquering empires also invested in forward defence structures, such as territorial walls, to hold back enemy raiders and in fortified structures garrisoned by troops to enable conquered lands to be permanently occupied. Ports were constructed and navies were built not only to engage the enemy at sea, but also to carry soldiers, their equipment, and supplies around the empire. It was one thing to create an empire and quite another to sustain it. The successful empire had to be efficiently administered. This required investment not only in public buildings and urban infrastructure throughout the empire, together with an effective form of communication, but also investment in specialized human capital. Successful empires required capable administrators as well as effective warriors.

Hence, investment in a successful conquest strategy was expensive and constituted a sizeable proportion of the national income of empires. Even during the *pax Romana* (AD 14–180), the armed forces alone absorbed about 58 per cent of central government expenditures (Goldsmith, 1987: 55). Clearly such investment would not be undertaken on a systematic long-term basis spanning many centuries unless there was also a systematic and competitive rate of return on war and conquest. What did this return involve? Conquest provided a steady increase in relatively scarce labour in the form of slaves, in fixed capital and land, in treasure, and in revenue from taxes imposed upon conquered territories. While part of the additional surplus was ploughed back into the continuing process of conquest, it was also used to increase the material standards of living of the empire's elite and to allow a rapid growth of population in the metropolis. In other words, the size and living standards of the successful conquest society could be increased beyond the limit imposed by neolithic technology, but only at the expense of the vanquished.

Ancient society chose to pursue the conquest strategy rather than the technological strategy because the expected and realized rate of return on warfare was far higher than that on new forms of production and economic organization. This was an economic decision aimed at maximizing material standards of living. The higher rate of return on conquest as compared to that on technological change arose because the existing world stocks of underused natural resources could be exploited by a successful conquest society employing the existing neolithic technology. Only once these natural resources approached exhaustion did the rate of return on investment in technological change become more attractive relative to that in war and conquest. As shown in Chapter 9, the technology strategy only began to be employed on a systematic basis in Europe during the high Middle Ages, culminating finally in the technological paradigm shift known as the Industrial Revolution.

A dependent strategy closely associated with that of conquest is colonization. Colonization takes place when an expanding society establishes an offshoot of itself in a new region and retains formal links with its satellite. This may be seen by the great powers either as an alternative to conquest or as part of the longer-term conquest process. Conquest does not necessarily imply colonization just as colonization does not necessarily imply conquest. If a conqueror merely takes over the ruling hierarchy, colonization need not follow, as in the case of Alexander in Persia, Cnut in Anglo-Saxon England,

and the British in India and Southeast Asia. And if a desirable region is either uninhabited or sparsely inhabited, colonization will not require conquest. But the threat of conquest in the face of resistance may be implied, and it may eventually occur in the future if there is any serious competition over resources between the colony and the native population, as in the case of Greek colonies in Sicily and southern Italy.

Generally speaking, colonization is a form of low-level conquest, in which the land of a less sophisticated society is taken over after just a few scuffles, and there is implicit or explicit threat of systematic large-scale violence if resistance persists. But to be effective it must also involve a programme of family multiplication as a supporting strategy. Often further resistance and violence is only avoided because of the decimation of native populations by diseases introduced by the intruders. Examples include the Spanish and Portuguese colonization of the New World in the early sixteenth century, and British colonization of North America and Australasia. Much of the implied threat of future conquest was bluff. It is remarkable that a handful of small European countries were able to establish large global empires at a surprisingly low cost through the threat of naval action, the establishment of relatively small garrisons of soldiers, some convicts, and, initially, a few boatloads of free settlers. Had the European bluff been called – particularly if coordinated worldwide – then the cost to the Europeans of making good the threat would, in many instances, have been greater than the benefit of the colonies to the mother countries. The bluff was successfully called in the eighteenth century by the colonists (if not the natives) of North America, and by many other colonies – such as those in India, Southeast Asia, and Africa – after the Second World War.

Provided the costs could be contained, the net benefits to the mother country of colonization were considerable. Some of these benefits are indistinguishable from those of conquest – such as slaves (Africa), plunder (precious metals from the New World), and taxes – at least in the early stages. In the case of less exploited colonies, the mother country was able to improve its domestic material living standards directly by exporting its mendicants and its criminals; and less directly through preferential access to new sources of raw materials and to colonial markets for its own domestic production. This was over and above the usual gains from free trade. In the longer term, however, as former colonies mature, even these gains disappear. But then investment is only undertaken on the expectation of returns within the lifetime of the decision-makers, not of their great-great-grandchildren.

CONQUEST-LED GROWTH

The central argument in this chapter is that during the development of each major civilization in the ancient world the conquest strategy was employed systematically to achieve a sustained increase in material standards of living beyond the level that could be generated by the neolithic economic system alone. In other words, economic growth – by which we mean a systematic increase in real GDP per capita – in the ancient world was largely conquest-led, although it was supplemented by the economies of specialization resulting from trade. This argument may come as a surprise to those who think of economic growth as being technologically led. Not only is it generally thought that sustained economic growth is a modern invention, but it is assumed that growth can only be a technological process in the wider sense of resulting from the application of new ideas to production and economic organization. To see growth in this way is to overlook the dynamic process that has dominated about 97 per cent of the history of human civilization. This is the very real cost of extrapolating the present onto the past. Yet while the conquest strategy led to the growth of successful conquest societies, it was largely a zero-sum game and did not lead to sustained economic growth on a global basis.

What is proposed here is that, for the civilization employing this strategy, conquest-led growth involves a dynamic process similar to that of technology-led growth. This similarity is fivefold. First, conquest-led growth is the outcome of a dynamic strategy involving a deliberate attempt to maximize the probability of survival and material advantage. The conquest strategy, like other strategies in different economic environments, is chosen on a benefit–cost basis from a range of alternative strategies. While conquest emerges in this instance as the dominant strategy, its success creates the opportunity for the development of subsidiary strategies such as commerce and technological change, which also contribute to the empire's prosperity. The viability of the subsidiary strategies, however, is heavily dependent upon the success of the dominant strategy.

Second, the systematic pursuit of this strategy generates a stream of net benefits that can be regarded as part of an empire's national income in just the same way as the net benefits from the application of new techniques. The net benefits include new productive units such as additional agricultural land; additional labour in the form of slaves and soldiers; additional fixed capital in the form of captured military equipment, irrigation systems, buildings, transport facilities, etc.; treasure; and additional tax revenue. The important point is that these captured resources become inputs for the generation of further production and further conquest. This is a self-sustaining process of change in which increases in GDP per capita are generated in a systematic way.

Third, to generate a perpetual stream of net benefits from conquest, a society must invest in specialized physical and human capital. This is identical to the prerequisite for technological growth. As discussed earlier, the physical capital includes military equipment and machinery, transport and communications, and public buildings; while human capital includes the skills required for planning and executing broad strategic ideas, for providing the necessary provisioning, for moving large numbers of men, horses, and

276

equipment quickly to various parts of the empire, for military campaigning and fighting, for governing newly acquired territories, and for the central administration of a growing empire.

Fourth, the conquest strategy, like that of technology, requires investment in new ideas. The successful conduct of war and conquest means keeping at least one step ahead of one's enemies. In the situation where two sides are equally matched in manpower, infrastructure, planning, tactics, and discipline, there will be a demand for new ideas. Those ideas will range from the strategy and tactics of war to the nature of military equipment and machinery, and the transport and supply of armies. Periods of intense competition between belligerents, as with economic competition, produces innovation. It is for this reason, as we saw in Chapter 9, that during classical antiquity the main type of technological change was for military rather than productive purposes. These ideas were a direct response to the dominant dynamic strategy of the day. Military innovation, like productive innovation, led to the dominant strategy being conducted more efficiently with a resulting increase in total factor productivity and hence of economic growth.

Finally, the systematic pursuit of the conquest strategy leads to an increase in population and living standards until, ultimately, this strategy is exhausted. The exhaustion of the conquest strategy – or, indeed, of any dynamic strategy – results from the excess of strategic marginal costs over marginal benefits, in other words from the failure of additional campaigns of conquest to cover their costs. This can result from either a reduction in the additional benefits from conquest as the number of unconquered urban societies decline in quantity and quality, or an increase in the costs of administration or transport. The strategic crisis – when the conquest society is suddenly thrown back upon its neolithic agricultural base – leads to a growth slowdown, stagnation, and downturn until a new or rejuvenated dynamic strategy is adopted. But, if the delay in the adoption of a new strategy is too great, the empire will collapse because the revenue demands of an overexpanded conquest society cannot be supplied by its neolithic economic system. The economic rise and fall of empires and civilizations, therefore, can be explained in terms of the systematic pursuit and eventual exhaustion of dynamic strategies.

There is, however, a major difference between technology-led and conquest-led growth. Technological change leads to a growth in real GDP per capita of both the civilization using this strategy and of human society as a whole – even if the innovating civilization is able to retain all the gains from their new investment. Conquest, however, is a zero-sum game. It produces an increase in real GDP per capita in the conquering country at the expense of the rest of the world. The conqueror gains at the expense of the victim. As it is a device not so much for creating new wealth as for redistributing existing wealth in a violent way, I have called it **zero-sum dynamic change** (ZDC) to differentiate it from modern technological dynamic change (TDC) and primitive environmental dynamic change (EDC).

But there are qualifications. Conquest can, and did, create some new wealth by focusing thinly distributed resources in the hands of a smaller, and more highly educated, proportion of the world's population who were likely to use it more efficiently. For example, a higher concentration of surpluses through conquest led to large-scale investments in irrigation works in Mesopotamia and Egypt which, in turn, led to economies of scale. This would not have been possible in smaller and poorer societies. The growth of large metropolises – such as Babylon, Nineveh, Memphis, and Rome in the Old World, and Teotihuacan and Tenochtitlan in the New World – on the proceeds of conquest also enabled a high degree of specialization and economies of scale to be achieved in manufacturing. Both would have increased productive efficiency. Finally, conquest was sometimes a vehicle for the transmission of superior ideas and technologies to other parts of the world, which, in the longer run, would have increased world living standards. It should be realized, however, that the majority of conquest empires in the Old and New Worlds emerged in regions where the technology and institutions of the conqueror were similar to those of the conquered. This is true for lands within the Fertile Crescent and around the Mediterranean of the Old World, and on the Mexican plateau of the New World. Conquest in these central regions of human civilization merely reallocated existing income and wealth. Only when the conquering empire slashed its way into regions that had not experienced the benefits of civilization before – such as Rome in Western Europe and the Incas in the tribal lands of South America – did conquest generate an expansion of technology. But even this should not be exaggerated. Productivity gains were largely restricted to urban technology, to more efficient institutions, and to large-scale organizations, because the agricultural technology of the conqueror was generally less suited to the physical conditions and climate of the barbarian lands. The light 'scratch' plough of the Romans, for example, was unable to handle the heavy but fertile lowland soils of northern Europe. Even in those limited cases where agricultural productivity did increase after the conquest, it was a once-for-all improvement and could not provide a basis for sustained economic growth. Only continuous conquest could do that. And, of course, against all this must be set the destruction caused by war in the shortrun. Conquest was, however, an effective dynamic strategy for successful military societies in both the Old and New Worlds.

Economic growth, therefore, is not just a technological process. It can be generated using other dynamic strategies such as conquest and commerce. Imagine the reaction of ancient man to the suggestion that material living standards could only be increased through technological change in the production of consumer goods and services. His puzzlement would have been no less than that of modern man faced with the proposition that conquest has been the main source of economic growth during all but an instant in the history of civilization. And could be again.

278

RIDING INTO BATTLE

The classical period for the conquest strategy was from the high point of the Sumerian civilization about 3000 BC to the collapse of the Western Roman Empire in AD 476 – a period embracing four millennia. During the first millennium or so of civilization regular but limited warfare was conducted between the city-states of Sumer, and economic gains including land and access to water supplies were made. But conquest was secondary to the technological dynamic strategy involved in constructing an urban society on new agricultural foundations and on commerce. After the classical conquest era, which ended with the fall of Rome, the small European kingdoms, like the early city-states of Sumer, fought savagely with each other. The economic gains of conquest in Western Europe, however, were limited because these kingdoms were quite equally matched. Hence the strategy of technology became just as important as conquest in the period before AD 1500. For medieval Europe the technological strategy provided a reliable longrun increase in material living standards, and the conquest strategy provided the opportunity for windfall gains.

From AD 1500 to 1700 conquest and colonization became important supporting strategies for many European countries, and the dominant strategy for Spain and Portugal. Finally, with the Industrial Revolution from the late eighteenth century, the technological strategy dominated, although from time to time the conquest strategy was involved in both Europe and the Asian–Pacific region. In Europe conquest emerged again during the Napoleonic Wars and during the First and Second World Wars; and in Asia during the 1930s and 1940s the Japanese employed a similar strategy. The Third World also suffered a further outburst of European colonization in the nineteenth century. Conquest since the Industrial Revolution, however, has depended heavily upon the dominant technology strategy and has prevailed only in short, self-defeating bursts.

The Mesopotamian empires

Both the ends and means of war and conquest are tied up with economic rather than political gains. Warfare, as we have seen, only replaced small-scale raiding activities when there was an economic surplus that could be used to finance military activities and that was worth fighting over. It is not surprising, therefore, that the earliest hard evidence for organized military activity on a large scale comes from the pioneering civilization of Sumer (O'Connell, 1989: 35). The civilization of Sumer emerged from the intense competition between the lower Mesopotamian city-states of Lagash, Kish, Ur, Erech, Suruppack, Larsa, and Umma. It was a competition involving regular inter-city warfare over land and access to water supplies (Reade, 1991:

33) and was similar to the later aggressive relationship between the Greek city-states and the small medieval European kingdoms.

In all three cases, war was used to obtain windfall gains rather than as a systematic strategy to increase material living standards, largely because the combatants were equally matched. In each historical case the combatants had to look to other strategies to increase systematically their material advantage. For the cities of Sumer it was technology and commerce; for the Greek cities it was commerce and colonization; and for the medieval European kingdoms it was technology and commerce. This intense competition in each historical case was not only the breeding ground for increasing living standards and the flowering of cultural activity, but also for the emergence of empires when the competitive forces boiled over into the rest of the known world. Interestingly, the gradual elimination of competitive forces, as the empires grew, saw a diminishing of the vigour of cultural activity.

In each historical case of intense competition between a large number of small 'states', ritualistic forms of fighting emerged. The phalanx was invented by the Sumerians but disappeared with the onset of the world's first empire (the Akkadian), and was reinvented by the Greeks two thousand years later. In medieval Europe the armoured knight on horseback played a similar role. These are examples of the wealthy ruling elite playing deadly war games, not examples of conquest and mass death conducted by entire societies. Warfare was limited by economic considerations. In highly competitive environments conquest was not sufficient to generate the regular and reliable surplus required to finance the instruments of mass death. The empires that finally emerged from these competitive cauldrons dispensed with such ritual – deadly as it may have been for the participants – and got down to the serious business of large-scale butchery out of which empires are made. The Sumerian phalanx gave way to armoured bowmen in the Akkadian and Assyrian empires; the Greek phalanx gave way to the sword-wielding Roman legionary, and the medieval knight yielded to the cannon and the gun. These were the weapons of mass death used by those who regarded war and conquest as a serious economic business, not just a game to relieve the boredom of earning an income at the 'office'.

Competition between the city-states of Sumer was temporarily constrained by the military successes of Sargon from Kish in central Mesopotamia. By defeating the cities of Sumer in the south and then turning north, Sargon was able to create the world's first empire which was administered from the relatively new city of Akkad (or Agade). Stretching from Syria and Anatolia in the north to the Persian Gulf in the south, and including the mountains as well as the plains, the Akkadian Empire flourished briefly between 2330 and 2230 BC. For the first time in the history of Mesopotamia the local rulers of the former city-states were transformed into governors who received their instructions from the imperial court (Reade, 1991: 51).

This was an empire based upon conquest. The taxes and tribute that were redirected to the new metropolis raised the living standards of the conquerors and provided the resources for Akkadian armies to penetrate into Syria and Anatolia in the north-west and Elamite Susa in the south-east. Sargon's military success was based upon the use of archers in place of the more dilettantish Sumerian phalanx, and greater use of the four-wheeled chariot largely as a shock tactic rather than a weapon of destruction. But like all the short-lived Mesopotamian empires, the Akkadian Empire depended heavily upon personal military leadership rather than institutionalized imperial bureaucracy. With the death of each Akkadian king, the new ruler had to suppress a rebellion and establish anew his right to rule. Naram-Sin, the grandson of Sargon, had to defeat a coalition of no less than seventeen Mesopotamian kings, and then resecure the empire's frontiers initially established by Sargon (Yoffee, 1988: 48). But, with the premature death of Sargon's grandson the Akkadian Empire collapsed and was overrun by tribesmen (the Guti) from the mountains.

How do we account for the brevity of the Akkadian Empire? Basically the empire was destroyed by the strategy that Sargon employed in its creation. In order to fashion an empire in Mesopotamia, Sargon had to master the forces that had created the pioneering civilization of Sumer. These forces were the intense competition between Sumer's city-states. As Sargon was either unable or unwilling to destroy these city-states completely, he merely succeeded in converting the internal competitive tension from a positive to a negative force as far as his empire was concerned. Instead of driving the technological and commercial advances as it had in the Sumerian civilization, competition became a dangerous centrifugal force that threatened to tear the Akkadian Empire apart. The only way this negative force could be constrained was through a successful conquest strategy, which could be used to placate Sargon's internal enemies. While Sargon's conquest strategy was successful, it was largely exhausted geographically by the time of his death. The reasons for this relatively rapid exhaustion of the world's first conquest strategy appear to be twofold. First, apart from the cities of Mesopotamia, there were few centres elsewhere in the region that would repay the cost of extensive warfare. Clearly Egypt was attractive, but too distant (as even the Assyrian Empire was to discover) to be an economically feasible target. Second, this pioneering conquest society had not had time to develop the infrastructure and logistics of long-range conquest and imperial rule.

Sargon's successors, therefore, had no option but to maintain the existing frontiers of empire against the surrounding hostile tribes. And they had to do this using only internal resources because, with the exhaustion of the conquest strategy, the inflow of outside resources abruptly ceased. Unfortunately for the Sargon dynasty, the attempt to extract more resources from within the empire merely inflamed the opposition from leaders in the former city-states. It was these growing internal forces of chaos that led to the collapse of the Akkadian Empire – a collapse exploited by the surrounding tribes.

For the next few centuries the cities of Sumer renewed their struggle for survival with one another, and with the surrounding nomadic tribes. From time to time relatively short-lived empires emerged, such as the Third Dynasty of Ur (2112–2095 BC) and those based in Isin, Larsa, and Babylon (particularly under Hammurabi, 1792–1750 BC), but each declined and fell as their conquest strategies were exhausted and they succumbed to incessant external competition. Eventually this region, like so many others, was caught up (about 1700 BC) in the whirlwind of the Indo-European horsemen of war, and in the end (about 1500 BC) the Sumerians were overwhelmed and absorbed by Semitic tribesmen.

Almost 900 years were to elapse before an empire greater than that of Akkad emerged. The Assyrian chance came with the clash of the Hittites (from modern Turkey) and the Mitanni (who were part of the Iranian push from Asia) over upper Mesopotamia about 1360 BC. They threw off the shackles of Mitanni domination and established their own small kingdom. In the early ninth century BC the Assyrian kingdom began to expand, reduced Babylon to a dependency, and by 825 BC had established a rapidly growing empire. By 670 BC the Assyrian Empire included not only the entire Mesopotamian region but also the eastern end of the Mediterranean including upper Egypt. Despite this amazing success, their decline was just as dramatic. Within a few decades of achieving their geographical limits, the Assyrians were forced to withdraw from Egypt, and in 612 BC after a successful rebellion by Babylon, supported by the Medes and Scythians on the northern border, their empire collapsed. The Persians who first emerged at this time became, within a few generations, the heirs to the Assyrian Empire together with Asia Minor and, temporarily, Egypt.

The Assyrian Empire (Figure 10.1), born from intense economic rivalry, was founded upon military innovation and a ruthless pursuit of the economic returns from conquest. Their success over a period of seven centuries owed much to the construction of a better organized and equipped army, based upon hierarchies of ten, and to considerable innovation in weaponry. At its height the Assyrian army employed a deadly combination of iron-armoured archers defended by shield bearers and armoured spearmen, mounted troops armed with bows – 'the deadliest weapon combination prior to the introduction of firearms' (O'Connell, 1989: 40) – and, from the late eighth century BC, the heavy two-wheeled chariot used as a fighting platform for bow-wielding aristocrats. This was an offensive force, employed with efficient ruthlessness, which few were able to resist. The Assyrians not only wanted to win battles, they also wanted to destroy their opposition and to acquire its wealth.

Such ruthless professionalism was the basis of the conquest strategy. It was aimed at maximizing the material gain that could be had through war. Assyrian seriousness of purpose, in contrast to the deadly dilettantishness of

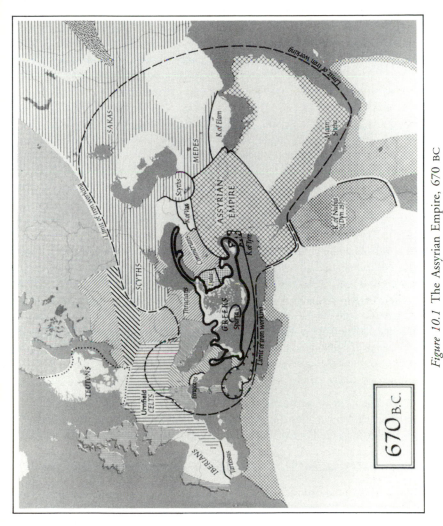

Figure 10.1 The Assyrian Empire, 670 BC

Source: Colin McEvedy, *The Penguin Atlas of Ancient History*, Harmondsworth, Penguin, 1967, p. 47. Drawn by John Woodcock. © Colin McEvedy, 1967. Reproduced by permission of Penguin Books Ltd.

the city-states of Sumer, is reflected in the way they went about destroying the cities of their opponents. To obtain additional treasure, slaves, metals, goods, food, and land, it was necessary not only to destroy armies but also to destroy cities. The Assyrians had learnt the secret that had evaded Sargon and his descendants. This is why the Assyrians, at least after 880 BC, invented siege machines that could dismantle city walls. The systematic slaughter and looting that followed was total war, not for terrorist but for economic purposes. Between 890 and 640 BC, wars occupied the Assyrians for a total of 180 years – three-quarters of the entire period. During this time the Assyrian army sacked Damascus (732 BC), Samaria (722 BC), Musasir (714 BC), Thebes (671 BC), and Susa (639 BC) amongst others. War for the Assyrian, as for the Roman, was a business not a game.

And it was a big business. As O'Connell (1989: 43) suggests, the costs of conducting war on this scale and regularity for almost seven centuries was far beyond the domestic resources of an agrarian-based urban society. Expenditures were massive, including expensive iron armour 'for thousands'; a large stock of war horses that had to be bred, fed, and transported; a number of massive siege machines that had to be carried to or constructed on site; together with thousands of soldiers that had to be fed, equipped, and paid. Such expenditures could only be made from additional resources acquired by conquest – resources that included treasure, slaves, horses, military equipment, metals, goods, food, and – of vital importance for an expanding empire based upon agriculture – land and other natural resources.

The conventional view of the Assyrian attitude to conquest is that it was undertaken for its own sake. Scholars argue, or imply, that conquest has an internal momentum that is driven by the aggressiveness of the male animal and financed by looting. When discussing the Assyrian destruction of enemy cities, O'Connell (ibid.: 43) says: 'each was a military victory but also a monument to the insatiable hunger that drove the beast'. And the military machine is viewed as a self-sustaining mechanism (ibid.: 43):

> To maintain its own sophistication the Assyrian military machine had to fight and keep on fighting. The enormous hauls of metal and slaves from the cities taken were the fuels which fed the economic fires of the military leviathan. As costs rose, so did the pulse of Assyrian history, which after 745 BC comes to resemble a vortex of destruction.

This explanation possesses an unreality akin to science fiction – of war for the sake of war, of conquest feeding conquest, and of the blood lust of the warrior driving history. This is a picture of bestiality and irrationality on a very large and very extended scale.

The argument and evidence in this book totally denies this type of interpretation. Human society is not driven by an irrational desire for death and destruction, and it is not a machine out of control, except possibly for relatively short and critical periods of collapse. Society is driven by rational objectives. Conquest for the Assyrians, as for the Macedonians and the Romans, was an economic strategy aimed at maximizing the probability of survival and material advantage in a highly competitive world. The proceeds from conquest were employed not only to fund further conquest – the main source of economic growth in antiquity – but also to increase the security and material standards of living of the empire's citizens. War for ancient empires was a business not a senseless terrorist activity.

It is misleading of historians to focus exclusively upon the destruction caused by the Assyrian armies – terrible as it was – as if this embodied the experience of the entire Assyrian population. While the soldiers of Assyria were involved in war, the large majority of the Assyrian population experienced peace, security, and a rising standard of living for almost 700 years. As far as the Assyrians were concerned, the conquest strategy provided a handsome rate of return on their considerable investment in this dynamic strategy – largely at the expense of their less successful but equally opportunistic neighbours. Death and destruction existed on the margins, but within the empire itself peace, security, growing prosperity, and culture blossomed.

While the Assyrian Empire lasted far longer than the Akkadian, it too eventually collapsed. What we need to discover is why the Assyrian Empire lasted longer than the Akkadian; what the forces were that finally brought about its collapse; and why this collapse occurred so suddenly in comparison with that of Rome a millennium later. There appear to be three main reasons for the greater longevity of the Assyrian Empire. The first is that Assyria was more successful than Akkad in subduing the lower Mesopotamian cities owing to the protracted severity of the conflict between Assyria and Babylon and the crushing victory of the former (Yoffee, 1988: 57). Assyria crushed its opposition ruthlessly by utterly destroying their cities and societies. Second, Assyria, with the advantage of being a 'second generation' rather than a pioneering empire, was able to develop more effective imperial infrastructure and bureaucracy. Consequently Assyrian armies were able to venture further afield, and newly conquered territory could be more easily assimilated into the empire. Third, there were many more urban centres in Anatolia, Syria, and along the eastern end of the Mediterranean – including the fabulously wealthy Phoenician Empire – in the early first millennium BC than in the late third millennium BC.

However, the conquest strategy eventually led to collapse – a collapse that occurred very quickly. There are three main reasons behind the Assyrian collapse. First, with the occupation of Egypt in 670 BC, the conquest strategy was finally exhausted; there were no further wealthy urban communities to conquer. Consequently the inflow of resources ceased abruptly and the imperial infrastructure and inflated living standards of the ruling elite had to be financed from within the empire. The growing burden of taxation together with the increasing oppressiveness of the regime led to a series of revolts within the occupied territories, particularly in Babylonia, at a time when the Cimmerians, Scythians, and Medes were pressing on the northern frontier. Second, the Assyrian imperial system, although much more effective than that of the Akkadian Empire, still had difficulty in integrating the conquered territories (Yoffee, 1988: 57–8). Third, and related to the last point, the Assyrians had overextended themselves when they conquered Egypt and ran down their financial resources to a precariously low level. The first of these explanations was responsible for the expansion of the Assyrian Empire drawing to a close and for creating severe internal problems, while the second two help to explain the rapidity of the collapse.

The Macedonian Empire

The story of the Macedonian Empire contains echoes of Mesopotamian experience some two millennia earlier: echoes of continuous and intense competition between large numbers of equally matched city-states, which provided the breeding ground for the emergence of empires. In the Greek world, deadly dilettantish contests between some 200 city-states – including Athens, Sparta, Corinth, Thebes, Laurium, Pylos, and Megara – contrast with the professional commitment to total warfare of the Macedonians. While the Greek states were deadly serious about their regular military contests, they were not committed to conquest as a dominant dynamic strategy. They were able to maximize their material advantage through the pursuit of commerce and colonization. In contrast, the Macedonians ruthlessly and innovatively pursued conquest as their dominant strategy.

Greek origins can be traced back to at least 1850 BC. By 1300 BC the early Greek kingdoms of Mycenae and Knossos, which were literate societies, had emerged and were on the offensive in Asia Minor (as told in Homer's immortal *Iliad*) and Cyprus. About 1100 BC the Achaean Greeks were overrun by the Dorians, who were illiterate barbarians from the north. The Ionian Greeks, who claimed to be pre-Dorian, retained control of the south-western coast of the Greek peninsula, the islands of the Aegean, and the west coast of Asia Minor. The Achaean Greeks in Cyprus were later (about 1000 BC) absorbed by the expansion of the Dorian Greeks.

The city-states of Greece evolved in the late eighth century BC from the illiterate tribal kingdoms that traced their origins back to the Dorian and Ionian Greek settlements. Over the following three centuries the urban institutions of these city-states, built upon an agricultural base, continued to evolve. Before 800 BC most of their citizens dwelt in farming villages, and only thereafter did true urban communities, pursuing trade and industry, emerge. While they dispensed with their kings and espoused democratic ideals, power in the early period resided in aristocratic hands, and occasionally – as at Sicyon (655–570 BC), Corinth (620–550 BC), and Athens (546–510 BC) – tyrants gained control.

While Greek city-states struggled with one another for economic advantage, generally in the form of additional farming land, they did not conduct total war, except towards the closing stages of the Peloponnesian Wars. As the Greeks did not employ conquest as a dominant strategy, owing to the existence of more cost-effective alternative strategies, they found it uneconomical to invest in the siege technology required to destroy the cities of their opponents. Their aim, in these circumstances, was merely to drive their rivals from the field of battle, not to totally destroy them nor to confiscate their livelihood.

The central military feature of Greek battles was the phalanx. As we have seen, this tactic was originally invented by the city-states of Sumer two millennia earlier. It was reinvented between 675 and 650 BC (O'Connell, 1989: 50), probably by the Dorian state of Sparta, and it replaced the deployment of heavy cavalry which was no match for the 'new' spear-carrying hoplite phalanx. In general, the phalanx was manned by the social elite who were sufficiently wealthy to purchase their own equipment. Only Sparta, which devoted itself to a military lifestyle, possessed a standing army because it saw its interests on the mainland. For the rest, war was a game played by the elite.

War was a serious game with occasional windfalls rather than a business for the Greeks, largely because, living in such a competitive environment so close to the sea, the strategic benefit–cost calculations favoured commerce and colonization rather than conquest. Even the windfalls of war were expropriated by the state in both Athens and Sparta, and were not regarded as the legitimate right of victorious commanders and their armies (Millett, 1995: 190; Hodkinson, 1995: 150). Pursuing the profits of trade, the Greek states discovered that it was relatively cheap to establish colonies around the Mediterranean. Greek traders became more adventurous in the eighth century, expanding east into the Aegean and Syria, south to Egypt, and west to Italy and Sicily. They traded their own craft products, wine, and olive oil, together with luxuries from the east, grain from the Black Sea region, and slaves and metals from Gaul. These trade contacts made it possible for the Greek city-states to specialize according to their comparative advantage, thereby increasing their efficiency and material standards of living. And, in the process, they discovered the ease with which colonies could be established.

Waves of Greek colonization occurred between 750 and 500 BC (Starr, 1991: 216). The main pressure for colonization was the competitive need to increase material advantage by city-states – particularly for Corinth, Chalcis, Eritrea, and Miletus – which suffered a shortage of good farming land. Clearly, colonization was a cheaper solution to this problem than conquest on the Greek mainland, particularly as the natives of Mediterranean lands were no match for the Greek hoplite phalanx. Sparta appears to have had sufficient productive land for its purposes and was able to exercise authority over the Peloponnese. Hence, it established only one colony, at Tarentum in

Italy. Greek cities were established around the shores of the Black Sea, along the southern coast of Asia Minor, at Cyrene in North Africa, along the southern shores of Italy and Sicily, and around the Mediterranean coast of France and Spain. While expansion of the Persian Empire throughout Asia Minor in the early fifth century overwhelmed Greek colonies in the east – at least until the expansion of Macedonia in the early fourth century – colonies in the western Mediterranean persisted until the expansion of Rome during the third century.

Through colonization the greater Greek community gained access to new natural resources and to areas that were vital sources of strategic materials (iron, other metals, and timber), resources (slaves), and cheaper food (wheat and fish). These colonial cities also facilitated the export of Greek wine, olive oil, and manufactured goods such as the famous red and black pottery. As colonization and trade grew, it was necessary to invest in better port facilities, warehousing, and shipping. It is generally acknowledged that between 750 and 500 BC there was, in the wider Greek world, a flourishing of 'the economic spirit' (Starr, 1991: 222). Colonization and trade were cheaper strategies for improving material living standards and for achieving economic growth than the strategies of conquest and technological change.

Yet, like the situation in Sumer some two millennia earlier, the early competitive balance between the Greek city-states began to shift menacingly by the end of the sixth century. This came about with the growing military dominance of Sparta in the south and the increasing ambitions of the Athenians following the Persian Wars. Sparta used its growing military strength in the late sixth century to establish military dominance over the Peloponnesians. Rather than destroy their neighbours, Sparta was content to reduce them to the status of dependent allies and to achieve a stability in Greece that would deter intending invaders. While this did not prevent the Persian invasions in 490 and again in 480 BC, it does appear to have assisted, together with the cooperation of Athens, in the successful repulsion of the invaders.

This demonstration of Greek military prowess may have contributed to the expansionist desires of Athens – owing to increasing problems in maintaining urban living standards from its own lands – by reducing the cost of conquest. Although Athens' attempt to extend its territories on the Greek mainland between 478 and 446 BC failed, it was successful in increasing its influence throughout the Aegean, around the western coast of Asia Minor, and along the approaches to the Black Sea, thereby giving access to the wheat-lands of Russia. Increasingly, conquest was becoming a more economically attractive strategy now that the scope for further colonization and trade was diminishing. The exhaustion of traditional dynamic strategies, therefore, placed increasing pressure on Greek material living standards and the ability to maintain their urban way of life. An alternative dynamic strategy was required.

By the mid-fifth century, the Greek world was no longer dominated by a large number of highly competitive city-states. Although each *polis* was theoretically independent, they had by now grouped themselves into four major blocks – the Athenian, Spartan, Corinthian, and Syracusan (Sicily). Despite the magnificent flowering of Greek culture in the fifth century – the golden age of classical antiquity – the economic signs were ominous. The alternative dynamic strategies to conquest that had been pursued over the previous three centuries were finally exhausting themselves. Colonization opportunities had, with the activities of Carthage in the west and Persia in the east, come to an end, and the scope for favourable trade was being squeezed in the west by Carthage and Etruria, in the north by Macedonia, in the east by Persia, and in the south by Carthage and Persia. Moreover, the technology strategy was too costly even to be considered. Increasingly the only option was conquest.

Attempts by Athens from 433 to 431 BC to extend its influence in the west at the expense of Corinth, a Spartan ally, eventually led a reluctant Sparta to declare war. This war from 431 to 421 was inconclusive, as Sparta could not match Athens at sea and Athens did not dare meet Sparta on land. Corinth was the overall loser in this contest between the leading Greek states. Continued economic expansionism by Athens led to an abortive and disastrous naval expedition to Sicily and to the resumption of war with Sparta, which ended with the total defeat of Athens in 404 BC and the extension of Spartan control over the Greek mainland. It is interesting that this struggle for economic power led to the only real innovations in Greek warfare – siege machines, new fighting ships, and a change in hoplite armour to enable greater mobility. These innovations arose, not so much from 'an agony of frustration' (O'Connell, 1989: 59), as from an increase in the potential benefits from conquest – for Athens the control of the Italian territories and for Sparta the control of the Greek mainland – and a reduction of the costs owing to the experience gained during the Persian Wars. But the spoils of war are not easily won by societies not accustomed to treating conquest as a business. Sparta's attempt after 404 to create an empire outside the Peloponnese led to defeat at the battle of Leuktra in 371, the subsequent secession of many of its mainland allies, and finally enemy invasion in 369 (Hodkinson, 1995: 146–7).

Under pressure from changing economic forces, the era of competitive city-states was breaking down. Yet Sparta's failure to achieve national unity left the door open to Macedonian conquest under Philip in 338. With Philip's assassination in 336, Alexander took over his father's plans for a Greek invasion of Persia. Alexander's war against Persia began in 334 and by 330 Darius, king of Persia, had been killed leaving his former empire for the taking. The success of Philip and Alexander of Macedonia was truly amazing. Within the space of a generation the Macedonians became masters not just of the Greek mainland but of the entire civilized world (Figure 10.2). During

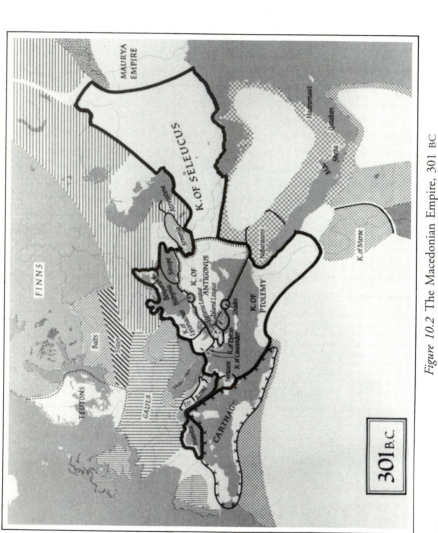

Figure 10.2 The Macedonian Empire, 301 BC

Source: Colin McEvedy, *The Penguin Atlas of Ancient History*, Harmondsworth, Penguin, 1967, p. 61. Drawn by John Woodcock. © Colin McEvedy, 1967. Reproduced by permission of Penguin Books Ltd.

this time their wealth increased exponentially. How do we account for this revolution?

A contrast is generally drawn by military historians between the conduct of war by the Greeks and the Macedonians. Until the final stages of the Peloponnesian Wars, Greek warfare was largely ritualistic (albeit deadly), whereas Macedonian warfare was conducted on a very professional basis. To the Greeks, war was a serious game, whereas to the Macedonians war was a profitable business. Accordingly, the Macedonians were more innovative in their weaponry and tactics, and invested more heavily in their military machine. They developed a new long-range phalanx, used heavy cavalry, and invented and built sophisticated siege engines and catapults. These weapons were mass-produced in large, state-run factories. They even employed some of the ancient world's greatest scientists – such as Archimedes of Syracuse – for the task (O'Connell, 1989: 65). And the Macedonians exploited these new military techniques ruthlessly to destroy their enemies for the purpose of 'self-enrichment' (Austin, 1995: 206–8).

One military historian (O'Connell, 1989: 57) has asked 'why it was that they [the Greeks] did not place greater reliance on [military] technological innovation'. His answer appeals to ideology:

> it seems the Greeks developed weapons and tactics suited to their own political, sociological, and psychological paradigms and, having done so, were essentially satisfied with them. Better weapons might have meant victory in certain instances. Yet winning outside the accepted military conventions implied the sacrifice of more deeply held values.

This suggests that attitudes to war are culturally determined, whereas all the evidence marshalled in this book shows that war, like all other dynamic strategies, is determined by fundamental economic conditions in all cultures. War for the Greeks was not the dominant economic strategy that it was for the Macedonians because other strategies were more cost-effective. Colonization and commerce were the major Greek strategies, and only when they had been exhausted, by the late fifth century, did Athens and Sparta begin to invest more heavily in military equipment and machinery. Before then the benefits of total war were not worth the additional costs. Macedonia, on the other hand, began its expansionary phase at a time when the only available dynamic strategy was that of conquest. The time for colonization and favourable trade had passed. Hence to the Macedonians conquest and growth were synonymous. Accordingly, they adopted conquest as their dominant strategy and were prepared to invest heavily in the necessary military technology and infrastructure. And the returns on this investment were astronomical.

The Roman Empire

The expansion of Rome, after the mid-fourth century BC, occurred in a world dominated by highly successful, military-based economic powers. In

291

the north Italic peninsula there was Rome's overlord, the cultivated Etruscans; in the south there were Greek colonies; in the western Mediterranean there were the Carthaginians; and in the east lay the vast Macedonian Empire. The only strategy that Rome could have employed in this crowded Mediterranean world was conquest, because the potential for colonization had been exhausted, the scope for advantageous trade was limited, and the benefit–cost calculus for technological change put it out of the question. Even the probability of success for Rome through conquest was extremely low. Rome, however, beat all the odds and, within 150 years, was master of the western half of the Mediterranean world. The critical question is: how was so much achieved in such a relatively short time?

Continuous settlement on the site of the city of Rome began in the mid-eighth century BC in a number of villages peopled by Latins. For the following few centuries this growing urban complex was ruled by elected kings, the last of whom were Etruscan. During this early period the Romans were involved in a desperate struggle for survival, as well as for plunder and land, with their neighbours, particularly with the warlike mountain tribes (Oakley, 1995: 12–14). In 509 BC the Roman Republic was established and Etruscan influence was thrown off. During the following Etruscan Wars the fledgling republic developed its military prowess, which was based upon a citizens' militia. After the capture of the Etruscan city of Veii in 396 BC, the citizen militia was transformed into a professional army receiving regular pay. But it was the sacking of Rome in 390 BC by the Gauls – who had sliced through both Etruscan and Roman defences – that brought about major military changes including the fortification of Rome, the admission of plebeians into the army, the replacement of the discredited spear-carrying phalanx with the sword- (*gladius*) and javelin- (*pilum*) carrying legionary, and the introduction of regular practice with both weapons. It was to be some eight centuries before Rome was again sacked.

The Roman army, which was mobilized for war on an annual basis from the late fifth century (ibid.: 14–16), became famous for its remarkable operational speed (a consistent 20 miles per day) based upon the construction of a paved road network (beginning in 312 BC with the Via Appia) throughout Italy and, later, the Mediterranean world. This mobility not only prevented opponents from regrouping, but enabled the Roman Empire to minimize the size of its army – often as small as 175,000 regulars at the height of its influence (O'Connell, 1989: 75). Needless to say, this network of roads and fortresses, which was unparalleled in the ancient world, was very expensive to construct and maintain. This was the basic infrastructure of the Roman conquest strategy, and it was used by soldiers not traders. Only a strategy that produced an acceptable and continuous rate of return on this investment could justify such large financial outlays.

The new military machine of the Mediterranean world paid good dividends. By 350 BC Rome had gained domination over the surrounding hinterland, and between then and 220 BC had conquered the remainder of the Italian peninsula beginning with the Latin League (340–338 BC) and ending with the Greek cities in the south. During this period the Romans demonstrated a determined professionalism and a systematic ruthlessness. In addition to the new fighting prowess of the legionaries, the Romans employed siege warfare, a strategy unknown to the Greeks at such an early stage of development. The Romans had begun as they meant to continue. If they were to succeed in such a highly competitive world, they had no choice.

Military historians usually argue that the Romans were not very innovative when it came to the use of war machines – that they borrowed heavily from others, particularly the Macedonians. Roman success, it is claimed, was due more to the professional manner in which these existing techniques were employed: 'they were used with a ruthlessness and an organizational mastery that were unprecedented, except perhaps by the Assyrians' (O'Connell, 1989: 76). Others (Starr, 1991: 466–7) even write about the 'dogged persistence of Roman leadership' and reveal that they refused to commit themselves to battle except when circumstances were favourable. Like the Assyrians and the Macedonians, the Romans regarded war as a lucrative business, in which foolish heroism was unprofitable. They also treated their opponents in a business-like, rather than a vengeful, manner: 'Beside looting their victims of movable property, the Romans commonly took about a third of conquered lands on which they settled colonies of Roman and Latin farmers' (Starr, 1991: 466). This land, known as *ager Romanus*, increased from 318 square miles in 510 BC to 735 square kilometres in 340 BC, and to 8,972 square kilometres in 264 BC – out of a total of 50,215 square miles for the entire Italian peninsula (Oakley, 1995: 12). And they exacted a combination of taxes and promises of troops. In return they provided both citizenship and protection for the conquered peoples of Italy (and after AD 212 of those throughout the empire) together with economic and political stability.

What was the motivation for this ruthless professionalism? One historian (O'Connell, 1989: 76) has claimed: 'Just as the predator kills with any means available, so did Rome. All were merely components to an end defined by political ambition.' Certainly the military efforts of Rome were merely a means to an end, but that end was economic rather than political. Conquest was a business pursued to achieve the materialistic ends of all Roman citizens. It is not possible to wage war systematically for some eight centuries merely for the political ambitions of the ruling elite. Wars are won by the foot soldier who is not fighting for political ideologies or for the political ambitions of an emperor in Rome. Rather, he and his generals are fighting for material gain. Whole societies, not just political leaders, wage war. And they wage war to improve their material advantage. In any case, what is political power other than the ability to control economic resources? And wealth was generally required in the ancient world to achieve political power.

From 264 BC Rome began a process of expansion and empire building outside Italy that lasted for four centuries. During this time Rome added about 1.8 million square miles to the size of its empire, or about 45,000 square miles each decade. This amounts to an average of 4,500 square miles for each of these 400 years – a truly remarkable feat in determination and persistence, which is hard evidence of Rome's absolute professionalism. And with this territorial expansion came a great flood of booty, taxes, and slaves into the metropolis; which increased Roman living standards and provided the basis for further conquest (Hopkins, 1980: 37–47). Rome's remarkable expansion began with the Punic Wars (264–41 and 218–01 BC) against Carthage, wars that left Rome in control of the western half of the Mediterranean, but which also left it near bankruptcy. What, in these straitened circumstances, should a risk-taking transnational military corporation like the Roman Republic do? While the answer seems to have surprised some historians, it would not surprise the business strategist. Starr (1991: 488) speaks for many historians when he exclaims with surprise:

> After the Carthaginian peace of 201, Rome had a multitude of problems. Much of Italy had been devastated, and large parts needed reorganization after rebellion and reconquest. The Gauls of the Po valley were virtually independent; the Romans held only the coast of Spain, which was far from tranquil. Financially the Roman state was in weak condition, and the Roman people were exhausted from the long war . . . Nonetheless the Romans at once turned east. Within 13 years Rome gained virtual mastery over the Hellenistic world.

Rome, like any great business enterprise, at once turned east in order to recoup the heavy expenditures involved in conquering the temporarily impoverished western Mediterranean. For an empire committed to increasing its material living standards through the conquest strategy, there was no other way to survive. From the fruits of war in the wealthy east, Rome was able to revive its economy at home and its empire in the west. So successful were they that, with the booty from the conquest of Macedonia in 167 BC, Rome was able to dispense with internal taxation until the time of Augustus some 150 years later (Levy, 1967: 65; Frank, 1940: 7; Hopkins, 1980). The entrepreneurs in this business of conquest included individual Roman generals as well as the Roman Republic. And their rapid success in the east – in the Hellenistic world – owed much to large-scale investment in military infrastructure and to the honing of Rome's military efficiency during the Punic Wars. Rome had become a very effective transnational military business.

War as business became even more entrenched in the society of Rome during the century and a half from 133 BC to AD 14. In this period, the strife-riven Republic/Augustan principate was able to conquer more territory than ever before. During these 147 years the area of the Roman Empire increased by a total of 1.08 million square miles, which averaged out to

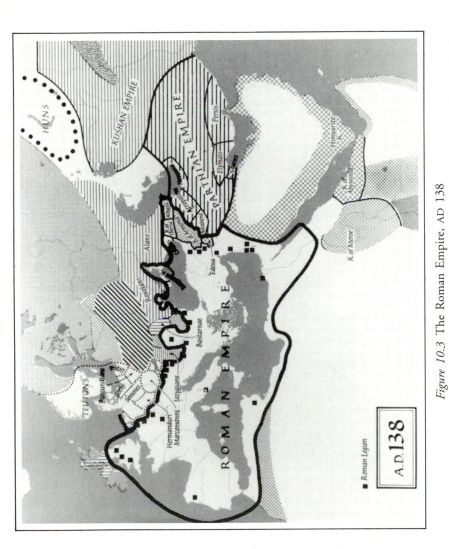

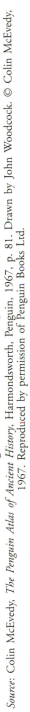

Figure 10.3 The Roman Empire, AD 138

Source: Colin McEvedy, *The Penguin Atlas of Ancient History*, Harmondsworth, Penguin, 1967, p. 81. Drawn by John Woodcock. © Colin McEvedy, 1967. Reproduced by permission of Penguin Books Ltd.

7,347 square miles a year – almost two-thirds greater than the average for the entire 400 years of empire expansion. In this period the military business of Rome transcended even the games of republican politics – of leadership crisis and civil war. And in this period Rome experienced an expansion of trade, a growth of Italian cities (and hence of economic specialization), an improvement in agriculture, and the development of a money economy (Hopkins, 1983). Hence, the prosperity achieved through the dominant strategy of conquest created the conditions in which other subsidiary strategies – that had been denied to Rome at the beginning of expansion back in the mid-fourth century BC – flourished and contributed to the increase in material standards of living. The success of the subsidiary strategies was highly dependent upon the success of the dominant conquest strategy. When it ended, so did theirs.

The years between AD 14 and 180 (Figure 10.3) are seen as the most peaceful and secure period that classical antiquity was to experience, despite the rebellions in Egypt and Judaea and the continual pressure on the borders from the barbarians. It is known as *pax Romana*. But in reality it was merely the quiet before the storm, the autumn before winter, the Roman Empire's 'Indian summer'. In this period – probably by AD 130 – the expansion of the Roman Empire finally came to an end, and an attempt was made to define and defend largely static boundaries. This period saw the 'crystallizing of its limits', with Rome extending about 3,000 miles (4800 km) from east to west enclosing a population of between 50 and 100 million. Yet these limits contracted slowly by about 500 square miles annually for the following three centuries until after AD 430, when the empire began contracting rapidly.

Starr (1991: 585) suggests that:

> The Empire inherited a policy of unlimited military expansion in which frontiers were fluid, but by the death of Augustus it had passed to a strategic defensive, in which it sought to hold what it had. Thereafter tributary kingdoms which had become pacified were occasionally annexed, but only minor military conquests occurred.

Why? The argument in this chapter is that during the first century after the birth of Christ the costs of additional conquests were beginning to exceed the derived benefits – that extra territory acquired through conquest was not paying for itself. A good test case for this argument is the Roman conquest of England, Wales, and southern Scotland from Claudius to Hadrian (AD 41–138). As Starr (ibid.: 586) informs us: 'This fringe area . . . never yielded enough revenue to meet the costs of the heavy garrison required to keep down the semicivilized British and to keep out the utterly uncivilized Picts in the Highlands.' Also the costs of central administration were escalating as the frontier of the Empire inched forward.

The Roman military business was bankrupt. State revenues that increased from 500,000 sesterces in AD 1 to 1,500,000 by AD 70 were largely exhausted a century later when Emperor Marcus Aurelius was forced publicly to auction state valuables, raise new and higher taxes, and reduce the silver content of the *denarius* to 70–78 per cent in order to defend Rome against the Germans (Tainter, 1988: 134–5). *Pax Romana* was merely a breathing space between the end of empire expansion and the beginning of a long, drawn-out process of collapse in which it remained to be seen whether an alternative dominant strategy to conquest could be developed before the empire gave way under its own weight now that it was thrown back on its neolithic technological base. And, in its existing condition, collapse it must, because the empire could only finance its swollen size and standard of living by continuous con-quest. The critical question was: could the costs of empire be cut back to match reduced revenues? These costs involved not only the imperial infra-structure and bureaucracy but also the size of the population and its material living standards – all of which exceeded the prevailing neolithic technological optimum. There were, however, too many vested interests which would suffer from this radical approach. Even if cost reductions could be achieved by a reduction in the size of the empire, a tactical retreat might have given encour-agement and economic support (in the form of abandoned resources) to Rome's enemies. There appeared at the time to be little alternative to defending the existing borders and hoping that a dynamic alternative would emerge.

But what were the possible alternative sources of prosperity? During *pax Romana* there was an increase in trade, based upon wheat from Egypt and Africa; wine and olive oil from Gaul, Spain, and Africa; and manufactured products from Italy. Trade also spread beyond the boundaries of empire into northern Europe, Africa, India, central Asia, and China. And this trade enabled further economic specialization both within, and of, the empire. But these positive trade effects could not, on their own, compensate for the demise of Rome's military business. Second, there was a wider dispersion of existing agricultural and urban technology throughout the Roman world. But it proved impossible to develop a new technological paradigm that was required to replace successfully the conquest strategy. As yet the benefit–cost calculus was not right, in part due to the nature of the factor-endowment ratio, and hence relative factor prices (there were still abundant supplies of natural resources that could be utilized within the existing neolithic technological paradigm) and in part due to Rome's monumental degree of specialization (in physical and human capital, and in organization) in the conquest strategy. Rome was locked into defending the remarkable achievements of its conquest strategy. Rather than investing in new industrial technology to achieve growth, the Romans, in their frustration, invested profits from trade and moneylending in landed estates to achieve social status. This was a sure sign of declining economic resilience.

Despite the relatively brief respite of *pax Romana*, the attempt to develop an alternative dynamic strategy to that of conquest therefore failed. The only prosperity achieved was of a precarious kind, as it was available only to the ruling elite. As Starr (1991: 589) says: 'by the second century this escalator [of prosperity] was slowing down, and those who stood on top were distinguished in style of dress, reserved seats in the theaters, and even a different scale of punishments in courts of law'. Also, financial difficulties were being increasingly experienced by various levels of government which, rather than cutting costs because of the influence of vested interests, increased taxes on those who had no political influence and devalued the currency. Between AD 60 and 200 the silver content of the *denarius* was reduced from over 90 per cent to under 60 per cent (Bolin, 1958: 210–11) and inflation rose accordingly, particularly affecting those on fixed incomes. Rome's conquest strategy had produced an economy in which the objectives of the ruling elite were achieved at the expense of the majority (80 to 90 per cent) of the population who were either urban workers, peasants, or slaves. Even as Rome made its long journey into night, the aristocracy led lives of luxury, while the vast majority of the people were poor and undernourished.

By the third century AD the failure to discover a viable alternative strategy to that of conquest led to economic and, hence, social and political decline. Population, hit by recurrent plague in AD 165–180 and 250–270, fell. So did economic production. Meanwhile, at the same time, the barbarians from beyond the frontiers – Germans in the north and the newly revived Persian Empire in the east – began to press in on the Roman Empire. To finance the defence of empire it became essential for governments to increase taxes, to requisition food and clothing, to demand free supply of administrative services from the upper classes, and to devalue the currency. While the inevitable collapse was delayed by the resourcefulness, the drive, and the ambition of many individuals and of an amazingly resilient culture, the empire was on a downward path experiencing barbarian incursions, civil wars, greater social rigidity, violence, and terrorism on the way. This economic decline was also reflected in considerable political instability, with twenty-two emperors and many more pretenders in just fifty years between AD 235 and 285. There was a decline in literacy and mathematical training leading to a reduction in effective government, including the abandonment of the census in Egypt after AD 250. Compounding these problems, former parts of the empire (such as Britain, Spain, and Gaul) achieved temporary independence in the mid-third century AD; revolts were experienced in various parts of the empire; and the military gained considerable independence – ironically only after the collapse of the conquest strategy. Towards the end of the third century the Roman state was even forced to abandon its traditional revenue-raising methods and to resort to coercive labour and barter (MacMullen, 1976). The forces of chaos were beginning to overwhelm the forces of order.

From time to time order reasserted itself and attempts were made to reform the organization of state and army (Diocletian AD 284–305 and Constantine AD 306–337), but this order was increasingly oppressive (where it was effective) and its tax imposts became intolerable, particularly as trade and industry declined throughout the fourth century. This was the cost of driving back the invading German and Persian armies, and in restoring the old frontiers. But it was a cost, in terms of a huge army (650,000 men) and bureaucracy (30,000 civil servants), that could not be supported in the longer term. Population, which had declined in the second and third centuries due to plague, failed to recover in the fourth and fifth centuries precisely because it had to adjust downwards to a level supportable by a neolithic economic system. This had major implications for agriculture, the military, and the bureaucracy, which experienced increasing problems in employing suitable labour. Coercion was increasingly, but ineffectively, resorted to in the last days of Rome (MacMullen, 1976). But nothing could alter the fact that a neolithic economic system could just not support such a vast conquest empire of up to 100 million people (Durand 1977: 269).

The first major crack in the edifice of empire occurred in AD 395, when it literally split into two halves: the Western Roman Empire centred on Rome and the Eastern Roman Empire centred on Constantinople. This was a final formal recognition of occasional dual rule that had existed since AD 364. While the east continued its urban-based lifestyle, central control in the west became increasingly ineffective as its oppressive demands increased. The economic and military response in the west was the development of a rural warrior nobility based upon large estates. The *villa* – the economic, social, and political focus of these large estates – became the centre of small-scale industry as well as the centre of local rural economy. Cities were of declining significance towards the end of the Western Empire. Those who worked on the land looked not to urban government but to the rural nobility for protection against predators both local (marauders) and imperial (tax collectors). To fulfil this economic, social, and political role, aristocrats fortified their villas and raised their own armies and, as Warren Hollister (1982: 25) tells us: 'Having deserted the cities, the aristocracy would remain an agrarian class for the next thousand years'. The development of local rural warlords was an effective, and logical, response to the decline of central responsible authority. And it became the economic bridge from the late Western Roman Empire to the Middle Ages. As Starr (1991: 697) writes:

> In many ways the western provinces were reverting toward the Neolithic level of simple food-production, but in doing so they were fashioning a network of stable, independent cells which could survive the withering away of the imperial machinery and the disappearance of a money economy in the early Middle Ages. These cells became the manors of medieval Europe.

Although Rome was finally sacked in AD 410, the first time in 800 years, the Western Roman Empire was not dissolved until AD 476. This collapse was an inevitable outcome of the exhaustion of Rome's dominant conquest strategy after AD 138, and the failure to develop a dynamic strategy to take its place. The breakthrough of Germanic tribes from beyond the northern frontier merely delivered the *coup de grâce*. Like all empires based upon the conquest strategy, the Roman Empire had got caught in a dead-end play. The attempt to use conquest as a way of achieving the objective of maximizing material advantage ultimately is self-defeating. Once the limits to this strategy are reached, where the marginal cost of conquest exceeds its marginal revenue, the system will cease to be dynamic and will eventually decline. And, ultimately, it will collapse because the superstructure of empire cannot be supported by the underlying neolithic economic system. In the case of Rome, this collapse took three centuries to work itself out, whereas in the cases of Akkad and Assyria, it took merely two to three generations. Rome's greater resilience can be accounted for by its more effective imperial structure and its greater financial and human reserves.

The conquest strategy ultimately led to a dead end, but it was responsible for providing Rome with a dynamic force that generated economic growth and prosperity for nearly eight centuries. Rome's collapse was inevitable only once this dynamic impulse had been exhausted and an effective replacement strategy could not be found. It is not correct to argue, as Tainter (1988: 150) has done, that 'collapse was in the end inevitable, as indeed it had always been'. There is no mathematical certainty about collapse, it just depends upon the availability of alternative dynamic strategies, not upon the 'complexity' of the sociopolitical system. In the time of Rome in the fifth century (unlike that of Britain in the eighteenth century), world population, given the prevailing agricultural technology, had not begun to press on natural resources to the point necessary to produce a major change in the technology strategy. The incentive to engineer a shift in the technological paradigm did not yet exist. Nevertheless, the collapse of the Roman Empire in the west cleared the ground for such a transformation when the economic conditions were finally appropriate, by removing an economic organization that for 800 years had specialized in the single-minded pursuit and defence of the conquest strategy, and by releasing in Western Europe those competitive forces that would forge a new economic structure capable of accommodating a new dominant strategy. As this failed to occur in the Chinese Empire – the old structure was not swept away and new competitive forces were not released – the Orient failed to embrace the technology strategy when the appropriate economic conditions finally emerged. While relative isolation may at times have been a blessing for China, in the longrun it was a curse.

The rise of Western civilization

With the collapse of Rome, Western Europe was left in the hands of the various Germanic tribes. In 528 BC this included the Visigoths in Spain; the Ostrogoths (under Theodoric) in Italy; the Franks (under Clovis) in Gaul; the Frisians, Saxons, Thuringians, Bavarians, and Lombards in what is now Germany; and the Angles and Saxons in Britain. These Germanic states 'vaguely prefigured the nations of modern Western Europe' (Hollister, 1982: 35). However, with the exception of Theodoric, the Germanic kings were unable to pick up the reins of Roman administration in these regions. They treated their kingdoms as personal estates, exchanging land for the support of their lay and ecclesiastical lords, and exploiting what remained for their personal use.

The earlier forms of imperial taxation broke down and direct administration was replaced by aristocratic fiat. As aristocratic warlords were rural-based, the old Roman urban centres declined in importance and only survived at all as centres of ecclesiastical administration. Hence, economic and effective political power resided with the landowning elite, both lay and ecclesiastical – an elite with both Roman and Germanic origins. In a world where central political control was weak, regional warlords, who were directly influenced by Germanic warrior traditions and values, emerged to dominate a system that was becoming increasingly local and self-sufficient. They supervised the great rural estates that were worked by slaves and semi-free workers, who became increasingly dependent upon their masters.

Over the following 500 years the foundations for the rise of Western civilization were laid (Figure 10.4). It was a process involving a pragmatic blend of the conquest and technological strategies, and it occurred in the context of a highly competitive environment. For two centuries after the fall of Rome, the Germanic tribes and kingdoms struggled violently with each other to lay claim to the former lands of the Roman Empire. These military bids for economic power were generally unsystematic and the successes were invariably short-lived. The first systematic European attempt to revive the ancient conquest strategy as a means of increasing material advantage was that by four generations of a family known as the Carolingians from Austrasia, the Germanic north-east of the Frankish kingdom. The Carolingians were powerful regional warlords who, in the Germanic tradition, attracted a following of warriors as vassals. As with earlier military forces based upon the central role of a dilettantish wealthy elite that supplied and maintained their own equipment, a distinctive heroic form of military organization emerged in Western Europe. In Sumer and Greece it was the phalanx, whereas in Charlemagne's kingdom it was the heavily armed and mounted knight (although there are many instances of knights riding to battle and dismounting to fight). The mounted knight, who emerged from a feudal economic system, was to dominate the nature of small-scale warfare that characterized the Middle Ages.

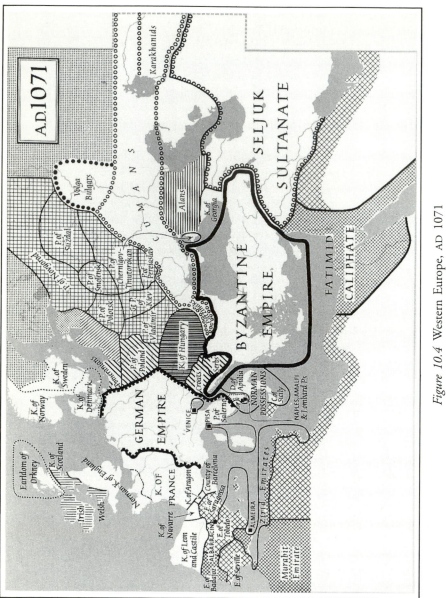

Figure 10.4 Western Europe, AD 1071

Source: Colin McEvedy, *The Penguin Atlas of Medieval History*, Harmondsworth, Penguin, 1961, p. 61. Drawn by John Woodcock. © Colin McEvedy, 1961. Reproduced by permission of Penguin Books Ltd.

The Carolingian rise to national prominence began in AD 687 when Pepin of Heristal led Austria to military dominance over neighbouring regions and, thereby, increased the family wealth and influence. His son Charles Martel was able to unite the Franks against the invading Muslims and to extend Frankish borders. Conquest brought in treasure and new estates from vanquished lands which were used to extend the wealth of the Carolingians and their followers. Charles was succeeded by his son Pepin the Short in 741, who in turn defeated the Lombards in Italy and drove the Muslims from Aquitaine.

Yet the greatest of the Carolingians was Pepin's son Charlemagne, who ruled a greatly expanded Frankish Empire that included modern France, north-eastern Spain, Italy north of Naples, western Germany, and Austria. Charlemagne, who was crowned 'Emperor of the Romans' by Pope Leo III in 800, together with the warrior elite that supported him, used conquest systematically to increase their wealth and income by regular plunder and acquisition of new lands. Warren Hollister (1982: 100) informs us that 'once Carolingian expansion was underway it fed on its own momentum. Conquests brought plunder and new lands with which the Carolingians could enrich themselves and reward their supporters.' This momentum, Hollister makes clear, was not conquest for the sake of conquest, but conquest for the sake of maximizing their material advantage.

Conquest was the most effective way of increasing prosperity (or achieving economic growth) in a world that was economically primitive and ineffectively administered. But in the Germanic world where society was held together by personal allegiance rather than by centralized bureaucratic control – a world in which any number of new regional warlords were waiting in the wings for their chance to gain centre stage – this way was unlikely to continue for long. Expansion through conquest had been exhausted before the breath in Charlemagne's body, and so his son Louis the Pious inherited an empire that could no longer pay for itself. Predictably, Louis was deserted not only by his father's supporters, who could no longer expect material rewards from the emperor, but also by his own sons who wanted a piece of the action denied to them by the new laws of succession that endorsed primogeniture. Civil war and fragmentation of the former empire occurred just at a time when Western Europe was being invaded by Saracens (Muslims), Hungarians (Magyas), and Vikings. As Hollister (1982: 101–2) aptly says: 'Carolingian expansion was like a snowball, growing as it rolled, rolling as it grew . . . Once the snowball stopped rolling it began to melt.' This is the fate of all dynamic systems, not just those fuelled by conquest. Human society in a competitive environment cannot stand still.

The other 'empire' created during the early Middle Ages was the German (or Holy Roman) Empire under the Saxon kings Otto I to III between 936 and 1002. At its height this empire included modern Germany, Austria, Switzerland, and Italy north of Naples. This was an empire built on conquest, but not with the object of funding further conquest. Unlike the Carolingian

303

Empire, it was effectively administered centrally using not aristocratic warriors, but leading bishops and abbots. As these clerics could not accumulate personal wealth to pass on to their heirs, there was no need to continue conquest to maintain their loyalty. In fact, clerics and intellectuals, as in the case of China, are generally contemptuous of warrior traditions and values. Associated with this new attitude in Europe to political rule was a flourishing of intellectual life in the court of the emperors – the 'Ottonian Renaissance' – of science, mathematics, philosophy, and literature. Hence the king, and his barons, were able to increase their incomes through careful management of their estates, trade (both with the North Sea and north Italian regions), and efficient management of the empire. This, in turn, was made possible by the economic changes that were taking place throughout Western Europe in the late tenth and early eleventh centuries.

What is striking about these economic changes is the role played in them by technological change. There are hints in the period from the eighth to the eleventh centuries that the foundations for a new dynamic strategy were emerging – a new strategy that might lessen the dependence upon conquest in order to increase material standards of living. While this was not strongly evident in the dynamic strategy of the Carolingians, it did influence the Ottonian approach, and is clearly evident in the growing prosperity of Anglo-Saxon England after Alfred the Great (871–899). Indeed, the success of this new strategy, in terms of growing prosperity, was in part responsible for the new wave of invasions in the ninth and tenth centuries by the Saracens from the south, the Hungarians from the east, and the Vikings from the north. Yet, while growing wealth attracted these outsiders, this same wealth properly managed enabled the Western Europeans to throw them back. Hence, after AD 1000 an emerging Western civilization was able to concentrate upon internal development without major external disruption – apart from devastating epidemics between 1347 and the late fifteenth century and beyond.

What these invasions did achieve, however, was the unification of kingdoms such as England and, to a lesser extent, Germany, together with the final development of feudalism (which had strong roots in the imperial past) in France. This form of economic and political system was to spread throughout Western Europe in the tenth and eleventh centuries, and to provide the basis for an intensely competitive system (discussed in Chapter 9) that gave rise to the new technological strategy. Even when feudalism began to decline after the eleventh century as central authority and security increased, and even as the fragmentation in France following the death of Charlemagne began to reverse itself, the legacy of a large number of small and highly competitive European kingdoms remained. This was the nursery of the new technological strategy.

By the mid-eleventh century, therefore, Western Europe was finding new ways of increasing the material living standards of its ruling elite. The vast majority of the population, however, lived at, or near, physiological

subsistence and were occasionally plunged below it, even resorting to cannibalism in their own families at times of extreme crisis (Hollister, 1982: 83).
This new strategy was necessary in a highly competitive system consisting
of a large number of small kingdoms that were fairly evenly matched. To
succeed in the struggle against war-like neighbours, it was essential to generate internal surpluses as the returns to conquest were uncertain, irregular,
and definitely limited. This new approach was well established by the beginning of the high Middle Ages.

While conquest was no longer the only dynamic strategy, it still occupied
an important place in the minds of the ruling elite in the high Middle Ages.
Certainly, conquest was pursued whenever the opportunity arose, such as the
Norman conquest of England and Sicily and southern Italy in the mid-
eleventh century, the crusades of the twelfth and thirteenth centuries (which
had economic as well as religious objectives, such as the acquisition of
territory and trading rights in the Levant and the sack of Constantinople in
1204), and the Hundred Years War of 1337 to 1453. At the beginning of
the high Middle Ages, the technological strategy was a way of obtaining the
surpluses necessary to finance wars of conquest. By the eleventh century, as
Hollister (ibid.: 139–40) says: 'Warfare was still commonplace, but it was
beginning to lessen as Europe moved toward political stability.' Actually it
was the emergence of internal economic progress based upon technological
change that produced both political stability and a growing strategic
alternative to conquest.

As the high Middle Ages unfolded, European societies experienced impressive rates of economic growth (in terms of real GDP per capita – see Chapter
9) which was able to satisfy, in part, the material objectives of the ruling
elites. War and conquest for Europeans, unlike for the Romans, were conducted between equals. It was, therefore, a highly costly strategy, in terms
of both direct expenditure on military activities and risk, which only occasionally brought windfall gains. It was equally capable of bringing windfall
losses. For the successful kingdoms, and each had its turn, war and conquest
became a bonus. And in order to gain access to the returns from conquest,
the combatants of medieval Europe invested in military technology that
included the pike against heavily armoured cavalry (Courtrai in 1302), the
longbow against mounted knights (Crecy in 1346, Poitiers in 1356, and
Agincourt in 1415), and the cannon against more traditional armaments
(Formigny in 1450 and Castillon in 1453) and fortifications (*CMH*, 1969,
vol. 8: ch. 21). What was becoming more important was the less risky and
more predictable returns that could be obtained from innovative economic
activity and trade.

By the beginning of the early modern period around 1500, trade, colonization, and technological change had emerged as the dominant dynamic strategies. Yet at the same time all European kingdoms were involved in determined

and costly military actions to extend their territories. Owing to the rapid growth of GDP per capita from the 1490s, the scale of warfare increased quite significantly from that during the stagnation of the previous century. Between 1495 and 1560 the main military struggle involved Spain and France who used Italy as their battleground, whereas between 1560 and the 1780s the main focus moved north, involving France and the various Germanic kingdoms with the occasional participation of the English and Dutch. While the borders between these kingdoms moved to and fro, no single country was able to achieve European dominance. And while economic gains were made from time to time, the effort required to secure these gains invariably left the would-be conqueror financially exhausted and other sources of income, from innovation and trade, were required to rebuild their political and military power. This period demonstrates quite clearly that, in a highly competitive environment where the combatants are fairly equally matched, there is no scope for the employment of the conquest strategy systematically to increase material living standards. To the contrary, the proceeds from the new dynamic strategies were used to fight these opportunistic wars. War had become a speculative activity.

From this time, the means of war changed dramatically as gunpowder replaced muscle power and as war machines became more complex and more expensive with guns and cannons replacing swords, bows, spears, and siege machines (van Creveld, 1989: 81–2). This did not result from a general return to the conquest strategy, however, merely from a rapid increase in real GDP per capita during the commercial era of the sixteenth century. The nations of Western Europe could now afford to conduct war on a larger and more expensive scale, and they adopted the necessary military technology to do so (Brady, 1991: 148–54). In turn these techniques were adapted to more peaceful activities on demand by the technology strategy in the centuries leading up to the Industrial Revolution.

Between 1495 and 1560 Spain did attempt to revive the ancient strategy of conquest and, in the process, came into conflict with France over Italy. After repeated attempts to occupy northern Italy, France was finally expelled by Spanish forces. By the time the Treaty of Cateau-Cambresis was signed, Italy was devastated and both France and Spain were financially exhausted. While Spain could console itself with its new kingdoms in the Mediterranean and in the Americas, France was forced to refocus its territorial ambitions from Italy to Germany.

For the next two centuries the main struggle for territorial gain through war revolved around the French and various Germanic kingdoms. The Thirty Years War (1618–1648), for example, involved a struggle between France, Austria, the various German kingdoms, and Sweden – with France and Sweden making the main gains. Then, at the end of the seventeenth century (1689–1697), England, Holland, Spain, and the Holy Roman Empire together defeated an attempt by the French to assume control of the Netherlands. This was followed by the War of Spanish Succession (1701–1714), during which Louis XIV of France attempted to secure the Spanish kingdoms left to his grandson, Philip of Anjou, in 1700 by the death of a childless king of Spain. The main beneficiaries under the concluding Treaty of Utrecht in 1713 were Austria (which received the Spanish Netherlands), Milan, Naples, Sardinia, and Savoy (which received Sicily). France had to be content with its pre-war borders and a bankrupt economy that took a generation to revive through alternative strategies.

Any ambitions that the Austrians had of building upon these military successes to create a European empire were thwarted by an anti-Austrian coalition involving France, Britain, the Dutch Republic, Spain, Bavaria, and Hanover. The resulting series of conflicts aimed at convincing Austria of its folly were not formally concluded until 1748. Even in the Germanic world, Austria would not remain unopposed as Prussia, in the 1750s, began a phase of territorial expansion that led to the Seven Years War (1756–1763) with Austria, and concluded with Prussia's acquisition of Silesia. And with Prussia's invasion of Poland, its economic power began to approach that of Austria. Hence after 300 years of conflict the map of Western Europe appeared little changed, despite the considerable costs involved in these military adventures. The only significant differences were the expansion of Western Europe east into Hungary and Poland, as Austria and Prussia began to exercise their growing economic power against less developed kingdoms. This intense military competition for economic resources is reminiscent of that on the plain of Sumer, and in the peninsula of Greece. Would it have a similar conclusion?

With the Industrial Revolution – the beginning of modern economic growth – the technological strategy finally emerged as the dominant and sustained dynamic strategy. This strategy, as we saw in Chapter 9, is the distinguishing characteristic of the modern world. Colonization and trade, although secondary strategies, have also been important but basically they are driven by technology. None the less, war has still been a major feature of European and world history since the Industrial Revolution. In Europe, major wars of conquest were pursued, ultimately unsuccessfully, by France from 1792 to 1814, and by Germany in the early and mid-twentieth century. And, as discussed in Chapter 9, global colonization was pursued with remarkable success by Europe between 1492 and the mid-twentieth century. But colonial wars were small wars (Parker, 1991: 194–5). In Asia, an industrializing Japan employed the conquest strategy with temporary success in the mid-twentieth century on the mainland of China and in Southeast Asia. But the highly competitive conditions of Western Europe did not have the same outcome as those in Sumer and classical Greece. Attempts at widespread conquest were unsuccessful because there was a new variable in the equation – the technological strategy.

European warfare in the modern period was, in most major respects, a continuation of the intense territorial struggle of the previous few centuries. In 1792 the Germanic world saw an opportunity to further its expansionist aims at the expense of its old enemy France, which was preoccupied with political revolution, by sending an Austro-Prussian army against Paris. To the amazement of the rest of Europe, the Austro-Prussian army was forced to withdraw and, by the end of the year, the French Revolution was on the offensive beyond its eastern borders. While this offensive was contained by an anti-French coalition in 1793, it burst out again in the following year in the Netherlands, beyond the Rhine, and in northern Italy. By the time a temporary peace treaty was signed in 1797, the republic had achieved in a few years what French kings had struggled unsuccessfully to achieve throughout the period 1495–1560. They had also discovered a young general of brilliance in Napoleon Bonaparte, who promised them an even more glorious and profitable future.

Over the following fourteen years, to 1812, France under Bonaparte succeeded in doing what no kingdom had ever done before – conquer the whole of western and central Europe. But in 1812 Bonaparte marched on Moscow, a march that was to bring him to final defeat at Waterloo in 1815. In the end the map of Europe looked much as it had in 1783 before the French Revolution. Even Bonaparte was forced to recognize that systematic conquest in a highly competitive world of equals – particularly when non-human resources can be replenished through the technological strategy – is difficult to achieve and impossible to sustain. He was not to know that this had been recognized respectively by Akkad and Athens some 4,000 and 2,000 years before.

The twentieth century provides two further European examples of attempted conquest. Prior to the outbreak of the First World War, the technology strategy enabled the nations of Europe to devote an even larger proportion of their GDP and an ever-greater technological sophistication to armaments and military infrastructure. Accordingly, the sophistication and cost of military hardware continued to increase on the land, on the seas and, for the first time, under the seas and in the air (van Creveld, 1989: chs 13 and 14). War had been taken to every part of man's environment. But they failed to appreciate – as they did not understand the lessons of the past – that, in a highly competitive environment of equally matched coalitions of combatants, an escalation of arms would merely increase the scale of destruction and carnage rather than provide any individual nation or coalition of nations with an advantage. Not surprisingly, between 1914 and 1918 the nations of Europe fought each other to a standstill with staggering losses of life – about 7.8 million troops – and capital on both sides (Bullock, 1993: 1068). The First World War, therefore, was a very costly demonstration of the highly competitive balance that had existed in Europe for a thousand years.

The formerly fluid alliances of European nations became more fixed in the generation prior to the First World War. By 1894 two major coalitions had formed – the Triple Alliance of Germany, which included Austria–Hungary and Italy, and the Dual Alliance of France and Russia. Over the following decade Britain associated itself more closely with France, reversing a military rivalry of centuries. This set of coalitions became more rigid during the final decade before 1914 with an easing of tensions between Britain and Russia over the Far East, and the emergence of a naval race between Britain and Germany (Kennedy, 1989: 321–30).

The unanswered question is: why did these fixed alliances emerge in a generation of peace, an unusual occurrence in European history? Formal alliances were required in the late nineteenth and early twentieth centuries to protect the unusually large gains that Western European nations had made from adopting the new dynamic strategy of technological change. What made the period after the 1880s different to that before is that rapid, technologically induced economic growth not only resulted in a greater stock of valuable physical assets that required protection – the ancient scorched-earth-and-retreat policy was no longer economically viable – but also led to a massive military build-up of personnel and sophisticated equipment which threatened to undermine the achievement of the technological strategy. Hence, for the first time in Western Europe, 'alliance diplomacy' became an essential art in the prevention of massive economic loss through war. The preservation of the technology strategy was of paramount importance.

But, as everyone knows, these alliances failed to prevent the outbreak of the most devastating war ever experienced in human society. Indeed, these alliances, while they did not cause the First World War, appear to have facilitated its onset and duration. The unstable element in Western Europe in the pre-war generation was the rapidly emerging power of Germany, whose industrial potential in 1880 was only 37 per cent of Britain's whereas by 1913 it was marginally superior (Bairoch, 1982: 292). Over this period Germany grew twice as rapidly as Britain, the world's first industrial nation (Offer, 1989: 321). Not surprisingly, a 'youthful' Germany pursued its expansionist aims (particularly in Europe) more aggressively, and appeared more willing to take risks, than those nations already at the top such as Britain and France (Kennedy, 1989: 274–5). Germany had much to gain and they had much to lose. Not only did Germany have territorial ambitions in the west, but it was also willing to support Austria–Hungary's ambitions in Serbia. In pursuit of these ambitions Germany initiated an arms race after 1910, the like of which had never been seen in Western Europe, and began preparing for the possibility of an economic blockade that would impact upon critical supplies of food and raw materials (Offer, 1989: ch. 23).

When Archduke Ferdinand was shot in June 1914, the descent into war took the path mapped out by the alliances that were meant to prevent such an occurrence. Austria–Hungary attacked Serbia; Russia began to mobilize against Austria–Hungary; Germany invaded France through Belgium (the Schlieffen Plan) before turning on Russia; France invaded Lorraine (Plan XVII); and Britain entered the war in support of Belgium. Only Italy wavered but later crossed over and entered on the side of the Allies. Why, we might ask, did each of the alliance signatories follow the conditions of their treaty so closely? Once the first move was made by Austria–Hungary, and given the well-known expansionist aims of Germany, the only way each of the alliance members could hope to protect their industrial wealth was to knock out the opposition before they had time to do the same. Victory, it was thought, would go to the swift. The conflict would be over before Christmas. Hence their industrial wealth would remain largely intact and there might even be some windfall gains for the bold.

But the war dragged on for more than four long, unprecedentedly destructive years and became, in the process, a global war. Why? Basically the answer lies in the relatively new dynamic strategy of technological change that had come to dominate Western Europe. Rapid, technologically induced economic growth enabled the formation of massive armies well supplied with sophisticated military technology. During the First World War, the Allies mobilized 40.7 million men and spent (in 1913 prices) $57.7 billion (Kennedy, 1989: 354). War on this scale was unthinkable before the era of the technological strategy. But nations that have adopted the dynamic strategy of technological change are able to sustain total warfare almost indefinitely, provided the economic base of each alliance is roughly equal – an outcome that had been ensured by a generation of 'alliance diplomacy' prior to 1914. Ironically, the equally matched economic coalitions that were meant to prevent war now prevented peace. What tipped the balance in favour of the Allies was the support given to them by their existing and former colonial empires.

By 1919 the millennial competitive balance had been destabilized by global war and by the peace conditions imposed by the victors. France, aided and abetted by its allies, attempted to take advantage of a defeated Germany – as the Germans had attempted to take advantage of a disorganized France in 1792 and in 1870 – to make good its wartime losses, to take back Alsace-Lorraine lost in the Franco-Prussian war, to take control of the Ruhr industrial area of Germany, and to impose punitive reparations. As is well known, this opened the way for the emergence of the conquest strategy once more – this time through the unleashing of irrational forces – despite the fact that in a technological age the conquest strategy is an anachronism. The costs of conquest are far higher than its benefits in a highly competitive world, which was clearly demonstrated during the First World War. While this was recognized by the Allies it was of little help, because the extent of the forces of irrationality unleashed in German society by the wrong-headed intervention of world leaders in 1919 was not understood until later. Those who had learnt the lessons of the First World War, but who did not appreciate the irrationality unleashed by it, were unable to prevent a further plunge into global war. Yet while Hitler's Germany was able to conquer Western Europe (with the exception of Britain) it, like Bonaparte's France, could not hope to retain its conquests in the face of a highly competitive world able to generate rapid increases in income through the technological strategy.

Hitler's attempt to conquer Europe should not be confused with the economically rational conquest strategy employed by pre-modern societies. Hitler's world view was thoroughly irrational. It was based not upon an analysis of existing economic forces but upon metaphysical considerations (Bullock, 1993: 150–6). His consistent aim was the revival of the German race both by 'purification' and by the achievement of greater living space, or *Lebensraum*, in Eastern Europe through conquest. Rather than the pursuit of material advantage, Hitler dedicated himself to the pursuit of racial supremacy. Conquest, therefore, was to serve a racial rather than a materialistic end.

Whenever there was a conflict in Nazi Germany between materialistic and racial objectives, it was the former that had to bend. To Hitler, the 'deciding forces in history' were 'politics, faith and will, not economics and material circumstances' (ibid.: 343). A few critical examples of this irrational approach include the assumption of control by Göring – who had no interest in economics – over rearmament and the economy in 1936; the decision in the summer of 1941 to exterminate all European Jews rather than recruit them as labourers; and the butchery and alienation of Ukrainian Slavs rather than assisting them to revolt against Stalinist tyranny (ibid.: 472, 873, 805).

Hitler's racial policies were pursued consistently, if not always openly, from their first expression in *Mein Kampf* in 1925 to the last testament dictated to his faithful secretary Bormann twenty years later (ibid.: 150, 955). Their clearest expression in a strategic sense, however, emerged from Hitler's discussion of his objectives on 5 November 1937 with his Chiefs of Staff (von Fritsel, Raeder, and Göring), his Minister of Defence (von Blomberg), and his Foreign Minister (von Neurath). At this meeting he declared Germany's pressing problem to be one of *Lebensraum* ('living space'), in which a 'racial community' of 85 million Germans were more densely settled in their existing territories than any other people, 'which implied the right to a greater living space'. Hitler went on to say that: 'the only remedy, and one which might seem visionary, is the acquisition of greater living space – a quest that has in every age been the origin of the formation of states and the migration of peoples' (ibid.: 598–9). This living space was to be sought in Eastern Europe rather than in overseas colonies, and it was to be achieved by 1943–1945 before Germany lost the advantage of its early rearmament programme. Further, he stressed that the German problem, which was not explained in any detail to potentially sceptical military officers, could not be resolved in any other way – not through world trade, autarky (self-sufficiency), or colonies. Characteristically, the prevailing dynamic strategy of technological change was not even mentioned. Just as Hitler's objectives were irrational, so were his methods of reaching them. As Albert Speer (1970:

473), more than a generation later, said of Hitler's final days: 'He had reached the last station in his flight from reality, a reality which he had refused to acknowledge from his youth.'

Hitler's irrational course of action for Germany was imposed from above, not built up from below as all rational dynamic strategies must be. It was a quest that ignored existing economic forces and the way individuals and families were responding to these forces by reducing the number of their children. Declining fertility rates in the interwar period (Cipolla, 1974) meant that German families would not have been able to populate the conquered territories in Eastern Europe even if its soldiers had been able to secure them permanently. This reality, however, failed to deter Hitler.

But if Hitler's quest was irrational, how was he able to come so close to achieving it? How was he able to come to power in a democratic country, and how did he achieve so much success prior to 1943? Hitler came to power in Germany because he was able to exploit cleverly the economic insecurity experienced in the Weimar Republic owing to the severity of both the 1919 peace settlement and the Great Depression. It must be clearly understood that in 1932 the electorate did not endorse the economically irrational policies outlined in *Mein Kampf*. Rather, they voted for a radical change to a political system that was unable to satisfy their materialistic objectives. Not only did middle-class support shift from the orthodox conservative parties to the radical Nazi Party, but working-class support transferred from the Social Democrats to the more radical Communist Party. In the uncertain circumstances of interwar Germany, this was an economically rational decision on the part of the electorate. Their mistake – at least by the 37.4 per cent that voted for the Nazi Party and the 14.6 per cent that voted for the Communists in July 1932 (and much the same again in November) – was not realized until after the first major defeats suffered by the German forces on the Russian front in 1943. But by then it was too late, because Hitler's political revolution had given him the power in the shortrun to impose his will upon the German people and to override their own materialistic objectives.

Ironically, Hitler's early diplomatic and military successes between the reoccupation of the Rhineland in 1936 and the Russian blitzkrieg in the summer of 1941 were largely due to the irrationality of his strategy. Between 1936 and the attack on Poland in September 1939, France and Britain made the understandable mistake of dealing with Hitler as if he were economically rational. In 1937, for example, the British attempted to divert Hitler from an aggressive advance into Europe by offering to return German colonies that had been confiscated during the First World War (Bullock, 1993: 585). But Hitler was not to be diverted from his historic task. Similarly, in September 1938 Britain and France thought they could satisfy Hitler by agreeing at the Munich Conference to the dismantlement of Czechoslovakia in favour of Germany. They only realized their mistake in September 1939 when Germany attacked Poland, but by then Hitler had achieved a military edge in Western Europe and could no longer be controlled by force. Even the pathologically suspicious Stalin thought he could buy Hitler off by supplying the raw materials that Hitler secretly sought, ironically, to invade the USSR. Stalin refused right up until the end to believe reports from his own sources that a German attack was imminent: the last train carrying Russian supplies to Germany left only hours before German armoured divisions rumbled across the Russian border on 22 June 1941 (Bullock, 1993: 778). Stalin realized his mistake too late to prevent the German army reaching the outskirts of Leningrad and Moscow before winter brought the onslaught to an end. In a fundamentally rational world irrationality can achieve stunning, if temporary, successes.

Despite its initial successes, Hitler's *Lebensraum* policy was doomed ultimately to failure, precisely because it was economically irrational. As history demonstrates quite clearly, only rational economic strategies have any chance of longrun success; but revealed objectives rather than outcomes are the test of rationality employed in this study. In this respect Hitler was determined to achieve German racial renewal through the exercise of political will, no matter what the prevailing economic reality. Therefore, despite Britain's failure either to give way before the Führer's fury, or to conclude a separate peace treaty, Hitler decided to fight a war on two fronts against a combined enemy which outgunned Germany in terms of raw materials, manpower, and industrial output. This was something Hitler had always vowed he would not do because he thought it was this mistake that had cost Germany the First World War. Had Hitler been economically rational, he probably would have attempted to reverse the disaster of 1914–1918 solely by diplomatic means, and certainly would not have invaded Poland let alone France or the USSR.

While Hitler's irrational *Lebensraum* policy should not be confused with the rational dynamic strategy of conquest pursued by pre-modern societies, it can be used – because of the amount of documentation available – to illustrate effectively the way conquest increases the GDP per capita of the conquering nation. The economic gains made by the Third Reich to the end of 1943 – gains that were at the expense of the occupied territories – were achieved through pillage, requisitioning, and forced labour (ibid.: 800–1). In the early stages, gains were made by pillaging, which involved 'grabbing stocks, machinery, raw materials, everything movable and carrying them off to Germany'. Later, requisitioning – a more effective and orderly form of pillaging – was instituted in the occupied territories. Local farms and factories were forced to meet quotas for production and delivery of goods to Germany on credit, under the pretence that financial settlement would be made after the war. In this way some 25 million tons of food from occupied Europe were delivered to Germany. It is claimed that between 1941 and 1943 these supplies 'increased the German civilian ration by between a fifth and a quarter while the population of the occupied territories, especially in the cities, went hungry' (Bullock, 1993: 800). Before the end of 1943, therefore, the German population had little reason to regret their decision to aid and abet Hitler's rise to power in 1932–1933.

Similarly, the export of raw materials from occupied Europe to Germany – particularly of oil, coal, and metals – initially aided Germany's rearmament programme and later contributed handsomely to its war effort. And this contribution would have been even greater had the Nazi economic system been less inefficient and its goals less irrational. The value of those unpaid deliveries amounted to 42 billion RM by September 1944 (or 43 per cent of NNP in 1938); and, according to Speer, something like 25 to 30 per cent of German war production up to July 1944 was supplied by the occupied Western territories and Italy (Bullock, 1993: 900; Mitchell, 1975: 785). Finally, workers – both male and female – from the occupied territories were forced to labour in German farms, mines, factories, and transport systems. Numbers of slave labourers increased from 300,000 in 1939 to over 7 million in 1944, by which time they made up about 20 per cent of the German work-force. Yet while the economic gains made by the Third Reich from conquest were similar to those made by ancient societies, the irrational nature of Hitler's strategy caused Nazi Germany to collapse only six years after embarking on this anachronistic course – somewhat less than the thousand years predicted by Hitler or almost achieved by ancient Rome and Assyria.

The encouraging feature of the second half of the twentieth century is that the Western nations appear to have recognized that conquest is not the best way to achieve their materialistic objectives. The West avoided the mistake of earlier generations by refusing to exploit ruthlessly both the collapse of Italy, Germany, and Japan after their separate defeats, and of the USSR and Eastern Europe in the early 1990s. The objective must be to retain the competitive balance between equally matched partners without forgetting the consequences of resorting to the conquest strategy, particularly now that we have discovered how to unleash the very forces that gave rise to the Universe. In man the Earth now has a worthy but dangerous adversary.

Chinese civilization

China has always puzzled Western observers. In particular, most have found it difficult to understand either why the Chinese Empire lasted so long – about 2,000 years from 221 BC to the early twentieth century – or why such a vital and technically advanced society between the eighth and twelfth centuries could have failed to invent an Industrial Revolution before a less advanced Western Europe. While the various dynasties rose and fell, a distinctive Chinese economic system continued to generate growth of both population and living standards, albeit in a fluctuating manner. A number of setbacks were experienced, but at no time in this long period could it be said that the Chinese economic system collapsed. It will be argued that this mystery can be solved when we understand the dynamic strategies pursued by the various Chinese dynasties. But first we need to survey briefly the historical experience of China (Fitzgerald, 1966; Elvin, 1973; Perkins, 1969; Spence, 1990).

At the risk of considerable oversimplification, the broad sweep of Chinese history from 1200 BC to AD 1800 can be divided, in terms of the strategic categories developed in this book, into four main periods. The first, which I have called the age of colonization of 1066–221 BC, roughly corresponds with the Chou dynasty; the second period, which I have called the age of consolidation, from 221 BC to AD 220, largely coincides with the Han dynasty; the third I have called the age of conflict, both internal and external, between AD 220–581; and finally there is the age of restoration between 600 and 1800.

The age of colonization (1066–221 BC) was dominated by regional warlords, who had the wealth and influence of European kings, intent upon conquest and colonization in order to bring the resources of what is now southern China into production under their control (Figure 10.5). While there was considerable internal competition between these warlords, particularly between 463 and 222 BC, the external pressure was not overwhelming as China was surrounded by less sophisticated societies – the nomadic tribes of Mongolia in the north, the 'wild mountain peoples' (ancestors of the Tibetans) in the west, and the primitive forest tribes of the south (Fitzgerald, 1966). Hence new resources could be acquired relatively cheaply through colonization, and there was no incentive to pursue a systematic conquest strategy. This period of intense internal competition generated considerable prosperity for the leading states together with a major cultural outburst of philosophy, literature, science, and technological innovation.

The age of consolidation between 221 BC and AD 220 was dominated by a successful attempt to achieve unity through central control and administration. This was the beginning of the Chinese Empire. There was, however, still considerable internal competition between large landowners, which generated an innovative and expansionist outlook. This was a period of prosperity, both in economic and cultural terms, and of continued expansion through colonization and conquest. China had conquered Turkistan by 51 BC, and between AD 73 and 102 its military forces had reached as far as the Caspian Sea and, possibly, the Black Sea. But as there was no external threat during these years and as the returns from external expansion did not meet the costs involved – the surrounding peoples did not live in wealthy urban societies – conquest was not pursued systematically and did not develop into a dominant dynamic strategy. Rather, this outward probing was the result of an adventurous spirit generated by internal competition.

The age of conflict, from AD 220 to 581, was the early forcing ground for innovation that finally emerged during the Sung dynasty. There are

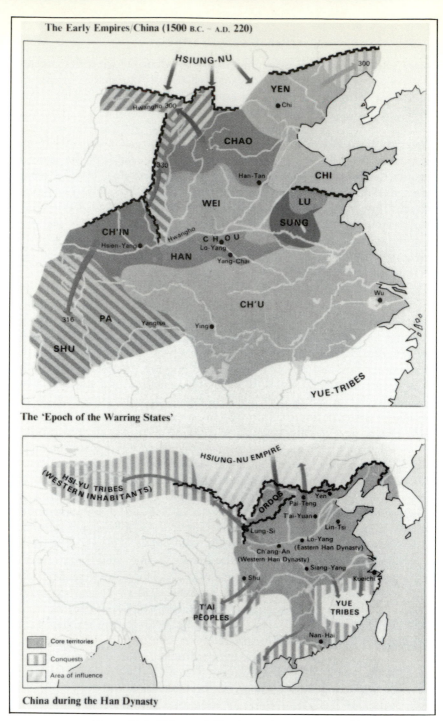

Figure 10.5 Chinese civilization, 1500 BC–AD 1644

Source: H. Kinder and W. Hilgemann, *The Penguin Atlas of World History, Vol. One*, Harmondsworth, Penguin, 1974, pp. 40, 226. Drawn by Harald and Ruth Bukor.

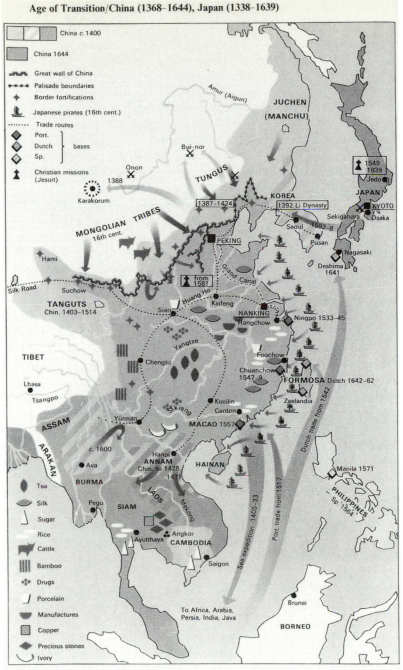

China during the Ming Dynasty, 1368–1644

parallels here with the intense competition within Europe that finally gave rise to the burst of technological change after 1750. Serious internal conflict broke out in this period between major regions in the north, south-east, and west of China. While the northern kingdom triumphed briefly between AD 265 and 316, it was overwhelmed by the Tartar invasions from the north. Between AD 316 and 581 the Tartars ruled the north, which had a population of about 30 million people. The former Chinese ruling elite moved south to dominate southern China with a population of about 20 million people (Fitzgerald, 1966). While there was constant border warfare between the various northern and southern regimes, no serious invasion attempts were made by either side, and there were long periods of stability. These regimes were ruled by wealthy warlords and there was considerable competition between them both in the regions (military) and at court (diplomatic).

The age of empire restoration, from about AD 600 to 1800, followed the conquest of the southern Ch'en dynasty by the northern Sui dynasty (Figure 10.5). In an attempt to regain the old unity – regarded as 'the right and normal state of the world' – central government authority and bureaucracy was re-established and later, in the Sung dynasty, a clear distinction was made between the civil and military spheres. There was a qualitative difference between the Sui–T'ang period (581–907) and the Sung period (960–1279) which were separated by fifty years of fragmentation that finally ended the last vestiges of aristrocratic decentralization. In the Sung civil bureaucracy, the scholar replaced the aristocratic warrior. To pay for this return to central-ization and to drive back the Manchurians it was necessary to increase taxes. The need for taxable surpluses generated the demand for technical innovation for which the Sung period is famous. Indeed the Sung dynasty coincided with a remarkable period of economic and cultural growth within a highly competitive context. It ended with a Manchurian invasion of the north in 1211 and a Mongol invasion taking all China in 1279. The nomads were attracted by the rapidly increasing wealth of Chinese society, and while their invasions brought the Sung prosperity to an end, they did not lead to economic collapse. The Ming restoration from 1368 to 1644 brought a renewal of economic and cultural prosperity, together with a remarkable outburst of overseas exploration in the years 1405 to 1433, which took massive Chinese fleets as far as the east coast of Africa – just preceding the European breakout after 1492. Once again the costs of this expansion, into a world less developed than itself, far exceeded the benefits and, therefore, it was brought to an end. Even the prospects of external trade appeared to be only marginally profitable. From this time forward China became increas-ingly introspective, isolationist, and relatively backward technologically. It experienced much population expansion but little economic growth, owing to the absence of serious internal and external competition – apart from the irritation of Mongolian tribes in the north and of Japanese pirates throughout the coastal regions – and to the oppressive control of an effective central administration run by scholars more interested in intellectual games than economic prosperity. By the seventeenth century we have the first evidence that population (120–200 million) was beginning to press upon natural resources, and by the nineteenth century that population (330–410 million) was outrunning those resources (Perkins, 1969: 16).

The usual arguments for the longevity of the Chinese Empire include the isolation of China from other advanced civilizations; the stabilizing influence of the Chinese bureaucracy; the unifying influence of Chinese language and culture; and the ability of China to stay at least one step ahead of its competitors in terms of technology, organization, and wealth (Fitzgerald, 1966; Elvin, 1973). While these elements are clearly important, they have not been integrated into a coherent argument that can successfully explain the divergent experience of China. The wider strategic argument in this book suggests that China's success in maintaining its empire derived from its dynamic strategy, and its dynamic strategy was a function of its economic environment both internally and externally.

We have seen that Rome attempted to maximize its material advantage by specializing in the conquest strategy. This was a rational response to an economic environment in which external competition was intense, and the expected rate of return on investment in conquest was considerably higher than that in trade and colonization and infinitely higher than that in technological change. Conquest's high rate of return derived from the wealth of surrounding urban societies in a crowded Mediterranean, and the low return from technological change resulted from the abundant supplies of natural resources relative to existing world population size that remained to be exploited by the existing neolithic technological paradigm. Once the conquest strategy had been exhausted, and as other replacement dynamic strategies could not be found, the Roman Empire collapsed.

China, on the other hand, was surrounded by vigorous but considerably less sophisticated, non-urban, and less wealthy peoples. In the period down to AD 1368 these outsiders provided a fair degree of competition to the point where they were able to occupy part of China for centuries at a time (and again in 1644 when the Ming were defeated by the Manchus), but they were never able to overwhelm the empire. It always managed to reassert itself. This external competition made it necessary for China to develop its military technology and to generate a surplus sufficient to defend its borders, at least before AD 1368, after which there was no serious external threat apart from the small-scale sporadic raids of nomads and pirates. But as the surrounding nomads did not possess sophisticated or wealthy urban societies, they were not worth plundering. In these circumstances the conquest strategy was only a profitable strategy for China's nomadic neighbours. We have seen how a number of westward probes, both by land and sea, demonstrated to Chinese satisfaction that the experiments were not worth their costs. Chinese military activity, therefore, was directed at defence rather than conquest.

The implication of this defensive stance is that the Chinese spent only as much on military activity as was thought necessary to keep the barbarian from the gate. We have seen, however, that they did not always spend as much as was required. Hence, the major dynamic strategy was not conquest, as it was for the more competitive Western civilizations, but either family multiplication as in the period before 1066 BC, or 'internal' colonization (in southern China) as in the period 1066–221 BC, or technological change as in the Sung period (960–1279). During those periods when external competition actually was intense – as in the first millennium after the birth of Christ – the Chinese adopted the technology strategy in order to develop a superior military infrastructure and, in the absence of systematic income from conquest, to generate additional internal surpluses from agriculture to finance the necessary military effort to defeat their enemies and maintain their frontiers. Clearly it was essential to generate internal economic growth through technological change in the Sung period because the defeat of China's enemies did not produce plunder (as in the West) and because the raising of taxes without raising economic surpluses led to well-documented riots (Fitzgerald, 1966). Hence, economic growth coincided with intense external competition, as during the Sung period; and the absence of economic growth coincided with periods of diminished external competition.

An additional reason for the absence of significant economic growth, except in the Sung period, was the nature of internal competition within the Chinese Empire. In the early proto-'feudal' period before 221 BC there was a considerable degree of competition between regional warlords. However, with the foundation of the Ch'in dynasty (221–206 BC), which first unified China, the 'feudal' structure was abolished and central control was established. In the long-running Han dynasty (206 BC–AD 220) the central administration was controlled not by aristocratic warriors as in the West, but by scholars, mainly the followers of Confucius. It is usually argued that this was done to resolve the problem of court intrigues (ibid.), but I want to suggest that it was the natural outcome of a society in which the dominant dynamic strategies were associated with internal development rather than with conquest. In all societies, those who controlled the dominant dynamic strategies also controlled government.

A major and enduring characteristic of China is that, after 221 BC, an amazing degree of unity was achieved by the imperial court in the face of strong regional centrifugal forces. And despite occasional successful takeovers – by the Manchurians in 1211, the Mongols in 1279, and the Manchus in 1644 – there was, in between, only modest external competition (Jones, 1981). This external competition was intermittent and not sustained. Contrast this with the experience of Western Europe after the fall of Rome. As we have seen, Europe consisted of a large number of small and highly combative kingdoms, which were surrounded by hostile and sophisticated societies. Europe, therefore, was subjected to continuous competitive pressure – and, hence, had to struggle in order to survive and conquer – between AD 500 and the mid-twentieth century, which produced the technological strategy that culminated in the Industrial Revolution. In China after the Sung period there was little comparable competitive pressure and hence little incentive to introduce new techniques of production. This is why the Chinese, pursuing their objectives rationally, adopted other dynamic strategies in these later years and, in the process, became technologically backward.

We need to look more closely at the dynamic strategies adopted by China. During earlier long periods of struggle by the Chinese to maintain or regain the old frontiers, the dominant strategy was technological change adopted in order to improve their military prospects and to increase their domestic surplus. During periods of external peace, the main strategies included family multiplication and colonization. While China from the time of the Han dynasty was engaged in some trade with Central Asia, India and, indirectly, the West – mainly exports of silk and tea – this trade was limited by China's isolation from other large urban centres. Hence commerce has never been a significant strategy for the Chinese. More specifically, during the period 221 BC–AD 1300 (and particularly 221 BC–AD 300 and AD 900–1300) a major strategy was family multiplication and colonization of the more sparsely settled south by the north (Elvin, 1973: 204). In the period before AD 300 this involved an attempt to absorb underused natural resources, whereas between AD 900 and 1300 it resulted from a more intensive use of natural resources by employing technological change. Only in the period 221 BC–AD 300, therefore, was family multiplication and colonization a major strategy in its own right. This redistribution of population produced an increase in GDP per capita as the balance between extensive and intensive use of natural resources changed towards the latter (ibid.: 211).

After the fourteenth century, however, with little systematic external competition, the dynamic strategy of family multiplication without colonization could not increase real GDP per capita, but neither did it reduce it before about 1800. Clearly a degree of technological fine-tuning, involving economic organization, production technique, and more efficient central control, was involved. But there was no incentive to continue the technological achievements of the Sung, both because the external threat had been reduced to manageable levels with invasion by the Mongols, and because better organization – something the Chinese were very good at – allowed the exercise of the traditional dynamic strategy of family multiplication. It is highly likely that, in the absence of European involvement after 1650, the population of China would have achieved a new equilibrium level, at least until some other moderate threat arrived. China's tragedy after the sixteenth century was that the European (and, later, Japanese) threat was not moderate. Because of the distance from which they came, initially in small numbers, the Europeans were regarded more as a curiosity than a threat. By the time this perception had changed in the century after the Industrial Revolution it was too late. And in the chaos that followed, the only possible dynamic strategy was family multiplication and the settlement of inferior land in the north-west, even though this meant a reduction in standards of living as population continued to press in on natural resources in the absence of technological change.

Why did the Chinese Empire last as long as it did? The answer is that China did not attempt to meet its objective of survival and prosperity through conquest which, as shown in the case of all Western empires (and in the case of all New World civilizations), must ultimately exhaust itself and lead to collapse because population and living standards achieve a size far above the technological optimum for a neolithic society. China did not follow the conquest strategy because, in the absence of surrounding urban societies, it could not. Had China been in a position to do so, the outcome would have been much the same as that for every other civilization in the Old and New Worlds – collapse. China attempted merely to maintain its borders by spending just enough on technological change in the military and economic spheres to achieve this purpose (not always successfully) and by pursuing the alternative strategy of family multiplication, combined with either colonization (before AD 1300) or technological and administrative fine-tuning (after AD 1300).

Yet while this strategy enabled the Chinese Empire to survive down to the twentieth century, it denied China the possibility of an internally generated Industrial Revolution. The reason, as we have seen, is that there was insufficient *sustained* external or internal (after 221 BC) competition to provide the necessary incentive for economic decision-makers to respond to changing factor prices (the falling prices of capital relative to natural resources) by adopting a new technological paradigm. This is not to say there was no internal or external competition, just that it was not of the same order of magnitude or duration as that in Europe. Mark Elvin (1973: 306–11) makes it abundantly clear that China had gone about as far as it could go with the old late-neolithic technological paradigm by 'the later eighteenth century'. By this time China had exhausted its supply of 'readily cultivable land' and, thereafter, had to turn to 'low quality land' in Manchuria, Inner Mongolia, and in the north-west. As a result, average farm yields in China declined by 22 per cent between 1821 and 1911 (Perkins, 1969: 27). The Chinese solution was not to invest in a new technological paradigm – as Britain did during the Industrial Revolution – but, as it had traditionally done, to bring population into a balance with natural resources. But this could only be achieved successfully in the complete isolation of Aboriginal Australia, rather than the partial and eroding isolation of the Orient. China's dynamic-strategic approach was radically different to that in Europe because the incentives facing it and, hence, its strategic benefit–cost calculus were different. It had nothing to do with underdeveloped institutional arrangements, particularly governmental, that are sometimes claimed to be sufficient for allowing economic expansion but not for economic growth (Jones, 1990: 16–21). Institutions respond in the longer term to the requirements of the dominant dynamic strategies – as they did during the Sung period – rather than acting as impassable barriers that can only be removed by political processes.

Strategic investment is, as I have attempted to show in this book, undertaken on the basis of benefit–cost calculations. Investment in the technological strategy will rise as competition – the need to struggle to survive – increases, and as the price of natural resources relative to the price of capital rises owing to the approaching exhaustion of the neolithic paradigm. Strategic investment has nothing to do with the *level* of GDP per capita – or of consumption demand – as Mark Elvin (1973: 312) suggests in his otherwise excellent book. Elvin argues that the great size of the Chinese economy meant that it was precluded from industrializing because the population pressure on natural resources reduced the level of consumer demand (GDP per capita) in China and because even the level of world demand was not sufficient to enable Chinese industrial production to exceed the threshold level required to introduce the Industrial Revolution. In Elvin's (ibid.: 314, 312) words, 'a given technology often demands a minimum scale of output if it is to be profitable', and 'the input–output relationships of the late traditional economy had assumed a pattern that was almost *incapable of change through internally generated forces*' (emphasis added).

In the light of my dynamic-strategy model, it is not possible to accept Elvin's argument (ibid.: 313–16) that China was caught in a 'high-level equilibrium trap'. He overlooks two crucial matters. First, that the pressure of population on natural resources in a competitive environment – as in the West – was a spur to the demand for a new technological paradigm. Strategic demand, which responds to relative factor prices under competition, is more important than the level of consumer demand. Ultimately China's misfortune was a lack of serious competition. Second, any new paradigm begins in a small way with the decision-making of local entrepreneurs and gradually transforms the entire economy, including the extent of the market for industrial products. Chinese, and even world, demand during and after a hypothetical Chinese Industrial Revolution would not be the same as before, as Elvin assumes. We have already seen that the Palaeolithic and Neolithic Revolutions were introduced with considerably lower levels of GDP per capita. In any case the level of GDP per capita, which is an outcome of the longrun dynamic process, merely influences the level of aggregate demand, not the level of strategic demand.

Strategic investment depends upon the benefit–cost calculations of investors who, in the late eighteenth century, were a small elite responding to profitability at the level of local markets and not to shifts in national aggregate demand. Such investments, therefore, are made initially in small (micro) areas of the economy and not at the national (macro) level. But if these investments are successful, they grow rapidly and are emulated by others until they figure large in the total economy. The Chinese economy was large and diverse. If the incentives provided by intense competition had been present, investment in new technologies in some sectors and some regions would have generated demands for inputs from other sectors and other regions, and these linkage effects would have multiplied through the economy, transforming it on the way. Aggregate consumer demand is the effect (indeed the object) and not the cause of strategic investment. It only has causal signif-icance in shortrun static analysis, not in longrun dynamic analysis. The great economist J.M. Keynes (1936), who redirected the concern of economics from the long to the shortrun, is largely responsible for this misapprehension (Snooks, 1993a: 404).

For China there was no deficiency of final demand, only an absence of incentives to develop a new technological paradigm. The only 'trap' was an inability to achieve the necessary threshold level of competition required to transform radically the Chinese strategic benefit–cost calculus and, hence, to transform strategic demand. When intense and sustained external compe-tition came from the West, it was too late to transform a society that had long specialized in order and stability. The response to the West could only come after the traditional dynamic strategy – family multiplication and reset-tlement – had been finally exhausted (by the mid-1950s), forcing China to undergo the painful process of remilitarization and internal reorganization necessary to enable the imitation of the European strategy of technological change. The opportunity and ability to create an unusual degree of order and stability accounts not only for the longevity of the Chinese Empire but also for its failure to generate its own Industrial Revolution.

Mesoamerican civilizations

What is fascinating about the various civilizations of the New World is that they emerged in total isolation from those of the Old World. While we are initially attracted to the cultural contrasts between these two distinct parts of human society, ultimately it is their fundamentally similar dynamic economic processes that continue to hold our interest. Much important research has recently been conducted – as summarized in Hammond and Willey (1979), Chase and Rice (1985), and Culbert (1991) – but we still know relatively little about the political economy of these various civilizations. Many conflicting interpretations of the rise and fall of Mesoamerican societies currently jostle with each other for recognition. I will argue that they can be resolved by using the dynamic-strategy model.

Much of this lack of consensus has to do with disagreement over the appropriate way to measure the progress of civilization – whether the indi-cators should be cultural, political, social, or economic. In this book it has been argued that the fundamental dynamic process of human society is economic, and that other dimensions, such as the cultural, social, and political, emerge from economic dynamics in a systematic way. Accordingly the appropriate measures of the rise and fall of civilizations are material living standards and population. While cultural historians, for example, may wish to challenge the view that Mayan society collapsed after the mid-ninth century AD, on the grounds that earlier cultural practices were continued down to the Spanish invasion, economic indicators suggest that such a collapse in core Mayan areas did occur and that former levels of population and living standards were never regained. But having said this, it must be admitted that currently available economic indicators are only approximate and cannot be used to map precisely the rise and fall of Mesoamerican civilizations.

Our analysis of the Old World has shown that the rise and fall of civilization resulted from the adoption and exhaustion of specialized dynamic strategies by materialistic decision-makers. The collapse of society is a function of the very forces that empowered the earlier expansion. While the available data are far from satisfactory, it is possible to interpret the rise and fall of two distinct Mesoamerican societies prior to the Spanish invasion: the Teotihuacan and the Mayan. While continuing research may change some of the details, particularly timing, the fundamental processes identified can be expected to pass the test of time. Aztec society, which was still in the early stages of its conquest strategy, was destroyed in the conflict between the Old and New Worlds in 1519 (Clendinnen, 1993). Similarly in South America the Incas, who thought they were on the verge of conquering the last bastion of civilization in what is now southern Colombia, were struck down by the Spaniards in the 1530s (Hemming, 1983). These societies will not, therefore, be examined here.

The classic stages of the civilizations of Teotihuacan and Maya overlap in time, but many of their characteristics contrast starkly with each other. Teotihuacan was a highly urbanized society in which the city of the same name dominated its sphere of influence. The city of Teotihuacan is located about 42 kilometres north-east of Mexico City (or the later Aztec city of Tenochtitlan) in the central Mexican highlands at a height of 2,275 metres (Figure 10.6). The geography of this region is semi-arid and the climate is temperate. At the city's peak between AD 500 and 600 its population was probably about 125,000 (Millon, 1988: 102). While this did not approach the city size of Rome (850,000), Constantinople (500,000), Alexandria, (600,000) or Antioch (400,000) in the Old World (Beloch, 1968), it was greater than any other city in the Basin of Mexico by a factor of twenty and in the Mayan lowlands (e.g. Tikal) by a factor of twelve.

The archaeological evidence suggests that prior to 150 BC, Teotihuacan consisted of several small villages covering no more than a few hectares with

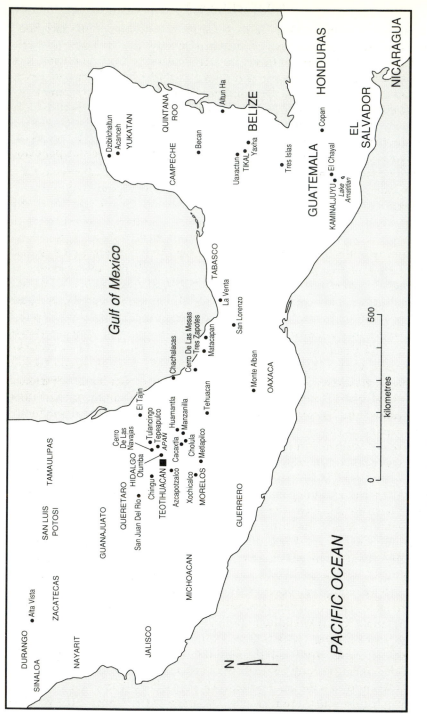

Figure 10.6 The ancient societies of Mesoamerica
Source: Drawn from data in Millon (1988).

a population of from 1,000 to 3,000 people. In the following 150 years, however, Teotihuacan grew at a rate faster than any other in its entire 900 year history. By about the birth of Christ, the city covered 6 to 8 square kilometres – about one-third of the peak reached in AD 150 when the Great Pyramid of the Sun had been built together with more than twenty temple complexes. During this period the city came to dominate the Basin of Mexico by including 85 to 90 per cent of the region's entire population. While substantial building occurred during the period AD 450–750, it consisted mainly of renovations and additions to existing monumental structures together with the construction of new residential compounds. A major industry was the mining, manufacture, and trade in obsidian blades and scrapers (Spence, 1984).

It has been estimated (Cowgill, 1979: 53–5) that population grew very rapidly – at 1.2 per cent per annum – between 150 BC and AD 1; began to decelerate from AD 1 to 150 ('still high but slowing rapidly'); and fluctuated around a flat trend between AD 150 and 750. The average population may have been about 30,000 to 40,000 for the period 150 BC–AD 1; 60,000 to 80,000 between AD 1 and 150; and 125,000 or more between AD 400 and 650. Hence this estimated population profile suggests rapid growth prior to AD 150 followed by a 'long plateau' until the society collapsed 'suddenly' in the mid-eighth century.

Such rapid population and urban growth during the 150 years prior to the birth of Christ implies a major breakthrough in Teotihuacan's use of dynamic strategies. As has been discussed elsewhere in this book, population growth in a viable society is a response to a successful dynamic strategy rather than a cause of it. The problem we face is insufficient evidence to demonstrate clearly what that strategy might be. What evidence we do have indicates the existence of both trade (Millon, 1988: 126–7) and warfare (Cowgill, 1979: 61–2). Such a sudden increase in population, however, is unlikely to have been caused by an expansion of trade. As will be shown in the next chapter, the rapid growth of trading nations – such as Achaean Greece, Tyre, Carthage, Venice, and, in the seventeenth century, Britain and Holland – is due to their central location usually on sea routes between at least two major trading areas, together with an ability to exploit such an advantage successfully.

Clearly Teotihuacan was involved in both local and long-distance trade, but this trade was limited by the absence of suitable draft and pack animals or of wheeled transport. Goods were carried by porter, who could transport a 40 kilogram load 25 kilometres per day. It has been estimated that for a 50-kilometre trip this would cost 16 per cent of the value of a load of corn and 33 per cent for a 100-kilometre trip. For modern peasant economies a one-third transport cost is considered excessively high (Culbert, 1988: 93). While dugout canoes could extend this range on rivers, their carrying capacity was not large. Economic trade in bulky items such as food, therefore, could be conducted over no more than 50–100 kilometres. Trade in more valuable items, however, was conducted over long distances. These items included consumption goods for the ruling elite (such as feathers, incense, ceramics, salt, exotic fur pelts, and precious metals and stones) and obsidian blades and scrapers (Hirth, 1984). With the exception of obsidian, which was widely used throughout Mesoamerica, these luxury commodities had little impact upon the economy. Obsidian, which has attracted much attention from archaeologists, was found in Mesoamerica only in a few sites, the chief of which were to the north-east of the Basin of Mexico over which Teotihuacan gained a virtual monopoly (Charlton, 1984). Yet while the production and export of obsidian blades and scrapers was an important industry – involving about 6 per cent of the city's population at its peak (Santley, 1984: 80–3) – it is unable to account for the rapid increase in population between 150 BC and AD 150. Also the obsidian industry developed, in significant part, in response to the demands of the military. As there were no innovations in transport, commerce would not have been a dominant dynamic strategy.

Neither is technological change the answer. Teotihuacan was a neolithic society and the agricultural techniques, including larger-scale irrigated farming, required to support urban development had been worked out between 500 and 150 BC (Cowgill, 1979: 53). There were no sudden increases in agricultural productivity and surpluses after 150 BC to support the process of urbanization. Even the main craft skills had emerged in village life prior to 150 BC. The main technical developments after this time were in monumental and residential building, and these were responses to an increase in material living standards rather than being a causal influence. Monumental building can be interpreted as investment by the ruling elite in political and social control so as to maximize their material advantage. Just as in the Old World's classical antiquity (Greece and Rome), technology was not a dominant but only a supportive strategy. That may have come later had not the Old World intervened suddenly and violently.

What does this leave? The only dynamic strategy that could account for the rapid increase in population between 150 BC and AD 150 was conquest. Conquest of neighbouring villages would have provided the labour required not only to construct and maintain the monumental buildings that impress even the modern visitor, but also to augment the rural labour force to feed this great city. Conquest would have provided the precious metals and stones used to finance these monumental public buildings and hydraulic schemes – even slaves have to be fed, clothed, and housed, and some materials have to be acquired through trade if they cannot be obtained locally. Conquest, or the threat of conquest, also would have enabled Teotihuacan to establish more distant garrisons or colonies to exploit mineral resources not available in the Basin of Mexico.

Sufficient evidence exists to support this conquest interpretation. Teotihuacan gained military ascendancy over the Basin of Mexico in the century or so before the birth of Christ and went on to control most of central Mexico (Spence, 1984: 87). It is also generally agreed that the

Teotihuacanos had a presence in some Mayan urban centres, that they probably interfered in Mayan politics, and even could have ruled some Mayan urban sites (Culbert, 1991: 315). This influence appears to have been strongest in the late fourth and early fifth centuries AD, and certainly extended back before this time. There is also evidence that the military forces of Teotihuacan were used to gain access to essential goods and mineral resources – such as obsidian, jade, copal, cacao, marine shell, and tropical feathers – in south Guatemala (see Figure 10.6), and to develop large-scale mining in north-western Mexico for supplies of cinnabar, haematite, limonite, malachite, and chert. This military outreach, however, did not extend beyond the seventh century AD owing to the ebbing of Teotihuacan power (Millon, 1988: 114–36). By the middle of the following century this great city finally collapsed, destroyed by force and fire, never to recover its former splendour.

If the available population estimates are approximately correct then Teotihuacan, by employing a conquest strategy, achieved its maximum population as early as AD 150, a level of economic development it was able to sustain for a further 500 to 600 years before its eventual collapse. Teotihuacan was able to achieve a degree of longrun stability, despite the fact that it had vastly exceeded its neolithic technological optimal size, because it was so successful in eliminating its local rivals in a world where long-distance campaigns were uneconomical. In a highly competitive world, the exhaustion of the conquest strategy after AD 150 would have led to a relatively quick onset of instability and collapse as the former conqueror attempted to maintain its frontiers against determined opposition. Teotihuacan, however, had destroyed its local opposition which it was able to dominate by virtue of its huge size. More distant neighbours, such as the central Mexican Plateau states of Cholula and Xochicalo and the lowland Maya, could not afford to put such large forces into the field nor maintain extended lines of supply with such primitive forms of transport. Therefore they were no real threat to Teotihuacan – at least not until it began to go into decline. In effect Teotihuacan had, by its initial military success, swept away its former competitive environment both internal and external. Its situation is closer to that of China after the final defeat of the Mongols in AD 1368 rather than to that of Rome after AD 130. Teotihuacan, like China, was able after AD 150 to bring its population into a state of longrun balance with its limited resources and to organize a stationary-state economy owing to an increasingly interventionist government. The forces of order completely overwhelmed the creative instinct of materialist man. In the process Teotihuacan lost economic resilience and ultimately became prey to internal and external forces of chaos.

This effectively demonstrates that diminishing marginal returns lead not to inevitable collapse, as some (Tainter, 1988: 195) have claimed, but only to equilibrium, as the classical economists told us in the early nineteenth century. How long this equilibrium is maintained depends upon the degree of competition, the reserves of the society, and the availability of other dynamic strategies. In a highly competitive environment the equilibrium will be only momentary, as it was for the Maya, because the gap between their over-expanded conquest size and the technological optimal size opened up dramatically before them at a time when their financial reserves had been exhausted by warfare. Collapse was sudden. Where competition is weak, and reserves are strong, as they were for Teotihuacan, the period of equilibrium, or more accurately stability, may be long and drawn out. But, ultimately, the end is the same.

In a world of greatly reduced competition, Teotihuacan certainly had the time to introduce a new dynamic strategy, but it lacked the incentive to do so. Had it adopted the technology strategy after AD 150, not only would the Teotihuacanos have survived beyond AD 700, as Western Europe was able to do, but they may have been in a position to launch their own attack against the Old World before 1500 (assuming they had also gained, through exploration, adequate immunity to outside diseases). But, of course, in the absence of the intense competition that prevailed in Europe from the same time such an outcome was not possible.

The core Mayan region (Figure 10.6) covered the lowlands of what is now the Yucatan Peninsula of Mexico, northern Guatemala, Belize, and small sections of El Salvador and Honduras. While the lowlands – at about 400 metres elevation – receive 1,000 mm of rain in the north and 3,000 mm in the south, most of the drainage is underground and permanent streams and rivers occur only on the fringes. The region supports tropical rainforests in the south and drier scrub forests in the north. This very different geography – and, hence, resource endowment – to that in the Basin of Mexico gave rise to a markedly different settlement pattern.

Mayan settlements of a scattered nature date back as early as 2000 BC. Over the next millennium these settlements multiplied as tribal groups – practising swidden (slash-and-burn) agriculture with maize, beans, and squash as the subsistence crops – increased their population, and migrated to unoccupied areas. By about 400 BC this technology had enabled the complete exploitation of the lowlands, and thereafter complex urban centres emerged (Webster, 1977). Even before the early classic period (from AD 250) some of these urban centres, such as Mirador and Tikal, were relatively large, at about 11,000 people, and possessed temples, shrines, and richly adorned residences for the elite (Haviland, 1969; Culbert, 1991: 311–12). This preclassic period also saw the emergence of kings who ruled the larger urban centres and exercised control over smaller centres.

During the early classic period (AD 250–600) the Mayan lowlands, in contrast to the Teotihuacan state, were dominated by a relatively large number of major urban centres of similar size and similar distance apart, which ruled over a hierarchy of other centres ranging from relatively large 'secondary centres' to small 'hamlets' and individual households (Cowgill, 1979: 53). The sphere of influence of Tikal, for example, had a radius of no more than 100 kilometres. In other words, unlike Teotihuacan in Mexico, no one centre dominated the Mayan lowlands. Instead it was held by a number of much smaller urban states, including no more than 40,000–60,000 people even in the late classic period, which were ruled by regional kings (Webster, 1977: 366). The important point to realize is that these various, equally matched centres produced a highly competitive environment which involved regular military conflict (Schele and Mathews, 1991). This situation is highly reminiscent of the competitive environments generated by the city-states of both Sumer and classical Greece. Such a comparison merely implies that the types of dynamic strategies adopted are likely to be similar, not that the cultural forms are necessarily the same.

The Mayan economic system was based upon relatively small-scale agriculture which began in small clearings on the fertile valley floors. But as population increased, this settlement extended up the valley sides through terracing and into the wetter lands through raised fields. This terrain made dispersed, small-scale farming the most efficient form of economic organization and, hence, the most effective form of political organization. The Mayan economic and political system contrasts with the centralized, larger-scale agriculture using extensive irrigation in the open semi-arid lands of the Basin of Mexico. This is similar to the contrast in the Old World between the large-scale, highly centralized, irrigated agriculture in Mesopotamia and Egypt and the small-scale, dispersed, agricultural system in Mediterranean countries such as Greece and Italy where good land was widely scattered. Both economic and political organization depend heavily on the nature of resource distribution and availability.

Economic expansion, rather than economic growth, is reflected in the very approximate estimates of population currently available. Culbert (1988: 89) has estimated that the population of the southern Mayan lowlands probably increased steadily – but not necessarily slowly (Webster, 1977) – between 2000 BC and AD 600, and 'explosively' between AD 600 and 830. During these last 250 years – the late classic period – population density may have reached 200 people per square kilometre over the entire region: 'a remarkable density for a Neolithic people'. This average was about four times greater than the number of people that could be supported by swidden agriculture, an indication of the role played by heavy investment in intensive land use (Culbert, 1973b: 72). But during the following century – the terminal classic period – there was wide-scale abandonment of urban centres in the core area (although in the northern regions some sites still flourished and cultural activities were maintained) and population 'declined to very low levels except for fairly small, quite well-defined areas'. Population in the core areas may have declined from 3,000,000 to 450,000 in just 75 years (Adams, 1973: 225). A more precise measure of this dramatic decline is the number of centres constructing dated monuments: in AD 790 there were nineteen, in 810 there were twelve, in 830 only three, and after 889 none (Culbert, 1974: 105).

The question that has preoccupied Mesoamericanists is how to explain the rise and fall of Mayan civilization. There are many theories but little agreement. To make sense of the course charted by Mayan society we must understand its dynamic process and the strategies that drove it. The available evidence suggests that before 400 BC the dynamic underlying scattered Mayan settlements, which employed the ancient swidden agricultural technology, was family multiplication and migration to new lands. No doubt they also engaged in small-scale raiding. By about 400 BC all available land had been occupied using the existing technology. This increased competition and led to improvements in rural technology, the construction of fortified villages and urban centres, the development of more sophisticated military skills, and the extension of trading networks. By the beginning of the early classic period (AD 250) there had emerged a highly competitive economic and military environment in which regional kings, located in major urban centres, conducted regular warfare aimed at securing additional territory, labour, and movable goods, and at securing trading advantages (Webster, 1977).

Owing to their roughly equal economic strength – economic resources in these tropical lowlands were relatively evenly distributed despite some diversity (Culbert, 1973a) – no one king was able to gain dominion over the entire area, although from time to time some were able to gain influence over neighbouring urban centres (Sanders, 1977: 296–7; Schele and Mathews, 1991: 245–50). As regional warlords were quite evenly matched, the gains from conquest could be regarded only as an occasional windfall and could not be relied upon to generate a sustained increase in material living standards. To achieve sustained economic growth it was essential, as in Western Europe, to continue to fine-tune their economic system; to experiment with terracing, irrigation, and raised-field agriculture; and to gain favourable access to tradable goods and to trading routes. It was during this period of economic growth that Mayan culture flourished, with writing – the only full Mesoamerican script – emerging in the third century AD.

The late classic period (AD 600–830) marks a major change in the use of dynamic strategies, as can be seen in the sudden and rapid increase in population. This new dynamic followed what Mesoamericanists have called a 'hiatus' in economic activity during the period AD 530–600. This hiatus was a period of transition when the old strategy of technological fine-tuning and trade experienced diminishing returns. During these years various Mayan 'city-states' struggled to gain ascendancy over one another – they struggled, in other words, to develop a new dynamic strategy: the fully fledged conquest strategy. While this strategic breakthrough by a few successful warrior kings prevented stagnation and collapse, it did not involve a major change of direction, for war had long been pursued as a subsidiary strategy.

332

It was the conquest strategy, therefore, that generated the sudden increase in population between AD 600 and 830. As argued earlier in the case of Teotihuacan, neither trade nor technology could have accounted for such an acceleration in economic development. The only persuasive candidate for this rapid change was conquest. This conclusion is borne out by the growing archaeological evidence for increased fortifications and military activity in the late classic phase – a period that coincided with the declining military influence of Teotihuacan (Chase and Chase, 1982; Culbert, 1991, Schele and Mathews, 1991). It is also supported by the persuasive arguments about the role of warfare in political development by Webster (1977).

How did the conquest strategies of the major Mayan centres, both within Mayan territory and against their neighbours, produce a population explosion as well as economic growth? My hypothesis is that a major objective of Mayan conquest strategy was to obtain additional supplies of cheap labour that could be employed to construct and maintain the highly labour-intensive clearing and large-scale earthworks – terracing, damming, and irrigation on hillsides and raised fields in the marshlands – that were necessary to increase agricultural productivity. This conquest-dependent increase in productivity permitted a rapid increase in population through family multiplication. Richard Adams (1980) has calculated, using radar mapping, that between 1,250 and 2,500 square kilometres of lowlands were serviced by Mayan canals. This was a labour-intensive infrastructure on a massive scale. While the required technology had been developed well before AD 600, it could not be introduced on a significant scale until sufficient surplus labour was available. Evidence suggests that the construction of those earthworks together with at least 180 kilometres of transport canals required approximately 500,000 labour-days to construct (Culbert, 1988: 96; Matheny, 1978: 192–5). Moreover, large supplies of cheap labour were required for the construction of ambitious public building programmes in the established urban centres (Culbert, 1988: 99–100).

Obtaining large supplies of excess labour is a major problem in decentralized, small-scale economic systems such as those that prevailed in the Mayan lowlands. The only way was through conquest. The evidence for increasingly destructive internal (Schele and Mathews, 1991) and external (Webster, 1977; Freidel, 1985) warfare is clear. Having constructed the large-scale earthworks and increased its agricultural productivity, Mayan society was able to expand its own population rapidly without reducing material living standards. In turn this larger population increased their military strength. The strategic circle was complete.

But how can we account for the collapse – in terms of living standards and population – of Mayan society? The argument throughout this book is that the collapse of complex societies results from the exhaustion of specialized dynamic strategies – thereby exposing the gap between the optimal neolithic size and their current overextended size – and a failure to replace them with other effective strategies before internal and, possibly, external forces of chaos overwhelm them. The limits of Mayan conquest strategy were reached quite quickly owing to the constraints imposed by their transport technology. Military supply lines were geographically restricted by the need to carry supplies and equipment using porters. Once these limits had been established through the equation of marginal strategic costs and benefits, major Mayan urban centres, which had become accustomed to the regular inflow of tribute of all kinds, would have experienced economic stress as the maintenance of rural and urban infrastructure had to be undertaken entirely from internal resources. The strategic circle was broken and Mayan society was thrown back on its neolithic origins. This would have led to the imposition of increased taxation on the population raised by increasingly oppressive means. Such an attempt to maintain a super-optimal population size would have placed considerable strain upon the living standards of its citizens, which can be seen reflected in the declining stature of Maya skeletons in the late classic period (Haviland, 1967; Willey, 1973). It would also have reduced the demand for the products of craft workshops. The combined effect of these forces made the major Mayan centres, which had expanded rapidly through conquest, vulnerable to considerable internal and external competition. Yet even before anarchy, the reduction of conquest 'revenue' may have been so significant that many Mayan centres were unable to maintain essential services (or, in more formal language, to cover average variable costs) and, hence, the only economically rational option was to abandon these urban sites.

The Mayan experience was very different to that of Teotihuacan, which had been able to eliminate internal and external competition. Mayan society, despite the emergence of a number of very successful conquest states, was highly competitive. It did not have time, unlike Teotihuacan, to attempt to develop new dynamic strategies. Any perceived weakness in the leading centres of Mayan society was sure to be exploited both from within and without. This is why Mayan society collapsed quite quickly after its conquest strategy had been exhausted, while Teotihuacan society kept the edge of darkness at bay for much longer.

The conquest-strategy interpretation developed here can be compared and contrasted with the interpretations of a number of Mesoamericanists. Webster (1977) and Tainter (1988) see warfare as playing a central role in the emergence of Mayan polity or 'sociopolitical complexity' rather than its economy, and view the collapse as resulting from the escalation of warfare rather than from its exhaustion as a strategy, as claimed in this book. Similarly Cowgill (1979), who recognizes the role of warfare in increasing population, views the collapse of Mayan society in political rather than my fundamentally economic terms. We all, however, reject the environmental interpretation of Mayan collapse (Culbert, 1988) – they not as categorically as myself.

Not only is there no evidence (Cowgill, 1979: 57) for significant environmental degradation, but this fashionably modern hypothesis totally ignores the ability of human decision-makers to alter their actions when their mistakes affect material outcomes. The environmental explanation of collapse is based upon simplistic, mechanical-engineering models in which, as there is no room for human flexibility and inventiveness, economic systems overshoot their targets, just like thermostatically controlled heating systems. How is it possible to take seriously a comparison between an automatic heating system and a dynamic societal system? Human societies attempting to maximize material advantage do not 'overshoot' in this mechanical way. This is a prime example of the danger of imposing fashionable current ideas on the past.

We must also reject eccentric hypotheses like those of Puleston (1979), which claim that the ideas of Mayan scholars about the cyclical nature of their past actually caused these long cycles to occur in reality. To the contrary, the great wheel of civilization in both the Old and New Worlds, as shown in Chapter 12, was driven by the vast majority of the population who were attempting to maximize their material advantage, not by a tiny minority of 'intellectuals' who had little direct influence on reality. The ancient pre-occupation with a cyclical view of life – in contrast to our own linear view – emerged from an observation of the dynamics of their own past; not the other way round.

Conquest has been a potent force in the Dynamic Society in the past. For ancient civilizations it was the central element in their economic growth and expansion. But those who committed themselves to this dynamic strategy also committed themselves to collapse, because ultimately the conquest strategy must exhaust itself, thereby exposing a grossly overextended society to the internal and external forces of chaos. Also the prosperity which was built upon conquest could not be passed on to successive civilizations – each conquest-driven civilization had to go through the same bloody process for itself. The curse of those who live by the sword was not to die by the sword but continually to reinvent the wheel of conquest. This was the eternal recurrence of classical antiquity, the force driving the great wheel of civilization.

The eternal recurrence was only broken with the emergence of the technological strategy in Western Europe. This was a long slow process that took place between the fall of Rome and the final triumph during the Industrial Revolution. Underlying the emergence of the technological strategy, in contrast to the Chinese experience, was the intense competition in Western Europe between a large number of small and equally matched kingdoms. As this competition precluded the use of conquest in a systematic way to increase material advantage, the combatants were forced to use other strategies such as commerce, colonization, and technology to generate the income needed to finance the struggle for survival. Eventually conquest became redundant.

But this did not prevent individual European nations attempting to conquer the rest, as demonstrated by the Napoleonic and the First and Second

World Wars. They were seeking not steady and systematic economic growth through conquest, as the ancients had done, but the sudden and risky windfall gains that it could bring in a modern technological world. What they did not realize was that technological change in a competitive environment confers not military superiority but rather a build-up in the potential for destruction and carnage. The benefits of wars of conquest in a competitive world are not worth their costs to any of the combatants. This has been clearly demonstrated in Europe this century. Henceforth the main danger is that through the interventionism of world politics, the existing competitive balance may be disrupted, irrational political forces be set free, and the horsemen of war be unleashed upon the Earth once more to create a whirlwind of thunder and dust that will block out the Sun.

11

CONJURERS OF COMMERCE

When thy wares went forth out of the seas, thou filledst many people; thou didst enrich the kings of the earth with the multitude of thy riches and thy merchandise.

(Ezekiel, XXVII, 33)

The merchant venturer is a skilful opportunist. Not content just to respond to favourable conditions he, through clever bargaining, creates his own opportunities. While he may be swept aside from time to time by the conqueror and the innovator, the merchant is quick to see his advantage and follows closely on their heels as they break new ground. At other times he is the very inspiration of society and is eagerly supported by the other two. If the rewards are high enough the merchant is prepared to take considerable risks and hardships. He will follow the camel trains across the deserts and over the mountains to strange lands in search of rare commodities in great demand such as silks and spices. He will undertake long and dangerous voyages on the seas where his cargoes are at the mercy of sudden storms, hidden reefs, and predatory pirates. He will fight to the bitter end rather than give up his favourable access to goods and markets. When the merchant is successful his riches are beyond the dreams of even the greediest kings. He has the power to conjure up riches out of the most unpromising economic circumstances. When he does so the entire society prospers and its culture reaches new heights – for he is the greatest of patrons. The merchant is the rider in Zechariah's fourth chariot.

Merchants have played a vital role in all the civilizations of mankind. Yet this role has changed with the prevailing economic conditions. When the benefit–cost calculus favoured conquest – as it did in the Akkadian, Assyrian, Macedonian, Roman, Mayan, and Aztec Empires – merchants played a subsidiary but vital role in economic prosperity. They were quick to take advantage of the new opportunities for trade that the expanding frontiers provided. When the calculus favoured technological innovation, as it has done since the

337

Industrial Revolution, merchants exploited the commercial opportunities provided by new productive processes, new commodities, and new methods of transport, communication, and ways of doing business. In these periods, when the dominant dynamic strategies were either conquest or technological change, the merchant's role has been an important but not a leading one. In these periods, commerce has been a subsidiary and supporting dynamic strategy.

Yet there have been other times when the economic calculus favoured the merchant and when commerce was the dominant dynamic strategy. Some of these times have been brilliant episodes in the history of human culture because prosperous merchants – merchant princes – have a propensity to be great patrons of the arts in a way that leading soldiers and innovating industrialists rarely are. While it is by no means universal, there has been a correlation between highly successful merchant venturing and the brilliant flowering of culture in all its manifestations – of art, architecture, music, and literature. This can be seen in ancient Mesopotamia, Minoan society, classical Athens, Venice and Genoa during the Italian Renaissance, and north-western Europe during the sixteenth century.

Merchants, probably because the princes amongst them deal in fine arts, have an appreciation of high culture of all kinds, and are active and enthusiastic patrons. In a particular sense the merchant has something in common with the artist – an ability to create something wondrous from the most unlikely materials. There is something of the magician about both. A society based upon commerce is a wonderful illusion, but an illusion that can suddenly evaporate at the very height of its achievement.

THE DYNAMIC STRATEGY OF COMMERCE

The commerce strategy involves the use of trade between regions and nations to generate economic growth. While most economic textbooks on the subject give the impression that trade just happens automatically between two regions if the necessary demand and supply conditions exist, it is in fact an activity undertaken by entrepreneurial merchants who perceive, or even create, profitable opportunities. The point I wish to make is that trade is a strategic activity undertaken by imaginative economic decision-makers who are willing to risk their capital to achieve profitable returns. In order to enhance their returns, merchant venturers will go to considerable lengths to negotiate or extract special privileges or monopolies.

What are the underlying economic conditions that make trade attractive to merchants? Profitable trading opportunities arise from differences between regions or nations – differences in natural resources, physical capital, human knowledge and skills, and technology. These differences ensure that the costs of producing goods and services will also differ between regions, which in turn provides the potential for profit that an astute merchant will attempt to exploit. By purchasing supplies of commodity x from region A that can produce it more cheaply than region *B*, and by selling it in region *B* where prices are higher, the merchant can make a profit provided transport and other costs do not entirely eliminate the price gap. In the process, the less efficient producers of commodity *x* in region *B* will go out of business and, over time, will begin producing commodity *y* in which their region has a comparative advantage. By purchasing stocks of commodity *y* in region *B* and selling them in region *A* where prices are higher, the merchant will make a profit, and will put producers of commodity *y* in region *A* out of business and they, in the fullness of time, will begin producing commodity *x* in which their region has a comparative advantage.

In pursuing his own material advantage, therefore, the merchant in this illustration is responsible for both countries specializing in the production of those goods and services in which they have a comparative advantage. Clearly, this leads to greater efficiency in the production of both commodities and to lower costs of consumption in both countries. Everyone is better off, particularly the merchant who was responsible for these commercial trans-actions. This is not an automatic process as economists usually imply. It occurs only because merchants, or middlemen, perceive an opportunity of buying cheap and selling dear.

Once the static gains from trade have been exploited, and real GDP per capita has been raised to a new and higher level, what is it that causes trade to continue to grow? Why move from this new and higher equilibrium level? There are a number of reasons. First, new resources of land and precious metals may be suddenly discovered – such as the Phoenicians discovery (1000 BC) of metal-rich Spain, the Athenian discovery of a rich new vein of silver at Laurion (*c.* 483 BC) and of the wheat lands of the Black Sea region, the Persian discovery in the first century AD of the Silk Route to China, the Spanish discovery in the sixteenth century of the land and mineral resources of the New World, and the British discovery of Australasia in the late eighteenth century. These 'discoveries' led to a sudden and rapid expan-sion of trade, initially exploited by the discoverers but quickly challenged by others owing to the rich returns they provided. While the extraordinary returns to trade were the motivating force in these discoveries, they were made and exploited by those civilizations or kingdoms that had successfully innovated in transport and communications, that had developed or purchased the necessary skills of navigation, and that had acquired the necessary naval and military power to gain trading concessions and to maintain them in the face of determined competition.

Trade will increase also as a result of technological change viewed in its widest sense. If the costs of conducting trade can be reduced, commerce will expand. This can be achieved through innovations in transport and communications and through improvements in the efficiency with which merchants go about their business (a reduction in transaction costs). These cost reductions may occur gradually via a large number of small changes, or they may occur by a smaller series of large steps. The historical examples are numerous and only a few will be nominated here. Innovations in sea transport were introduced by the Egyptians, Minoans, Phoenicians (Edey, 1974: 33–48), Greeks (Warry, 1980: 17–19), Spanish (Greenhill, 1988: 67–9; Scammell, 1981: 26) and British (Pollard and Robertson, 1979). As far as overland transport was concerned, donkeys were used from about 3000 BC; camels were introduced in the twelfth century BC; horses were being used in China to pull waggons by 250 BC; and railways were introduced by Britain in 1825. Major canals were dug in Egypt (Necho's Canal connected the Nile with the Red Sea) in the fourth century BC, in China about 220 BC, in Egypt (Suez) in 1869, and in the middle Americas (Panama) in 1914. Markets have also changed dramatically over time. In the pioneering civilizations of Sumer, Egypt, and Minoan Crete it is clear that temples and palaces organized the systematic collection and distribution of goods, although there were also private exchanges of goods and services (Reade, 1991: 61). The Greeks are thought to have been the first to develop public marketplaces, initially based upon barter, but from the sixth century BC (at least), based upon coins (Starr, 1977: 108–17). Interestingly, in Western Europe this trend was reversed from 1500 when public pitched markets began to be phased out in favour of private transactions (Jones, 1993).

Finally we should consider the role of new commodities in stimulating trade. This has occurred throughout history, but has only become systematic and sustained under the technology strategy since the Industrial Revolution. Once again examples are numerous and diverse and begin with stone tools about 2 million years ago (East Africa) and include ceramics and sculpture (Czechoslovakia) 27000 BC, pottery (Japan) 11000 BC, copper objects (Anatolia) from about 7900 BC, painted pottery (Iran) 6600 BC, printed textiles (Anatolia) 6500 BC, wheel-thrown pottery (Mesopotamia) 4000 BC, bronze objects (Eurasia) 3000 BC, glass objects (Egypt and Mesopotamia) 1400 BC, iron objects (Anatolia) 1250 BC, steel objects (Cyprus) 1100 BC, blown glass (Syria) 50 BC, and clockwork (China) AD 725 (Calder, 1984). And so on down to the present. Since the Industrial Revolution there has been an exponential increase in the number of new consumer goods that the rest of the world feels unable to live without. The list is well known and will probably be endless. Technological change, therefore, is a major driving force in the expansion of trade. In view of the dynamic strategy argument presented in this book, the main direction of causation in the innovating country since the Industrial Revolution has been from technology to trade, but there is also a feedback from trade to technology. The conjurers of commerce have been overtaken in the modern world by the maker of the wheel.

Commerce-led growth

How does trade generate economic growth? We need to consider both the static and dynamic gains from trade. The static gains include both ordinary and extraordinary returns to a given change in the conditions of trade, and the dynamic gains are the outcome of these returns over time. First there are the ordinary gains from trade that are usually discussed by economists in a comparative static framework – by comparing two equilibrium positions – rather than a dynamic framework. As already illustrated, trade between two regions occurs because both will be better off by specializing according to their comparative advantage and by trading with each other than if they both attempted to produce and consume all products. They will be better off after trade than before, because they can focus their resource endowment on the production of what they do best, and because they may also be able to achieve economies of scale. The gains from trade will not be equally divided between the two regions but will depend upon the economic bargaining power of each, which will be expressed through the terms of trade (the price of x relative to the price of y). These are the ordinary static gains from trade that economists have discussed ever since Adam Smith published *The Wealth of Nations* in 1776. They are usually invoked against tariff protection and in support of free trade. Yet, while they lead to an increase in GDP per capita, it is a once-for-all increase and will not lead to a sustained increase – it will not generate economic growth.

What economists do not discuss when considering the static gains from trade are, what I will call, the extraordinary gains from trade that are captured not by the two regions engaged in trade (in our earlier illustration), but by a third group that specializes in merchant venturing. While our merchant venturer, like the neoclassical economist, is also an advocate of free trade, he is not an advocate of free access by all merchant venturers to this trade. Our merchant venturer wants to maximize trade but also to minimize competition between merchant venturers. He wishes, in other words, to gain privileged – hopefully even exclusive – access to interregional markets. If this can be achieved, our merchant venturer can raise his fees for service and can earn extraordinary profits at the expense of both trading regions. To achieve this, our merchant venturer will need to be outside all regions/countries involved in the trade that he wishes to facilitate, otherwise they will attempt to improve their gains by forcing him to reduce his. Ideally he will want to belong to a separate community or society of merchant venturers, such as that of Venice between AD 1000 and 1797, in order to negotiate and protect his exclusive access to interregional markets. Societies specializing in merchant venturing in this way will pursue commerce as a dominant dynamic strategy in order to increase their material living standards over time – in other words, to achieve economic growth.

How do merchant societies gain special access to international markets? Location has always been an important consideration. Those cities, regions, or kingdoms that are fortunately located on major trading routes by sea or land have been able to exploit this advantage by extracting a surplus (or 'economic rent') over and above a normal market return on trading activities through monopoly pricing. Some of those cities in the path of trade are able to improve their economic position by persuading their neighbours – either by providing a vitally needed service such as military support, or by the threat of conquest – to grant them trading privileges or even monopolies. This is where the conjuring skills of the merchant come to the fore. As we shall see, some cities with virtually no natural resources have been able to build up large and prosperous empires using little more than the skills of diplomacy or sleight of hand. They have been able to create castles in the air out of little more than their native wit. Such conspicuous fortunes created quickly in this way constitute a two-edged sword. It is a strategy that generates a rapid and substantial increase in real GDP per capita, but it also attracts the unwanted attention of outsiders who are keen to break into the privileged circle either by military action or by seeking the support of powerful patrons. Intense military struggles, as we shall see, have emerged regularly in history between cities and kingdoms competing for the extraordinary gains that can be made from commercial monopolies.

How can these gains from trade be viewed from a dynamic perspective? Or, in other words, how does trade generate rapid and sustained economic growth? The economic theoretic answer to this question is not particularly helpful. As we have seen, the static gains from trade are limited – once a country has specialized according to its comparative advantage there will be no further improvement in efficiency. There are, however, a number of indirect effects of trade that can generate economic growth (an increase in real GDP per capita) as well as economic expansion (an increase in real GDP). In the first place, involvement in trade can lead to the accumulation of large surpluses that can be made to work for the successful commercial nations. If these surpluses are invested in new domestic industries using the latest technology, or used to set up financial institutions, they can serve to increase material living standards, particularly if they form the basis for further trade, as was done in the cities of Flanders and northern Italy during the Renaissance. Second, international trade has in the past been an important vehicle for the dissemination of technological knowledge, which can be used by the recipient countries to increase productivity and hence economic growth. This can be seen in the cases of Achaean Greece, Phoenicia, and Western Europe. Third, international trade can provide a country with the financial capital, physical capital, raw materials, and skilled labour required in the growth process. Fourth, and very importantly, trade provides a non-destructive form of competition – although this can degenerate into military conflict – that encourages innovation and economic progress.

Finally, international trade may spark off a number of changes within a country that could produce economic growth. The opening up of world markets, for example, may lead to the expansion of industries many times greater than would have been possible on the basis of domestic demand alone. While this might merely produce economic expansion, there are a number of ways in which it can also lead to economic growth. If population increases rapidly in response to trade with at least no reduction in average living standards, trade-induced economies of scale may be reaped. Also trade-induced expansion may lead to the discovery of new resources – particularly of precious metals and stones – that will generate further rounds of economic growth. This, as we have seen, has been important in the past. But mineral booms are always transitory. Sooner or later mineral deposits are exhausted and the economic growth based upon these finds comes to an end. Sustained economic growth requires a continual search for new or rejuvenated dynamic strategies.

Trade, therefore, has been employed by most countries to provide a boost to their material standards of living, and by a fortunate few to generate spectacular longrun economic growth. Because an economic system founded upon neolithic agriculture could provide only a relatively low-level base for real GDP per capita, trade was a particularly important dynamic strategy before the Industrial Revolution. If the income generated by a neolithic system is spread fairly evenly over the entire population – as in classical Greece where the peasant holdings were as small as 4 hectares and the largest holdings were in the vicinity of only 30 hectares (Starr, 1977: 123) – the standard of living even of the elite would not strike us as being very satisfactory. In a closed system, the only way for the elite to improve their standard of living is by using their power over the vast majority of the population to extract all the surplus above subsistence levels. This was possible in the irrigation economies of Egypt and the Near East, but not on the Greek peninsula, because only in the former was the land amenable to large-scale production using forced labour. If the elite wished to increase its living standards further, or to increase the size of their class at the existing standard of living, they had to adopt either the conquest or the commerce strategy. If the commerce strategy was chosen (on a benefit–cost basis), extraordinary surpluses could only be generated by achieving monopoly access to traded goods and markets.

When countries have adopted commerce as their dominant dynamic strategy, technological change and conquest have usually been employed in a supporting role. The large monopoly gains from trade have been used to build up powerful navies – as in Tyre, Carthage, and Athens in classical antiquity, Venice and Genoa after AD 1000, Spain and Portugal during the sixteenth century, and Britain and the Dutch Republic during the seventeenth century – and powerful armies – as in Mesopotamia and the Islamic nations. These military forces were used by the trading nations to maintain and further their commercial interests. Technological change was also used to develop better means of land and sea transport, and to build the urban centres with their supporting industries in which the merchant venturers have flourished. Even family multiplication has played a supporting role by providing the manpower to establish colonies along major trading routes and near to sources of the major trading commodities. There have been times, therefore, when

343

the merchant has dominated the soldier, the innovator, and the head of family.

The end of commerce-led growth

While commerce-induced prosperity and growth can be spectacular, it cannot be sustained indefinitely. Sooner, rather than later, this dynamic strategy exhausts itself and either economic growth comes to an end or new strategies are substituted. Civilizations based upon the dynamic of commerce have generally flowered brilliantly for a time then disappeared without trace. The major exception was Britain, which became prosperous on trade in the sixteenth and seventeenth centuries and was able to find a successful replacement strategy in the eighteenth and nineteenth centuries – namely, the Industrial Revolution (Snooks, 1994b: ch. 1). But they had the good fortune to be in the right place at the right time.

The problem with the commerce strategy is that economic growth is only sustained while trade is expanding. As soon as trade ceases to *grow* so does real GDP per capita. And if trade actually declines before a new strategy has been developed, real GDP per capita will also decline. In a given historical era the scope for further expansion of markets is always limited. And the favoured position of any leading commercial power is likely to be undermined at any time. The extraordinary gains from trading monopolies can collapse overnight as a result of one or more of the following developments: the discovery of new trading routes; technology introduced by other nations in transport, communications, and finance that provide an advantage over the established monopolists; the exhaustion of a mineral bonanza; the saturation of new markets for a particular set of commodities; a change in the balance of political support for the competitors; a change in the balance of military power.

CONJURERS ON CENTRE STAGE

The merchant first appeared on the world stage during the early Mesopotamian civilizations to exploit trading opportunities with the surrounding nomadic peoples, between the city-states of the plain and, possibly, with other civilizations on the Nile and Indus. By 2200 BC each of the Old World's three literate civilizations contained about three-quarters of a million people. They supported twelve towns with populations of between 10,000 and 15,000 people: of which six were located in Sumer, four in Egypt, and two in the Indus Valley (McEvedy, 1967: 26). From excavations for this period we know that these civilizations imported gold, ivory, lapis lazuli, carnelian beads, copper, silver, timber, stone bowls, pots, and dates; and that they exported grain and manufactured products. Trade in some of these items was taking place in Mesopotamia by at least 4000 BC (Reade, 1991: 45).

344

The early Mesopotamian cities flourished because they developed a technology that could control the rivers and convert the sand into grain, which in turn could support urban craft activities and supply the basis for a profitable trade with other regions. Sometimes this trade had to be protected by the establishment of colonies as strongholds against those who were tempted to divert some of the growing prosperity to themselves. On the basis of this trade, cities like Ur at the head of the Persian Gulf and Susa on the overland route to Iran grew prosperous. Right from the very beginning of civilization a favourable location conferred extraordinary profits.

The manner in which Mesopotamian inter-city and international trade was organized is still a contentious issue. In Sumer, for example, the archaeological evidence suggests that city temples and palaces were responsible for organizing and financing much of the trade, and it is silent about the role of private merchants. At one time this was taken to mean that trade was publicly organized and that a private merchant class did not emerge until the Old Babylonian period after 2000 BC (McEvedy, 1967: 26). It is now thought that private merchants were operating in the earlier Sumerian period both on their own account and as agents for the various monarchs, but that they did not achieve dominance until later (Crawford, 1991: 150). According to Aubet (1993: 85):

> It is known that since the middle of the third millennium, private commercial transactions took place in Mesopotamia, in which a very advanced system of accounting in terms of gold and silver was developed, particularly in long-distance trade. At the same time, there is clear evidence that the temple and the palace devoted themselves very early on to making profits by practising usury or acting as bankers. All this means that much of the trade in Mesopotamia was organized by and for the state, coexisting with private traders.

Private merchants, therefore, appeared early in human civilization, and by about 4,000 years ago had come to dominate the dynamic strategy of commerce. They also came, through their economic success, to dominate political, social, and religious life. We are told (ibid.: 87) that:

> In western Asia . . . the merchant enjoyed enormous social prestige. In government circles, the merchant always had a high social status, shared in the profits of the palace and occasionally formed part of the royal family. Only thus can we appreciate the significance of the hymn to Enlil, the chief god of the Sumerian pantheon, who is addressed as 'merchant (*dam-gar*) of the vast land'. So the rank of the merchant is comparable with that of a god, which would be unthinkable if the merchant had been a subordinate or had not belonged to a dominant class.

Such was the importance of the dynamic strategy of commerce to early neolithic civilizations.

For four millennia Mesopotamia was at the very centre of east–west trade in the Old World. In the beginning this probably involved trade between the Indus Valley and Egypt with products such as ivory and spices. By 1600 BC this trade had been extended by the Achaean Greeks to include southern Italy and beyond; and by at least 900 BC Egypt was trading directly with the Indus Valley through the Red and Arabian Seas. By 700 BC the Phoenicians and classical Greeks had extended this trade to Spain, Gaul, and even England in search of metals. And during the first century BC, Mesopotamia had intermittent contact with China via the Silk Route.

These trading roles were played out by the Middle East and Egypt until the European breakout in the late fifteenth century AD, beginning with voyages around the Cape of Good Hope to India by the Portuguese Vasco da Gama in 1497–1498 and Cabral in 1500. Further explorers reached the East Indies (the 'Spice Islands') in 1512, China in 1513, and Japan in 1543. This direct contact with the Orient by Western Europe made the more costly overland routes to India and China redundant. Although overland trade did not cease entirely, by 1600 European trade with the Orient via the Levant was the subject of history. The Middle East and the Mediterranean ceased to be the centre of world trade. But during these four millennia, merchants from the cradle of civilization grew prosperous. Even when it was not the dominant dynamic strategy – the Akkadians, Assyrians, Babylonians, and Persians pursued conquest rather than trade – commerce contributed to the prosperity of the region and gave rise to flourishing cities such as Antioch, Babylon, Seleucia, Ravy, Hatru, Istakhr, and then later under the influence of Islam, Kufa, Baghdad, Hamadan, Wasit, and Tabriz. In the tale that unfolds in this chapter, however, we will follow the fortunes of the merchants of the seas.

The ancient Greek world

Commerce before 2000 BC was conducted largely upon the great rivers that supported civilization – the Tigris, Euphrates, Nile, and Indus – and overland using donkey trains. The first extensive trade by sea began in the Mediterranean with the mysterious Minoan culture that flourished on Crete between 2000 and 1400 BC. The Minoans developed an extensive trading empire in the Aegean Sea which included not only commerce but also the establishment of colonies on various islands (including Rhodes) off the coast of Asia Minor, and possibly even on the Greek mainland (Castleden, 1990: 120). While this area was the centre of their trading operations, the Minoans also traded with Egypt and the Levant. Indeed, they held a monopoly on east–west trade which extended to Italy and beyond. It was this monopoly that enabled the Minoans to earn extraordinary surpluses and, thereby, to rise above the base level income provided by a neolithic agricultural system in this pre-Greek society.

346

The Minoans exported pottery (the finest in the world), bronze and lead figurines, gold and silver vessels, military equipment, textiles and clothing, wine, olive oil, and other raw materials; and they imported slaves, tin, emery for drilling and polishing stone bowls and vases, obsidian, copper, amber, lapis lazuli, ivory, alabaster, amethyst, and carnelian. These imports came largely from Cyprus, Syria, Afghanistan, Babylon, Egypt, and Europe, as well as the Aegean (Castleden, 1990: 118–200). While their dominant strategy was commerce, they appear to have protected their trading empire with military force. This needs to be stressed because earlier studies of this society portrayed the Minoans as a peace-loving people at one with nature and their fellows. While fortifications may not have been constructed in Crete, it is now thought that they used forward defence in the form of a powerful navy. Certainly they possessed arms, armour, chariots, and warships (ibid.: 122, 162–5, 18–20). This trading empire supported a relatively prosperous and vital culture that appears to have been less innocent and peaceful than the traditional wisdom has claimed. As Castleden (ibid.: 178) demonstrates: 'The Minoans were sensual aesthetes and visionaries with bloodstained hands, and possessed of a much fiercer, darker, grimmer and more exotic beauty than we hitherto imagined.' How could it have been otherwise in a highly competitive world in which trading monopolies could be maintained only through military force?

How did the Minoans organize their economy and their trade? The available archaeological evidence, which is biased towards large-scale public infrastructure, suggests that in Minoan (and Egyptian) society at this time, kings and priests played a significant role in the economy and in trade (ibid.: 7). But this does not mean that private merchants were crowded out by bureaucrats. To the contrary. What we know about the motivation of bureaucrats suggests that they would not have been as enterprising as individuals trading on their own account. Hence any commercial nation that conducted trade privately would have an advantage over those trading bureaucratically. In these circumstances a bureaucratic commercial system would not last long – certainly not some four centuries.

The stark reality of the timeless struggle for survival was brought home to the Minoans by the Mycenaean invasion of Crete during the fifteenth century BC. From 1400 BC the new centre of trade and culture, generally regarded as a mechanical copy of the highly original Minoan culture that they displaced, shifted to the mainland. Between 1400 and 1100 BC the Mycenaeans traded widely in the eastern half of the Mediterranean (Figure 11.1). They became heirs to the Minoan monopoly of east–west trade, and they established colonies in the 'heel' of Italy and in southern Sicily (Burn, 1966: 46). There is abundant evidence that, as we would expect, the Mycenaeans were a warlike people who, when not trading, were raiding Hittite cities along the coast of Asia Minor (Starr, 1991: 109). The most famous battle they fought was the siege of Troy, which gave rise to those great epics the *Iliad* and the *Odyssey*.

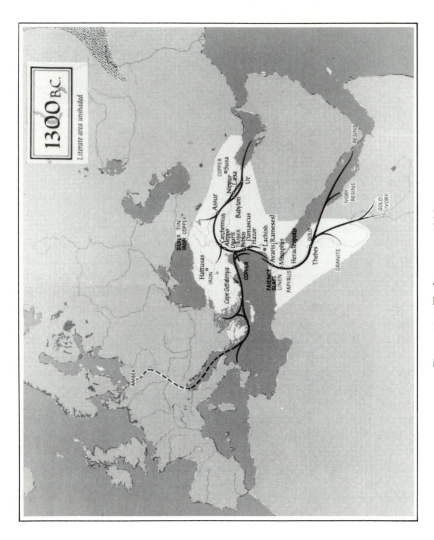

Figure 11.1 Trade routes, 1300 BC

Source: Colin McEvedy, *The Penguin Atlas of Ancient History*, Harmondsworth, Penguin, 1967, p. 35. Drawn by John Woodcock. © Colin McEvedy, 1967. Reproduced by permission of Penguin Books Ltd.

But like all expansionary societies operating within a competitive environment, there comes a time when the dynamic strategy is driven to exhaustion and the competitors waiting in the wings and watching for their chance on centre stage move in. By about 1300 BC Mycenaean trade with Sicily and Italy ceased, that with the Near East declined, and, as a result, their economy appeared to lose momentum (Burn, 1966: 49). About 1200 BC they came under attack from the northern tribes known as the Dorian Greeks, and Mycenaean society collapsed entirely soon after 1100 BC, thereby plunging Greece back into the Dark Ages.

With the demise of Mycenaean civilization, the Greek mainland became largely isolated from the rest of the world. As usually happens when central authority collapses, small tribal groups, ruled by regional warlords calling themselves kings, emerged. These tribes eked out a rural subsistence living by farming and nomadic grazing. From this primitive base the economic, social, and political characteristics of classical Greek civilization evolved during the few centuries after 1100 BC.

Commerce, together with colonization, was the dominant dynamic strategy in classical Greece. This strategy facilitated the economic expansion and growth achieved during the 'age of expansion' from 800 to 500 BC, and continued to underpin the prosperity of Greek society during the 'golden age' of Greek culture during the fifth and fourth centuries. War also played a role. In the highly competitive tribal environment existing before 800 BC military prowess became essential for survival and, during the age of expansion, war was employed to protect Greek colonies. But towards the end of the fifth century, by which time the commerce/colonization strategy had exhausted itself, conquest became increasingly important as a dynamic strategy in its own right.

Throughout this book I have argued that the neolithic agricultural foundation of ancient society provided only a limited standard of living. At this time the cost of introducing a new technological paradigm – as occurred with the Industrial Revolution some 2,500 years later – was prohibitive. In order to generate higher material living standards than the neolithic ceiling allowed, it was necessary to adopt a strategy such as conquest, or commerce often with the support of colonization. This was particularly important for Mediterranean countries such as Greece. While the irrigated valleys of Mesopotamia and Egypt were relatively productive and could generate surpluses of grain to support wealthy urban centres, the mountainous and stony lands of Greece – with small scattered plains of productive soil – were less accommodating (Starr, 1977: 40–1). Geographic conditions in Greece required farming on a smaller scale than in the Middle East. This meant that a larger proportion of the population, perhaps in the vicinity of 80 to 90 per cent, were involved in subsistence farming.

To achieve higher living standards, even at an early stage in the evolution of Greek society, it was necessary to employ other strategies that would

349

generate greater surpluses and give access to richer natural resources. This accounts for the early importance of both commerce, which under monopoly conditions could provide a quick surplus, and of colonization which could give access to richer resources elsewhere. Although the Greeks faced a new competitor in the southern Mediterranean – the Phoenicians, who will be discussed in the next section – they were able to recover the monopoly of northern east–west trade formerly held by the Mycenaeans and Minoans. This monopoly enabled the emerging Greek civilization to crash through the ceiling on living standards imposed by their agricultural system. The waves of colonization that occurred after 750 BC in the Aegean and Black Sea region and, particularly, in southern Italy and Sicily helped to protect that trade but also gave the various Greek cities direct access to richer resources than were available on the mainland. These colonies provided the cheap grain required to build up specialized, non-rural activities in the mainland cities, while trade generated demand for the products of urbanization. Urbanization on the scale achieved in Greece would not have been possible without commerce and colonization.

But commerce came before colonization, despite the traditional arguments to the contrary (Starr, 1977: 63). The important point to remember about commerce is that it can be used to generate high returns in the shortrun, particularly if special access to markets can be achieved. The process of colonization on the other hand, which requires an increase in population through family multiplication, takes longer to arrange – at least a few generations. But once colonies have been established, they can lead to an even more rapid increase in commerce. Colonization is also a more costly strategy because it requires a greater commitment to military support, particularly if the underlying threat of conquest is challenged by the local peoples. As was discussed in Chapter 8, colonization is a special case of the family multiplication strategy which is required when the stocks of freely available natural resources in the known world have been fully claimed. Greek colonization did not arise from overpopulation, as is often claimed (Burn, 1966: 81, 86), but rather from the dynamic strategy of family multiplication with the specific intent of establishing colonies. Overpopulation is not a problem in dynamic and developed societies, only in those experiencing crisis. As we know, classical Greece was perfectly able to control its population size (ibid.: 43–4).

While natural resources can be systematically accessed by colonization, there is also the lottery of accidental discovery. This is a matter of luck rather than strategy. The luck of the Athenians was to discover new deposits of silver at nearby Laurion in 483 BC, which helped to finance the build-up in its naval power at a time when colonization and commerce were slowing down and Athens was beginning to seek new strategies. This windfall helped Greece both to defeat the invading Persians at Salamis and to protect the trade routes to the Black Sea which provided essential food supplies. By the mid-fourth century, however, the mines were exhausted, trade was no longer an engine of growth, and the Athenians were experimenting with a new strategy — conquest. But this is taking the story ahead far too quickly.

We need to consider in more detail the role of commerce. The main centres of Greek trade were Athens, which dominated commerce in the Aegean, the Black Sea, and the eastern end of the Mediterranean (where they competed with the Phoenicians), and Corinth, which developed trading and colonial links with Italy and, later, Syracuse in Sicily, which dominated trade in the Italian peninsula and the routes to Gaul and England (and competed with the Carthaginians). Traded goods included raw materials and manu-factured products. Greece imported tin, copper, silver, gold, and wool from Europe; papyrus, linen, and glass from Egypt; resins from Arabia; iron, woollen textiles, and timber from Asia Minor; copper from Cyprus; and wheat and fish from the Black Sea region. Greek exports included slaves, wine, oil, pottery, and, increasingly, a variety of manufactured items (Starr, 1977: 64–70; McEvedy, 1967: 54).

But more important than the range of goods involved in the trade centred on Greece was the monopoly they had upon the northern east–west routes. This monopoly generated the extraordinary profits that were used to build up Greek urban industries and Greek military power. As Chester Starr (1977: 76–7) confirms:

> I must reiterate the inescapable view that trade was profitable . . . it would not be too much to claim that Hellas could never have attained a relatively advanced economic structure without its overseas trade. Once these social and economic developments had occurred, the major Greek centers were then dependent on its continuance.

Greek merchants commissioned local manufacture of the goods they knew would sell in bulk, largely in Western markets. Added to this, the increasing inflow of foreign manufactured goods encouraged imitation in Greek work-shops. And imitation led eventually to Greek improvements and innovations. At this time the Greek artist-craftsman had no peer.

By acting as a hub of trade between the Near East and Europe, Greek ports became exchange centres for new ideas throughout the known world. In the period before 600 BC they, unlike their Phoenician counterparts, exceeded the expertise of craftsmen in the Near East. As Starr (ibid.: 82) says:

> In this respect, i.e., technological change, the age of expansion was a period of extraordinary progress. It is not too much to say that from somewhat before 800 down to 500 the Greek world acquired the stock of technical skills and methods on which it, and the Romans there-after, normally relied for the rest of ancient history.

Greek craftsmen became highly skilled in the working of iron, gold, silver, general metal work, pottery, textiles, sculpture, and masonry. The growth of urban industry was an outcome of trade and in its turn contributed to further trade.

A rough attempt to measure the comparative expansion of Greece in the seventh and sixth centuries has been made by Chester Starr (ibid.: 37–8, 192). On the basis of the number of temples and statues built in these two centuries, he suggests that economic activity in the sixth century may have been greater than that in the seventh by a factor of three. He also suggests that during the fifth and fourth centuries this rate of economic change slowed. While this measure is very crude and cannot distinguish between economic expansion (increase in real GDP) and economic growth (increase in real GDP per capita), the suggestion that economic change increased in an exponential way between 800 and 500 BC and then declined in the 'golden age' and beyond appears consistent with the qualitative evidence. Certainly trade increased rapidly until the sixth century, and the periods 800–600 and 600–500 saw the application of foreign technology and local innovations respectively. This would have generated economic growth as well as expansion prior to 500. But once the limits to trade expansion had been reached and innovation had ceased, economic growth would have ground to a halt. It is at this point that the conquest strategy became a viable option.

A further Greek innovation that would have contributed to economic growth down to about 500 BC was the emergence of public markets. Initially public markets involved exchange through barter, but by the mid-sixth century these markets had been monetized. This institution would have contributed to Greek prosperity by reducing the (transaction) costs of the way urban societies conducted their business. The Greek public market enhanced the economic freedom of individuals and influenced the emergence of Greek political individualism, or democracy. (This will be discussed in a future book.)

It is a reflection of the importance of trade in the Greek economy that a wide range of social groups, including the aristocracy (at least before 600 BC) was involved. This occurred even in Sparta, the most military of Greek states, in the early period. Starr (ibid.: 51) documents in detail the aristocrats involved, and explains:

> upper-class participation in colonization and trade is evident, for over-seas ventures required surplus resources in the form of food, seeds, animals, and metals. In the eighth and seventh centuries what other elements in Greek society could have provided this surplus, or could have dared to risk it abroad?

Curiously, he claims that while the aristocrats were interested in economic gain, they were not rational maximizers. He argues that they acquired wealth only in order to participate in the political and social activities of their class. They were, as I suggested in Chapter 6, political rather than economic men. His story about Greek aristocrats is that, as a class, they were intimately involved in the development of trade before 600 BC, but thereafter they withdrew and left this activity, which they now despised, to non-aristocratic groups and to foreigners while they themselves became involved in politics and war (ibid.:191–2).

In fact, aristocratic involvement in overseas trade before 600, their withdrawal between 600 and 500, their later condescending attitude to commerce, and their involvement in politics and war thereafter, is clear evidence that Greek aristocrats as a class were indeed economically rational. The aristocrats, with their modest surpluses (the largest holdings were only about 30 hectares), entered trade when monopoly returns were high, but as these returns were increasingly challenged by the Carthaginians in Sicily and elsewhere in the western Mediterranean, as other groups in Greek society entered commerce, and as trade and the potential returns from it ceased to grow (Millett, 1983: 47; Mossé, 1983: 54), they withdrew from commerce to attend to their landed incomes by extracting a greater surplus from the peasantry (Starr, 1977: 163) and by exploring the possibilities of conquest. Greek aristocrats were economically rational throughout the entire period 800–330 BC. The only change was in the dynamic strategy that they employed to maximize their material advantage. This consistent explanation of motivation contrasts with the inconsistency in Starr's argument (ibid.: 192) that

> [i]t could also be argued that economic concerns really did bulk larger in the minds of the upper classes until the fifth century, when the economic structure of the advanced Greek *poleis* had become well established; thereafter they devoted a larger part of their interest to political contention and the aristocratic way of life.

This suggests that their fundamental motivation rather than their strategy changed suddenly around 600 BC. No persuasive explanation is given for this change.

The Phoenicians in the Mediterranean

The collapse of Achaean Greek civilization left a commercial vacuum in the Mediterranean that the Phoenicians – particularly those at Tyre centrally located on the coastal strip of Palestine – were able and willing to fill. When the Achaean Greeks were at their height, the 'Phoenicians', as they were only later to be called, were totally insignificant as an economic force. Thereafter they emerged rapidly to become the undisputed leaders of the commercial world along the eastern, southern, and western coasts of the Mediterranean for almost a millennium. Only in the Greek sphere of the central northern Mediterranean were they absent.

Phoenicia is of considerable interest because it was the first society to come to prominence solely through pursuit of the commerce strategy – a strategy that led to the establishment of colonies as well as trading posts. As we have seen, classical Greece employed commerce, colonization, and conquest. Curiously, little is known about the Phoenicians, apart from their invention of the alphabet, because little of their civilization has been unearthed. Much of what we do know comes from the unflattering accounts left by their competitors – even the name by which we know them was given by the Greeks (Aubet, 1993: ch. 1).

The Phoenicians were a Semitic-speaking people known to their neighbours as the coastal Canaanites. Around 1200 BC they experienced a major crisis as both Philistine and Israelite tribes invaded their territory (ibid.: 21). When subsequently they began venturing into the wider Mediterranean world between 1200 and 1100 BC, they were referred to by their contemporaries as 'Phoenicians' (Harden, 1963: ch. 3). The main eastern Phoenician cities were Tyre, Sidon, Aradus, Byblos, and Barytus (now called Beirut), which were never fashioned into a formal political unity, although in the ninth century Tyre assumed control over Sidon (Aubet, 1993: 37). This is a rare example of a purely commercial society. Within a remarkably short space of time these Canaanite coastal traders had transformed themselves into energetic seagoing merchant venturers with trading stations throughout the southern half and eastern end of the Mediterranean. They saw their opportunity in the collapse of both the Achaean Greek and Hittite civilizations, and in the decline of Egyptian influence over the Levant – and they grasped it with both hands. This was the way in which the Phoenicians could increase their wealth and prosperity above that based upon neolithic farming, specialized craft activities, and coastal trading.

Phoenician merchant venturers spread throughout the Mediterranean during the period 1000–700 BC, reaching Cyprus, Rhodes, and Crete in the north, and extended south along the northern coast of Africa to the Pillars of Heracles (Straits of Gibraltar), and to Malta, Sicily, Sardinia, Corsica, the Balearic Islands, and, most importantly of all, Spain. Owing to the presence of the Etruscans in Italy and the Greeks in the Aegean, the Phoenicians failed to make inroads into these areas. On all these routes the Phoenicians established trading posts about every 50 kilometres, which was the distance their sailing ships could travel each day. They also established towns at some sixteen sites along the North African coast (including Carthage c. 814 BC), and at four sites in Spain, with others on all major Mediterranean islands. It is thought that the Phoenicians only settled (as opposed to traded with) Sicily around 700 BC, when the growing number of Greek colonies in southern Italy and Sicily began to threaten their commercial routes (Edey, 1974: 72). In contrast to the Greeks, commerce was the sole dominant dynamic strategy for the Phoenicians. This commercial expansion required considerable investment in infrastructure, involving 'an enormous deployment of means of transport, human material, equipment and personnel' (Aubet, 1993: 76).

It is difficult to reconstruct the precise nature of this commercial enterprise. The most recent examination suggests that private trade was involved

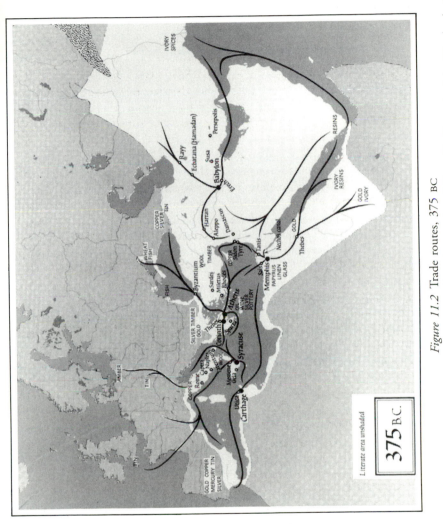

Figure 11.2 Trade routes, 375 BC

Source: Colin McEvedy, *The Penguin Atlas of Ancient History*, Harmondsworth, Penguin, 1967, p. 55. Drawn by John Woodcock. © Colin McEvedy, 1967. Reproduced by permission of Penguin Books Ltd.

in this westward expansion from the beginning, but that it developed along-side public enterprise by Phoenician kings and under their protection. Maria Aubet (ibid.: 95–6) writes:

> In the Near East in general, and in Phoenicia in particular, public trade and private initiative, almost always associated with the search for profits and the desire for gain, were perfectly complementary. It was a synchro-nous process . . . in which the palace needed the private merchant as much as the trader needed the protection of the palace.

From the ninth century BC private initiative became increasingly dominant. Accordingly, the ruling elite of Phoenician cities, including the king and the leading citizens, were part of a merchant oligarchy. Phoenician society and religion – Melqart, the god of Tyre, was the patron of shipping and trade – were fashioned by the dominant dynamic strategy of commerce.

The Phoenician cities, particularly Tyre, held a monopoly of trade for three centuries on the Levantine routes. From the ninth century BC, Tyre began expanding territorially eastwards into Syria, an experiment that continued until the Assyrian armies were on the march during the second half of that century, after which they had to be content with commerce without conquest (ibid.: 37–41). They traded their own manufactures (textiles; dyed cloth, particularly the famous royal purple; glass; and metal work) and primary produce (timber; wine; and oil) in exchange for linen, papyrus, gold and ivory from Egypt; wool from Anatolia (Asia Minor); copper from Cyprus; and resins from Arabia (McEvedy, 1967: 44). The steady growth of this trade certainly increased the prosperity of Tyre; and increased its population to about 30,000 (Aubet, 1993: 29). However, it was the discovery of metals (including silver, copper, and tin) in southern Spain, possibly as early as 1000 BC, that made this emerging trading empire fabulously wealthy for its time. Spain was the source of the world's first metals bonanza, and the Phoenician monopoly ensured their prosperity because it generated extraordinary profits. In fact, everything that went through Phoenician hands, as did most of the east–west trade in the southern Mediterranean, earned them an attractive commission. Very rapidly they were able to build up large surpluses. Monopoly access to markets brings quick profits. According to Aubet (ibid.: 98), 'Tyre was famous among her neighbours and contemporaries for her extraordinary riches and economic power'. It was this fact that excited the prophecies of doom from the Old Testament prophets Isaiah (eighth century BC) and Ezekiel (early sixth century BC).

But large surpluses also generate problems – how to use them to best advantage, and how to stop others from appropriating them. Most successful trading societies invest their surpluses in manufacturing activities and in lending at high rates of interest. The Phoenicians were no exception. Not only did Tyre possess the funds to establish urban industries but, being at the very centre of the known world, it was an exchange-house of ideas on

356

new products and new methods of production. They began by trading in valuable goods such as gold and silver jewellery, ivory and metal objects, and later graduated to establishing workshops in their own cities to produce similar commodities for established markets. By cutting out foreign craftsmen, and thereby lowering costs, the Phoenicians were also able to develop new markets. In fact, they appear to have been more interested in producing large quantities of existing goods for a mass market than in producing entirely new goods. Experts suggest that Phoenician craftsmanship, while exacting and skilful, was, unlike contemporary Greek craftsmanship, derivative in design (Edey, 1974: 58–9).

However, Phoenician craftsmen did excel in the dying of cloth and in the working of wood and stone. Both Tyre and Sidon were famous throughout the known world for their expensive purple cloth, the dye for which came from a shellfish called murex that was harvested in local coastal waters. So popular was this cloth with the wealthy that its production continued even after the fall of Tyre to Alexander in 332 BC, and it was purchased as late as AD 800 by Charlemagne (ibid.: 61). Similarly, their craftsmanship in timber and stone was much in demand. Phoenician craftsmen were said to have been employed by David and Solomon, kings of Israel, to construct a palace, the great temple, and a fleet of merchant ships (ibid.: 60–2). Moreover, the Phoenician trade in metals led them to develop their well-known skills in working copper and iron. While they were not interested in pioneering new products and methods they were amongst the most skilled employers of industrial techniques in the known world – techniques needed to maintain Phoenicia's commercial lead.

The other problem faced by societies able to create wealth relatively quickly, almost out of thin air, is their attractiveness to predators. Tyre was so conspicuously wealthy that the expanding Assyrian Empire demanded, and received, tribute for over 250 years from about 880 BC. The Phoenicians, however, were able to bear the impost and probably regarded it as the cost of the commercial privileges they enjoyed. In effect, it was an alternative to investing in a strong army, which was out of the question in such close proximity to powerful, land-based empires. Better to pay tribute to the Assyrians and suffer the indignity of Babylonian (572–559 BC) and Persian (from 539 BC) authority than to be completely destroyed. The Phoenicians also used their commercial surpluses to provide naval aid to their Persian overlords in the wars with the Greeks between 490 and 480 BC. This not only ensured continued Persian 'protection', but also could have eliminated a major commercial competitor. Unfortunately for Tyre, the Greeks inflicted a crushing defeat on the Phoenician navy at Salamis and, through Alexander, they had their vengeance with the final destruction of Tyre in 332 BC, which brought eastern Phoenician society to an abrupt end.

Away from the centre of world power in the western half of the Mediterranean, the Phoenicians did take more aggressive steps to protect their commercial interests (Figure 11.2). In relative isolation the Phoenician colony of Carthage (meaning new city) probably established about 814 BC, was able to build up its military strength without attracting retribution from powerful neighbours. Actually, in the beginning the Carthaginians needed to achieve a degree of military strength for defence against the Libyans, and to protect their overland routes in Africa. The main threat in the western Mediterranean, however, was Greek colonization of southern Italy and Sicily, which began from 750 BC. To combat this threat, Carthage established its own colonies in Sicily before 700 BC and formed an alliance with the Etruscans against the Greeks from about 600 BC. This military competition escalated, and in 550 BC the Carthaginian general Mago defeated the Sicilian Greeks using mercenaries and established the Magonid dynasty that lasted for 150 years.

While the Carthaginians later suffered defeat at the hands of the Sicilian Greeks, the greatest calamity was experienced when they came into conflict with the rapidly emerging Republic of Rome. As discussed in Chapter 10, the First Punic War (264–241 BC) was fought and won at sea by the Romans, who had no previous naval experience. As a result of this surprising loss, the Carthaginians were expelled from Sicily. The Second Punic War (218–201 BC) was brilliantly conducted but finally lost by Hannibal the Great (there were several Hannibals in Carthaginian history) – the second generation leader of the 'Barcid Dynasty' that established itself in Spain about 237 BC – on the Italian peninsula. The Third Punic War in 149–146 BC led to the complete destruction of Carthage and the end of a remarkable and wealthy commercial civilization that had existed for almost a millennium.

Where did Carthage go wrong? They had begun well and been relatively successful against the Greeks. But that was a fight between two societies pursuing the commerce strategy. Both used the proceeds of trade to protect and extend their own commercial interests. As Carthage's trading profits were probably greater than those of Greece because of its monopoly over the mines of Spain, it could hold its own against the more warlike Greeks, even though it used less highly motivated mercenaries. The conflict with Rome was entirely different. Commercial Carthage made the mistake of pitting itself against a society committed to the dynamic strategy of conquest. The Romans treated war and conquest as a business in the way that the Carthaginians treated trade as a business. Both were equally committed to maximizing their material advantage, but they used different means to do so. War to the Carthaginians was merely a tool with which to protect and further their commercial interests. While the Carthaginians could out-trade the Romans, they could not out-fight them. Mercenaries are no match for an innovative citizen army bent upon consistent success in its chosen profession. The exception, of course, was the military-based 'Barcid dynasty' that emerged in Spain. But this was a brief (237–202 BC) if brilliant exception in a thousand years of Phoenician history.

This fascinating – indeed classic – confrontation between two entirely different dynamic strategies had an inevitable outcome. It was a conflict involving the world's most successful commercial society against what was about to become the world's most successful conquest society. As suggested above, the eastern Phoenicians based on Tyre took a more realistic approach and went to great lengths (and considerable expense) to avoid the clash between commerce and conquest. They emerged in an area that had long been dominated by powerful conquest societies – Akkadian, Assyrian, Babylonian, and Persian – and recognized the futility of such a confrontation. Ironically, by trying to avoid conflict they became a province of the Persian Empire and, hence, an object of prey for the Macedonian king Alexander the Great, who was pursuing the new Greek strategy of conquest with unparalleled success. The eastern Phoenicians ended doing exactly what they had attempted for so long to avoid – confrontation with a powerful enemy on land. But they did so with grim and deadly determination.

In contrast, the western Phoenicians some 186 years later deliberately became involved in a commerce–conquest confrontation initially because they did not have overpowering neighbours and, later, because they failed to realize that the Romans would soon become even more powerful than the Assyrians had been. In the end neither their eastern nor western spheres had much choice. There is little that a commerce strategy can do against a conquest strategy, whether you see it coming or not. But both east and west faced the end in the same way – they resisted to the last man, woman, and child. The Phoenicians ended as they had begun – with a stubborn determination not to give a foreigner a bargain.

The rise of Western commerce

The lesson of this confrontation between commerce and conquest was not lost upon the victors. For the next six centuries Rome ruthlessly pursued the conquest strategy and came to occupy much of the known world. Nevertheless, although conquest was the dominant strategy underlying Rome's economic growth and expansion, trade, largely arising from conquest, was important in contributing to general prosperity (Pucci, 1983). Until the establishment of Constantinople in AD 324, the main centre of trade in the empire was Rome – a city that grew not from commerce, however, but from conquest – which drained strategic metals (tin, iron, copper, silver, gold, mercury) from Western Europe, and essential foods (wheat and fish) from the Black Sea region, north Africa, and Egypt (Garnsey et al., 1983). In contrast, the other major cities of the empire, Alexandria and Antioch, were established by Greeks and owed their prosperity to commerce. Alexandria was the centre of trade between Rome and India, while Antioch was the centre of trade between Rome and Mesopotamia and beyond.

This pattern of trade continued until the Roman Empire split into its western and eastern spheres. Thereafter two new trading systems emerged based upon Rome and Constantinople – the former turning west and the latter turning east – which disrupted the broader east–west commerce that had flourished for two millennia. While the overall returns from empire trade must have declined, Constantinople appears to have gained most from these new arrangements. Rome, however, was now denied its previous access (enjoyed since the second century BC) to grain supplies from the Black Sea and Egypt, which were absorbed by Constantinople and were only available to Rome when in surplus and, even then, at a higher price than previously. Rome had to make do with wheat from the old Carthaginian region of Africa as little agricultural surplus was generated at this stage by Europe. Rome also lost the valuable tribute of the east. Yet it did have one major bargaining advantage, the metal supplies of Europe. Nevertheless, Rome's economic position was severely diminished by this political split, which reduced its ability to withstand the growing forces of chaos from within and without.

Constantinople was able to continue after the collapse of Rome in AD 476 because of its control over the trading routes throughout the Black Sea and eastern Mediterranean. But as trade of the Eastern Empire was not expanding and, hence, real GDP per capita was not increasing, this was merely a holding operation. In the face of an exhausting dynamic strategy, eventual collapse was inevitable. Trade became less favourable from the seventh century AD because of the growing forces of Islam throughout Mesopotamia, Palestine, Egypt, North Africa, and Spain. While Constantinople continued to control the sea routes, the Muslims took charge of the land. Particularly damaging was the loss of grain from Egypt and Carthage, which forced the Byzantine Empire to rely increasingly upon food from the Black Sea region. There was some compensating expansion in the west owing to the growing overland trade with the North Sea trade bloc, but as trade overall was not expanding from the eighth century, neither was economic growth. The Byzantine Empire was losing economic resilience – losing the power to survive in a competitive environment.

Even when trading opportunities arose in the west with the growing economic power of the European kingdoms, the Byzantine Empire was not able to take advantage of them. In order to ensure naval support from the emerging maritime powers – Venice and Genoa – it had to give away the valuable trading rights of the entire empire. For the last few centuries of the empire's effective existence, down to AD 1204, most of its trade, and the prosperity that went with it, was the monopoly of the north Italian maritime cities. Fittingly it was Venice who organized the empire's dismemberment and disposal during the misnamed Fourth Crusade. After all, Venice had long since conjured away the most profitable parts of the empire's commerce. Even the re-emergence of the Byzantine Empire in 1261, and its continuation until 1453, was not to alter that significantly.

The maritime Republic of Venice

Five centuries after the collapse of Rome, Western Europe – a former back-water of human history – was on the move. The last society that rose to wealth and power solely on commerce, Tyre, had expanded from the eastern end of the Mediterranean to the west, setting up trading posts and colonies in Western Europe. From the tenth century AD, the maritime cities of Venice, Genoa, Pisa, and Amalfi began to prosper through trade and to expand eastward throughout the Mediterranean, even establishing colonies in the old Phoenician homeland. The cycle of commerce and economic growth had come full circle.

Venice, at the end of the Middle Ages, was one of the wonders of the world. It was the most wealthy city in Europe, and it displayed its wealth conspicuously in the rich accoutrements of its upper class and in the fine public buildings, churches, and private palaces – all opulently decorated and furnished – hovering miraculously above the lagoons off the northern Italian coast. This was the greatest example in history of the conjuring art of commerce.

Venice was more than a remarkable city. The republic at its height also held considerable territory in northern Italy, along the Dalmatian coast, along the east and south coasts of the Greek peninsula, together with Crete. Its ships traded throughout the Mediterranean tapping into the rich commerce of the Levant, throughout the Black Sea where they linked up with the caravans on the Silk Route from China, throughout the Aegean and Adriatic Seas and, later, around Spain to the Netherlands. They operated large financial institutions that were mainly absorbed in Venice's own commercial and military interests. They were the Western bulwark against the Turks. They were even responsible for the temporary break-up of the Byzantine Empire. In 1500 they were at the very peak of their wealth, power, and influence. And all this had been achieved throughout the course of five centuries by a group of refugees from a few swampy islands solely through the dynamic strategy of commerce.

Who, 500 years before, could have imagined such a miraculous rise to wealth and power? At the beginning of the second millennium AD Venice was a small if vital community living on a number of small lagoons at the north-eastern head of the Adriatic sea. These lagoons were occupied in AD 568 by refugees escaping the Lombard invasion of northern Italy. In the early centuries some Venetians traded in the Mediterranean, but most of the Levant trade entering the Adriatic was carried in Greek and Syrian ships. At this time the Venetians specialized in trade with northern Italy and along the Dalmatian coast (Lane, 1973: 5). Venetian trade with northern Italy and beyond was based upon a free-trade agreement granted in AD 840 by the Western emperor. But they were under formal control of the Byzantine emperor, from whom, in exchange for naval support, the Venetians received trading privileges in the

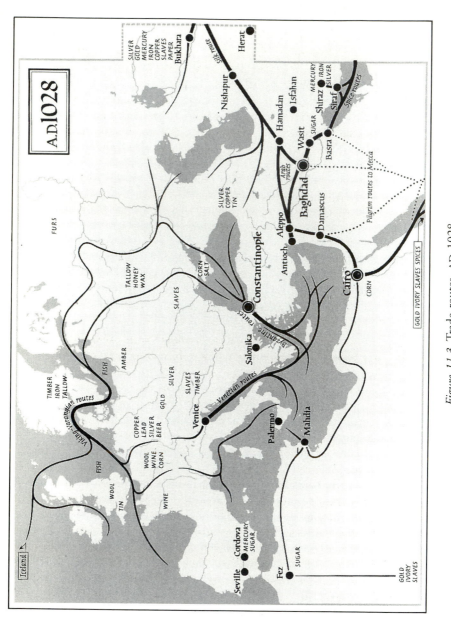

Figure 11.3 Trade routes, AD 1028

Source: Colin McEvedy, *The Penguin Atlas of Medieval History*, Harmondsworth, Penguin, 1961, p. 59. Drawn by John Woodcock. © Colin McEvedy, 1961. Reproduced by permission of Penguin Books Ltd.

Adriatic. This was very similar to the role played by Tyre in the Persian Empire. The ultimate privilege was granted to the Venetians by the Byzantine emperor in 1082 by which they gained, in return for naval aid against the Normans in Sicily, complete freedom of trade throughout the empire, the right to own commercial facilities in Constantinople, and freedom from all customs duties (Luzzatto, 1961: 52). This formalized their major role in east–west trade (Figure 11.3) and gave Venice complete victory over its commercial rivals such as Genoa and even merchants of the Empire. While Venice had no natural resources of any kind, it saw an opportunity to exploit the growing wealth of Western Europe and the declining power of the Byzantine Empire, and it had the wit to succeed. This was an exercise of the very highest art of the commercial conjurers – of being able to create fabulous wealth and culture virtually out of nothing. From the swamps princes came.

On the eve of the First Crusade in 1095 the future Venetian course that would carry them to the heady heights of the 1480s had been set. Venice had already established itself as an important centre of commerce between the Levant in the east, Constantinople at the hub of the old empire, and the North Sea via the new German Empire in the west. The subsequent history of Venice – and, indeed, that of the other urban centres of northern Italy – can be characterized as rapid expansion and economic growth between the First Crusade of 1095 and the Black Death of 1347, fluctuating growth between 1347 and the 1480s, and stability and *relative* decline between the 1480s and 1600.

Venice's opportunity for large-scale expansion and growth came with the First Crusade. But it was an opportunity almost lost. Warships and transports were needed to carry the crusaders, their horses and equipment, and supplies of food and fodder from Western Europe to Palestine. Also, large financial loans, which were to be paid back handsomely with plunder from the Levant, were required. Venice was slow to exploit this opportunity, partly because she was conscious of the emperor's suspicion of the Latin occupation of former imperial territory, and partly because Genoa was a more convenient point of departure for most crusaders (ibid.: 72–3). Genoa and Pisa, however, were eager to gain a foothold in the Venetian trading sphere and willingly provided transport and naval support during the successful sieges of Antioch and Jerusalem. In return they received not only special trading privileges but also property rights in these cities. Naturally this was more than the Venetians could cope with, and in 1100 they sent a fleet of 200 ships to Jaffa for the assistance of Godfrey of Bouillon in return for 'a church and a suitable site for a market in every city subsequently taken by the crusaders, and . . . immunity from taxes and the right of wreck throughout the Kingdom of Jerusalem' (ibid.: 73). This was worth even the displeasure of the emperor.

Owing to the great success of the First Crusade, and to the continuing assistance given by the northern Italian maritime powers, many Venetian, Genoese, and Pisan colonies were established throughout Syria and Palestine.

The crusade leaders were willing to grant to the merchant states a quarter of a town (in a few cases even an entire town), or a single street, or a certain number of houses, together with legal protection. This enabled the Italian merchants to establish trading facilities in the Levant and to get on with their commercial activities, and even to collect feudal dues from the native inhabitants. In later years Italian migrants settled permanently in these Levantine cities. By 1100, therefore, Western Europeans were firmly established in the former Phoenician homeland that had, nearly 2,000 years before, established similar colonies in Western Europe. There was even a similar division of spheres of influence. Just as the Greeks had specialized in northern Mediterranean trade and the Phoenicians in the south, so the Venetians kept to the north (at least until 1200) and the Genoese and Pisans focused upon the south.

But if the nationality of the merchants had changed, the commodities following the east–west routes were much the same. The pattern of commerce seemed timeless. From the Levant came the familiar spices, silk, cotton, perfumes, precious stones, arms, slaves, and paper that originated in Persia, India, China, and Syria; these in return for the more mundane commodities from Europe including timber, woollen cloth, and metals. At first the European merchants confined themselves to the coastal regions of the Levant but later, in the mid-thirteenth century, some Europeans, like the Polos, penetrated into Mongolia and China. Finally, if briefly, the West reached the fabled Orient. More significantly, the stories these few told of the mysterious East encouraged other Italian explorers (from Genoa) to attempt to reach China by sailing west from Spain. Although they were not successful, failure conferred a most acceptable second prize – the fabulously wealthy Americas.

While the First Crusade had brought great material returns to the European invaders, if only in the shortrun, it hardly fulfilled the objectives of Pope Urban II to assist the Christian Eastern emperor in his struggle against the Islamic Arabs and Turks. The crusaders may have been against the forces of Islam but they were most definitely for themselves, not the Byzantine emperor. This conflict of economic interests – the crusades were not about religion – led to the souring of relations between Venice and the Byzantine Empire and led to the loss of the Venetian monopoly, confiscation of Venetian property throughout the empire, and riots against Venetian citizens in Constantinople.

Venice, however, obtained its revenge. In 1202 Venice hijacked the Fourth Crusade called by Innocent III against Islam and redirected it against the forces of Constantinople. With the fall of Constantinople in 1204, Venice received about one-quarter of the empire – mainly along the Greek coast together with Crete and most of the Aegean Sea – and it led to the creation of the Latin Empire. Venice was also guaranteed complete freedom of commerce throughout the new Latin Empire. The transformation was truly remarkable. A tiny maritime community that was formally under the control of the Eastern Empire was, through prosperity created by the conjurers of commerce, able to arrange for the empire to be dismantled and for itself to become one of the major beneficiaries. The brilliance of this achievement was little diminished even when the Byzantines, who retreated to their Asian territories to form the Empire of Nicaea, retook Constantinople in 1261. While their old enemy Genoa made some temporary gains, most of these were later retrieved by Venice.

Over the next 150 years the maritime cities of Italy, and particularly Venice, experienced a substantial expansion of trade under very favourable conditions. At this time they controlled not only the trade between Egypt/Levant and Europe, but also commerce in the Aegean and Black Seas. By 1300 ships from Venice and Genoa were sailing regularly to that other European centre of trade and urbanization – the Netherlands. This central role in the expanding commerce between a growing Western Europe and the East brought Italian merchants extraordinary profits, which fed the economic growth of the maritime republics and the living standards of their populations. These surpluses were also used to establish financial institutions and to commission Italian manufactures. In turn, this led to the growth of wealthy inland cities in northern Italy such as Milan, Verona, Bologna, and Florence, which shared in the wealth and cultural attainment of the maritime cities. The Italian Renaissance, therefore, was built upon the prosperity arising from the skilful employment of the dynamic strategy of commerce.

Prosperity, however, was not evenly spread across the face of Italy, even in the north. The rural areas, where farming was conducted either on great estates or highly fragmented small tenant holdings, were largely unaffected by urban prosperity (Luzzatto, 1961: 165–6). Farmers continued to use the old technology and old forms of organization, much of which survived into the mid-twentieth century. Why? Because the rate of return on investment in trade-oriented urban activities – including textiles and metal manufactures – was higher than the net return to a transformed agricultural system. That had to wait for the technological paradigm shift known as the Industrial Revolution. The time was not yet ripe in the thirteenth and fourteenth centuries, as the old neolithic technological paradigm had not been exhausted. At this stage there were other, more economic ways of increasing real GDP per capita.

The second phase, one of fluctuating growth, began with the Black Death of 1347–1349 (during which up to 60 per cent of the population of Venice, which was about 120,000, perished) and continued to the end of the Middle Ages. Population recovery took place in fits and starts owing to the continuing presence of plague which haunted the lagoons. Even by 1500 the population was only about the level reached in 1300, rising to 190,000 in the 1570s. But further outbreaks of pestilence in 1575–1577 and 1630–1631 reduced the population on each occasion by about one-third (Lane, 1973: 18–19). To make matters worse, it was a period increasingly disrupted by war with its chief commercial rival Genoa. This was a sure sign that the limits of the commerce strategy were being progressively approached. Genoa and Venice first clashed in the mid- and late thirteenth centuries, when Genoa challenged the supremacy of Venice in the eastern Mediterranean. Initially, this conflict was expressed in acts of piracy, attacks on each other's colonies, and pitched battles at sea. But by the fourteenth century this struggle for commercial supremacy became more serious and determined. In the 1350–1355 war the Venetians not only employed mercenaries from Greece and Dalmatia to man about one-third of their galleys owing to the impact of the Black Death on their population and the reluctance of the remainder to forgo the good life, but they also escalated the war by involving the Catalans, a rising maritime power with no love for the Genoese, their nearest competitors. Yet as the combatants only met on the seas, their contests, although expensive, were unlikely to be conclusive. This war, however, signalled a change of intent.

The conflict of 1378–1381 started in the usual way as a trade war but ended as a grim struggle for survival. Aiming a death blow at the very centre of Venice, Genoa was only stopped on the sand bars close to Chioggia by English and Italian mercenaries. Death in Venice was only a few hundred metres away in June 1380. Venice had only just survived, but the cost of war, which dragged on to 1381, led to financial exhaustion: the state of Genoa, so close to victory, collapsed never to rival Venice again. From the late fourteenth century, therefore, Venice had finally emerged victorious from its long struggle with its old rival in commerce. But it was a close thing.

While these trade wars severely drained the financial resources of Venice, the large profits that could be conjured up from commerce enabled the republic to recover quickly in the fifteenth century. Skilful as always, Venice exploited a series of temporary monopolies in the trade of key products and monopolies arising from the control of the galleys in which trade was carried. But the golden age had passed. While Venetian trade was maintained, it no longer increased at a rapid rate. Accordingly, growth of real GDP per capita must have slowed over the longer run and fluctuated in the shortrun as new temporary monopolies were won and lost (Lane, 1973: 185). The commerce strategy of Venice, which had served it well for more than four centuries, was showing definite signs of exhaustion.

In these circumstances it was not surprising that the Venetians began to search for new dynamic strategies. Early in the fifteenth century Venice turned to conquest, financed by the proceeds of commerce, on the Italian and Dalmatian mainlands (Brady, 1991: 150). The usual scholarly argument is that Venice wanted to secure its supplies of food and raw materials, and to control the northern passes to north-west Europe (Lane, 1973: 225–7; Luzzatto, 1961: 150). This would hardly have been necessary for an energetic trading nation. It certainly had been unnecessary for Venice in the preceding five centuries. Food can be (and was) imported freely and other commodities and services exported; one does not have to control the trade routes in order to participate in commerce; in any case, there was always the sea route to north-western Europe.

It was not the right to trade that Venice was pursuing but rather the right to extract extraordinary profits from this mainland commerce as its trade elsewhere had stagnated. Venice employed the conquest strategy to do so, but not just to gain extraordinary profits from commerce. They also extracted conquest tribute from the mainland cities and from rural properties. This view challenges the conventional wisdom that Venetian conquest on the mainland was independent of their commercial activities, and that the nobility only became interested in obtaining land in Italy after it had become available through conquest. Luzzatto (1961: 154), for example, reverses the true relationship when he says:

> The conquest of the mainland clearly did not cause the Venetians to turn away from commerce. Nor, as we have seen, did it suddenly start them buying up land, for this they had always done. There can be no doubt, however, that by flooding the market with the properties of dispossessed despots and rebels, the conquest did encourage the Venetian nobility to acquire large estates . . .

In fact, conquest was pursued because commerce was no longer highly profitable.

There is an interesting parallel between the way the conquest strategy was pursued by Venice in the fifteenth century and by other commerce strategists in the past. Like Carthage, Venice employed mercenaries to undertake its wars because, like Carthage, Venice was having trouble effecting a transition between the dynamic strategies of commerce and conquest. As we have seen, it is possible to win wars against other commercial powers – Carthage against Greece, Venice against Genoa – using mercenaries. But when faced with nations specializing in conquest, the probability of success is low. Venice was to discover this, at considerable cost, for itself.

After 1494, when France and, later, Spain invaded Italy, Venice faced aggressive competitors that had been fighting each other, and outsiders, on land for a thousand years. As the economic power of these kingdoms increased during the late Middle Ages, they were more than a match for Venice. Surprise is usually expressed at Venice's seemingly irrational involvement in wars on the mainland. Luzzatto (ibid.: 150), for example, says:

> The effect of territorial conquest was to embroil Venice in the ceaseless wars of the Italian states, wars which not only compromised and complicated the life-and-death struggle with the Turks, but frequently imposed still heavier financial sacrifices than the Turkish war itself.

What is not realized is that Venice, faced with an exhausted commerce strategy, was attempting to employ the only alternative strategy capable of boosting real GDP per capita in the shortrun – conquest. Venice had over the centuries become addicted to 'quick fixes'.

Trade, however, had ceased to be a 'quick fix'. The period after 1500 saw the absolute decline in commerce outside the Adriatic, particularly with the Levant (Luzzatto, 1961: 152). Venice was being increasingly challenged on the seas by the Spanish and the Turks, and was gradually becoming a second-class maritime power. Increasingly, Venice was unable to compete with the woollen textiles and metal manufactures produced in north-west Europe. By the mid-sixteenth century, Venetian ships no longer sailed to the Netherlands, and by 1600 Dutch and English ships were sailing freely throughout the Mediterranean. But the most obvious sign that the Mediterranean maritime powers were fading from prominence was the regular use by north-west Europe of the new routes around the Cape of Good Hope to India, the East Indies, and China. The new opportunities in trade were to be found in the New World, not the Mediterranean. Venice's problem was that after the fifteenth century, and particularly after 1600, it could not compete with the new maritime powers, particularly the Dutch Republic, England, and France. While Venice had been conjuring up wealth out of trading monopolies, north-western Europe had been transforming its agricultural and urban economies to provide a more firmly based wealth. They had begun experimenting with the new technological strategy. Like the morning mists over the lagoons, the conjurer's illusion was dissipating under the glare of a more substantial dynamic strategy.

Venice soon discovered the futility of a conquest strategy in Italy. After a series of costly wars in the early sixteenth century, it decided in 1529 to pursue a policy of neutrality in the hope of retaining the territory it had won in the early fourteenth century and almost lost in the early fifteenth century through rashly pursuing further conquest. For Venice, conquest was not a good substitute for commerce. And in 1718 it concluded a peace treaty with the Turks, which ended the life-and-death struggle in which it had been engaged for centuries. Between 1718 and 1797 Venice was finally at peace with the world.

In rejecting the conquest strategy, Venice decided in the sixteenth century to focus upon building up its economic power from within by improving its mainland agricultural base as north-western Europe had done and developing its manufacturing industries by, for the first time, tariff protection and by specializing in the production of luxury commodities. On the mainland it developed commercial products of rice, silk, and wheat, which it was able to export. This was a major transformation from its commercial heyday when Venice was a net importer of food. In the city itself, manufacturers specialized in the production of woollen textiles, silk textiles, lace-making, leatherwork, jewellery, arms, soap, and printing in which it became one of the leading centres in Europe. This new technological strategy provided the basis for a growing population on the mainland, increasing from 1.5 to 2.0 million between 1550 and 1770, if not in the city, which stabilized at about 140,000 people. It also generated a modest but steady growth of real GDP per capita.

Gone were the heady days of rapidly increasing prosperity and of the life-and-death struggle for survival and material and cultural glory. In their place was a peaceful and steady prosperity. Yet this was a sign not of new life but of impending death. The Venetian Republic was unable to withstand the all-conquering Napoleon in 1797 who, ironically, 'traded' the remains of this once great commercial power for the Belgian provinces of Austria.

Commerce in north-western Europe

For the first time in about three millennia the dynamic strategy of commerce in the civilized world shifted from the Mediterranean to the North Sea. For the first time since the beginning of civilization the Mediterranean was no longer the centre of the world. History turned to north-western Europe.

With the collapse of Rome in AD 476 the economic communities of Europe turned in on themselves and trade withered. Slowly these economic communities consolidated and began turning outwards again. By the eighth century there was a revival of trade in Europe, centred not only on Venice in the south but also on the North Sea. Frisian traders and seamen travelled throughout the North Sea, the English Channel, and along the great rivers of the mainland, carrying wine, beer, salt, oil, glass, wool and woollen textiles, metal work, and amber in their small but agile wooden ships (McEvedy, 1961: 42).

By the eleventh century the major kingdoms of north-western Europe had grown in economic strength and, as a result, trade became far more extensive (Figure 11.3). The major traders were the Vikings in the west, extending even into the Atlantic to Ireland and Iceland, and the Varangians in the east, reaching into the Baltic and along the great Russian rivers as far as the Black Sea. Viking traders carried raw wool from England to supply the Flemish cloth industry, as well as wine, beer, fish, salt, and metals, while the Varangians traded fur, slaves, fish, tallow, honey, and wax. This trade was evidence of an increasing prosperity in north-western Europe which in turn led to the spread of hamlets, villages, and towns across the rural landscape. Yet, at this stage, the traders were just as likely to extract goods by force as by exchange.

By the thirteenth century, however, commerce was in more professional hands. Flemish merchants had come to dominate trade in the west, and German merchants – the forerunner of the Hanse – controlled trade in the east. In the west, wool from England and woollen textiles from Flanders formed the centre of this trade. Other goods involved in European commerce included wheat (England and France), wine (France), tin (Cornwall), other metals such as iron, copper, lead, silver, and gold (Germany), and timber, furs, tallow, honey, wax, and slaves (Russia) (ibid.: 58, 72). With increasing agricultural prosperity, expanding trade, and growth of manufacturing, the first substantial towns of Paris and Cologne emerged. Unlike the former Roman towns which were imposed upon Europe, they emerged from the economic foundations of a new society. The two commercial systems of Europe, one in the north and the other in the south, interacted via the over-land route through Germany.

Europe, at the end of the Middle Ages, was the centre of a very extensive trading system that had strong links with the Levant, Africa, India, and China. The northern and southern centres of this wider system – respectively the North Sea and northern Italy – were linked not only by overland routes but also by ships from the Mediterranean. The focus of the North Sea system in the 1480s was the wool trade, in which the Dutch played a major part. In this trade England's role had changed from that of principal supplier of fine raw wool to that of manufacturer of woollen cloth which was 'finished' in the Low Countries. The Netherlands now imported their raw wool, of a lower quality, from Spain and Ireland. As before, the German Hanse held a monopoly of the Baltic–North Sea trade, the basic part of which was the westward flow of cheaper grain and an eastward flow of textiles. Apart from the shipment of coal from Northumberland, the other traded goods were much the same as in earlier centuries. This vibrant commercial system had emerged in the fourteenth and fifteenth centuries following the Black Death. From the prosperity of this trade, held in check only by the continuing attendance of pestilence, a number of new towns emerged, including Antwerp, Brussels, Ghent, Bruges, London, and Lübeck. This development in adversity formed the basis of a phase of commercialization that prepared the way for the Industrial Revolution.

The limited opportunities for generating economic growth and prosperity in this period, owing to the continuing outbreaks of plague throughout Europe, led some kingdoms to consider the conquest strategy. If it was not possible to reap the rewards of investment in technological change in agriculture and industry, one could still attempt to exact tribute from one's neighbours. England, for example, attempted to increase its material living standards by conquest in France during the Hundred Years War. This gave England access to the feudal dues of the territory it held in south-west and northern France. But it was a strategy that faded in significance once the deadly grip of pestilence was gradually released after the fifteenth century.

Between the 1490s and 1600 north-western Europe experienced a golden age of prosperity (Figure 11.4) owing to the pursuit of the commerce strategy (Van der Wee, 1990; 1994: 5; Monro, 1994). For over a century trade flour-ished, populations grew in a sustained way for the first time in two centuries, and material living standards grew rapidly (see Figure 12.7). What accounted for this remarkable change? There were two important causal events: the break-out of Western Europeans into the rest of the world (the ultimate cause), and the temporary abatement of plague. In Chapter 9 we saw how, from 1492, the Spanish and Portuguese had discovered the New World of the Americas. This opened up a vast supply of natural resources that were

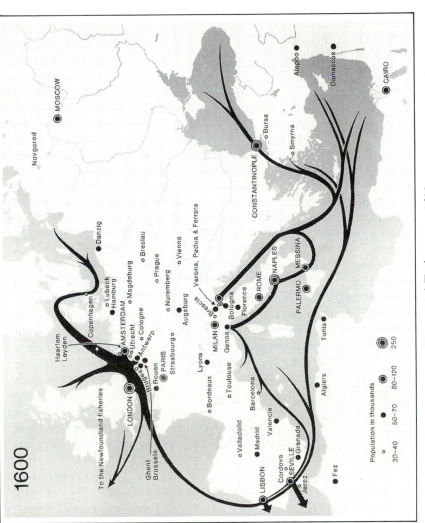
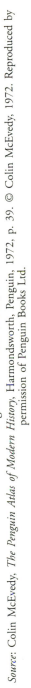

Figure 11.4 Trade routes, 1600

Source: Colin McEvedy, *The Penguin Atlas of Modern History*, Harmondsworth, Penguin, 1972, p. 39. © Colin McEvedy, 1972. Reproduced by permission of Penguin Books Ltd.

eagerly exploited by the Western Europeans. Mineral wealth in the form of gold and, later, silver was first to attract the attention of the *conquistadores*, followed by land for farming. In addition, the Portuguese successfully exploited the West African coast, there was a revival of silver and copper mining in central Europe, and the Baltic grain trade flourished (Van der Wee, 1994).

In the first half of the sixteenth century American gold flowed in ever larger quantities into Spain until, by the middle of the century (see Figure 11.5), it was surpassed by flows of silver that eventually peaked in the 1590s (Ball, 1977: 190–2; Barrett, 1990: 238). This flow of treasure was such a temptation that English monarchs secretly commissioned 'privateers', such as Francis Drake and John Hawkins, to divert some of it to Britain (Seaman, 1981: 221–2). While the impact of this inflow of bullion on Spain was expansionary but inflationary, for the rest of Europe it generated a considerable and sustained increase in effective demand by Spain and its colonies for manufactured products, food, and raw materials. Although Spain attempted to prevent other countries supplying both its own manufacturing requirements and those of its colonies, the policy was self-defeating because of its inflationary effects – too much money chasing too few goods. English and Dutch goods not only got around tariff barriers, but found their way into Spanish ships bound for the New World (Ball, 1977: 192). As Spain could not meet this rapid demand, its bureaucrats had to turn a blind eye to official policy.

Not only did the suppliers of manufactured goods and grain to Spain prosper from the urgency of this new demand, but the merchants who handled this trade – together with the trade with Asia made possible by the inflow of bullion from the Americas (Tracy, 1990: 3) – made extraordinary profits. The major merchants and manufacturers who benefited handsomely were in London/England and Amsterdam/the Dutch Republic. Antwerp in Flanders, which had previously been the leader in the North Sea trade, lagged behind largely because of its domination by Spain. The population of London as a proportion of the total English population, for example, rose from 2.0 per cent in 1500 to 4.9 per cent in 1600, and the city and its surrounding area became increasingly wealthy.

The prosperity of the Dutch and English in the late sixteenth century is reflected in their move into the Mediterranean to trade directly with the Levant. This move bypassed Venice completely. The north had finally surpassed the south. They also entered into direct trade with the Orient by forming their East India companies early in the seventeenth century. In this way the Dutch and English gained direct access to the spice trade that even the Venetians, or indeed the Phoenicians before them, had been unable to achieve. To gain special concessions and monopolies is all part of the commercial conjurer's art – the art of creating wealth out of virtually nothing – and to maintain them usually means war. The English and Dutch were

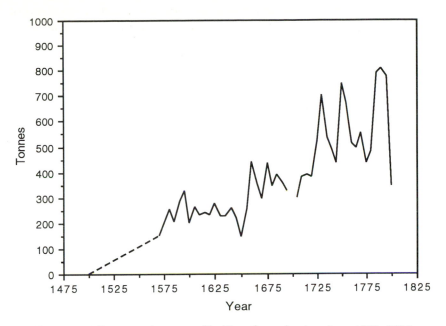

Figure 11.5 European imports of bullion from the Americas, 1500–1800
Source: Drawn from data in Barrett (1990).

no exception. Until they both discovered they had more to fear from France than each other, they were continually at each other's throats. It is interesting that these East India companies, as well as their respective countries, were able and willing to go to war to defend their trading interests (Tracy, 1991: 2).

The effects of the commerce strategy on the economic prosperity of north-western Europe can be seen most clearly in Holland, in the Low Countries before the revolt against Spain after 1568 (Van der Wee, 1993: 17), and particularly in England which was more isolated from the ravages of war in continental Europe. It can be seen from my great-waves diagram (Figure 12.7) that between 1492 and 1561 English real GDP per capita increased very rapidly at 1.6 per cent per annum, and between 1562 and 1601 at the still respectable rate of 0.8 per cent per annum. This can be placed in historical context by a comparison with growth rates during the Industrial Revolution, which ranged from only 0.4 to 0.5 per cent per annum over shorter periods of time. Hence the commerce strategy worked its wondrous effect upon English prosperity as it had for Venice and Phoenicia in earlier centuries. But by 1601 the golden era of commerce for England was over. English living standards stagnated until about 1630, after which they began growing again but much more slowly (0.15 per cent per annum) to 1700, and then at double this rate (0.31 per cent per annum) from 1700 to 1760. But even eighteenth-century growth was modest. In Holland, where 30 to 40 per cent of the population of the Netherlands lived, the growth of GDP per capita accelerated during the period 1580–1650 but stagnated thereafter (van Zanden, 1993: 270); and in Flanders and Brabant the period of most rapid growth, 1500 to 1560, was followed by half a century of stagnation to 1610 owing to the Revolt, and then by slow but steady growth to 1760 (Blomme and Van der Wee, 1994: 91).

What brought the golden age of commerce in north-western Europe to an end just as it appeared to be settling in for the long term? Why did not England use the commerce strategy for as long as Venice and Phoenicia? The reasons are complex. On the one hand there was a reversal of the conditions that had generated this mercantile boom – the end of the precious metals bonanza until a recovery in the second half of the century (Figure 11.5), and the renewed tightening of pestilence's deadly grip for one last time. On the other hand, it was difficult for the most advanced Western European kingdoms to squeeze much more from the existing late neolithic technological paradigm which was approaching exhaustion. Further commercial expansion depended upon a major technological paradigm, shift, which occurred after 1780 in England in the form of the Industrial Revolution. The commercial age in north-western Europe was briefer than those for Venice and Phoenicia because there was less room for economic manoeuvre in the seventeenth century within a technological paradigm that was now some 10,000 years old and approaching its limits.

The end of the mercantile boom was heralded in the 1590s by the peak of silver flowing into Spain from the New World. The wellsprings of the golden age were beginning to dry up at least for the following few generations. Not surprisingly, Spain was the first to feel the effects of this change, particularly as it was compounded by bad harvests in the 1590s and outbreaks of plague in 1599–1601, and again after the turn of the century, particularly 1627–1631. Spain's population, which had peaked by 1590, began to decline alarmingly and, by the mid-seventeenth century, was almost back to the level of 1500 (ibid.: 193–4). A major prop for the prosperity of the sixteenth century, therefore, had fallen away in the early years of the seventeenth.

Spain's experience was not unique, and some have argued that the first half of the seventeenth century saw 'an almost universal crisis' emerge in Western Europe (Ball, 1977: 194). Serious outbreaks of plague were suffered by England in 1603, 1625, and 1665 (the last 'great plague') when between one-sixth and one-quarter of London's population perished; by the Netherlands in 1623–1625, 1635–1637, and 1663–1664; by Italy in 1630 and 1656; and by France particularly during the decade after 1628 (Seaman, 1981: 348; Ball, 1977: 195). These outbreaks of pestilence combined with the effects of the Thirty Years War from 1618 to 1648 – when Germany lost about 40 per cent of its people – made serious inroads into the population of Europe which declined throughout the second half of the seventeenth century. It also disrupted agricultural and industrial production, as can be seen reflected in the rise of grain prices to famine levels in southern Europe and the widespread decline in the output of manufacturing (Ball, 1977: 195, 199).

Clearly, this crisis must have adversely affected the volume of trade conducted by the merchants of Western Europe. While the trade data are incomplete, they do indicate disruption in the first half of the seventeenth century. Seville, which had an effective monopoly on commerce with the Spanish Indies until about 1630, suffered a fall in the value of its trade from the 1590s and a fall in its tonnage after 1610, and particularly after 1621 from which there was no recovery. Dutch shipping tonnage to the Baltic fell moderately after 1600, rose briefly from 1611 to 1620, and fell severely thereafter. Danzig customs fell by one-third in the mid-1620s. Exports of cloth to the Baltic by the Dutch fell sharply after 1619, as did that of the English after 1620, with further falls for both in the second half of the 1620s. England's wider trade in woollen 'short cloths' fluctuated in the early seventeenth century and fell by one-third between 1614 and 1620, never to recover (Davis, 1973: 53; Ball, 1977: 196–8). There was also a fall in industrial production during the first half of the seventeenth century, particularly in Italy and central Europe (Van der Wee, 1988: 370–3).

England, however, was more fortunate than most because it held aloof from continental conflicts such as the Thirty Years War. Hence, its merchants were able to take advantage of what trade was available, particularly after 1630 in southern Europe owing to the decline in Italian industry (Davis, 1973: 7). Moreover, English craftsmen were able to meet the demand for the new draperies, which were lighter and cheaper than the declining trade in short cloths. Also after 1660, growing English influence in the east and west led to an expansion of trade with India and the East Indies (textiles, tea, dyestuffs) and with the New World (sugar and tobacco) (Monro, 1994: 181). These developments account for the slow but steady increase in English real GDP per capita after 1630.

An analysis of England's exports in 1700 lays bare the nature of its trade. While about 50 per cent of exports were woollens and 20 per cent consisted of manufactures, food, and raw materials, as much as 30 per cent were re-exports of New World commodities such as tobacco, sugar, spices, and calicoes (Davis, 1973: 7). In other words, a growing part of English commerce was concerned with the handling of goods produced elsewhere. This was a boon to England's merchants, but not to its manufacturers. And it is why London, the centre of commercial activity, continued to grow more rapidly than the nation throughout the seventeenth century. Between 1600 and 1700 the population of London grew from 200,000 to 575,000, while the population of England increased from only 4.066 to 5.027 million (Bairoch et al., 1988: 33; Mitchell, 1988: 7). This meant that the proportion of

England's population living in London more than doubled from 4.9 to 11.4 per cent during the seventeenth century.

The first half of the eighteenth century saw a renewed expansion of trade between Western Europe and the rest of the world as their colonies grew in population and wealth. Not only were these colonies an important source of natural resources as they had been in the sixteenth and seventeenth centuries, they were also a growing source of demand for Western Europe's manufactures. While they continued to supply vast amounts of precious metals, although at increased costs as the mines became deeper, European colonies were also becoming important sources of luxury food and raw materials now that the vast land resources were being more effectively exploited. Yet, we should not overestimate the importance of this trade, because prior to the Industrial Revolution late-neolithic technology did not allow the generation of large food surpluses owing to relatively low agricultural productivity levels. Large agricultural surpluses were not generated until the early to mid-nineteenth century and beyond. Colonial exports in the eighteenth century were dominated by luxury goods such as furs, sugar, tobacco, spices (particularly pepper), and cheap Indian cotton textiles. But this luxury trade did generate growing purchasing power in the colonies for European manufactures and for slaves.

While commerce in the eighteenth century did increase steadily, it was not the basis for a great boom in Western Europe (Steensgaard, 1990). Nevertheless, European merchants who were able to gain special privileges and monopolies, as through the East India companies, became very prosperous. The country to gain most in the first three-quarters of the eighteenth century was England, which in 1763 gained sole control of the eastern half of North America, a monopoly over India in the 1760s when the French and Portuguese (apart from the toe-hold in Goa) had been expelled, and a strategic presence in the West and East Indies and in Africa. The importance of this, at a time when marginal returns from fine-tuning the English late-neolithic economic system were declining rapidly, can be seen reflected in the growth of real GDP per capita of about 0.3 per cent per annum. This is a growth rate as fast as that achieved during the first half of the Industrial Revolution, but only a fraction of the rate of growth of 1.6 per cent per annum achieved during the golden age of the commercial strategy. It is clear that without the benefit of trade in the eighteenth century the English economy would have stagnated.

Towards the Industrial Revolution

The golden age of the sixteenth century was the last great flourish of commerce as the dominant dynamic strategy in history. Even the modest expansion of commerce that had occurred during the first half of the eighteenth century was exhausted by the 1770s. Where was the Dynamic Society

376

to turn? The upper limit of the late-neolithic technological paradigm had been reached (which is only detectable with hindsight), and the strategy of colonization had largely been played out. There were two possibilities – conquest or a great shift in the technological paradigm.

To the French, who in 1760 were smarting from colonial losses to the British and who were experiencing internal social problems, conquest seemed to be the obvious choice. A French invasion of Britain was planned in the west of Scotland and the south of England, but before it could be executed the British navy fortuitously destroyed the French fleet. A further attempt by the French to involve the Spanish as an ally in their plans also failed, and they were forced to give up control of Canada in exchange for the return of former possessions in the Caribbean that had been snatched earlier by the British. Later, revolutionary France was more successful and, as we saw in Chapter 10, made amazing if temporary gains of conquest on the Continent under Napoleon Bonaparte.

Britain, on the other hand, while happy to meet force with force, made no attempt to secure territory on the European mainland even after Napoleon's defeat. While they appeared satisfied with their extensive colonial acquisitions, this satisfaction would not have lasted had they not been able to transform the technological foundations of their society through the Industrial Revolution. They would not have remained satisfied because their economy would have stagnated, as it was showing signs of doing between 1760 and 1780 with real GDP per capita growing only at the rate of 0.1 per cent per annum. Eventually this would have driven the British to adopt the dynamic strategy of conquest. The implications of this probability are examined in the final chapter.

But the historical record shows that Britain embraced the technological strategy which gave birth to the Industrial Revolution. This was a complex change which emerged from a process of technological and commercial trans-formation that had been taking place in Europe for over a thousand years. It was the first technological paradigm shift in the world in 10,000 years – the first, indeed, since the Neolithic Revolution of the Fertile Crescent. From this time on, trade was to be driven by the technology strategy. It became more important to gain monopolies over newly innovated products and processes than over the access to markets.

Trade clearly is still important and feeds into the growth process, largely through the diffusion of ideas (Kenwood and Lougheed, 1983: 13), but it is not the dominant strategy of Western civilization. Small nations – such as Singapore – can still prosper through commerce, but they will never become great powers in the way that Greece, Tyre, Carthage, Venice, or mercantile England were able to do. The great powers of today and the future are those who derive economic rents from pursuing the technology strategy and trading the new products of that strategy. The conjurer has been displaced by the maker of the wheel.

12

THE DYNAMIC SOCIETY

A sea of forces flowing and rushing together, eternally changing,
eternally flooding back.

(Nietzsche, *The Will to Power*, 1885)

*It was early morning and the sun had yet to break through the swirling
mists. The rowers were straining at their oars against the rushing currents
that drew their pentekonter ever closer to the rocky Lydian shore. As the
oars hit the angry sea in unison the narrow craft surged into the waves.
But as they were lifted again in sheets of fine spray whipped by the wind
into grimacing faces, the endangered vessel was dragged back by the under-
current towards the menacing rocks. Standing at the stern of the warship,
a lone figure watched this deadly drama as the company of fifty warriors
battled against the flooding seas. Time after time his beleaguered vessel rose
and fell in a circular motion on the waves without making progress. If
only a wind would spring up from the east, he thought, to drive the waves
offshore taking us away from this deadly coastline. Will we ever be able to
escape these earth-binding forces and, like Icarus, soar into the heavens?
Will Daedalus ever grant us that power? Abruptly his thoughts were cut
short by the sudden loud cracking of breaking timber.*

What has made us as we are? This is history's most puzzling question. In order
to answer it, we need to discover the driving force in human society together
with the process by which it has been transformed over the past 100,000 years.
Many scholars – natural scientists, social scientists, historians, and philosophers
– have, as discovered in Chapter 5, attempted to answer this question of
questions. Because of its complexity, most scholars have resorted to an almost
endless list of factors that appear to have a reasonably persuasive claim to at
least some influence. Few have attempted to build a general model to explain
human dynamics throughout time, and there has been no consensus about
either the pattern or the process involved. Most see the fortunes of human
society as being determined by forces outside the ambit of man.

As the book is one long argument, an attempt will be made in this chapter to draw its many threads together in order to provide a picture of the dynamic pattern of human society and to construct an existential model – a model of existence rather than a model of deductive thought – that can explain it. This model is concerned with the driving force in human society and the dynamic processes by which it has been radically changed since the emergence of *Homo sapiens*. It is a model that places man, and the dynamic strategies that he employs to achieve his objectives, at the centre of human progress. It attempts to explain the three great dynamic mechanisms in human society over the last 2 million years – the great dispersion, the great wheel of civilization, and the great waves of technological change that have finally broken through the eternal recurrence of war and conquest. A more formal presentation of the dynamic processes revealed in this chapter will be taken up in a future work.

THE PATTERN OF DYNAMIC CHANGE

To provide an overview of the human odyssey we need to sketch the outline of change in – or timescapes of – the Dynamic Society. As these timescapes are the outcome of the dynamic process, they provide valuable insights concerning the underlying dynamic mechanisms. They are the 'pictures' of dynamic change that need to be examined using the general model developed in this chapter. Only by employing this tripartite system of analysis – timescapes, existential model, dynamic mechanisms – can we fully under-stand the Dynamic Society.

The most readily available evidence for the dynamics of human society is the size and change in populations. From the sixteenth century in Europe it is possible to provide fairly reliable annual estimates of population (Cipolla, 1974; Wrigley and Schofield, 1981). Before then estimates are only available at irregular intervals, and can only be regarded as very rough, particularly as we go further back in time and include non-literate societies that did not record their activities other than in their archaeological remains. But if we wish only to draw approximate profiles of global and regional population, rather than focusing upon detailed figures, we can push back estimates of population to about a million years ago. Evidence on the growth of material living standards, as measured by real GDP per capita, is even more difficult to obtain. Until recently GDP estimates were only available back to 1688, and only for England. Since then I have estimated GDP per capita for England back to 1086 using that amazing set of national accounts compiled by William the Conqueror in Domesday Book (Snooks, 1990a; 1993a; 1994c). Using different and more approximate methods, others are now attempting to do the same for other European countries, at least back to 1500 (Blomme and Van der Wee, 1994). While it does not appear to be possible to obtain direct estimates of GDP for earlier periods, my published estimates can be used to draw implications about the relationship between GDP per capita and population for earlier civilizations.

Human populations

Global population has increased from about 0.125 million people a million years ago to 5,400 million people today. This change has taken place in three main phases (see Figure 12.1 – this entire period can only be represented on a double log graph): the period before the Neolithic Revolution when population expansion had been made possible by a new hunter/gatherer technology (the Palaeolithic Revolution); a period of much more rapid growth from the Neolithic Revolution to the peak of Roman hegemony; and another burst of expansion since the Industrial Revolution. Population expansion, therefore, increased rapidly following each technological paradigm shift, and in each case slowed down as the paradigm approached exhaustion. This suggests that over the extremely longrun, population and technology are involved in a step-like relationship, and that technology is driving this relationship.

Figure 12.2 (which is a more conventional semi-log graph on which growth rates are represented by the slopes of the lines) shows the growth of global population over a shorter period of 8,000 years – the period since the Neolithic Revolution. While it is quite clear that global population has grown at an exponential rate (i.e. a positive compound rate of its initial size) of

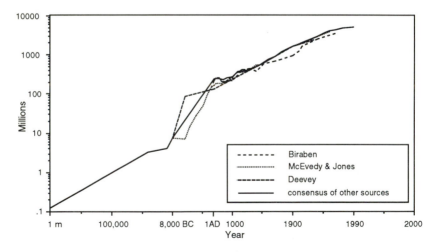

Figure 12.1 World population – the last million years

Sources: Drawn from data in Biraben (1979); Deevey (1960); McEvedy and Jones (1978); Calder (1984), Cipolla (1974), Clark (1977), Durand (1977), Livi-Bacci (1992); and UN (1973).

about 0.06 per cent per annum, it has fallen far short of Malthus' 'geometric rate', by which he meant a doubling each generation that would have required a compound rate of 3 per cent per annum for each of these 8,000 years! While it is true that the rate of population growth was greater from the Second World War than it has ever been in the past, this rate of increase has been slowing since about 1970. Also, Figure 12.2 shows that the *rate* of population growth has not been increasing progressively, but has fluctuated considerably throughout the history of human civilization. Population growth was particularly rapid from the beginning of urban society to the high point of the Roman Empire; but from the time of Christ to about AD 900 it slowed appreciably; then its rate increased briefly between AD 900 and 1300, only to fall again, this time in absolute terms, until 1500; there was another burst in the sixteenth century followed by stagnation in the seventeenth century and slow growth in the first half of the eighteenth century; thereafter, global population accelerated – with a few slumps – until the end of the third quarter of the twentieth century. It is highly likely that as the Third World industrializes, global population will enter another period of much slower growth. Cameron (1989) calls these population waves 'logistics'.

In the light of these data it is completely misleading of the ecological engineers in *Beyond the Limits* to imply that the global economy is currently experiencing a rate of growth of population that is Malthusian in character. They give this impression in a number of ways. First, their explanation of exponential growth – which, as we can see in Figure 12.2, can vary from low to high rates – is peppered with examples that show a doubling each

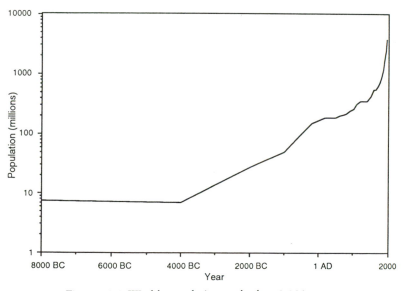

Figure 12.2 World population – the last 8,000 years
Sources: as for Figure 12.1

period. They even say (Meadows *et al.*, 1992: 16): 'That is exponential growth, doubling and redoubling and doubling again'. True, but it may take many periods of time (or generations) to do so. The fact is that modern global population has not been able to achieve a doubling in a generation. And there is every reason to expect that the existing rate will decline in the future. Second, the ecological engineers give the impression that exponential growth of population at the higher rates is automatic and inevitable, purely because population is capable of reproducing itself. The truth is that it can, and has, taken place at low rates both in primitive societies and in the modern developed world. Third, they dismiss the reduction in the rate of growth of global population between 1970 and 1991 from 2.1 to 1.7 per cent per annum by saying 'but it does not mean that population growth is anywhere close to levelling off' (ibid.: 24), and by immediately switching the discussion from *rates* to *absolute increases* in population. The fact is that world population *is* growing exponentially – i.e. by a positive compound rate – but it is currently about *half* the rate required for a doubling each generation, and it will decline further as more regions of the world adopt the technology of the Industrial Revolution and beyond.

It is difficult to obtain population data over long periods for individual ancient civilizations. What has been obtained is shown in Figure 12.3, which focuses upon the Near East, Egypt, Greece, and Rome. While these data do not show the shorter-term fluctuations in population, they do outline the general rise and fall of individual civilizations. The pattern that emerges is of rapid growth in the early stages of the civilization, followed by stagnation and, eventually, rapid decline. The population for the eastern civilizations of India and China are also shown in Figure 12.3. As these civilizations continued in one form or another down to the present, they do not decline dramatically, although they do stagnate for long periods of time. Finally, Figure 12.4 presents the available population estimates for the Mesoamerican civilizations. They demonstrate an even more rapid rise-and-fall cycle than the ancient civilizations of the Old World, owing to the particularly acute impact upon them of Old World conquest and disease, although a few, the Olmec, Teotihuacan, and the Mayan civilizations, emerged, flourished, and then collapsed in isolation.

While population data for this early period can be used to show the broad trends in the economic expansion of human society, they cannot indicate shorter fluctuations. For this we need to seek other data, such as the expanding geographical area of the Roman Empire and the detailed archaeological evidence on the rate of construction of urban centres in the Mayan civilization. These data have been presented in Figure 12.5 and can be considered as broadly representative of longrun economic fluctuations in both the ancient Old and New Worlds. The data on the geographical expansion of the Roman Empire (Figure 12.5a) suggest that the great conquest cycle in

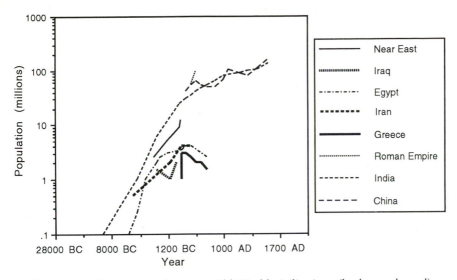

Figure 12.3 Population of ancient Old World civilizations (both axes logged)
Source: Drawn from data in Beloch (1968), Durand (1977), and McEvedy and Jones (1978).

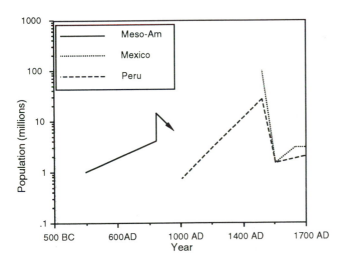

Figure 12.4 Population of ancient New World civilizations (both axes logged)
Sources: Drawn from data in Calder (1984), and McEvedy and Jones (1978).

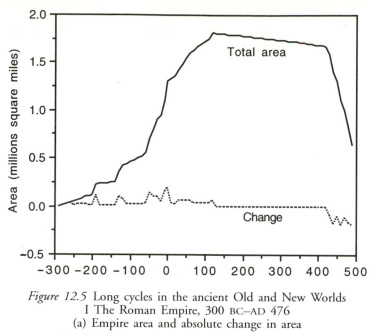

Figure 12.5 Long cycles in the ancient Old and New Worlds
I The Roman Empire, 300 BC–AD 476
(a) Empire area and absolute change in area
Source: Data for total area from Taagepera (1968: 171).

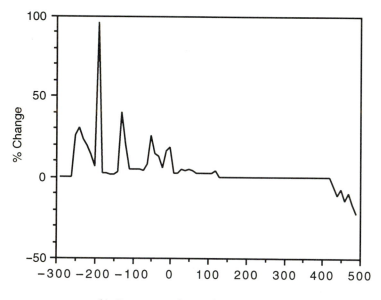

(b) Percentage change in empire area
Source: Calculated from (a) above.

384

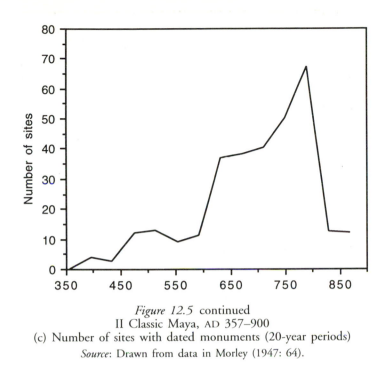

Figure 12.5 continued
II Classic Maya, AD 357–900
(c) Number of sites with dated monuments (20-year periods)
Source: Drawn from data in Morley (1947: 64).

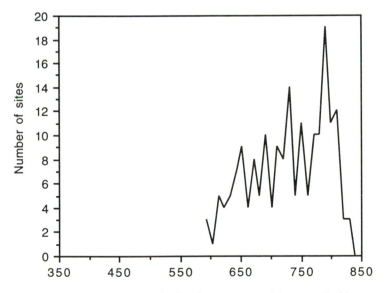

(d) Number of sites with dated monuments (5-year periods)
Source: As for (c) above.

the Old World was about 320 years in duration between 250 BC and AD 120. Of particular interest is that during these great waves of 320 years there were six marked subcycles of conquest, averaging one every 50 years (Figure 12.5b). For the New World, the data on construction of dated monuments at classic Mayan sites (Figure 12.5c) suggest great waves of about 240–250 years. More detailed construction evidence on Tikal, one of the major Mayan cities, confirms this, with the centre of the city undergoing dramatic changes every 200 years or so (Jones, 1991: 121). It is also interesting to realize that the Maya themselves thought their society experienced regular great cycles every 256 years (Puleston, 1979: 63). And within these great waves of the New World were long cycles averaging about 50 years, and within these were medium cycles of about 20 years. As can be seen from Figure 12.5d, for the lowland Maya between AD 600 and 790 there were four long cycles ranging from 40 to 60 years, which averaged 50 years.

The past millennium has witnessed the remarkable rise of Western civilization. To understand what this implies, the populations of Europe and Britain are compared with that of China over the period 1000 to 2000 in Figure 12.6. The interesting feature of this comparison is the close parallel between the three population series. Each describes three great waves of economic change. On average these great waves are about 300 years in duration, although no precision for a regular cycle can be claimed. Peaks were achieved between 1200 (China) and 1300 (Europe and England), about 1600,

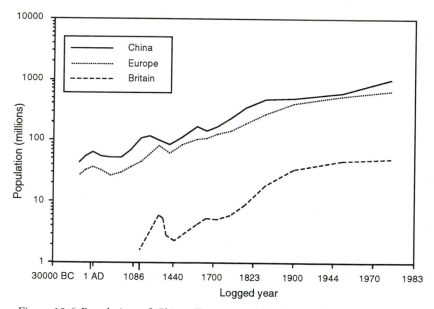

Figure 12.6 Population of China, Europe, and England – the last 2,000 years
Sources: Drawn from data in Biraben (1979), Durand (1977), McEvedy and Jones (1978), and United Nations (various years).

386

and the present; with troughs around 1400 and the 1650s. Since the Second World War, however, there has been a divergence, with Europe's (including England's) rate of population growth levelling off while China's has entered a new phase of expansion.

The close parallels between the population profiles of east and west during the past 1,000 years suggest a considerable degree of interaction between England and Europe, and even some (largely non-economic) interaction between Europe and China. More important, however, were the general economic paradigmatic conditions they shared. We have already seen how the Black Death, which began in China in 1331, had reached western Eurasia in 1346, and Western Europe by 1347. In a similar way a new disease, possibly measles, which emerged in China in AD 162 had found its way to the heart of the Roman Empire by AD 165; while – reversing the direction – another new disease, possibly smallpox, began in the Roman Empire in AD 251 and appeared in China about AD 317. These diseases, which were carried along the overland trade routes, clearly had an impact upon population cycles. But more importantly, China and Europe were experiencing similar interrelationships between population and natural resources, owing to similar sizes of populations and available land. As they were both agricultural economies many of their entrepreneurial responses were also similar. Only in the last 300 years did their dynamic strategies diverge markedly owing to very different competitive environments.

This uniformity in the great waves of population growth is very interesting. It suggests that the conditions, the responses, and the shocks were similar over a large part of the Old World during the past millennium. It is also evidence that the dynamics of human society is systematic and not random. If demographers such as Lee (1973; 1993) and his ilk – who argue that human society is largely driven by the impact of accumulated random shocks on population – had been correct, we would expect to see considerable regional variation in demographic fluctuations. The accumulation of local shocks, therefore, would give very different population fluctuations in Europe when compared with China.

The evidence presented here on the process of longrun economic expansion is fascinating. It suggests that, in both the ancient and post-ancient eras in major regions throughout the world, economic change has taken place via great waves of roughly 300 years in duration. There is even a hint that shorter cycles – the long wave – of about fifty years existed in the ancient Old and New Worlds. While no precision should be claimed for the regularity of both these 'great waves' and 'long waves' owing to the random impact of external shocks – which are capable of distorting any regular internal economic rhythms – their persistence down through the millennia and throughout the globe is difficult to ignore. It is of particular significance that they emerge even when dynamic strategies as different as conquest (Rome and Maya) and technological change (Western Europe) are employed. The overwhelming implication of this evidence is that the economic decision-making of materialist man is eternally rhythmic in nature and transcends time, space, and dynamic strategy.

Material living standards

Within Western Europe, the parallels between the great population waves of England and the Continent are quite remarkable, particularly as England is quite small demographically (16 per cent) in relation to Western Europe. There have been three great waves over the past 1,000 years and their peaks and troughs are coincident. In terms of the relationships between resources, population, and technology, Britain and the rest of Europe were clearly operating in very similar ways within the same highly competitive environment and against a background of common economic conditions. They were also subject to similar major shocks, and were closely integrated through the exchange of commodities and resources. As both societies appear to have been pursuing broadly similar dynamic strategies in similar circumstances, we would expect the processes and outcomes also to be broadly similar, particularly as England was more representative of what has happened in Western Europe over the past millennium than any other individual kingdom. We have seen in Part III that Western European countries experienced similar changes in institutional arrangements and production techniques between the heyday of feudalism in the eleventh century and the emergence of mercantile capitalism in the sixteenth and seventeenth centuries, and that the Industrial Revolution, which emerged in the late eighteenth and early nineteenth centuries in England, had spread to Western Europe by the early to mid-nineteenth century and to Eastern Europe later in that century. Further we know that the Black Death of 1347–1349 and the debilitating epidemics that followed had a similar impact throughout Europe. We would expect, therefore, to discover a similar pattern for GDP and GDP per capita in both England and Western Europe *as a whole* (but not, of course, with all its less representative component parts). Hence my estimates of English GDP and GDP per capita since the eleventh century can be used as a rough proxy for the emergence of Western civilization. England, the leader in this dynamic process, epitomizes and encapsulates, more than any other European country, the rise and maturation of Western civilization.

Figure 12.7 shows the relationship between population, GDP, GDP per capita, and prices for England – and through it Western civilization – for the period 1000 to 2000. The three great waves of economic change demonstrate a number of similar and contrasting features. The first feature they have in common is that population only increases in the longer term when living standards (or GDP per capita) are either growing or, at least, not falling. As soon as living standards do begin to fall, so does population. This is a very important discovery, because it has much to tell us about what is driving these great waves. But more of that later.

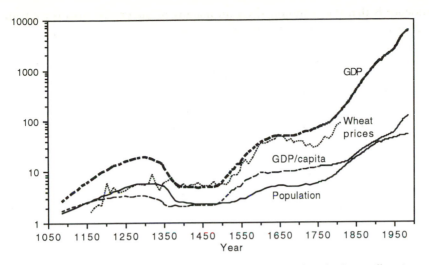

Figure 12.7 Great waves of economic change in England – the last millennium
Note: Log scale on vertical axis
Source: G.D. Snooks, *Economics without Time*, London, Macmillan, 1993, p. 257.

Second, each great wave is characterized by a period in which relatively high rates of growth of GDP per capita were achieved. Growth rates as high as 0.6 per cent per annum were achieved for the period 1086 to 1170, which implies a doubling of living standards every 117 years; and as high as 1.6 per cent per annum for the period 1492 to 1561, which implies a doubling of living standards every forty-four years. All this took place within the technological paradigm bequeathed by the Neolithic Revolution; shaped by the classical civilizations of Sumer, Greece, and Rome; and fine-tuned by the emerging European civilization. By 1500 the sophistication of the economic system of the West had surpassed that of the ancients (Mokyr, 1990: 55) By 1700, in terms of real GDP per capita, it was about double that of Augustan Rome or Periclean Athens (Goldsmith, 1987: 19). The Europeans, and particularly the English, showed how much further the old economic system could be taken after 1500. While Western Europe also dabbled with varying degrees of success in commerce and colonization (especially Britain) and conquest (especially Spain, Portugal, and France), they kept their technological change option open (unlike the ancient world). In turn, this offered new prospects for colonial expansion.

The three great waves also provide a number of interesting contrasts. The first of these concerns the first two waves. In both cases, England's population at the upper turning points of 1300 and 1650 was about 5.5 million, whereas real GDP per capita in 1650 was higher than that in 1300 by a factor of 2.8. In other words, the population downturn in the second half of the seventeenth

389

century occurred, not because of a mechanical relationship between population and natural resources, but because economic decision-makers, in the face of the emerging exhaustion of the old technological paradigm, were not prepared to allow population growth to erode the advances in living standards made during the sixteenth century. Population change, in other words, was part of the dynamic strategy of materialist man, rather than man being the plaything of demographic forces driven largely by external random shocks. Second, for the first time in European history, population growth began to stagnate at a stage – during the second half of the twentieth century – when GDP per capita was growing at unprecedented rates. While this was made possible by continuing technological change under the new industrial paradigm, it underlines the fundamentally important point that population growth is merely part of the dynamic strategy of man; it is not his master.

The third contrasting feature is the role played by the technological strategy in each of these three great waves. Expansion during the period 1000 to 1300 was based upon the adaption of classical agricultural technology to the different climatic and geographical conditions of northern Europe. This enabled an expansion of agricultural settlement to previously unsuitable areas, and an increase in productivity, at least until 1200. At the same time, factor markets for labour, land, and capital emerged in response to fundamental economic forces, thereby improving organizational efficiency. By 1300 these dynamic strategies of extensive and intensive natural resource use had been exhausted. The second great wave began with considerable energy in the 1490s once the economy had been released from the vice-like grip of pestilence and it was fuelled by the organizational and technical changes that had taken place during the previous century, the economic outcomes of which had been suppressed. During the sixteenth century Western Europe fully exploited the possibilities inherent in the Neolithic Revolution by employing the commerce strategy. It carefully fine-tuned the economic/political/social possibilities that had been handed down by earlier civilizations; it took regional specialization and trade about as far as it could go within this old framework; and it enjoyed the supernormal profits of commerce. But by 1800 it stood at the crossroads. The only way forward was to achieve a major shift in the technological paradigm. Had the Industrial Revolution not occurred, then Western Europe's real GDP per capita would not have increased further and may have declined following a scramble for arms.

While our data for earlier civilizations do not permit a similar discussion of fluctuations in population and real GDP per capita, it is reasonable to speculate that great waves of economic change occurred as dynamic strategies were implemented and ultimately exhausted, followed by further waves as new strategies were adopted or old ones rejuvenated. We are encouraged to do so by the great waves of about 200–300 years recorded in the physical expansion of ancient societies (Figure 12.5). We can also speculate that living standards increased during the early phases of each upswing owing to the progressive adoption of technical ideas from earlier civilizations; to a growing specialization as trade links were developed; to economies resulting from growing scale; and to the improvement of organizational forms. But we should not overemphasize this matter, because the major dynamic strategies in the ancient world were conquest and commerce, which provided relatively easy gains for private adventurers and for the state. So seductive were these easy gains that the improvements in GDP per capita achieved by each civilization – Sumer, Greece, and Rome – were not greatly surpassed by those that came later. Using fairly rough procedures, Raymond Goldsmith (1987: 19) was unable to detect any advance in real GDP per capita between Periclean Athens and Augustan Rome. Each newly emerging civilization began with a lower standard of living than its predecessor and, while they eventually caught up with them, they did not go much beyond their predecessors – at least not permanently – because of the attraction of the cheaper and more temporary gains from conquest and commerce. For example, Roman GDP per capita at the end of the Augustan period (AD 14) was double that in England in 1086 but, after the commercial expansion of the sixteenth and seventeenth centuries, only half that of England in 1688 (Snooks, 1993a: 196). Had it not been for the Industrial Revolution, however, England's living standards would have fallen again with the exhaustion of its commerce strategy, which might have encouraged England to pursue the only remaining strategy of conquest (a possibility discussed in the final chapter).

Our examination of these Dynamic Society timescapes suggests that we need to construct a model to explain four outstanding characteristics. We need to explain the great steps in the progress of human society that occurred with the Palaeolithic (hunting) Revolution 1.6 million years ago; the Neolithic (agricultural) Revolution 10,600 years ago; and the Industrial Revolution just over 200 years ago. We need to explain the rise and fall of civilizations over the past 8,000 years. We need to explain the great waves of economic change that occur within each civilization whether ancient or modern. We need to explain the paradox that, while each individual civilization appears to have experienced a growth in living standards (or GDP per capita), there has not been a significant increase in basic living standards from one civilization to the next over time prior to the Industrial Revolution. Only by employing the ephemeral strategies of conquest and commerce were civilizations able temporarily to transcend the basic living standards made possible by the existing technological paradigm. And we need to explain a process that quite clearly is neither random nor 'chaotic' as some have suggested recently (Radzicki, 1994).

AN EXISTENTIAL DYNAMIC MODEL

What are the characteristics of a truly dynamic model? A dynamic model will focus upon processes as well as outcomes. These processes will involve interactions between fundamental economic forces such as relative factor prices, decision-makers in competitive environments, the strategies they adopt, and the impact of those strategies on the material fabric of society. A dynamic model will be self-starting and self-sustaining, subject only to *passive* inputs (sunlight, oxygen, etc.) from the physical world. And the dynamic system will respond positively and creatively to shocks from outside the system. External shocks will be of two types: minor shocks – such as floods, droughts, or unusually cold or hot seasons – that produce oscillations in economic activity but which are relatively easily overcome; and major shocks that are generated by organic rather than physical systems – such as invasions and epidemics – that will destabilize the system and may even contribute to collapse. Such a model can be constructed from an examination of longrun historical processes. In conjuction with the above timescapes, our general existential model of the Dynamic Society can be used to explain the mechanisms by which the society of primitive man has been transformed into modern society. A brief summary of the model developed here was provided in Chapter 1. What remains to be done is to discuss it in more detail and complexity.

The model consists of four interrelated elements and one external and random force:

1 the competitive driving force of materialist man which provides the model with its self-starting and self-sustaining nature;
2 the dynamic strategies, including family multiplication, technology, commerce, and conquest which, in a competitive environment, are employed by economic agents through investment in strategic infrastructure to achieve their objectives;
3 the competitive dynamic tactics of order and chaos used by individuals and groups of individuals to capture the gains made by the Dynamic Society;
4 the constraining effect provided by the eventual exhaustion of dynamic strategies, which in individual societies may lead to strategic crisis and collapse, but in global human society leads to technological transformation; and
5 a system subject to random shocks both minor (droughts, floods, etc.) and major (wars, disease, etc.).

Hence the very longrun driving force arises from the nature of man – indeed of life itself – in competitive circumstances, and the wave-like process by which the transformation of society is achieved is due to the creative use of various dynamic strategies and the ultimate exhaustion of those strategies. The constraints, in other words, arise from the very sources of expansion and growth, are internal to the model, and are relative rather than absolute. We need to discuss these matters in greater detail.

1 Essentially, the overwhelming desire on the part of mankind for survival and for the maximization of material advantage leads to a choice of dynamic strategies that are strongly influenced by the degree of external competition faced by a particular society. It is this process that I have called **dynamic materialism**. The degree of external competition determines the framework within which the costs and benefits of adopting various dynamic strategies are evaluated. Think of societies being distributed along a **global scale of competitiveness**, with those societies experiencing a very high degree of competitiveness at one extreme, and those societies experiencing no external competition at the other extreme. Other societies will be located between these extremes. For the purposes of this analysis, we need to divide the world into two parts – the Old World of Europe, Asia, Africa, and Australia on the one hand and the New World of the Americas on the other – and construct a scale of competitiveness for each. After the initial migrations from Siberia to the Americas, which began at least 40,000 years ago, both parts of the globe were effectively isolated from each other by rising seas (about 15,000 years ago) and acted as separate worlds. We can call our comparative device, for convenience, the Old World scale and the New World scale. Societies at the highly competitive end of the Old World scale include the classical ancient civilizations and Western European countries, while the best example of a closed society is Aboriginal Australia. Other societies in Eastern Europe, India, and China range between these two extremes. On the New World scale of competitiveness are the Mesoamerican civilizations at the highly competitive end, with the Inuit (Eskimos) and Tierra del Fuegans at the isolated end. Various North and South American cultures can be distributed along the scale between these extremes.

If the society in which we are interested is at the highly competitive end of the scale, it will pursue any one of the four dynamic strategies, whereas if at the non-competitive end, it will choose only the family multiplication strategy if unused resources are abundant, or the family planning strategy – a static rather than a dynamic strategy – if all natural resources are fully utilized. Both choices are rational in that they are directed at maximizing the probability of survival and material returns given the perceived costs and benefits of alternative strategies. The closed society will rate the costs of the technology, commerce, and conquest strategies as too high and the benefits too low to bother adopting them. They opt for a quiet life, a risk-averse life. On the other hand, the open society has to fight for its very survival and, therefore, will be prepared to adopt a high-cost strategy if it provides a competitive edge in the struggle for life and prosperity.

2 Once an open society decides to opt for a dynamic strategy – which is the typical case for human society or, indeed, for life – there is a range from which to choose. This choice is largely influenced by the factor

endowments of natural resources, labour, and capital and, hence, the rela-tive prices – either implicit or explicit – of these factors, together with the relative entry costs of various strategies in a competitive world. In Chapter 8 we discussed the mechanism – the **strategic imitation** mechanism – by which individual investment projects are transformed into dynamic strategies for entire societies. Where natural resources are relatively abundant and, hence, relatively cheap, the family multiplication strategy will be employed. This involves extending the family influence by reproduction and migration to adjoining areas. If, however, all natural resources are fully utilized at a given level of technology and there is growing competition for these resources (i.e. where land is relatively expensive), a society has three dynamic options. It can pursue the *dominant* strategies of technology, conquest, or commerce, which are generally supported by one or more subsidiary strategies. The technology strategy involves increasing productivity by applying 'new' ideas to production and economic organization (hence, technological change is demand-determined); the conquest strategy (which may also involve colonization) involves acquiring private and public income and labour supplies (slaves) through military activity; and the commerce strategy involves capturing a disproportionately large share of the gains from trade through monopoly pricing. The choice of strategy will be strongly influenced by the relative benefit–cost possibilities of these strategies, the time horizon (discount rate) of the society, and the amount of infrastructure that already exists for the pursuit of one or other of these strategies. To implement the chosen strategy, economic decision-makers invest in the necessary infrastructure required to achieve their objectives. In doing so they expect to receive a competitive rate of return on their investment. The actual rate of return will determine their future decision-making. If successful, a dynamic strategy will, in its initial phases, generate increasing returns to scale, which will lead to increasing rates of economic growth. Eventually it will come to play a dominant role in the society. Hence the dynamics of human society result from the strategic demands of economic decision-makers in a competitive environment rather than the fortuitous removal of supply-side barriers (Jones, 1981; Kennedy, 1989) and/or the impact of external shocks (Lee, 1993), both of which are fashionable in scholarly circles.

Those individuals and societies that employ an appropriate dynamic strategy or combination of strategies gain a competitive advantage, achieve their objective of survival, and are well on the way to maximizing their material advantage. Those that employ an inappropriate strategy, or employ it inefficiently, are either eliminated by the victors, as has occurred throughout life on Earth, or are reduced to slavery or poverty. In a competitive environment the incentive to succeed, therefore, is intense. And the victors pass on their dynamic strategy both in substance and form to later generations, just as the strategies – largely of conquest – of classical antiquity were passed from Sumer to Assyria to Greece to Rome and beyond (although it became clear with the dramatic fall of Rome that other strategies might be required in the future). These historical dynamic strategies, which were discussed in Chapters 8 to 11, are summarized in Table 12.1. The dominant dynamic strategies range from family multiplication in palaeolithic society to conquest and commerce in ancient neolithic societies, and to technology in modern society. This general pattern is broken only by societies that experienced varying degrees of isolation, leading to family planning in Australia for the 20,000 years before British settlement, central control in Teotihuacan for the 600 years of effective isolation before its collapse after AD 750, and family multiplication and central control in China from AD 1368 to 1800, its phase of self-imposed exile. Table 12.1 also shows the main subsidiary or supporting strategies. Technology is the chief of these owing to the demands made by all dominant strategies for more efficient strategic infrastructure. Commerce has also played an important supporting role to dominant strategies throughout space and time in the Dynamic Society.

What are the political and social outcomes of the dynamic strategy process? Those that control the dominant dynamic strategies also gain effective power in society either directly, by participation in major societal organizations, or indirectly, through their influence on political and social representatives. These strategic leaders include the head of the kinship group in the family multiplication society, the warrior in the conquest society, the merchant in the commerce society, and the entrepreneur in the technological society. The dynamic strategy drives the sociopolitical structure.

3 Within a particular society, individuals and groups of individuals will employ a range of tactics to capture as many of the gains made by the Dynamic Society (from their dynamic strategies) as possible. Those in power will attempt to impose order on their economic rivals (both internal and external), whereas those ambitious individuals without economic and political power will attempt to create chaos in order to topple the ruling elite. I have, as discussed in Chapter 7, broadly categorized these efforts as the **dynamic tactics** of order and chaos. The order category will involve various tactics aimed at maintaining and exploiting the *status quo*, ranging from rent-seeking to the imposition of restrictive regulations, tariffs, and ideology; and the chaos category will involve tactics aimed at disrupting the existing order ranging from deregulation and reform to protest and rebellion (including radical ideology). Those who are best able to handle competitive conditions tend to opt for chaos, in which they have a comparative advantage, and those who are least able to handle competition opt for order. As we have seen, there is a gender dimension here. Every society at any point in time is involved in a struggle between the forces of order and the forces of chaos. A healthy society is able to achieve a balance

Table 12.1 Strategies of the Dynamic Society – the last 2 million years

Society	Dominant strategy(ies)	Subsidiary strategy(ies)
1 Palaeolithic, 1.6 myrs–10,000 BP	family multiplication	technology
2 Aboriginal Australian		
• before 20,000 BP	family multiplication	technology
• 20,000 BP–AD 1788	family planning	technology
3 Sumerian	technology/commerce	conquest
4 Akkadian	conquest	commerce
5 Assyrian	conquest	commerce
6 Achaean Greek	commerce	colonization/conquest
7 Classical Greek	commerce	colonization/conquest
8 Persian	conquest	commerce
9 Phoenician		
• Tyre	commerce	colonization
• Carthage	commerce	colonization/conquest
10 Macedonian	conquest	technology/commerce
11 Roman	conquest	commerce/technology
12 Venetian/Genoese	commerce	colonization/conquest
13 North-western Europe		
• before AD 1100	conquest/commerce	technology
• 1100–1500	technology/commerce/ conquest	technology
• 1500–1760	commerce/colonization	conquest
• 1760–	technology	colonization/commerce/ conquest
14 Islamic		
• Arab (before AD 1200)	conquest	commerce/technology
• Ottoman (before AD 1500)	conquest	commerce
15 Chinese		
• 1066 BC–AD 221	colonization	'conquest'
• AD 221–1368	defence/technology	family multiplication/ colonization
• AD 1368–1800	family multiplication	central control
16 Mesoamerican		
• Teotihuacan		
• 800–150 BC	family multiplication	commerce/technology
• 150 BC–AD 150	conquest	commerce/technology
• AD 150–750	central control	commerce
• Mayan		
• 2000–400 BC	family multiplication	commerce/technology
• 400 BC–AD 500	commerce/technology	conquest
• AD 600–830	conquest	commerce/technology
• Aztec	conquest	commerce/technology

Source: see text, Chapters 8–11.

between these forces. However, those societies in which the forces of order dominate, become inflexible and unenterprising (as in the former USSR); whereas those societies in which the forces of chaos gain the upper hand and order cannot be restored (as in Yugoslavia in the early 1990s) will tear themselves and their physical environment – both manmade and natural – to pieces. It should be clear that the forces of order and chaos are tactics employed by materialist man to influence the distributional outcomes of the dynamic strategies. The significance of the dynamic tactics is that if they get out of balance, the resulting instability renders a society vulnerable to outside take-over bids.

4 The force constraining the expansion and growth of human society is not the supply of resources, natural or otherwise, but the exhaustion of its dynamic strategies and the inability to replace them with new strategies. This operates through the declining rate of return on the investment of time and resources in the dominant dynamic strategy. Unless new strategies are adopted, or old strategies rejuvenated, a society will eventually grind to a halt – at least temporarily. This will occur when the marginal return to the dominant strategy is equal to its marginal cost. In other words, when an extra unit of investment in conquest, commerce, or technology only just pays for itself. At this stage there is no incentive to undertake any further investment. This is what I have called the **strategic crisis**. This will produce a number of outcomes. In an individual society that is relatively stable it will produce a downturn in economic activity that will provide the incentive to introduce new strategies or to revamp old strategies as the basis for a further long upswing, thereby generating a cessation of the downturn and the beginning of a new upswing. But if a large revenue gap suddenly emerges, as at the end of the conquest strategy, or if the forces of order and chaos are badly out of balance, or if no alternative dynamic strategies are available, this downturn may eventually lead to collapse, particularly if it coincides with a major external shock such as war or disease. If, on the other hand, this exhaustion of dynamic strategies is experienced on a global scale, then it will ultimately lead, as past experience has shown, to a technological paradigm shift, which we know as the Palaeolithic, Neolithic, and Industrial Revolutions.

An interesting question is how the 'strategic' crisis can be reconciled with the Malthusian population crisis as an explanation of turning points. The answer is that the strategic-crisis hypothesis – strategic exhaustion – encompasses the Malthusian hypothesis – natural resource scarcity – and in the process completely transforms it. In the Malthusian hypothesis, population – which is seen as beyond the control of human agents who appear determined to maximize reproduction rather than material living standards – is treated as an exogenously determined force which outstrips the productivity of agriculture, owing to the scarcity of natural resources, and brings economic growth to an end. In the strategic-crisis hypothesis, population growth is endogenously determined, as it is a response to man's dynamic strategies, and is brought to an end when these strategies have been exhausted. It is not primarily the pressure of population on resources but the exhaustion of ways of releasing the development potential of natural resources that brings expansion temporarily to an end. In other words, the dynamic mechanism of decline is based upon diminishing returns to dynamic strategies and not to scarce resources. Population expansion is not a determinant of the crisis – which is a strategic crisis – but a response to it. The Malthusian crisis is a special case of the strategic crisis, which often emerges when a society has been overwhelmed by the forces of chaos and the only dynamic outlet is family multiplication.

The process of collapse also requires further explanation. Collapse is here defined in economic terms as a permanent and unsustainable reduction in both real GDP per capita and population. Of particular interest is the collapse of advanced ancient societies which, prior to this traumatic event, were able to increase their population and GDP per capita beyond the levels dictated by a neolithic technology, through conquest or commerce. With the final exhaustion of either the conquest or commerce strategy, the revenue structure of the society collapses but the cost structure remains largely unchanged. There emerges a dangerously large **strategic revenue gap** which, in the absence of alternative dynamic strategies, imposes great pressure on the society to reduce its size and living standards. But such a retreat is not a practical possibility, owing to the heavy fixed investment in infrastructure – including grossly over-expanded urban centres – of either a conquest or commerce kind. While it is theoretically possible to reduce variable costs, such as payments to soldiers, bureaucrats, and urban unemployed – it is just not practicable, owing to the pressing need to defend fixed capital from external attack and to prevent social unrest at home. This is an example of the forces of order attempting to control the forces of chaos.

Consequently, our ancient society is thrown back on the internal resources of a neolithic economic system to fill the strategic revenue gap between a conquest (or commerce) cost structure and a neolithic technological revenue structure. With the end of military expeditions, *total* conquest income falls to zero. In this situation there are two possible paths that can be followed but both lead to collapse. First, the increased taxation, currency devaluation, coercion, and oppression that follow from this strategic revenue gap, as the ruling elite attempt to maintain their real incomes while real GDP per capita is falling, lead to the generation of internal tension, rebellion, and political instability. Finally the entire society collapses with opportunistic neighbours picking up the pieces. Second, even if the forces of chaos do not overwhelm those of order, eventually the neolithic economic system will be unable to provide the essential services required to maintain the urban society. In other words, our society will not be able to finance even the average variable costs let alone the average fixed costs of civilization, and the infrastructure will deteriorate. Voluntary abandonment of the metropolis, as appears to have happened in Mesoamerica, becomes the only viable economic option.

It will be clear that in my dynamic model the collapse of human societies is an outcome of changes in fundamental economic forces operating through the dynamic strategies, not the outcome of institutional problems arising from social complexity. It is true that institutional problems reinforce the fundamental problems, but they are largely a reflection of the exhaustion and non-replacement of the dynamic strategies. They have nothing to do with complexity. Hence issues of information processing and the breakdown of social order may be part of the detailed *narrative* of collapse but they do not play a fundamental *causal* role. The point of this book is that the dynamics of human society is driven by fundamental economic forces – the 'primary dynamic mechanism' – and that institutions respond to these forces – through the 'secondary mechanism' – rather than driving them. The relationship between these primary and secondary mechanisms will be the subject of a future book.

5 The broad outlines of this dynamic process have been summarized in Figure 12.8, which is a simple diagrammatic model of the Dynamic Society. While there are induced feedback effects of real GDP per capita on strategic investment, of the dynamic strategies on resource endowment, and of institutional change on the competitive environment, the overwhelming causal influence arises from materialist man and his dynamic strategies. In a competitive environment materialist man invests in the most efficient dominant dynamic strategy. This leads to a change in capital, population, natural resources, and productive efficiency, which is accommodated by induced changes in the institutional structure. In turn, these economic and institutional changes generate increases in real GDP per capita. This process provides the Dynamic Society with its upward momentum. The mechanism by which this growth force is transformed into very longrun fluctuations – either the great wheel or the great linear waves – involves strategic investment driving the society towards the strategic ceiling, which leads to a crisis that has a negative impact upon real GDP per capita. The outcome – renewed growth or collapse – will depend upon the relative strength of the strategic possibilities on the one hand and the forces of order and chaos on the other.

Finally consideration should be given to the determinants and role of institutional change in this model (Figure 12.8). The broad longrun institutional framework is driven by the dynamic strategies of materialist man, while the shortrun structure is provided by the interacting forces of order and chaos. For example, in the case of the Roman Empire, it was the dynamic strategy of conquest that drove the longrun development of their military, political,

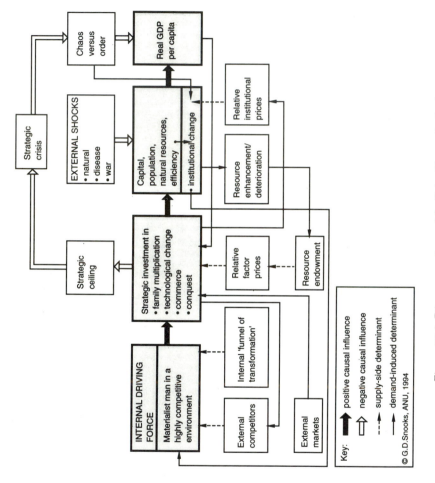

Figure 12.8 Diagrammatic model of the Dynamic Society

Chaos versus order

Real GDP per capita

Strategic crisis

EXTERNAL SHOCKS
• natural
• disease
• war

Capital, population, natural resources, efficiency
• institutional change

Relative institutional prices

Resource enhancement/ deterioration

Strategic ceiling

Strategic investment in
• family multiplication
• technological change
• commerce
• conquest

Relative factor prices

Resource endowment

INTERNAL DRIVING FORCE

Materialist man in a highly competitive environment

Internal 'funnel of transformation'

External competitors

External markets

Key:
→ positive causal influence
⇒ negative causal influence
---- supply-side determinant
---→ demand-induced determinant

© G.D.Snooks, ANU, 1994

and social institutions; while the struggle between those who attempted to retain control of Rome's conquest business (forces of order) and those who wanted to take it over (forces of chaos) determined shorter-term changes such as the growing polarization between an increasingly oppressive bureaucracy and the growing power of regional rural warlords in the empire's final days. But while the demand for institutional change is driven by dynamic economic forces, the choice of direction is influenced, on the supply side, by the transactions costs of the various alternative structures. The most efficient of these alternatives, in the light of similar decisions made in the past, will be chosen by rational decision-makers.

This argument about institutional change, arising from the dynamic analysis of the above pages, is a major departure from the supply-side analysis of the conventional wisdom (North, 1990). Douglass North, the pioneer of historical institutionalism, views institutional change as an outcome of changing property rights and transaction costs influenced by exogenously determined population change. According to this view, institutional change is a major dynamic force in the emergence of Western capitalism rather than a response to a more fundamental dynamic. I am not arguing, however, that institutional change does not play a role in the Dynamic Society, just that it is driven by more fundamental forces. As portrayed in Figure 12.8, institutional change, driven by the dynamic strategies of materialist man, has an impact upon real GDP per capita and an induced feedback effect upon his competitive environment. The progress of human society is driven by the 'primary dynamic mechanism', while institutional change is the outcome of the 'secondary dynamic mechanism' driven by fundamental economic forces.

THE THREE GREAT MECHANISMS OF THE DYNAMIC SOCIETY

We are now in a position to use both the timescapes and the existential model to identify and explain the three great interlocking mechanisms of the Dynamic Society that have been operating over the past 2 million years. The general model, derived from our detailed historical examination, generates separate but related processes of economic change in different historical circumstances. But even these different circumstances are related to one another by an overarching global dynamic structure. That dynamic structure is provided by the great technological paradigm shifts (as reflected in Figure 12.9) that have been occurring at geometrically diminishing intervals since the emergence of mankind, in the form of the Palaeolithic (hunting), Neolithic (agricultural), and Industrial (modern) Revolutions. Within this global dynamic structure the dominant mechanisms of change have been the 'great dispersion' during the palaeolithic era; the 'great wheel of civilization' which operated between the rise of Sumer and the fall of Rome in the Old

World, and the rise of the Olmecs and collapse of the Aztecs in the New World; and the 'great linear waves of economic change' that have broken the eternal recurrence of the ancient world and allowed the Dynamic Society to take the high road to material prosperity. Each of these mechanisms has carried human society towards the upper limits of the prevailing technological paradigm.

The dynamic structure: the great technological paradigm shifts

As we saw in Chapter 9, the process by which technological paradigm shifts emerge is accelerating in a geometric fashion. The interval between the Palaeolithic and Neolithic Revolutions was about 2 million years, and that between the Neolithic and Industrial Revolutions was about 10,000 years. The time taken for the technological shifts to occur involved hundreds of thousands of years for the Palaeolithic, 4000 years for the Neolithic, and 100 years for the Industrial Revolutions. And the time taken to transmit each of these new paradigms around the known world was about 1.2 million years for the Palaeolithic, 3,000 plus years for the Old World Neolithic, and 200 plus years for the Industrial Revolutions. A similar pattern of acceleration was discovered in the great waves of life examined in Chapter 4, with each wave being about one-third the duration of the one before. In human society, as in life itself, the pace of change is accelerating. The reason is that both genetic change and technological change involve processes in which the outputs of one paradigm become the inputs of the next paradigm, because both life and human society are continuous living systems. As the thread of continuity has never been broken, neither system has had to return to the beginning. We can expect societal change to continue accelerating into the future.

The development path implied by the great technological paradigm shifts can be illustrated by reference to Figure 12.9 which, for obvious reasons, I have entitled the **great steps of human progress**. This figure refers to all societies in the known world. To clarify the process involved, I have truncated the horizontal time axis. In reality, most of the figure would have been taken up with the distance between the Palaeolithic and Neolithic Revolutions, with most of the change occurring along the right-hand vertical axis. Figure 12.9 is designed to show two things: the stepped profile of *potential* real GDP per capita at the global level made possible by the three paradigm shifts (heavy line); and the more gradual increase in *actual* real GDP per capita (broken line). As can be seen, potential GDP per capita increases relatively steeply – becoming more steep as we approach the present – but is then stationary for much longer periods of time which diminish geometrically over time. On the other hand, actual GDP per capita increases only gradually to the potential ceiling and describes a more wave-like development path. This catching-up process by actual GDP per capita is driven by the three great mechanisms discussed above. While there will be long periods when actual income

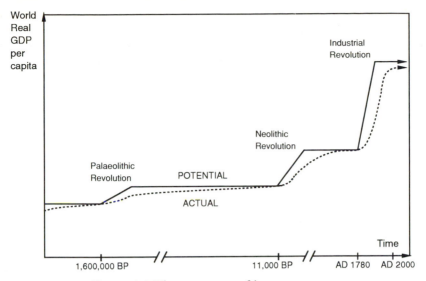

Figure 12.9 The great steps of human progress

approaches the potential ceiling, there will be other periods when it moves away again. Eventually, however, when the current technological paradigm has been fully utilized, actual income will press persistently against the potential ceiling. This is when the next technological revolution takes place.

Our model can explain the technological paradigm shifts in human society. It is a process that begins at the regional level and, later, spreads throughout the world. It begins in a region which is at the leading edge of the existing technological paradigm, such as the Rift Valley in East Africa at the dawn of mankind, or the Fertile Crescent in the ancient Old World or the Mesoamerican isthmus in the ancient New World, or England just before the Industrial Revolution (see Figure 8.2). In such a region, the exhaustion of all dynamic strategies, including the existing technological strategy after a long process of fine-tuning, will call forth a radically new set of technical ideas that causes a shift in the technological paradigm – a technological trans-formation. The reason for the paradigm shift is the continuing drive of economic agents in a highly competitive environment together with funda-mental change taking place in factor endowments – and relative factor prices – of natural, human, and physical resources. In particular, the price of natural resources rises sharply relative to all other factor prices; and of the others, the price of labour rises relative to the price of capital. Hence, there are powerful incentives to substitute capital for labour, and to invest in radically new techniques that will both save on old natural resources and exploit new natural resources. If human society somehow misses this obvious and rewarding possibility – although we have never failed to do so in similar

403

circumstances in the past – it will tear itself apart as regional warlords attempt to exploit the growing global instability and chaos. There is no standing still in a competitive world; no acceptable alternative to the Dynamic Society.

Each technological paradigm with its associated dynamic strategies provides the conditions that determine the characteristic optimum size for the economic systems that flourish within it. This optimum size can be defined in terms of both population and real GDP per capita. The optimum size of economic systems in the palaeolithic paradigm was very small, consisting of forager bands of about twenty-five people operating within tribal structures of about 500 people. While normal nutritional standards were perfectly adequate and leisure standards were relatively high (hunting and gathering occupied about five hours per day), their consumption of services from durables – such as housing, transport, communications, large-scale entertainment, welfare, etc. – was very low. This placed a low-level restriction on their total consumption and made them vulnerable to natural disasters.

In the neolithic paradigm, owing to an ability to produce sizeable surpluses, the optimum size of economic systems increased dramatically. Urban centres based upon agricultural hinterlands supported from 5,000 to 30,000 people depending upon the region and stage reached in the neolithic era, and operated within spheres of influence with as many people again. But by adopting the dynamic strategies of conquest or commerce, neolithic cities in the Old World increased to 400,000–1,000,000 people in empires that could be numbered in tens of millions (the Roman Empire in AD 14 had a population of about 54 million), while in the New World the population in cities reached 100,000–200,000 in empires of millions of people. While the normal nutritional standards of the majority of the population may have been little higher and their leisure standards much lower than those in the neolithic period, their consumption of services from durables (including better storage and distribution of food during natural disasters) was much higher. The ruling elite, however, were vastly more prosperous than tribal leaders in neolithic society. Overall, real GDP per capita had risen dramatically but the equity of distribution had fallen.

In medieval Western Europe, the fine-tuning of the neolithic technological system inherited from classical antiquity appears to have generated a marginal increase in the optimum size of regional capitals from about 30,000 in the early neolithic period to about 50,000 (the size of London) in 1500. This optimum was only transcended at this time by leading cities in conquest kingdoms (e.g. Paris 230,000) and major commercial regions (e.g. Milan 100,000) (Bairoch et al., 1988: 283). After the European breakout, city size quickly transcended the neolithic optimum through the returns from conquest and commerce. By 1700 the largest cities in Western Europe were London (570,000) and Paris (500,000). Yet cities of this size could not have been maintained in the face of an exhausting commerce strategy had it not been for the Industrial Revolution which transformed the optimum city size. London, for example, increased its population to 2.23 million in 1850, 6.62 million in 1900, and 10.4 million in 1985.

It is not clear that economic systems in the modern technological paradigm have achieved their optimum size. Populations of modern affluent cities can exceed 10 million people (the size of ancient empires), while developed nations can exceed hundreds, and ultimately thousands, of millions. In these developed nations real GDP per capita has not only reached very high historical levels but it is far more equitably distributed than before the Industrial Revolution. And it continues to grow.

The great dispersion

The first great mechanism driving our technological paradigm shifts was **the great dispersion** of the palaeolithic era. This involved the adoption of the extremely slow but very effective dynamic strategy of family multiplication and migration to enable greater control over unused natural resources. These resources were utilized through a hunter–gatherer technology. As we saw in Chapter 8, the great dispersion of modern man (*Homo sapiens sapiens*) – and there had been earlier dispersions of more primitive species such as *Homo erectus* – probably began in Africa about 100,000 years ago. By 40,000 BP most of Europe, Asia, Australia, and possibly both North and South America had been occupied (see Figure 8.1).

Once established in these new regions, hunter–gatherer societies continued to pursue the family multiplication strategy until, about 10,600 years ago in the Old World and 8,000–7,000 years ago in the New World, the palaeolithic ceiling of potential GDP per capita was reached. This occurred in particularly favourable areas that I have called **funnels of transformation** (Figure 8.2). These were narrow necks of land through which relatively large numbers of people passed and where competition was relatively high. With the exhaustion of the palaeolithic technological paradigm in these areas, the incentive was generated for a new technological breakthrough – the Neolithic Revolution. What started in these funnels of transformation spread slowly but steadily throughout the known world until all known natural resources were fully exploited and pressures mounted for a new paradigm shift into the agricultural era.

The great wheel of civilization

The mechanism driving the technological paradigm shift between the neolithic and modern eras was the **great wheel of civilization**. Each rotation of the great wheel brought the Dynamic Society closer to the limit of the old neolithic paradigm through population expansion and the transmission of ideas. It is a process of economic change in which each cycle begins anew. It is a process underlying the rise and fall of civilizations. There is no continuity between one great economic cycle and the next. Instead of being an ever-accumulating series of waves, the ancient mechanism of change is an ever-recurring wheel of rise and fall; of the phoenix emerging once more out of the ashes; of Sisyphus beginning once more to roll his rock up the mountain side. The reason for this eternal recurrence is that the great wheel of civilization is driven by the dynamic strategy of conquest. The conqueror must rebuild his empire anew on each and every occasion. Only through the great linear waves of economic change, which are driven by Daedalian technological change, can the great wheel be broken and human civilization be set free to soar with Icarus. But this escape may not be permanent. If we forget how we broke away from the eternal recurrence we will be doomed to join it again. The great waves of progress can always give way to the great wheel of conquest.

Why is it, most interested observers ask, that the great civilizations of antiquity were able to achieve so much in intellectual, political, social, administrative, and military terms, but so little in economic terms? In particular, why is it that the material standard of life did not increase significantly from the peak of one civilization to the next? Why did each successive civilization have to begin at roughly the same economic level? Why was the success of each ancient civilization specific to that civilization? Why wasn't ancient success cumulative? This multilayered paradox is resolved when we think of the period 5000 BC–AD 476 not in terms of the failure of the ancients to ride the great linear waves of economic progress, but in terms of their success in driving the great wheel of civilization.

The great wheel of ancient civilization rotates slowly in historical space without gaining the technological traction required to drive it upward from the plain of Sumer into the surrounding hills of GDP per capita. In Figure 12.10 four great wheels of economic growth have been depicted, each of which represents a single ancient Western civilization in a series of succession – that of Sumer, Assyria, Greece, and Rome. While the diameters of the wheels are slightly different owing to a marginal improvement in living standards over time as military and organizational structures became more efficient, they have a common axis which is fixed by a shared technology. That technology is a rotational two-field agricultural system based upon use of a light 'scratch' plough drawn by livestock, together with a system of irrigation. This economic system emerged from the Neolithic Revolution and the pioneering urban society of the Sumerians. While there were marginal improvements in this basic economic system between 3000 BC and the birth of Christ, little violence is done by assuming that the axis (AB) is fixed. It is important to bear in mind that while the 'great steps' diagram operates at the global level, the 'great wheel' diagram operates at the level of the individual society.

How does the great wheel diagram work? Somewhat arbitrarily, I have identified three main phases through which the wheel of each civilization

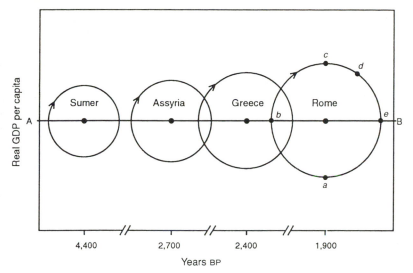

Figure 12.10 The great wheel of civilization

slowly rotates in a clockwise direction. Each great rotation takes from one to two millennia. Time on the horizontal axis is not continuous and only the central value has been noted for chronological convenience. We start at the low point of the wheel. The origin *a* of each civilization is small and unimpressive and, with the exception of Sumer, the pioneering civilization, it is overshadowed by its predecessor. But despite its unimpressive origins, there exists a transforming internal energy. This vitality is born of a competitive environment in which individuals struggle to live and prosper. As this internal energy is translated into economic expansion through family multiplication, the incipient core of a new civilization borrows ideas and techniques from its predecessor and applies these to its expanding society. Owing to this process of strategic imitation, real GDP per capita begins to grow, and the great wheel begins to turn slowly anew. Once our emergent civilization has borrowed all it can from the past, the wheel has reached point *b*, the maximum level of real GDP per capita that can be generated from the neolithic economic system common to the ancient world.

This is a critical point at which the great wheel could stop and even rotate back again. The most cost-effective way of maintaining positive economic growth in ancient societies – of continuing the upward swing of the great wheel – is through the adoption of conquest as the dominant dynamic strategy. A fortunate few, such as the Achaean Greeks and Phoenicians, were able to increase material living standards beyond this base level through commerce. But even here the conqueror was never far away. In the earlier phase of expansion driven by family multiplication, our emerging civilization came into conflict with neighbouring groups and was forced to develop an

407

effective military capability. To maintain momentum beyond point *b* a civilization needs to undertake large-scale investments in the skills and infrastructure of systematic war and conquest (and, for a few, commerce). This is the beginning of an increasing specialization in the dynamic strategy of conquest. As the net benefits to conquest begin to flow into the metropolis, the great wheel rotates slowly in a clockwise direction taking our new dynamic civilization with it into the higher altitudes of real GDP per capita. While it is not possible at the global level for real GDP per capita to exceed this ceiling (called 'potential' in Figure 12.9), individual societies employing either the conquest or commerce strategies can do so at the expense of other societies.

There are always limits to any dynamic strategy. Eventually the conquest strategy will be exhausted as the growing costs of extending and maintaining the empire absorb much of the benefits that it generates. More specifically, we can expect that beyond a certain stage in the expansion of empire, the marginal returns – that is, the net benefits generated by each step in the process of conquest – will begin to decline and, eventually, will be reduced to zero. At this stage the benefit to be derived from any further act of conquest will be totally absorbed by the cost of achieving it. As shown in Chapter 10, the Roman Empire reached this point with the conquest of Britain. This is the point at which the conquest strategy becomes totally exhausted. In terms of our great-wheel diagram, the rotating wheel has reached its highest point *c*.

It is not possible for human society in a competitive environment to stand still. If the old strategy has been exhausted and a new strategy cannot be quickly initiated – a very difficult achievement for a strategically specialized society – the great wheel will continue its journey in a clockwise direction, this time downwards. Once the empire has reached its furthest boundaries, self-interest will suggest to the empire leaders that, if it is not profitable to expand further they should at least attempt to maintain what they have achieved. What they usually fail to realize is that the empire is a dynamic entity. Its very existence depends upon the ability to continue to expand. The stationary state is not possible for a conquest society in a highly competitive environment because it is thrown back upon a neolithic economic system which is only able to deliver a real GDP per capita of AB in Figure 12.10. What is really required for survival is a reduction of real GDP per capita, population, and infrastructure to the optimum levels dictated by the neolithic economic system. But this is never acceptable to the old conquest society, which, because of its self-interested nature, wishes to maintain the *status quo*.

Any attempt to stabilize frontiers imposes severe strains upon the whole structure as conquest revenue and resources cease to flow into the metropolis. While the conquest cost structure is largely fixed, even in the longrun, the revenue structure reverts to the neolithic level. This requires additional taxes to be raised in an increasingly oppressive way on existing estates, which plays into the hands of those wishing to reap the whirlwind of chaos. Eventually, rebellions will erupt from within, which in turn will make it increasingly difficult to handle the usual pressures from without. The great wheel will continue to rotate towards *e* and beyond as the economic system grows increasingly inefficient; as the government panics, becomes increasingly oppressive, and undermines the monetary system; and as resulting inflation further erodes the real value of incomes. Those predatory societies waiting in the wings for their chance on centre stage will detect the empire's growing internal problems and will attack with renewed energy. Ultimately the forces of chaos from within and without will overwhelm the forces of order and the empire will collapse. Or the metropolis will just be abandoned because it is no longer an economically viable option once basic services can no longer be provided – once average variable costs can no longer be covered. The great wheel will have completed its slow rotation and will have come to rest. It is time for a new civilization to emerge from the ashes of the old – a time for the great wheel to begin rotating anew – for there is never any shortage of opportunists.

Each successive civilization represented in Figure 12.10, which relies upon the old neolithic economic system, will go through the same circular process. The great wheel will rise and fall, but will be unable to achieve traction. In this way each civilization will experience a process of sustained increase in material standards of living, possibly achieving periods of high rates of growth. But one should not be misled by the bold outlines of my great wheel diagram. The process of growth will not be smooth like the circumference of a circle – rather, it will fluctuate, with rapid growth leading to minor crises, followed by periods of temporary downturn and decline. In the Old World the great (non-linear) wave was about 320 years in duration, while it was about 250 years in the New World. There is, therefore, a wave within the circle.

The economic achievements of conquest, while impressive, cannot pass from one civilization to the next. They are specific to the conquering civilization, as each successive empire has to go through the process of conquest for themselves. Unlike progress achieved through technological change, it is not transferable. The circular development paths of each civilization in Figure 12.10 share the same axis. But each major ancient civilization is greater than the last and it carries the existing technology and economic organization to even more distant parts of the world until, eventually, global natural resources approach full utilization, the existing technological paradigm approaches exhaustion, and the signs of a new technological dawn begin to appear. This is the eternal recurrence of ancient civilization. Nietzsche (1968: 1067), initially a classical scholar, wrote about the 'world of the eternally self-creating, the eternally self-destroying, this mystery world of the twofold voluptuous delight . . . without goal, unless the joy of the circle is itself a goal'. And again: 'everything becomes and recurs eternally – escape is impossible!' But there is an alternative to Nietzschean affirmation of eternal repetition – technological change. Through technological change it is possible to transfer economic progress from one society to another without calling upon the horsemen of war. It is possible, through the technology strategy, to break into the great wheel of civilization and create the great linear waves of economic change.

The great linear waves of economic change

The Industrial Revolution not only ushered in a new technological paradigm, it also began a new era in which linear, if fluctuating, economic growth was possible. While the Neolithic Revolution gave rise to the eternal recurrence, the Industrial Revolution provided the means to convert the internal energy of dynamic materialism into continuous economic progress. This continuous progress has been transmitted through great linear waves of economic change that had their beginning about 1,000 years prior to the Industrial Revolution (see Figure 12.7). But the period of the Industrial Revolution was a critical watershed. Had it not been successful, the great wheel of civilization would have re-emerged. It has, as we know, been successful and the surging great waves of economic change are carrying society ever closer to the technological ceiling imposed by the industrial paradigm which, as before, will be transcended by a post-industrial technological paradigm.

What we need to consider here is how the mechanism of the great linear waves – and the smaller cycles it contains – are generated. Such an analysis should be able to explain not only the great waves of Western Europe over the past millennium, but also those operating within the great wheel of civilization detected in Figure 12.5. These great rhythms of the Dynamic Society emerge not from a particular time, place, or dynamic strategy, but from the eternal nature of the internal driving force – from materialist man in his competitive environment. The mechanism I have in mind is that cycles at various levels – from 3 to 30 years – are generated by the application and exhaustion of dynamic strategies. While the shorter-term cycles of three to twelve years are only of marginal interest here, they form the basis of the 'long waves' of about forty to sixty years. The smaller cycles can be accounted for by the cyclical pattern of investment in individual *projects* (rather than strategies) and technologies that are driven by the shortrun plans of economic agents, together with the subsequent exhaustion of those plans through declining marginal returns. The coordination of these investments by large numbers of economic decision-makers is determined by levels of entrepreneurial confidence in the economy. The main projects, involving new technologies, at the beginning of the upswing generate linkages that stimulate imitation in the Schumpeterian fashion.

More important are the longer cycles, which during the last century have been approximately forty to sixty years in duration (Solomou, 1987), as they are the basis for the 'great waves' of 300 years. There is no need to insist on perfectly regular cycles, just that there are long cycles of varying length –

410

which in the modern (and ancient) period appear to be about fifty years in duration – through which economic growth proceeds. These longrun cycles involve the coordinated investment plans of a generation of innovative economic agents and their imitators, which are ultimately exhausted by the second generation of investors following in the footsteps of their 'fathers' and living off the easy gains. Our second generation is able to achieve success by investing in existing successful activities rather than in new and more risky innovative projects. In effect, their plans are imitative rather than innovative, but they are rational in benefit–cost terms. Ultimately, however, the investment criterion deteriorates, the rate of return falls, and speculation becomes a major 'investment' activity as the second generation continues seeking the easy returns. As a result of this 'second-generation' effect, productivity declines, the economy stagnates, economic institutions are bankrupted, and the economy turns downwards into either sharp depression or extended recession. Only when the exhausted investment plans have been abandoned, only when the overextended 'first-generation' industries and technologies have been reconstructed, only when new or rejuvenated investment plans have been devised can the economy begin a new phase of longrun development. Inevitably the same pattern of innovative investment, imitation, over-expansion, speculation and depression will recur. Collective memory is short, but in any case it is never as powerful as the optimism of materialist man.

This strategic-demand model is seen as revisionist. It is advanced as a replacement for the traditional supply-side explanation of the long Schumpeterian cycles of about fifty years. Usually the long cycles are linked to the emergence of new technological ideas rather than to the strategic demand for these ideas. And even these supply-side forces are treated as exogenous to the model. Where demand is considered at all, it is final demand for consumer goods, which in reality is merely an outcome, not a cause, of strategic demand. W.W. Rostow, for example, has associated the long cycle with the emergence of five technological 'revolutions' involving a number of leading sectors: 1780s–1830s, cotton textiles, the steam engine, coke iron; 1840s–1900s, railroads and steel; 1900s–1960s, automobiles, electricity, chemicals; 1970s–, microelectronics, biotechnology, new industrial materials, lasers. These 'revolutions' are seen solely as the outcome of supply-side forces. Rostow (1990: 550) explains: 'Our approach is to impose a stable demand function over time, and to represent the introduction of new sectors into the economy as occurring due to a falling supply price associated with improving levels of technological knowledge.' Increasing technological knowledge is left unexplained, while the demand function, which is assumed to be stable, concerns final demand not strategic demand. This traditional type of 'model' explains little.

The 300-year cycles that have been detected above in the ancient Old and New Worlds and during the rise of Western civilization have been generated by large-scale dynamic strategies that are accumulations of the shorterrun

411

investment projects and lifetime investment plans. In turn, these are all part of the attempt, possibly extending over about four to eight generations, to exploit the potentialities of a major dynamic strategy such as conquest or technology advancement. In this dynamic process the opportunistic investment plans of individual decision-makers are transformed into the dynamic strategy of society through the 'strategic-imitation' mechanism (the microeconomic mechanism discussed in Chapter 8), and are supported by the emergence of a ruling elite sympathetic to this strategy. The upswing of the 300-year cycle will be punctuated by shorter cycles of the type briefly discussed above. After a number of generations (say three to six) a particular strategy, or combination of strategies, becomes 'locked in' owing to its initial success, to the growing ossification of societal institutions as the forces of order gain the upper hand, and to the 'second generation' effect of looking to the easy gains. Eventually the dynamic strategy is exhausted, and the returns to large-scale societal investment will decline, stagnate, and even become negative. At the same time, population and GDP per capita reach a peak and then begin their ritualistic descent. During the course of the extended contraction, which may last for two or three generations, old inflexibilities are removed and new ways are found to fine-tune the economy to take further advantage of the existing technological paradigm. This fine-tuning may involve further organizational change and, if the existing paradigm is neolithic, better agricultural techniques, and greater specialization owing to an expansion in, and sophistication of, international trade. These developments pave the way for further large-scale investment in a new strategy extending over many generations and a new longrun upswing in the Dynamic Society, until, in their turn, these new possibilities are exhausted.

It will be clear that these great-wave downturns are not a response to Malthusian crisis. They are not Malthusian for two reasons. First, they are not determined primarily by excessive population growth – which is a response to dynamic strategies – or by absolute limits to the supply of natural resources, but by the exhaustion of the prevailing dynamic strategy. Second, Malthusian effects are *not* long-term in nature but only short-term, owing to the rapid adjustment of population to the growth of food supplies (Malthus, 1970: 77–8). A long-term Malthusian crisis is an impossibility because the population will self-destruct. It is incompatible with the great-wave contractions that have existed for up to a century or more. As suggested earlier, this analysis of longrun downturns in terms of strategic crises is more general than the Malthusian analysis, and can be thought of as encompassing it as a special case that emerges only in a collapsing society.

Finally, do not expect to find statistical evidence of precisely regular cycles at any level. While the internal dynamic mechanism identified here would produce fairly regular cycles in a vacuum, these dynamic rhythms are distorted by the frequent but random impact of external shocks. Yet there is enough evidence throughout time and space to confirm the existence of

412

this endogenous cyclical process. Unfortunately, these externally caused irregularities have been seized upon by some empiricists as evidence that human society is driven by unsystematic exogenous forces (Lee, 1993; Solomou, 1987: 169–71).

Dynamic mechanisms and philosophical ideas

The analysis in this book suggests that dynamic economic processes are the prime mover behind cultural change in human society. This is particularly evident in man's changing philosophical view of life on Earth. It will be argued here that the various dominant dynamic strategies in the past have been largely responsible for shaping man's views about the nature of human history and even about the nature of time in the natural sciences.

It is generally acknowledged that while modern man embraces the idea of continuous progress or linear time, ancient man viewed life as essentially cyclical involving a process of creation, growth, decay, destruction, and recreation – a process of eternal recurrence. Richard Morris (1985: 10–11), for example, writes that ancient scholars

> believed that history followed cyclic patterns, and that there was a sense in which time could be thought of as being circular. We, on the other hand, habitually think of time as something that stretches in a straight line into the past and future.

But we can go further than this and identify three broad categories in the history of ideas on this issue that coincide with the palaeolithic, neolithic, and the modern eras.

During the palaeolithic era man's view of life was dominated by endless repetition (Eliade, 1971: ch. 1). Cycles of birth, death, and rebirth were celebrated in rituals involving the alternation of day and night, phases of the moon, seasons of the year, and recurrent floods and droughts. My argument is that the symbolism of the rituals celebrating endless repetition were not, as usually thought, a direct response to the rhythms of the natural world – which are obviously present in all eras – but rather a response to the economic dynamic of palaeolithic society, which was the substance of cultural reality. The dominant dynamic strategy of palaeolithic society – family multiplication and migration – was endlessly cyclical involving birth, growth, decay, death, and rebirth. All within the family of man. It was this dynamic process that dominated their daily lives and enabled them to survive and maximize their material returns as individuals and families. This, rather than the more esoteric activities of observing the night skies and predicting the phases of the moon and the seasonal solstices, shaped palaeolithic man's attitudes towards life. More esoteric knowledge was the occupation of a tiny minority of religious experts. The natural cycles in the physical world, however, provided a rich source of symbolism.

A more elaborate view of life was fashioned in ancient, or neolithic, societies in both the Old and New Worlds. In the Old World, both east and west, life was thought to go through a process of very long, endlessly recurring cycles determined either by cosmic forces, the constellations, or by the world's creator. One particularly influential view in antiquity was the 'Chaldean doctrine' popularized in the third century BC by Berossos' *Babyloniaca*, spreading throughout the Hellenic world and thereafter to the Romans and Byzantines. As Mircea Eliade (1971: 87) writes,

> According to this doctrine the universe is eternal but it is periodically destroyed and reconstituted every Great Year (the corresponding number of millennia varies from school to school); when the planets assemble in Cancer ('Great Winter') there will be a deluge; when they meet in Capricorn (i.e. at the summer solstice of the Great Year) the entire universe will be consumed by fire.

This great year was thought to be some 36,000 years long (Morris, 1985: 18). Some versions of this circular view, which were held by the Stoics and some Neoplatonic philosophers, saw each cycle as being a faithful repetition of the last, right down to the smallest factual detail (ibid.: 19–21). Also in China the idea of eternal recurrence, with a world cycle of 23,639 years, was central to Taoism. In India cosmic cycles of 12,000 divine years, or 4.32 million ordinary years, was a fundamental tenet of Hinduism. These cosmic cycles contained cycles within cycles, of which the smallest was, interestingly enough, 360 years. Buddhism and Jainism also accepted this pan-Indian doctrine of cyclical time and, I was pleased to discover, compared it to a wheel with twelve spokes (Eliade, 1971: 115–16).

In the New World, the various Mesoamerican civilizations also saw life as a succession of long recurrent cycles. According to the Maya, history repeated itself regularly and endlessly. At the end of each historical cycle of 256 years, history was expected to repeat itself. Dennis Puleston (1979: 63) explains:

> It is clear that the Maya conception of historical repetition did not entail an exact replication of past events but rather a conformance of history to certain underlying, predictable patterns as revealed in the katun prophecies. The prophecies, in turn, seem to have been largely based on an accumulation of recorded history.

Each great cycle was a process of creation, growth, destruction, and re-creation. The Aztecs also saw life as passing through similar cycles of creation and recreation. But they believed, as some pessimistic ecologists do today, that their civilization was the fifth and final creation. And the only way to prevent the setting of the fifth and final sun was through continuous human sacrifice (Thorne and Raymond, 1989: 250). Owing to their brief history, they focused upon the long cycle rather than the great wave, which by their reckoning was fifty-two years (Morris, 1985: 22).

414

Once again I will argue that this cyclical view of life which existed throughout the ancient world, both Old and New, was not a matter of psychological or religious necessity (to master the 'terror of history') as claimed by Eliade (1971: ch. 4); nor was it a response to the rhythms of the natural world. Rather, it was an outcome of the dynamic economic process that they all shared. As we have seen, in ancient societies the conquest and commerce strategies generated the great wheel of civilization which shaped their view of the world – past, present, and future. The world view of ancient man was grounded in economic reality. The explanation of the perceptions of life, therefore, is to be found not on the mountain tops but in the plains.

It is usually argued that the Judaeo-Christian tradition gave rise to the idea of linear or continuous history (Morris, 1985: 22): in effect, that the new world view was a product of cultural forces. God created the world which will continue to develop according to His will until the coming of the Messiah, who will bring history to a close. It is possible to interpret this theocentric view of history not as linear but as a single cycle which has its beginning and end in Christ the alpha and omega of the world (Gould, 1987: 21). Even so, within this religious tradition there were some – such as St Irenaeus of Lyons, St Basil, St Gregory, and St Augustine – who held the linear view of history while others – such as Clement of Alexandria, Minucius Felix, Arnobius, and Theodoret – held the older cyclical view (Eliade, 1971: 143–4). This competition between two Christian schools of thought continued throughout the Middle Ages down to the seventeenth century, after which the linear view became more influential and finally triumphed during the nineteenth century – the century of Darwin and the social Darwinists (or more correctly the social Lamarkists – Bowler, 1988: 39–40). Needless to say there were reactions against the triumph of progress, most notably by the classical scholar Friedrich Nietzsche, who attempted to revive the idea of the eternal recurrence of antiquity.

Clearly, the Judaeo-Christian tradition was not responsible for the dramatic change in the interpretation of history, because it harboured both views until at least the eighteenth century. And of course, in ancient society there had always existed a sense of historical narrative – as evidenced by the monuments marking events within the various dynasties of both the Old and New Worlds – even if this was embodied in the wider view of eternal recurrence. The most plausible explanation of the emergence of the idea of progress in history and life during the eighteenth and nineteenth centuries in Western Europe was the emergence at that time of the dominant dynamic strategy of tech-nological change. Through the Industrial Revolution, Western civilization has been able to break into the great wheel of civilization to create the great linear waves of economic change that have ever since produced systematic and linear economic growth. This view is diametrically opposed to the conventional wisdom which suggests that the emergence of the idea of linear time was responsible for the emergence of our modern technological civilization! Consider the claim of Richard Morris (1985: 85): 'It has been suggested by a number of writers, that the reason a technological society developed only in the West was that only the West possessed the concept of linear time.' This is a clear statement of the unsupportable view that ideas drive the Dynamic Society. It is also factually incorrect, as the technological origins of the West can be traced back to the early Middle Ages (Chapter 9); and the Sung Dynasty in China achieved a remarkable degree of technological change and economic growth from the tenth to the thirteenth centuries.

The transformation from the ancient to the modern economic dynamic had a profound effect not only upon scholars who, over the past few centuries, have generally thought in terms of continuous progress rather than recurrence, but also upon the willingness of others to accept these ideas. Any idea, no matter how profound, that is of no use to the Dynamic Society will just fade away. The idea of evolution or progress only became widespread during the first half of the nineteenth century, as can be seen in the approaches of Charles Lyell to geology, Charles Darwin to biology, and archaeologists to prehistory. Of the latter, Bruce Trigger (1978: 61) informs us that '[t]he main accomplishment of archaeology at this period was to document that technological progress, rather than degeneration or cyclical processes was the most prominent feature of human history'. While there is always an internal momentum in the development of ideas, they only become widely accepted if they are reinforced by what is happening in the real world around us. And in the real world of Victorian England evidence of economic 'progress' was abundantly clear.

Currently the ecological engineers are challenging the idea of progress. They believe that we can defy economic gravity and create an eternally stationary society if we place ourselves in their hands. While we shall return to this daunting possibility in the final chapter, it should be emphasized here that the Dynamic Society cannot stand still in a normally competitive environment – it cannot defy economic gravity. It must continue to change technologically or revert to the eternal recurrence. Their ideas, like those of the ancients, will not be sustained in the face of continued economic growth.

A new model to explain the dynamics of human society has been developed in this chapter. It is a model that emphasizes the role of economic agents who employ alternative dynamic strategies in order to achieve a competitive edge in the eternal struggle for life and prosperity. These dynamic strategies involve the extensive use of natural resources through reproduction and migration; the intensive use of existing resources through technological change; the acquisition of new natural, physical, and human resources through warfare; and the capture of commodities and financial resources through monopoly pricing in commerce. In this dynamic process, mankind is the driving force, and other variables, such as population, capital accumulation, and technical and organizational ideas, respond according to its decision to employ the most cost-effective strategy. The entrepreneurial use of dynamic strategies, and the inevitability of their exhaustion in a finite physical world, can explain the cyclical development of human society at a number of different levels. It can explain the technological paradigm shifts, the great wheel of civilization, and the great linear waves of economic change that have enabled the Dynamic Society to escape the eternal recurrence. This approach also highlights the similarities between the Dynamic Society and the dynamics of being which were investigated in Part I.

The dynamic model developed in this chapter can be used not only to explain the development path of human society in the past, but also to provide answers to some of the big questions currently being asked about the future. Is the Dynamic Society currently on a collision course with the natural environment? Will the outcome be collapse for both human society and the ecology? Are the ecological engineers correct that the only hope is, with their guidance, to achieve the stationary state? Or is there another way? These issues are explored in the final chapter entitled 'Edge of darkness?'

13

EDGE OF DARKNESS?

Bring me my bow of burning gold!
Bring me my arrows of desire!
Bring me my spear! O clouds unfold!
Bring me my chariot of fire!
(Blake, *Milton*, 1804–1808)

Out of the west came an irresistible force. A force of burning ambition. A chariot of fire. Its name was Alexander. Crossing the ancient rivers of the Euphrates and the Tigris, Alexander emerged on the plain of Gaugamela due north of the great city Babylon. Here he was confronted by a multi-national host assembled by Darius, king of the Persians. These forces of reaction included warriors – some of whom were mounted on wondrous animals such as elephants and camels – recruited from the many lands under the Persian king's control. Darius had chosen the field of battle carefully, even levelling the ground for his scythed chariots which he gambled would slice through the Macedonian phalanx. But the Greek chariot of fire was not so easily extinguished. Alexander, by using innovative strategy, was victorious and Darius, who had been watching from a position of safety, wheeled his chariot round and fled. Darius' retreat from this unstoppable force ended in the vale of death, and the Eternal City in all its splendour was Alexander's for the taking.

This journey of exploration is approaching its end. We have travelled through many lands over very long periods of time. It is now necessary to take stock of what we have seen and learned. It is time also to peer through the mists into that distant land in which none of us can travel – the future. We cannot go there but we can look at it through the lens of the past. Some major options are looming up before us, and we need to ensure that we make the right choices. We should not be diverted by those who are risk-averse – those riders in the chariot of retreat.

What have we seen and learned in the many strange lands of the past? First and foremost we have discovered that human society, like life, has an

418

internal dynamic which, in a competitive environment, *must* find expression in continual change. We have discovered that the existential model developed in Chapter 12 to explain the dynamics of human society can also be used with little modification to explain (Chapter 4) the dynamics of life in general. Basically, the dynamics of life is an economic rather than a scientific problem, involving proactive rather than passive individuals. As Darwin's model of biological evolution was based largely upon the theories of the classical economists, it can be encompassed by the more general dynamic model of the development of life constructed here.

We have seen that economic change proceeds in a number of predictable ways. There are three great dynamic mechanisms – the great dispersion, the great wheel of civilization, and the great linear waves of modern growth – of which the latter two are relevant to the future of human society. These three mechanisms have operated within a dynamic framework provided by the great technological paradigm shifts that have emerged in human history in an accelerating way. Over time, the intervals between these paradigm shifts and their duration have been shortening in a geometrical fashion, and have never failed to emerge when the old paradigm was exhausted. There is no reason to suppose that they ever will, driven as they are by the materialistically inventive spirit of mankind. They are indeed eternal. Possibly the greatest error we can make is to place unnecessary obstacles in their way in the mistaken belief that the signs of their coming are the signs of a collapsing ecology. Owing to their relevance to the future, we need only focus here upon the ancient and modern dynamics.

It is essential to realize that the modern pattern, involving a longrun increase in real GDP per capita via the great linear waves of economic change, is not inevitable. The Dynamic Society is capable of regressing back to the ancient pattern of eternal recurrence. The prevailing great wave could, under certain prescribed circumstances, become the great wheel of future civilizations. The key to the future resides in the technology strategy. If we lose power over this we will be plunged back into the zero-sum strategies of the ancient past. Until we finally recognize this possibility, the danger of retrogression will always exist.

Most observers appear totally unaware of this possibility. In fact, many natural scientists and ecological engineers are adamant that, if growth-inducing technological change is not brought to an immediate halt, our civilization will collapse. Some, as we saw in Chapter 6, are convinced that the world economy has already gone beyond the limits of the environment to sustain further economic and population growth. This can be translated into the terminology used in this book as meaning that the technological paradigm introduced with the Industrial Revolution is approaching exhaustion. Whether this is so has yet to be determined. It is illuminating, however, to see how our approaches to the same 'problem' differ. The ecological engineers claim that further growth beyond these natural resource limits will cause the entire ecological system to collapse. They demand, therefore, that the world immediately take steps to achieve the stationary state. In contrast, my analysis of the Dynamic Society suggests that further growth-inducing technological change is required to crash through the ceiling of the present technological paradigm. Failure to do so will end in the eternal recurrence of war and conquest.

How sound is the analysis of the ecological engineers? The critically important answer is that there is a fundamental flaw in their methodology. It is invalid to use computer simulation models in the analysis of non-marginal, longrun economic change. This technique is only valid when examining marginal changes in the shortrun and, even then, it is an *ad hoc* approach that does not focus on processes, only outcomes. The ecological engineers do not appreciate that by eliminating the technology strategy – the hallmark of the modern paradigm – it is not possible to continue to work within a model of this paradigm. On the one hand, they dismiss the very foundations of the modern paradigm – growth-inducing technological change – and, on the other, they base their simulation procedure on the observed behaviour of a few variables (such as population, resources, food, industrial output, and pollution) from that paradigm over the past generation or so. Logically it is not possible to do both, unless you are prepared to assume heroically and ahistorically that the nature of mankind, which is genetically determined, will suddenly be transformed. They assume that materialist man, who negotiated Western civilization through the Industrial Revolution, will, beyond the year 2000, be transformed into cultural man. No longer will mankind attempt to struggle for survival and the maximization of material advantage. This assumption may be convenient but it is denied by the entire history of the human race.

The only way to determine what might happen in the future to a world in which growth-inducing technology strategy has been outlawed is to employ what I have called historical dynamic modelling. This involves the use of the existential model of the Dynamic Society developed in Chapter 12 to simulate the future scenario envisaged by the ecological engineers. The outcome will be highly disturbing to those who have placed their faith in the policy prescriptions of the radical ecologists.

BEFORE 2000: A WORLD WITHOUT THE INDUSTRIAL REVOLUTION?

We cannot model the distant future, as some appear to believe, because we do not know what the next paradigm shift will involve. But we can model the past. To gain some insight regarding what would happen in the future if the technology strategy were denied, we should ask what the world would be like in AD 2000 if the Industrial Revolution – the modern technological paradigm shift – had not happened. In this way it is possible to compare the modelled outcome with what actually happened between 1760 and 2000. The world beyond 2000 cannot be meaningfully modelled if we eliminate the dominant dynamic strategy of technological change, because the recent past cannot be used validly to test the backward simulated results of the model (the method used to check the 'predictive' ability of the computer model). By employing historical dynamic modelling, however, we are not confined to the present economic dimension, nor do we need to assume heroically and ahistorically that the nature of mankind has suddenly been transformed after being genetically shaped for 2 million years by the struggle to survive in a competitive world.

The modern world described by the ecological engineers in *Beyond the Limits* is similar to the historical circumstances of Western Europe in 1700 just prior to the Industrial Revolution when natural resources were being rapidly depleted. In the name of resolving current ecological problems they are asking us to eliminate economic growth by using technological change in a sustaining rather than a transforming way. We can model this problem historically by showing, in a logical way, what would have happened if the technological paradigm shift known as the Industrial Revolution had not happened. This may appear to be a daunting task, but provided we are willing to go far enough back in time, it is quite manageable. By taking an extremely longrun approach to the modern period, we can throw light on even the most complex issues. The value of the historical approach is that it can tackle the big issues that are completely beyond the reach of the deductive approach employed by both the economist and the ecological engineer.

A more limited counterfactual proposition – both in time and scope – has been examined recently by Joel Mokyr (1993b: 119–20). He asks: what would the level of GDP have been in 1830 if population and resources had grown at their actual historical rates while, at the same time, there had been no increase in productivity? This is *not* the same as testing whether there had been no Industrial Revolution. While three alternative assumptions for the savings ratio are employed by Mokyr, no attempt is made to take into account historical events such as the Napoleonic wars or bad harvests. This limited counterfactual exercise is not very helpful – other than to *illustrate* that if, in a *ceteris paribus* world, you hold one variable constant the outcome will change – because it is not based upon a realistic economic or, better still, a historically determined model. It is unrealistic to assume that the world's leading economic and maritime power would have continued to increase its population in the face of significantly declining living standards over a period of three generations without embarking upon a compensating campaign of conquest.

What was the position in which England, one of Europe's most advanced economies, found itself around 1700? As can be seen from Figure 12.7, the population and real GDP of England had been static for about half a century, real GDP per capita had grown little (0.1 per cent per annum) for about a century, and rural prices had been falling for fifty years. This had come after an amazingly energetic upswing in the sixteenth century, which was the last hurrah of the late-neolithic technological paradigm. After a thousand years of fine-tuning, the capacity for further increases in productivity from this paradigm had come to an end. The natural resources of England had been used as intensively as the existing paradigm allowed. And the commerce strategy, which had fuelled this final growth surge and enabled England greatly to exceed the optimum size dictated by the late neolithic technological paradigm, was now largely exhausted. England now appeared to be at the crossroads. In the absence of a new dynamic strategy, it would face a strategic crisis that would definitely lead to a severe downturn and possibly to collapse. Other countries in Western Europe were also approaching the same state in which England now found itself. What road would they take?

As we know with hindsight, Britain – followed closely by France, Belgium, USA, Germany, and so on – went through a technological transformation later known as the Industrial Revolution. The question we wish to answer here is: what would have happened in Western Europe and, hence, the rest of the world, if this technological transformation had not been possible owing to 'an act of God'? History provides us with two possible scenarios, of which only one matches the conditions prevailing in Western Europe in the eighteenth century. The two possibilities arise from widely different competitive environments – one is the case of virtually no external and limited internal competition, and the other is the case where both external and internal competition was intense.

The prime case of a society experiencing little or no external competition is Aboriginal Australia before British settlement in 1788. As shown in Chapter 8, it is generally accepted that the first human inhabitants migrated to Australia from Southeast Asia at least 60,000 (possibly 100,000–140,000) years ago. The original inhabitants, who were reinforced by ripples of new arrivals, appear initially to have occupied the northern coast of Australia and then, through family multiplication and continued migration, moved round the coast (reaching 'Tasmania' after 2,000 years), possible only then moving inland. As these new arrivals faced an abundant supply of resources in a land both accessible and moderate of climate, it is reasonable to expect that expansion would have reached the maximum rate possible in a palaeolithic society, particularly as there were no natural predators. Hence, the main phase of population growth would have occurred during the first half of the period before British settlement, rather than the last few millennia as some have claimed. Also, the method of gradual settlement in a land with no natural 'funnel of transformation' would have minimized internal conflict. As we saw in Chapter 8, the archaeological evidence suggests that by 20,000 years ago all parts of Australia had been inhabited and the continent's natural resources were fully exploited with the available palaeolithic technology.

The relevant question is: why, once all resources had been fully exploited using a palaeolithic technology, did not a neolithic revolution, involving settled agriculture and urban centres, occur? The answer can be found in the absence of significant external and internal competition in Australia 20,000 years ago. As Australia was effectively isolated from outside competition, particularly after the final rising of the seas from 15,000 to 5,000 years ago and as the pattern of settlement minimized internal competition, there was no incentive to introduce a Neolithic Revolution. The costs of doing so would have far exceeded the perceived benefits, particularly as Australian Aborigines were unable to factor into their calculus the eventual British invasion some 20,000 years in the future. Only by controlling the size of their families through abortion and infanticide and bringing their population into longrun equilibrium with the changing stock of natural resources could Aboriginal Australians prevent their living standards from falling. It is quite likely that the Aboriginal population of some 20,000 years ago was about the same as in 1788, around 1 million people. This was a major achievement, as few societies have ever been able to strike this delicate balance without collapse. Of course, 'longrun equilibrium' is not the same as 'stagnation', as population would have fluctuated gradually in accordance with changes in climate and the rise and fall of the seas, which influenced the amount of land available for hunting.

While longrun equilibrium between population and natural resources is possible in the absence of significant external and internal competition, this was not the situation in which the kingdoms of Western Europe found themselves in 1700, or in which we find ourselves today. Western Europe had been a cauldron of intense internal and external competition throughout the previous millennium. There are, as we have seen, numerous historical examples in the ancient world of intensely competitive environments which can be drawn upon to construct a more realistic scenario for Western Europe between 1700 and 2000. Basically they fall into two main groups. First, there is the group involving highly competitive city-states which, while involved in regular warfare, also exploited economic activities such as commerce and colonization to improve their living standards. Examples include the civilizations of Sumer and Greece. In these civilizations, war – while a serious and deadly activity – was not employed as the dominant dynamic strategy, as there were always other economic opportunities to be exploited more cheaply.

Second, and of more relevance to our hypothetical construct in Europe around 1700, are the city-states or kingdoms that could only improve their prospects at the expense of their neighbours because various economic opportunities in trade and migration had been crowded out by larger neighbours. Examples include Assyria, which in about 1300 BC was crowded out by the Hittites, the Mitanni, the Aramaeans, and the Kassite kingdom of Babylon. The only way to expand and prosper was through conquest. This gave birth to the Assyrian Empire from about 911–612 BC. Another example is the kingdom of Macedonia under Philip (382–336 BC) and his son Alexander (356–323 BC), which was hemmed in by the Thracians and Illyrians in the north, the Greeks in the south, the Persians in the east, and the Carthaginians in the west. These societies monopolized available commerce and colonization. Expansion, therefore, meant conquest. By 323 BC the empire of Alexander extended from the Greek mainland in the west to the Indus Valley in the east, and the upper Nile in the south – an empire based upon war.

Our final and most famous example in this group is Rome. When the Roman Republic was established in 509 BC, it was a tiny city-state surrounded by highly successful civilizations: the Etruscans in the north of Italy (whose domination Rome had only recently thrown off) and beyond them the Gauls; the Greek world extending from southern Italy and Sicily in the west to the Greek peninsula in the east (and beyond them the fabulous Persian Empire); and the Carthaginian Empire in the western Mediterranean. In such a crowded Mediterranean world, colonization and the easy gains from trade were precluded. The only prospect for expansion and prosperity was through war and conquest. Rome's probability of success was low. But they rose to the challenge and took control of Italy by 220 BC, of the western Mediterranean after the defeat of Carthage in 201 BC, and of the Hellenistic world by 167 BC. This expansion through conquest continued for another three centuries until stagnation set in and Rome finally collapsed in AD 476.

In the light of this historical experience, what prospects lay ahead in 1700 for a Europe denied the possibility of an Industrial Revolution by 'an act of God'? Clearly, the first possibility considered – the achievement of longrun equilibrium between population and natural resources at a given level of technology – was not possible. This required an absence of external competition, as in Aboriginal Australia before 1788, and a long slow process of adjustment to an initial abundance of natural resources using a palaeolithic technology (that prevented the accumulation of surpluses). For a thousand years Western Europe had been surrounded by aggressive and highly competitive neighbours, including the Muslims in the south, the Turks in the south-east, the Poles and Russians (and beyond them various dynamic Asian nomadic societies) in the east, and the Vikings in the north. And within Western Europe competition between the large number of small kingdoms had been extremely intense. Only the economic safety valves of technological change and commerce had prevented the earlier emergence of large-scale conquest as a reality.

After 1492 the intense internal conflict in Western Europe broke out into the rest of the world, with Spain and Portugal leading and, after 1600, with the Dutch, English, and French following. While, this breakout of the Western Europeans might have been expected to lead to a reduction of competitive pressure within Europe, this was not the case. As well as expanding into the

New World, Spain also embarked upon a campaign of conquest within Europe which, after a long clash (1495–1560) with France over northern Italy, led to a modest Spanish empire in the western Mediterranean, Sicily, and Italy. Over the next two centuries the European struggle for territory continued north of the Alps and centred on wars between France and the various Germanic kingdoms. These inconclusive conflicts included the Thirty Years War (1618–1648) between France, Austria, various Germanic kingdoms, and Sweden; the struggle for the Netherlands (1689–1697) between France and a coalition of England and the Dutch Republic; the War of Spanish Succession (1701–1713) between France, Austria, and Savoy; and the Seven Years War (1756–1763) between Prussia and Austria.

Not only did internal conflict appear to intensify in the period after 1500, but the European breakout carried it to the rest of the world, with conflict between the Dutch and both the Spanish and Portuguese in the Americas, Africa, India, and Southeast Asia; between the British and French in North America; and between the British, the Portuguese, and Dutch in Africa and Southeast Asia. Clearly, in the face of this intense military competition within and without Europe, the stationary state predicted by classical economists in the early nineteenth century was a spectacular flight of fantasy. It contradicted the historical experience of the previous thousand years, in failing not only to comprehend the role of military competition, but also to realize that sustained economic growth was a characteristic feature of European experience. And, more surprisingly, it denied the changes taking place around them in the very midst of the Industrial Revolution.

Could the opening up of the New World through colonization and trade have provided an outlet for these competitive forces? Possibly in the short term, but it would only have postponed the development of a new global empire through conquest. It is important to recognize, however, that the benefits from colonization of the New World by late-neolithic powers were limited. Apart from the initial windfall gain from plunder which had multiplier effects throughout Western Europe, there would have been little generation of new wealth from Mesoamerica because both the conquered and conquerors were neolithic societies. Indeed, the specialized late-neolithic technology of Europe, fine-tuned over a thousand years for the climate and soils of northern Europe, is unlikely to have been as appropriate in the shortrun as the home-grown technology of Mesoamerica. Admittedly, the contrast between the two technologies was greater in North America and Australasia, but we should not exaggerate the net gains to be made. The more spectacular gains from colonization occurred in the nineteenth century *after* the Industrial Revolution had significantly increased the productive potential of these new regions. Remember also that trade would have been conducted in sailing ships, rather than steamships. Once the easy gains from colonization and trade had been exhausted, the kingdoms of Western Europe would have been at each others' throats again in deadly earnest.

In the absence of the Industrial Revolution at a time when the neolithic technological paradigm was completely exhausted and the leading European nations had expanded well beyond their optimum size, the combination of competition within and without Europe would have provided, in a relatively short period of time after the mid-eighteenth century, overwhelming incentives for conquest on a scale that not even the emperors of Rome could have dreamed of. Conquest would have begun in Europe – possibly through a combination of the two most wealthy maritime powers, England and the Dutch Republic, who together in 1697 had managed to thwart France's ambitions in the Netherlands – and would have spread quickly to the rest of the world. The great wheel of civilization driven by war and conquest would have begun to turn once more.

The Industrial Revolution, therefore, almost certainly prevented the beginning of a new phase of conquest – a retrogression to the ancient dynamic mechanism – that would have included not only Europe but the rest of the world. Within a new world empire based upon conquest, there would be little generation of new wealth, except as the natural resources of the New World were brought into the late-neolithic process of production. As already suggested, the scope for increased productivity for these new regions in a pre-industrialized world was not very great. As in the Roman Empire, global economic growth would be extinguished. There would be, however, a redistribution of existing wealth in favour of the conquering empire, with a reduction in the wealth and income of the conquered regions. Conquest is a zero-sum game: material living standards of the conqueror would have increased through deprivation of the vanquished. Within the new global empire, wealth and income would be monopolized by the aristocratic military elite and, hence, income would become even more inequitably distributed than it had been in 1700. Similarly, population growth in the metropolis would be supported by the inflow of material returns from the conquest, while at the margins of empire population would fall, or at least be maintained at a significantly lower material standard of living. World population would probably have peaked at about 900–950 million, a level actually achieved in 1800. Here then is a world in which global population increase and economic growth have been eliminated and in their place have been substituted world domination and immiserization through conquest. Not a happy trade-off.

The historical role of the Industrial Revolution (i.e. of technological change and continued economic growth) can be seen clearly in the contrast between the world as we know it now and our hypothetical late-neolithic world for the year 2000. It would be a world based upon an agricultural system inherited from the ancient world (although adapted to various regional differences around the world) in which human (particularly slave) and animal power dominated. Urban industries would be based upon labour-intensive craft activities, and transport would depend upon animal power on the land and windpower on the seas. The political and social system would have regressed from its mercantilist form in 1700 to one based upon an aristocratic warrior elite. Wealth and income would have become more highly concentrated in the hands of the few who drove the conquest-oriented system. And there would be no significant increase in global real GDP per capita. Also, the cultural system built upon this economic base is, as suggested in Chapter 11, unlikely to have been particularly glorious. Conquerors do not make great patrons of the arts. If such a system lasted as long as the Roman Empire it would exist until the year 2500 or beyond.

BEYOND 2000: A WORLD WITHOUT GROWTH?

The above exercise in historical dynamic modelling clarifies the current debate about whether the developed world has exceeded the limits to growth and whether the elimination of growth-inducing technological change will be beneficial to human society and to the ecology. It suggests that to deny the dominant growth-inducing technology strategy – which could only be achieved through some sort of global dictatorship – would not eliminate the attempt of materialist man to maximize material advantage, but merely divert it into other less acceptable strategies.

Human nature is, as shown by our study of the past, unchanging. As we have seen, it is genetically determined, and education has not been able to modify it fundamentally. If the study of history tells us anything it tells us this. Hence if the ecological engineers are serious about eliminating growth, they will have to change their methods. Rather than attempting to inform and persuade the citizens of the world, who will continue to pursue their economic advantage, they will have to persuade some potential eco-dictator to place a ban on economic growth and population increase.

If this could be achieved, what would be the outcome? Our historical model provides an unambiguous answer. Human nature is constant, but the dynamic strategies employed to achieve human desires are variable. If growth-inducing technology could be banned, economic decision-makers would merely seek out other strategies. The key question is: what dynamic strategies other than technological change will be available to us in the future? What about the commerce strategy? As we saw in Chapter 11, modern international trade is driven by technological change which generates new products and new preferences. Hence, if growth-inducing technological change is elimi-nated, there will be no further *increase* in trade; it might even decline from present levels. And in the modern competitive world there is little chance for favoured nations to gain monopoly access to markets or extraordinary profits from new products. What about the colonization strategy generally associated with trade in the past? The era for establishing new colonies has long since passed because of the widespread nationalistic feeling generated by growing economic and, hence, political independence. Future colonization of the type achieved in the past could only be gained through large-scale military action, as was attempted by Hitler in the 1940s.

Quite clearly the only remaining dynamic strategy is war. In this future scenario, where growth is eliminated by coercion, there would be war between the dynamic strategists and the oppressive global power. Any global power that outlawed the technology strategy would need to be prepared to fight hard and long. The outcome would be disastrous for the world, particularly if it involved nuclear weapons, plunging it into a darkness from which it might never emerge.

The ecological engineers, like Aztec priests of the fifteenth century, see mankind approaching the edge of darkness and, at all costs, want to hold human society back from that edge. While the Aztec priests attempted to do so by continuous human sacrifice, the high priests of ecology want to pluck out the very heart of the Dynamic Society. If the ecological engineers were successful in their quest, they would actually push us all into the abyss of war and conquest. Even if a stable outcome eventually emerged, the great waves would have been replaced by the great wheel – the eternal recurrence of war and conquest – and all existing wealth would be focused in the hands of the warrior elite in the successful conquest state. Not only would this dramatically increase inequality within and between regions, it would, ironically, have an infinitely worse impact upon the physical environment than the current technology strategy both because of the impact of war and because of the removal of the population safety-valve normally provided by technological change.

Such an extreme outcome is probably highly unlikely, not through lack of intention but lack of persuasiveness by those who would hold us back. It is unlikely that the ecological engineers will ever be able to convince either individuals or global organizations to pursue policies that will minimize the probability both of survival and of material advantage. Only an irrational eco-dictator would even attempt to do this. Yet irrational dictators have emerged in the past during great economic crises: who in 1925, for example, believed that Hitler would actually implement the plans outlined in *Mein Kampf*? Similar crises in the future are not impossible, particularly if we turn our face against economic growth. The point which needs to be made is that even if the ecological engineers were successful, their very success would generate substantially more misery and damage to society and ecology than their failure. This conclusion, however, should not be seen as a criticism of all those genuine environmentalists who are rightly concerned with both the environment *and* human society, but rather as a warning to those who may not realize that the radical engineering of society in the name of the ecology is not compatible with human freedom and well-being.

It is more likely that the ecological engineers will be only partially successful. But by persuading even a significant proportion of individuals and global organizations that the historically familiar signs of a technological

428

paradigm approaching exhaustion are instead the signs of a world teetering on the edge of darkness, they may do considerable and unnecessary damage. Through costly and unnecessary government intervention at the national and global levels, they may contribute both to the weakening of Western civilization by suppressing the role of independent regions in the development of new technologies (Chapter 6) and by reducing its economic resilience, and to the delay in any future technological paradigm shift. This may be enough to create an economic crisis that will set free once more the irrational forces of destruction. A future paradigm shift is necessary not only to increase average material standards of living beyond the late-industrial technological paradigm level but also to distribute them more equitably between nations, just as the Industrial Revolution provided greater equality between social groups within nations (Snooks, 1994b: chs 1 and 3). The history of humanity over the past 2 million years gives us every confidence that such a transformation – the fourth so far – will be forthcoming.

In Chapter 9 it was shown that the distance between paradigm shifts and their duration has been declining in geometric fashion. The time taken for the technological shifts to occur involved hundreds of thousands of years for the Palaeolithic (c. 1.6 myrs ago), 4,000 years for the Neolithic (10,600 years ago), and 100 years for the Industrial (c. 1760) Revolutions. This suggests that the next paradigm shift could begin soon and could be completed in no more than a generation or so. The future revolution, as history has suggested, will release population from the present natural resource limits and, as a result, actually *reduce* environmental degradation. This is because it will no longer be necessary to push natural resources to their limits with an increasingly restricted technology, and because higher levels of real GDP per capita in the Third World will lead to a levelling-off of population, as has already occurred in developed nations (United Nations, 1991). Existing projections for the Third World, which show continued increases in population, although at a declining rate, over the next 150 years, are based upon the economic system of the present paradigm. Under the future paradigm these projections will be no longer relevant and will have to be revised downwards. This occurred in developed countries after the Industrial Revolution. The present concerns about overpopulation and environmental degradation, therefore, will be overcome by the future technological paradigm shift. This conclusion is not wishful thinking, because it is based upon an analysis of human society over the past 2 million years. But this is not to say that we should abandon attempts to protect the environment, just that we should not allow this remedial action to derail the Dynamic Society into the abyss of war and conquest.

What will the fourth technological paradigm shift bring? To answer this question would be like attempting in 1750 to say what would unfold from the Industrial Revolution. While there were signs to be read in the mid-eighteenth century, such as the growing use of fossil fuels, there was no way to tell where it would all end. Yet we can speculate sensibly about a central feature of all economic revolutions – the source of energy. The first revolution saw the extension of human energy with the use of more efficient tools; the second revolution saw the partial substitution of animal, water, and wind energy for human energy; and the third revolution saw the substitution of thermal energy based upon fossil fuels for both human and animal energy. It appears highly likely that the fourth revolution will involve the substitution of solar energy for fossil-fuel energy. This will resolve, for all practical purposes, the problem that increasing entropy (the outcome of depletion of natural resources and the generation of wastes) – based upon the second law of thermodynamics (Ekins, 1994: 291–2) – might ultimately pose for the dynamics of human society. From the fourth revolution, physical constraints upon growth will be limited only by the flow of solar energy.

We can avoid blundering over the edge of darkness only by pushing beyond the limits of the existing technological paradigm as we have always done. To shrink back from doing so by rejecting growth-inducing technological change – as the ecological engineers maintain that we should – is to risk plummeting into the abyss of war and conquest. By crashing through the limits of an exhausted late-neolithic technological paradigm, the Industrial Revolution enabled us to escape from the eternal recurrence of conquest that had always dominated civilization. When we finally reach the ceiling of the late-industrial paradigm we will need to shrug off those who would hold us back, out of ignorance, fear, or self-interest, and break out into a new paradigm. There is no acceptable alternative. The history of the Dynamic Society is an optimistic story, and will continue to be so if we choose to ride the chariot of fire rather than the chariot of retreat.

The end of the Dynamic Society? There is no end towards which it is inexorably progressing. There is no final destination. Only continuous journeying. While human life continues to cling to the Earth, the forces driving human society will never be exhausted, as they are fuelled by an unending desire to survive and prosper. And as there is no limit to human desires there can be no end to scarcity, no end to economics or materialist man. The last man *is* the first man. The Dynamic Society, therefore, has no end or beginning. It is an eternal entity. The Eternal Dynamic Society.

GLOSSARY OF NEW TERMS
AND CONCEPTS

As *longrun dynamics* is a new area of study, it has been necessary to develop and employ a range of new terms and concepts. To assist the reader, these terms and concepts have been brought together and briefly defined in this Glossary. When a new term or concept is first mentioned in a chapter it has been printed in bold type. Italics in the Glossary have been used to indicate that additional concepts are also defined here.

Collapse. See *strategic crisis*.

Commerce strategy. Commerce, like conquest, has been used by ancient societies to lift its populations and real GDP per capita above the optimum levels dictated by the neolithic *technological paradigm*. Through monopoly access to markets and commodities, commerce empires have been able to grow and prosper in the most remarkable way. But the cost of this rapid growth is eventual collapse, because once the commerce strategy has been exhausted the empire superstructure cannot be financed from internal sources. This strategy is closely associated with colonization which develops in order to facilitate the commerce strategy. Also see *dynamic strategies*.

Conquest strategy. This is the main *dynamic strategy* employed by ancient societies to increase their size – in terms of population and material living standards – above the optimum determined by the neolithic technological paradigm. Conquest is a zero-sum game with the conqueror growing at the expense of the vanquished. The ultimate cost of this strategy, however, is collapse, because once it has been exhausted the former conquest society is thrown back upon its neolithic economic system which cannot support the structure of empire. Also see *zero-sum dynamic change*.

Dynamic materialism. This is the term coined in this study to encapsulate the process by which economic decision-makers attempt to achieve their materialist objectives in a competitive environment by adopting the most cost-effective *dynamic strategies* and *dynamic tactics*. The essential components of dynamic materialism are a typically competitive environment in which mankind struggles against other species and its own kind for scarce natural resources in order to survive and prosper. Those circumstances bring out a heightened ambition, together with an aggressive and creative energy, in what has been called here *materialist man*.

Dynamic strategies are those strategies employed by decision-makers attempting to maximize the probability of survival and prosperity. In the Dynamic Society these strategies include *family multiplication, conquest, commerce*, and *technological change*. The adoption of any one of these strategies will depend upon factor endowments and, hence, relative factor prices, and will require investment in specialized infrastructure. This investment generates a stream of positive net returns. Economic growth, therefore, is strategy-led. A dominant dynamic strategy will be pursued until it has been economically exhausted, which will occur when the marginal cost of this strategy equals its marginal revenue. This leads not to *collapse* but to equilibrium.

Dynamic strategy model. This is the name given to the model used in this study to analyse the dynamics of human society. It focuses upon the role of economic decision-makers who attempt to maximize the probability of their survival and material prosperity by investing in a range of dynamic strategies including *family multiplication, conquest, commerce*, and *technological change*. This model has also been employed to explain the dynamics of life before the emergence of mankind, by which individual life forms 'invest' in the dynamic strategies of reproduction, predation, symbiosis, and genetic change. In both applications of the model the dynamic strategy employed is that which is most cost-effective.

Dynamic tactics are the methods employed by *materialist man* to gain a disproportionately large share of the surplus generated by the Dynamic Society. Essentially they involve a clash between the *forces of order and chaos*.

Economic distance is a key concept in the 'concentric spheres' model of human behaviour developed elsewhere (Snooks, 1994a: 50–1) and used in this book. In this model the individual is at the centre of a set of concentric spheres that define the varying strength of cooperative relationships between him and all other individuals and groups in society. The strength of the economic relationship between the central individual and any other individual or group – which could be measured by the economic distance between them – will depend upon how essential they are to the maximization of his utility. Those aspects of the central individual's objective function that require the greatest cooperation – such as the generation of love, companionship, and children – will be located on spheres with the shortest economic distance from the centre (and vice versa). This is a simple economic model, but it can explain the nature of human relationships where complex genetic models (Dawkins, 1989: 91) fail completely.

It also explains economic decision-making in the household as well as the market sectors and in human society throughout space and time.

Economic expansion refers to economic change not encompassed by the concept of *economic growth*. It is defined (Snooks, 1994a: 127–9) as an increase in the number of households (or family units) without any increase in real household income or *Gross Community Income* (*GCI*). This can occur either by bringing unutilized natural resources into the system of production, or by a more intensive use of existing resources through technological change, or both. The family or household is the source of economic expansion. In short, economic expansion is household multiplication.

Economic growth is defined as a change in *Gross Community Income* (*GCI*) per household rather than the more conventional measure of GDP per capita (Snooks, 1994a: 25–7). It is contrasted with *economic expansion*. In order to avoid confusion at both the analytical and communication levels it is essential to restrict the use of this term to the above concept. It is most unfortunate that recently the term 'intensive economic growth' has been used for the above concept and 'extensive growth' has been used for what is really economic expansion rather than economic growth. In fact economic expansion (i.e. an increase in the numbers of households and population) can arise from both the extensive and intensive use of natural resources. Invariably authors who employ this confusing terminology lapse into the use of the summary term 'economic growth' without qualification.

Economic resilience is the command nations have over material goods and services, and is measured by GDP per capita. It is a measure of society's ability to compete and survive, and should be contrasted with the concept of quality of life, which has little to do with survival in the longrun. Economic resilience is the power of nations, and of human society itself, over longrun survival.

Environmental dynamic change (EDC) is economic change achieved through the dynamic strategy of family multiplication. This involves an increase in the number of family units (households) for the purpose of gaining greater control over unused natural resources with a given state of technology (Snooks, 1994a: 127). It leads to population increase and migration and is the basis of the 'primitive dynamic' that has been called here the *great dispersion*, which in palaeolithic times led to the occupation of all continents except Antarctica by modern man. This dynamic mechanism has involved *economic expansion* without *economic growth*. Also see *zero-sum dynamic change*.

Existential models are empirical models of reality – or models of existence – and can be contrasted with the logical or deductive models of physics and economics, which are merely constructs of the mind. Deductive models are powerful tools that can be used selectively in the reconstruction of dynamic processes, but are limited by the range and complexity of issues they can examine. As existential models are based upon dynamic *timescapes*, they can liberate us from the limitations of deductive thought. They set free the imagination to range over the actual patterns of existence. And in these patterns we can see the dynamic processes of reality.

Family multiplication strategy. This is the oldest *dynamic strategy* known to mankind – a strategy it has in common with other animal species. It involved the exploitation of unused resources through procreation and migration to new regions. By increasing the size of the extended family and gaining a greater control over natural resources, the family head was able to achieve his objectives of survival and the maximization of material advantage. This was the force that drove the primitive dynamic which has been called here the *great dispersion*.

Forces of order and chaos. These are the *dynamic tactics* employed by *materialist man*. Any healthy and viable society must achieve a balance between these forces and those who employ them. The forces of order arise from the strong desire of those in authority, or those with a substantial economic interest in the existing system, to impose order by encouraging or forcing other people to conform to their values. The forces of chaos, on the other hand, arise from an equally strong desire on the part of those who do not have a stake in the system to disrupt and overthrow the existing order. These forces, therefore, are used as *dynamic tactics* within society (rather than *dynamic strategies* by society) by individuals and groups who hope to capture an unequal share of the surplus generated by the Dynamic Society.

Funnel of transformation. This is a physical environmental factor that helped to determine where the Neolithic Revolution would occur when the palaeolithic technological paradigm was approaching economic exhaustion. In the Old World this was the Fertile Crescent and in the New World it was the Mesoamerican isthmus. It is highly likely that the Rift Valley of East Africa played a similar role in the Palaeolithic Revolution (the shift from scavenging to hunting). These were corridors of heightened competition, appropriate resources, and exchange of ideas through which peoples from several continents had to pass. They were the sites of technological revolution and the sources of its transfer to the rest of the known world.

Genetic paradigm shift. Once the introduction of new genetic 'ideas' in a dominant species has reached its limits – once the existing genetic paradigm has been exhausted – there will be a collapse in the dominant species as it has no further dynamic options at a time when it is being challenged by other aspiring species. Such a collapse, which may be reinforced by external shocks, will lead to the emergence of a new set of dominant species. This can be thought of as a genetic paradigm shift, which is the biological equivalent of a *technological paradigm shift* (which involves a collapse not of the human species but of the old economic system). It gives rise to the genetic profile known in the natural sciences as 'punctuated equilibria'.

Global scale of competitiveness. This concept was developed here to explain the general approach to *dynamic strategies* adopted by various societies in both the Old and New Worlds. The degree of external competition determines the framework within which the benefits and costs of adopting various dynamic strategies are evaluated. Think of societies being distributed along a global scale of competitiveness (or openness), with those societies experiencing a very high degree of competitiveness (openness) at one extreme, and those societies experiencing no external competition (closed societies) at the other extreme. Other societies will be located in between. We need two scales, one for the Old World and another for the New World. A society at the highly competitive end of the scale will pursue one of the four strategies of *family multiplication, conquest, commerce*, or *technological change* depending on which is most cost-effective in achieving the objectives of *materialist man*. At the non-competitive extreme, a society will choose only the family multiplication strategy if unused resources are abundant, or the family planning strategy – a static rather than a dynamic strategy – if all natural resources are fully utilized. Both choices are rational in that they are directed at maximizing the probability of survival and material returns, given the perceived benefits and costs of alternative strategies. It is this scale of competitiveness that has determined the basic strategic approach of societies to economic change, and hence the order in which they have passed through the great paradigm shifts.

Great dispersion, The. This was the first great mechanism driving the *technological paradigm shift* – between the palaeolithic and neolithic eras. It involved the adoption of the extremely slow but very effective *dynamic strategy* of *family multiplication* and migration to enable greater control over unused natural resources and hence a greater probability of survival and prosperity. These resources were progressively utilized through a hunter–gatherer technology.

Great linear waves of economic change. This is the dynamic mechanism of the modern technological era. Eventually the modern paradigm will be exhausted, and this will open the way for a future great step in human progress. It is a mechanism fuelled by the technological strategy. The Industrial Revolution not only ushered in a new technological paradigm, it also initiated a new era in which linear, if fluctuating, economic growth is possible. While the Neolithic Revolution gave rise to the eternal recurrence – the *great wheel of civilization* – the Industrial Revolution provided the means to convert the internal energy of *dynamic materialism* into continuous economic progress. This continuous progress has been transmitted through the great linear waves of economic change of about 300 years in duration.

Great steps of human progress. This describes the millennial step-like increase in global potential material living standards made possible by the great *technological paradigm shifts*. There are relatively brief periods – known as the Palaeolithic, Neolithic, and Industrial Revolutions – when the potential for material living standards increases relatively sharply, separated by vast intervening periods. During these intervening periods, actual material standards gradually approach the potential levels set by the prevailing technological paradigm. While actual living standards can never exceed the potential at the global level, individual societies can exceed this technologically determined level at the expense of other societies through the strategies of conquest or commerce. While the technological ceiling level was static, the response of human society was dynamic. This resembles the profile of genetic change known by the term 'punctuated equilibria', which should not be confused with the *great waves of biological life*.

Great waves of biological life. These trace out the surging progress of life over the past four billion years. There have been four great waves of life encompassing the eras of blue-green algae (2,200–700 myrs), of newly emergent animal life (700–250 myrs), of the dinosaurs (250–65 myrs), and of mammals and man (65 myrs to the present). These great waves of life, which have been accelerating over time, have been generated not just by genetic change but by all the *dynamic strategies* (including also reproduction, symbiosis, and predation). It is important not to confuse the great waves with the profile of genetic change known as 'punctuated equilibria'.

Great wheel of civilization. This was the mechanism driving the technological paradigm shift between the neolithic and modern eras. It was the dynamic of ancient society. Each rotation of the great wheel brought the Dynamic Society closer to the limit of the old neolithic paradigm through population expansion and the transmission of ideas. It is a process of economic change in which each cycle of ancient society begins again anew. It is the mechanism underlying the rise and fall of ancient civilizations. It is the eternal recurrence of the ancient world driven by the dynamic strategy of conquest which, for a time, enables individual societies to exceed the global living standards determined by the ancient technological paradigm. The conqueror must rebuild his empire anew on each and every occasion. The only escape is through the technological strategy via the *great linear waves of economic change.*

Gross Community Income (GCI) is a measure of total economic activity that takes place in both the household and market sectors on an annual basis. It is an extension of the concept of GDP to the Total Economy. It is a term coined in Snooks (1994a: 17).

Longrun dynamics involves an approach to the study of economics that focuses on the process of change over significant periods of time (generations, centuries, millennia). The benefits of this approach include the identification of some of the larger issues that emerge from dynamic change in society, and an understanding of the real-world dynamic process. Longrun dynamics is an area of economics that is largely ignored by the theorist because it is too difficult to handle mathematically, but it is an area that the analytical historian can and should make his/her own. In this study, 'longrun' is a single word for an important concept in materialist history – a single word to raise the editorial hackles.

Materialist man is a central concept in the analysis of the Dynamic Society. Materialist man is related, yet very different, to the economists' concept of *Homo economicus.* Rational economic man is not a dynamic force in society, but rather an abstract collection of preferences and rational choices concerning consumption and production. Economic theorists have divorced these behavioural outcomes from more fundamental human motivational impulses. Hence economic man is disembodied and has no real-world substance – he is little more than a cardboard cut-out. Economic man is merely a useful analytical device to achieve shortrun equilibrium solutions.

Materialist man on the other hand is a real-world decision-maker who attempts to survive and, with survival, to maximize material advantage *over his lifetime.* This does not require perfect knowledge or sophisticated abilities to calculate rapidly the costs and benefits of a variety of possible decision-making alternatives, just an ability to gather sufficient real-world information to make sensible cost-effective decisions. It does not require decision-makers to maximize in every situation (which is always self-defeating) but just over the course of a lifetime. To do so implies progress over time. It does not mean that every individual acts in this way, just that the large majority do. It does not mean that mistakes in conception and execution are never made, just that they lead to corrective action. Materialist man is a realistic dweller in a dynamic world. I have earlier (Snooks 1994a: 46–51) called this concept 'dynamic economic man' in contradistinction to the economists' 'static economic man', but now believe that an entirely new term is required for a very different type of decision-maker.

New economic revolution. This event occurred in the West during the generation following the late 1940s. Its main characteristics involved a major, technologically induced shift from manufacturing to service activities, together with a major change in the gender structure of labour demand that caused a rapid increase in the market participation rates of 'married' females after a century of stasis. In turn this led to a shift in the balance between consumption and fertility in the household, which caused a reduction in the size of the Western family from five to three people – the first significant and sustained reduction in the entire history of human society. It has taken place within the industrial technological paradigm initiated by the Industrial Revolution.

Strategic crisis. A strategic crisis occurs when a civilization's dominant dynamic strategy is economically exhausted. This point is reached when the marginal costs of the dominant strategy equals its marginal revenue. Owing to the highly specialized nature of the dominant strategy, rapid switching to other strategies is not possible. Crisis is, therefore, inevitable. The approaching strategic crisis leads to a slowing down of the upswing and eventual downturn. Any future recovery must await the rejuvenation of the old strategy or the development of entirely new strategies. Collapse will only occur if the old dominant strategy, such as conquest or commerce, led to the expansion of the civilization beyond the optimum size dictated by the prevailing technological paradigm. Collapse follows the rapid emergence of the *strategic revenue gap* between the revenue capacity of the existing technological paradigm and the cost structure of a conquest /commerce empire. The speed of the collapse will depend upon the level of global competition.

Strategic-crisis hypothesis. The strategic-crisis hypothesis encompasses the Malthusian hypothesis. In the Malthusian hypothesis, population is treated as an exogenously determined force which outstrips the productivity of agriculture and brings economic growth to an end. In the strategic-crisis hypothesis, population growth is endogenously determined as it is a response to man's dynamics strategies. Hence population expansion is not a determinant of the crisis but a response to it. The Malthusian crisis is a special case of the strategic crisis that emerges only when a society has been overwhelmed by the forces of chaos.

Strategic demand is a central concept in this study. It refers to the demand by decision-makers who are investing in dynamic strategies – *family multiplication, technological change, commerce,* or *conquest* – for the ideas and resources required to implement these decisions. It is a response in a competitive environment to changes in fundamental economic forces, such as relative factor prices. In the model developed in this book, strategic demand plays the major determining role in the dynamics of human society. It is contrasted with the currently fashionable supply-side models, and with Keynesian models that focused upon aggregate demand.

Strategic imitation. This is the microeconomic mechanism by which the investment projects of individuals, who attempt to exploit new changes in fundamental economic conditions, are transformed into the *dynamic strategies* of nations or even of civilizations. It owes its origins to that remarkable faculty of human beings to imitate the successful actions of their peers in order to gain access to the supernormal profits earned by 'strategic innovators'. This faculty appears to have emerged in the evolutionary process and is akin to herd instinct in the animal kingdom. It is the mechanism by which human desires are translated into material advantage.

Strategic revenue gap. This concept is central to the explanation in this book of why ancient civilizations collapsed once they had exhausted their dominant and highly specialized dynamic strategy. The only way ancient societies could exceed the optimum size, in terms of population and material living standards, dictated by their neolithic economic system, was through the dynamic strategies of conquest and commerce. The problem was that once these strategies had been exhausted – at the point where their marginal cost equalled their marginal revenue – and the stationary state was temporarily achieved, the society was thrown back upon its neolithic revenue structure while being forced to retain the old empire cost structure. Reduction in population, material living standards, infrastructure, and territory to the neolithic optimum sizes was not feasible and, hence a large strategic revenue gap emerged. As ancient societies were unable to adopt the technological strategy, owing to its prohibitive costs in a world of underused natural resources, it was impossible to fill this gap. Attempts to increase taxation, reduce welfare, and resort to inflationary currency devaluation merely increased the *forces of chaos* which ultimately led to the collapse of the society.

Technological strategy. This strategy is the dominant dynamic of modern society and, in the past, has been employed by economic decision-makers to transcend exhausted technological paradigms. It was at the very centre of the Palaeolithic (hunting), Neolithic (agricultural), and Industrial (modern) Revolutions or *technological paradigm shifts*. And it will be the dominant dynamic strategy of the future. Unlike the conquest and commerce strategies, it leads to an increase in material living standards not only for its host civilization, but for human society as a whole.

Technological dynamic change (TDC). In societies where all natural resources are 'fully' utilized with the existing state of technology (in its broadest sense), *economic growth* and *economic expansion* can be regarded as component parts of a wider dynamic process of economic change called here technological dynamic change (TDC). The balance between growth and expansion will depend on the nature of the aggregate production function in a particular society at a particular time, which in turn will be influenced by the internal dynamics (family fertility and consumption) of the household (Snooks, 1994a: 127–34). TDC is the outcome of employing the technological dynamic strategy. It is contrasted with environmental dynamic change. This is the basis of the 'modern dynamic' which has generated the *great linear waves of economic change.*

Technological paradigm shifts. The progress of human society takes place within a dynamic structure defined by the great technological paradigm shifts in which growing resource scarcity is transcended by mankind breaking through into an entirely new technological era, thereby opening up extended possibilities for further economic growth. This involves the introduction of an entirely new set of techniques, skills, institutions, and outcomes. There have been three great technological paradigm shifts in human history: the palaeolithic paradigm shift when hunting displaced scavenging; the neolithic paradigm shift when agriculture displaced hunting; and the industrial paradigm shift when urban centres displaced rural areas as the major source of growth. This has generated the *great steps of human progress.*

Timescapes are those portraits of reality provided by a visual representation of longrun quantitative data. These portraits emerge from the statistical record of the course taken by both biological life and human society over vast expanses of time. They include the *great waves of biological life* and the *great linear waves of economic change.* They show us the nature of real-world relationships; and seeing is the beginning of understanding. They provide a glimpse of dynamic processes operating in life and in society, and they are the building blocks of *existential models* (Snooks, 1994a).

Zero-sum dynamic change (ZDC). While *technological dynamic change* (TDC) involves an increase in material living standards for both the society employing the technological strategy and for human society as a whole, zero-sum dynamic change (ZDC) benefits the dynamic society at the expense of the rest of human society. ZDC results from a dominant society employing either the conquest or the commerce (in contrast to trade) strategies. This was the basis of the 'ancient dynamic' which generated the eternal recurrence of war and conquest that has here been called the *great wheel of civilization.* In fact even ZDC may generate some increase in global material living standards owing to the concentration of resources in the hands of those who are able to employ them more efficiently owing to economies of scale and more sophisticated organizational and human capital skills, but only if it is greater than the material losses inflicted by war. Also see *environmental dynamic change* (EDC).

REFERENCES

Abel, W. (1980), *Agricultural Fluctuations in Europe: from the thirteenth to the twentieth centuries*, London, Methuen.

Adams, R.E.W. (1980), 'Swamps, canals and the locations of ancient Mayan cities', *Antiquity*, 54, pp. 206–14.

Adams, R.E.W. (1973), 'Maya collapse: transformation and termination in the ceramic sequence at Altar de Sacrificios', in T.P. Culbert (ed.), *The Classic Maya Collapse*, Albuquerque, University of New Mexico Press, pp. 133–63.

Adams, R.E.W., (ed.) (1977), *The Origins of Maya Civilization*, Albuquerque, University of New Mexico Press.

Adelman, I. (1987), 'Simulation models', in J. Eatwell, M. Milgate, and P. Newman (eds), *The New Palgrave: a dictionary of economics*, London, Macmillan, vol. 4, pp. 340–2.

Alvarez, L.W., W. Alvarez, F. Asaro, and H.V. Michel (1980), 'Extraterrestrial cause for the Cretaceous–Tertiary extinction', *Science*, 208, pp. 1095–108.

Ashton, T.S. (1948), *The Industrial Revolution 1760–1830*, London, Oxford University Press.

Attenborough, D. (1993), 'Springbok of the Kalahari', BBC programme on ABC television, 'Wildscreen', 11 November.

Aubet, M.E. (1993), *The Phoenicians and the West: politics, colonies and trade*, New York, Cambridge University Press.

Austin, M. (1995), 'Alexander and the Macedonian Invasion of Asia: aspects of the historiography of war and empire in antiquity', in J. Rich and G. Shipley (eds), *War and Society in the Roman World*, London & New York, Routledge, pp. 197–223.

Bairoch, P. (1982), 'International industrialisation levels from 1750 to 1980', *Journal of European Economic History*, 11, pp. 269–333.

Bairoch, P., J. Batou, and P. Chèvre (1988), *The Population of European Cities, 800–1850: data bank and short summary of results*, Geneva, Droz.

Ball, J.N. (1977), *Merchants and Merchandise: the expansion of trade in Europe, 1500–1630*, London, Croom Helm.

Barrett, W. (1990), 'World bullion flows, 1450–1800', in J.D. Tracy (ed.), *The Rise of Merchant Empires: long-distance trade in the early modern world, 1350–1750*, Cambridge, Cambridge University Press, pp. 224–54.

Barro, B.J. and P.M. Romer (1990), 'Economic growth', *NBER Reporter*, Fall, pp. 1–5.

Beaton, J.M. (1983), 'Does intensification account for changes in the Australian Holocene archaeological record?', *Archaeology in Oceania*, 18, pp. 94–7.

Becker, G.S. (1976), 'Altruism, egoism, and genetic fitness: economics and sociobiology', *Journal of Economic Literature*, 14 (3), pp. 817–26.

Becker, G.S. (1991), *A Treatise on the Family*, enlarged edn, Cambridge, Mass., Harvard University Press.

Beloch, J. (1968; orig. pub. 1886), *Die Bevölkerung der griechisch-römischen Welt*, Rome, 'L'erma' di Bretschneider.

Benda, J. (1959; orig. pub. 1927), *The Betrayal of the Intellectuals*, Boston, Beacon Press.

Benton, M. (1985), 'Mass extinction among non-marine tetrapods', *Nature*, 316 (29 August), pp. 811–14.

Bergstrom, T.C. (1995), 'On the evolution of altruistic ethical rules for siblings', *American Economic Review*, 85 (1), March, pp. 58–81.

Biraben, J.-N. (1979), 'Essai sur l'évolution du nombre des hommes', *Population*, 34 (1), pp. 13–24.

Birdsell, J.B. (1957), 'Some population problems involving Pleistocene man', *Cold Spring Harbor Symposia on Quantitative Biology*, 22, pp. 47–70.

Blainey, G. (1975), *Triumph of the Nomads: a history of ancient Australia*, South Melbourne, Vic., Macmillan.

Blomme, J. and H. Van der Wee (1994), 'The Belgian economy in a long-term historical perspective: economic development in Flanders and Brabant, 1500–1812', in A. Maddison and H. Van der Wee (eds), *Economic Growth and Structural Change. Comparative Approaches over the Long Run/Croissance économique et mutation structurelle. Comparaisons dans le long terme: Proceedings, Eleventh International Economic History Congress, Milan, September 1994*, B13, Milan, Università Bocconi, pp. 77–96.

Bolin, S. (1958), *State and Currency in the Roman Empire to 300 A.D.*, Stockholm, Almqvist & Wiksell.

Boserup, E. (1965), *The Conditions of Agricultural Growth: the economics of agrarian change under population pressure*, Chicago, Aldine Publishing Company.

Boserup, E. (1981), *Population and Technology*, Oxford, Basil Blackwell.

Boucot, A.J. (1983), 'Does evolution take place in a vacuum? II', *Journal of Paleontology*, 57 (1), pp. 1–30.

Boulding, K.E. (ed.) (1973), *The Economy of Love and Fear*, Belmont, Calif., Wadsworth.

Bowdler, S. (1977), ' The coastal colonization of Australia', in J. Allen, J. Golson and R. Jones (eds) *Sunda and Sahul: Prehistoric Studies in Southeast Asia, Melanesia and Australia*, London, Academic Press, pp. 205–46.

Bowler, P.J. (1988), *The Non-Darwinian Revolution: reinterpreting a historical myth*, Baltimore & London, The Johns Hopkins University Press.

Brady, T.A. (1991), 'The rise of merchant empires, 1400–1700: a European counterpoint', in J.D. Tracy (ed.), *The Political Economy of Merchant Empires*, Cambridge & New York, Cambridge University Press., pp. 117–60.

Bridbury, A.R. (1962), *Economic Growth: England in the later Middle Ages*, London, Allen & Unwin.

Britnell, R.H. (1995), 'Commercialisation and economic development in England, 1000–1300', in R.H. Britnell and B.M.S. Campbell (eds), *Commercialising Economy*, Manchester, Manchester University Press, pp. 7–26.

Buckle, H.T. (1894), *History of Civilization in England*, 3 vols, London, Longmans, Green & Co.

Bullock, A. (1993), *Hitler and Stalin: parallel lives*, London, Fontana.

Burn, A.R. (1966), *The Pelican History of Greece*, Harmondsworth, Penguin.

Butlin, N.G. (1983), *Our Original Aggression: Aboriginal populations of southeastern Australia, 1788–1850*, Sydney, George Allen & Unwin.

Butlin, N.G. (1989), 'The palaeoeconomic history of Aboriginal migration', *Australian Economic History Review*, 29 (2), pp. 3–57 [corrected figure, *AEHR*, 30 (1), 1990, p. 92].

Butlin, N.G. (1993), *Economics and the Dreamtime: a hypothetical history*, Melbourne, Cambridge University Press.

Calder, N. (1984), *Timescale: an atlas of the fourth dimension*, London, Chatto & Windus, The Hogarth Press.

Cambridge Medieval History (1969), vol. 8, Cambridge, Cambridge University Press.

Cameron, R. (1989), *A Concise Economic History of the World: from paleolithic times to the present*, Oxford/New York, Oxford University Press.

Campbell, I.H., G.K. Czamanske, V.A. Fedorenko, R.I. Hill, and V. Stepanov (1992), 'Synchronism of the Siberian Traps and the Permian–Triassic boundary', *Science*, 258, pp. 1760–2.

Carson, H.L. (1975), 'The genetics of speciation at the diploid level', *American Naturalist*, 109, pp. 83–92.

Castleden, R. (1990), *Minoans: life in Bronze Age Crete*, London & New York, Routledge.

Charlton, T.H. (1984), 'Production and exchange: variables in the evolution of a civilization', in K.G. Hirth (ed.), *Trade and Exchange in Early Mesoamerica*, Albuquerque, University of New Mexico Press, pp. 17–42.

Chase, A.F. and P.M. Rice (eds) (1985), *The Lowland Maya Postclassic*, Austin, University of Texas Press.

Chase, D.Z. and A.F. Chase (1982), 'Yucatec influence in terminal classic northern Belize', *American Antiquity*, 47 (3), pp. 596–614.

Chen, G., J.A. Tyburczy, and T.J. Ahrens (1994), 'Shock-induced devolatization of calcium sulphate and implications for K-T extinctions', *Earth and Planetary Science Letters*, 128 (3–4), pp. 615–28.

Cipolla, C.M. (1974), *The Economic History of World Population*, Harmondsworth, Penguin.

Cipolla, C.M. (1976), *Before the Industrial Revolution: European society and economy, 1000–1700*, London, Methuen.

Clapham, J.H. (1949), *A Concise Economic History of Britain from the Earliest Times to 1750*, Cambridge, Cambridge University Press.

Clark, C. (1977), *Population Growth and Land Use*, 2nd edn, London, Macmillan.

Clark, M. (1985), 'Manning Clark', in R.M. Crawford, M. Clark, and G. Blainey, *Making History*, Fitzroy, Vic., McPhee Gribble/Penguin Books, pp. 55–67.

Clendinnen, I. (1993), *Aztecs. An Interpretation*, Cambridge, Cambridge University Press.

Cloud, P. (1988), *Oasis in Space: earth history from the beginning*, New York & London, W.W. Norton & Company.

Collard, D. (1978), *Altruism and Economy: a study in non-selfish economics*, Oxford, Martin Robertson.

Coombs, H.C. (1993), 'Who owns the intelligentsia?', *Australian Business Monthly*, February, pp. 116–19.

Cowgill, G.L. (1979), 'Teotihuacan, internal militaristic competition', in N. Hammond and G.R. Willey (eds), *Maya Archaeology and Ethnohistory*, London & Austin, University of Texas Press, pp. 51–62.

Crafts, N.F.R. (1985), *British Economic Growth during the Industrial Revolution*, Oxford, Clarendon Press.

Crawford, H. (1991), *Sumer and the Sumerians*, Cambridge, Cambridge University Press.

Crawford, M. and D. Marsh (1989), *The Driving Force: food in evolution and the future*, London, Mandarin.

Culbert, T.P. (1973a), 'Introduction: a prologue to classic Maya culture and the problem of its collapse', in T.P. Culbert (ed.), *The Classic Maya Collapse*, Albuquerque, University of New Mexico Press, pp. 3–40.

Culbert, T.P. (1973b), 'The Maya downfall at Tikal', in T.P. Culbert (ed.), *The Classic Maya Collapse*, Albuquerque, University of New Mexico Press, pp. 63–92.

Culbert, T.P. (ed.) (1973c), *The Classic Maya Collapse*, Albuquerque, University of New Mexico Press.

Culbert, T.P. (1974), *The Lost Civilization: the story of the classic Maya*, New York, Harper & Row.

Culbert, T.P. (1988), 'The collapse of classic Maya civilization', in N. Yoffee and G.L. Cowgill (eds), *The Collapse of Ancient States and Civilizations*, Tucson, University of Arizona Press, pp. 69–101.

Culbert, T.P. (ed.) (1991), *Classic Maya Political History: hieroglyphic and archeological evidence*, School of American Research Advanced Seminar Series, Cambridge, Cambridge University Press.

Cunningham, W. (1882), *The Growth of English Industry and Commerce*, Cambridge, Cambridge University Press.

Darby, H.C. (1977), *Domesday England*, Cambridge, Cambridge University Press.

Darwin, C. (1979; orig. pub. 1859), *The Origin of Species by Means of Natural Selection or the Preservation of Favoured Races in the Struggle for Life*, New York, Avenel Books (orig. London, J. Murray).

Davis, R. (1973), *English Overseas Trade 1500–1700*, London, Macmillan.

Dawkins, R. (1986), *The Blind Watchmaker*, Harlow, Longman Scientific & Technical.

Dawkins, R. (1989), *The Selfish Gene*, Oxford & New York, Oxford University Press.

Deevey, E.S. (1960), 'The human population', *Scientific American*, 203 (3), pp. 194–204.

Desmond, A.J. and J. Moore (1991), *Darwin*, London, Michael Joseph.

Dicke, R.H., P.J.E. Peebles, P.G. Roll, and D.T. Wilkinson (1965), 'Cosmic blackbody radiation', *Astrophysical Journal*, 142, pp. 414–65.

Dietz, R.S. and J.C. Holden (1970), 'The breakup of Pangaea', *Scientific American*, 223 (4), pp. 30–41.

Dingle, A.E. (1988), *Aboriginal Economy: patterns of experience*, Melbourne, McPhee Gribble/Penguin.

Domar, E.D. (1946), 'Capital expansion rate of growth and employment', *Econometrica*, 14 , pp. 137–47.

Durand, J.D. (1977), 'Historical estimates of world population: an evaluation', *Population and Development Review*, 3 (3), pp. 253–96.

Easteal, S. (forthcoming 1995), *The Mammalian Molecular Clock*, Austin, R.G. Landes.

Eccles, J.C. (1989), *The Evolution of the Brain: creation of the conscious self*, London & New York, Routledge.

Edey, M.A. and the editors of Time-Life Books (1974), *The Sea Traders*, New York, Time-Life Books.

Ehrlich, P.R. and A.H. Ehrlich (1990), *The Population Explosion*, New York, Simon & Schuster.

Ekins, P. (1994), 'Limits to growth', in G.M. Hodgson, W.J. Samuels, and M.R. Tool (eds), *The Elgar Companion to Institutional and Evolutionary Economics*, Aldershot, Elgar, vol. 1, pp. 289–98.

Eldredge, N. (1986), *Time Frames: rethinking of Darwinian evolution and the theory of punctuated equilibria*, New York, Simon & Schuster.

Eldredge, N. and S.J. Gould (1972), 'Punctuated equilibria: an alternative to phyletic gradualism', in T.J.M. Schopf (ed.), *Models of Paleobiology*, San Francisco, Freeman, Cooper, pp. 82–115.

Eliade, M. (1971), *The Myth of the Eternal Return: or, cosmos and history*, Princeton, Princeton University Press.

REFERENCES

Elliott, D.K. (ed.) (1986), *Dynamics of Extinction*, New York, John Wiley & Sons.

Elvin, M. (1973), *The Pattern of the Chinese Past*, London, Eyre Methuen.

Erickson, E.E. (1973), 'The life cycle of life styles: projecting the course of local evolutionary sequences', *Behavior Science Notes*, 2, pp. 136–60.

Finley, M.I. (1985), *The Ancient Economy*, 2nd edn, London, Hogarth.

Fisher, F.J. (1954), 'Commercial trends and policy in sixteenth-century England', in E.M. Carus-Wilson (ed.), *Essays in Economic History: reprints*, London, E. Arnold.

Fitzgerald, C.P. (1966), *A Concise History of East Asia*, Melbourne, Heinemann.

Fleming, R. (1991), *Kings and Lords in Conquest England*, Cambridge, Cambridge University Press.

Forbes, R.J. (1958), *Man the Maker*, London, Abelard-Shuman.

Forrester, J.W. (1961), *Industrial Dynamics*, Cambridge, Mass., MIT. Press.

Forrester, J.W. (1968), *Principles of Systems*, Cambridge, Mass., Wright-Allen Press.

Forrester, J.W. (1973), *World Dynamics*, 2nd edn, Cambridge, Mass., Wright-Allen Press.

Foster, J. (1994), 'Biology and economics', in G.M. Hodgson, W.J. Samuels, and M.R. Tool (eds), *The Elgar Companion to Institutional and Evolutionary Economics*, Aldershot, Elgar, vol. 1, pp. 23–9.

Frank, T. (1940), *An Economic Survey of Ancient Rome*; vol. 5: *Rome and Italy of the Empire*, Baltimore, Johns Hopkins Press.

Frech, H.E. (1978), 'Altruism, malice, and public goods', *Journal of Social and Biological Structures*, 1(2), pp. 181–5.

Freedman, W.L. *et al.* (1994), 'Distance to the Virgo cluster galaxy M100 from Hubble Space Telescope observations of Cepheids', *Nature*, 371, (27 October), pp. 757–62.

Freidel, D.A. (1985), 'New light on the dark age: a summary of major themes', in A.F. Chase and P.M. Rice (eds), *The Lowland Maya Postclassic*, Austin, University of Texas Press, pp. 285–309.

Fukuyama, F. (1992), *The End of History and the Last Man*, New York, Free Press.

Gamow, G. (1952), *The Creation of the Universe*, New York, Viking.

Garnsey, P., K. Hopkins, and C.R. Whittaker, C.R., (eds) (1983), *Trade in the Ancient Economy*, London, Chatto & Windus.

Goldman, M.I. (1983), *U.S.S.R. in Crisis: the failure of an economic system*, New York, Norton.

Goldsmith, R.W. (1984), 'An estimate of the size and structure of the national product of the early Roman Empire', *Review of Income and Wealth*, Series 30, pp. 263–88.

Goldsmith, R.W. (1987), *Premodern Financial Systems: a historical comparative study*, Cambridge, Cambridge University Press.

Gould, S.J. (1982), 'Is a new and general theory of evolution emerging?', in J.M. Smith (ed.), *Evolution Now, a Century after Darwin*, San Francisco, W.H. Freeman, pp. 129–45.

Gould, S.J. (1987), *Time's Arrow, Time's Cycle: myth and metaphor in the discovery of geological time*, Cambridge, Mass., Harvard University Press.

Graham, R.W. (1986), 'Plant–animal interactions and pleistocene extinctions', in D.K. Elliott (ed.), *Dynamics of Extinction*, New York, John Wiley & Sons, pp. 131–54.

Grant, M. (1976), *The Fall of the Roman Empire: a reappraisal*, Radnor, PA, Annenberg School Press.

Greenhill, B. (1988), *The Evolution of the Wooden Ship*, London, Batsford.

Grove, J.M. (1990), *The Little Ice Age*, London & New York, Routledge.

Groves, C. P. (1994), 'The origin of modern humans', *Interdisciplinary Science Review*, 19 (1), pp. 23–34.

445

Gur, R.C., L.H. Mozley, and E. Gur (1995), 'Sex differences in regional cerebral glucose metabolism during a resting state', *Science*, 267 (27 January), pp. 528–31.

Hacker, B. (1968), 'Greek catapults and catapult technology: science, technology and war in the ancient world', *Technology and Culture*, 9, pp. 34–50.

Hall, A.R. (1983), *The Revolution in Science, 1500–1750*, 3rd edn, London & New York, Longman.

Hamilton, W.D. (1964), 'The genetical evolution of social behaviour', *Journal of Theoretical Biology*, 7, pp. 1–52.

Hammond, N. and G.R. Willey, (eds) (1979), *Maya Archaeology and Ethnohistory*, London & Austin, University of Texas Press.

Hannah, L. (1993), 'Cultural determinants of economic performance: an experiment in measuring human capital flows', in G.D. Snooks (ed.), *Historical Analysis in Economics*, London & New York, Routledge, pp. 158–71.

Harden, D. (1963), *The Phoenicians*, London, Thames & Hudson.

Harrison, P.D. and B.L. Turner, (eds) (1978), *Pre-Hispanic Maya Agriculture*, Albuquerque, University of New Mexico Press.

Harrod, R.F. (1939), 'An essay in dynamic theory', *Economic Journal*, 49 , pp. 14–33.

Hartwell, R.M. (1963), 'The standard of living', *Economic History Review*, 2nd series, 16 (1), August, pp. 135–46.

Harvey, P.D.A., (ed.) (1984), *The Peasant Land Market in Medieval England*, Oxford, Clarendon Press.

Haviland, W.A. (1967), 'Stature at Tikal, Guatemala: implications for classic Maya demography and social organisation', *American Antiquity*, 32, pp. 316–25.

Haviland, W.A. (1969), 'A new population estimate for Tikal, Guatemala', *American Antiquity*, 34, pp. 429–33.

Hayek, F. A. (1952), *The Counter-Revolution of Science: studies on the abuse of reason*, Glencoe, Ill., Free Press.

Hayek, F.A. (1988), *The Fatal Conceit. The errors of socialism*, London & New York, Routledge.

Hemming, J. (1983), *The Conquest of the Incas*, London, Penguin.

Hilton, R.H. (1983), *The Decline of Serfdom in Medieval England*, 2nd edn, London, Macmillan.

Hirth, K.G. (ed.) (1984), *Trade and Exchange in Early Mesoamerica*, Albuquerque, University of New Mexico Press.

Hobsbawm, E.J. (1963), 'The standard of living during the Industrial Revolution: a discussion', *Economic History Review*, 2nd series, 16 (1), August, pp. 119–34.

Hodges, H. (1970), *Technology in the Ancient World*, London, Allen Lane, The Penguin Press.

Hodkinson, S. (1995), 'Warfare, wealth, and the crisis of Spartiate society', in J. Rich and G. Shipley (eds), *War and Society in the Roman World*, London & New York, Routledge, pp. 146–76.

Hollister, C.W. (1982), *Medieval Europe: a short history*, New York, Alfred A. Knopf.

Holt, J.C. (1982–85), 'Feudal society and the family, I to IV', *Transactions of the Royal Historical Society*, London.

Hopkins, M.K. (1978), *Conquerors and Slaves*, Cambridge, Cambridge University Press.

Hopkins, K. (1983), 'Introduction', in P. Garnsey, K. Hopkins, and C.R. Whittaker (eds), *Trade in the Ancient Economy*, London, Chatto & Windus, pp. ix–xxv.

Hubble, E.P. (1929), 'A relation between distance and radial velocity among extra-galactic nebulae', *Communications to the National Academy of Sciences*, 15, pp. 168–73.

Hubble, E.P. (1934), *Red-shifts in the Spectra of Nebulae*, Oxford, Clarendon Press.

Hubble, E.P. (1958), *The Realm of the Nebulae*, New York, Dover.

REFERENCES

Jacoby, G.H. (1994), 'The universe in crisis', *Nature*, 371, (27 October), pp. 741–2.

John, A.V. (1980), *By the Sweat of their Brow: women workers at Victorian coal mines*, London, Croom Helm.

Jones, A.H.M. (1964), *The Later Roman Empire, 284–602: a social, economic and administrative survey*, 3 vols, Oxford, Basil Blackwell.

Jones, C. (1991), 'Cycles of growth at Tikal', in T.P. Culbert (ed.), *Classic Maya Political History: hieroglyphic and archaeological evidence*, Cambridge, Cambridge University Press, pp. 102–27.

Jones, E.L. (1981), *The European Miracle: environments, economies and geopolitics in the history of Europe and Asia*, Cambridge, Cambridge University Press.

Jones, E.L. (1988), *Growth Recurring: economic change in world history*, Oxford, Clarendon Press.

Jones, E.L. (1990), 'The real question about China: why was the Song economic achievement not repeated?', *Australian Economic History Review*, 30 (2), pp. 5–22.

Jones, S. (1993), 'Search, specialisation, and the decline of the pitched periodic market in English economic history', ANU Economic History Seminar, October.

Kadish, A. (1989), *Historians, Economists, and Economic History*, London & New York, Routledge.

Keesing, R.M. (1975), *Kin Groups and Social Structure*, Fort Worth, Holt, Rinehart & Winston.

Kennedy, P.M. (1989), *The Rise and Fall of the Great Powers: economic change and military conflict from 1500 to 2000*, London, Fontana.

Kenwood, A.G. and A.L. Lougheed (1983), *The Growth of the International Economy, 1820–1980: an introductory text*, London, Allen & Unwin.

Kenyon, J. (1993), *The History Men: the historical profession in England since the renaissance*, 2nd edn, London, Weidenfeld.

Keynes, J.M. (1936), *The General Theory of Employment, Interest, and Money*, London, Macmillan.

Keynes, J.N. (1891), *The Scope and Method of Political Economy*, London, Macmillan.

Kinder, H. and W. Hilgemann (1974), *The Penguin Atlas of World History*, vol. 1: *From the Beginning to the Eve of the French Revolution*, Harmondsworth, Penguin.

King, G. (1936), *Two Tracts by Gregory King* (edited by G.E. Barnett), Baltimore, Johns Hopkins Press.

Knott, J.W. (1994), 'Road traffic accidents in New South Wales, 1881–1991', *Australian Economic History Review*, 34 (2), pp. 80–116.

Lach, D.F. (1977), *Asia in the Making of Europe*, vol. 2: *A Century of Wonder*, Chicago, University of Chicago Press.

Landels, J.G. (1978), *Engineering in the Ancient World*, Berkeley, Calif., University of California Press.

Landes, D.S. (1969), *The Unbound Prometheus: technological changes and industrial development in western Europe from 1750 to the present*, London, Cambridge University Press.

Landes, D.S. (1983), *Revolution in Time: clocks and the making of the modern world*, Cambridge, Mass., Belknap Press of Harvard University Press.

Lane, F.C. (1973), *Venice, a Maritime Republic*, Baltimore, Johns Hopkins University Press.

Langdon, J. (1986), *Horses, Oxen, and Technological Innovation*, Cambridge, Cambridge University Press.

Lawson, T. (1994), 'A realist theory for economics', in R.E. Backhouse (ed.), *New Directions in Economic Methodology*, London and New York, Routledge, pp. 257–85.

Leakey, R.E. (1981), *The Making of Mankind*, New York, E.P. Dutton.

Leakey, R.E. and R. Lewin (1992), *Origins Reconsidered: in search of what makes us human*, London, Little Brown.

Lee, R. (1973), 'Population in pre-industrial England: an econometric analysis', *Quarterly Journal of Economics*, 87, pp. 581–607.

Lee, R. (1993), 'Accidental and systematic change in population history: homeostasis in a stochastic setting', *Explorations in Economic History*, 30 (1), pp. 1–30.

Levi, M. (1988), *Of Rule and Revenue*, Berkeley, University of California Press.

Levy, J.P. (1967), *The Economic Life of the Ancient World*, Chicago, University of Chicago Press.

Livi-Bacci, M. (1992), *A Concise History of World Population*, Cambridge, Mass. & Oxford, Blackwell.

Lovejoy, C.O. (1981), 'The origin of man', *Science*, 211, pp. 341–50.

Loyn, H.R. (ed.) (1989), *The Middle Ages: a concise encyclopaedia*, New York, Thames & Hudson.

Luzzatto, G. (1961), *An Economic History of Italy: from the fall of the Roman Empire to the beginning of the sixteenth century*, trans. by Philip Jones, London, Routledge & Kegan Paul.

McCloskey, D.N. (1976), 'English open fields as behaviour towards risk', *Research in Economic History*, 1, pp. 124–70.

McCloskey, D.N. (1981), 'The industrial revolution 1780–1860: a survey', in R. Floud and D. McCloskey (eds), *The Economic History of Britain since 1700*, vol. 1: *1700–1860*, Cambridge, Cambridge University Press, pp. 103–27.

McCloskey, D.N. and J. Nash, (1984), 'Corn at interest: the cost of grain storage in medieval England', *American Economic Review*, 24, pp. 174–87.

McEvedy, C. (1961), *The Penguin Atlas of Medieval History*, Harmondsworth, Penguin Books.

McEvedy, C. (1967), *The Penguin Atlas of Ancient History*, Harmondsworth, Penguin Books.

McEvedy, C. (1972), *The Penguin Atlas of Modern History (to 1815)*, Harmondsworth, Penguin Books.

McEvedy, C. and R. Jones (1978), *Atlas of World Population History*, London, Allen Lane.

MacMullen, R. (1976), *Roman Government's Response to Crisis, A.D. 235–337*, New Haven, Yale University Press.

Maddison, A. (1982), *Phases of Capitalist Development*, Oxford, Oxford University Press.

Maddison, A. (1994), 'Explaining the economic performance of nations, 1820–1989', in W.J. Baumol, R.R. Nelson and E.N. Wolff (eds), *Convergence of Productivity: cross-national studies and historical evidence*, New York, Oxford University Press, pp. 20–61.

Malthus, T.R. (1970; orig. pub.1798), *An Essay on the Principle of Population; and, A Summary View of the Principle of Population*, Harmondsworth, Penguin.

Marx, K. (1957–61; orig. pub. 1867–94), *Capital*, 3 vols, Moscow, Foreign Languages Publishing House.

Matheny, R.T. (1978), 'Northern Maya lowland water-control systems', in P.D. Harrison and B.L. Turner (eds), *Pre-Hispanic Maya Agriculture*, Albuquerque, University of New Mexico Press, pp. 185–210.

Mayr, E. (1963), *Animal Species and Evolution*, Boston, Belknap Press/Harvard University Press.

Mayr, E. (1991), *One Long Argument: Charles Darwin and the genesis of modern evolutionary thought*, London, Allen Lane, The Penguin Press.

Meadows, D.H., *et al.* (1972), *The Limits to Growth: a report for the Club of Rome's project on the predicaments of mankind*, New York, Universe Books.

Meadows, D.H., D.L. Meadows, and J. Randers (1992), *Beyond the Limits: confronting global collapse, envisioning a sustainable future*, Post Mills, Vt, Chelsea Green.

Meyer, M.A. (1991), 'Women's estates in later Anglo-Saxon England: the politics of possession', *Haskins Society Journal*, Studies in Medieval History, ed. R.B. Patterson, III, pp. 111–29.

Mill, J.S. (1848), *Principles of political economy*, London, Parker & Co.

Mill, J.S. (1875), *A System of Logic. Ratiocinative and Inductive*, vol. II, London, Longmans.

Millett, P. (1983), 'Maritime loans and the structure of credit in fourth-century Athens', in P. Garnsey, K. Hopkins, and C.R. Whittaker (eds), *Trade in the Ancient Economy*, London, Chatto & Windus, pp. 36–52.

Millett, P. (1995), 'Warfare, economy, and democracy in classical Athens', in J. Rich and G. Shipley (eds), *War and Society in the Roman World*, London & New York, Routledge, pp. 177–96.

Millon, R. (1988), 'The last years of Teotihuacan dominance', in N. Yoffee and G.L. Cowgill (eds), *The Collapse of Ancient States and Civilizations*, Tucson, University of Arizona Press, pp. 102–64.

Mises, L. E. von (1958), *Theory and History*, London, J. Cape.

Mitchell, B.R. (1975), *European Historical Statistics, 1750–1970*, London, Macmillan.

Mitchell, B.R. (1988), *British Historical Statistics*, Cambridge, Cambridge University Press.

Modelski, G. (ed.) (1987), *Exploring Long Cycles*, London, Frances Pinter.

Moir, A. and D. Jessel (1989), *Brain Sex: the real difference between men and women*, London, Michael Joseph.

Mokyr, J. (1990), *The Lever of Riches: technological creativity and economic progress*, New York, Oxford University Press.

Mokyr, J. (ed.) (1993a), *The British Industrial Revolution: an economic perspective*, Boulder, Col., Westview Press.

Mokyr, J. (1993b), 'Editor's introduction: the new economic history and the Industrial Revolution', in J. Mokyr (ed.), *The British Industrial Revolution: an economic perspective*, Boulder, Col., Westview Press, pp. 1–131.

Monro, J.H. (1994), 'Patterns of trade, money, and credit', in T.A. Brady, H.A. Oberman, and J.D. Tracy (eds), *Handbook of European History, 1400–1600*, vol. I, Leiden, Brill, pp. 147–95.

Morley, S.G. (1947), *The Ancient Maya*, Stanford, Stanford University Press.

Morris, R. (1985), *Time's Arrow: scientific attitudes towards time*, New York, Simon & Schuster.

Mossé, C. (1983), 'The "world of the *emporium*" in the private speeches of Demosthenes', in P. Garnsey, K. Hopkins, and C.R. Whittaker (eds), *Trade in the Ancient Economy*, London, Chatto & Windus, pp. 53–63.

Mulvaney, D.J. (1987), 'The end of the beginning: 6,000 years ago to 1788', in D.J. Mulvaney and J.P. White (eds), *Australians: to 1788*, Broadway, NSW, Fairfax, Syme & Weldon, pp. 74–112.

Nelson, R.R. and S.G. Winter (1982), *An Evolutionary Theory of Economic Change*, Cambridge, Mass., Harvard University Press.

Nichols, J. (1994), 'Language at 40,000 BC', paper presented to AAAS Annual Meeting, San Francisco, 21 February.

Nietzsche, F. (1968; orig. pub. 1901), *The Will to Power*, trans. W. Kaufmann and R.J. Hollingdale, New York, Vintage Books.

North, D.C. (1981), *Structure and Change in Economic History*, New York & London, Norton.

North, D.C. (1990), *Institutions, Institutional Change, and Economic Performance*, Cambridge & New York, Cambridge University Press.

North, D. and R.P. Thomas (1973), *The Rise of the Western World*, Cambridge, Cambridge University Press.

Oakley, S. (1995), 'The Roman conquest of Italy', in J. Rich and G. Shipley (eds), *War and Society in the Roman World*, London and New York, Routledge, pp. 9–37.

O'Connell, R.L. (1989), *Of Arms and Men: a history of war, weapons, and aggression*, New York & Oxford, Oxford University Press.

Offer, A. (1989), *The First World War: an agrarian interpretation*, Oxford, Clarendon Press.

Pagan, A. (1993), 'Real business cycle models: a selective survey', seminar paper, Canberra, Economics Program, RSSS, Australian National University, April.

Parker, G. (1991), 'Europe and the wider world, 1500–1700', in J.D. Tracy, (ed.), *The Political Economy of Merchant Empires*, Cambridge & New York, Cambridge University Press, pp. 161–95.

Penny, D., M.A. Steel, P.J. Waddell, and M.D. Hendy (1994), 'Quantitative evaluation of large DNA data sets: the "Out of Africa" hypothesis', paper presented to the Australasian Conference on Archaeometry, University of New England, Armidale.

Perez, C. (1985), 'Microelectronics, long waves and world structural change: new perspectives for developing countries', *World Development*, 13 (3), pp. 441–63.

Perkins, D.H. (1969), *Agricultural Development in China, 1368–1968*, Edinburgh, Edinburgh University Press.

Persson, K.G. (1988), *Pre-industrial Economic Growth*, Oxford, Blackwell.

Peters, R.H. (1991), *A Critique for Ecology*, Cambridge, Cambridge University Press.

Phelps, E.S., (ed.) (1975), *Altruism, Morality, and Economic Theory*, New York, R. Sage Foundation.

Phillips, J.R.S. (1988), *The Medieval Expansion of Europe*, Oxford, Clarendon Press.

Piper, J.D.A. (1982), 'The precambrian paleomagnetic record: the case for the proterozoic supercontinent', *Earth and Planetary Science Letters*, 59 (1), pp. 61–89.

Pollard, S. and P. Robertson (1979), *The British Shipbuilding Industry, 1870–1914*, Cambridge, Mass., Harvard University Press.

Ponting, C. (1991), *A Green History of the World*, London, Penguin Books.

Popper, K.R. (1957), *The Poverty of Historicism*, London, Routledge & Kegan Paul.

Popper, K.R. (1966), *The Open Society and its Enemies*, 2 vols, 5th edn, London, Routledge & Kegan Paul.

Popper, K.R. (1972), *Objective Knowledge: an evolutionary approach*, Oxford, Clarendon Press.

Pritchard, J.B. (1950), *Ancient Near Eastern Texts Relating to the Old Testament*, Princeton, Princeton University Press.

Pucci, G. (1983), 'Pottery and trade in the Roman period', in P. Garnsey, K. Hopkins, and C.R. Whittaker (eds), *Trade in the Ancient Economy*, London, Chatto & Windus, pp. 105–17.

Puleston, D.E. (1979), 'An epistemological pathology and the collapse, or why the Maya kept the short count', in N. Hammond and G.R. Willey (eds), *Maya Archaeology and Ethnohistory*, London & Austin, University of Texas Press, pp. 63–71.

Quale, G.R. (1992), *Families in Context: a world history of population*, New York, Greenwood Press.

Radzicki, M.J., 'Chaos theory and economics', in G.M. Hodgson, W.J. Samuels, and M.R. Tool (eds), *The Elgar Companion to Institutional and Evolutionary Economics*, vol. 1, pp. 42–50.

Rampino, M.R. (1992), 'A major late Permian impact event on the Falkland plateau', abstract, *EOS: Transactions of the American Geophysical Union*, 73(43), October, p. 336.

Rathbone, D. (1991), *Economic Rationalism and Rural Society in Third-Century A.D. Egypt*, Cambridge, Cambridge University Press.

Rathbone, D. (1994), 'Ptolemaic to Roman Egypt: the death of the *dirigiste* state?', *Production and Public Powers in Antiquity B1: Proceedings, Eleventh International Economic History Congress, Milan, September*, Milan, Università Bocconi, pp. 29–40.

Raup, D.M. and J.J. Sepkoski (1982), 'Mass extinctions in the marine fossil record', *Science*, 215 (19 March), pp. 1501–3.

Reade, J. (1991), *Mesopotamia*, London, British Museum Press.

Renfrew, C. and P. Bahn (1991), *Archaeology: theories, methods and practice*, London, Thames & Hudson.

Roberts, R.G., R. Jones, N.A. Spooner, M.J. Head, A.S. Murray, and M.A. Smith (1994), 'The human colonisation of Australia: optical dates of 53,000 and 60,000 years bracket human arrival at Deaf Adder Gorge, Northern Territory', *Quaternary Geochronology (Quaternary Science Reviews)*, 13, pp. 575–83.

Romer, P.M. (1986), 'Increasing returns and long-run growth', *Journal of Political Economy*, 94, pp. 1002–37.

Rosenberg, N. and L.E. Birdzell (1986), *How the West Grew Rich: the economic transformation of the industrial world*, New York, Basic Books.

Rostow, W.W. (1960), *The Stages of Economic Growth: a non-communist manifesto*, Cambridge, Cambridge University Press.

Rostow, W.W. (1990), *Theorists of Economic Growth from David Hume to the Present: with a perspective on the next century*, New York, Oxford University Press.

Round, J.H. (1964; orig. pub. 1895), *Feudal England. Historical Studies on the Eleventh and Twelfth Centuries*, London, Allen & Unwin.

Samuelson, P.A. (1983), 'Complete genetic models for altruism, kin selection and like-gene selection', *Journal of Social and Biological Structures*, 6 (1), pp. 3–15.

Sanders, W.T. (1977), 'Environmental heterogeneity and the evolution of lowland Maya civilisation', in R.E.W. Adams (ed.), *The Origins of Maya Civilization*, Albuquerque, University of New Mexico Press, pp. 287–97.

Sanders, W.T. (1984), 'Formative exchange systems: comments', in K.G. Hirth (ed.), *Trade and Exchange in Early Mesoamerica*, Albuquerque, University of New Mexico Press, pp. 275–9.

Santley, R.S. (1984), 'Obsidian exchange, economic stratification, and the evolution of complex society in the Basin of Mexico', in K.G. Hirth (ed.), *Trade and Exchange in Early Mesoamerica*, Albuquerque, University of New Mexico Press, pp. 43–86.

Scammell, G.V. (1981), *The World Encompassed: the first European maritime empires c. 800–1650*, Berkeley & Los Angeles, University of California Press.

Schele, L. and P. Mathews (1991), 'Royal visits and other intersite relationships among Classic Maya', in T.P. Culbert (ed.), *Classic Maya Political History: hieroglyphic and archeological evidence*, Cambridge, Cambridge University Press, pp. 226–52.

Schumpeter, J.A. (1934), *The Theory of Economic Development: an inquiry into profits, capital, credit, interest and the business cycle*, Cambridge, Mass., Harvard University Press.

Seaman, L.C.B. (1981), *A New History of England 410–1975*, London, Macmillan.

Slipher, V.M. (1914), 'The radial velocity of the Andromeda Nebula', *Lowell Observatory Bulletin*, no. 58, pp. 56–7.

Snooks, G.D. (1990a), 'Economic growth during the last millennium: a quantitative perspective for the British industrial revolution', *Working Papers in Economic History*, no. 140, Canberra, Australian National University, July.

Snooks, G.D. (1990b), 'Arbitrary decree or rational calculation? The contribution of Domesday Book to economic history and economics', *Australian Economic History Review*, 30 (2), pp. 23–49.

Snooks, G.D. (1993a), *Economics without Time: a science blind to the forces of historical change*, London, Macmillan.

Snooks, G.D. (ed.) (1993b), *Historical Analysis in Economics*, London & New York, Routledge.

Snooks, G.D. (1994a), *Portrait of the Family within the Total Economy. A study in longrun dynamics: Australia, 1788–1990*, Cambridge, Cambridge University Press.

Snooks, G.D. (ed.) (1994b), *Was the Industrial Revolution Necessary?*, London & New York, Routledge.

Snooks, G.D. (1994c), 'Great waves of economic change: the Industrial Revolution in historical perspective', in G.D. Snooks (ed.), *Was the Industrial Revolution Necessary?*, London & New York, Routledge, pp. 43–78.

Snooks, G.D. (1995), 'The dynamic role of the market in the Anglo-Norman economy and beyond, 1086–1300', in R. Britnell and B. Campbell (eds), *A Commercialising Economy? England 1000–1300 AD*, Manchester, Manchester University Press, pp. 27–54.

Snooks, G.D. and J. McDonald (1986), *Domesday Economy: a new approach to Anglo-Norman history*, Oxford, Clarendon Press.

Sokoloff, K.L. and B.Z. Khan (1990), 'The democratization of invention during early industrialization: evidence from the United States, 1790–1846', *Journal of Economic History*, 50, pp. 363–78.

Solomou, S. (1987), *Phases of Economic Growth, 1850–1973: Kondratieff waves and Kuznets swings*, Cambridge, Cambridge University Press.

Solow, R.M. (1956), 'A contribution to the theory of economic growth', *Quarterly Journal of Economics*, 70, pp. 65–94.

Speer, A. (1970), *Inside the Third Reich: memoirs*, London, Weidenfeld & Nicolson.

Spence, J.D. (1990), *The Search for Modern China*, London, Hutchinson.

Spence, M.W. (1984), 'Craft production and polity in early Teotihuacan', in K.G. Hirth (ed.), *Trade and Exchange in Early Mesoamerica*, Albuquerque, University of New Mexico Press, pp. 87–114.

Stafford, P. (1994), 'Women and the Norman Conquest', *Transactions of the Royal Historical Society*, London, pp. 221–49.

Stanier, R.Y., M. Doudoroff, and E.A. Adelberg (1963), *The Microbial World*, Englewood Cliffs, NJ, Prentice-Hall.

Stanner, W.E.H. (1965), 'Aboriginal territorial organization: estate, range, domain and regime', *Oceania*, 1 (36), pp. 1–26.

Starr, C.G. (1977), *The Economic and Social Growth of Early Greece, 800–500 BC*, 4th edn, New York, Oxford University Press.

Starr, C.G. (1991), *A History of the Ancient World*, 4th edn, New York, Oxford University Press.

Stebbins, G.L. (1982), *Darwin to DNA, Molecules to Humanity*, San Francisco, W.H. Freeman.

Steensgaard, N. (1990), 'The growth and composition of the long-distance trade of England and the Dutch Republic before 1750', in J.D. Tracy (ed.), *The Rise of Merchant Empires: long-distance trade in the early modern world, 1350–1750*, Cambridge, Cambridge University Press, pp. 102–52.

Stubbs, W. (1880), *The Constitutional History of England in its Origin and Development*, 3 vols, Oxford, Clarendon Press.

Suzuki, D.T. (1990), *Inventing the Future*, Sydney, Allen & Unwin.

Suzuki, D.T. and A. Gordon (1990), *It's a Matter of Survival*, North Sydney, Allen & Unwin.

Swan, T.W. (1956), 'Economic growth and capital accumulation', *Economic Record*, 32, pp. 334–61.

Taagepera, R. (1968), 'Growth curves of empires', *General Systems*, 13, pp. 171–5.

Tainter, J.A. (1988), *The Collapse of Complex Societies*, Cambridge & New York, Cambridge University Press.

Temple, R.K.G. (1989), *The Genius of China: 3,000 Years of Science, Discovery, and Invention*, New York, Simon & Schuster.

Thorne, A. and R. Raymond (1989), *Man on the Rim: the Peopling of the Pacific*, North Ryde, NSW, Angus & Robertson in association with ABC Enterprises.

Tracy, J.D. (ed.) (1990), *The Rise of Merchant Empires: long-distance trade in the early modern world, 1350–1750*, Cambridge, Cambridge University Press.

Tracy, J.D. (ed.) (1991), *The Political Economy of Merchant Empires* (Studies in Comparative Early Modern History), Cambridge/New York, Cambridge University Press.

Trigger, B.G. (1978), *Time and Traditions: essays in archaeological interpretation*, Edinburgh, Edinburgh University Press.

Trivers, R. (1985), *Social Evolution*, California, Benjamin/Cummings.

Tullock, G. (1978), 'Altruism, malice, and public goods', *Journal of Social and Biological Structures*, 1 (1), pp. 3–9.

Tylecote, A. (1992), *The Long Wave in the World Economy: the current crisis in historical perspective*, London & New York, Routledge.

United Nations (1973), 'History of world population growth', in *The Determinants and Consequences of Population Trends: new summary of findings on interaction of demographic, economic and social factors*, New York, United Nations, pp. 10–32.

United Nations, Dept. of International Economic and Social Affairs (1991), *World Population Prospects 1990*, New York, United Nations.

United Nations (various years), *Demographic Yearbook*, New York, United Nations.

Vail, P.R. and R.M. Mitchum, Jr. (1979), 'Global cycles of sea-level change and their role in exploration', *Proceedings of the Tenth World Petroleum Congress*, vol. 2.

Van Creveld, M.L. (1989), *Technology and War: from 2000 BC to the present*, New York, Free Press.

Van der Wee, H. (ed.) (1988a), *The Rise and Decline of Urban Industries in Italy and in the Low Countries (Late Middle Ages–Early Modern Times)*, Leuven, Leuven University Press.

Van der Wee, H. (1988b), 'Industrial dynamics and the process of urbanization and de-urbanization in the Low Countries from the late Middle Ages to the eighteenth century: a synthesis', in H. Van der Wee (ed.), *The Rise and Decline of Urban Industries in Italy and in the Low Countries (Late Middle Ages–Early Modern Times)*, Leuven, Leuven University Press, pp. 307–81.

Van der Wee, H. (1990), 'Structural changes in European long-distance trade, and particularly in the re-export trade from south to north, 1350–1750', in J.D. Tracy (ed.), *The Rise of Merchant Empires: long-distance trade in the early modern world, 1350–1750*, Cambridge, Cambridge University Press, pp. 14–33.

Van der Wee, H. (1993), *The Low Countries in the Early Modern World*, Aldershot, Variorum.

Van der Wee, H. (1994), 'Urban industrial development in the Low Countries during the late Middle Ages and early modern times', *Working Papers in Economic History*, no. 179, Canberra, Australian National University, September.

Van Zanden, J.L. (1993), 'The Dutch economy in the very long run: growth in production, energy consumption and capital in Holland (1500–1805) and the Netherlands (1805–1910)', in A. Szirmai, B. Van Ark, and D. Pilat (eds), *Explaining Economic Growth. Essays in honour of Angus Maddison*, Amsterdam, North-Holland, pp. 267–83.

Warry, J.G. (1980), *Warfare in the Classical World: an illustrated encyclopaedia of weapons, warriors, and warfare in the ancient civilisations of Greece and Rome*, London, Salamander Books.

Watson, J.D. and F.H.C. Crick (1953), 'Molecular structure of nucleic acids: a structure for deoxyribose nucleic acid', *Science*, 171, pp. 737–8.

Webster, D.L. (1977), 'Warfare and the evolution of Maya civilization', in R.E.W. Adams (ed.), *The Origins of Maya Civilization*, Albuquerque, University of New Mexico Press, pp. 335–72.

White, K.D. (1984), *Greek and Roman Technology*, Ithaca, NY, Cornell University Press.

White, L. (1962), *Medieval Technology and Social Change*, Oxford, Oxford University Press.

White, T.D., G. Suwa, and B. Asfaw (1994), '*Austraopithecus ramidus*, a new species of early hominid from Aramis, Ethiopia', *Nature*, 371 (22 September), pp. 306–12.

Willey, G.R. (1973), 'Certain aspects of the late classic to postclassic periods in the Belize Valley', in T.P. Culbert (ed.), *The Classic Maya Collapse*, Albuquerque, University of New Mexico Press, pp. 93–106.

Witt, U. (ed.) (1992), *Explaining Process and Change: approaches to evolutionary economics*, Ann Arbor, University of Michigan Press.

Witt, U. (ed.) (1993), *Evolutionary Economics*, Aldershot, Hants, England/Brookfield, Vt, E. Elgar.

Wrigley, E.A. and R.S. Schofield (1981), *The Population History of England, 1541–1871: a reconstruction*, London, Edward Arnold.

Yoffee, N. (1988), 'The collapse of ancient Mesopotamian states and civilization', in N. Yoffee and G.L. Cowgill (eds), *The Collapse of Ancient States and Civilizations*, Tucson, University of Arizona Press, pp. 44–68.

Yoffee, N. and G.L. Cowgill (eds) (1988), *The Collapse of Ancient States and Civilizations*, Tucson, University of Arizona Press.

INDEX

Darwin 83; and ancient civilizations 423; and ancient Greece 59, 280, 286, 287, 288, 289–90, 349; and ancient Mesopotamia 279–82; and Assyrian Empire 423–4; avoidance of *see* isolation, negative strategies, specialized niche strategy, trade protection; between Islamic civilization and the West 61; between life forms 2, *see also* struggle for survival; between Venice and Genoa 363, 364, 365, 365–6; between Venice and north-western Europe 368; and Carthage 294, 358; and China 315, 318, 320, 320–1, 322, 324; and choice of dynamic tactics 395; and commerce strategy 332, 341; comparison of China and Western Europe 320–1, 387; comparison of Roman Empire and medieval Western Europe 254; and conquest strategy 254–5, 271, 301, 423–4, 426; and cooperation 179–80; and counterfactual model of the Industrial Revolution 422–5; defined 240; and demand for chemical nutrients 26–7; and dynamic strategies 23–4, 87, 392, 399, 435; and dynamic tactics 392; and dynamics of life 83, 86–7; and European breakout 259–60, 424–5; in existential model 392; and factor endowment 240; in first dynamic sequence of life 89; and funnels of transformation 405, 434; and genetic change 90; global level of and speed of collapse 438; high degree of *see* open societies; and hunter–gatherer societies 51; and Industrial Revolution 264; and innovation in Sung Dynasty China 315, 318; and institutional change 399, 401; lack of *see* closed societies, isolation; and longrun equilibrium, population and natural resources 423; and Macedonian Empire 286, 423–4; and materialist man 176, 187, 392; and Mayan civilization 330, 331, 332; and medieval Western Europe 253–5, 280, 300, 304; and medieval Western Europe and technological change 247, 254, 301; military and stationary state 425; and monopoly, and

conquest strategy 271; and palaeolithic societies 187, 271; and predation strategy 90; and rise of Western civilization 301; and Rome 291–3, 424; for scarce resources *see* economics; in second dynamic sequence of life 89–90; and shift to industrial paradigm in Western Europe 259; and specialist niches 87, 89; and stationary state 187; and strategic choice 253–5, 393; and strategic crisis 438; and strategic investment 323–4; and Sumerian civilization 279–80; and symbiosis strategy 90; and technological paradigm shifts 227, 240–1, 258–9, 403; and technological strategy 122, 254, 301, 304, 335; and Teotihuacan civilization 329–30; and trade 332, 342; and urbanization 53–4; and war 53–4; and Western Europe 259–60, 264, 307, 423–6; and Western Europe and technological strategy 258–9, 335; *see also* dynamic materialism; global scale of competitiveness; markets; monopoly; struggle for prosperity; struggle for survival
computer simulation models 103–10; of ecological engineers 135–6; and economics 114–15; *see also* mechanistic models of human society; 'World2' and 'World3'
concentric spheres model of human behaviour: an economic model 432; at individual and aggregated levels 182; contrasted with Marx's dialectical materialism 181, 181–2; contrasted with Rostow's stages-of-economic-growth hypothesis 181, 182; and cooperative relationships 432; and decision-making in household and market 433; defined 432; and genetic models 432; and materialist man 180–2; and political man 182–3
conquest: and civilization 272; and diffusion of technological paradigm 241; economic viability of 272; and great waves and subcycles of 386; and modern world 314; in Western culture 272
conquest empires 395; collapse of 438;

and forces of order and chaos 408–9; and stationary state 408; and strategic revenue gap 408–9, 438, 439

conquest-led growth 275–8; contrast with technology-led growth 277; defined 276; prerequisites of 276–7; as zero-sum game 277; *see also* conquest, zero-sum game; zero-sum dynamic change

conquest strategy 4, 209, 270–336, 394; and Achaean Greek society 396; and Akkadian Empire 280–1, 396; and ancient civilizations 391, 423–4, 431, 436; and ancient Greece 280, 286, 287, 349, 395; and Arab society 396; and Assyrian Empire 282–6, 284–5, 285–6, 395, 396; and Athens 288, 350–1; and Aztec civilization 325, 396; and Carolingians 301, 303; and Carthage 358, 367, 396; and Chinese civilization 314–24, 396; choice of 274, 276; collapse of 431; and colonization 274–5, 394; and commerce strategy 276, 343, 347, 357, 359, 367; and competition in medieval Western Europe 254–5; and competitive environments 271, 426; and counterfactual model of Industrial Revolution 421; and culture 427; defined 273, 431; diseconomies of in modern world 244; as dominant strategy 272, 274, 276; and economic growth 5, 11; exhaustion of 60, 254–5, 284–6, 296–7, 335, 408, 431; exhaustion of and forces of chaos 335; exhaustion of and strategic revenue gap 397; and existential model 392, 432; and France 306–7, 377, 389, 425; and German (Holy Roman) Empire 303–4; and Germanic kingdoms (17th–18th centuries) 425; and the great wheel of civilization 406, 407, 407–8; and investment in 273, 273–4, 274, 276–7; and Macedonian Empire 122, 286, 289–91, 396; and material living standards 5, 11; and material living standards in ancient civilizations 254, 270, 272–8, 284–5, 431, 436; and material living standards in palaeolithic societies 271; and maximization of individual utility 183; and Mayan civilization 60, 333, 396;

and medieval Western Europe 254–5, 280; and Mesoamerican civilizations 324–35; and the Mesopotamian empires 279–86; and Minoan civilization 347; and monopoly 260, 271; and Mycenaean civilization 347; and Neolithic and Industrial Revolutions 241–2; and neolithic technological paradigm 431; and north-western Europe 396; and open societies 435; and Ottoman Empire 396; and palaeolithic societies 271; and Persian Empire 396; and the Phoenicians 357, 357–8; and population 431; and Portugal 389; and predation strategy 8; and Rome 291–300, 319, 395, 396, 399, 401; and ruling elite 274, 297–8; self-defeating nature of 300; and Spain 306, 389, 425; and Sparta 289; and strategic crisis 277; and strategic demand for ideas 202, 203; and strategic revenue gap 300, 408, 439; as subsidiary strategy 279–80, 305–8, 310, 335–6, 343, 347, 396; and Sumerian civilization 279–80, 395, 396; and technological paradigm shifts 241–2; and technology 251–2, 278; and technological strategy 246–7, 274, 276, 279–80, 307, 308, 310, 440; and Teotihuacan civilization 328–30, 396; transmission of 394–5; and transmission of ideas 278; and Tyre 359; and urbanization 278; and Venice 360, 361, 366–7, 368; and Western civilization 300–14; and Western Europe 305–6, 335–6, 424; and zero-sum dynamic change (ZDC) 431, 440; zero-sum nature of 209, 276, 277, 426; *see also* conquest empires; dynamic strategies; eternal recurrence of war and conquest; war

conservative ideology: and forces of order 185, 395

continental drift 28–30; and isolation of life forms 29, 30

continuing economic growth: and Industrial Revolution 268, 410, 435–6; *see also* great linear waves of economic growth

continuing technological change: and environmental degradation 247; and Industrial Revolution 239, 243–4,

395, 397; theories of the dynamics of 99–136; timescapes of 440
humanism: opposed by environmentalism 110
hunter–gatherer societies: collapse of 225; competition among and natural resources 51; and environmental degradation 51; and economic resilience 232; family economy of 227–37; and family multiplication strategy 225, 405; and gender division of labour 228; and the great dispersion 48, 435; in New World 405; nuclear family in 228–31; in Old World 405; and physical environment 51; and population change 380; technology of 48, 227–8, 380, 405, 435; and war 54, 179; *see also* forager bands; tribes
hunting: displaced by agriculture 440, *see also* neolithic paradigm shift, Neolithic Revolution; shift from scavenging to 434, 440, *see also* palaeolithic paradigm shift, Palaeolithic Revolution; and technological strategy 440
hunting revolution *see* Palaeolithic Revolution

ice ages 33–35
ideas 8, 201; demand for by materialist man 124, 438; and desires 204, 207; and driving force of human society 206–7; and dynamic strategies 88, 124; and economic growth 10–11; exchange of and funnels of transformation 434; and human evolution 143; independent power of in theories of dynamics of human society 101, 102; intellectuals on 206–7; new, and survival 48; strategic demand for *see* strategic demand for ideas; and technological strategy 244; transmission of and neolithic technological paradigm 436; *see also* genetic ideas; philosophical ideas; technological ideas
ideology: and dynamic tactics 131, 133, 185; and redistribution of wealth 131; *see also* conservative ideology; radical ideology
imitation: and diffusion of technological paradigms 241; *see also* strategic

imitation
imitation effect 212; *see also* strategic imitation
Inca civilization 325
India: on global scale of competitiveness 393; population of 382, 383
individual life forms: collapse internally generated 77; competition among 22–3, 69; and cooperation 23; and desires/instincts 84; and driving force of life 23; driving force of 2, 6–7, 9; and internal struggle 44–6, *see also* disease; and physical environment 22, 25–6, 73–4; *see also* decision-making individuals
individualism: interaction with cooperation in maximization of individual utility 180; *see also* competition
individuals: driving human evolution 143; *see also* economic man; materialist man
inductive method: and biology and materialist history 15
Industrial Revolution 5, 401; characteristics of 62; and city size in Western Europe 404–5; and classical economists 425; and climate change 35; and colonization of New World by Western Europe 425; and commerce strategy of north-western Europe 377; and competition in Western Europe 264; and continuing technological change 264; and continuous economic progress 410, 436; counterfactual model of a world without 420–7; diffusion of 109; and dynamic materialism 436; and Eastern Europe 388; and economic resilience 264; and England 388; and eternal recurrence of war and conquest 6, 426, 430; and exhaustion of neolithic technological paradigm 62; and existential model 391; and factor endowment 262, 265; and fossil fuels 262, 263, 265, 266; and gender division of labour 215–16; and great linear waves of economic change 410, 435–6; and great steps of human progress 436; and the great wheel of civilization 410; historical role of 426; and industrial